Anchors and Eagles

Paul L. Adkisson

SECOND EDITION

Order this book online at www.trafford.com/06-2728
or email orders@trafford.com

Most Trafford titles are also available at major online book retailers.

Note for Librarians: A cataloguing record for this book is available from Library and Archives Canada at www.collectionscanada.ca/amicus/index-e.html

ISBN: 978-1-4251-6391-4

We at Trafford believe that it is the responsibility of us all, as both individuals and corporations, to make choices that are environmentally and socially sound. You, in turn, are supporting this responsible conduct each time you purchase a Trafford book, or make use of our publishing services. To find out how you are helping, please visit www.trafford.com/responsiblepublishing.html

Our mission is to efficiently provide the world's finest, most comprehensive book publishing service, enabling every author to experience success. To find out how to publish your book, your way, and have it available worldwide, visit us online at www.trafford.com/10510

www.trafford.com

North America & international
toll-free: 1 888 232 4444 (USA & Canada)
phone: 250 383 6864 ♦ fax: 250 383 6804
email: info@trafford.com

The United Kingdom & Europe
phone: +44 (0)1865 722 113 ♦ local rate: 0845 230 9601
facsimile: +44 (0)1865 722 868 ♦ email: info.uk@trafford.com

10 9 8 7 6 5 4

II

This book is dedicated to all seafaring men
and in memory of the most extraordinary sailor
I had the pleasure of serving with:

Ronald Fields Pinnell (aka "Pinhead")

and especially to
Toni

for her persistence, her devotion and her unfaltering support
in the making of this book

IV

CONTENTS

Preface

Anchors and Eagles, based on fact, contains remarkable descriptions of experiences lived and shared during one man's twenty-year career while in the U.S. Navy. Appropriately, the title was selected with the knowledge, and as a reminder, that a sailor is constantly confronted with or surrounded by one or the other. "Anchors" are the collar device worn by chief petty officers, the highest graded enlisted men, and "eagles" are not only worn on the rating badges of petty officers of all grades; eagles are the distinct collar device worn by Navy captains, the highest-ranking line officers below flag grade.

Understandably, the life of a sailor is so varied that there can be no main characters in this story other than the author himself. A sailor meets new shipmates with each set of transfer orders. Sometimes paths do cross, but seldom do old shipmates find themselves stationed together again at future commands. A sailor is more apt to retain civilian friendships acquired during his travels, since the probability is likely that he will periodically return and renew those acquaintances. There is also a strong feeling of trust while in civilian company, when military discipline can, for brief periods of time, be set aside. The life of a sailor is not necessarily a good life, but it has its rewards — some planned or anticipated, others totally unexpected. The story also explores the down side of such a life.

Anchors and Eagles describes situations that affected the interface, understanding, conflict, and cooperation between officers and enlisted men of all grades. No book or story relating to the Navy way of life would be complete without including humor along with the more serious aspects. *Anchors and Eagles* does so. The story takes one individual from his final few days of high school adolescence into the U.S. Navy. It describes his mistakes, his learning experiences, and the changes that took place in his attitude and maturity as he traveled to many foreign countries. It includes peacetime and wartime experiences.

1

Anchors and Eagles includes numerous WestPac (Western Pacific) deployments. Each deployment was a completely different experience, some more rewarding or more exciting than others, each unique in itself.

The story describes how the accomplishments and performance of enlisted men were seldom recognized or commended in a manner deserving of their efforts; how work accomplished during off-duty hours as well as during normal working hours, to ensure that all ship movement commitments were met, was taken somewhat for granted by those who were not "hands-on" participants. It depicts hardworking enlisted men, not expecting a great deal of gratitude, frequently allowing their inner frustrations to become more outwardly apparent as they relaxed ashore, well away from their usual work environment.

Mothers, wives, other relatives, and friends of seafaring men learned to expect noticeable changes in habits and personalities as a result of the experiences they shared during deployments. A great deal of maturing always occurred during those periods of time when the men were alienated from their homes and families as dictated by military needs. Some men became fathers and were unable to be present at that most important time in their lives. While they were under the pressures of military rule and discipline, their travels took in some of the most exotic ports of the world, where they met and mingled with real "natives." New and lifelong friendships were permanently established while old acquaintances were being renewed. These men learned a great deal about the customs and traditions of peoples of different races as they made honest attempts to learn unusual words and difficult phrases in local tongue-twisting languages. They shopped at some of the world's most famous bargainers' paradises, where they purchased souvenirs to display and give as gifts upon returning home. They participated in the nightlife, witnessed the daytime beauty of magnificent Oriental landscapes, and marveled at architectural wonders. They talked with street beggars and saw the crippling results of malnutrition in children and adults alike. They lived and felt the uneasiness of being alone in unfamiliar surroundings while at the same time experiencing a warm and receptive hospitality from the people of the host countries. As seagoing men they saw thousands of miles of ocean, were subjected to severe weather conditions, and lived with anxieties only a sailor truly understands. They all aged while they gained wisdom through invaluable experiences. Upon each return to the United States they expressed their experiences in their own special way. The trinkets and stories they brought with them were a very real part of their lives, and they always looked forward to sharing these with the most wonderful and cherished people in the world: their loved ones at home.

There is no intention on the author's part to claim or insinuate that his particular experiences were commonplace, rather that they were unique to him and to numerous situations he was personally confronted with, or became knowledgeable of, over a career spanning twenty years. Some of the names of individuals contained herein have been changed, and some have been intentionally omitted.

It was the friendship, encouragement and conduct, the leadership, guidance and performance by the men with whom he most closely associated himself while on board the USS *Colahan*, coupled with the understanding and fair treatment awarded him by the Commanding Officer, CDR C. L. Keedy, Jr. that established the foundation upon which the author built a highly successful and satisfying career in the U.S. Navy.

1

THE BREAK

No doubt my anxieties, limited experiences, and problems as a seventeen-year-old were shared by an infinite number of youths. However, to me they were unique and compelling. My high school grades were unworthy of commendation and were not commensurate with my actual innate abilities. My outside interests went little beyond the occasional gratification sanctioned by Hope, my first romantic encounter at an age far too young for explicit detail, and my untrustworthy 1932 Chevrolet sedan needed a new transmission. The cold, dreary January weather so common to the San Joaquin Valley contributed to my restless mood.

Dan and Richard, two classmates and close friends had recently been sworn into the Naval Reserve. On occasion they stopped by my home, proud in their uniforms, which impressed me considerably. Al, Gary, and I, who made up the balance of this close group, wanted desperately to join Richard and Dan, and be part of the same reserve unit. I was reluctant to make such a decision. How would my overprotective and restrictive parents react?

It was much more than just the desire to be with my friends that made me want to join the Navy. It was the need to break away, to sever weakened and straining family ties. I wanted to reach out and participate in the real world. Being a member of the reserves could not possibly satisfy my thirst for dramatic change. I had to do more. So I called my friend Gary. He answered the telephone on the first ring.

"Hello."

"Hey, Gary, what say we join the regular Navy instead of the reserves?"

Gary's immediate and unhesitating response shocked me: "Okay, Paul."

I was experiencing a strange sensation throughout my body, quite unfamiliar. I experienced a moment of fear as his words echoed through my mind, as though each cell of my brain was rejecting what I wanted to hear.

"I really mean it, Gary."

"Sure, I really mean it too. I'll sign up with you."

Our conversation came to a rapid end. There were other calls to make. The importance and potential impact of such a decision should spread as quickly as possible to the others in our group, so that they, too, might share in the excitement of such a venture.

Richard, probably the most carefree in the group, was easily persuaded. Al was hesitant, more concerned about his family ties than the rest of us. Dan, who was known for his ability to exercise good judgment, seemingly equipped with greater foresight than the rest of us, preferred to continue his education. Four of us, intent on pursuing the challenge, would approach our parents each in our own way.

I waited until evening, sitting restlessly at the large living room couch situated just inside the front door. I was well concealed and separated from the dining room and adjoining kitchen, where my parents were talking. My thoughts were troubled as I scanned my surroundings.

At the far side of the room, the open-hearth fireplace somehow took on the appearance of being much larger than usual and glared back at me. To the left, sitting silently without life, was the bulky black-and-white console TV set, our main source of family entertainment. *I doubt that we will get much use out of you tonight,* I thought. *I will be the one to provide the entertainment on this occasion.* To my right the upright piano sat proud, as the senior member of all household furnishings, shadowed by venetian blinds that partially hid the outside world from view. Finger-marks were faintly visible where someone had brushed the thin layer of dust on the piano top. I wondered how my mother with her meticulous housekeeping habits had managed to overlook such a condition.

I heard the click of the dining room light switch and awakened from my thoughts to the realization that it was after dusk and my moment of truth would soon come. The light from the dining room reached through the invisible barrier of my fear and beckoned me. It was time.

I stood erect, my muscles tense, as I took that first awkward step into my future. My mother and father had moved to the dining room and were

5

carrying on a conversation about the neighbors' dog and the new litter of pups to which it had recently given birth. Both parents seemed to be in good spirits; there was nothing obvious about their frame of mind that might interfere or distract from the importance I had placed on the discussion to follow.

My approach was hesitant and clumsy, yet straightforward and to the point. Even as I spoke, questions raced through my mind. What would I do should they refuse me? Would I become angry or belligerent? Why should they refuse such a request? Even if they were to refuse, I would surely find another way. My heart pounded; my legs weakened. I was almost incapable of carrying my own slim 155-pound frame body and was barely aware of my own voice as I blurted out, "I want to join the Navy!"

My mother, the youngest of eleven children and consequently the victim of continuous hand-me-downs, shared a very close relationship with her family during her youth. A proud woman of forty-four, Mom was relied upon to participate in activities outside the immediate home environment, even knowing such involvement was seldom acknowledged to a desirable level of appreciation. The genuine concern for the education and welfare of her only two children was obvious through her volunteer efforts at many school functions. How sad that such interest was more often than not mistaken by me as artificial, a means of ensuring we were constantly under her watchful eye. It would be difficult to determine just how, when, or where she developed her somewhat domineering attitude; however, on occasion it was manifested without the patience and understanding of which she was otherwise so capable.

Dad, at fifty-seven, was exceptionally active. He had been raised under strict supervision, his father having been a minister. Apparently, my grandfather had insisted on complete religious harmony within their family circle. Dad never over emphasized his own personal religious beliefs but nonetheless provided me with the knowledge needed to decide for myself what my preferences and beliefs would be. He was never the affectionate type; however, I always knew that he admired and loved me. It was not in his nature to show an open display of affection for either of his children. His more obvious and deeply felt love was for my mother. Knowing I was a product of that love meant very little to me. Blinded by his infatuation, my father seldom, if ever, took sides even in the most remote sense if it might have meant disagreeing with my mother's wishes. He relied heavily

6

on Mom as having the final say in decisions and family policy. This was especially true of decisions about my activities. It was common to hear him say, "Go ask your mother." Seldom would my mother say, "Go ask your father," at which times I was inclined to believe he had already been told how to respond — the decision already final. I was very envious of Jack, my older brother, as I desired total equality in any and all dealings with our parents. That could not have been possible. It was most difficult for me to accept the fact that Jack was two years my senior and therefore had extra privileges. Time and again I was told, "When you are your brother's age you can . . ," or, "Wait until you are your brother's age." I realized I would never have similar privileges as long as I lived under the same roof. I would never be my brother's age!

There was never a time during my youth that I can recall being hungry or without proper clothing. Yet I know there must have been times my parents went without in order to provide Jack and me with quality as well as quantity. We had all our needs plus many things considered luxuries that would probably have been more fully appreciated by less fortunate families. I had a pleasant childhood, but I no longer considered myself a child. I longed to be accepted and treated as an adult. My statement was cold and abrupt.

"I want to join the Navy," and I held my breath as my parents absorbed each word, not wanting them to misunderstand the importance of what I had said.

Mom spoke first, then Dad.

"You want to do what?"

"Why would you want to do something like that?"

There was no display of shock or disbelief as I had expected. Somehow they must have known, but how? Nonetheless, they seemed quite prepared.

I felt uneasy and fearful. I knew that I had been abrupt, but what could I possibly say that would be acceptable and cause an immediate favorable response without having to expose my inner feelings? I did not want to create a scene that might cause them to refuse permission for the sake of showing their authority.

Too many times during my youth I was denied things other youngsters my age were allowed. Too many times misunderstanding parents had disappointed me — and I could not afford to allow it to happen on this occasion.

Would my eyes betray me in some display of resentment as I searched for an explanation that would win them over?

"The GI Bill. I want to get in before the GI Bill expires so I can complete my education after I get out," I blurted out.

Deep inside I was screaming *I want to go, to get out of here and be on my own! Why do you question my desires when they concern my life and my future?*

The GI Bill was the crutch on which I leaned heavily. That was something parents could believe in without having to face the reality that their adolescent son wanted desperately to be on his own.

We stood at the halfway point between the dining room and the living room in silence. The muffled breathing of the gas floor furnace took precedence over all.

"Are you sure that is what you want?"

What? Is there a chance that Mom, the dominant decision-maker, is actually showing a favorable possibility? Have I won without having to battle, without ridicule? Is it possible that I am being tested, being offered an opportunity to reconsider? Do they actually doubt my sincerity?

"I am positive. I really want to join the Navy."

No further explanation was necessary. Much to my immediate relief, they both gave me their blessing.

I wished that my parents had shown similar understanding on other occasions. The distinct impression I could not help but have, knowing how I had been raised up until that time, was that they were going to benefit by my decision just as much, probably more, than I was. They would no longer be responsible for me — and with Jack attending college they would, for the first time since my brother and I were born, have the house to themselves.

Three days later, Gary, Richard, Al and I satisfactorily completed the battery of tests at the Navy Recruiting Office. We all qualified. What a wonderful feeling. Within a day I would quit school. That same week I would be sworn into the U.S. Navy!

The next day, my final day at school, the delayed realization that my decision had been acceptable to my parents finally hit home. I felt exceptionally light on my feet and devoid of worries. *This is great,* I kept whispering to myself. *I'm on my own at last.* I firmly believed I had spent a lifetime accomplishing nothing and for the first time I was actually doing something adult that I sincerely felt compelled to do. The crisp December air tasted clean, and I filled my lungs to capacity with each breath and exhaled with anticipation of each breath to follow. The acuteness of my hearing exaggerated all sounds around me, as though I were experiencing some new sense for the very first time. The quadrosymphonics of distant horns as vehicles acknowledged their own existence, the chirping in and out of unison of multitudes of birds, and the grating of dried leaves as they inched their way through the otherwise empty streets and gutters adjacent to the school, were practically foreign to me in this new experience of my own senses. The combined confusion of unrelated conversations intermingled with occasional laughter of students across the campus was of little significance. The winter chill was thwarted by an abundance of inner warmth kindled by a radiance of self-satisfaction.

Was I really free? Were the bonds that held and compelled me about to sever the final threads? How strange that questions about my future did not factor into the glorious pool within which my imagination was swimming wildly.

The task of informing teachers and counselors of my immediate withdrawal from school was fun. I was almost defiant in my approach and took pleasure in letting it be known I would no longer be guided by the rules governing students. I impressed no one other than myself by exhibiting such an attitude, but it gave me a sense of satisfaction that I gloried in. I was pleased knowing that I would be fully responsible for myself without having to contend or compete with existing peer pressure. I knew that the discipline of the Navy would far surpass that of school, but the belief that I would be treated as a man for complying made me believe that the transition could only be welcomed and for the better.

It was January 20, 1955. The weather was exceptionally favorable with no overcast and unlimited visibility. Most good-byes had been said. Gary, Richard, Al, and I boarded the Greyhound bus at the Bakersfield Bus Depot not knowing if or when we would return. We could see our parents standing alongside the bus, tears streaming down our mothers' cheeks with forced smiles unevenly suspended on their quivering lips. Friends, girlfriends, and neighbors waved their final farewells as the roar of the diesel engine drowned out whatever pleasantries were being exchanged. And there was Linda. Sweet, innocent Linda stood silent. Her flawless brown hair flowed gracefully to her shoulders. Her beautiful dark brown eyes sparkled through a thin film of protective moisture, completely composed with her own special half-smile. She was more beautiful than I had ever seen her, yet for the first time since our acquaintance she was of lesser concern. Surely I would return for Linda at another time.

Little did we realize the Greyhound bus had already been filled to capacity before we were quite literally herded on board. Our suitcases were jammed in the center aisle, readily available for us to straddle and use as the hard and uncomfortable seats they would serve as should we choose to sit instead of stand. I chose to stand, not really caring about the lack of seating accommodations but more concerned that the bus round that first bend, severing the final thread binding me to the life I had known and grown to despise.

The bus lurched forward; we looked at each other almost laughingly.

"Here we go," I said.

Gary followed with; "We're off."

Ever so slowly we crept down the ramp to Eighteenth Street, made that first left turn, and headed east toward Highway 99.

"I'll bet they follow in their cars for a ways," remarked Al.

"Yeah, they'll want to make sure we don't fall out or something."

"Or got on the wrong bus," quipped Richard.

We all laughed as we looked at one another sheepishly. The final thread was about to part. All that remained were the physical examinations and, most important, the swearing-in ceremony that was to take place within twenty-four hours.

I found myself wondering how my parents would cope with major holidays that year, Christmas in particular since it would be the first since my birth that they would probably celebrate without me. I knew how they had always focused their attention on making Christmas very special for my brother and me, and that it would be a difficult holiday for them without having their "baby" around. My thoughts reversed as I considered the possibility that they might be just as concerned about me having to spend Christmas away from the only home I had ever known. Thoughts of Christmas and all of the joy and festivities the season brought with it quickly vanished as I regained the more dominant considerations of my current situation.

The bus trip would be uneventful. Highway 99 was not new to any of us. We had all traveled a portion of the route on previous trips with our parents. Those passengers fortunate enough to be seated blocked roadside scenery from our view. We tried to pass the time by making conversation, but even that was somewhat futile. Subjects that interested us and we would

10

have enjoyed talking about were far too personal, and we dared not discuss them with strangers so near. We were already the focal point and didn't feel the need to attract further attention.

I broke what had become an uncomfortable period of silence even knowing we all knew the answer to my question before boarding: "I wonder how long it will take?"

"I'd guess about three hours," Gary stated with an obvious certainty.

"Let's see. That will put us there about noon."

"Right, Rich, that's really an intelligent deduction," chuckled Al, "How did you manage to figure that out?"

Several more minutes passed before Gary made the most reasonable remarks of the journey: "I sure hope we stick together during boot camp. Wouldn't it be cool if we all got stationed together?"

Al, with his typical negative outlook disregarded the possibility. "Fat chance of that."

"I dunno; I guess we could ask," Richard faked a unique dumbness.

I was involved with my own inner thoughts but knew that I should make some effort at participating in the conversation. My rather futile attempt at humor was an indication of my youth and inexperience. "I wonder if they'll start giving us shots today? And what about that square needle!"

We had all been forewarned, sometimes jokingly, sometimes almost believably, of the agonies and suffering all sailors must endure; but the square needle had to be the worst possible experience that could happen to a man. Having any kind of a needle injected into one's left testicle was hard to imagine, but a square one at that just had to be the absolute pinnacle of torture.

Gary's head jerked around abruptly and he half-snapped, with obvious uncertainty, "Aw, come on Paul. You know that's a bunch o' bullshit."

Simultaneously we all bent slightly forward with pained expressions crowding the smiles from our lips. The chance that we would be subjected to such an ordeal did exist in our imaginations no matter how hard we tried to show disbelief. No doubt we would find out!

Realizing that by this time most passengers were aware of our intentions on joining the Navy, I spoke loudly, with more clarity, and changed the immediate subject. "Hey, can you guys swim?"

I asked the question jokingly of the group but looked directly at Gary. Several months prior I had played a role in preventing a tragedy by helping to pull him from an irrigation canal in which he nearly drowned.

11

"You know, that's a heck of a big canal we're gonna be floating around in."

Richard's follow-up; "Yeah, and there's no crawfish. Just sharks," did not amuse Gary.

Al's attempts at humor never did quite succeed, but he always gave it his best shot. "And I hear they are attracted to redheads."

Gary came back at Al with lightning speed. "You got it all wrong pal. They like big noses and you've got a blue ribbon winner."

We all laughed again and tried to look as conspicuous as, in fact, we were. We spoke of Sandra and Paula, the two sweethearts of the group. At one time or another each of us had tried gaining favors from them. Well, all but Al. Al was seldom around when we had female companionship on our minds. We talked of the many fun-loving, honest times shared with Edna, Carol and Bert.

"Do you think they'll write to us?" Richard asked.

"Sure, who else would they write to!" I responded.

Gary interjected, "We'll probably have so many chicks chasing us around the world we won't have time to answer if they write."

Our brief conversations were short and choppy and probably made little or no sense to those around us. No subject lasted for any noticeable duration.

Several more minutes passed during which we were not capable of communicating. Only the steady roar of the bus and the uncoordinated squeaks and groans of well-used interior bus furnishings interrupted what would otherwise have been total silence. Someone several rows toward the front of the bus shattered the unusual calm with an unfortunate sneeze that immediately triggered the loud, unmistakably clear, rasping sound of passing gas. Without hesitation and without thinking, I blurted out, "There must be a sailor up there." I could feel the blood rushing to my face, embarrassed at the total lack of response. I immediately followed with, "I wonder if sharks are equally attracted to red faces." Only a small handful of passengers were amused.

The bus continued south on Highway 99, stopping briefly several times at Greyhound depots along the way. As we entered the San Diego city limits we knew that it would only be a matter of minutes before we would reach our destination: the Naval Training Center, AKA boot camp.

NTC, the Naval Training Center, San Diego, California, had its inception in 1916 when Mr. William Kettner, Congressman from the Eleventh Congressional District of California and spokesman for the San Diego Chamber of Commerce, interested the Honorable Franklin D. Roosevelt, then Assistant Secretary of the Navy, in establishing a naval training activity on the shores of San Diego Bay. Due to the nation's entry into World War I, further development of this plan was postponed until 1919, when Congress authorized acceptance by the Navy of the present site of the training center. The original grant consisted of 135 acres of highland donated by the San Diego Chamber of Commerce and 142 acres of tideland given by the City of San Diego. Construction work began in 1921, and on June 1, 1923, the U.S. Naval Training Station, San Diego, was placed in commission under the command of Capt. (later Rear Admiral) David F. Sellers, U.S. Navy.

At the time of its commissioning in 1923 the station bore little resemblance to its current size or arrangement. At that time Camp Paul Jones housed the entire population of the station and the maximum recruit strength was 1,500. The period of recruit training was then sixteen weeks.

During the 1920s the Recruit Receiving and Outgoing Units were housed in the Detention Unit, known as Camp Ingram, which consisted of a group of walled tents adjacent to the south boundary of Camp Paul Jones. Until Camp Lawrence was completed in 1936, recruits spent their first three weeks of training under canvas in the Detention Unit.

In 1939 a construction program was commenced that within three years was to increase the capacity of the station fourfold. This expansion went hand in glove with a large-scale program of harbor improvements by means of which the channel and anchorages in San Diego Bay were deepened and 130 acres of filled land were added to the eastern boundaries of the station. By the end of 1941, when the Japanese attacked Pearl Harbor, Camp Luce had been completed and the construction of Camps Mahan, Decatur, and Farragut was already well under way. Virtually all this construction work was completed by September 1942, when the capacity of the station had reached its wartime peak of 33,000 men, 25,000 of whom were recruits. The period of recruit training during World War II varied between three weeks and seven weeks.

In April 1944, the Secretary of the Navy changed the status of the training station to that of a group command and redesignated it the U.S. Naval Training Center, San Diego. Under the Center Command were established three subordinate commands: the Recruit Training Command, the Service School Command, and the Administrative Command.

The years immediately following World War II saw a considerable reduction in population of the training center despite a postwar expansion of the service schools, and by the end of 1949 the population of the center had dropped to a twenty-year low of 5,800 men. Six months later, when the Communists invaded the Republic of Korea, an immediate expansion of all Naval training activities took place, and by September of 1950 the center was again operating at nearly full capacity.

During the early months of the Korean conflict it became apparent that the demand for trained personnel in the rapidly growing Pacific Fleet would require further expansion of this training center. Accordingly, steps were taken by the Navy Department to reactivate Camp Elliott, formerly a World War II Marine Corps training camp. On January 15, 1951, Camp Elliot was placed in commission as Elliot Annex of the Naval Training Center for the purpose of conducting the primary phases of recruit training. In March 1953, in line with the planned reduction in size of the Navy, training at Elliott Annex was discontinued and it was placed in an inactive status. During its first two years of operation, over 150,000 recruits received training there.

Late in 1952 projects were approved to convert some recruit barracks into classrooms and to extend training facilities by construction of a permanent recruit camp on the undeveloped training center land lying to the south and east of the estuary. The six converted barracks went into service as recruit classrooms in April 1953, and upon completion of construction work on the new camp the NTC filled out its boundaries of 435 acres.

As the bus entered San Diego Naval Training Center we heard shouts of, "R and O!" coming from all directions. My first thoughts were that we were being welcomed. I had no idea "R" and "O" really represented the lowest possible form of Navy life, the new recruit, arriving for "Receiving" and "Outfitting." We would be called R and O by every sailor sworn in before us. It didn't matter if they had been sworn in that very morning; they were "senior" and therefore had "privileges." I thought I had escaped living under special rules once I left the home where my brother had been privileged with special treatment. The abruptness of such similarity awakened me to a reality I had not anticipated. I was soon to realize the full impact of

"RHIP": "Rate" ("Rank," in reference to officers) by all means did "Have Its Privileges."

As we exited the bus we were warmly welcomed by a uniformed man. I had absolutely no idea what significance the uniform he was wearing represented, nor did I understand what the stripes on his sleeve meant. Regardless of his obvious kind and sincere nature, we all instinctively knew that he was in charge. I heard someone call him "Chief" but thought that to be some kind of a nickname or slang. I remember thinking to myself, *I wonder if I am going to wear a uniform like that?*

Chief politely told us to remain as a group and to follow him closely so as not to become separated because we might miss out on being sworn into Uncle Sam's Navy. In no way was I going to miss out on that. I could hardly wait for that moment of triumph to come.

Gary, Al, Richard, and I were no longer the only ones in the group. There had been other busses off-loading equally excited young adults, and we were all forming one larger group of about seventy. Of course the four of us tried to remain as close to each other as possible, making it more likely we would remain together during our basic training.

The entire group followed Chief inside one of the many buildings, where, much to our surprise and delight, we were advised that the swearing-in ceremony was to take place immediately. Chief told us to stand at attention, hold up our right hands, and repeat after him. I was bursting with excitement and a sense of pride, knowing that the ceremony I was about to participate in would change my life dramatically. I had no concept of the magnitude of change that was to take place, not just over the next few days and weeks, but ultimately over the twenty-two years that were to follow.

In unison we repeated: "I, [each stating his own full name], do so solemnly swear . . ." The crazy thought passed through my mind: *What if I give the wrong name? Will I later be able to say I was never sworn in?* "... that I will support and defend the Constitution of the United States against all enemies, foreign and domestic; and that I will bear true faith and allegiance to the same; and that I will obey the orders of the President of the United States and the orders of the officers appointed over me, according to regulations in the Uniformed Code of Military Justice. So help me God."

Chief said, "Congratulations; you are now on active duty in the United States Navy. Conduct yourselves accordingly."

Gary, Al, Richard, and I looked at each other a bit dumbfounded. Simultaneously we congratulated each other with no thoughts or considerations of just what was to come next.

One member of our group half-hollered, "Hey Chief, when do we eat?"

The previously soft-spoken chief, in a deep rasping voice that actually shook the walls, roared with ferocity, "Who in God's fuckin' hell told you that you could speak while standing at attention?"

I knew that the final thread, the umbilical that had, up until that precise moment been attached to my previous life, had at last snapped with a resonance I would never forget. I was, at last, in the U.S. Navy!

2

ATTENTION

There were neither rest periods nor time for sleep that first night on the base. Indications of dozing or any other hints or evidence of fatigue were quickly discouraged by whoever was responsible for issuing orders to our group at the time. Without exception we were required to follow all orders, many of which we thought to be ridiculous at the time but for which we later gained respect and understanding. Whatever experiences we may have shared during our school days offered little similarity to that with which we were then confronted.

The decision had been final; there was no turning back. We were there to become a very real part of the U.S. Navy, and we were to remain under the direct control and supervision of our Company Commander, Chief Sellers, until graduation.

Everything that was to take place over the next twelve weeks involved standing in one line or another. Usually we could expect the lines to be formed by company, one company squad following another. Other times lines were formed alphabetically. By virtue of having a last name that began with an *A* I frequently found myself at the head of the line. Others were therefore provided the opportunity to observe and benefit by my unfortunate mistakes. The issuance of uniforms was accomplished alphabetically. Being one of the first to receive parts of the uniform did not provide me with any privilege over the selection.

"Well now, sweetie, you look like this size should fit you," was the typical comment by the issuers. And who were the issuers? Other "boot campers" that were probably several days senior to us.

Not only did I think the garments were probably the wrong size, I didn't even know what some of them were. Each of us, one following another, processed through the uniform issue area filling up our first unit of issue, our "seabag" — that heavy-duty canvas bag that we would live out of for several of the following days. After the entire company received their uniforms we assembled on a "grinder," an area resembling several tennis courts in size, usually used for marching or for calisthenics. As Chief Sellers called out the names of each uniform item, we counted how many units of each we had been issued, making certain we had neither more nor less than that amount authorized. I found this particularly confusing because I had never heard terms like *mattress cover, tie-ties/clothes stops, dungarees, jumpers,* and *skivvies.* I vividly recall thinking to myself, *How am I supposed to know how many skivvy shirts I have when I don't even know what the damn things are?* I tried desperately to see what those around me were counting before I made a move. Even that got me in trouble.

"What the hell are you doing, sailor? You better snap out of that daze and get with the program."

I was significantly relieved when my count was confirmed as correct. I worried unnecessarily about what the punishment might have been had I miscounted one thing or another. The threat of being "put" or "placed on report" was always present. It carried with it the threat of a full spectrum of punishment possibilities, each fully detailed within the military justice system.

Once our uniforms were counted, recounted, and then confirmed as having been properly accounted for, we shouldered our full seabags and marched to a large, empty room inside an adjacent building. There we were each first issued a cardboard box about the size of an orange crate and second we were required to strip naked. We then packed the garments we had stripped ourselves of, everything we owned that was identifiable as civilian in nature, into the boxes that had been provided. There were two exceptions: wedding bands and religious devices, such as crucifixes and Saint Christopher's medals, that would normally be worn on a chain around one's neck.

I really got an education as I watched those around me packing up their personal property. We were told that our "civvies" and other personal belongings would be sent to our parents (or wives) and we were given the opportunity (and encouraged) to toss offensive items that might be considered questionable by our loved ones, into the center of the room. Almost every one of us shed at least one condom. There were French ticklers, all kinds of pornographic materials, weapons, letters, and some things that I couldn't even identify. We never questioned or discussed the destiny of those sensitive belongings.

At some point in time we were marched directly to an area of tables where we were separated into two groups. One group cut name stencils while the other group picked up small pots of thick white and black indelible ink and stencil brushes. One group was responsible for stenciling all clothing and the other group was responsible for ensuring the correctness of names and service numbers on the finished stencils. (At that time service numbers consisted of seven numbers — some years later Social Security numbers replaced the seven-number system). The artistic abilities (or the lack thereof) of those doing the stenciling were immediately obvious. Some of the names were stenciled such that they were nearly illegible. Garments had to be stenciled specifically at designated locations. Dungarees were clearly stenciled in large letters so that we could be easily identified by name; shirts were stenciled across the back, trousers on the back above the left pocket. This procedure was also changed some years later such that the stenciling of names was done in a manner so as to conceal rather than display them. Dress uniforms were stenciled on the inside, well concealed; blue trousers and jumpers, inside at the belt line. Skivvy shorts, shirts, and socks also had to be stenciled. Stencils provided the only means by which individuals could identify their own garments. We were each then provided with one final issue of our own complete set of stencils to keep for future use.

Some recruits had been issued the older and far more in demand "thirteen-button" dress uniform trousers instead of the newer zipper-fly, side-pocketed type. The older thirteen-button front-flap style was a much sharper-looking, certainly far more "sailor"-looking uniform. It did lack front pockets, an acceptable inconvenience satisfied by better looks, fit, and comfort. Admittedly, the thirteen-button trousers were a real hassle when it came time to relieve oneself. I was issued the newer trousers, with zipper fly and side slanted pockets. All of us were truly surprised to find that bell-bottom trousers were *not* authorized! Neither were uniforms tailored to fit the body, and there were no side zippers on jumpers. Tailored uniforms went by way of "the old Navy"; trousers of the (then) modern Navy had pillared pant legs, which were the same circumference, the same diameter, from the crotch to the bottom of the trousers. I was lucky in that one of the men who didn't care about style swapped his thirteen-button-style trousers for mine.

19

Patch-pocket Seafarer-style dungarees were also in high demand, whereas the side-pocket-style dungarees were considered to be something less than seaman-like. I was destined to wear the side pocket style until I could afford to buy Seafarers quite some time later.

Marching was not difficult, although occasionally I would find myself out of step. It was the march commands that caused the most confusion. Everyone, at one time or another, whether we were actually on the march or standing in place, simply forgot which way was right and which way was left. Giggling at someone's failure to turn or face the ordered direction was never dealt with lightly by the chief. He simply blamed everyone for such stupidity and threatened to stencil RIGHT and LEFT where we would be constantly reminded of those directions in the future.

Several classmates were proficient at calling cadence and did so at every marching opportunity. We all "harmonized" the simple yet effective words that assisted us in keeping in step. The closer we were to another marching group, the louder we would get. The words to each tailored verse were simple:

"Oh, I know a gal who lives on a hill;
She won't do it, but her sister will.
Sound off, ONE, TWO,
Sound off, THREE, FOUR.
Cadence count ONE, TWO, THREE, FOUR,
ONE, TWO — THREE FOUR!

"Your boots are shiny; your leggings are tight;
Your balls are swinging from LEFT to RIGHT.
Sound off, ONE, TWO,
Sound off, THREE, FOUR.
Cadence count ONE, TWO, THREE, FOUR,
ONE, TWO — THREE FOUR!

"Oh, I don't know, but I've been told
That Eskimo pussy is icy cold.
Sound off, ONE, TWO,
[and so on]."

Even the chief allowed us a little fun with cadence calling. He would go so far as to encourage it as long as it kept us in step.

One of the most important things we all had to learn was how to live and get along with others in a military organization. Life and living conditions in the Navy differed greatly from anything any of us had known in civilian life. Learning to live together in close quarters as members of a military unit was one of the major missions of recruit training. It was next to impossible finding the time or the place where one could relax with any reasonable or expected privacy.

What an experience it was learning how to fold clothes the Navy way. Nothing had a top or a bottom. Each garment did, however, have a "pussy," and the pussy always had to be in a certain position! We folded, refolded, and re-refolded each garment until all of the pussies met with the chief's personal approval. We joked about the size of some of the pussies. Chief Sellers taught us that the pussy must always be kept as clean and as tight as possible — that large dirty pussies were not only sloppy and undesirable; they were absolutely unacceptable! We quite readily agreed with the chief.

We had all undergone somewhat of a preliminary physical examination before our induction, but we were told that we were also expected to undergo a far more comprehensive exam. Sometime during that first day or two, after once again being required to strip, we were marched barefoot from one phase of physical examination to a multitude of others. I was embarrassed having to bend over and spread my "cheeks." During my youth I had never experienced an examination for hemorrhoids or a hernia, nor had my prostate checked. I didn't even know what the doctors were looking for, yet they probed deep within each and every crevice, feeling the most sensitive and private parts of our bodies, while explanations of any kind were never offered. We did as we were told without hesitation, without exception, and without question. The humiliation would not have been so apparent had it not been aggravated by the fact that there was absolutely no privacy. We were just a lot of young men standing in several lines, each in full view of one another. We were all "privileged" to view each phase of processing to which those ahead of us were subjected. That didn't make it any easier, knowing what to expect when it came our turn.

21

The physical would not be complete without the accompanying dental exam. I was fortunate in that my teeth were in excellent condition. Unfortunately, such was not the case for a good percentage of other recruits. Those with dental needs had to return for additional work, sometimes several times over a period of days or weeks for more fillings, tooth extractions, or other dental needs. Regardless of whatever discomfort they might have felt following those appointments, they were not excluded from other processing requirements. They simply had to press on that much harder to make sure that they did not fall behind. To fall behind usually meant a transfer into another boot camp company and having to repeat portions of training. Late graduates were therefore delayed in reaching their final destination in the "real" Navy, something everyone wanted to avoid if at all possible.

I do not recall exactly how the group was divided into different boot camp companies. I was disappointed because Gary was the only one of the original four that was placed in another company. At every opportunity Richard, Al, and I teasingly accused or in some manner insinuated that only those individuals found to be illiterate or dysfunctional beyond acceptable limitations were placed in "that" company; that company being reserved for "slow learners."

It became apparent that the overwhelming majority of recruits within our group were less educated and of questionable integrity. They were, without a doubt, the meanest-looking bunch I had ever been in such close contact with. For the most part, they were older and their long hair, visible scars, and challenging expressions were enough to tell me that I had better be very careful. I learned that most of that remarkably rugged-looking group was from East Los Angeles, and it was a reasonable assumption that they were more than likely well experienced in street fighting. As a youngster I was cautioned frequently by my parents not to associate with such individuals. Yet there I was, knowing that the situation I was in would require that I consider everyone around me as more than casual acquaintances. We would all be learning together, marching together, eating, drinking, and in essence, sleeping together.

Rapidly, with extraordinary haste, everything that we were being confronted with or exposed to in the course of our processing and training became unpredictably jumbled up and extremely confusing. No sooner would one aspect of processing near completion than another would begin. I was amazed at the ability and relative ease a small handful of the group showed as they rapidly became fully acclimated to most of the new experiences with which they were confronted. Their acceptance of military rule, familiarity with their surroundings, and knowledge of the military structure in general made me feel much more inferior and insecure. I wondered why I was having what I perceived to be exceptional difficulty where others adapted with such ease. Since I was not raised within or around a military environment, I failed to consider the very real possibility that those few who appeared so exceptional just might have been military dependents. In fact, I later found that to be the case. They were, therefore, already well conditioned to an environment I found to be quite foreign.

We all spoke English, though there were some who spoke with unique accents. But everyone understood one particular word, a word that provided instant emphasis to whatever the subject might have been at the time. The use of the word *fuck*, or a variation thereof, was the chief's primary means of motivating us.

"What the fuck do you think you are doing?"; "Just who the fuck do you think you are?"; and "Don't you know what goddamn fuckin' attention means?" were all common questions that I found impossible to answer to the chief's satisfaction. Getting caught daydreaming brought on a real deluge of even more impressive four-letter words, for some of which I later found new meaning.

The word *fuck*, not foreign to my vocabulary since I was a youngster, was, as far as I was concerned, used far too frequently by my peers as well as by the chief. It was always used as a means of emphasizing or expressing absolute, unquestionable authority. Quite remarkably, sometimes the word was used three or more times within a single sentence.

Being constantly deluged with so many four-letter words couldn't help but rub off on those of us hearing them. Most of us became accustomed to speaking in a manner similar to that which we were most often subjected, in terms of four-letter words that for some strange reason began to make more sense out of an otherwise lackluster conversation. The failure to use at least occasional four-letter words was actually looked upon as a sign of weakness. It didn't take me long to realize that showing any signs of weakness was dealt with immediately and severely, not just by our instructors, but also by our peers. I had to show my strength in words, as I lacked the more desirable physical attributes others were "blessed" with. I felt that I had to make the best of my ability to swear, as my skinny, underdeveloped body and baby face features seemed to invite unnecessary harassment by bullies.

The part of processing that each of us hated equally was that first haircut. That was the real turning point for the "birds of a feather" friendships that had been developing. The Los Angeles crowd was one group that consistently fought anyone and everyone, and there was the all-other group. The haircut requirement was almost "miracle"-inducing. The roughest, toughest, meanest of them all became like the biblical Samson without their hair. Instantly changes in personalities became apparent; egos were shattered and quickly far more acceptable human beings evolved.

The reluctance I previously felt at developing additional friendships began to dissipate. Other than the fact that most of them were much huskier or taller than I was, I found that there were few other noticeable or significant differences. The selective gang-oriented relationships rapidly became a thing of the past. The group, the entire company, became a family that worked together and stood up for one another. God have mercy on anyone from another company that ventured forth in even the slightest effort to create a problem with someone from our company. (We, on the other hand, felt that it was all right for us to cause problems with the "boots" in other companies.) I surprised myself when I realized that not only had I been accepted by those individuals who had, just days before having their hair cut appeared totally ruthless, but I had also willingly accepted them as my trusted friends.

Religious preference was not addressed other than the fact that all recruits were required to attend services of one denomination or another. Gary, Richard, Al, and I were faced with a unique situation. Even though we had been friends through grade, junior high, and high school, we had never questioned or discussed our own religious beliefs. None of us were enthusiastic about attending services, especially since we were then faced with the realization that each of us was of a different faith! Al was Jewish, Gary was Catholic, Richard was a Christian Scientist, and I was Methodist.

Our decision was in total agreement and was practically instantaneous. Together, as the team we had entered the Navy, we agreed that we would attend a different service each Sunday, thereby not only retaining our close friendships, but in doing so also becoming more educated and more familiar with each other's religious upbringing and beliefs. That practice not only tightened the already tight bond of friendship we had enjoyed for years; it instilled within each of us a mutual respect for each others' religion. We actually poked fun at different aspects of each service we attended, always standing firm on our individual convictions. We found humor in the question: "Which God are we going to see this Sunday?" instead of "Which church?"

Any time there are groups of relatively confined individuals there are bound to be times when tempers flare. So it was within Company 046, the company to which I was assigned. The term *smoker*, new to my vocabulary, took the place of *fight*. When two individuals elected to fight out their differences, someone would shout, "Smoker!" The result was very similar to hearing someone shout "Fire!" except that instead of causing the area to be evacuated, it encouraged observer participation.

More often than not smokers took place in the "head," the restroom. We enjoyed watching the fights, though few of us ever wanted to be actual participants. It was a type of recreation that provided brief opportunities for us to transfer our thoughts and energy away from our prison-like environment. I can't help believing that the change of pace, regardless of the cause, was good for most of us. No one ever suffered serious injuries. I found it strange how such activities cemented friendships that would not have otherwise been possible between rivals.

It had never entered my mind that I would be responsible for washing my own clothes — and *only* in the manner prescribed: by hand. Every evening we were required to wash each piece of clothing we had worn that day. We hauled water by bucket from spigots a short distance away from the clothes wash area. There, at specially constructed cement platforms, we used "kayak" brushes, heavy-duty fiber brushes, to scrub our clothing inside and out. Then using clothes stops or tie-ties, short shoestring-like strands of woven cotton, we attached each garment to clotheslines. Depending on weather conditions, we could usually count on all of our freshly washed garments to be dry "enough" within twenty-four hours. In the event of rain or heavy fog we were given a little slack and did not have to remove the clothing from the clothesline the day after washing it.

Some of the guys tried to beat the "must wash" system by wearing the same clothing more than one day. Inevitably that ended in failure because inspections were held twice daily; once in the morning while we were wearing dungarees and once in the afternoon while wearing "blues" or "whites." The inspecting officer was always Chief Sellers and it was extremely rare that any discrepancy, whether clothing being soiled, improperly creased, or out of place, escaped his eye.

In what we considered emergency situations we were quite successful covering small smudges or stains with chalk. Chalk, incidentally, was considered contraband. It was absolutely forbidden for recruits to have *anything* that had not been properly issued. Therefore, not only was chalk unauthorized, if a recruit was found in possession of it, he was under threat of being charged with having "misappropriated government property." The threat of being charged for any offense, particularly misappropriation, carried with it a high probability that the offender would suffer some kind of severe penalty as prescribed within the Uniform Code of Military Justice (UCMJ). There was no penalty for doing something wrong — the only penalties issued or carried out were for getting caught! With that, there were some chances that we thought we had to take in order to successfully complete boot camp.

As I think back, it becomes obvious that our ingenuity was expected, silently encouraged, and more likely than not it was admired. Most assuredly we had actually been taught how to improvise should the need present itself once we became a permanent part of the fleet. The tools or devices we used to improvise with, such as chalk, we easily obtained by being alert to our surroundings and cautious in our manner of approach.

"Captain's Mast," nonjudicial punishment, was handled by our Company Commander, Chief Sellers. That meant one or another type of extra duty, usually night marches (with M-1 rifle) or extra guard duty. At the time we thought of all offenses as serious; however, in reality there was not, to my knowledge, a single recruit in Company 046 that was either charged with or convicted of a truly serious offense. Minor infractions were few and far between and were dealt with fairly.

The routine began to take on a reasonable semblance of order after about three weeks. Reveille sounded at 0500 — "ZERO FIVE HUNDRED," *not* "5:00 AM" as a civilian would say. There would no longer be an AM or a PM. We learned something we already knew but didn't really know how to routinely express. The twenty-four-hour day was, in fact, a twenty-four day, and we would express the time as it really was. Thus 1:00 AM became the first hour of the day and was known as 0100 hours; 1:00 PM became the thirteenth hour, therefore 1300 hours; 2:00 PM became 1400 hours; and so on. Strange that it was difficult to grasp at the time yet made so much sense. Military time could leave no margin for error.

Zero Five Hundred (hours) came early! It always seemed to be, and sometimes actually was, just minutes after going to bed. There were no exceptions to reveille. Everyone had to get up and go through the morning ritual of what was commonly known as the four S's. "Shit, shower, shampoo, and shave."

Next we made up our bunks and assembled outside with no time to spare. We then marched to the mess hall, where all companies seemed to arrive simultaneously, each trying to wedge its way in front of others as we were being lined up for breakfast. The idea was to get there early, to allow time for a brief break after breakfast — however that never seemed to work out. Nothing took place without first forming one or more lines. The routine was nearly always the same. We would hurry up and then wait, hurry up and wait.

I complained about the food along with everyone else, but we all knew that the food was actually quite good. Whoever complained the loudest was probably eating more than the rest of us.

No one, to my knowledge, ever skipped a meal. It would have been near impossible to skip a meal since we were all required to march to the mess hall as a group and we were required to assemble as a group after each meal at the mess hall.

Regardless of the amount we ate at one sitting, we were always hungry when the next meal came around. I immediately began gaining weight. Not flab, but honest-to-goodness well-formed muscle. I began to have hopes of losing my skinny frame before graduation.

Following breakfast, while assembled, we were given our daily orders. We followed specific routines for each day of the week. Usually calisthenics followed breakfast, sometimes with, sometimes without our rifles. Then we marched wherever we were told, always with rifle in hand. Following an hour or two of vigorous marching and rifle calisthenics we reported to our first class of the day.

Each of us had our own issue of *The Blue Jacket's Manual* (the BJM, as it became known to us), our primary learning tool. There were many other training aids but we were consistently taught to use and live by the BJM. It contained the basics by which we were all required to govern our lives.

Navy terminology, ship identification, differences and similarities in terms such as *bow line* (the forwardmost line at the bow of a ship) and *bowline* (a form of knot). We learned how to identify the wide variety of insignias and devices that were worn on the collars, shoulders, and sleeves of Navy personnel and of the rating structure that differentiated "rate" (a Navy enlisted person's pay grade) from "rating" (a specialty within a rate) and "rank" (an officer's pay grade). There were variations of command ceremonies, shipboard telephone talking procedures, and navigation to learn, and the difference between Officers' Country (their staterooms and the wardroom), CPO Country (chiefs' living spaces and their mess hall), and enlisted berthing compartments. There were eye-opener classes on the prevention, reporting of, and care for different diseases — VD in particular. There were classes on safety devices, safety precautions, safety valves, safety this and safety that, and rules of good seamanship, and on and on ... but always with extreme emphasis on remaining alert while standing "watch." Shipboard compartmentation, a numbering and lettering system that was designed to give each compartment an "address," was confusing. Once understood, it provided an easy-to-follow system of finding any designated compartment. For example, on ships built prior to 1949, C-217-A identified a compartment in the C, or after, part of the ship, on the second deck below the main deck, starboard side, which is used for supply and storage. Ships built after 1949 have a similar system that contains the deck number, frame number, relation to centerline of the ship, and the use of the compartment.

To facilitate more practical demonstrations of many subjects the USS *Recruit*, appropriately nicknamed the *Neversail*, an almost-full-scale model of a destroyer escort, was constructed on the base for use by all recruits. On board this land-locked ship practical exercises were held in many shipboard functions, including stationing personnel for getting underway and for anchoring, the handling of mooring lines, compartmentation, and the manning of watch and battle stations.

It was difficult staying alert during class sessions, especially following rigorous field training. The problem was not always apparent to us, but our tired bodies sometimes mistook "sit and learn" time as "relax and doze" time. More than one time I found myself standing at the back of the classroom holding my rifle high above my head with both hands — one form of punishment instructors issued when one was known to be anything less than totally alert. No one ever went to sleep in that position.

We learned that walls were "bulkheads," that there were no stairs on a ship, only ladders; an overhead, not a ceiling; a deck, not a floor. There was a bow and a stern, and one was topside or below-decks (or down below). We learned the differences between "chocks," "cleats," and "bollards." We learned about "boat davits" and the difference between a "hatch" and a "scuttle." There were so many new terms added to my vocabulary I couldn't help but become somewhat confused at times.

We attended classes on military chain of command and on the rating structure. I think those classes were the most difficult for me to grasp. I even had some problems differentiating between officers (commissioned by Congress) and enlisted personnel. Being told there were two specific titles for addressing each of seven different enlisted rates and yet another ten specific titles for each of the line officer grades was scary at best. I found it nearly impossible to remember the differences between officer specialty collar devices. I couldn't distinguish a chaplain from a doctor, a supply officer from a warrant officer. I was absolutely lost. My buddies would try to help me only to laugh at my ignorance at identifying military ranks and specialty fields. I did eventually learn, but it took far greater effort than I ever exerted toward any subject matter during my school years in civilian life.

There were classes on knot tying, military etiquette, ship silhouette and aircraft identification, and damage control. We practiced fighting actual fires, and we had to prove that we could swim — or at least remain afloat for a specified period of time. We learned the right and wrong way to salute, when and where to salute, and why a salute was or was not required. We learned how to challenge the approach of an unidentified person and how we were to conduct ourselves should we become prisoners of war.

We became familiar with naval history, the names of Paul Jones, Preble, Decatur, Farragut, Nimitz, Halsey, and other naval heroes in whose honor the camps, buildings, and streets of the training center were named. The single phase of training that really grabbed my attention the most, and woke me up to the realization that I might someday need to rely upon skills or knowledge acquired during boot camp training, was the tear gas experience.

Groups of about fifteen at a time assembled inside a cemented "gas chamber" and were told to "don gas masks." After a few minutes of listening to Chief Sellers ramble on about nothing significant (during which time, and without our knowledge, the chamber was being filled with tear gas), he told us to remove our masks and *walk* to the exit hatch. It was like being hit with a sledgehammer right between the eyes as we experienced tear gas for the first time. I found myself, as were others around me, flailing my arms ridiculously in front of me, trying to push the invisible cause of my pain and choking away from me.

Another most important and memorable phase of training was the day at the Firefighting Center where we learned the chemistry of fire and the basic principles of combating it. Under the watchful supervision of trained firefighters we put out serious fires under simulated shipboard conditions as we gained valuable experience in the proper use of the OBA (Oxygen Breathing Apparatus).

Weekly we marched to the barbershop whether we needed haircuts or not. After two weeks we realized that haircuts also meant inoculations. First the haircut, then straight to the "dispensary" for shots. Sometimes we would get up to three shots at one time. The cholera shot always caused the most pain. It was almost comical watching as shots were being given, because there was just enough time after the injection for one to get his jumper about halfway on before the gripping pain started. There was no way out of getting shots, absolutely no exceptions. I was very concerned because I knew that I was highly allergic to tetanus vaccine. I had been warned frequently by my parents that I had almost died from a tetanus shot, and that another shot of the same would more than likely kill me. Each time we lined up for inoculations I asked what kind of shots we were getting — only to be told to "Shut up and quit complaining." I was more than concerned, more aptly I was downright scared — but my fear didn't slow down the process. I took my shots right along with everyone else. Quite some time later I was told that all recruits with known sensitivities to drugs, including allergic reactions, had been identified as part of their induction processing and that necessary precautions had been taken accordingly. I shall always believe it was wrong and unnecessary to intentionally cause those recruits known as being susceptible to allergic reactions to suffer such anxieties, particularly where the consequence of a simple mistake could have resulted in a death.

As for the square needle: well, it wasn't really square after all, but in any and every description I may have given of it, or may give of it in the future, it will always be perfectly square and every bit as uncomfortable as one might imagine.

Attending Sunday church services was one of those mandatory things I never quite understood, unless it was just one more means of conditioning us to accept and follow orders. We could attend the chapel of our choice — but there was to be no lying around the barracks (or anywhere else) during services. On one occasion Gary, Richard, Al and I made the daring decision to "cut" church services. We'd been good little boot campers and were deserving of some kind of a break. So one particular Sunday we intentionally violated one of the rules and spent the hour and a half, that was supposed to be for God, out of site in hiding. Later that same day a lot of boot camp companies were directed (via public address system) to report to one of the grinders "for an immediate briefing." There was a lot of guesswork as to the reason(s) for the briefing. Most of us believed it was because there had been a lot of recent unrest brought about by Communist factions participating in boundary disputes, sometimes pushing their differences to warlike skirmishes where neighboring governments were in disagreement. The general consensus made a great deal of sense; we were being called together to be updated on the United States' policies as related to international unrest — and of course we would have our boot camp training shortened to the degree we would probably all be immediately dispatched to support and defend our country. We were going to war!

When all of the companies were properly assembled, the Base Commander stepped forward and took the microphone in hand. He had a very somber look about him, and it was obvious that the news was not going to be good. After a few tense moments had passed, during which this high-ranking officer scanned each and every one of us, he cleared his throat and spoke. His remarkably clear voice, intensely amplified, immediately grabbed our attention.

"It has come to my attention that some of you have decided not to attend church services as ordered. My staff has collected the names of those of you who did not attend services today."

My mind went numb and I could feel my body shaking for fear of whatever consequences I was soon to suffer.

Damn, why can't there be a war or some kind of disaster instead of this? I thought.

"Those of you who skipped services will take two steps forward and stand fast," the Base Commander continued.

I looked at Richard, hoping for some sort of sign not to worry, but instead saw something of a mirrored frightened image of myself.

Shit, he's just as scared as I am, I thought to myself.

The decision to step forward or not had to be an individual one. Stepping forward meant admitting a blatant violation of orders — and there was always the possibility that I (or we) just might have gotten away with it. We all knew, or at least we had been taught and had reason to believe, that admitting our guilt also meant quick and potentially severe punishment, a black mark that would probably follow us throughout each of our enlistments.

My reluctant but firm decision was to remain where I was, to stand tall and look as honest (and churchgoing) as possible. About a dozen recruits very sheepishly took those two steps forward and were looked upon with outrage and disgust by everyone around them. Al was one of those that stepped forward. I couldn't see Gary so I didn't know what action he had taken.

All of the Company Commanders then took the names of the admitted guilty and promptly delivered them to the Base Commander. After a brief but deliberate comparison between the names of those who had stepped forward and the names he already had, the Base Commander again cleared his throat and read the names of those who had stepped forward. He then, much to my disbelief and disappointment, said, "The individuals whose names I have just read [long pause] will become fine sailors and can consider themselves men for having the courage to step forward."

I don't think I ever felt more uncomfortable in my life. The obvious insinuation was that those of us who had not stepped forward were less than men and our futures were questionable at best.

"I shall now read," the Base Commander continued, "the names of those of you who not only disregarded your orders, but are also something less than honest individuals. Company Commanders will conduct Captain's Mast and award appropriate punishment to the following individuals in accordance with the Uniform Code of Military Justice."

I hated myself! Why couldn't I have been a man and step forward? And there was Al, for God's sake, standing proud as a peacock. I envied Al for that. He had "balls," I didn't. Then came the names. As each name was called I knew that mine, Richard's or possibly Gary's would be next. Our names were never called, but we suffered just as badly as if they had been. None of us ever missed religious services again.

Mail call was something we all lived for. Receiving letters from loved ones and friends really helped to keep our spirits up. A few of the guys did receive infamous "Dear John" letters, but mostly letters were full of love and concern for our well being. Finding the time to respond to those letters was sometimes difficult. There were so many duties that kept us busy. We had to practice our knot tying; we had to study the contents of the BJM and practice the "sixteen-count manual of arms" with our M-1 rifles. And we had to memorize all of the "General Orders," the set of eleven basic orders that were devised as constant reminders to members of all branches of military service that we were always to perform our duties responsibly and professionally.

At various times, and usually when least expected, we were confronted by one instructor or another with, "Tell me General Order Number Four," or any other number that came to their mind. Even though there were only eleven General Orders, occasionally the question, "What is General Order Number Twelve?" was asked. The response had to be immediate and unfaltering: "To make damn sure we know the other eleven, sir!"

Legally the term *sir* only applied when addressing an officer, however we were required to treat all instructors as officers as long as we were in training. That made nearly everyone we came in contact with equally deserving of the "sir" recognition.

General Order would remain the primary rules that would govern our basic military duties throughout our enlistments; for me that would come to mean over twenty years.

Returning to mail call for a moment, as it truly was one of the few daily occasions to which we all looked forward. At one time or another each of us had significant news from home that we enjoyed sharing even though very little of that news was equally interesting to those with whom we shared it. We didn't care if someone's neighbor had the flu or if Cousin Jane ran off with someone from a neighboring town. But we did care when something we could all relate to was shared. Such was the case when somewhere near the halfway point of boot camp one member of our company received his draft notice. At first he showed concern that he might be in some kind of trouble because he could not report for induction into the Army as ordered by the President of the United States. After a little thought, and some prompting by several boot camp "sea lawyers" (those who always knew more than anyone else), he tore the notice up and said, "Fuck 'em. I hope they think I'm a draft dodger. I hope the FBI spends the next four years searching the globe for me." We could all laugh at the FBI search, but the thought of having beaten the Army draft system was good news. It was something we had all done — with or without an official notice of induction.

We all waited impatiently for the sixth week to arrive knowing that each of us had earned a single day of "liberty." It was commonly referred to as "Cinderella liberty" because we had to be back in our barracks no later than 2400 hours that same day. Since I had informed my parents of the occasion, they opted to drive some three hundred miles to meet me at the training center and spend the day with me. I asked several of my friends if they would like to accompany me, however they had to stand "duty" or they had other plans. I managed to get in touch with Gary and he agreed to spend that day with me. My parents, in turn, invited his mother to accompany them to San Diego.

Gary and I prepared for their visit with far greater care than we had ever prepared for any inspection. We wanted to look our exceptional best, extremely proud of the fact that we were in the military service. This was our first real opportunity to show off our "service dress blues." We wore our whitest of white hats, our glossiest spit-shined shoes, and our lint-free, absolutely spotless dress blues. With our shoulders pulled back, chests high, we didn't walk but rather proudly strutted directly to the visitor's area where we knew our parents would be waiting.

Our parents approved of our obvious physical changes, and soon they realized that our attitudes had also matured noticeably. We were no longer the same schoolchildren that up until six weeks prior had relied almost entirely on their guidance. We were governed by and fully accepted a completely different set of rules and regulations that in reality would have lifelong effects on our lives and the lives of just about everyone with whom we would ever come in contact.

Our knowledge of the real Navy, the Navy beyond the gates of boot camp, was practically nonexistent, yet we described "our" Navy like we had been born and raised by it. We had barely experienced six weeks of recruit training, but we thought we knew just about all there was to know. How very wrong we were.

Gary and I enjoyed our first off-base experience as active duty sailors by sharing a picnic lunch and walking through the magnificent Balboa Park Zoo. We talked about the more interesting phases of our training, special occurrences or experiences, and some of our expectations. It was an enjoyable outing that ended all too quickly. After we said our farewells at the main gate, it was back to the military routine for us.

We had to walk or march everywhere. Walking alongside someone required marching in step with one another. Only those of us attending boot camp were required to abide by this "rule"; graduates had their choice of keeping in step or not. Since it was rare that a recruit went anywhere alone, we all got plenty of practice marching.

On our way back to our respective barracks, Gary and I walked across the many grinders and talked about our day of liberty. Understandably, recruits were not authorized the privilege of having an automobile on the base — so as Gary and I marched toward the barracks area we had to respond to one recruit's challenge after another. Each company had its own barracks and at least two recruits on guard duty outside. Recruits guarded dumpsters, walkways, grassy areas, and anything else the Company Commander required. It didn't matter that one guard was sometimes within whispering distance of another; each carried out his duty and challenged Gary and me as we approached, "Halt. Who goes there?" followed by: "Advance to be recognized."

We heard the same challenge time after time; each time having to identify ourselves and prove our authority to be there. Proper identification consisted of announcing our names and showing our ID card and liberty card. It took close to an hour to walk about four blocks. Gary was more fortunate than I because he arrived at his barracks first.

That six-week point was valued for another important reason. Prior to that point in time recruits were not allowed to enter the Navy Exchange, or the "Gedunk." We finally had earned the privilege of purchasing some items, like candy and cigarettes, but only in limited quantities. Those privileges had been earned but could easily be revoked if not protected. That meant we had to make sure there were no, or at least an absolute minimum number of, discrepancies found during all future inspections.

Chief Sellers was a good Company Commander. He looked after us and tried his best to teach us well. But his good side was not to be tampered with, nor was he one easily taken advantage of. He was never reluctant to issue swift punishment whenever someone violated the rules.

On one occasion Chief Sellers caught the daytime guard smoking while on duty. To a recruit, that was considered a fairly serious offense. Nicknamed because of his size, Moose had to stand up on the clothes wash platform, light up a full pack of twenty cigarettes, and smoke them all at the same time. The punishment was that he had to do that with a washbucket over his head! As a reminder to the rest of us that violations would not be tolerated, we were all required to witness the punishment as Moose gagged to the point of throwing up. The chief told Moose in no uncertain terms that should he repeat the offense, he would find himself eating the cigarettes after smoking them to stubs. Chief Sellers *always* carried out his threats — and we actually admired him for it. When we did well, treatment was good. When we did not do well, we were punished accordingly.

The final six weeks passed quickly. Classroom time became shorter and our time spent out on the grinder became longer. We were being thoroughly acclimated to the strenuous routine we would be subjected to during graduation ceremonies. It was not unusual to see recruits pass out from overexertion while involved in routine as well as more strenuous physical exercise.

As boot camp neared an end, our hair once again became an important factor, at least in our own eyes. It was humorous watching as we all tried desperately to train whatever growth we had accumulated since that first "scalping." We did not think of it as fair when some of the guys' hair grew at an amazing rate while others' hardly grew at all. Regardless of the amount of hair on our heads, it was somewhat comforting to know that the friendships that had developed during those weeks of close confinement would remain intact. It was an interesting phenomenon, how the length of one's hair had at one time played such a role: Those with the longest hair had the worst attitudes and were to be feared. They could be counted on as the meanest and the strongest — their hair made them that way. Had it not been for that first close cropping we were all subjected to, very few friendships would have developed. We had become a very tight group of close friends, never dreaming that after graduation our chances of being stationed together or even seeing each other again were practically nil.

Graduation Exercises

Graduation day came about without any significant problems. Many parents were there to witness the graduation exercises. It was a hot day and as expected the usual number of recruits passed out from overexertion.

Immediately following the exercises we marched back to our barracks where we eagerly awaited the issuance of our "orders." As the result of various interviews, aptitude tests, and individual backgrounds, we had been recommended individually for specific assignments. I had been recommended, in writing, and I was absolutely sure that I would receive orders to attend Aviation Machinist School at Norman, Oklahoma.

Orders were issued to each of us. A couple of the men were shocked and disappointed upon receipt of orders that would keep them right there, at San Diego Naval Training Center, not as recruits but as staff members, supposedly an honor but in fact a nightmare. No one wanted to stay there! Equally despised, a couple of men were ordered to naval air stations right in or near their hometowns, precisely from where they were trying to get away!

Richard and Al graduated as Seaman Apprentices and received orders to attend technical schools.

Gary graduated as Fireman Apprentice and received orders to a destroyer stationed at San Diego.

I also graduated as a Fireman Apprentice and received orders to a destroyer that was somewhere in the Far East on operations with the Seventh Fleet. Aviation Machinist School was not to be my assignment as "planned."

3

UNDERWAY

My first set of official orders was confusing. I was directed to report to Treasure Island Naval Shipyard, California "FFT" (For Further Transfer). FFT meant that my ship was somewhere else — more than likely on the opposite side of the Pacific Ocean as a part of the Pacific Fleet.

So what is a fleet?

Rudy C. Garcia, Chief Journalist, provided an excellent description in the April 1957 issue of *All Hands, The Bureau of Naval Personnel Information Bulletin*. The following is extracted from that article:

Everybody talks about it: "The power of the Fleet. He's a Fleet Sailor. Fleet shore duty." You read about it in newspapers, magazines and other periodicals. But what does everybody mean by "Fleet?"

The "fleet," according to one definition in *Webster's New International Dictionary*, is "a number of war vessels under a single chief command; also, the collective naval forces of a country."

Here's what it means so far as you and we are concerned. Let's start at the very top. The U.S. Fleet is the Operating Forces of the U.S. Navy. The Fleet, in both the Atlantic and Pacific, forms the naval power of the U.S. and it is the sole reason for the existence of the rest of the United States Navy.

The major Fleet commands in the U.S. Fleet are the Pacific Fleet, the Atlantic Fleet, the Naval Forces, Eastern Atlantic and Mediterranean. The Pacific Fleet includes the Seventh Fleet, the First Task Fleet, the Naval Forces Western Pacific and sea frontiers and the area support commands.

The Atlantic Fleet includes the Second Task Fleet, the Operational Development Force and sea frontiers and base support commands. The

Operational Development Force tests and evaluates new weapons and equipment for service use.

For operating purposes, a Fleet may be divided into a number of Task Commands. For administrative purposes, such as transfer of enlisted men, the various types of ships that go into making a Fleet are grouped according to type. Destroyers are under Commander Cruisers and Destroyers Pacific (ComCruDesPac) or Commander Cruisers and Destroyers Atlantic (ComCruDesLant). Take a ship under ComCruDesPac for example. When the ship from this type command joins the Seventh Fleet, in the Far East, it is under the operational control of ComSeventh Fleet. Yet that same ship and its crew remains under the administrative control of ComCruDesPac.

Because of the many varied jobs that may be assigned to a Fleet, it is often necessary to subdivide them into Task Forces, composed of several types of ships, depending upon the job the force is to perform. This task force may include aircraft carriers, battleships, cruisers, amphibious craft and auxiliary vessels such as tenders, oilers and supply ships.

When a Fleet is large enough and its duties are extensive enough to require division into many task forces, it is usual to form the forces into Task Groups. Task groups are of a more temporary nature than task forces and are usually dissolved after each particular assignment.

Task groups are assigned numbers according to the particular force of which they are a part. For example, Task Force 72 may have a task group assigned to a special mission and its designated number may be Task Group 72.3 Task groups may be further subdivided into task units and task elements. Take TU 72.3.1. Spelled out, this means Task Unit 1 of Task Group 3 of Task Force 2 of the Seventh Fleet.

Then there are type commanders, divisions and squadrons. The very basic unit of vessels by type is the division, and quite frequently two divisions are joined to form a squadron. The term "squadron" may also be applied to an organization of minor strength, whose commander operates under "detached" orders or directly under the instructions or orders of the Chief of Naval Operations.

There are also two other Fleets which you hear a lot about and which are also components of the operating forces. These are the Atlantic and Pacific Reserve Fleets. Known as the "Mothball Fleets," these ships provide a great reservoir of ships ready to be put into active service on short notice.

Another Fleet in the U.S. Navy, which is also a part of the operating Forces, is the Military Sea Transport Service (MSTS). This Fleet, which is the largest ocean shipping organization in the world, transports personnel and cargo of the Department of Defense. [At this time there were 265 ships, including escort aircraft carriers, cargo ships, passenger ships, and tankers.]

There, basically, are the U.S. "Fleets" as they were in the mid-1950s.

I reported to the OOD (Officer of the Day) at Treasure Island as ordered and was told that as soon as transportation was available I would be on my way to the Orient. While waiting for that transportation I was required to "muster" (report to a designated location) several times each day, when and where I was assigned a variety of duties. I found that Navy terminology prevailed everywhere. I swabbed, laid wax, and buffed the barracks deck. I scrubbed bulkheads and cleaned in and around the barracks head. I was surprised to find that taps and reveille were strictly enforced. I was wrong (as usual) in thinking that those rules were strictly for boot camp.

Quickly I became acutely aware of the distinction, the policies of separation that were designed to keep officers and enlisted personnel in their own rightful and respective places. There was an "officers' head" and an "enlisted head," as if one or the other of us did our bodily functions uniquely different. There was an "officers' pool" and an "enlisted pool"; apparently we swam differently too. There was an area known as "Officers' Country," where the grass was greener and enlisted personnel dared not traverse. Later I would find that the boundaries were also enforced at military beaches, where the signs clearly spelled out: OFFICERS ONLY or ENLISTED AREA. Notice AREA instead of ONLY when referencing the "lowly" enlisted member. In time I would find that wherever such rules could be invoked, they would be.

After several days of thinking I had been permanently sidetracked, I found my name posted on a flight roster; destination Barbers Point, Hawaii, FFT. I was excited at the thought that I might spend several days in Hawaii waiting for another flight to "somewhere" in the Orient.

A group of us, those destined for Hawaii or farther west, boarded a small twin-prop cargo plane that was primarily utilized for carrying mail. We were seated in hanging strap-like seats, backs to the bulkhead. The center of the airplane was stacked with mailbags; everything was strapped down securely with heavy-duty cargo netting. To my recollection I had never been more uncomfortable.

The (approximate) eleven-hour flight to Hawaii was terrible. The constant roar of the engines was deafening. Cramping at least, extreme discomfort at best, was experienced by everyone other than the crew. Periodically, during times of severe turbulence, I truly feared for my life. The thought crossed my mind how unfair it would be to die in an airplane crash as a sailor, never having served on a ship.

The sun had not yet risen, but it was already very hot and humid when we landed at Barbers Point, Hawaii. The silhouetted palm trees were absolutely beautiful against the dawn sky. I was really impressed, totally enthralled, as nature's first rays of sunlight revealed the beauty of my surroundings. I had heard of Hawaii and had read articles about the island paradise. I'd seen pictures of Waikiki Beach, but I had never dreamed I would ever be there actually experiencing it for myself.

I had not slept during the long flight, but the excitement of being on a tropical island, in a true paradise, overrode any exhaustion I might have otherwise felt. The thought of swimming at Waikiki Beach and the possibility of meeting a young Hawaiian beauty during my stay created an additional, newly acquired excitement. I wanted to perform my assigned duties quickly in hopes that upon completion I would be able to venture beyond the main gate and do all that I could do in whatever time I was allowed.

Another short-lived daydream! Those of us that had not reached our final destination were told not to leave the flight line. Our next flight was scheduled to depart within several hours. What a disappointment. On the brighter side was the fact that the flight-line Gedunk was open twenty-four hours daily, so we had a place to sit and snacks to munch on. Those two benefits did help relieve our hunger pains, and the time appeared to pass more quickly.

I had thought Hawaii was hot and humid, but on April 22, when I reached my final (flight) destination and disembarked the aircraft somewhere in the Philippines, I learned the true meaning of hot and humid. It was like stepping into an oven — indeed, it was actually difficult breathing. The requirement that I wear full dress blues while in transit made the discomfort that much worse. My uniform rapidly became soaked with perspiration.

I was one of a small group that was then transported by bus to the Sangley Point Receiving Barracks. The barracks was constructed in a manner that was supposed to resemble something in line with more ancient marine shipboard conditions.

Imagine, if you can, about a dozen toilet seats all in a single row, about a foot of open space between each seat, the entire row in open view without benefit of privacy partitions, and an open trough of running water extending the full length about a foot below the seats. Kind of a communal outhouse — but worse! The discomfort caused by extreme heat and terrible humidity was compounded by an obvious nose-grabbing lack of ventilation. Then of course there had to be an occasional smart-ass who would, when several individuals were seated, come along with a large wad of lighter-fluid soaked toilet paper; light it and drop it in the trough at the source of flowing water. By not being alert to such a prank one could suffer some significant and painful burns. The burning paper floated within inches of each toilet seat, extremely near to that very sensitive part of one's body that protruded below the seat, and would as an absolute minimum burn all the hair from those butts and balls that remained in place. Oh, a big joke as for the perpetrator and for some of those who had been around long enough to know what to expect. Some men were angered as they managed to jump clear of the flames, but most of them just grumbled some form of profanity while they scoffed at the prankster's attempt to catch them off guard. I was happy to learn that I would only have to remain there a single night.

The following day an even smaller group of us was once again transported by bus on to the receiving barracks at Subic Bay, a two-story World War II screen-enclosed wooden structure. Conditions were not quite as bad as they had been at Sangley Point, but things were not significantly better either. There was no such thing as air conditioning although it was very much needed. The dust-clogged screened windows kept the mosquitoes out, but they also restricted the already-small amount of airflow available for ventilation.

Almost immediately after arriving at the barracks we were directed to report to the Disbursing Officer to convert whatever American money we had. We were told that it was a very serious offense to be caught anywhere in the Orient with American greenbacks (Hong Kong being the exception). Our currency was converted to Military Payment Certificates, similar to Monopoly money and commonly referred to as MPC. Our coins were also converted to this strange paper currency. Each denomination was a different color and a different size for ease in identification. MPC could then be exchanged for the local currency at legitimate exchange booths on the base. MPC could also be exchanged for foreign currency off base on the black market at a rate lower than that for greenbacks. The rule was; exchange your money for the local currency on board your ship or on the base prior to exiting the main gate. The convenience, coupled with the higher off-base rate, attracted just about everyone to engage in illegal exchanges at one time or another. Far more often than not, money exchanged illegally was done so as a convenience, not as a profitable endeavor. Converting American green-backs on the black market brought a very high exchange rate — as much as four times the authorized rate. The larger the bill denomination, the higher the rate, an extremely profitable venture for those who never got caught. Severe penalties were imposed upon those who did get caught.

Periodically all MPC was called in to exchange for newly issued MPC. The intent was to discourage the local foreign nationals from accumulating large quantities of MPC and/or engaging in illegal currency transactions by keeping them guessing as to when the new MPC might be issued.

While waiting for my ship, or for some other mode of transportation that would get me to it, I was assigned temporary duty on a tugboat where I spent the next couple of days on my hands and knees in unbelievable humid heat chipping rust and paint off the tug's corroded deck. The Bos'n Mate First Class, Petty Officer in Charge of the tug, the "skipper," as it were, was more of a first class jerk in my opinion. He had no patience with me and simply disregarded the fact that I had not yet had ample time to acclimate myself to the local weather conditions. He demanded more of me than of his own crew so that they could take advantage of the slackened workload I so conveniently provided. I had enough boot camp in me to know that I was, without question, to do as I was told. Fortunately, I knew by my own en route experiences that I would probably not be assigned to the tug for long.

Just across a short bridge at the edge of the base (a military reservation at that time) there was a small community known as Olongapo; the only liberty town available to sailors and most of it off limits to the military. I was told that the town was filthy dirty, the roads were unpaved, only a few of the dozen or so bars were equipped with fans (none had air con-ditioning), and they were all filled with ugly women. I was also told, and

43

was somewhat shaken by it, that the Huks, the Filipino headhunters who comprised a good portion of the communist insurgence, periodically kidnapped sailors. The victims of such foul play were later found dead in a jungle or up on some mountainside with sacks filled with hungry rats tied over their heads. Others were found with their stomachs gutted and their testicles stuffed down their throats. I just didn't know what to believe, but the sources of information seemed quite reliable. Anyway, I was exhausted at the end of each day, and off-base liberty in such a primitive environment was not something in which I wanted to participate. As long as I had any say in the matter, I was going to make sure my balls remained hanging right where they belonged!

When I was released from my duties on board the tug at the end of my third day, I decided to wash my dirty dungaree uniforms. I had no idea how long I would remain attached to the base, but I did know that I would be best received with clean working uniforms when I arrived at my destination. So, for the first time since graduating, I relied on my boot camp training. I got a bucket, some soap powder, and tackled the task of scrubbing my dungarees. Within seconds of having submerged my dungarees in the hot soapy water, certainly insufficient time to scrub the ground-in rust and paint chips from them, I heard my name along with those of three others announced on the public address system. We were all directed to report to the Chief Master at Arms immediately. My first logical thought came as a question: *What have I done wrong this time?*

I left my trousers soaking in the bucket and rushed to the office of the Chief Master at Arms. As soon as I entered his office and identified myself, he spoke quickly with authority and urgency.

"Get your shit together now and report to the USS *Twining* immediately!"

I tried to explain that I was in the process of washing my clothes by hand and that my new dungarees were soaking in hot soapy water, but the chief didn't care about that.

"The goddamn ship is getting underway, and you and those other three men better get your asses on board before it does! It wouldn't go well for you to miss movement since that would, among other things, mean you'd remain under my fuckin' control," he snarled at me.

I returned to the barracks, shoved everything haphazardly into my seabag and headed toward the piers. Somewhere between the barracks and the pier I met up with the other three guys. It was something of a relief finding that they were also E-2 apprentices. What a clumsy bunch we were. It was a combination of fear and ignorance that caused me to intentionally leave my wet dungarees behind, still soaking in soapy water, just waiting for someone to come along and "claim" them.

The chief had been absolutely right. Deckhands aboard the USS *Twining* were preparing to toss off the mooring lines in preparation for getting underway.

One by one our small group of four requested permission to board. The last of the group crossed the brow just in time to see it removed. Within seconds we could feel the ship shiver as the propellers churned in the water, forcing the ship away from the pier. What a thrill! I was actually going to sea on a Navy vessel; I could finally consider myself a sailor!

The four of us, Bob, Cary, George, and I, were surprised to learn that we were all heading for the same ultimate destination; the USS *Colahan* (DD-658). We were all Fireman Apprentices fresh out of boot camp and we had just about everything in common: We knew absolutely nothing about what was going on and we were constantly being ridiculed by everyone around us — officers and enlisted men alike. We were clumsy in all that we said and did. Sailors around us took interest in making us feel totally worthless. How wrong of us to have thought that when we donned our second stripe, that first promotion from recruit to apprentice, and were actually at sea on a naval vessel, we would be considered as equals, as full-fledged sailors.

We found that we were not to be accepted as crewmembers or as friends while temporarily attached to any transit carrier. Ship's Company, generally all members permanently assigned to any ship or station, were, much like opposing sports teams, rivals to crew members of all other ships or stations. Outsiders such as us were nothing more than that. Outsiders — and an inconvenience! It would be quite some time before we would be treated as equals in even the slightest manner. We received no guidance and no companionship other than that which we shared among our small group of four. Immediate questions such as "Where is the head?" and "Where are we supposed to eat?" were either ignored or responded to in some form of ridicule. "Didn't you learn a goddamn thing in boot camp" and, "I ain't your fuckin' mommy," were the most frequent responses.

The best part of being in transit on board the USS *Twining* was that we were not told to "turn to," sailor's lingo for work. The worst thing was that we were required to wear our white uniforms instead of dungarees. To this day I do not understand why whites were required of us, unless it was to make sure all other crewmembers could easily identify us as temporary passengers. Everything we brushed against instantly became one more unsightly smudge on our already-unkempt uniforms.

Since there were no empty bunks on board, or at least no one told us if there were, we slept on the main deck, wrapped around our seabags in a most uncomfortable fashion. Our boot camp white inspection uniforms rapidly became more than a disgrace. Lack of sleep and the constant ridicule by everyone around us had me almost convinced that I'd made a terrible mistake. This Navy just wasn't all that I thought it would be, nor was it even similar to what I had been taught it would be.

After an exceptionally long five days at sea, the *Twining* pulled into Manila Harbor where she tied up alongside the *Colahan*, my final destination.

Even though the previous few days had been on board an identical class destroyer, it was not until that moment, during my first observation of my new home, that my boot camp training of ship types was recalled. I thought of the things I had learned about destroyers and I wanted very much to see that which I had learned, to have it all proven to be factual as quickly as possible — that destroyers were designed to, and were capable of protecting carrier task forces and amphibious forces from air, surface, and submarine attack; they could track down and destroy submarines in hunter-killer operations; they were capable of attacking enemy surface forces, and they were valuable in providing missile or gunfire support in instances of attacks on shore targets.

I had also learned that the large power plants and very light armor gave destroyers high speed and maneuverability in combat. They were easily damaged by relatively light hits, and they had a short operational range when they were without benefit of refueling and replenishing support at sea.

Destroyers outnumbered all combatant ships in the fleet. Most were launched during World War II and were "updated" through Fleet Rehabilitation and Modernization (FRAM) programs. The *Colahan* was, from her exterior appearance, the most beautiful ship in the fleet! In time my opinion would change.

All naval vessels are designated by "class." The first of any particular design is normally the class of all ships to follow that are of the same design. The USS *Colahan* was a 2100-ton "FLETCHER (DD-445) Class Destroyer" built in 1942-43 by the Bethlehem Steel Company, Staten Island, New York. She was named in honor of CDR Charles Ellwood Colahan, who was born in Philadelphia, Pennsylvania, on October 25, 1849. Commander Colahan experienced a well-rounded naval career aboard various ships in both the Atlantic and Pacific and assumed command of the newly commissioned USS *Cleveland* in March 1903. On March 11, 1904, he died at his home in Lambertville, New Jersey. The USS *Colahan* was capable of steaming at speeds in excess of thirty knots (about thirty-six miles per hour) and was equipped with five-inch guns, 40mm guns, torpedoes, depth charges, and hedgehogs (small forward-fired weapons used during anti-submarine attacks). The *Colahan* was placed in commission on August 23, 1943.

The four of us, Bob, Cary, George, and I, after having gained permission to leave the *Twining*, crossed the brow between the two ships and each of us, as we were trained to do, requested permission to board the *Colahan*. Naively I knew that we would be welcomed aboard and we would be treated with admiration, having successfully completed boot training and having already become seafaring sailors. Of course I was wrong again. The OOD, while shaking his head in some kind of disbelief, reluctantly granted the permission necessary for us to board.

"Look at you! Don't you have any pride in yourselves? You people are unbelievable."

He went on and on, suggesting we were unworthy of further comment but nonetheless continuing to give us a tongue-lashing we weren't prepared for and we sure as hell didn't feel we deserved. Finally, after listening to all the different methods of expressing total disgust at our appearance, we were escorted to the Engineering Department berthing compartment where we were given verbal orders. After we cleaned ourselves up we were to once again report for duty, but this time in accordance with Navy regulations; appropriately presentable. We were also told that the ship would be getting underway immediately.

As one awkward moment passed, another would invariably present itself. Once again we found ourselves at the mercy of a very biased crew. The head was secured for cleaning, and the "head cleaner" would not allow us access. Our feeble explanation that we had been ordered to cleanup and to present ourselves to the OOD immediately didn't bother the cleaner. Instead, he took great pleasure in knowing that we were not at all in control of the situation. In fact, he knew that he was totally in control. Improvise we did. We took birdbaths with the assistance of a "scuttlebutt" (drinking fountain) and quickly changed uniforms; that would have to do. Each of us "extracted" the clean whites that we had, at some time in the past, jammed into our seabags. They had remained white but they were wrinkled beyond anything acceptable. After looking each other over and commenting on each other's unacceptable appearance, we decided that we might just as well get it over with.

U.S.S. Colahan

USS *Colahan* — *Fletcher* Class Destroyer — April 1955 to December 1958

What we didn't know, didn't learn, or had simply forgotten was that the OOD would no longer be stationed on the main deck where we had boarded not more than an hour before. The OOD had restationed himself on the bridge, where the Captain normally positioned himself whenever the ship was entering or leaving most ports. The Captain was there as overseer;

he listened to the orders given and watched to make sure correct procedures were followed as the ship was being maneuvered.

This time, as we started to enter what we knew to be the Captain's domain, the bridge, the OOD quickly, almost politely, directed us to report to E Division berthing for further assignments.

Once we realized that E Division was the same as Engineering, we had no difficulty finding our way there.

Our assignments consisted of where we would berth, which lockers were available for us in which to stow our uniforms and other belongings, and where to go for further assignment(s).

Bob, Cary, and George were all assigned to the forward engineroom.

I was assigned to the after engineroom where I would soon learn the duties, responsibilities, and skills of a "snipe" (engineering personnel) and how I could best prepare myself, and what the requirements were, before I would be considered eligible for promotional consideration. That process, although expanded upon significantly, would remain fairly constant throughout my nearly four-year tour of duty aboard *Colahan.*

My first thorough look at the berthing compartment really set me back. Hadn't I just spent an unduly amount of boot camp time learning the importance of cleanliness? Yet the berthing space I was looking at, the space I was to live and sleep in, was an absolute mess. It smelled of every conceivable foul odor; the metal deck was rusty and was covered with cigarette butts, discarded newspapers and other unidentifiable trash. It was also hot and humid. Bunks were not made up, towels hung haphazardly from bunk chains, and dirty clothing was strewn about everywhere even though there were two heavy-duty laundry bags that hung conveniently behind the compartment ladder well; one for white things, clothing and "fart sacks" (sheet-like mattress slipcovers), and one for dungarees and socks. At the time I didn't find it unusual, however later I found that the engineers' berthing compartment was the only compartment not furnished with a scuttlebutt. There did not appear to be any similarity between what I had been taught and what I was seeing firsthand. I had never lived in such an environment and found myself wondering how long I would have to contend with such living conditions.

MM2 (Machinist's Mate Second Class) M.D. Adams, the Petty Officer In Charge of the after engineroom, had selected me out of the group of four new apprentices. He said that he selected me because I was the huskiest. To me, that was one fine compliment.

Adams was his own person. The "system" was not necessarily something he felt obligated to follow; rather it was his goal to satisfy all after engineroom and associated engineering requirements through fair and equitable leadership. Adams didn't just exercise authority; he truly led by example. He was never reluctant to get his hands dirty, and he was always available with good advice. He provided me with the first significant sign of real fairness and understanding within the system. It was Adams' influence, his outstanding leadership, his acceptance and understanding where needed, and his personality that I would eventually pattern a good portion of my military career after. First, I had to grow up physically, mentally and militarily.

MD, as Adams was frequently referred to, was probably never aware of the absolute dedication, loyalty, and respect he had from all who knew him; particularly those directly subordinate to him. He quite simply did things his way — and his way was always right. Everyone could see that MD's decisions were, whether or not in strict compliance with Navy regulations, without exception fair and always in the best interests of all concerned.

Reveille came early that first morning on board the *Colahan*. The boot camp bugle call I had grown to hate had been replaced by the shrill, ear-piercing whistle of a boatswain's pipe. The boatswain's pipe was the tool that called our attention to all immediate requirements or functions. It was the prerequisite to the passing of verbal communications over any loudspeaker or intercommunication system. Each whistle, more appropriately each "call," had a meaning in and of itself, reveille being but one. Calls were piped to signal the crew to attention, for meals, for starting or securing from special details, to call all hands to battle stations and many other functions. I finally saw the reasoning and some significance to the Navy tradition that "sailors shall not whistle."

After breakfast that first day I reported at "quarters for muster and inspection" as directed on the 1-MC (the primary intercommunication system) with everyone else assigned to E Division. (Within several months *E* was redesignated *M* at which time E became the Electrical Division and M became the Machinery Division.) My place of muster was all the way aft, on the starboard side of Mount 55 (five-inch gun mount).

50

The purpose of muster was obvious; to take a roll call/head count and determine whether anyone had fallen overboard during the night. Machinist's Mate Chief Rogers conducted muster (inspection was not enforced to any noticeable degree), any special instructions or information was passed on, and then he issued the order to "secure from quarters."

So what was I supposed to do then? Everyone except me knew where to go. I heard "Turn to" piped, but since no one gave me any direction, I just wandered around on the fantail for a minute or two and then went back down to the berthing compartment where I found a nice row of footlocker tops that could easily accommodate my stretched out body — and I lay down. I was just starting to doze when I was abruptly and rudely awakened. I knew instantly that I had once again done something wrong. One of the after engineroom men had grabbed me by the back of my shirt and yanked me off the locker tops onto the deck. He was outraged as he yelled directly into my face, "Who in the fuck do you think you are?"

I had heard the question so many times it was beginning to make a great deal of sense. I was beginning to wonder just who the "fuck" I was, too. I looked up rather dumbfounded, not knowing just what was going on, and another deluge of questions, appropriately interjected with "fuckin' this" and "fuckin' that" bombarded me. I could feel tears forming in my eyes from having had my feelings hurt, embarrassed at my ignorance, but I knew instinctively that I had better shape up right away or otherwise be labeled a crybaby.

I tried to explain that I really didn't know where I was supposed to go, but that just didn't fly.

"Did you ever hear of the after engineroom?"

Obviously I had.

"Well, get your dumb boot camp ass down there where you belong *haiyaku*."

Haiyaku? I didn't know of the word's origin, but it didn't take much imagination for me to figure out that it meant either "now," "quick," or "or else."

I delivered my dumb boot camp ass (actually a fairly accurate description, all considered) to the after engineroom, where MD was waiting. He did not believe my explanation and called me a "gold brick" (slang for "goof-off," derived from the belief that real gold bricks do little more than lie in one place gathering dust). Then MD provided me with an armload of old rags and directed me to clean out the "snake pit."

51

My very first shipboard work assignment, more punishment than anything else, was having to wipe up all the oil and accumulated dirt and trash from the open area under the main engine reduction gears, otherwise known as the snake pit. The job wasn't all that bad until you consider the combination of confinement, discomfort, lack of adequate lighting, and the grease and oil I was standing in and quite literally surrounded by.

The following morning and practically every Monday through Saturday morning thereafter, quarters for muster, securing from quarters, and turn to were automatically followed in robot fashion, regardless of whether the ship was underway or in port.

I got the answer to my question of how long I would have to live in the filthy berthing compartment real fast. Within a couple of weeks after reporting aboard I was assigned the added duties of compartment cleaner. Chief Rogers told me that I was to make sure the decks were clean, as debris and trash would no longer be tolerated. Compartment occupants were responsible for making their bunks, and "gear adrift" (anything not properly stowed) would be turned in; available for claim by the rightful owner if he was willing to accept the consequences. I was supposed to report the names of all individuals who failed or refused to comply with the rules.

I hated compartment cleaning! I got on everyone's "shit list" as I turned in their names for one infraction or another. Of course I became selective in whose names I turned in; no sense in losing those few friendships I had managed to acquire. I was berthed with, and subsequently had to deal with individuals in all pay grades up to E-6, first class petty officers, and none of them accepted my explanation that I was "just trying to do my job" when I turned in their names. I learned quickly that it was easier on everyone, particularly me, if I picked up after the petty officers instead of reporting them.

There was a good side to being assigned as compartment cleaner. During working hours, the ladder leading down into the berthing compartment was triced up. That is, being hinged at the top, it was swung upward and tied to the overhead by the bottom rung. In the triced-up position no one could enter or leave the compartment. In theory this allowed the compartment cleaner(s) unrestricted and uninterrupted access to all areas that were in need of attention. In fact, it allowed for brief periods of uninterrupted relaxation completely out of sight, certainly out of reach of superiors, since the compartment cleaner was the only one who could release the ladder from its triced-up position and lower it back to the deck.

Chief Rogers was known more for his flashlight than anything else. He *always* had his flashlight in hand. He shined his light everywhere, looking into dark corners, between machinery, up in the overhead, and down in the bilge. We used to joke about the chief and his flashlight. We would mimic him, always searching for that unknown "thing," being sure to shine our imaginary flashlights directly on the overhead incandescent light bulbs — to make sure they were on! We had actually seen Chief Rogers do precisely that. He didn't seem to have the ability to focus on anything without benefit of his handy flashlight.

At sea four watch stations were required in the after engineroom: top watch, throttleman, lower-level watch and messenger. My first watch standing assignment was that of messenger. At first that didn't make much sense to me. Why assign someone who doesn't know much about anything to undertake the task of going places he can't find and/or doing things he doesn't know how to do? Actually, that was precisely why such an assignment was given to the apprentice. It forced me to learn real shipboard compartmentation, that of *Colahan* instead of the boot camp *Neversail*. It required that I learn my way around the main engine machinery as I documented on record forms the temperatures, pressures, water and oil levels of all associated machinery. It forced me to learn when the readings I was taking were within specifications and when they were approaching some limitation. I was not to delay in bringing questionable observations or indications of potential problems to the attention of the top watch, he being responsible overall for the effective and efficient operation of the engineroom as a whole. Not only did it make me a more reliable member of the team; it made me feel responsible.

Periodically, as an added but necessary precaution and as positive verification that the plant was, in fact, operating correctly, the top watch would check on the reliability of the messenger by spot-checking temperatures, pressures, and levels. The messenger watch was also responsible for sweeping the entire engineroom at the end of each four-hour shift and had to dump the "shit can" regardless of how little trash might have accumulated during the shift.

There was also the task of making a fresh pot of coffee for the oncoming watch regardless of the time of day or night. Sometimes, when I was running late, I used the boiling water from the deaerating feed tank, the

"DA tank," as it was more commonly referred to, as a short cut, a time-saver. I never worried about boiler water carryover, the degree of dissolved chemicals that carried with them a high probability of causing diarrhea in those who drank the coffee. The dilution factor was sufficiently high that there was no real concern about serious side effects from the ingestion of my specially prepared brew. I didn't exactly make up the shortcut — I was taught it! It came with the steam cycle lesson that needed to be learned before consideration for promotion to E-3.

The steam cycle was not all that difficult to learn: the boiler, as the name implies, boiled the water that formed steam — the steam provided the means of turning main engine turbines, generator turbines, and other auxil-iaries — the condenser converted the steam back into water, or condensate as it was — condensate pumps pumped the water from the "hot well" of the condenser up into the DA tank (where most of the remaining noncondens-able gasses were removed) — and finally, feed pumps pumped the water back to the boiler where the cycle started all over again.

Periodically chemicals were added to the boilers to prevent scale build-up, primarily calcium and magnesium, and to cause excess "sludge" to fall to the bottom of the boiler where it could be procedurally removed without shutting down the plant.

Watches were stood in four-hour shifts, normally four hours on watch and eight hours off. During the off hours, depending on whether those hours were during the normal workday (0800 to 1600) or not, we were required to do the routine tasks of cleanup and minor maintenance in and around the engineroom. The 0400 to 0800 watch really had it tough. That meant they had to stand two four-hour watches during other than work-ing hours plus they had to work in the engine room during the eight-hour workday. Sixteen hours a day in the engineroom was a most unpleasant experience. Weekly the watch would be "dogged," which meant two two-hour shifts between 1600 and 2000 instead of one four-hour shift. While underway, engineroom personnel could count on working sixteen hours a day, one week out of every three. Also while underway, maintenance was somewhat limited because most systems were necessary to the operation of the main engines. Only where backup systems were available or where systems could be safely bypassed could maintenance be performed.

Water, oil, and steam leaks were commonplace and kept us all busy finding and repairing them. Steam leaks made the space more uncomfort-able and contributed significantly to water shortage problems. I would find myself chasing the mysterious disappearing water problem throughout my naval career.

There was always work to be done. If it wasn't maintenance, it was preventative maintenance. And then there was always "paintwork" that had to be washed and deck plates that had to be scrubbed and wire-brushed.

Every Friday was "field" day, the day when just about everything got a thorough cleaning. All the "brightwork" (brass and copper pipes, valves, and fittings) had to be shined with nothing other than brightwork polish. At sea Fridays meant the "lowly" enlisted men would work harder than any other day of the week. I use the term *lowly* only because that was exactly how we were treated by most of those in the officer ranks. Anyone wearing a Dixie-cup white hat, the instantly identifiable enlisted sailor's hat, was considered to be sneaky and was not to be trusted.

It was almost comical watching the younger, inexperienced officers as they exercised their authority. Their word was absolute and final; it was the law. Failure to carry out their every wish and command would always end up costing valuable liberty time when the ship was in port.

But I'm getting ahead of myself. The first day or two at sea, underway, found many a man hanging over the side. Seasickness was to be expected of many sailors, at least on that first day out. Pork chops or some other greasy food was invariably served that day, probably because it was easier to bring it back up than it was to keep it down. The inability for some men to get topside or to the head fast enough made many confined spaces, including the berthing spaces, smell atrocious. That caused even more men to get nauseous. Then there were always those who would intentionally try to make others sick by pretending to be sick, allowing chewed-up foodstuff to drool out of their mouths or feigning the gagging stage just before vomiting. Trying to get rid of the stench was a task no one wanted, particularly those individuals who were not responsible, but someone had to do it.

Officers seemed to remain out of sight that first day out. That was because officers did not get sick — or so went the saying, and no enlisted man could confirm otherwise.

I found that shipboard food on board the *Colahan* left a lot to be desired and was no comparison to that which I had grown accustomed to while attending boot camp. And of course many meals had unique but descriptive names that eliminated any need to elaborate on the menu. For breakfast we frequently ate "SOS" (shit on a shingle), a Navy variety of creamed beef on toast, or "creamed foreskins on toast," a similar concoction that was made with chipped beef instead of ground beef. I liked SOS but found the other too much like chewing salty cardboard. Periodically, especially during rough weather, a meal of "horse cock" could be depended on, that being a variety of sliced lunchmeat, usually tough as shoe leather and saltier than the ocean itself. I was amazed at how some of the men actually liked the stuff and gorged themselves with it at every opportunity.

At first, life at sea was interesting simply because everything was new and foreign to me. "Boot" was to be my name for an undetermined period of time.

It took no time at all to understand why destroyers were, and are, called "tin cans." They continuously bob up and down as they rock port and starboard; seemingly capable of twisting snakelike with unexpected jerking motions. The sea didn't have to be rough for the ship to conduct its tin can mimic as it sliced its way through the ocean. At times one could observe the entire bow or stern completely underwater as the ship rode out the larger, rougher swells.

During the more extreme rough weather all hands were ordered to remain clear of the main deck at which times the designated route while traveling forward or aft became via the 0-1 level (one level above the main deck). I found it, as did many others, far more convenient to violate the directed route and use the main deck, but to do so with extreme caution. Waves varied in size and were completely unpredictable. It was more luck than anything else when those of us that elected to take our chances made it any noticeable distance without being knocked against a bulkhead, or at least getting a thorough soaking from a wave that wasn't supposed to be there. There were many minor injuries suffered as a result of violating the 0-1 level order, but they were never reported. Captains Mast, or simply "Mast" (of which I would learn a great deal), almost always meant swift, though not always accepted as fair, punishment. To admit violating standing orders almost always meant Mast.

Shipboard personnel were assigned to segregated berthing corresponding to their department. Within each department there could be several divisions. Most tight and lasting shipboard friendships were between personnel of the same division. Each department of the ship was under a "Department

Head," an officer who was responsible for its organization, training, safety, security, material conditions, maintenance, cleanliness and the conduct and performance of all his assigned personnel.

On the *Colahan*, some of the departments were identified as Operations, Navigation, Weapons (Deck), Supply, Medical, Communications, and Engineering. As a result of fleetwide directives, the Engineering Department consisted of "E," electrical and interior communications; "M," engineroom (my assignment); "B," fireroom (boiler room); and "R," shipfitters. The crew separated all groups into two more easily recognized, more distinct groups, commonly known as "snipes" or "deck apes," depending on whether they were assigned duties below decks or topside.

"What the hell are you doing up here, snipe?" and, "Get back down in your hole where you belong," were common expressions, always given and taken in jest. Rarely did a deckhand venture into the depths of a fireroom or engineroom. Not out of fear, simply out of knowing how terribly hot and noisy it was down there. Temperatures varied from very hot to extremely hot, usually exceeding 150° F in many parts of the enginerooms and firerooms.

Most snipes were truly proud of the severe and uncomfortable conditions under which they were required to work. There was always the friendly argument between engineroom and fireroom personnel as to which group really had it the worst, each having absolute respect for the other's working conditions, neither wanting to be in the other's shoes.

Snipes as a whole were a tough bunch; something I definitely wanted to be considered a part of. I decided right away that I would become a "MM," Machinist's Mate. At that time I had absolutely no idea just how demanding it would be to accept the responsibilities and fulfill the obligations required of the Machinist's Mate rating. My admiration for M.D. Adams no doubt played a significant role in that decision.

It was not exactly difficult being accepted as a member of the same division, yet friendships were not easily cultivated. Most of the men that I was closely associated with were considered old-timers. *Everyone* outranked me!

As a newcomer, I was assigned to all of the "shit details" such as Head Cleaner, Compartment Cleaner, and every "working party" that was "called away" (announced over the 1-MC). It was easy to determine who the lowest rated personnel were — they were always the ones to show up when special details were necessary.

Once or twice a week, depending on whether or not the Ship's Laundry was up and running, and then depending on the backlog of clothing stacked up at the laundry room/compartment, I had to help sort and distribute clean laundry. Rarely was the laundry dry when it was returned to the compartment for sorting, but everyone was required to stow it in their lockers nonetheless. During the process of washing and drying, blotches of rust and other fixed stains were frequently picked up, causing permanent discoloration to our clothing. No one, other than those who actually operated the Ship's Laundry, ever used the free service it provided to clean their inspection or liberty uniforms.

Marcel, one stripe ahead of me at the time, became my best friend. He was from Brussels, Belgium, and I was fascinated by his ability to speak French. Marcel exhibited all the best traits of a young man his age. He was clean-cut, reliable, and intelligent. He was competent and resourceful. I was especially impressed at how well Marcel could relate to his superiors and how much he was admired by everyone. He and I would spend practically all of our waking hours together, either working in the engineroom or simply sharing spare time together. I never grew tired of his interesting stories and the manner he had of describing them. Sometimes his stories were of his childhood but for the most part he told me of his first impressions and experiences in the United States where he invariably found himself in some uncomfortable situation because of his inability to speak English. Marcel spent a lot of time teaching me simple words and phrases in French. Sometimes I was able to intentionally twist his native language into vulgar expressions just to see his reaction. I enjoyed exercising my ability to embarrass Marcel when I would swear one form of vulgarity or another in French at shipmates who had absolutely no idea what I was saying. I also took great pleasure in ridiculing and laughing at Marcel when he did his best to scold me for my antics.

Marcel, because of his readily but unfortunate acceptance of my unique, sometimes warped sense of humor, became my target. I would intentionally do little things to frustrate him. I would hide tools he was working with and then watch as he frantically searched the area for them. I would "accidentally" spill something on his cleaning station, slip steel nuts or washers into his coffee when he wasn't looking, hide his white hat when I knew he would soon be going topside, and on and on... .

Marcel was something of a glutton for my crude sense of humor. I could always con him out of a cookie or candy that he had received from home. Then I might do one of any number of repulsive things with it. At times I rubbed such goodies on my crotch and then immediately tossed them back in with the rest. Or I might take a bite, express how disgusting it tasted, and throw it on the deck, or I might even spit it out and tell him not to ever give me any of his crappy-tasting junk from home again. Usually he would become angered. Then the next time he showed up with some kind of homemade goodies I would humbly approach him, practically beg him to forgive my previous totally uncalled for act, and promise faithfully that I would never do such a thing again. Repeatedly, time and again, Marcel would buy my story only to see me pull it off again, guffawing boisterously at each repeat performance.

There was one instance, when I was standing alone on the main deck just gazing out over the ocean, and Marcel came along. I told him I was out of "smokes" and asked him politely if I could borrow one. After checking his pack, he found that he was down to his last cigarette, but in keeping with his normal generosity, Marcel offered it to me. I told him I'd rather not take his last cigarette, that I could do just as well without, and that he should save it for himself. No, Marcel insisted that I take that last cigarette — so I did, then immediately tossed it overboard into the ocean.

"See, I told you I could do without," I said as I laughed at my wide-eyed totally dumbfounded friend.

How lucky I was that Marcel was such a quiet person and that he rapidly got over just about any form of anger, disgust, and distrust. Tolerant as he was, I know that there had to have been times when I must have pressed him close, or maybe even beyond his remarkable patience.

Marcel was great to be with at all times but particularly when I wanted to apply myself properly. He was never willing or receptive to any participation relative to activities associated with my "other" side. That side, briefly described above, will be expanded upon later.

Shipboard conservation of fresh water was constantly stressed. The ship's evaporators were not capable of keeping up with demand. By directive, twenty-five gallons per man, per day, was the allowable ration. That allowance was more theory than enforceable, but most of the crew made honest attempts at conserving. Lavatory sinks were equipped with spring-loaded hot and cold spigots to make it more difficult, practically impossible, to waste water. Anyone seen taking too long in the shower was ridiculed or reprimanded by subordinates as well as superiors. Taking a "Navy" shower was an absolute must. That required individuals to quickly shut off the shower water immediately after wetting down; soap themselves and scrub themselves without benefit of running water. Then, once thoroughly scrubbed, they could turn the water back on and quickly rinse off. There was no privacy and there were no shower curtains, so water usage was easily observed. While in port, particularly when there was a rush to the showers in preparation for liberty, we had to step outside the shower stall to do our soaping and scrubbing down while others stepped in and wetted down. There could be a dozen or more men trying to shower at the same time, and there were but two shower stalls in the engineers' head! Quite a sight to see.

As an added precaution in the continuous effort at conserving fresh water while at sea, showers were normally secured except during specific hours. We did not have the luxury of showering at our convenience. In fact, there were times when there was such a shortage of fresh water that the showers were secured "until further notice." That meant anywhere from a day to a week, depending on how quickly we could recover our shortage.

The shut-off valve for securing fresh water to the after head was conveniently located in the overhead directly above the main generator in the after engineroom. Convenient for those of us assigned to that space because we could access fresh water in the middle of the night if we thought it was necessary. There was a sense of defiance among engineroom personnel in that since we made the water, we ought to be able to use a little more of it. A sense similar to that which the cooks lived by; they cooked the food and therefore were privileged to eat as much as they wanted — as often as they wanted.

Personnel assigned to the after fireroom used another strategy and somehow managed to keep it a secret. By tapping into the pressurized feedwater system, the system used to provide water directly to the boilers, they rigged their own shower — showerhead and all! I learned of their "ingenuity" when I became suspicious after seeing several fireroom personnel going down into their "hole" with their "douche kits" (toiletry items) under arm, some wearing "flip-flops" (shower shoes), and some even more conspicuously carrying their towels. They were fresh and clean when they emerged minutes later. My suspicions were confirmed when I conducted my own little investigation.

Interestingly, feedwater could not be rationed; its use and replenishment were determined by boiler demand. Excessive use was always attributed to leaky safety valves, steam leaks, low pressure drains backing up, or some other plant-related deficiency or malfunction. The truth was, it was easier to waste the more critical feedwater than it was to waste fresh water. The crew simply suffered when the feedwater supply got too low because fresh water distilling ceased until feedwater was adequately replenished. Fair? Not at all, but those with the knowledge and access always served themselves first and best in one way or another.

The command, realizing the need for supplementing fresh water demands, authorized saltwater showers — an innovative step in the right direction. The saltwater that was tapped off the ship's fire main system was an inexhaustible supply that was provided directly from the ocean. That system was always pressurized for the purpose of fighting fires, and diverting such a small flow to the shower stalls was easily accomplished without detriment to fire fighting capabilities.

Saltwater showers were not at all bad when patrolling in tropical waters. The idea was to rinse off as much sweat and grime as possible with saltwater and then scrub with Lava soap, the best known soap capable of providing a lather under such conditions, and rinse off using the same saltwater system. There was no such thing as wasting saltwater since the ocean was so conveniently available. Very little fresh water was then needed for the final rinse.

Once in a while, while in port, uninformed members of the crew were found cooling off exuberantly in the refreshing coolness of a saltwater shower. That is, until they were explicitly and mockingly informed of the fact that they were really showering with polluted harbor water! The look of panic, of utter disbelief, confirmed that such had never entered their minds.

At sea, heavy tropical rainsqualls might last a few seconds, a few minutes, or sometimes longer. When the ship was on freshwater hours and the makings of a squall was evident, crewmen, snipes in particular since they were prone to being the grimiest, would rush to their lockers, grab a bar of soap, and run naked up on the main deck to shower in the tropical rain. When timed right, it was a refreshing means of cooling down while at the same time getting rid of an accumulation of sweat and grime. Such rainsqualls had their own uncanny ability at precision timing. The heaviest of rain would invariably stop abruptly when there were an abundance of naked bodies, all thoroughly soaped down. Almost instantly, assisted by the never-ending heat of the tropics, the soap would harden to a grease-like film. Some men preferred to wait for the next squall to rinse off while others elected to seek more immediate relief that was provided by saltwater showers. Dried salt on the body wasn't nearly as uncomfortable as dried soap.

Berthing spaces were not equipped with air conditioning. Instead, air was sucked from topside via ventilation fans and forced through duct headers that split into numerous branches of ventilation ductwork. Air exited just above deck-level at several locations within each berthing compartment. The compartments were hot, especially considering the hot humid air that was being drawn upon to service the spaces. Even at night the volume of airflow was insufficient to make living conditions comfortable.

I was one of the few who was lucky enough to have one of the ventilation ducts pass beside my bunk. With just a small modification, a little ingenuity, some of us were able to make living conditions only slightly but noticeably better. Regardless of how we improvised, we had to use good common sense. We had to make sure that whatever we did was as inconspicuous as possible while at the same time provide a practical means of added air circulation. For example, I cut a hole approximately two inches in diameter out of the five-inch duct to allow some air to escape. That, in and of itself was insufficient, however by sticking cardboard into the hole a portion of the airflow was easily diverted to my face and chest. It was like having my own private air conditioner as the diverted air evaporated the perspiration from my body. Any such modifications were very illegal, but those of us who took it upon ourselves to make them were usually quite successful (in not getting caught). Had it not been for those who were greedy, those who cut a hole too large and tried to divert too much or all of the air flow through any given duct, it's doubtful there would have been any action taken to restore the ductwork. As it was, periodically the "tin benders" (shipfitters) would make their rounds and patch all of the holes they could find. No one, to my knowledge, ever suffered a severe reprimand for the illegal modifications — probably because the discomfort without such minor alterations was known to be very real.

At night, when the berthing spaces remained unbearably hot and humid, I, as did many others, took my blanket topside and slept on the main deck. A favorite place was under the five-inch gun mounts where six or seven men could easily be accommodated, with the gun mount itself providing a bit of protection in the event of rain or strong winds. I liked sleeping under the midship torpedo racks. Sometimes during the night the ship would enter rainsqualls and everyone sleeping topside would have to scramble for more appropriate cover; usually that meant their own bunk. More than once I banged my head on the torpedo racks when I was abruptly awakened by unexpected rain.

The messenger watch was always responsible for locating and waking up oncoming watchstanders. This was particularly burdensome since many times the relieving watchstanders were sleeping topside in unknown locations. Then, somewhat unfairly I thought, the messenger was invariably blamed when the watchstanders were relieved late. Messengers could not leave until all members of the watch station had been properly relieved. I learned quickly that I had better start looking early if I expected to be relieved of my messenger duties on time.

With the calling of the oncoming watch came the potential for unexpected perils. The task of waking someone up was somewhat perilous at best. I never knew what to expect, although I learned quickly to be prepared at all times for the unexpected. Everyone had their own waking-up personality, and some were downright ornery. Waking someone up with the beam of a flashlight directed in their eyes was reason for just about anyone to come out of their bunk swinging. Then there were those who just didn't want to wake up — or wanted to lie there until they knew that they would be late, knowing that the fault would always rest on the shoulders of the messenger. I became accustomed to hearing variations of, "Yeah, yeah, I'm awake. Now get the fuck out of here before I shove that goddamn flashlight up your ass."

There were other proven ways to awaken those who made it most difficult on the messengers. I couldn't believe my eyes when I watched a senior petty officer pour a mixture of cigarette butts, ashes, and water down the gaping mouth of one of those hard-to-wake individuals. That worked remarkably well and I told myself that I would never place myself at risk of the same thing happening to me. The recipient of that really rude awakening was never a problem after that.

Mid-Rats, midnight rations, were not provided on the *Colahan*. Appetites were quite alive and well in the middle of the night, especially for the mid-watch: midnight to 0400. It was a watch that didn't allow for sufficient sleep either prior to or following the watch.

Usually around one or two in the morning, I, as well as other messengers, would be "dispatched" on search-and-retrieve missions. The search was for food, any kind of food. Returning empty-handed was not exactly in any messenger's best interest, since the older hands knew that there was food out there someplace; it was just a matter of finding it. Getting caught by anyone other than another messenger was another matter. It was considered a serious offense to steal food rations. It was also illegal to have food down in the engineering spaces because theoretically and perhaps in fact, it would attract cockroaches and other vermin. But the desire for some kind of nourishment was overwhelming. We used to joke about attracting roaches. It sounded like a pretty good idea; we would then have another source of nourishment to fall back on when food was not to be found.

The midnight search for food had to be done with extreme care, usually without benefit of a flashlight since that would most assuredly attract unwanted attention. The spud locker on the 0-1 level was not always a sure bet, but it was always a good bet. It was normally kept locked, but with a little ingenuity, provided the locker was full enough, there were ways to gain access and squeeze a few out.

Potatoes were not a favorite food, but they were acceptable and easy to prepare. They baked quickly when placed next to a main engine steam line. Once in a while, when scrounging around the mess decks, I'd really luck out. Cooks and mess cooks were not the most careful individuals, and they sometimes left canned goods of one kind or another in plain view. Other times they neglected to lock the storage cabinets. I was always "praised" when I returned with cans of fruit.

Marcel would invariably comment on our eating habits under such conditions. Once while we were taking turns scraping chunks of peanut butter out of a can with our fingers, wasting no time in consuming the treat without benefit of bread or crackers, Marcel's question made us laugh as he considered our etiquette from another prospective: "I wonder what they'd say back home if they saw us eating like this."

Silverware was not always available. Having it in one's possession clearly meant that it had been taken from the mess decks, misappropriated, and relocated to some unauthorized location. The rule was relaxed to the extent that one spoon, a sugar spoon, was allowed in any space that was authorized a coffeepot; spaces in which watchstanders were required.

One time, when I proudly returned with a can of olives, something different for a change, I was ridiculed.

"What in the hell are we going to do with this crap?" I was asked.

When I responded with, "Eat it," my facial expression and tone of voice made it clear that I was *not* referring to the olives. Realizing the effort I had put into my search and having returned with what I thought of as a great find, my choice of words and expression clearly showed that I meant "eat shit!" I caught a rapid and unexpected backhand from an engineroom vengeful "bad ass" for that.

On very rare occasions, someone somehow managed to steal a few eggs. Cooking them also required a bit of ingenuity. A #10 can, properly modified to fit snugly over a hot-plate, provided for an acceptable skillet. We could improvise for cooking oil, when it was not available, by using a very thin coat of 2190-TEP, the readily available oil used to lubricate just about all engineering machinery. Did it taste bad? Palatable it was not, but doctored with enough salt and pepper it could be made acceptable. The problem it created, diarrhea, was always considered worth it. Once, while standing the mid-watch, we had all the makings for French-fries. We had cooking oil, the real stuff. We had a #10 can — no modifications necessary. We had the hot-plate and we had potatoes. With great anticipation, mouths watering, we washed and pealed the potatoes. Potato slices were placed in a standard Navy soup bowl for safe keeping while the oil was being heated on the hot-plate. As I held the bowl above the preheated oil, preparing to carefully shake the potatoes therein, the bowl slipped from my hand and plunged into the oil. The hot oil spilled over the sides of the can onto the hot-plate and instantly flashed into a roaring fire. We all scrambled for extinguishers but before we could put the fire out, noticeable damage had been done. All of the white-painted asbestos insulation around the piping above and around the hot-plate was thoroughly blackened. Some paint was blistered badly. Hunger was no longer an issue. The entire watch section chipped in and worked feverishly the remainder of the shift. After washing, scraping, and sanding as much as we could, to get rid of the more obvious damage, we repainted the entire area. The air ejectors, used for removing noncondensable gases from the main engine condenser, and everything above them, sparkled with a brand new paint job.

The following morning, after quarters, the chief paid a visit to our space. He highly commended us for our initiative, for having improved the appearance of the engineroom without being directed to do so — during a time other than normal working hours! We acknowledged his ability to recognize our efforts and accepted his praise. Why not? Undeserving as it might have been, recognition and praise were appropriate in the eyes of the beholder, the chief!

There was yet another "taboo" source of food that was tapped occasionally: emergency rations. Granted, anyone caught could expect a rapid court martial. Emergency rations were precisely that, not to be touched unless dire emergency conditions existed, like being shipwrecked at sea without any other source of nourishment.

Emergency rations were conveniently stored on lifeboats and life rafts and in other difficult, though not impossible to access, locked stowage areas. They consisted primarily of "C-Rations," "hot-cans" containing precooked foods such as hamburger, spaghetti, soup, and the like. The hot-can containers were actually double cans. The inside can contained the food product while the surrounding can was filled with a chemical catalyst agent. The procedure was simple. The inner can was opened first, usually with the aid of someone's very unsterile pocketknife. Holes were punched around the top of the outer can, and plain water was slowly poured through the holes into the chemicals. The catalytic reaction was immediate, and the extreme heat generated heated the inner "meal" quickly. Emergency rations were actually quite good, considering the lack of anything better around. Heartburn was the inevitable result of consuming hot-can meals, but rarely did anyone dare complain about that. None of us ever seriously considered the most remote and unlikely possibility that by satisfying our midnight hunger with emergency rations we might someday find ourselves at the mercy of the sea without food.

There were other activities to help occupy the four hours of the midwatch. We shined our shoes, and we washed socks and white hats with boiling hot water obtained from the DA tank. The handrails surrounding the entire space were used as drying racks for any item(s) of clothing. It was a viable alternative to the problem of white hats and socks "disappearing" when they were sent to the Ship's Laundry. And of course we would spend a great deal of time telling stories of our youth, our girlfriends, schools we had attended, places we had lived, and just about anything in general that we had experienced pre-Navy.

Even though we were not required to wear white hats while on watch in the engineering spaces, there were some men who did. White hats were quite flexible, especially after the newness had worn off. So those of us who wore them did so fashionably — imaginatively — upside down, twisted, and otherwise modified to fit individual personalities. I modeled mine by first turning the sides down, like a bucket over my head; then I curled the bottom of the rim upward from the back to a point about three-quarters of the way toward the front. It was not an exact replica but did take on the appearance of a Robin Hood hat.

I also followed suit when I realized that some of the men had tied their work shoelaces into a knot instead of a bow. At first I thought it was out of ignorance, but I quickly realized there was time saved by not having to tie them in a neat little bow every time the shoes were put on. It was like wearing modified sandals; just slip them on and be on my way. Where time was of the essence, during drills for example, shoes tied in that manner were most appreciated.

Some of the old-timers had "steaming lockers," named so because of their location; surrounded by steam lines down in the engineering spaces. It was an earned privilege that was based strictly on seniority and longevity. Usually steaming lockers were standard upright lockers that were mounted wherever room permitted and where they would not distract from the surrounding appearance. Any form of additional storage space was always in demand, since berthing compartment lockers rarely provided enough space for all of the personal belongings we would like to have stowed. Even the distribution of berthing compartment lockers was based on time and pay grade. E-6s and E-5s usually claimed upright lockers, highly preferred because of how easy they were to access. Footlockers were not easily accessible — retrieving desired items of clothing or other things usually meant digging through a heap of disheveled belongings.

There were many sea stories and sea-related fables some of the guys liked to tell and others were willing to listen to. There were a lot of stories about sailors having been saved by whales, porpoises, and giant sea turtles. And there were stories of the albatross, the largest web-footed seabird that was considered good luck when observed at sea by seafaring men of long past. They were believed to be a sign that land was near. That might have been true at one time; however, I found that albatrosses were known to follow ships from continent to continent, regardless of weather conditions, watching patiently for anything eatable that was thrown overboard as they rode the wind currents. They seemed to know that an abundance of leftover food would be thrown over the fantail of a ship at sea at least three times every day.

Albatrosses have the remarkable ability to glide just inches above the water, gracefully following the ocean's swells. It seemed that they had the ability to glide indefinitely without so much as the slightest flapping of their wings. As dusk approached, the birds mysteriously disappeared, probably resting up for the night after settling on the water; floating instead of flying during hours of darkness. Weather conditions did not noticeably discourage those magnificent birds; they were there regardless of typhoon conditions or calm seas.

A few sailors liked to fish off the fantail. It was extremely unlikely that they would ever catch anything — even when the ship was moving slowly. The huge dual screws, the ship's propellers, churned the water enough to discourage any fish from approaching near enough to the ship from the stern. On the other hand, seagulls were quite willing to swoop down into the ship's wake, even settle on the water, and grapple for any kind of food scraps that were thrown overboard.

It didn't take a great deal of imagination for a couple of crewmen to figure out a new "sport," that of fishing for birds! It was simple. Just pack bread or any other kind of foodstuff around a hook and cast out over the fantail. The hungry seagulls were always anxious to eat anything that floated — so the "fishermen" needed only to keep their bait on the water's surface long enough for their "prey" to take it. It was not a frequent occurrence; however, there were times when birds were caught by this means. Once hooked, the bird would immediately take to the air. Cruel? No doubt — but a more unusual sight would have been hard to imagine, that of a fisherman attempting to reel in a flying bird instead of a fighting fish. The "thrill" of catching a bird never lasted long. I am not aware of any bird that was ever reeled all the way in. After a brief but intense struggle, the birds always snapped the fishing line and flew away. When the Skipper found out about such activities he put an immediate stop to it. Fantail fishing was not stopped; it was simply reserved for the purpose of catching fish.

I was captivated by all that the sea had to offer. I was always amazed at the beautiful blue-and-purple flying fish and at their ability to fly above water, running on their tail fins on top of the water for unbelievable distances between periods of flight. Sometimes they would fly right up on board the ship, usually crushing their heads upon impact against the ship's superstructure. Whales, the largest living creatures in the world and perhaps the most graceful, were truly things of beauty, absolutely spectacular, especially when they would break the surface in preparation for a dive. I cannot adequately describe the beauty as a whale's huge tail swoops slowly and gracefully out of the water, dripping with remnants of the sea, the *V* of the tail widely spread and pointing directly downward, then slowly submerge back into unknown depths of the ocean below. From time to time an abundance of porpoises would show up in some sort of formation and glide gracefully alongside the ship for hours at a time. Occasionally we would see glass and cork fishing floats, sea turtles, and indistinguishable pieces of debris floating by.

I particularly loved watching the sunsets. Depending on weather conditions, sunsets ranged from the very plain and drab disappearance of the sun over a gray horizon to the far more spectacular multicolored prismatic rays of sunlight as they shone through clouds of every dimension from a sky brightly filled with variations of orange and red. I saw sunrises that were equally spectacular.

For as far as the eye could see, I saw millions of Portuguese man-of-wars with their purple fins providing sails by which the wind guided them. I experienced fearsome electrical storms lighting up many a night sky accompanied by the deafening roar of thunder, always a significant reminder of just how insignificant man is in comparison to the world around him. Not quite as astounding or breathtaking, but of great interest and eye-catching, was the dull luminous glow from the water surrounding the ship's hull forming an eerie trail of bright green phosphorus that illuminated the ship's wake as she steamed peacefully into the darkness of the night.

4

FIRST IMPRESSIONS
AND THE REALITY OF
WESTPAC LIBERTY

The date was May 19, 1955, and I was as anxious as anyone to set foot on dry land. It was fairly early in the morning, shortly after breakfast, when the Bos'n pipe sounded "Attention" and I heard the word passed over the 1-MC.

"Now set the special sea and anchor detail for entering port."

All hands assigned to the duty section for that day had to report to special watch stations and provide assistance in maneuvering the ship into port. The other two sections, once they were relieved, were free to clean up in preparation for going ashore on liberty. Liberty in Japan!

For several days prior to our arrival at Sasebo, Japan, MD and a couple of other petty officers had teased me about how they were going to "hit the beach" with me and get me "stewed, screwed and tattooed in the nude," among other things. I prepared for the greatly anticipated experience in a manner unequaled in the past; this would truly be a new adventure for me.

I took a Navy shower, probably using just a little more water than usual. The need to conserve water was not taken quite so seriously when everyone knew we were entering port where fresh water was readily available and plentiful. I shaved with extra care, making sure I didn't nick myself as I usually did when I was in a hurry. Once all of my personal hygiene needs were met, I rushed to the berthing compartment to finalize my liberty preparations.

After selecting my very best pair of whites, I dressed as if preparing for a boot camp inspection. Several petty officers poked fun at how I was preparing — that I would probably have all the girls in Japan chasing after "super-clean cherry boy-san." "Cherry" anything meant that the subject was either in perfect condition, untouched, or virginal. "San" was the polite suffix added to the end of any term describing a male or female. Even though I knew I was being teased, the thought of being chased by girls in a foreign country, the possibility of actually getting laid there, made my adrenaline pump as never before. Once again came the call of the Bos'n pipe followed with: "The uniform of the day for all hands topside is undress whites. Now all hands not actually on watch fall in at quarters for entering port."

It seemed that hours passed as I stood at quarters with my division. Having to remain at attention as the ship slowly inched its way into the harbor was tedious. My attention was focused on the remarkable beauty of the Japanese landscape, particularly one landmark that had been appropriately nicknamed "Jane Russell Hill" for its shapely bust-like appearance.

The nearer we maneuvered the ship into the harbor, the more we became surrounded by an ever-increasing number of small Japanese boats; most were carrying from one to three passengers, all waving flags or holding signs welcoming us to Sasebo and inviting us to whatever establishment they represented; usually bars and nightclubs. Signs such as FREE DRINKS and SEXY LADIES were predominant.

Once the small boats cruised within throwing distance, the Japanese occupants, all wearing their biggest smiles and waving excitedly, threw packets of cards, matches, and plastic cigarette holders, each item imprinted with simple directions to their places of business. Some variation of "You please come my place" was usually squeezed into whatever other message they wanted to convey. Misspelled words were common and humorous, but they too provided additional stimulation to my young and impressionable interests. By one means or another all "solicitors" managed to get their messages across to us.

Finally, as we were approaching the pier, from the 1-MC came the words: "Now secure from quarters." Clearing the main deck of unnecessary personnel made it easier for deck hands to handle mooring lines in the process of getting the ship safely tied up alongside the pier.

I eagerly watched whatever I could see from inside the after berthing compartment hatch. Absolutely everything was interesting and exciting. Talk about stimulation, I was totally engulfed by curiosity. I wanted to get off the ship and experience the land I had heard and read about. And of course I wanted to see the beach where MD had promised we would go.

"Now, liberty call. Liberty commences for Sections 2 and 3, to expire on board at 2400 for enlisted men and at 0600 for all hands tomorrow morning, May 20, 1955. The liberty uniform for enlisted men is service dress whites with ribbons; for officers and chief petty officers, khakis with ribbons or appropriate civilian attire. Now liberty call."

Finally, there it was, the word all of us in liberty sections were waiting to hear!

As previously planned, MD and a couple of other pals of his met Marcel and me on the quarterdeck. I watched each of them present their ID card and liberty card to the OOD, request permission to leave the ship, and salute the flag on the fantail as they stepped from the ship onto the gangway (brow) leading ashore. I didn't want to make any mistake that might cause the OOD to consider denying me my liberty. Bathing suit under arm, in the most perfect posture that I could muster, I approached, requested and was granted permission, and departed the ship following closely behind my leaders.

Numerous base taxis were readily available to transport individuals or small groups wherever they wanted to go. "Base cabs," those that were authorized to enter and exit the base, were easily identified by the green bubble taxi sign mounted on top. They were also slightly larger than other cabs. Base cab drivers were only supposed to accept Japanese yen for their fare — which was not always convenient. Periodically cab drivers were called into the dispatch station to turn in whatever Japanese yen they had accumulated. Their funds had to balance with their meter readings — there was very little allowance for a variance. The system of payment was designed to help keep American MPC out of black-market circulation off base. Sailors were never reluctant to pay the drivers in MPC when they had nothing else, but that took a bit of persuasion. Japanese drivers knew that they would be subject to severe penalties, above and beyond the loss of the base taxi contract, if they were caught manipulating or commingling funds. And since they were known to be tested periodically for their honesty, by representatives of the Naval Investigative Service, the drivers exercised a great deal of caution. Cab fare paid in MPC usually ended up with the passenger being shortchanged as a result of the conversion factor, especially when, more often than not, the paying passenger had been drinking or was new to the country. There was also an expected gratuity to be paid since the driver violated the rule to satisfy the passenger's request.

Another not so frequently used method of shortchanging that was practiced most often at the base clubs, particularly at the EM (Enlisted Men's) Club, was when servicemen were given change in obsolete MPC, absolutely worthless paper. Seldom did the recipient of that rip-off realize he'd been taken until the next time payment was being made for something else. Then it not only proved to be quite aggravating; it was also embarrassing. It was practically impossible to identify the perpetrator. To the newcomer in Japan, "they" really did all seem to look alike. When positive identification could be made, the accused person would become totally indignant and would flatly deny any wrongdoing.

They would say, "No, no, you terribry wrong. You mistake. Me never cheat you rike that."

There is no "L" sound in the Japanese language, the sound of "R" being about as close as most of them could pronounce. Most frequently the more direct response to being accused was: "Why you talk talk bad thing me?" Rarely did the victim recover his loss. It was something of a game that sailors just didn't seem to comprehend and were usually incapable of winning.

I was fascinated by the moneychangers; the usual first stop en route to off-base liberty. They were, regardless of the country we visited, the most nimble-fingered individuals in the world. The normal procedure was for us to stand in single-file lines, each line terminating at an individual money change booth and each booth occupied by one female moneychanger. They could count money faster than lightning — and with unbelievable accuracy; rarely did they make a mistake. We always recounted our money for fear of being shortchanged since our eyes were never able to keep up with the moneychanger's count.

Our next step was an attempt to instill deep within our minds the current exchange rate so that we could make purchases without having to labor over whether or not the price was fair. Some men carried small calculators — but the downtown shops also had their own. Shop proprietors were never reluctant to shove their calculators in front of potential shoppers in an effort to show them firsthand how honest they were in offering remarkable bargains.

Immediately after converting some money into Japanese yen (360 yen to the American dollar), the five of us squeezed into two base cabs and agreed to meet somewhere downtown "on the strip."

The drive, kamikaze style, was enough to awaken the dead — then scare them back to death. Driving on the "wrong" side of the road was confusing enough, but the cabbies drove as if they were not only immune to accidents, they were not required to abide by traffic laws — assuming there were some.

In reality, the drivers were probably more proficient than they were dangerous. Granted the fact the cabs were small in size, the cabbies were uncanny at their ability to maneuver their vehicles through the tightest of spaces, in the most congested of traffic, and between any and all other obstacles — at unbelievable high rates of speed! To top that off, the already initiated sailors, those more familiar with Japanese ways, encouraged drivers to go faster by using Japanese words the drivers were sure to understand: "Haiyaku" (Hurry up), coupled with promises of "Takusan okane" (Lots of money) to those drivers who responded favorably.

Once we arrived safely somewhere downtown, we paid the driver and began touring the area. I must have been about as wide-eyed as any child during a first visit to an ice-cream parlor. Everything that I saw was interesting and unique.

We had been walking for twenty minutes or so, just window-shopping, marveling at all the wondrous things available to buy, when I said one of the stupidest things a sailor could ever ask: "So when are we going to the beach?"

At first, dead silence as I was looked upon with absolute disbelief. Then came the unmistakable roar of laughter that could only mean I had said something terribly wrong.

"You dumb fucker — you *are* on the beach! Damn, Ad, [my newfound nickname], you'll never be a sailor if you don't even know when you're on the fucking beach."

So there on that day, in the faraway country of Japan, in the town of Sasebo, I learned that one did not necessarily have to be "at" the beach. Being "on the beach" was, quite simply, anywhere off of the ship on land.

Liberty, to most young inexperienced sailors in the Orient, meant drinking just about anything intoxicating. There were no age limits or restrictions for the consumption of alcoholic beverages off-base. This opened the door to experiences some sailors were not totally prepared to undertake. On-base, strict adherence to the "over twenty-one" rule applied. It became necessary for those of us desiring to partake in alcoholic beverages to do our drinking off-base, where we had the "adult" freedom to do so. We could become totally intoxicated while also being overwhelmed by the vices provided by other attractions — beautiful, shapely, desirable women included.

In time, once I had overheard enough sailor talk, I knew that a "steamer" was any individual capable of drinking as much or more, staying out as late or later, being as obnoxious or more obnoxious, than those men who had already proven themselves. To be known as a steamer was the liberty-time goal of many sailors. Being able to keep up when, in fact, it was long past time to give up mistakenly made me think such individuals were to be admired and respected. Being the last one standing, being the last to leave, and having the final word were all marks of distinction carried by that relatively few known as steamers. For whatever reason sailors do stupid things, I wanted that distinction. Quite by chance — unknowingly and unintentionally — I began working at it that very first liberty.

In accordance with MD's leadership and direction, our first planned destination was the Jungle Club. But as the club came into view, I became separated from the group, momentarily distracted by a group of rickshaw drivers. It didn't take much persuasion, recognizing the fact that I was a typical young horny sailor, when one of the drivers spoke.

"Hey, Joe, you rikee pretty gir[l]? You ride my rickshaw, go prenty good time."

The price was not negotiable up front.

"No, no, you check-check first, you rikee for sure, you pay."

So I accepted the offer that had been made by one of the rickshaw drivers and climbed into the seat without the slightest knowledge as to where I was — where I was going — or whether I would ever be capable of finding my way back.

Within minutes we were at a place that looked more like a private residence than a house of ill repute. In fact, it probably was a residence. The girl inside was probably a friend or relative of the driver, or she may have been under contract with any number of rickshaw and/or taxi drivers. Once I saw the young school-age appearing girl, probably about my age, the driver pulled me to the side and said, "OK, you rikee you pay 400 yen, number-one short time." That sounded like a bargain to me. Three hundred sixty yen to the dollar meant an hour of sexual pleasure for about $1.11.

"Sold," I said.

The girl and I wasted no time getting in the bed and I immediately began working off my otherwise perpetual erection.

At some time during the hour I was there, the girl asked me how much I had paid.

"Four hundred yen."

She showed signs of being somewhat surprised.

"Why you pay so much?"

Until she said that, I thought I had the bargain of a lifetime. Once I explained and she realized that the rickshaw driver had also taken his finder's fee, she was satisfied that the price had not been inflated. I thought the price was just about perfect; reconfirmed when I found that the price had also included the round-trip fare back to my starting point. The very same driver had patiently waited for me just steps from the house.

After being returned safe and sound, feeling a little drained of energy but otherwise ready for whatever experience was next to come, I relocated MD and the rest of the group where they had previously planned to be: at the Jungle Club. They were all a bit angry at me for having disappeared, but after I explained to them that I had been "window-shopping" in close proximity, they relaxed — perfectly satisfied that I had not taken any unnecessary chances; I had not been out of line. It would not have been wise for me to brag about my escapade since they had, to some degree, accepted responsibility for me when they first took me under wing.

The Jungle Club was my first introduction to, my very first experience at, a nightclub. The booths were well padded and the décor was plush. The hostesses were absolutely gorgeous and were instinctively driven to please male clients; whether that meant simple conversation or serving them drinks. At that juncture, I didn't know if there were other pleasures that could also be included or negotiated.

Marcel and I were both interested in one particular girl. We had been watching her intently and had brought her very feminine and favorable attributes to each other's attention. We agreed that she was by far the most beautiful girl in the club. The girl was small in comparison to American women, yet built proportionately perfect. The tiny black mole on her right cheek was truly a beauty mark that made her that much more distinctive and seductive. She was sitting alone just a couple of booths away from us and seemed to be daydreaming.

Marcel leaned just slightly forward over our table, his unintentional disclosure that he was going to approach her. Without hesitation I quickly jumped to my feet and rushed toward her table.

"Paul, you sonofabitch... ." Marcel fumed.

As I slid into the semicircular booth she was occupying I politely asked if I could join her. Her simple, "Sure," started my heart pounding. Marcel glared at me. I didn't have the slightest idea as to what I should say or do next. I heard my awkward voice ask if she wanted to share some champagne with me — and I was a bit startled with another immediate, "Sure."

I had tasted champagne at home as a youngster, but the stuff we were served tasted more like ginger ale. It was sweet and easy to swallow.

My reluctance to engage in conversation was due to a distinct shyness I had acquired years earlier, coupled with the fact I had been a bit overwhelmed having been so readily accepted by such a beautiful treasure of the Orient. But conversation did evolve as the beverage we were sharing loosened my tongue and gave boost to my otherwise-lacking courage.

I learned that her name was Takiko and that she was a hostess at the club. She spoke very good English and willingly provided answers to all of my questions. She took the time to teach me a few simple Japanese words and made sure I was capable of pronouncing them correctly. I was a gentleman and Takiko could not have been more of a lady.

I wanted to remain at the Jungle Club for the rest of the evening, enjoying my new feeling of freedom. I also had something of a remote thought in the back of my mind that I might get lucky with the lovely creature that was sitting closely, even romantically, beside me. But as luck would have it, and to Marcel's delight, MD insisted that we move on to greener pastures. I promised Takiko I would return the following evening.

77

"You come back tomorrow, we make [l]ove my prace, ne?" she whispered in my ear.

I could not believe what I had heard, yet the promise was real and very exciting. After several assurances from her that what she had whispered was precisely what she meant, I got up to leave.

The erection bulging in my pants was uncomfortable, and I silently prayed that it would go unnoticed in the dim lighting of the club — subside completely by the time we crossed the floor to the exit. I couldn't help but visualize how great it was going to be getting rid of that erection, as many times as possible, the following night. Thinking such thoughts reinforced, with that much more strength, the already-rigid erection I was experiencing. It was not going to go away!

At the exit Takiko giggled as she looked down at my pants. She spoke as she very gently rubbed by bulging crotch with both of her hands.

"You no forget, tomorrow I take care, ne?"

I thought to myself, *What part of heaven is Japan?*

Later that same night, after we had once again settled at another equally impressive club, Club Kokusai, MD did his best to caution me about my drinking.

"Slow down, Ad — this Jap beer is green and it'll sneak up and getcha."

Other shipmates had other ideas as they unanimously voiced a different opinion, one of uncalled for encouragement: "Aw, leave Ad alone; he's a steamer and can handle it."

I beamed as I ordered another — and another. It didn't take long before the room began to swirl around me and I knew that the inevitable was about to take place. I rushed to the head.

Many Japanese rest rooms were communal, male and female combined — and were used by both genders simultaneously. Such was the case at the Kokusai. Relatively few downtown rest rooms were equipped with wall-mounted urinals. Most toilets were mounted at floor-level, directly over septic tanks, usually without benefit of running water. Whether one was throwing up or squatting over an elongated *benjo*, both were awkward and were not easily performed by Americans. Squatting behind a tree, with no container to aim for, would have been easier.

While throwing up in a "regular" toilet was never a pleasant experience, having to get down on hands and knees with one's face within inches of a *benjo*, so close to the filth and stench it emitted, was a situation only a sailor would undertake. I was such a sailor that night. Unfortunately, the position of my upper torso, head lowered and butt up, provided just enough downward angle, aided by gravity, for my liberty card and my ID card to slip from my jumper pocket. Both fell directly into the waste matter below. Without hesitation I did the unthinkable, what no reasonable person would ever consider doing. I rolled up my sleeve, reached in, and retrieved them. Those two cards were my tickets ashore, and there was no way that I was going to abandon them.

That first liberty ended up a total disaster for me. Few sailors, if any, have been sicker or felt worse. I remember being assisted; probably I was carried to, and "poured" into, a taxi with "friends." Upon return to the ship I was helped across the brow and somehow managed to obtain permission to board. That night I ended up sleeping in my "pajamas" (fully clothed) on some locker tops for the few remaining hours before reveille.

MD worked me harder than ever the following day. He knew that my muscles were stiff from head to toe, my stomach muscles in particular, and that I was suffering my first and potentially the worst hangover I would ever suffer throughout my entire life. He instilled within me a bit of wisdom, a standard that I would not only live by throughout my military service but continued to practice throughout my years of employment: *Work hard, play hard — there is time for each — never commingle or become confused by which takes priority.*

My failure to realize that I had to stand duty the following night meant that my promise to return to Takiko at the Jungle club had to be broken. I did not know that by special request "exchange of duty" was an option that was usually approved; someone else could have stood my duty that night. I stood my duty knowing that the next night, the third and final night before the ship would depart from Sasebo, I would receive Takiko's undivided attention. I thought of little else during those twenty-four hours of duty.

I was well prepared for liberty that third afternoon when liberty call was announced. What I wasn't prepared for was what I learned when I arrived at the Jungle Club. First, one of the club hostesses told me that Takiko had waited faithfully for me the previous night. She had lied to her "station boyfriend" (permanently shore-stationed boyfriend — her bread and butter) so that she could be with me.

"I'm sorry; I had the duty. Where is Takiko?"

My question was answered nonchalantly; "She no work tonight, she home with station boyfriend."

I was one terribly disappointed sailor!

The ship departed bright and early the following morning, when by directive and of necessity shipboard routine resumed. There was little time for anything else to occupy my mind. I did spend a great deal of what little free time I had writing letters to family members and friends. I wrote far more letters than I ever received — but that, according to the old-timers, was to be expected. I was supposed to disregard my disappointment when letters were not answered. After all, I was a sailor; one who would sooner or later adjust to the realization that loneliness was always a seagoing partner.

I had more of an inquisitive mind than my peers, and I was far more adventurous. I was known to take chances many others would not take. For instance, I ate and drank whatever the locals were eating and drinking. I would not hesitate to venture inside establishments that didn't exhibit the eight-by-ten-inch blue **A** in their windows. The **A** designated those places that served food or beverages to be "Class-A" establishments. Theoretically, that meant all of the establishments displaying the sign had been thoroughly checked out by American authorities and were considered safe and sanitary. All other establishments were off-limits to members of all branches of military service. I can say unequivocally many of the off-limits establishments were as safe or safer than some of those qualified to display the blue **A**. I'm not saying that visiting off-limits establishments was acceptable behavior. I'm sure that some of the chances I took were far from safe, some were absolutely unacceptable. I was very lucky not being victimized in one way or another while taking such chances. In retrospect, I was the perfect example of a fool, but even knowing that, as a direct result of my chance taking I did gain invaluable knowledge of people and places. I saw and lived situations few other sailors experienced, many of which will be described in detail later.

Our next port call, June 8th, was Yokosuka, Japan. Unfortunately, the ship struck a whale as we were entering the harbor. The sharp superstructure of the bow sliced deeply into the whale's side, assuring it could not possibly survive. In no time at all there were literally dozens of small Japanese boats heading toward the severely crippled mammal. They were coming from all directions, deliberate in their objective, determined to retrieve whatever they could salvage of the whale's remains. There was nothing the Captain or crew of the *Colahan* could do about the situation other than continue on course toward Yokosuka.

Yokosuka provided a great deal more in the choices of nightlife than Sasebo, all of which were within walking distance of the base. Several blocks from the Yokosuka Naval Base main gate was the Club Alliance, something between an Enlisted Men's Club and a YMCA, where a can of ice-cold American beer cost a dime. One night a week, "Nickel Night," beer flowed "freely." At a nickel a beer few sailors departed the club cold sober. Cigarettes cost a dime a pack at the club — considered expensive in comparison to the ninety-cent-a-carton shipboard price. A saving of a penny a pack meant an extra package of twenty cigarettes when bought by the carton.

The more compact "stand bars" were cozy and enjoyable even though they lacked the availability of entertaining hostesses. They were small bars with very little room in which to maneuver; sometimes horseshoe-shaped and sometimes a straight bar. Most of the stand bars were not much larger than a typical large Western-style walk-in clothes closet. Regardless of the type, size, or shape of the bar or nightclub, the price for drinks remained fairly consistent. There was never the need to bicker or barter over the price of any beverage since everything was already more than reasonable.

"Souvenir Street" was very near to the main gate and was more commonly known as "Black Market Alley." Sooner or later all sailors were sure to find themselves somewhere along that narrow strip. *Everything* imaginable could be found for sale on one side or the other of the two or three blocks Souvenir Street had to offer.

It didn't take me long to learn how to barter. The first price was at least double the acceptable price, sometimes triple. The smart shopper would test the market, shop around and learn what the going prices were, then make his purchase at the store or from the vendor offering the best deal. Cameras, camera equipment, and electronic devices were the exception, where haggling over the displayed prices seldom resulted in a discount.

Beautifully lacquered music/jewelry boxes, decorative and impressive china dishes, personalized coffee mugs, engraved cigarette lighters, and paintings, were commonplace and could be purchased at truly bargain prices. Grampus fishing rods and photo albums were also plentiful and were favored over other souvenirs. "Dirty" (pornographic) pictures, actual color photos, usually depicting forty-eight positions of sexual intercourse, were openly displayed in most of the small souvenir shops. The same pictures were printed on silk scarves and handkerchiefs, all for sale at near give-away prices.

Downtown department stores, well off the souvenir strip, had fixed prices — and sold their commodities as cheap as a shopper could expect — but it wasn't fun shopping without the haggling process.

Also for sale were several variations of *Baby-san* joke books. They provided near perfect examples of the humorous side of Japanese and U.S. Navy relations. Baby-san, the adorable cartoon character of the books, represented the typical Japanese girlfriend of the typical American serviceman; sailor most frequently. She found herself in every possible awkward predicament, always miraculously managing to escape. Baby-san was a *cho-cho*, a butterfly, as she "serviced" as many boyfriends as she could get away with. The jokes, far more accurate than imagined, showed her remarkable ability and ingenuity in covering her tracks, never getting caught. Baby-san knew what ships were in port and what ships were at sea — she knew when ships would enter port and when they would depart — and she had at least one boyfriend on each ship. She knew which boyfriend was likely to show up and she tried desperately to always have the right guy's picture proudly displayed when he arrived. The switching of pictures at different times of the day was sometimes necessary in baby-san's very disciplined life. She never ran out of excuses. She provided logical and believable answers for every conceivable situation that took on the appearance of her being or having been unfaithful. The *Baby-san* series of joke books was a favorite of all sailors. We could all relate to her; we all knew a Baby-san!

Every evening, as the sun began to fade, Black Market Alley came to life. All of the shops were lit up like Christmas; lights of all shapes and colors would flash their welcome-to-my-place message and they were quite effective in attracting attention. The prostitutes (businesswomen, as they preferred to be called) were on every corner, available by the hour or by the night. The services of the hookers were also negotiable; the lovelier and shapelier girls were sure of getting and receiving the highest offers.

"Hey, Joe, you like fuck my sister?"

82

Such offers were prevalent and were usually proposed by youngsters barely out of, or perhaps still in, grade school. Within all referrals to their sisters was the guarantee that they were "cherry." Cherry girls would willingly lose their virginity if the price was right, and they would lose it several times every night... .

Sailors who managed to make it from one end of the strip to the other without accepting offers of one kind of sex or another would sometimes be accused of preferring men to women. If that was the preference, it too could be arranged. Drugs were also available but were not as openly and brazenly offered. Tea was usually substituted for marijuana, and no one ever complained. To whom would they submit their complaint?

Overnight "chits," or passes as they were also known, a privilege usually approved for more seasoned sailors and automatically authorized for officers, were not that easily obtained by enlisted men at the bottom of the pay scale. Chiefs also had to request overnight authority. An approved overnight chit assured there would be no penalty for returning to the ship after midnight (Cinderella liberty).

There were times, particularly after a ship's party when alcohol had a manner of changing one's priorities, when men would approach the Captain himself and ask for his written authority to remain ashore overnight. The skipper was fair game — and could be approached ashore in hopes he would approve such requests. I never knew the man to turn anyone down. He probably should have in instances where individuals had already consumed more than their share of booze, but the skipper knew that his refusal would have added significantly to the probability of an unnecessary scene. Tempers were far too easily provoked toward the expiration of liberty and oftentimes innocent bystanders suffered the consequences. It was unlikely an angered sailor would take it out on the Captain — but frustrations were very apt to be vented on nearly anyone else.

You never saw a surlier bunch of hungover sailors than in the mornings at liberty boat landings. Most sailors, although there were exceptions, tried to either drink all night or have sex with their newfound female "acquaintances" all night. Occasionally there were those that not only tried to but probably did accomplish both goals. In any event, it was more than obvious that those (excluding the far more gentlemanly officers) who remained ashore overnight while in the Orient, were totally exhausted in the morning.

On their behalf I will also say that they were probably the hardest bunch of workingmen too. Overnight privileges were in high demand, and those few individuals who, for whatever reasons, would not carry their share of the workload, could expect to be denied future requests for such approval.

Marcel and I were fortunate, since most of our requests for overnight liberty were approved. Once, when we both had "overnighters," we spent the entire evening at a submariner's hangout, the White Hat, a small bar in an alley behind Club Alliance. Instead of taking advantage of the overnight privilege we had been granted, we decided to return to the ship.

As we turned the corner from the alley and stepped onto the sidewalk to head "home," we saw an exceptionally well-dressed, very shapely, very classy Japanese lady approaching. She was not soliciting — but rather minding her own business walking on the sidewalk. I'm sure there were plenty of decent Japanese women, but they were the exception in areas frequented by sailors. I asked the lady where she was going and she very politely told me she was going to get something to eat. We asked if we could accompany her, and she said no. We offered to buy her meal, and she again said no. Marcel and I figured we had nothing to lose. After all, we did have overnight passes. So we persisted and kept on walking with her, Marcel on one side, I on the other.

It was a rare opportunity; we had actually met a nice, decent Japanese woman and we were not ready to give up on making her acquaintance without exerting a little more effort. She tried to discourage our obvious efforts, but we refused to listen. Finally, after walking several blocks into an area that was probably off-limits, she stopped in front of a small sushi bar. Marcel and I figured that was the end of the trail for us and we were fully prepared, though not entirely willing, to give up.

Marcel and I were pleased beyond expression when that beautiful woman reluctantly, yet graciously, allowed us to sit with her while she ate sushi. She offered to share her meal, and I accepted — only to find that the unusual taste was not entirely to my liking. I had never tasted sushi; rice and raw fish wrapped and rolled in seaweed and sliced into one-inch pieces. The unusual flavor was different from anything I had ever tasted, not at all what I had expected.

As the woman continued to eat, I assured her that we would pay for her meal. With a slight bow forward and over her plate of remaining sushi she politely and humbly thanked us. Then, when I knew she was finished eating and that she was about to get up, I quickly rushed to hold the door open for her. I thanked Marcel for his initiative in paying for the meal and immediately closed the door. Marcel's somewhat muffled, "You sonofabitch," was expected.

Taking advantage or otherwise tricking Marcel was never planned in advance; situations just presented themselves — and I acted accordingly.

Marcel quickly paid for her meal and joined us outside. Very much to our surprise and delight, Pat (her Americanized name) invited us to stay at her home for the night.

Pat's home was beautiful. It was a typical Japanese house with clouded-glass sliding doors leading into a small foyer, an area that was reserved for the removal of outside footwear and for the donning of house slippers. We removed our shoes and put on the guest slippers she provided. After sliding another set of paper-windowed doors we entered the home proper.

Without any other exchange of words, absolutely no discussion whatsoever, Pat grabbed my neckerchief and spoke.

"You sleep my bed; he sleep Midori bed."

It never entered our minds that there might be another female living with Pat. And even though we each probably had visions of making it with Pat, we really didn't expect to sleep with female companions that night. Buddha, or some form of spiritual entity, was most assuredly looking favorably upon us.

I was ravished beyond the point of consent that night. Raped? Perhaps so, at least to some degree. Pat simply would not leave me alone — but exhausted as I was, I "allowed" the activities to continue not knowing whether I loved it or wanted it to stop. She made sure I was absolutely and positively satisfied in every respect, arousing me as frequently as my hormones would allow and then satisfying my sexual needs as they had never before been satisfied. I found myself once again wondering just what part of heaven Japan occupied.

Early the following morning Marcel and I kissed our new friends, our unexpected lovers, good-bye. We promised to return that same night and headed back to the ship. There was never a mention of money or payment for services by either Pat or Midori. Marcel and I really hit the jackpot that night.

We knew that no one would ever believe us, so we kept that unbelievable story to ourselves. It was suspected, however, due to our exceptionally happy mood as we worked that following day, that either something spectacular had happened the night before or we were planning on something remarkable happening while on liberty that night. Both suspicions were completely accurate.

Liberty call commenced at 1600 hours, and Marcel and I were first in line to go ashore. We spent the whole day buying an impressive assortment of souvenirs. It was still daylight when we knew we could no longer carry anything additional and therefore made the decision to go directly to Pat's place.

Without hesitation Pat welcomed us back into her home. Pat and Midori radiated with happiness; they were genuinely anxious for us to return, overjoyed to see us. They giggled and laughed and embraced us as they talked quickly to one another in Japanese. Reality set in when they started thanking us in English — thanking us for all the wonderful gifts, the impressive assortment of "presentos" we had brought them.

I had never seen two people lose their composure quite so rapidly as when we explained that there was nothing for them, that everything was for us or for our families in the States. Then, as only an ugly American would do, I laughed at their disappointment, at their having considered us as thoughtful and generous. I went further, well beyond the limits of good judgment.

"We're not here to give; we're here to receive."

Marcel was the only one to appreciate my warped sense of humor as he laughed with me — only to break it off with the same spontaneity as he then accused me of being cruel. Pat and Midori then understood the real reason we were there.

Both girls then admitted that they worked at Club Florida, a bar on Souvenir Street, and that if we expected to sleep there we would have to pay just like everyone else. That clearly meant we would have to go to the bar, buy them more ladies' drinks (usually colored water or tea) than anyone else, and then meet them later. A donation of some monetary value was also expected. We told the girls we would think about it, gathered up our belongings, and headed back to the ship to stow them. We then "hit the beach" again to do some steamin' of our own. I ended up staying at Hotel Green Heights that night.

Hotel Green Heights was a house of prostitution. It was nestled up on a hillside on a piece of prime property that provided a beautiful view overlooking a portion of Yokosuka and the harbor. Surrounding homes were poorly constructed but were attractive, and the occupants were friendly. I could sense their disapproval of the business that was being conducted at the hotel, but they didn't voice it openly. Quite the contrary, they made me feel safe, comfortable, and welcome whenever they saw me on "their" hill. It was there, at Hotel Green Heights, that I met Kimiko; a very attractive "businesswoman." She became the only Japanese girl I was truly interested in sleeping with. Kimiko was far more than a professional; she was an absolute detailed perfectionist.

The hotel *mama-san*, the common term for all house madams — also used as a polite term when addressing older women, particularly store proprietors, was in absolute control of her girls. All negotiations were conducted through her, and her price was final. The girls received 50 percent of whatever Mama-san agreed upon. Prices were based on how close it was to payday, whether it was for a "short-time" (an hour or less) or for an all-night session, whether the girl was in demand or not, how frequent the client patronized the place, how many ships were in port, and other factors. Prices ranged anywhere from 400 up to 1,000 yen; somewhere between a dollar and three dollars in U.S. currency. Considered quite a bargain to those who indulged.

Kimiko became a very good friend and I became quite fond of her. It was not always a sexual thing — we would sit and talk for hours about any subject and we could sleep together without having sex. Unlike other girls at Green Heights, Kimiko was allowed to take walks up and around the mountain areas with me. There was a real sense of trust that Kimiko and I shared, and we were always totally honest with one another. There were times, whenever Kimiko was not in need of money, that she would give me back her 50 percent "commission." I always knew that there could be no viable future for us much beyond that which we had already shared, but Kimiko always preferred to believe that some miracle would eventually tie us together for life.

Kimiko and I did manage to keep in touch by mail as well as in person for about twelve years. Periodically she made honest efforts to get out of the profession, only to return time and again to the lifestyle she knew best.

Marcel and I spent many hours walking the back streets of Yokosuka. The scenery was truly breathtaking. Trees and shrubs were emerald green, and the homes were picturesque. There were mountain trails embedded with stone pebbles and a number of steep stairways leading up the mountainsides to brightly colored religious statues, shrines, and pagodas. Everything looked as if it had jumped right out of the pages of *National Geographic*. We spent a lot of time taking 35mm slide photographs and 8mm movies around the area. How else could we prove that something other than the strip existed and that we had actually been to, and had observed with our own eyes, those beautiful and impressive outlying areas?

Once when Marcel and I were walking up in the foothills, we both clearly saw the upper portion of a beautiful Buddha statue, in among surrounding trees and other greenery, some distance above us. It did not appear to be too far, so we decided to follow the trail for a closer look. When we believed we had hiked a distance proportionate to where we thought the statue should be, we found ourselves thoroughly confused. The statue of Buddha was nowhere to be seen. We conducted what we both considered a reasonably thorough search of the area but we couldn't locate it. When we finally gave up and began retracing our steps back down the hillside we maintained a constant over-the-shoulder vigil but we never again caught sight of what we both knew to be there. The mystery of the disappearing Buddha remains "unsolved." Imaginary? I think not.

Many sailors took chances smuggling booze on board when they returned off liberty. Any attempt to do so was dangerous, since most attempts were foiled by the OOD. The OOD and the POOW (Petty Officer of the Watch) closely scrutinized the lower pay grades for illegal contraband.

I got brave one night and decided to smuggle two pints of whiskey on board. I really didn't like the taste of whiskey, I'd not yet acquired the taste, but I wanted to prove to my closest peers that I could pull it off. On that occasion I had forgotten that the *Colahan* was tied up "out in the stream" next to an "AD," a destroyer tender. That meant I not only had to cross the tender's quarterdeck, I would also have to make it successfully across two other destroyers tied up between the tender and the *Colahan*.

"Foss," another member of the after engineroom gang and friend of mine, was with me that night. Foss had far more scruples than I; he was a more serious individual, much less apt to go against the grain of any rule or regulation. That's not to say Foss didn't enjoy his liberty ashore or that he didn't have a sense of humor, as he most assuredly did. He was more inclined to behave himself, do his job the best he could, complete his enlistment without any unnecessary hang-ups, and get on with his life. Foss was one of those individuals that was admired by everyone with whom he came in contact.

The two pints of whiskey were a little more than I could conceal comfortably, so I asked Foss if he would carry one for me. Without the slightest hesitation Foss showed me his very broad grin and politely told me he would not! He knew that I was going to have a problem getting both bottles on board, but he was not about to be my accomplice. I was disappointed but not angry. He was true to his character; I should never have asked such a favor of him.

As we proceeded up the gangway steps to the tender, I began to have second thoughts. I asked Foss his opinion, if I should discard the two bottles into the ocean.

"Do what ever you want," was his uncommitted, somewhat-expected reply.

I made sure the two pints were as inconspicuous as possible, both tucked tightly beside each other in front of my stomach, half under my trouser belt line and half beneath my jumper. I looked a little plump but otherwise not too identifiable as one smuggling booze aboard. As we continued climbing the gangway, I could feel myself becoming more and more nervous. There were already several sailors that had been pulled aside by the OOD for violations of one kind or another.

I breathed my first sigh of relief when the OOD on the tender granted me permission to "cross." Similarly, I was granted permission to cross the two destroyers, and in practically no time I found myself requesting permission to board the *Colahan*.

"Permission granted."

As I boarded I could feel the two pints slipping lower into my trousers and I knew that there were very few steps remaining before one bottle or the other would become visibly apparent — or worse yet, slip all the way down my pants leg. Instead of attempting to walk the distance from the quarterdeck (midship) aft to the berthing compartment, I decided it best to climb down the engineroom ladder, it being conveniently located right there at the quarterdeck. Foss continued on his way to the berthing compartment, not wanting to take on the appearance of having anything to do with my activities should I suffer the misfortune of being caught.

The first couple of steps down the ladder I knew I was in trouble. I could feel both bottles slipping lower into my trousers. I had to take turns pushing one after the other back up while continuing to descend the fifteen or so steps of the vertical ladder. My somewhat spastic movements could only have appeared suspicious to the engineroom watch as well as the topside POOW as I made my way down the ladder. Just as I stepped from the ladder onto the deck plates of the engineroom upper level, one of the bottles slipped all the way down my pants leg and fell out onto the deck.

"What's that?" I heard the topside petty officer yell down.

"It's my Bible, pal, don't worry about it." I quickly scooped it up, concealed it under my partially hunched-over body, and hobbled out of his view. Concerned that the petty officer was going to investigate further, I immediately hid both bottles inside a large emergency first-aid chest that was mounted adjacent to the electrical switchboard.

"Didn't sound like a Bible to me," I heard him say as he descended the ladder; "Let's have a look-see."

I kept walking away, my back to my adversary, toward the opposite side of the engineroom. With each step I pretended to be more and more inebriated as I wobbled back and forth into the handrails and surrounding machinery. When the petty officer caught up with me and demanded to see my Bible, I slobbered as I spoke in short, muffled, unintelligible phrases and feigned a state of total drunkenness. Finally, my last dramatized act of defiance was that of slowly sliding down the side of the bulkhead to the deck plates — passed out drunk!

I heard the petty officer grumbling, "I give up," as he turned around and left what he must have thought of as nothing more than a pathetic crumpled-up pile of useless being. Within a minute or two my rival was gone and I was back on my feet celebrating. It had been a very close call, but I had, on my very first attempt, successfully smuggled two pints of whiskey on board. I would, in time, recover my treasures and celebrate on board instead of ashore — a venture that was dangerous, even more so than that of smuggling it aboard.

About a week after departing Yokosuka, we pulled into Hong Kong Harbor, the most popular R & R port in the Orient.

By this time I had experienced the three modes of standing engineering duties: "main plant," "auxiliary," and "cold iron." Underway we were always in the main plant mode, with one or both main generators providing electrical power throughout the ship. Anchored, it was optional, main plant or auxiliary, depending on how soon we expected to get underway and what the power requirements were. The auxiliary mode meant switching from the main steam plant requirements of underway operations to the much smaller auxiliary plant requirements of a single generator. The cold iron mode, favored by all snipes, was only possible when we were tied up alongside another ship or facility capable of and willing to provide the ship with an external source of electrical power. Since we were going to anchor about a mile or so out in the bay, the decision was to go on auxiliary, with the "rainmaker" (evaporators) on the line. Being "on the line" meant in operation or in use.

Similar to the small-craft welcoming party we were greeted with at Yokosuka, but to a greater extent, the boats that had accompanied us as we entered port continued to circle us. They not only displayed their welcoming banners and pelted us with souvenir packets; they also carried cargoes of beautiful women, each representing a live advertisement of the quality and availability of female companionship and where we should go to get the best at the cheapest price.

Being anchored out required that all hands be transported by water taxi from the ship to shore. The Captain's Gig, usually engineered by a snipe, provided the Skipper with his own private water transportation. The cost for a water taxi was very little and could be met with a bar of soap or a pack of cigarettes. Since that was dealing in illicit trade it was also considered dealing in the black market, so those who elected to make payment in that manner had to be exceptionally cautious.

The ride by water taxi to shore was usually uneventful and took about fifteen minutes. The return trip, if taken late at night with a lot of drunken sailors, usually meant bloodshed. Booze and sailors just didn't mix well. It didn't take much, sometimes no provocation at all, for someone to take a swing at anyone or anything within swinging distance. The fights could be depended on, and I learned quickly to use a great deal of caution and keep my distance from potential troublemakers while at the same time maintaining a tight fist to use when necessary. There were always a few "bad asses," those who were either easily provoked or made it a practice to intentionally become provoked. They were the ones who enjoyed picking on the unsuspecting. They usually opted to sucker punch their targets, thereby realizing a quick and easy victory, at least making a win more likely.

It really was unsafe taking the last water transportation, liberty boat or water taxi, but there were always those, like me, who thought more of the extra liberty time ashore than of the possibility of being beaten or thrown overboard. Officers used better judgment and were seldom seen taking that last water taxi at the expiration of liberty for enlisted men. They not only had the option of taking an earlier boat; they could also take a later one without penalty. Unlike "Cinderella Liberty" enlisted men, their overnight privileges were valid everywhere.

There were any number of reasons that could or would provoke a fight — some valid, others not. I recall one incident in particular where, had a vote been taken, I would have voted provocation indeed. It was quite late at night, a duty night for me, and it was shortly after having been relieved from the watch at midnight. I had just climbed into my "tree," my bunk, and I heard someone groaning in a nearby bunk. I looked one tier of bunks across from mine and watched in shock and disbelief as the drunk sailor lying face down pulled his mattress from under his face, and "puked" directly into the face (and open mouth) of the sleeping sailor directly below him! The fight that ensued was short-lived as the drunk received just punishment for what he had done.

Hong Kong, a British Crown Colony (at that time), was strictly a liberty port and it provided the only real break in shipboard routine during the scheduled six-month WestPac cruise. This was the port everyone was anxious to visit. Not only did it mean maximum liberty hours; it meant ample opportunity to buy even more exotic souvenirs. Tailor-made clothing and footwear, hand-made form-fit boots, were always in demand.

Tailor shops were all similar in their sales techniques. They all had stacks of magazines and reams of pages that had been torn from recent issues of American fashion magazines, all depicting every imaginable type and style of clothing. All tailor shops had nice, comfortable lounge chairs for potential clients. But the one thing I found profoundly different about Hong Kong tailor shops was the fact that they all served booze — and it was always free! *Any* kind of booze. Any kind and any brand, imported or local. If they didn't have it right there, they'd send a runner to get it. Since I was not really interested in buying clothing, I took advantage of the free drinks. Proprietors knew precisely what they were doing, as they practically required clients to accept their offer of free drinks. Clients began to feel an obligation to buy something. And those who had already placed orders were influenced to buy more. I was no exception and was subsequently persuaded to buy a cashmere sweater.

As for Marcel? Well, Marcel did his thing and suffered tremendous ridicule the rest of his time on board the *Colahan*. Marcel was a true admirer of the King: Elvis Presley. Marcel probably had every record cut by Elvis, but his admiration went even farther. Not only did he like the clothing Elvis wore; he also liked the color of that clothing. So my very good friend was measured and fitted with an Elvis look-alike suit, large lapels and all. Marcel always stood his ground in that the color was salmon, but we all swore it was pink! It was not until years later, well after I retired from the Navy, that Marcel actually admitted that he probably made a mistake when he made that purchase. Yes, Marcel, and everyone but you knew it all along.

Marcel and I enjoyed touring out-of-the-way areas together. Once we hired Jackie Poon, a thin, undernourished-appearing but decent Chinese man, to show us around Hong Kong. The tour included watching two young Chinese girls making love to each other in the back room of some fleabag hotel. The girls, not at all provocative, first screwed each other with a double-ended dildo, then proceeded to show their skill at inserting eggs into their vaginas and their ability to pop them out quite some distance into some observer's white hat. The show was meant to entice us, to get us hot and horny, and then for us to catch a "short time" with one of the available hookers. It didn't work with us. Our idea was to see the "show" and get on with the tour — which we did.

Live lesbian shows or acts were fairly common, and a lot of sailors paid the price and watched them. With the right amount of money, a sailor could witness, even participate in, just about anything he could describe, including watching a woman having sex with a dog, a horse, or just about any other available animal!

Jackie Poon, Marcel, and I took the Peak Tramway, visited Madam Butterfly's respectable home, and swam at Repulse Bay. Jackie showed us other sights and made his personal recommendations as to which bars or establishments we should patronize. For his time, his effort, and his noteworthy advice we shared in providing him with a significant monetary bonus. Jackie did not expect that and he was very appreciative.

The following day I had the duty and I couldn't find anyone with whom to swap, so I was stuck on board and had to stand auxiliary watches. Since the evaps (evaporators) were on the line, watches had to be stationed in Main Control, the forward engineroom. At that time I had absolutely no experience or training on the evaps. When it came time for me to stand my watch I was given a five-minute hands-on lesson.

"If the water in the sight glasses goes up, close those valves a little. If the water goes down, open the valves a little."

I'll never forget his final words: "When the tanks are full, call the chief and let him know."

With that training and those instructions, I relieved the watch, thereby accepting the responsibilities that went with it. I did precisely what I was told and maintained proper water levels in the sight glasses. A couple of hours into my watch I felt a real sense of satisfaction and the stress of operating the evaps seemed to disappear, especially when I realized I had successfully filled all of the tanks. I called the chief.

What I wasn't, but should have been told by the off-going watch, was a matter of extreme importance; *which* tanks I was to fill. My orders had been clear; I had been told to fill *the* tanks.

There were "feedwater" tanks and there were "freshwater" tanks that the evaps were capable of distilling directly into. Bear in mind the fact that the only source of water from which to distill was always the ocean. Under a vacuum system of distilling, water temperatures remain well below that point normally associated with boiling. That might not seem too important to the casual reader; however, add in one other significant factor; the fact that Hong Kong Harbor was, and probably always will be, one of the most polluted harbors in the entire world. Bacteria of every known disease, some probably unknown, pollutants of every conceivable source, dead animals, including human remains, were all known contaminants in Hong Kong Harbor. And they were always plentiful.

The chief came down the ladder rather nonchalantly; not a care in the world. Sticking out of his back pocket was a "fuck book," a paperback novel, the main source of shipboard entertainment (and perhaps education) all chiefs seemed to partake in, usually while the rest of the crew worked. I'm sure he was just as anxious to get back to his book as I was to have the evaps secured.

"So you think you're all topped off, huh?" The chief glared over his glasses and spoke with a tone that seemed to question my ability to reason. His voice carried with it the distinct hint that I might have lacked the ability to determine the accuracy of tank levels, that they may or may not have actually been full.

"Yeah, Chief, everything's full. Can we shut this thing down now?"

"Okay." He then followed up with another question. "How 'bout fresh water? How much fresh water do we have?"

What a stupid question. Hadn't he just asked, and hadn't I clearly answered; everything was full?

"I just told you, Chief, *everything* is full."

"Godammit, Ad, I'm talking about the freshwater tanks."

"So am I, Chief."

The chief looked me square in the eyes and said, "Ad, you ain't telling me you topped off them fuckin' freshwater tanks, are you?"

"Yeah, Chief, like I said, all the tanks, fresh and feed."

I know today what I didn't know then. That chief saw his life flash before him, he saw his military career going right down the drain, and all because of me.

"Jesus Christ, Ad, what the fuck are you tryin' to do, kill the whole fuckin' crew? Don't you know you can't distill to freshwater tanks in port? And this is fuckin' Hong Kong Harbor for Christ's sake."

I stood there totally dumbfounded. I knew I'd done something terribly wrong, but I did not fully comprehend the magnitude or seriousness of the problem I had created.

I never saw that chief move as fast as when he started running up the ladder. He stopped briefly halfway up, turned, and yelled his orders at me with unmistakable clarity. "Ad, you better start drinking as much fresh water as you can. Half of this crew is gonna die because of you, and by God you better die with them. Now you keep your fuckin' mouth shut about this until I tell you otherwise!"

Clearly the chief was going to cover up my mistake. Equally clearly, it was *his* ass he was covering, not mine.

The chief took immediate steps to secure all fresh water throughout the ship. No drinking water, no showers, no cooking water, no fresh water for any purpose whatsoever. Freshwater tanks were consequently dumped into the harbor. Most of the crew was ashore on liberty, so the steps the chief had to take affected relatively few. The skipper, obviously and appropriately siding with the chief, made immediate arrangements for the purchase and delivery of fresh water by barge. As an added precaution, as that water was being pumped to the ship, it was heavily chlorinated to kill any remaining contaminant residue within the freshwater system.

I was never reprimanded for my mistake. How could I have been? That would have let the cat out of the bag. The skipper did not need the makings of a mutiny on his hands and elected to keep the entire matter under wraps. I'm not so sure of the wisdom in that decision, even though there were no treated ailments as a result of my unintentional mistake — my ignorance, as it was. That incident was perhaps the single most influential occurrence, which caused me, from that day forward, to take all matters as related to the process of shipboard qualification dead seriously. I always imposed significantly more stringent qualification requirements on anyone that I either personally trained or in any way shared in that responsibility.

The next day Marcel, Bob (another snipe), and I got an early start and we went directly to Repulse Bay. We hadn't been there very long when our attention was directed toward three very attractive Oriental women sitting alone on the beach not too far from us. Two of the three went into the water while the other remained stretched out on a towel. Bob and Marcel went into the water and were immediately accepted as water playmates, so I figured the remaining girl would be equally receptive to my advance. I was wrong. She simply told me right up front that she was not interested in my company. I returned to my own towel and sat there pouting for a few minutes, then went back for attempt number two. Strike two! I watched as "my" girl went into the water. It became obvious to me, as she floundered around in the shallow water, that she did not know how to swim — that I had a third opportunity to get to know her. I went directly to her and asked if I could help her learn how to swim. Instantly, as if she were an old and very dear and trusting friend, she jumped into my arms.

"For sure? You teach me?"

OK, Paul, do it right, I said to myself. *This little darling just might make my day a little brighter.*

Kim-Kim was half Chinese and half Portuguese, a perfect combination that resulted in a woman of genuine beauty, absolutely gorgeous, more so than anyone else I had ever met; centerfold material of the highest quality. Not to shortchange the other girls, as they too were exceptionally beautiful.

Kim-Kim was fun to be with, and she made me feel welcome even though my purpose was supposed to be that of swim instructor. I found that as I held her up in the water she didn't seem to mind when my supporting hand or hands wandered a little bit off the fulcrum. Matter of fact, I began to think she was enjoying my toying hands just as much as she seemed to be enjoying the swim lesson.

The six of us remained playing in the water for about an hour, after which we accompanied the girls to their towels where we immediately asked if we could see them again — soon. Just as quickly they answered yes in their own anxious way. They quickly followed up with additional information: the fact that they all lived conveniently together across the channel on Kowloon Peninsula, in an area at that time considered part of a Communist sector and consequently off-limits to American sailors. Kim-Kim gave me her personalized "business" card, thereby providing me with her full name as well as her home address.

Marcel, Bob, and I went into the men's locker room to wash off the ocean's salty remnants and to put on our uniforms. When we returned, the look of absolute disappointment that was clearly on the face of each of the three girls was unmistakable. They had never considered the possibility that we were anything other than officers. But there we stood, our distinct uniforms identifying us as undesirable enlisted men. In their eyes were the thoughts that we were probably broke, typically uneducated, and more than likely, troublemakers. Why shouldn't we be thought of as such — or even behave as such? After all, every book ever written, every movie ever produced, every conversation ever based on a sailor's behavior clearly depicted enlisted men as anything other than honorable.

"You are not officers?" one of the girls asked.

"Not hardly," I said.

Actually, they had unknowingly paid us quite a compliment in thinking we were officers and gentlemen. Apparently, we had conducted ourselves appropriately while in their company. It must have been that conduct that gave them the courage to stick to their agreement to see us again the following day — but with the emphatic stipulation that we show up in civvies, not in uniform! They didn't want us to ruin their reputations! That seemed fair enough to us; after all, we *couldn't* show up in uniform at a place off-limits to sailors.

Fortunately for us, the proprietor of the Saint Francis Tailor Shop (where we had already made purchases) was more than sympathetic to our plight. He suited each of us in tailored suits that had been ordered and paid for by civilian tourists. We were told that we could change clothing there at the tailor shop the following morning and that we would have to have the clothing back by closing time (well into the night) that evening.

The next day, immediately after changing into civvies, we rushed to the ferry landing. We were pleasantly surprised to learn that there were no authorities, no Shore Patrol or other enforcement agency, there to question the purpose or legality of persons boarding the Five Star Ferry, the usual transportation across the harbor to Kowloon. As Hong Kong was a free port, tourists from any country were welcomed. Also, a good portion of the population, other than the Chinese, comprised Caucasians and was indistinguishable as to their native homeland. So we blended right in, paid for our tickets, and boarded the ferry.

The trip was short and in no time we were setting foot on "forbidden" territory. The excitement of seeing our lady friends was nothing in comparison to the excitement in knowing we had exercised poor judgment and were probably in violation of any number of rules and regulations. We made ourselves appear as nonchalant and inconspicuous as we were capable.

We arrived at Kim-Kim's place around noon and were received respectfully. Each of the three girls had their own separate bedroom, and we were immediately segregated, a male and a female to each. Once we were separated it became apparent that it was time to get serious, time to negotiate. We had not contemplated what we then learned — the three "ladies" were actually hookers! Kim-Kim wanted immediate payment, up front, before anything else could be considered. No conversation, no beer drinking, nothing.

Kim-Kim's dismay was apparent when I showed her all of my money. "Is that all you have?"

I told her yes, even though I always kept a few extra bucks safely tucked away in my shoe just in case some unexpected need presented itself.

Once we had all come to some monetary arrangement with our "mates," we regrouped together in something similar to a living room; an area quite small and crowded in comparison to Western standards. We were served beer and snacks, purchased by the girls but paid for with our money. After comparing notes, we knew that all three girls were disappointed in their pre-performance earnings, but since we were already there they probably figured that a little income was better than no income. Besides, we were a sure thing.

The girls took pleasure in showing us some revealing photographs that confirmed their reputation and stature beyond any possible doubt. Those girls weren't just hookers; they were exceptionally high-class call girls. They had pictures taken with public and political figures of different nations, compromising pictures taken of them with well-known wealthy tourists, and pictures taken with very famous movie stars. Kim-Kim had served as the steady girlfriend of one particular movie star while he was starring in a very well known movie that was filmed in Hong Kong. Marcel and I jokingly discussed the possibilities of stealing some of the photographs and using them for the purpose of blackmail. The movie star, now deceased, was a strong consideration.

After a reasonable period of time, perhaps an hour or so, I took Kim-Kim's hand and led her back into her bedroom. I was not surprised to find that she was a most remarkable woman in bed. No wonder her talents were in demand by worldly rich and famous persons.

After another exhausting hour or so of sublime sensual and sexual pleasure, we once again mustered in the "meeting" room. Bob just ranted and raved about his beauty, how he had eaten her well and proper and how much she had craved more and more of his remarkably "talented tongue."

"Jesus, Bob, just think about how many cocks you just sucked 'by proxy.'"

Bob really didn't care.

Marcel wasn't talking and never did. Neither did I, until now.

It was getting late rapidly, late for three American GIs in Kowloon. Bob, suffering with a sudden case of diarrhea, needed to use the bathroom as we were preparing to leave.

After a few minutes had passed, Marcel and I heard Bob emit a painful yell from the bathroom. He said he was all right, but when he came out just moments later, holding his head, blood was noticeably visible as it oozed from under his hand and formed a small trickle down the side of his head.

I neglected to mention that Bob was a bit clumsy and rather tall. Banging his head seemed to be something of a pastime, especially down in the engineroom where there was not a lot of headroom.

As Bob was getting up from the toilet he had banged his head on the corner of a cabinet directly over him and had acquired a nasty gash in his scalp. One of the girls gave him a small glass container of something that resembled iodine and suggested that he return to the bathroom and treat the wound. As Bob was unscrewing the cap he accidentally dropped the container on the bathroom sink, where it shattered instantly. The contents splattered in all directions, not just in and around the sink, but all over one side of the brand-new borrowed suit trousers he was wearing.

As soon as the bleeding stopped and Bob got himself cleaned up (except for the permanently stained tailored trousers), we kissed our "sweethearts" goodbye, promised to return another time, and headed back to the ferry.

We were safely on board the Five Star Ferry, about halfway across the channel on our way back to the Hong Kong side, when, for whatever reason sailors do stupid things, Bob, no longer in his nonchalant, inconspicuous mode, threw one of the life-rings overboard — a really dumb thing to do. No one said anything, even though the incident had not gone unnoticed. We almost believed Bob was going to get away with it, until the ferry was fully docked. In an instant Bob was apprehended by the Hong Kong police. Bob was extremely lucky in that each of us had the foresight, almost a policy, to carry hidden funds while on liberty. We combined all of our funds and were able to buy Bob's way out of a potentially serious situation. Then all we had to worry about was what fate awaited Bob at the tailor shop.

Marcel and I wedged Bob in between us as we awkwardly entered the shop. Somehow we managed to get back to the dressing room where our uniforms were without Bob's stained attire being noticed. After quickly but neatly folding the borrowed clothing, making sure no stains were visible, we changed into our uniforms and approached the proprietor. We thanked him profusely and, as the saying goes, we got the hell out of there.

The remainder of the evening we did a little bar-hopping as we discussed and rediscussed our experiences of the day at each stop. We had "gotten away" with everything, clean and simple. Yet there were still some elements of concern regarding the damaged clothing. Having made a purchase at the tailor shop meant documentation; records of our names and what ship we were stationed on. Bob pretended to shrug it off, but we knew he was worried about it. He figured the worst thing that could happen would be that he would have to pay for the suit. We figured differently. If the proprietor filed a complaint, it wouldn't take a very intelligent Commanding Officer to determine we had been in violation of standing orders; not to wear civvies. And, of course, we could all have been charged with other offenses as well.

That evening we planned on returning to the ship a little earlier than usual, since the following morning the ship would be getting underway early. But our plans were temporarily interrupted.

Pinky's Tattoo Parlor, boasting perhaps the most reputable tattoo artist in all of Hong Kong, was on the way back to the ship, so why not pay it a visit? I knew that sooner or later I'd have my body permanently and colorfully adorned for life by being tattooed, thereby proving my manhood along with maintaining the tradition of seafaring men. That decision resulted in a serious and irrevocable mistake that I have regretted my entire adult life.

I thumbed through multitudes of pictures, variations of every conceivable tattoo "art," some of which was remarkably detailed. I screened Pinky's catalogs and photographs, unsure of precisely what I was looking for but intent on finding it that day.

Not all sailors have tattoos. In fact, it was, and may still be, a violation of Navy regulations to get one. Penalties were seldom imposed unless the tattoo depicted some form of obscenity and was visible while fully clothed — or some medical complication developed as a result of having been tattooed. Painful skin infections caused by dirty needles were difficult to cure; the massive variety of germs (in Hong Kong) had built up some degree of immunity to those medicines that were most readily available. Such infections invariably ended up permanently scarring or altering, sometimes completely destroying the tattoo during the healing process. The danger of contracting syphilis or some other venereal disease via dirty needles was also a very real danger.

Sailors had, and probably always will have, a strange imagination when it comes to selecting the tattoo of choice. There is no limit as to what they will have permanently imprinted or where they will have it imprinted on their bodies. It is exhibitionism at its peak, and many sailors reveled in it. It would take a book to fully describe the never-ending variety of tattoos I personally observed. The more common varieties of tattoo were found above the nipple of each breast and included, but were not limited to, HOT and COLD, LEFT and RIGHT, PORT and STARBOARD, and SUGAR and CREAM. Other favorites included spider webs and/or hinges on the elbows, shoulders, and knees; daggers on forearms; LOVE on the knuckles of one hand and HATE on the other; snakes of all varieties; the head or full body of a black panther; flowers; and the names and dates of port calls. The more ridiculous included flies or other insects on one's penis; a dog chasing a rabbit up one's anus; similarly a snake disappearing from view. There was the fairly common tattoo of a rooster hanging by a noose, always tattooed on one's leg anywhere below the knee so that "I'll bet five bucks I've got a cock hanging below my knee" was a sure winner.

I remember one young sailor as he proudly displayed his freshly tattooed forearm to a group of crewmen. It was a true work of art; a beautiful red rose with the words IN MEMORY OF MOM on a cross nestled within its petals. He thought a great deal of his mother but should have taken into consideration the fact that she was still alive and well. He thought it meant *Thinking of you, Mom.* No wonder sailors are usually thought of as something less than intelligent human beings. They sometimes have a tendency to prove it.

So there I was at Pinky's and within a few minutes I made my selection; the decision to be tattooed had long before been made, so it was time to get on with it.

Pinky himself was the artist. He simply glanced at the picture I pointed out and set about the task of fulfilling my request. After he shaved most of the hair off of my right forearm, it was thinly coated with petroleum jelly. Pinky had a palette of different-colored inks in one hand and his electric tattooing gun in the other. He went right to work without benefit of stencil or presketch. The artwork was made with the vibrating needle directly into the skin of my forearm; any mistakes would be immediate and permanent. It was painful, though not unbearable; more the combination of discomfort, the awkward position in which I had to hold my arm, and the knowledge of the act itself that caused me to begin feeling nauseous. Pinky placed an ice pack on the back of my neck and continued with his work. The entire process, from start to finish, probably took no more than forty-five minutes. The finished product was perfect. It was unmistakably clear, colorful, and admirably detailed!

The flying dragon permanently "etched" in my forearm afforded me with a distinction of which I was at one time quite proud. I can no longer say that. The terribly faded and practically indistinguishable tattoo remains to this day. It is rare that anyone can recognize it as anything other than what it has become: an old faded blotch of an unidentifiable tattoo.

Early the following morning, as all divisions were making preparations for getting underway, I was down in the engineroom. Someone from topside yelled down the hatch, "Hey, you got a Bob, a Paul, and a Marcel down there?"

Someone acknowledged that we were there.

"There's a guy from some tailor shop on a boat off the starboard side that wants to see one of them."

Instant fear. *Why couldn't we have gotten underway earlier?* The three of us decided to face the situation together so we all responded. Just as we feared, it was the proprietor himself — but why was he smiling? He was holding a fairly small package, carefully wrapped, that he wanted one of us to retrieve. Bob leaned over the lifeline and accepted the package. He tore open the wrapping, and there inside were three standard Navy issue bathing suits, the ones we had, in our haste, inadvertently left at the shop. We grinned from ear to ear as we looked at each other, and we laughed as we thanked him for having been so thoughtful. We knew that he had not yet unfolded the stained trousers and that our worries were no longer of immediate concern.

From Hong Kong we returned to Yokosuka, where we entered the shipyard for a minor overhaul; some much-needed maintenance and upgrades to many operational systems and related components. We would remain in dry dock the better portion of the six-week "upkeep," a period of maintenance and refurbishing. That meant a lot of hard work, but it also meant a lot of liberty. More important, it meant our final port before we were scheduled to cross the ocean and head for the "Big Island," home, the good old U.S. of A.

There was nothing unusual about setting the *Colahan* on the blocks in the drydock basin, but it was nothing less than amazing watching as the shipyard workers constructed the intricate web-work of bamboo side supports and the surrounding scaffolding. I had never seen anything like it. I knew that bamboo had great strength characteristics, but I never dreamed it could be used in such a manner or to such extremes.

An unbelievable number of Japanese workers scrambled their way up and around the scaffolding as they scraped and sandblasted the hull in preparation for fresh paint. Japanese shipyard workers were not at all unlike a colony of ants; each individual knew precisely where he was going and what function he was going to perform when he got there. They were a hardworking group, and the result of their customary manner of working in unison and harmony was impressive. They proved themselves capable of accomplishing more in a couple of hours than the crew could have done in a day, at a cost nowhere near that which it would have been had the work been performed in the United States.

About halfway through the shipyard period, Marcel and I were denied weekend passes. We wanted to visit Tokyo and we knew that a single day would not allow us ample time to see or do all the things we might have done, given more time. The disapproval was expected — enlisted men were never granted more than a day of liberty at overseas locations. So we were disappointed but not discouraged; we were intent on taking the train to Tokyo anyway.

Purchasing the tickets at the train station wasn't too difficult. The word *Tokyo* was the same in Japanese as in English. Finding the right train was a little bit more of a challenge. We showed our tickets, printed entirely in Japanese characters, to numerous non-English-speaking Japanese travelers who would in turn rattle off some meaningless gobbledygook, thinking we would understand. Fortunately, each time we were given directions we were also shown by the pointing of a finger which way we should go.

The first train we boarded was the wrong one. Immediately upon boarding, Marcel showed his ticket to one of the passengers and there was no mistake about his effort to alert us. His panicked expression and his hand waving and finger pointing let us know that we had no time to spare in getting off that train and getting on the right one!

The train ride, which provided for standing room only, was fascinating even though it was a bit uncomfortable. We enjoyed seeing the countryside, which was more often than not studded with numerous rice paddies of various shapes and sizes. It was a welcome change from the usual liberty endeavors we were accustomed to.

We marveled at the precision executed at the many stops along the way. Immediately, whenever the train stopped, the doors would slide open. Simultaneously, like hordes of insects, people scrambled and squeezed in between each other as they hurried on their way; some coming, some going, others standing fast. Everyone knew that the train system operated on a very precise timetable, and they knew to stand clear of the doors just seconds before departing for the next station. Doors slammed shut and the train departed, only to repeat the procedure over and over at each of the many stops en route.

Luck was with us, as one of the passengers convinced us that we were at our destination. But we were somewhat baffled. Our surroundings, unfamiliar as they were, were obviously not comparable or compatible with what we had believed Tokyo would consist of. There were no signs in English, so we again showed our tickets to one party after another until we understood what was going on. We had not been told, or at least not in English, that we would have to change trains in Yokohama.

Marcel and I were getting quite a kick out of not really knowing where we were, and we joked about getting lost and of the possibility that we might end up unintentionally taking the weekend off without permission.

Tokyo was totally unlike the liberty ports of Sasebo and Yokosuka. It was actually quite similar to any stateside metropolis, except for the obvious lack of signs in English. After a brief "tour" of the area and we were satisfied as to the makeup of the city, we made our way by taxi on to the U.S. Army base where we visited briefly with a friend of mine; a captain in charge of Special Services. At first I found it a little awkward, not knowing whether to address him as "Captain" or by his first name. He dismissed the "Captain bullshit" quickly, and we got on with our visit.

The return trip to Yokosuka was a repeat performance in reverse. We considered ourselves seasoned travelers because we had already traveled the route and we were no longer the least bit afraid of the unknown. We still had to rely on being assisted by accompanying passengers to make sure we changed trains at the right place and that we did not somehow fail to disembark at the Yokosuka station.

That trip to Tokyo was the first of what was to become many adventurous trips into remote and sometimes-hostile areas that I knew nothing about, many times having to rely heavily on the advice and directions given to me by total strangers. The consequences of taking such chances were not always favorable.

Some sailors, for whatever reasons, never went ashore. I don't know if it was out of fear of the unknown, mingling or associating with a different race, catching some kind of disease, getting lost, or what. I knew that one of those men was tight-fisted money-hungry. For him, going ashore would have meant putting a dent in his savings. All in all, they were a rare group of four or five individuals who, in my opinion, were a bit strange. Self-imposed restriction was "crazy." I could only imagine it to be nothing less than imprisonment — with fewer privileges! I questioned one of that group, a cook, as to what his reason was for never leaving the ship.

"I've got everything I need right here."

"Jesus, man, don't you ever get horny?"

"Listen, Ad, there ain't no piece of ass on this earth that's any better than fuckin' a chunk of raw liver."

I didn't ask him any more questions. Nor did I eat liver again while he was a member of the crew.

Another shipmate, one I came across in the head, swearing profusely as he proceeded to shave his eyebrows, told me why he never intended on going ashore again. "Somehow" he had been "invaded" by tiny critters, crabs, and they had made their home in the hair on his head and in his eyebrows. No way was he ever going to be humiliated that way again. I laughed heartily at his misfortune and assured him that in no time at all he'd be back "over there" gathering friends and relatives of the crabs he was in the process of getting rid.

Crabs, as bad or worse than lice, were disgusting little creatures, and at one time or another most sailors had a problem with them. That's not to say everyone was shacking up with the locals. It was unlikely and rare, but crabs *could* be acquired from an inhabited toilet seat — on board ship as well as ashore. They were easily picked up ashore while sleeping on unchanged or dirty linen. In any event, they were nasty little things and anyone known to have them was tagged as having slept with the wrong party, regardless of how they were actually acquired.

Snipes had a way about making the best of just about any situation. The in-port work routine could be manipulated to whatever degree one's imagination might allow. Jim, one of the older and more experienced E-3s that didn't seem to care whether or not he was ever promoted, had a knack for humor. He would sing songs that related to our tasks, songs that made a great deal of sense as they provided an alternative to the frustrations of work. One of his favorite songs, I'll call it "Copaltite," always brought smiles and laughter to an otherwise-serious bunch of workers. Copaltite was an adhesive sealant, as was Gasket Goo. If the project at hand didn't call for one, it probably called for the other. Either would have been equally effective on just about anything that needed an airtight or moisture-proof seal. Jim's song, simple and to the point, went like this:

"Oh, zee Copaltite,
Oh, zee Copaltite.
Do you use zee Copaltite?

No, I use zee Gasket Goo!
Gasket Goo?
Yes, I do!
Oh, zee Copaltite,
Oh, zee Copaltite."

Another favorite was sung to the tune of "Down in the Valley," conceived by Ike, another well-liked snipe who was also blessed with the ability and the desire to share his sense of humor.

"Down in the bilges,
The bilges so low,
Hang your head over;
Hear the bilge water flow."

Liberty was important, a priority of sorts to the vast majority of enlisted men. It was really the only opportunity to relax well away from the confines of most military rule. Actually, we were subject to military discipline at all times, twenty-four hours a day, whether or not we were on a military installation. It was the surrounding environment provided while away from military command that would eliminate the stress, the awareness of the otherwise presence of authority and military law. Having one's liberty revoked was not always fair play. The Exec (Executive Officer) loved to revoke liberty. The following explains just one of his tactics.

Sailors were expected to donate whenever asked to do so. Several times a year, prior to the establishment of the Combined Federal Campaign, we were asked to give a fair amount of our measly and well-deserved pay to one charity or another. The going rate was a minimum of one dollar each, regardless of pay grade. It was an irritant to all of us, having to contend with command pressure at those times. I decided I had given enough to charity and I would no longer donate any portion of my pay; I would keep my money for my own best interests.

Every two weeks payday rolled around. Chiefs were paid in the CPO quarters, officers were paid in the wardroom, and the rest of the crew lined up alphabetically on the port side of the ship and walked single file down to the mess decks, where, after having properly filled out and presented a "Navy Pay Receipt," also known as a pay chit, we were paid in cash. The pay chit was scrutinized by several Ship's Office personnel before payment could be made. Any discrepancy on the chit resulted in it being immediately torn in half. A misspelled word, a missing comma, an illegible signature, smudges, wrinkles, and creases or folds were considered reasons for denying payment. Since discrepancies had to be corrected, that meant starting all over. More than once I had to go back to the end of the line and get paid along with other "stragglers."

My last name, beginning with *A*, placed me at the front of the pay line. It was one of those "donate-to-the-local-charity" paydays, Navy Relief to be precise, and I was intent on keeping all of my pay. My pay chit was carefully "researched" by the string of office personnel, and payment was made. Sitting adjacent to the Paymaster, with his hat turned upside down on the table to receive donations, was the hateful and ever-smirking Exec. I tried not to make eye contact as I walked past him, quickly stuffing all of my pay into my pocket as I departed. I was proud of myself, having had the courage to keep what was rightfully mine. I gloated when asked by my buddies how much I had donated.

"Not a red cent!"

That afternoon at 1600 hours, liberty call sounded as usual. I got all spruced up and reported to the Liberty Card Petty Officer to get my liberty card, anxious to hit the beach. The petty officer was as perplexed as I was when he found that my card was not with the rest of them. I went to the Ship's Office, where I was told the Exec had my card.

My opinion of the Exec stems from my own observations and believable hearsay. The man, a lieutenant commander, was despised by most officers as well as enlisted men. He was ruthless in most of his actions and he thoroughly enjoyed reprimanding everyone with whom he came in contact. He would, without exception, find fault of one kind or another, everywhere he went. The Exec ruled by dictatorship and fear. Men would turn around and go in any alternate direction rather than approach or pass him. We all stayed clear of him as much as we were able.

I was faced with a major decision, whether or not to enter Officers' Country in hopes of recovering my liberty card. I'd been man enough so far, and since the Exec's stateroom was just around the corner from the Ship's Office, the decision was instant committal to proceed.

I could feel myself shaking, not violently but noticeably, as I knocked on the Exec's door. There was no response from within. I knocked a little harder.

"Enter," came the distinct voice of authority from behind the closed door.

I entered.

"What do you want?" He glared at me.

I wasted no time getting right to the point. "Sir, I was told at the Ship's Office that you have my liberty card."

"Yes Adkisson, I have your liberty card." He intentionally didn't elaborate, preferring to see me squirm as I searched for a way of communicating more directly my purpose in being there.

Again I was to the point. "May I have it?"

"Adkisson, you did not donate to Navy Relief this morning, did you!"

My follow-up response was a logical question to which I already knew the answer. "Is that why you have my liberty card?"

"Yes, Adkisson."

I was provoked but chose my words carefully. "I didn't know that I had to buy my liberty, sir."

"You know it now, Adkisson."

I hated hearing him continuously repeat my name. He would remember it, and the likelihood of my being subjected to future harassment was being compounded. I reached under my jumper, retrieved my wallet, pulled out a dollar bill, and handed it to him. The Exec, always smirking, first took my dollar then spoke. "No, Adkisson, it's five dollars now."

Red-faced and angry, I paid!

Sailors were frequently coerced for donations back then. Fortunately, after enough complaints were elevated to higher authority, that practice was, by directive, discontinued.

Not to be too negative or misleading, there were many instances of assistance that were provided willingly. For example, during the year 1956, ships and men of the Atlantic Fleet, like their shipmates ashore and in the Pacific, maintained the spirit of goodwill and brotherhood so traditionally a part of the Navy. There was the $7,500 check presented by the USS *Coral Sea* (CVA 43) to Hungarian relief; the submarine USS *Irex* (SS 482) played host to 230 orphans and indigent children in Mediterranean ports; the USS *Becuna* (SS 319) carried donated clothing to the needy children of Europe; the destroyer USS *Charles S. Sperry* (DD 697) off-loaded a statue of Comdr. John Barry at Wexford, Ireland, as a gift from U.S. citizens to the Irish; the LSTs USS *Whitfield County* (LST 1169) and *Windham County* (LST 1170) donated 120 pints of blood to the Red Cross; and on March

18, when an emergency call was put out by the Norfolk hospital for blood donors to save the life of a young girl, more than 200 officers and enlisted men from the U.S. Amphibious Base at Little Creek, Virginia, responded.

But getting back to the underhanded tactics followed by the *Colahan's* Executive Officer: On one occasion he placed me on thirty-days VD restriction, punishment awarded those individuals unfortunate enough to have contracted one strain or another of venereal disease.

(*Note*: In the Navy, punishment is "awarded" the same as decorations and commendations. The term *award* quickly took on a new meaning to me, since my awards, for a time, were more often than not, *un*rewarding.)

I did not have VD! I was suffering from prostatitis, an infected prostate gland. Just because I had a urinary discharge, not contagious, not even uncomfortable, it provided the Exec with sufficient reason to restrict me and to openly and publicly post my name on the "VD Roster" along with those who actually had some form of communicable sexually transmitted disease. Since officers were immune to, or at least never contracted, VD, their names were not posted. So they would want us to believe. But we knew of instances where officers did contract VD, even though their names were not posted. The Exec knew that there were, and he probably relied upon, those crewmen who delighted in advising friends and loved ones back home of the names contained on that infamous roster.

I took the only retaliatory action I could think of at the time, a dangerous decision but one that I believed to be precautionary as well as preventative and curative in nature.

The corpsman striker was known to hide the key to Sick Bay up in the overhead just outside the door in a maze of hydraulic lines and electrical cables. Similarly, although unrelated, men were known to stash small bars of soap in the overhead above the showers just in case they forgot to take their own. The corpsman striker was a lazy E-3 who really didn't give a damn about responding to the needs of his sick shipmates. Having to carry the Sick Bay key on his person was just another inconvenience to him. Late one night I borrowed the key from its hiding place and let myself into Sick Bay. I conducted a rapid search with my flashlight, and in no time at all I had a large bottle of penicillin and a couple of bottles of tetracycline; both known to cure just about any kind of venereal disease. In fact, there was a period of time when penicillin pills were actually distributed at the quarterdeck — for those who intended on engaging in sexual activities

110

while ashore as well as for the after-the-fact participants. I then had all the medication I would ever need to make sure I would never be faced with the humiliation of VD restriction again. I learned years later of the potential damage I could have done to myself by taking such medication without proper foods and liquids.

During my twenty-plus years of naval service, I came in contact with officers of all sizes, shapes, and colors, of all grades and from all backgrounds; most were college-educated, some were appointed from enlisted ranks, and I observed a wide variety of temperaments. I can say with absolute certainty my opinion of that Executive Officer places him at the absolute bottom of the barrel, unworthy of the respect the uniform and devices he wore received. The man himself deserved no respect whatever. Words cannot adequately describe the contempt held by nearly all of the men on board *Colahan* for this poor excuse of a naval officer. His name is not worth the ink it would take to disclose.

5

HOMEWARD BOUND
LIFE AT SEA

It was August 1955, and the *Colahan* was on her way home. For the old salts it was all routine, just one more day at sea. For the "Black Gang," the snipes, it meant back to eight hours of daily work plus the four to eight hours on watch and eight to twelve hours off watch underway routine. For some it meant minimal or no watch-standing duties. For example, the doc, Chief Hospitalman Sturtevant and his "strikers," (persons E-3 and below working toward or "striking" for advancement in a particular rating), were not required to stand watches. Sick Bay was open for treatment during normal working hours. That was considered enough duty for them since they also had to respond at any hour of the day or night, whenever the need for their expertise existed.

Machinist's Mate Packett, the husky first class in charge of the forward engineroom, was disliked by practically everyone subordinate to him as well as many of the men senior to him. Packett would lumber along, huge gorillalike hands swinging to his sides, palms facing backward instead of inward, always glaring provokingly at anyone in his path. He ruled much the same as the Exec, but with brutality along with fear and authority. Packett used his threatening size and strength as effective weapons, quite successfully intimidating everyone of a lower pay grade as well as some of higher pay grades.

Packett had a habit of thumping subordinates right between their eyes or on the back of their heads with his huge, hard-as-rock knuckles. He'd go so far as to kick certain individuals on their head or in their face as they climbed the engineroom ladder and attempted to exit through the main-deck topside hatch.

Packett never hesitated to carry out his threats of bodily harm when anyone around him didn't measure up to his demands or expectations. I was lucky in that I did not work directly under him. It took very little, even the simple act of a subordinate being in Packett's presence, to aggravate him. The few times that I was directly under his control I was very careful not to intensify whatever aggravation my presence caused him.

I had already developed a strong hatred for Packett, but I secretly vowed to "get him" one way or another when I saw him carry out a significantly cruel act. Without any provocation, just one more means by which he showed those around him that he was "bad," he proceeded to kick a small puppy through a deck scupper, a drainage outlet, sending the puppy overboard to sea where it was destined to drown. His boisterous comment, "We don't need no fuckin' dogs on board," cemented my vow to someday get even. It didn't matter that animal mascots of any kind were not allowed on board. Many things that were not allowed could be found if a thorough-enough search was conducted.

Every couple of days the ship crossed a time zone at which time all ship's clocks were advanced an hour, usually during the mid-watch. No way would the Exec shorten working hours by advancing clocks during the day. When we crossed the International Date Line the Exec made sure we had an extra working day, not an extra Sunday. I was told that just the opposite held true when the *Colahan* was en route to the Far East when the Exec made sure Sunday was skipped when we crossed the date line, and the clocks were set back during working hours, thereby adding an hour to the already-lengthy workday.

Snipes had it tough and the whole crew knew it. Engineering spaces were hot and the air was heavy, always smelling of lube oil and fuel oil.

Once in awhile when deckhands got caught wasting fresh water, the punishment awarded would be for them to stand one or more watches manning the evaporators down in the forward engineroom. Not only did they gain a new appreciation for the life of a snipe, they also gained an appreciation for the manner in which fresh water was distilled.

Snipes, while they enjoyed observing the apparent torment suffered by deckhands as they manned the Evaps, took a very strong exception to the notion it was punishment. If it was punishment, and snipes were routinely assigned evaporator watch, what were the snipes being punished for? After enough complaints, the Exec determined that it was *not* punishment and it was *not* extra duty. He concluded that it was "cross-rate training" and that it was not only needed, it was necessary to ensure the ship's readiness for operations at sea! What a bunch of baloney! But as one considers the source, it becomes understandable that such a poor example of naval leadership would make that determination.

As previously described, sailors frequently slept on the main deck rather than suffer from the heat and poor air circulation down below in the berthing spaces. I neglected to mention that this practice was an irritant to the Exec, probably because it provided a brief period of something approaching relief or comfort for some crewmen. As was previously mentioned, heavy and unpredictable tropical rain squalls were fairly common during the day — but they also occurred at night. Put the three together, men sleeping on the main deck, heavy rain, and the Exec, and what do you have? Executive opportunity! The Exec was believed to intentionally change the heading of the ship in the middle of the night for the purpose of chasing and entering rain squalls, knowing full well the main deck would get a thorough wash-down; all hands sleeping there included. That man was beyond the ornery stage. He was, in my opinion, either a pathological fanatic or a sadist about causing misery whenever and wherever he could; Captain Bligh reincarnated?

Periodically drills of one kind or another were conducted. Fire, man overboard, flooding, and of course General Quarters were common. Some drills, such as man overboard, were welcomed by snipes because the normal work routine was interrupted while all hands not assigned special details reported to their assigned place of muster for a head count. General Quarters, Battle Stations, was the worst for snipes because their assignments were, far more often than not, down in the engineering spaces. It got particularly uncomfortable down there when the drill included the simulation of nuclear, biological, or chemical agents present. In those instances, all ventilation had to be secured and the engineering spaces became unbearably hot. We took turns sneaking up the port ladder to crack open the only hatch not visible to topside personnel, enabling us, for a moment, to gulp in several breaths of fresh air. The Exec probably had multiple orgasms during such drills, especially if he fully understood the impact they had on those of us assigned to an engineroom or a fireroom.

114

Since there was a shortage of engineroom personnel, my first battle station assignment was that of a "telephone talker" in the after engineroom; an assignment that would normally require a good understanding of everything transmitted and received. I had not yet grasped many of the engineering terms and I did not understand much of what I heard. I quickly found that saying "repeat" over and over was not acceptable to the other phone talkers. I was embarrassed when I heard comments such as: "Hey, dumb shit, did you copy?" M.D. told me to disregard their derogatory remarks and to do the best I could. He reminded me that in my position as phone talker I could easily become directly or indirectly responsible for an unnecessary casualty. Just as easily, I could be instrumental in the recovery process of a casualty — but only if I understood and passed information accurately.

"You'll be a lot better, we'll all be better off, if you continue to ask for a 'repeat,' regardless of the number of times, until you fully understand, rather than pass on something that is wrong or of no value," he told me.

I realized that instead of being dubbed "dumb shit" I should more appropriately have been commended for letting them know I didn't understand what they were saying. I had, up until the time Adams talked to me, pretended to understand on many occasions. I had not considered the possibility of contributing to some kind of disaster — but luck had been with me and conditions were such that I got away with it.

It did not take long before I became just as familiar with engineering terms and conditions as anyone else. Instead of fearing incoming messages, I looked forward to exercising my proficiency as a phone talker.

During "GQ," General Quarters, any number of drills were conducted; Battle Stations was but one. If the five-inch guns were not actually fired, live ammunition was not handled and the midship's "dummy loader" was used for practice. The dummy loader provided an excellent means of practicing loading on a replica of the huge five-inch guns without the use of black powder. It allowed for maximum practice loading a solid five-inch dud projectile, fifty-five pounds or so of solid brass, without any danger of explosion. It was, for all practical purposes, a safe mode of practice. Safe, that is, until my buddy Bob accidentally dropped one of the practice projectiles, blunt end first, on his foot!

115

There can be no doubt as to the pain Bob felt; his foot was crushed — few bones remained intact. There was little that could be done immediately, other than provide him with painkillers and get him to his bunk. I had never seen anyone suffer such agony. Bob's foot turned every color of the rainbow, and every little movement, regardless how slight, was sheer torture to him.

For one reason or another a cast could not be put on Bob's foot — perhaps because of the severe swelling. Knowing how medication was dispensed back then, I seriously doubt that Bob was prescribed as much painkiller as he should have been. But who am I to say? I just cannot imagine anyone being in such obvious pain without greater efforts being exerted by the attending medical "professional" toward the further reduction, or even the complete elimination of pain. What made Bob's situation worse yet was the fact that he had to use the head from time to time. The crutches he had been issued were of little value to him while he was ascending or descending the ladder between the berthing compartment and the main deck where the head was. Imagine trying to climb a ladder on crutches as the ship bobbed up and around like a cork, maintaining one's balance under such conditions. Then imagine Bob slipping while halfway up the ladder and instinctively although unintentionally catching himself on that unprotected crushed foot! That was precisely what I saw happen, and poor Bob almost passed out from the excruciating pain. I cannot imagine how he must have felt when the chief "medic" provided him with the "comforting" advice that he was not to worry, that the bones would eventually heal themselves. He was probably told to continue taking APCs, a form of aspirin, and to "take it easy... ." That was the typical advice that was given to sailors regardless of their complaint or the significance of their malady. We expected that advice and made fun of it. The common expression that "anyone capable of dispensing APC's qualifies as a corpsman" was not necessarily true, but it seemed to make a lot of sense.

A reasonable period of shipboard time had passed, and I thought I was fitting in, progressing as a sailor, at a satisfactory pace. But I began to feel more frustrated at all the negative and derogatory terms to which I was being called or referred. Thinking back, I know that I was being "tested" just like any other newcomer. The ridicule was not all that bad, in fact it helped me find my way. My attitude was being changed, not by choice but rather of necessity.

Perhaps the biggest change came over me one night at the end of a mid-watch. I was standing messenger watch duties, and it was about 0330 hours, time to call the relieving watch. I awakened all the watch reliefs and returned to the engineroom. One by one the reliefs showed up as 0345 approached, the time all reliefs were supposed to be on station.

My relief, a rather husky guy with just a little more time in the Navy than I had, was the only one who failed to show up on time. I returned to the berthing space, where I found him, still in his "pad," sleeping comfortably. This time I made sure he was awake before I returned to the engineroom to wait for his late arrival. I had to make extra rounds and record readings for my yet-to-arrive relief since readings had to be taken hourly. His being late was bad enough, but having to take his readings for him irritated me that much more. Even after I finished taking the readings, he still hadn't shown up. I made another trip to the berthing space, and there he was, still curled up in his bunk. This time I shook him more violently and told him I'd already taken his first set of readings and to get his butt down in the "hole." Having gained some "smarts," I stood right there beside his bunk and made sure he was on his feet before I returned to the engineroom. Ten more minutes passed and the other watchstanders began chuckling and ridiculing my inability to wake up my own relief. I headed back toward the compartment a fourth time. This time I found him admiring the reflection of his freshly combed hair in a mirror above one of the sinks in the head. I asked him why he thought his appearance was more important than relieving me on time.

Through a wise-ass grin, his words were clear: "If you don't like it, Ad, you ca—"

I did not allow him to finish his sentence, and I vented my frustrations with a vengeance as my tightened fists pounded away at him with every ounce of strength I could muster. Blood splattered in all directions as I repeatedly, with surprising accuracy, battered his face as rapidly as I could. The mirror he had been looking into was shattered as the back of his head smashed into it, and I kept on swinging. He ended up half crouching against the outer bulkhead, hands flailing around in a belated effort to protect himself from the onslaught he himself had provoked. I stepped back, clearly the victor, and assessed (marveled) at the beating I had delivered. It was at that precise moment that I realized my ability to be aggressive. It was a new sensation, and I liked it. It came as something of a surprise, the realization that I had been the brunt in many instances where, had I been more aggressive, I may very well have been admired instead of ridiculed. I

117

knew from that day forward that I would no longer be subjected to unnecessary ridicule, nor would I continue to take unwarranted threats from the so-called badasses on board.

My relief, thoroughly thrashed, made his way to his feet, and I prepared to continue fighting in the event he made the slightest aggressive gesture. He did not.

"I've had it, Ad, you busted my nose and I ain't gonna stand my watch now."

Busted? I thought of it more in terms of having been remodeled. I returned to the engineroom and told the group what had happened. Only after each of them, one at a time, went to and inspected the blood-splattered head did they congratulate me: "It's about time you acted like a man," and, "So the pussycat finally turned tiger." But the comment I liked most was to the point and simple: "Well done, Ad."

I stood the remaining portion of the messenger watch that night, but I had a satisfied smile on my face the entire time.

The word spread quickly of my aggressive action that night. It was a rarity thereafter that I was intentionally ridiculed for anything other than things for which I would have expected to be reprimanded or ridiculed. I had gained a welcomed respect by my shipmates.

It was not always easy selecting friends. It was more the process of becoming accepted by someone else. I had to be the one chosen as a friend rather than the one doing the choosing. I don't remember just how I became a friend with Tom Mundy. Tom was about as daring as a sailor could be. More accurately, he was the ultimate instigator. Tom was always willing to participate in just about any activity to gain attention, legitimate or not. The more chancy, the more likely he would be willing to become actively involved.

Tom feared no one and he was respected by almost everyone. Some of that respect was deserved while some was generated out of fear. He was a hardworking individual and he believed in doing the job right. Sometimes Tom could be overly cocky. At those times he became somewhat short-fused as he allowed his temper to take charge. Tom simply would not take any insolence from anyone, especially when he was ashore and had consumed a few beers.

I admired Tom, and some of his more admirable characteristics rubbed off on me. He was a natural leader, one who was easy to follow — I admired that. Eventually he became one of my best friends. If I wanted excitement, I'd hook up with Tom knowing full well anything could, and probably would, happen. If I wanted to stay out of trouble, I'd hook up with Marcel.

Tom, having been assigned to the fireroom, was also part of the Black Gang. He had been aboard several months longer than I, and his duties were a little more demanding. Everyone assigned to either of the enginerooms knew that fireroom personnel worked harder — but we always argued to the contrary. It was as hot or hotter, smelled as bad or worse than the engineroom, and without question was, or at least took on the appearance of being, far dirtier. There was a never-ending attempt by fireroom personnel to wash the thin layer of black fuel oil from the surface of nearly everything within the space.

Boiler maintenance was also a difficult, demanding, and never-ending job. Perhaps the easiest task associated with boiler maintenance was the sampling of boiler water, conducting tests to make sure the chemical content of the boiler water was within specific limits. Chemicals were added as needed to maintain the water chemistry, thereby reducing scale buildup, foaming, and erosion among other things.

Tom, a little smarter than the usual lower-rated fireroom snipe, put his mind to work when he learned how to conduct boiler water hardness tests. The procedure required the use of 190 proof (95 percent pure) ethyl alcohol. Ethyl alcohol, strong as it was, was consumable. Add Tom's ingenuity and imagination to the availability of ingestible alcohol, plus the availability of a Coke dispenser down on the mess decks, and the Secretary of the Navy's regulation denying alcoholic beverages for other than medicinal purposes was instantly bypassed. The funny thing was, ethyl alcohol came in five-gallon containers clearly marked POISON; each container displayed the large customary skull and crossbones on the attached label. No doubt about it, ethyl alcohol certainly would kill if consumed in excess.

The five-gallon containers were stowed in the most difficult to access place on board, all the way forward beneath the forecastle, at the bottom of the Bos'n Locker, the lowest hold on the ship; as if sailors were too lazy to climb several levels down a ladder, having to open a couple of access hatches en route, in order to obtain not the beverage of choice but certainly the beverage of availability.

Tom nicknamed the stuff Lucy, partly because ethyl had the sound if not the spelling of a girl's name and partly because I Love Lucy was a very popular television program, a title most fitting to our situation too.

Tom and I did not abuse our "privilege" of access to Lucy. It was not an every-night occasion. Rarely, when we determined we were deserving of a special break, we'd toss a coin to determine who was going for Lucy and who would get the Cokes. Then we'd meet topside someplace where we had an unrestricted view of everyone coming in our direction. The ocean was always conveniently available for the disposal of evidence should the need arise.

There was a distinct danger, well beyond getting caught, as to the consumption of Lucy. It was extremely potent and had to be carefully "rationed." We never indulged in more than two drinks each. Even that seemingly insignificant quantity bordered on excess.

The secret of our periodic after-hours cocktail parties was carefully guarded. It would have been disastrous had it been divulged or discovered by anyone incapable of "social drinking." So our infrequent cocktail hours were enjoyable and relaxing — and secretive. We managed to keep it that way by allowing only a very few of our closest and most trustworthy friends in on it.

Movies, the major source of entertainment while at sea, were shown nightly on the fantail or in the mess deck compartment. During rough seas or inclement weather the crowd gathered in the mess hall. While the crew had their own movies, chiefs and officers watched movies in the chief's mess and in the wardroom, respectively. Movies were seldom of the best quality, and rarely were we privileged to see anything recently released. "Shit kickers," westerns, were always favored over love stories and comedies. At sea, particularly ships within a squadron, but also other passing U.S. Navy vessels, usually took advantage of whatever opportunities there were to swap movies.

The nightly movie commenced at or before dusk whether it was shown down on the mess decks or topside on the fantail. Nearly all sailors smoked and the ones that didn't had no choice in the matter. They had to contend with a smoke-filled compartment or choose not to watch the movie when it was shown on the mess decks.

When the movie ended, it was comical watching men exit the top of the stairwell leading to the main deck. They were temporarily blinded by the darkness of the night, their eyes having already been fully acclimated to the mess decks and passageway lighting. Those that didn't have the convenience of a flashlight would feel their way, one hand stretched out in front, the other swinging to one side.

Tom and I, whenever we felt a little ornery, would make sure we were in the area when the movie ended, our eyes fully adjusted to whatever light the night provided. We harassed the men in any number of childish but effective ways. It was easy walking right up to within inches of an unsuspecting victim's face and then turning on a flashlight directly into his eyes. The unexpected glare blinded him to an even greater extent, thereby further guaranteeing that the victim would not be able to identify his "assailant(s)." We would take any number of annoying actions, to include thumping them on the forehead, punching them in the stomach, and/or grabbing them and swinging them around so as to further disorient them as best we could in the time allowed — and then we would quickly "disappear" up or down a nearby ladder before they could regain their night vision. There was always the possibility that others might come along and expose our identities via the use of their own flashlight(s), so we had to "hit and run" expeditiously. We took an even greater pleasure in aggravating the men on nights "Darken Ship" was ordered, a condition under which absolutely no light of any kind, including the light of a match or a cigarette, was allowed topside. We were smart enough not to make it a nightly practice; no sense taking a chance on somebody setting us up and catching us in the act.

If Tom and I were not up to one form of harassment or another, there were other elements that could be, and many times were, more effective in causing some degree of discontent or discomfort among the crew.

Once, when the sea was relatively calm and a movie was being shown on the large canvas screen mounted on Mount 55, on the fantail, a huge unexpected wave came crashing over the starboard lifelines right into the movie-watching crowd. It was always a bit humorous when someone received an unexpected soaking; however, in this instance it was very nearly disastrous. It is hard to imagine the sight, and far too difficult to describe with understandable clarity, but when that huge wave hit us we were totally at its mercy. We were helplessly tumbled over and between each other; flailing our arms around wildly in hopes of grabbing onto something stationary as we were washed with tremendous force into the port lifelines. It was not immediately known whether anyone had been washed overboard, but since the possibility did exist, the Exec called all hands to Quarters for muster.

Allow for a brief explanation of two types of muster: 1) "Quarters," where all hands not actually on watch mustered for a head count topside; and 2) "On Station," where all hands mustered on their watch station, in their berthing compartment, or in their working space. In bad weather, muster would normally and sensibly take place "On Station."

That particular night, with the strong possibility that one or more men had been washed overboard, our ruthless and contemptuous Exec, perhaps intentionally, called for the muster at Quarters, topside! All hands, willingly or not, did precisely as we were instructed. My place of muster, with my division, was on the fantail to the starboard side of Mount 55. It was dark, it was cold, and many of us were soaking wet. All we wanted was to get the muster over with and get below where we could dry off.

Right in the middle of the head count, another wave of the same or stronger magnitude came crashing over the starboard lifelines and provided a crushing blow directly into my group. I was thrust down and under the gun mount where I was instantly immobilized, the breath having been completely knocked out of me. I also suffered a nasty gash to my left hip, where I had smashed into one of the gun mount hold-down bolts. I do not know to this day who "scooped" me up and carried me to safety, but I do recall thanking him for his assistance. That second wave had actually washed a couple of men overboard, but both had managed to cling onto the lifelines and were able to scramble back on board.

There was another call for muster, but the second time it was, with better judgment, ordered to take place On Station. As if some sort of miracle had protected each of us that night, the entire crew was accounted for and safe.

The mess hall was utilized for activities other than eating and watching movies. After meal hours it provided a place for the men to write letters and to play checkers, chess, cards, and other entertaining games of chance and skill. It was a gambler's paradise even though gambling for money was illegal; in theory it was forbidden. Those who gambled paid no attention to the rules that forbade it. Hundreds of dollars, even thousands on occasion, and numerous IOUs changed hands nearly every night. Gamblers were somehow immune to normal sleep requirements and were known to gamble all night long, yet they somehow managed to carry out their daytime duties without a noticeable problem.

There was a period of time during which I ran a "bank," an activity that was also forbidden but was practiced by a relatively few men who had extra funds. In other words, I was something of a loan shark. Exorbitant interest rates were always charged for loans, regardless of who was running the bank; usually seven dollars in return for a five-dollar loan — fourteen dollars for ten dollars, and so on, with payment in full by the debtor expected on the following payday. Return rates became double (or even triple) the loaned amounts while in Hong Kong. Many times the borrower(s) would simply pay off the interest and allow the principal to carry indefinitely. I was always happy to negotiate such an agreement, especially when the interest was for a larger amount since I quickly recovered the original loan, sometimes many times over, when interest-only payments were made. I was also selective as to whom I made loans; some crewmen were bad risks and I made it a practice to know who they were. I was not normally selective as to pay grades, and I made loans to anyone, up to and including chiefs. "Motorcycle," a chief nicknamed for his ability to seemingly be everywhere at the same time, was the only person I ever loaned money to that I did not charge interest. But that was only because my fireroom buddy, Tom, had asked that favor of me. Officers were off-limits — too much probability of their communicating the illegal activity to higher authority.

Collecting the debts was seldom a problem. Since I was usually at the head of the pay line, I stationed myself where everyone had to pass me after they were paid, outside the view of the Paymaster, my little black book with names and account balances tightly gripped in my hand.

I loaned a steward twenty dollars at the twenty-eight-for-twenty dollar rate. A couple of days later, prior to payday and unbeknownst to me, he was transferred off the ship. I was not too happy at the loss but simply shrugged it off as a bad loan. As my rather typical good luck would have it, several months later he was transferred right back to the *Colahan*. Payday I˙was standing at my usual point of collection, waiting for him in particular. He walked directly to me and fanned out his entire payday income, a rather large amount of money, and he told me to take whatever he owed. He fully expected me to take $100 or more. I reached into the stack of bills and removed a single "twenty." I told him that even though I was not entirely satisfied with the twenty, I was willing to accept it, but that he was never to approach me for a loan again. That news, that I was a fair "banker" traveled quickly to those known to borrow — and my loan sharking business immediately got better than ever!

Getting food from the galley to the mess deck was a bit of a problem. The galley was just forward of midship on the main deck. All food had to be hand carried from the galley down to the mess deck in "gunboats," large stainless-steel containers, not to be confused with the dictionary's definition of the same term: "armed craft of shallow draft." The stairwell leading to the mess deck was steep and narrow and was difficult to descend even when both arms were free. Regardless of how calm the sea was, and it was seldom calm, the ship never stopped bobbing and rolling. Mess cooks had to make their way from the galley, by way of the main deck, down the stairwell ladder to the serving line, both hands gripping overfilled gunboats all the way. The heavy salt spray from the ocean was easy for them to stagger through, but the possibility of solid and unexpected waves breaking over the side of the ship, hitting them full force, was of far greater concern and a very real danger. Frequently, and understandably, food was spilled along the way, especially soup and other preparations that had a tendency to slosh around easily. When the sea was extremely rough, too rough to prepare "hearty" meals, let alone for the mess cooks to manhandle, we could depend on horse-cock sandwiches as our primary staple, sometimes for several consecutive meals.

Officers and chiefs were more fortunate. Officers had their own stewards and their own galley. Their meals, far more palatable I might add, were prepared within a few steps of where they were served — far less chance of an accidental spill. CPOs were normally provided with rations out of the main galley; however, they had another option not available to the rest of the crew. They were privileged with having their own refrigerator and their own food cache. They could improvise or supplement meals to their own satisfaction.

Actually, the food served to crewmen was not entirely bad. It was not nearly as good as that provided at boot camp, but taking into consideration the facilities available for preparing meals, it was probably about as good as could be expected.

There were certain foods we could plan on, such as onion soup at the noon and evening meals, baked beans and hard-boiled eggs for breakfast on Saturdays, eggs to order only on Sundays, and corned beef that was tougher than shoe leather. There was always plenty of milk, though it was not always chilled to a desirable degree and occasionally it soured before it was served. Bread, prepared and baked on board while at sea, was coarse and in no way resembled the soft fresh bread available in civilian supermarkets. Steak? When "steak" was served it was of the absolute lowest quality and was little more than chunks of chewy gristle, but, even as we bitched and complained, we ate it.

It was rare that I did not leave the mess hall with a full stomach. There were times that I didn't get my fill, but only because of one or the other of the following reasons: I was too lazy to go to the mess hall; I didn't want to take a chance on getting wet in rough or rainy weather; I was too late and the mess was secured; I didn't like what was being served; I was too busy or I didn't want to clean up; I didn't want to change into the Uniform of the Day (in port only); or I had a food stash of my own — another violation.

Regardless of repeated warnings of the potential consequences, sun-bathing was a dangerous yet favorite pastime. Severe burns from the tropical sun were not frequent, but they did occur. Sunburn, to the degree it limited an individual's work capabilities, was a punishable offense. Only those with truly severe burns ever complained. Snipes, considering the heat and humidity of the spaces in which they worked and lived, suffered as much or more from sunburn than most other crewmen. Sunbathing activities diminished and eventually stopped as the ship distanced itself from the tropical zone.

Those of us new to the ways of the sea, unworthy of recognition as seafaring sailors, continued to live and learn by hands-on experiences. As a messenger, I was sent to other parts of the ship to retrieve nonexistent things, such as a left-handed monkey wrench, so many feet of water line, a relative bearing among other imaginary things; always returning empty-handed with the knowledge I had once again been made something of a fool.

I observed and sometimes participated in other irritating and sneaky get-even tactics. When I knew, or at least believed I wouldn't be identified as the culprit, I would fill condoms with warm water and carefully place them alongside certain sleeping individuals, usually those who had at one time or another taken advantage of my innocence or inexperience. I knew that sometime during their sleep, or for sure upon waking up, they would roll over and the condoms would break. Other times, but always while my intended target was sleeping, I would tie his shoelaces together in tight knots. Other times, when I was lucky enough to get away with stealing a couple of raw eggs, I would crack them directly into someone's shoes, a sure way to grab his immediate attention at reveille. I continued playing my typical dumb self when asked if I knew anything about the activities. What made the whole thing more worthwhile, the truly greatest satisfaction to me, was when everyone else joined in and laughed at the wide variety of indignant reactions that inevitably resulted from my somewhat cowardly yet clever methods of get-even harassment.

I was disappointed when I was singled out at Quarters one morning and told that it was my time for mess cook duties. For some reason I had thought that I was going to be bypassed, that I was more important as a snipe, that the skills I had acquired would demand my retention by M.D. Adams. This was not the case.

I reported to the cook as directed, and my duties were briefly described. Basically, I would do exactly as I was told — without question and without complaint — and I would wear whites during my assignment there. It was something of an abrupt awakening to find that I was taking orders from someone not nearly as understanding or as tactful as M.D. had been.

First, I had to move all of my belongings out of the engineers' berthing compartment and into the mess cooks' compartment. Fortunately, the mess cooks berthed above the starboard shaft alley, in the compartment directly forward and within a few feet of my previously assigned bunk. That made the move a little more acceptable, since it was so convenient.

I was already familiar with the mess cooks compartment because as a messenger I had to climb down into the port and starboard shaft alleys hourly to check the propeller shaft bearings for overheating and for proper lubrication. The shaft alleys provided access to the very bottom of the ship, where bearings and struts provided necessary support to the propeller shafts at the point of penetrating the hull. Leakage through the huge propeller shaft packing glands also had to be monitored closely, as they were the only device(s) between the open sea and the ship's interior.

It irritated the mess cooks when engineroom messengers entered their compartment to perform their checks of the shaft alley. It was noisy opening the scuttle, and the light emanating therefrom was a nuisance. As a mess cook, I learned what it was like to be the "irritatee" rather than the "irritator."

The starboard shaft alley was also a favorite hiding place for those of us that didn't want to participate in certain working parties.

I hated mess cook duties. It meant getting up long before reveille, setting up the serving line before each meal, and then having to serve the crew. The duties varied in that sometimes I was assigned to the scullery, the real pits.

Scullery duties consisted of scraping, cleaning, and washing the dirty trays as they were "deposited" at the scullery window. There was a garbage container available for the crew to scrape their trays into; however, there was always more to be scraped off before the trays could be rinsed and then sent through the dishwashing and drying mechanisms. It stank in the scullery and it was hot and humid; much the same as it was in the engineroom. The deck was slippery with greasy foodstuffs, and I found myself spending just as much time sliding back and forth across the deck as I was cleaning trays and utensils. Then, after the entire crew had been served, I had to clean not only the scullery but also the mess decks too.

I began to think of the life of a sailor as that of one who would always be chipping, scraping, washing, sweeping and swabbing, rinsing, shining, preparing for and unpreparing from, and on and on.

My whites rapidly became stained beyond cleaning, and I knew it was going to cost me a bundle to replace them. There were no special allowances for mess cook uniforms.

Making "breakouts" was another mess cook chore. The cook was responsible for making out his list of everything he needed for the upcoming meal, and the mess cooks were required to haul it out of stowage and up to the galley. Everything had to be done within time limits, since meal hours were so strictly adhered to. Mess cooks did not stand watches but they had little free time to spare. When they weren't actually working, they were either trying to, or they were, sleeping.

Mess cooking was a onetime assignment, and with that knowledge everyone managed to complete their tour without complaining excessively. There were better things to look forward to; the period of leave I had earned and hoped to take early in September when we returned to San Diego.

6

BECOMING A SAILOR

I could reasonably plan on remaining in and out of San Diego, California, for approximately six months before the next overseas deployment. The first month, I requested and was granted two weeks' leave. It was an interesting leave, far away from the duties and responsibilities to which I had grown accustomed. I enjoyed showering my family with the souvenir gifts I had purchased in the Far East. My father was particularly proud of his new three-piece Grampus fishing rod, each piece carefully mounted and encased in a lightweight wooden carrying case. My mother was pleased and proud of her new ninety-six-piece set of Noritake china, a bamboo design of the finest quality available in Japan at that time. My brother thought of the wooden carved facemask from the Philippines as one of his most unique possessions. Linda, my hometown sweetheart, was delighted with the cashmere sweater I had purchased in Hong Kong, but she was understandably disappointed, and we were all a bit taken aback, when she showed us the inside of the neck where the clearly marked tag read: MADE IN U.S.A.. I was embarrassed at not having seen the tag sooner, and I was upset at having traveled all the way to Hong Kong to buy a garment that had been made in the United States. Linda made me feel a little bit better when she reminded me that it was "the thought" that mattered.

I spent a good portion of my leave telling my family and friends of my experiences; although some of my stories were toned down while others, to add a little spice, were exaggerated. Many details had to be left out for fear my family might think that I had become somewhat corrupt or otherwise unwholesome; that my Navy peers were misleading me.

I had seen and done things that were considered taboo. I had participated in unacceptable behavior, but even more disturbing was the fact that I

128

had developed an attitude unique to myself. I no longer felt that I had to do everything precisely in line with my parents' wishes; I felt that my wishes, rightly or wrongly, were of equal or greater importance. I had learned to make my own decisions and I had become man enough to stand by them.

When I returned to the *Colahan* at the expiration of my leave I thought that my period of absence had served to sever whatever responsibilities I had as a mess cook, so I reported for duty with engineroom personnel. It was only a day or two before Machinist's Mate First Class Packett realized that I was back. The instant he realized that I had failed to report back to the mess decks for the remainder of my "tour" there, he made sure that I thoroughly understood my obligation to complete my time as a mess cook and sent me on my way.

There was one, and *only* one good thing, as far as I can recall, about mess cook duties; we all had "open gangway" liberty. There were no night duties or watches to stand, so we could go ashore every night. The obvious problem with that was the lack of sleep we suffered when we took advantage of open gangway. No one ever went ashore for just a few minutes. Having that freedom was a great privilege overseas whereas it seemed to be of less value while in the States.

My exposure to the "enhanced" adult lifestyle of the Far East had spoiled me. In the States I was still an underage adolescent with no adult privileges. Wearing the uniform made me proud, but I could not understand why, as a member of the military and willing to fight and die for my country, I was considered too young to drink a beer, too young to vote! At that time the age of majority was twenty-one and that age constraint was as strictly enforced on military installations as it was off.

I spent most of my time ashore walking somewhat aimlessly around town. There was one place some of the younger underage sailors liked to frequent, that sold "near beer," a nonalcoholic beerlike beverage. I felt more grown up sitting at the bar, even knowing the beverage was probably comparable to, or in the same category as, soda pop. I never saw the place void of the younger sailors and marines that enjoyed the adult environment — without adult beverages.

There was always Balboa Park to stroll through, and of course there was the spacious and truly interesting San Diego Zoo. Also, small groups of the younger guys pooled their incomes and then rented apartments.

Periodically I'd get invited to one of those places where I, like the guys who rented them, thoroughly enjoyed the privacy and the refuge the apartments provided.

If there was no booze or snacks of one kind or another available, we would scrape together a few bucks and buy whatever provisions we were in need or desirous of. Obtaining alcoholic beverages from a liquor store was never a problem. If a proprietor wouldn't sell it to us, and we couldn't get one of the older salts to buy it for us, we'd simply ask someone on the street, usually some drunk or a vagrant. For a dollar or less they would buy and deliver whatever we wanted. All they wanted in return for the favor was enough money to buy a bottle of cheap wine; usually Thunderbird or its equivalent.

I was very happy to return to the engineroom upon completion of my mess cook assignment. It was rather obvious how much I enjoyed working on and around the heavy-duty machinery. It was tedious and nonrewarding work, but we all worked together and most of us got along great.

The younger and less experienced officers, the administrators, were not much older than the younger enlisted men. The perception was that they only knew how to direct; without regard for, or understanding of the real or potential problems that were related in one way or another to their demands. They expected absolute and immediate compliance when they were dealing with younger enlisted men. Sometimes it was comical watching the younger officers, the ensigns in particular, as they voiced their authority for little or no apparent reason other than to hear themselves practice giving commands; thereby impressing no one other than themselves.

Officers, like enlisted men, did not always stop to evaluate what they were about to say. There was nothing wrong with an officer laughing at something improper or out of context that an enlisted man said — but woe unto the lowly sailor who laughed at anything an officer did or said; unless he was telling a joke, and then we laughed even when the joke fell flat. All too often inexperienced officers disregarded one of the most powerful principles of military leadership; their intended role of setting an example. Sometimes they simply forgot that they were supposed to look smart, remain military in appearance, and that they were to be understanding before their influence could be positive in nature.

Chiefs, far more often than not, were thoroughly experienced leaders and were equally demanding of adherence to the orders they issued, however they were far more likely to be fully cognizant of any consequence that might result. In simple terms, it was easier to follow the more understanding or sensible orders issued by a chief. They had been where we were, they had done what we were doing, and they had proven themselves through years of experience.

Certainly chiefs were, in the eyes of most enlisted men, hated and admired at the same time. We hated them because they had privileges we lacked, they wore uniforms similar to those that officers wore, and they seldom got their hands dirty; but most of all because it was nearly impossible to fool them. They truly were, as they have always been traditionally referred, the "backbone of the Navy."

Liberty was not considered with the same priority in the States as it was in the playgrounds of the Orient. During the six-month period of stateside operations many crewmen attended schools of relatively short duration. Most of the training was accomplished during the daytime, and classes were attended on the base, away from the ship, usually during working hours. In one way or another all Navy or Navy-sponsored schools further improved the attendees' ability to perform productively. There were courses on leadership, firefighting, and damage control; short courses in electronics, navigational systems, and weaponry; engineering courses on welding, brazing, and soldering; and courses on human relations. Most courses were considered extracurricular, and the time it took to attend them usually provided minimal interference with shipboard duties.

There were also lengthy technical schools where attendance required that individuals be temporarily transferred, sometimes thousands of miles from the ship's homeport. The technical schools were in great demand because they not only taught fundamental principles, they also provided in-depth training on the more intricate details; the physical internal workings of most shipboard components. Usually, upon satisfactory completion of a technical school came a well-deserved promotion.

I was offered the opportunity to attend the very comprehensive Machinist's Mate School at Great Lakes Naval Training Center on the shore of Lake Michigan, but out of ignorance I turned it down. I wanted to remain on board the ship where I could gain hands-on knowledge and experience, on-the-job training. I should never have turned down such an opportunity. School graduates were far more competent and dependable than those who did not attend and those who for whatever reason failed to graduate. Promotion exams were taken right out of the school curriculum. Also, graduates were more likely to be favorably recommended to participate in promotion exams for the next higher pay grade. They had a distinct edge as a result of their training and they were far more likely to pass any future in-rate exam.

Interestingly, all who participated in and passed promotional exams were not necessarily promoted. There was a quota system. The more critical the rating, the more openings there were for promotions. The overloaded deck ratings, particularly the Boatswain's Mate rating, usually had the least number of promotions authorized. The snipes, particularly the Machinist's Mate rating, usually had one of the highest number of promotions authorized. Regardless of the quota system, promotions were always more likely among those who completed one or more of the many technical schools that were offered.

So, by my own misguided choice, I turned down the opportunity to attend the much-in-demand Machinist's Mate training and struggled to keep up with the demanding engineroom workload. With so many snipes off at school, demands placed upon me increased noticeably.

In port it wasn't too bad, but underway the personnel shortages were far more evident. Watches were no longer four hours on and eight hours off; it became mandatory to designate a two-section watch bill instead of the usual three. At times we had to stand four hours on duty and four hours off, or the more preferable but equally demanding six hours on and six hours off. In either case, it was a twenty-four-hour-a-day routine for as long as the ship remained at sea.

Periods of time at sea usually ranged from one week to three weeks, sometimes longer. Working hours remained unchanged, so snipes could depend on a minimum of twelve hours a day down in the hole. Tempers became short, and fights between men of different divisions became more frequent. Snipes were a tough bunch, but we still took exception knowing that most crewmen stood but one four-hour watch a day, sometimes less. It was not wise for the luckier ones to ridicule us. At the right time, the right place, whoever was being harassed would eventually make sure that whoever was doing the harassing would feel the impact of a tightly gripped fist to his nose — or an unexpected backhand across his face. Such fights were short, usually ending in a minute or less.

Fights between men of the same division were less frequent, but when they did occur they were more apt to last longer. Sometimes two men would continue fighting off and on over a period of days.

I had a distinct hatred for Dan'l, a Machinist's Mate third class. He was thin, a little shorter than I, extremely feisty, and he took a great deal of pleasure making my life as miserable as he possibly could. Dan'l would challenge me at every opportunity. He would threaten to "kick ass" (mine) for little or no reason; always bragging that he had boxed "golden gloves" and that he could "drop" me "like a used condom."

Once, down in the engineroom, while Dan'l was perched over the scuttlebutt like some kind of vulture, and I was in need of replenishing my sweat-drenched body with the water he wouldn't allow me near, through his own special challenging smirk he asked me, "What say there, Ad, do you like me?" Then, before allowing me to answer honestly he immediately followed with; "If you tell me you don't like me, I'm gonna work you over like you wouldn't believe!"

Since it was not my desire to be worked over, I exercised my better judgment and I did not answer truthfully. I didn't want a confrontation with Dan'l, yet secretly I was hoping he would eventually go one step too far, maybe take that first swing. I wasn't sure that I would come out of it unscathed, but I began to welcome the opportunity to find out. Dan'l was no dummy; he knew just how far he could go without crossing the line, the point beyond which I would no longer contain myself. He continuously pushed me just so far, instinctively stopping just prior to the point where I might have responded physically; possibly with a violence he didn't really want to test. At that time I was willing to exercise restraint.

It would probably come as a surprise to Dan'l if he knew the degree of admiration I had for him as to his courage in standing up to Packett. Whenever the two of them met while ashore, there was bloodshed. Dan'l would invariably end up being badly worked over, but he always gave it his best shot. Nor did Packett come out of those ordeals totally unmarked.

With October 16, 1955 came my first promotion. I had successfully passed a fairly simple shipboard exam designed to test my knowledge of engineering space fundamentals; primarily the how and why of the main propulsion plant steam cycle and associated auxiliaries. I was proud having been promoted to pay grade E-3 and I quickly sewed on my FN (Fireman) stripes. The promotion did not provide for cutting me any slack as far as the workload was concerned, but wearing three stripes instead of two allowed me to blend in as one of the crew instead of standing out as a two-stripe boot camper. There were some men in pay grade E-3 that were also wearing one or two hash marks; each hash mark representing four years of military service, not necessarily all Navy time.

I was aware, although I never really understood why, that there were some men who **did** not care about being promoted. Some were happy knowing their mandatory military service was being served and that they would be honorably separated at the end of their enlistment. Even some of the "lifers," as careerists were termed, were content adding hash marks instead of promotion chevrons, knowing that each hash mark meant four more years vested toward lifetime retirement income. And there were those who were just as content with the knowledge that they had shoes on their feet, a place to sleep, and three meals a day.

It was my goal to be promoted as quickly and as frequently as was allowable by Navy regulations, even though I had absolutely no intention on making the Navy a career. I wanted to serve my time, honorably, and get out.

It was probably the sincere interest and the effort that a small group of us exerted toward getting ahead that motivated most of those who previously didn't care. I was seldom seen without some kind of study course in hand, not just the required courses, but every course I could take that was in any way related to engineering and/or leadership.

The satisfactory completion of designated courses was mandatory before anyone could be recommended to participate in the Navy-wide promotion exams. Each course consisted of a dozen or so lessons; each lesson required the completion and mailing of answer sheets to a designated grading authority. After grading, the answer sheets were returned to the candidate(s). Any lessons failed had to be repeated.

I did not believe in the correspondence course system of learning, so I used a system more suitable to me whenever possible. I did not believe in learning only that which was contained in the course. Following a course through step-by-step procedures, answering only those questions believed important enough to require answers, meant that I would probably overlook or ignore a lot of other significant information. So I cheated! I copied the corrected answers from someone else's previously graded lessons, intentionally marking a few answers incorrectly, and then, after mailing my answer sheets off I studied my head off. I studied only that which I knew I needed to study, disregarding or rapidly skimming over everything that I already knew. I studied the minor as well as the major details. Whenever I finished a course "my way," I had a thorough knowledge of everything it was designed to teach! I took pleasure in challenging shipmates to open my course book(s) to any page and ask me questions on any subject. Rarely did I not know the correct answer. I used this method of studying very successfully throughout my military career. Since I was learning far more than the average sailor, certainly more than was expected, I never considered it cheating. Quite the contrary, I considered my method of study a far more effective means of acquiring that knowledge essential to all phases of military training; technical and professional.

Fireman Andrews, also known as "Arkie," was another motivating factor in my effort to advance. Arkie was one of those two-hash-mark E-3s who, for a time, thought more of his hash marks than of advancement stripes. He believed, and tried very hard to enforce his own rule(s), that petty officers second class *and* sailors with two hash marks had head-of-the-line privileges — particularly when it was a chow line.

Arkie was an interesting individual and seemed to get along well with just about everyone. He was one of the more knowledgeable FNs, having been assigned to engineering for years instead of the few months or lesser number of years with which other E-3s were credited. Since Arkie had the most time credited to his military service and since he was qualified to stand all of the engineroom underway watches (with the exception of top watch), he was given the title "Leading Fireman," a title indicating some degree of power and one of which Arkie was quite proud. The fact that his title got him out of some of the more menial tasks and allowed him to drink coffee along with the petty officers while the rest of us worked made him gloat with pride. We, in turn, looked upon his "situation" as disgusting; anything other than desirable. Those of us in pay grade E-3 knew that we had progressed a mere two steps out of boot camp and those few individuals who remained stuck in that pay grade over a long period of time, as Arkie had, were either ignorant or they were not carrying their share of the load. Being rewarded for failing promotion exams, or for intentionally refusing to participate in those exams, was in opposition to any rules of fair play and/or traditional expectations.

Arkie appeared to be far more comfortable hanging out with men nearer his age, regardless of their pay grade. He was something of a pet to Packett. Arkie was usually seen following Packett around like a puppy and unintentionally, or perhaps intentionally, took on some of Packett's less than admirable personality and mannerisms. Whatever it was, if it was good enough for Packett, then it was good enough for Arkie. Snipes of all pay grades poked fun at how Arkie's nose was buried so far up Packett's ass that it would break off if Packett ever turned a sharp corner.

I think Arkie realized that his stature was at stake when he saw my peers and me studying so hard. The handwriting was there — some of us younger guys were going to pass him up if he didn't buckle down and put forth greater effort. There was no argument as to his ability; he had the competence and he deserved to be promoted. All he needed was to pass the exam.

Whether it was me or someone like me that helped Arkie realize his potential, assisting in getting him interested in being promoted, I was glad and I welcomed him as someone worthy of competition. In fact, Arkie was promoted to Machinist's Mate third class (E-4) and on to second class (E-5) while I was assigned to *Colahan*. It wasn't until then that he realized he was not only petty officer material, he really enjoyed having and exercising the responsibilities that went with it.

Perhaps one of my biggest disappointments during my entire military career was when Arkie was promoted to MM2, Machinist's Mate second class, and I was not. Arkie, justifiably so, became a grade senior to me.

A good portion of my shipboard time while stateside was spent on machinery maintenance. Engineroom personnel were routinely assigned work from the PMS (Preventive Maintenance Schedule). There were pencil zincs and zinc plates that had to be replaced in all machinery cooled by salt water. Without sufficient zinc available, electrolysis would erode machinery internals. Bearings that were found worn near or outside acceptable tolerances were replaced. Old packing was replaced with new packing whether needed or not. Clearances of one type or another were checked on nearly all machinery, and corrective action was taken to maintain, in some instances restore, those clearances to within allowable specifications. Damaged lagging pads were replaced with new. There were literally hundreds of gauges throughout the engineering spaces; each one had to be removed and calibrated periodically.

136

Not PMS-related, but nonetheless work requiring time and effort, was the never-ending procedure of chipping and painting; wire brushing and polishing; adding something to, or draining something from whatever needed it; and washing paintwork. Systems suspected or known to have leaky valves had to be isolated; the valves subsequently removed and sent to a repair facility for corrective maintenance. There was always work of one kind or another to be accomplished; we *never* caught up.

Blacks, or "niggers" as they were more commonly referred to by most, were not well received by the predominantly white crew; Machinist's Mate first class Packett in particular. I fell in line with the majority, and without justification I also began to think of blacks as niggers.

What a shock it was when MM1 Boyd, a rather stocky African-American, reported aboard and was assigned as Petty Officer in Charge of the after engineroom. It had only been a few years since by executive order the military service had been desegregated, and racial relations were not exactly favorable. Prejudice and racist attitudes were common — even though they were not supposed to be condoned. Having to associate with a "nigger," having one in our midst seemed bad enough, but having to work for one was a tough pill to swallow.

Boyd wasted no time in getting our attention. He was not, nor were any of his orders, to be taken lightly. Boyd was demanding and strict; he knew precisely what he wanted accomplished, and he knew how to go about getting it done. Little by little we began to disregard the color of Boyd's skin. It did not take long before we began to realize that Boyd was not only one of us; *he was probably the best one of us.*

Boyd's approach to leadership was similar to M.D.s, and he gained more and more respect with each passing day. Boyd had the ability to calculate exactly how much work each of us was capable of doing during the workday and he accepted nothing less from any of us.

We all had our shortcomings, or bad habits, and Boyd was no exception. His irritating and noticeable habit was that of saying "ya know" several times within the content of single sentences. We picked up on that quickly, and when Boyd wasn't around we would mimic him in our conversations; always making sure to include "ya know" in between every two or three words. But Boyd had wasted no time in gaining our absolute respect, and our foolish mockery of his only noticeable bad habit made us realize that we truly had accepted him as one of us.

137

Boyd proved that he was capable of sharing a bond of friendship, even as he exercised his leadership skills. On one such occasion, when the entire after engineroom gang was in the process of comparing our tans, Boyd stuck his arm right there in the middle of ours and said, "I win, ya know."

Tools, of the variety needed, were a luxury we normally did without. But Machinist's Mate first class Boyd's requests for tool purchases were, for reasons that befuddled us, always approved. He had special tool bins constructed so that inventories were more easily and efficiently conducted. The strictest control over the issue and receipt of tools was adhered to at all times. Boyd conducted inventories of all tools twice daily — once prior to the issuance of any tools and then again at the end of each workday. No one left the engineroom at the end of the day if there was a single tool out of place or missing! The tool bin was not to be closed and locked until it was 100 percent in order.

On occasion it was frustrating for us when a tool inventory came up short. Accusations would run the gamut, each of us placing blame on someone else. But Boyd would just stand there, his teeth clenched together, jaw tight, and demand that we find the missing item(s). Sooner or later (more often sooner) someone would locate the missing tool. More often than not it was recovered from the bilge where someone had carelessly dropped it and then failed to retrieve it.

In a matter of weeks, because of Boyd's insistence and persistence, we had the smartest-looking engineroom in the entire squadron, perhaps in the entire fleet! First Class Packett fumed at the realization that he had been clearly outdone by a "fuckin' nigger," the only manner in which Packett was ever known to refer or describe African-Americans.

Different ships (commands) within as well as outside our own squadron heard of the *Colahan's* sparkling clean after engineroom. Captains, commanders, and chiefs came from other ships and inspected our space, sometimes departing annoyed with the realization that their spaces were nowhere near comparable. They in turn would send their leading petty officers over to show them that the transition from typical engineroom to outstanding engineroom was an achievable goal.

Boyd impressed me as one of the finest examples of military leadership I ever came across throughout my career. Not only was he dedicated and loyal to the Navy; he exercised that same dedication and loyalty to the men subordinate to him. In time, I would incorporate much of Boyd's perseverance and tolerance into my own approach toward exercising effective leadership.

Time seemed to pass more quickly as I became more acclimated to my Navy surroundings. I began thinking more and more about my high school sweetheart, and in January 1956, we were married.

My married life and my military life were distinctly different. I tried very hard to keep them separated, never wanting to mix the two. I do not believe it would be appropriate nor would it be of significant interest to document both lifestyles within the pages of this book since it has always been my intention to detail only my military experiences. There was conflict between my married life and my Navy life, and my married life lost that battle.

Shipboard rumors were sometimes fabricated just to pass the time. I learned to disregard just about everything that was not documented in one way or another. There was, however, one believable rumor that got my attention. Fairly reliable sources had it that petty officer first class Packett was given some extremely favorable treatment when he took his test for promotion to CPO (E-7). It was rumored that he was not only allowed to leave the testing area several times in order to look up some of the answers to test questions, he was also allowed to take all the time he needed without regard to normal test-time limitations. Understandably, Machinist's Mate first class Packett did pass, and he was selected for promotion.

On the day of his promotion Packett was in rare form. At that time I knew very little about what the CPO initiation consisted of, but I was hoping it would take its toll when it came Packett's turn. It was around midnight when a very drunk, newly initiated Chief Packett returned to the ship. His new CPO uniform was badly soiled, his tie had been cut off at the halfway point, he reeked of alcohol, and he was more belligerent than I had ever seen him. Packett stumbled around the berthing compartment, made his way to his locker, and was intent on vacating the space of his belongings without further delay; his new home having become CPO quarters. The noise he was making was uncalled for, and most of it was intentional. He wanted everyone in the compartment to be aware of his presence and that he had become a chief petty officer.

Boyd was the only one to complain. "Hold it down, Packett; there's people trying to sleep here."

Packett immediately responded, "It's *Chief* Packett, you fuckin' blue-gummed coon, and don't you ever forget it."

Packett rambled on with a few more choice four-letter expletives, all directed at Boyd, and all as derogatory as could be. Boyd exercised his usual good judgment and said nothing more. Everyone in the compartment followed Boyd's lead, no one complained further but we were all wide-awake and fully cognizant of Chief Packett's activities. Too bad, I remember thinking, that it wasn't Boyd having been promoted to chief instead of Packett. It probably would have been Boyd if he had met the time in grade eligibility requirements that were in effect at that time.

Boyd did eventually have his opportunity at competing for chief, and he was promoted. I'm sure he was a fine CPO and I'm only sorry that I never served with him during the time he wore "the hat." The CPO hat was commonly referred to as "the hat;" therefore, those who earned or wore "the hat" were chiefs.

It was customary on board most ships to transfer newly advanced CPOs as soon as possible after they were promoted. That made Packett's promotion worthwhile since the *Colahan* would be well rid of him — for good, I hoped. I never saw Chief Packett again after his transfer. He may have turned himself around, and he just might have become a better person as a chief. I certainly hope so, but I know it would have been extremely unlikely.

"Underway training," six weeks of strenuous exercises at sea, was always a significant training period prior to every overseas deployment. During that time all shipboard systems were tried and tested and then tried again. General Quarters, Battle Stations, was called at any time of the day or night; sometimes several times during the day, and sometimes right in the middle of a meal (with the Exec's blessings no doubt). Radical maneuvering exercises were accomplished along with gunnery drills. When the five-inch guns fired, especially Mount 53 located on the 0-1 level directly over the after engineroom, it was hazardous to those of us in that space. Debris of all types, including fibrous asbestos dust from cracked or damaged lagging pads, and broken incandescent light bulbs, flew in all directions, rapidly filling the engineroom with a dusty smoglike appearance. Such conditions made breathing difficult.

Underway training was tedious and it was a real strain on everyone, snipes in particular. The heat and discomfort of the engineering spaces could not be felt or understood from the bridge. As long as the ship was moving, engineers and the main propulsion plant were considered to be alive and well by the command.

It was during that first year that I began to hate the military way of life. If there was a way to irritate the "lifers," those individuals with career intentions, I enjoyed doing it. I began to think that only the uneducated, only those that lacked the ability to succeed in the civilian world, would remain on active duty for more than one enlistment. I was confident that I was no dummy and I certainly didn't fit my own stereotypical description of what a career-minded sailor was, so my plan was simple. I would do my time and get out. There was no way I would ever allow myself to be placed in the same category as that of a lifer!

7

WORK HARD; PLAY HARD

It was April 1956, a little over a year had passed since I joined the Navy, and my opinion of the Navy way of life continued to deteriorate. I was developing an unhealthy attitude of diminished respect for authority of any kind, and I took little or no pride in my appearance. I began to think more and more about the day I could thumb my nose at the Navy as a proud civilian. Somehow I managed to retain the dedication and pride I had in my work and I continued to do as I was told. I shudder to think of the things I might have considered doing to the machinery, short of sabotage, had I not enjoyed my work. For example, the improper installation of packing rings to pump shafts would have caused little more than excessive leak-off but would also have become a significant contributing water shortage factor. Similarly, the improper installation, or the installation of damaged "flexitallic gaskets" (steel gaskets with compressible metal and asbestos inserts designed to seal steam line flanges), would have allowed for steam leaks, another cause of water shortage; but of equal consequence would have been the increase in temperature and humidity of the entire engineroom. Any job that was not tackled with professional zeal eventually had to be redone, which added unnecessarily to the already-demanding workload required within the space.

Strange, as I think back, how important it was to each of us, regardless of our attitude toward Navy life, how we worked together under such adverse conditions, and we always did our assigned jobs to the very best of our abilities. Rarely did we have to redo work that was not accomplished properly in the first place. It did happen, but it was a rare occurrence.

Once the underway training phase was completed and both ⌐
crew had satisfactorily proven their worthiness and readiness, the *Colahan*
was tied up alongside one of the many piers at the San Diego Naval
Shipyard. Final preparations were made for the long and strenuous journey
across the ocean; another WestPac deployment to the Far East would begin
within a couple of days. The ship was in good shape, and since there was
very little maintenance in need of attention, the crew was afforded ample
time to prepare. We took on our own personal provisions; snacks, reading
materials, uniform items, writing materials, the most recent photos of our
loved ones, and just about anything that would tend to make our time at sea
a little more comfortable and enjoyable, and make the time seem to pass
more quickly.

Understandably most of the married men took leave during the final
days in port. They wanted to share as much of the remaining predeploy-
ment time as possible with their families. It was an emotional time for
everyone. Some of the men were overanxious to return to the Orient, while
others were deeply saddened with the realization that they would soon be
leaving home. For me, it was a mixture of many emotions. I would miss my
family; however, the excitement of the Orient was also in my blood. I had
thoroughly enjoyed most of my overseas experiences and I looked forward
to picking up right where I had left off.

Without any unexpected delay, the *Colahan* got underway as scheduled
and she immediately headed west. Our first stop, primarily to refuel but
also to give the crew a short R and R break, was Pearl Harbor, Hawaii. It
was Cinderella liberty for all enlisted men under the grade of chief. I was
terribly disappointed knowing my activities, whatever they might have consisted of, would have to be curtailed early enough to get me back to the ship
before midnight. The general distrust of enlisted men and the preferential
treatment received by officers and chiefs, regardless of the fact that such
treatment was passed off as earned privileges, were significant contributing
factors in the growing contempt I had for the Navy.

The *Colahan* remained four days alongside the pier at Pearl Harbor.
She was scheduled to depart on April 16, 1956, a date that I would always
remember as having been one of the most important days of my life in the
Navy.

Marcel and I could hardly wait to go ashore that April 15th, the day pri-
or to our departure. We had big plans. At liberty call we presented ourselves
in our sharpest white uniforms, and immediately upon disembarking we

headed straight to Hotel Street; the strip, also known as "Shit Street." We were a day premature, but with the knowledge the ship was getting underway on the sixteenth, and since we had both been recommended for, participated in, passed, and were to be promoted on the sixteenth (and proud as we were, beyond description), we decided to promote ourselves a day early. We were to become E-4s, petty officers, and we needed to change our rating badges accordingly.

All of the tailor shops in Honolulu carried military insignia, patches, and collar devices for all branches of the service. Marcel and I stopped at the first tailor shop we came to and had the necessary changes made to our uniforms. The three red FN stripes were removed and were replaced with a "crow," an eagle over a single *V* chevron, the lowest of petty officer grades but that first major step of recognition and achievement.

One Very Proud 3rd Class Petty Officer
That First Significant Promotion — April 16, 1956

"So who should we write up first?" I jokingly asked Marcel.

Writing someone up was slang for placing someone on report for one violation or another, and was usually exercised by petty officers. The threat of being written up was *always* present.

"If you don't shape up, I'll write *your* ass up," was his prompt response.

144

We spent the day walking around, periodically voicing our admiration for each other's brand-new crow, and eventually we ended up relaxing at Kuhio and Waikiki Beach. We were both underage, so the sharing of a toast, one consisting of alcoholic beverage, in recognition of our newly acquired petty officer status, was out of the question; at least for the time being.

Marcel and I had no idea of the distance it was back to the ship, but we made the decision to walk it anyway. It was a long, tiresome walk; quite a few miles, but it was also refreshing. Our conversation varied as we walked, but we always returned to the most important subject of the day, our promotion(s) and the new crows we were wearing. In our minds we had already become NCOs, noncommissioned officers, and we had been promoted without benefit of the Commanding Officer's blessings.

Interestingly, the U.S. Navy was the only branch of military service that considered enlisted men in grades E-4 and above as NCOs. All other branches, probably with greater insight, only considered grades E-5 and above as such. The only reason I mention that fact is because Navy NCOs in grade E-4 were not always allowed access to NCO clubs. Sometimes NCO clubs of other services were cooperative and they relaxed their own rule for the benefit of sailors. In time, we learned where we were accepted and where we were not. Conversely, the Navy had PO (Petty Officer) Clubs that welcomed other branches of the service in pay grades E-4 and above.

The following day Marcel and I, among others, were congratulated and officially recognized in the POD, the Plan of the Day, as having been promoted to the next higher grade. Marcel and I were officially Machinist's Mates third class. Tom Mundy was promoted to BT3, Boiler Technician third class. It was great hearing our names read at Quarters that morning. It was equally a tremendous letdown when we reported to the engineroom and were immediately told by one of the senior petty officers that as far as he was concerned we were nothing more than overpaid Firemen, that we had not gained one thread of knowledge overnight, and that we would continue to do basically the same work. In our minds we thought that we had proven ourselves before we were recommended for advancement, but then we found that it was necessary to prove to an even greater degree that we truly were worthy of the brand new crows we were wearing.

At the time I felt insulted, but later I realized that it really was important, proving one's ability to perform adequately and effectively as a petty officer. I did, however, promise myself that I would never be so tactless during my military service as to insinuate that anyone having been promoted was anything other than deserving of it. Overpaid or undeserving? Never! Sincere congratulations would *always* be in order.

Our next port, another fueling stop but one that would last no more than four hours in duration, was located 1,300 miles northwest of Honolulu; Midway Island.

Midway had little to offer the aspiring tourist. The atoll, only six miles in diameter, consists of two islands totaling twenty-eight square miles. It is interesting to note that such a small area contributed so greatly to the outcome of World War II. The Battle of Midway, June 4-6, 1942, resulted in a severe defeat for Japan. There the Japanese lost four aircraft carriers and suffered heavy losses in men and planes. Keeping the Midway Islands, a strategic fuel depot between Japan and the United States, proved to be one of the decisive naval victories and the turning point of the war.

At the time of our visit at Midway, the Navy maintained a small base there, consisting of a radio relay center and weather station. Along with the primary fueling operations, the islands provided a home for several hundred Navy personnel and their dependents. The absolute isolation provided little more than a place to bask in eternal summer, surrounded by crystal clear waters and tropical breezes.

Prior to entering port, all of the heads were secured; a precaution to make sure no waste of any kind would be pumped into the sea surrounding the islands. Anyone having to "go" between the time the ship entered port and the time it was securely tied up alongside the pier would have to "hold it."

Tom Mundy's refueling duties included taking fuel oil soundings, checking tank levels in preparation for taking on fuel, and carefully monitoring the tanks as they were being filled. Fuel tank sounding tubes were located all over the ship, a couple were in the aft head (which was roped off for entering port). I was standing at the top of the port engineroom ladder, at the forward entrance to the head, when Tom, on his way to his refueling station, was stopped by Seaman Mac. Mac, an E-3, the man responsible for roping off the hatch thereby properly securing the head, was quite insistent that absolutely no one could enter. Tom bristled when Mac spoke.

"You can't go in there."

Mac really didn't understand. He didn't realize that Tom had to enter the head to take soundings. Tom, not having the time to discuss the fueling operation or associated safeguards along with other requirements, simply made his situation known in as few words as possible. There was not a whole lot of time to spare.

"I have to go in there."

"No, you can't," was not what Tom wanted to hear as he began spreading the rope-lined barrier wide enough to squeeze through; completely ignoring Mac's "orders." Somewhat demanding, the younger and less experienced seaman grabbed Tom's shoulder and tried to restrain him. Tom instantly swung around and with lightning speed and in rapid succession he planted several well-calculated punches to the surprised seaman's face and body.

"Now don't try to stop me again," was Tom's good and smartly heeded advice.

Shortly thereafter that same seaman, Mac, told me, "I'm gonna get him."

"You're gonna get who?" I asked.

"You know who. I'm gonna get all you white motherfuckers."

Without hesitation I bolted toward Seaman Mac. But Hollister, a seaman I had not noticed, quickly grabbed me from behind, pinned both of my arms to my sides, and for the moment rendered me nearly helpless. I saw Mac as he viciously swung a "dogging wrench," a metal pipe used for tightening hatches, in my direction — and I felt a terrible pain as it smashed into my head, resulting in a fairly deep gash to my scalp. Blood began streaming down both sides of my face as I struggled with desperation to free myself from the bear-hug clench by which I was being restrained. Within seconds others in the area pulled Hollister away from me and I angrily made my way to Sick Bay where the doc proceeded to sew me up.

I had not landed a single punch, and I was furious. It angered me even more knowing that Hollister was probably no match for me. Then, to top off whatever humiliation I already felt, I found that I had been placed on report for *assault*. I knew that I would be standing in front of the Captain within a few days at which time my punishment would be determined. I was sure to lose some valuable liberty time for an offense I had not, by any reasonable definition, committed. As far as I was concerned, if I committed assault then surely Mac committed nothing less than attempted murder. But Mac was also charged with assault; aggravated assault. The difference being that I never made physical contact whereas he had.

Several days later Seaman Hollister told me that the reason he had held me was because he was trying to break up the fight. I accepted his explanation, but only in order to avoid another confrontation. In my heart I knew better — it was a two-on-one situation where I was being held by one individual while another one beat me.

Midway island was little more than an airstrip and a fuel storage depot. The island is flat, not much above sea level, the climate very similar to that of Hawaii, and there are plenty of palm and coconut trees. Surrounding the island is an ocean of beautiful clear water. It was, and probably remains, an island inhabited by thousands of black-footed albatrosses, otherwise known to sailors as "gooney birds." Beautiful in their ability to fly, gooney birds represented poetry in motion as they swooped and turned, gracefully catching every breeze on their wings. Be that as it may, the gooney bird on the ground was a different story altogether, and a hilarious one at that. All left feet, they portrayed a scene of tangled toes and awkward wing flapping during takeoff and a series of nose-dives, somersaults, tailspins, and thuds upon landing. Gooney birds made their homes and nesting grounds anywhere on the island they pleased; Midway was, at that time, a sanctuary and breeding ground for more than 200,000. It was a serious offense to harass them in any way, which was just a little too much to ask of young, inquisitive sailors. The birds were fun to watch. More fun to chase. Their wingspans were so wide that in order to become airborne it took almost more effort than they were capable of exerting. They would try and try to get up enough speed, then they'd trip over their own wings, tumbling over them time and again. They appeared to be the most clumsy of God's creatures while on the ground, but in flight they were glorious, a sight to behold. They were graceful beyond comparison as they soared on the winds for hours on end. But they were also a hazard to arriving and departing aircraft.

Tom, always inclined to test the system to some degree, managed to capture one of the birds. He couldn't quite hold onto the beak of his catch and subsequently received a nasty peck on the back of his hand. I'm sure Tom has fond memories of that bird whenever he looks at the permanent scar that bird rendered him.

Midway Island also provided for a refreshing break at an outdoor beer garden. There we were, thousands of miles out in the middle of the ocean with nothing but gooney birds around us, yet we were required to wear our white liberty uniforms if we expected to visit the beer garden. Did that make sense? Not at all. Did we do it? You bet we did! I never questioned why age restrictions were not imposed there; probably because of the very

148

short period of available shore time allocated to the crew during the refueling procedure.

Some of the men preferred taking a short dip in the ocean; others shopped at the very small Navy Exchange or the Gedunk — alternative activities that were authorized while on Midway.

We crossed the International Date Line one day out of Midway as we entered the "Realm of the Golden Dragon." Those who had never crossed the date line were issued wallet-size identification cards that acknowledged the fact they had crossed that invisible line. There was no celebration and no initiation. The only significant event was the date; it being advanced by one day.

Typhoons were an expected rage of the sea, and we knew that we were in for one before we would experience liberty again. The sky began showing its first signs of trouble as it darkened from light blue to shades of gray and deep purple. The small whitecaps began forming larger swells, and the slow, comfortable swaying of the ship quickly became roller-coaster rising and plunging dips accompanied by pronounced jerking motions as the ship listed more and more heavily to port and to starboard.

The normal work routine usually remained uninterrupted by typhoon conditions; the sea had to be extremely heavy, a potential danger to all hands, before the work routine was either slackened or called off.

It was not easy sleeping under typhoon conditions. Even the old salts, fully acclimated to the sea, found it difficult getting sufficient sleep.

The bunks that were provided for the crew were not built for comfort. Most were constructed of a conduitlike frame, with heavy-duty meshlike wire that provided the bottom support for the mattress. They were compact in length and width; shorter than some men, definitely not tailored for individual comfort. Bunks were mounted three high. each bunk was secured to brackets on one side and hung by two chains on the other. Outboard bunks, those mounted against the port or starboard bulkheads, were singles; there were no bunks mounted directly beside them. Inboard bunks were two abreast. All bottom bunks hung barely above the deck-mounted foot-lockers, a burdensome obstruction to the men as they gained access to their personal belongings.

We all had our own system of counterbalancing the awkward motions of the ship as we tried to find just the right position, one that would allow for enough comfort long enough to fall asleep. Some men lay spread-eagle with their arms dangling on both sides of their bunk, legs spread with feet gripping the outer edges of the bunk frame. Some wrapped their arms around supporting bunk chains while others lay on their sides, head and feet stretched as far as possible to one side with their butts as far to the other side as possible. The heavier a person was, the less he was apt to roll.

Head-to-foot sleeping was mandatory, under the guise or belief that the germs being breathed out by one person would not be breathed in by the person in the adjacent bunk. With a compartment so crammed full of bodies, the air being breathed was well mixed, so if there were germs to be spread there was little likelihood that the head-to-foot rule did much to reduce the probability of cross-contamination. Sleeping in that manner probably did as much to create problems as it did to prevent the spread of germs, especially to those unfortunate enough to be sleeping two abreast, within inches of each other, as opposed to those that had walking space between their bunks.

Personal hygiene differed from one individual to another. Most of us did our best to keep our bodies clean, and we used deodorant liberally. However, the feet of a few individuals emitted an unbelievable foul odor, distinctly different from the expected, the more common, almost but not quite acceptable, odors caused by farts, bad breath, dirty clothing, and sweat. The stench of "rotting" feet was brought to the odor producer's attention as quickly as it was detected, but corrective action was never immediate. It was no wonder that officers seldom ventured down into the enlisted berthing spaces. To those who were not accustomed to such surroundings it must have added significantly to their already-predominant belief that enlisted men were beneath them, animal-like, something other or less than human.

The typhoon condition that we were experiencing, although never gaining the strength we expected, did prevent certain types of maintenance from being performed. The deck force could not work on the main deck, as it was awash with salt water and rainwater. For snipes, painting was difficult, though not impossible. The black gang, snipes, we being below decks and well protected from the elements, performed maintenance and cleanup; but the work area we covered was scaled down noticeably. During the worst of inclement weather conditions, our workload consisted primarily of washing down paintwork. It didn't matter if we spilled a little soapy water — that simply provided a situation and a reason to clean an area larger than might have otherwise been planned.

Typhoon conditions always created problems on the mess deck. We picked up our silverware and our trays at the start of the mess line and we were served portions as we made our way along the line. It was something of a balancing act, trying not to spill the food from the tray while we cautiously made our way to the mess deck.

It was never wise to tease or ridicule the mess cooks during rough weather; they were more apt to overload your tray with food substances that were most apt to slosh around. During rough weather the serving line and the mess decks were understandably littered with food and were extremely slippery, dangerously so.

Finding a place to sit was easy during typhoon conditions because many of the crew preferred skipping meals. Once we were safely seated, we had to hang onto our trays with one hand and eat with the other when we were able to let go of the table with that other hand long enough to take a bite. Food had a tendency to spill from one man's tray into the tray of the man sitting alongside or across, sometimes into each other's laps. That did not provide an atmosphere conducive to good relations. Fights broke out; trays filled with portions were invariably overturned on the unfortunate underdogs.

Those who were prone to become seasick would rush from their tables in their attempt to get topside, in hopes of emptying their stomachs over the side. Usually they made it; sometimes they did not. When they couldn't hold it down they heaved right in their tray, or on the table or the deck. The sight and smell had a tendency to trigger similar actions by other men. Under such conditions only the truly hungry strong-willed sailors had the fortitude to remain on the mess decks very long.

Rough weather actually provided a form of recreation down in the engineroom. The top watch had the distinct privilege of riding the metal rag-bin (or rag-can) back and forth across the steel deck plates as the ship rocked in every possible direction. The rag-can, (normally used to store wiping rags) with "rider," skimmed around the deck like a carnival bumper car, the rider always managing to spin around and prevent damage to equipment by absorbing the shock of collision with his feet. It didn't take a great deal of skill, but it did require an awareness as to the dangers the rider might encounter were the rag-can to take an abrupt and unexpected change of direction.

By the time of my promotion to MM3, I had gained some experience on the lower-level watch station. As a petty officer I was expected to qualify on all stations, including that of top watch. I would not actually be assigned to stand the duties of the top watch, just to qualify for the watch station in the event everyone senior to me was incapacitated.

The duties of the lower-level watch station meant added responsibilities. Instead of merely taking the readings and having someone else evaluate them, I would do my own evaluating and, time permitting (not an emergency situation), make recommendations or suggestions to the top watch that might improve the efficiency of the plant. Primarily my duties consisted of monitoring oil levels, water levels, and temperatures associated with the machinery down there. It also meant shifting from steam pumps to electrical-driven pumps, or vice versa, whenever required.

There was no phone communication from the upper-level to the lower-level, only a two-and-a-half-inch diameter brass "voice tube" that extended from the upper-level handrail to about five and one-half feet above the lower-level deck plates; about ear-level to the lower-level watchstander. Anyone on the upper-level could get the attention of the lower-level watchstander by ringing a bell that was electrically activated by pressing a button mounted on the upper-level handrail next to the voice tube.

I learned from experience that the voice tube was also an excellent means of harassing the lower-level watchstanders. As frequently as I thought I could get away with it, especially when Marcel had the lower-level watch, I did my dirty deed. First I rang the bell. Marcel, mouth close to the voice tube, would yell his acknowledgment with, "Aye?" or "Yeah?" I would then intentionally rattle off something senseless, something that sounded urgent but completely indistinguishable, knowing that good ol' conscientious Marcel would immediately come back with, "Repeat." I also knew that Marcel would then have his ear pressed tightly against that voice tube to make sure he would understand the repeated communication over the roar of the engineroom machinery. I then poured water down the tube! Marcel never thought it was all that humorous. I considered it absolutely hilarious; especially knowing how many times he had repeatedly fallen victim to one form or another of my intimidating deeds. Yet Marcel always got over his frustration (not anger) quickly. Little did he realize that it was his ability to quickly regain his self-composure that motivated me to continue my absurd activities.

After I had become thoroughly familiar with the lower-level watch station, I was moved to and trained on the main-engine throttle board as throttleman. That position was just one step below that of top watch, and with it came a great deal of added responsibility. The throttle board was the master monitor of the engineroom. Gauges on the board provided immediate access to information relative to all critical machinery throughout the space. There were gauges that measured oil, water, and vacuum pressures, main and auxiliary steam pressures, pressures at different points in the main-engine turbines, and a wide variety of temperatures throughout the plant. And there was the all-important annunciator, the unit that received orders of speed and shaft/propeller rotational direction from the bridge, and then transmitted verification back to the bridge as the orders were acknowledged and responded to by the throttleman. A tachometer monitored the port propeller shaft in revolutions per minute.

I enjoyed the responsibilities and the activities of my assignment as throttleman. Not only was I responsible for maintaining the proper speed and direction of the after engineroom main-engine turbines; I had to become knowledgeable and proficient in taking immediate corrective action as the result of any simulated or actual casualty to the plant. Throttleman became my permanent watch station for most of my remaining time aboard the *Colahan*.

Time passed more quickly standing throttleman watches because I could engage in conversation with the top watch who was usually seated on the rag bin right next to the throttle board. Whenever possible, it became a question-and-answer session between the top watch and myself. I wanted to pick the brain of the top watch to gain valuable information that I could use. I also wanted to impress others with my knowledge of the plant and its systems. Actually, I wanted to know more than the top watch! I wanted to challenge him on his knowledge of the machinery for which he was responsible.

M.D. Adams had always encouraged me in my quest for knowledge, whereas most other top watches wouldn't participate in my "game." I took pleasure in memorizing many propulsion plant specifications. For example, I knew how many tubes there were in the main condenser as well their length, diameter, and wall thickness. I knew how many disks there were in the lube oil purifier, I knew how many gallons per minute each pump was capable of pumping and the number of revolutions per minute at which they were designed to operate most efficiently. I knew the high and low limitations within which all engineroom equipment had to remain, and I was aware of significant clearances that had to be maintained as well as what action had to be taken when they were found to be outside those specifications.

Admittedly, at that particular time most of my engineering plant knowledge did me absolutely no good other than to provide me with the self-satisfaction of knowing interesting or unique things, trivia, that most engineroom personnel did not know (and probably did not care to know). As an E-4 I could not put my knowledge to practical use since it was not required or expected of anyone in my pay grade.

Work time and watch-standing time at sea were augmented to some degree with imaginative pranks that we played on one another. Some pranks intentionally tested the competence of watchstanders. Since watchstanders were thoroughly trained on different actions to take under a wide variety of circumstances, I took pleasure in shutting the isolation valves to different gauges — then standing back and watching to see what the response would be when it was observed by my intended victim. Loss of lube oil pressure to the main-engine reduction gears required the immediate stopping of the main-engine turbines; loss of main steam pressure required cross-connecting steam between the two enginerooms. Other actions might require tripping the turbo generator or starting or stopping a variety of machinery. To protect myself from accusations of tampering or of participating in a form of sabotage, I always made sure that other watchstanders, with the exception of the targeted victim, were also well aware of what I was doing. That was by no means a guarantee that nothing could go wrong, but it was a form of insurance that the victim would far more likely be stopped before he took unnecessary, irrevocable, or even damaging "corrective" action.

I recall targeting MM1 Boyd as he stood one of his many top watches. I convinced Marcel to manipulate the weight-loaded pressure-regulating valve that governed oil pressure and flow to the main-engine reduction gears. I was the throttleman. Marcel did his part well, and I pretended to ignore the dramatic fluctuation of the oil pressure gauge on the throttle board. Boyd's eyes nearly popped out when he saw the needle on the gauge flicking back and forth from far too much pressure to insufficient pressure. I never saw a man move as fast as he moved when he made it from the upper-level to the lower-level in two giant leaps. Marcel had not seen Boyd's rapid departure from the upper-level, so I flailed my arms and yelled at the top of my voice to get his attention. Within seconds, but what seemed like minutes, Marcel looked at me with a grin from ear to ear. But he saw that somewhat panicked look on my face and he knew that something had gone wrong. He immediately turned from his jovial self into someone that looked terribly sick. Marcel ran to the throttle board where I quickly described Boyd's action. We just stood there waiting for Boyd to come back up from the lower-level, where he was, no doubt, analyzing or troubleshooting the lube oil pump. We could have saved ourselves a lot of unnecessary work had we the courage to tell Boyd about our prank. As it was, we feared his anger and how he might vent whatever frustration he felt. For the next several hours Boyd had the entire engineroom gang searching for oil leaks and anything else that might have caused the fluctuation and momentary loss of lube oil pressure. Since Marcel and I were the only ones in on the prank, we never told others that we had created the appearance of a lube oil problem, the one that had somehow mysteriously corrected itself. Marcel and I also decided that at no time in the future would Boyd be tested again. He was considered off limits from any and all such activities from that day forward. In fact, we wouldn't even entertain the thought of playing any engineering related tricks on anyone as long as Boyd was around ... period.

Everyone became a target sooner or later. I made it a habit to check all of the gauge line isolation valves as a first step when there were indications of a problem. Most of the time such indications were accurate and there really was a problem that a minor adjustment corrected. Other times I was also a victim. Depending on my mood at the time, I usually laughed it off with those who so cleverly fooled me — rarely did I become angered at those responsible. It all depended on what corrective measures I had taken prior to the realization that I had been the victim of a prank.

The freshwater isolation valve to the after head, the one previously described, provided a means of getting even. It was easy allowing just enough time for the victim to wet down, to get fully lathered, and then shut off the water supply to the showers. Two or three minutes was sufficient time for the soap to dry out before turning the water supply back on. Sometimes I would cycle the water off and on more than one time, always making sure the "on" time provided little more than a drizzle and only for a few seconds. It was anybody's guess as to who would get even last, and how he might accomplish it. Revenge was sweet, even commendable, when it was cleverly exercised by a fertile imagination and was divvied out with substantial ingenuity.

During long periods of time away from home, usually during WestPac deployments, many crewmen had their heads shaved. They didn't do so out of any kind of spite; they just didn't want to be bothered having to comb it. Beards were not allowed on the *Colahan* even though it was obvious that other commands, ships and stations, did allow them. Other ships also authorized seventy-two hour weekend passes while the longest weekend pass allowable on the *Colahan* was limited to forty-eight hours; and that was only allowed when the ship was stateside. The lack of consistency, each ship and each command having its own set of rules, made it that much harder for me to accept much of what I was forced to contend with. Whatever was authorized elsewhere was either allowed to some lesser degree or disallowed entirely on board the *Colahan*. We had an Exec who thought his primary responsibility with regard to the morale of the crew was more theoretical than factual. Apparently he did his job inversely because as a direct result of his policies we had the worst morale imaginable, probably fleetwide.

Shipboard raffles were illegal unless they were organized and overseen by the command. That didn't stop the crew from having unauthorized raffles; it only limited the variety of prizes that we could offer to cash, or things other than special liberty. Material things such as cameras and binoculars were commonly raffled off by crewmen; tickets, or chances as they were most commonly referred, sold out most expeditiously when the prize being offered was cash. Our chances sold for anywhere between a dollar and five dollars each, and were sold in lots of either fifty-two or sixty per raffle item, depending on whether we were using the clock or a deck of cards in determining the winner. When the fifty-second chance was sold, someone was chosen at random to pick a card from a fresh deck, and there was an instant winner. When the sixty-chance method was used, bets were made as to when some significant thing would occur, such as what minute of the hour the next unscheduled drill might be called, or what minute of the hour the revolution counter on the propeller shaft tachometer would roll over to all zeros.

In the instance of the counter zeroing, which was seldom — perhaps two or three times a year — it was customary for the throttleman on duty to buy his watch section a round of drinks at the next liberty port. The throttleman would always try to get a naïve, less-than-alert relief just prior to the event so that the relief would be stuck with carrying out the tradition.

Anchor pools, sixty chances per pool, were usually coordinated by the command and cost between $5 and $20 per chance. The winner was determined by the official time recorded; the exact minute that either the anchor was dropped or the first line was secured ashore. The winner of a $5 pool received $250, while $50 went into the Ship's Recreation Fund. The winner of a $20 pool received $1,000; $200 went to the recreation fund.

Another source of money for the Rec fund came from the selling of liberty and special liberty passes that could be used while in port. This system was another hard pill for me to swallow. According to Navy regulations, liberty was something a person earned. The most useless, lowest-graded, know-nothing, do nothing sailor could buy his way ashore, whereas the hardworking, dedicated, dependable sailor who preferred to save his money would have to remain on board and carry the "liberty hound's" share of the workload along with his own. Fair? Not at all! But I was learning rapidly that the Navy way was not at all the fair way. It was a way, to be determined at any given time, by any given individual of greater authority, as the appropriate and acceptable way at that particular moment. It could be initiated at any time, it could be denied later, and it could be reinstated at the whim of authority. I hated it!

During night watches while underway, weather permitting, the after engineroom top watch usually allowed "unauthorized" topside breaks. That is, he allowed all watch stations, one at a time, to vacate their post and take short breathers topside, out of the heat. Sometimes those breaks were extended up to thirty minutes or more. Those that remained below watched over the unmanned watch station. The refreshing coolness of the night air was always welcomed.

Late in April, we arrived at our first real WestPac liberty port; Yokosuka, Japan. I no longer needed to rely on anyone's advice or guidance since I had been there before and I remembered much of the area. I was anxious to live the more adult fun-filled life that was available and affordable to me in the Orient. I was also anxious to show Kimiko, of Hotel Green Heights, my new crow.

The day of our arrival I had the duty. We were told that we would be required to remain anchored out in the harbor the first few days, so we had to remain steaming in the auxiliary plant mode with the main-engines shut down. I was not happy knowing I couldn't go ashore that first day, but it didn't matter all that much since we were scheduled to remain in port for about three weeks.

It was early evening that first day and I was hanging out in the Electric Shop, the same location as the mess cooks' berthing compartment only on the port side of the ship instead of the starboard side. It was a convenient place to socialize with other snipes yet it was rarely utilized by more than two or three individuals at a time.

I was sitting on the workbench reading a letter when someone stepped through the hatch and quietly said, "Hi Paul."

I was shocked when I looked up and saw Gary, my hometown buddy and one of the four that had joined the Navy together, standing there in his liberty uniform.

"So whatcha doin'?" Gary's typical never-excited, always-relaxed tone of voice questioned me.

I jumped to my feet and grabbed his hand and shared a grip that transmitted the true friendship we had for each other.

Gary just happened to be on the main deck of his ship, also anchored in the same harbor, when he saw my ship entering port. He recognized the ship's hull number, 658, as that of the *Colahan*; the ship I had received orders to upon graduation from boot camp. Gary had taken one liberty boat from his ship to shore — then caught another liberty boat that delivered him to the *Colahan*. His intuition had been correct; I had "the duty" and had not gone ashore. We had a lot of things to talk about, mostly the things we missed at home but also of our Navy experiences. I introduced Gary to Marcel, and the three of us visited for a couple of hours. After we made firm plans that the three of us would meet ashore the following day, Gary departed.

Marcel, Gary, and I did meet the following day as planned. Our first stop was at a bar to toast our good fortune in having run across each other so many thousands of miles away from home. We swapped sea stories, each of us trying to outdo the story just told with something of greater interest. We had a group picture taken by one of the many photographer vendors and paid in advance for our copies, not knowing whether or not we would ever see the finished product. We also entrusted our shoes to one of the numerous "traveling" shoeshine boys, also without guarantee (other than the boy's word) that we would ever see our shoes again. The picture and shoes were returned about an hour later; shoes glistening with an unbelievable gloss, and our souvenir photographs clearly showing the three of us, happy as could be, sitting at a table behind three tall bottles of Nippon beer.

We then walked the strip shopping for some appropriate souvenirs, stopping from time to time for another tall beer. With each new bar came a new group of gorgeous girls, all of them telling us how much we resembled movie stars and would we please buy them some drinks. Sometimes we did, depending on their approach and how beautiful they were.

I was amazed at the vast number of beautiful women, and how they all managed to live and work so close by Navy bases, until I realized they were there for the money and would do just about anything to get it. There were also those who were looking for a ticket to the United States. There was a distinct lack of ugly girls; too much eye-catching competition.

Marcel, "Buck" and Me

It didn't take long before the alcohol took charge and the joint decision was made to stop shopping and to quench our thirst with liquid refreshment instead. So we settled in at one of the smaller bars and continued guzzling the local brew. Shortly Marcel excused himself from our table, complaining of stomach problems, and he headed for the *benjo*. After about fifteen minutes Gary and I became concerned at Marcel's failure to return, so we went to the *benjo* looking for him. There he was, sitting on the toilet, trousers pulled down below his knees, his head hanging almost to his lap as he groaned unintelligibly. Marcel was sick!

Gary and I were feeling great. We were just getting wound up, and we wanted Marcel to join us. We tried unsuccessfully to get Marcel back to his feet as he let it be known that he was sick and he sure as hell wasn't at all in the mood to participate in our follies. What else was there for us to do except vent our disappointment by ramming our fists through the plasterboard inner walls of the head? We decided that wasn't good enough, not nearly sufficient damage, so we proceeded to rip chunks of the plasterboard off of the wall, covering Marcel with some pieces as we tossed other chunks about haphazardly. Plaster dust was everywhere; in our eyebrows, in our hair, and all over our uniforms.

"Oh, God, Paul, not again," came Marcel's weak voice through the plaster dust that was so evenly suspended in the air around us. "Oh, Jesus, oh God no," he muttered as Gary and I continued our outlandish act of destruction.

Gary and Me In Yokosuka, Japan

"What the hell, Gary, guess we better leave Marcel and get the fuck out of here."

160

Upon hearing my comment Marcel immediately pulled himself together. He was not sick enough to take the blame for the destruction in which Gary and I had so enthusiastically participated.

The whites we were wearing probably saved our butts; we brushed the dust out of our hair, and the remaining evidence was barely visible on our white uniforms. Lucky for us we were not wearing blues! We strolled out of the place as if nothing was wrong, but as soon as we were back in the street our feet picked up a rapid pace and we disappeared into the crowd.

Marcel had enough. He called it quits and headed back to the ship. Gary and I soon found another small but comfortable bar where we decided to "drop anchor" for the rest of the evening. In between gulps of beer all we could do was laugh at our earlier escapades, and we could only hope that Marcel was all right and that he had found his way back to the ship without any unexpected problems.

Gary kept eyeing the many full whiskey bottles that were sitting on display shelves behind the bar. It didn't take long — the very instant the bartender turned his back for a moment too long, Gary grabbed one of the bottles and tucked it conveniently under his jumper. It was time to move on once again. About a block down the narrow street Gary removed the cap and took a healthy gulp from the bottle. He immediately spit out what he was able to keep from swallowing and he began swearing; "Damn Gooks, cheatin' bastards. It's nothing but friggin water."

Gary swung the bottle around, intentionally sloshing its contents over anything and everything within range. He made sure the Japanese-driven minicabs, that were slowly making their way through the crowd of street pedestrians, received their fair share of the odorless and colorless liquid.

We were out of control that night. Fortunately we didn't end up in jail. When our time ashore approached its end, we found ourselves at the Fleet Landing where we said our farewells, and boarded liberty boats going in different directions. Gary headed home, to CONUS, the Continental United States, the following morning; his six-month deployment had ended, whereas mine had just begun.

I was saddened the following morning as I watched Gary's ship heading out of the harbor toward the open sea. We had never before shared in a comparable adventure. I really missed the companionship that came with the friendship we had acquired so long before. I had, before that moment, taken his friendship far too much for granted. I waved my final farewell, my good-luck gesture, in his direction knowing full well he would not be able to see it.

Within a couple of days the *Colahan* moved from anchorage to one of the many docks at the Yokosuka Naval Shipyard where we would remain for two weeks. Engineers looked forward to securing from auxiliary steaming and shifting to shore power; going on "cold iron." Otherwise, it was business as usual.

Friday was always "Field Day," and the entire working day was devoted to cleaning everything that could be seen, but did not move. We made a very strong soap solution with a mixture of boiler compound, sulfamic acid, and powdered soap, in buckets of hot water — a very strong chemical solution that removed or dissolved just about everything other than paint. It provided the perfect cleaning solvent for washing everything in the engineroom, and its use eliminated the need to scrub hard. Our unprotected hands suffered as a result of using the strong solution; usually the skin dried and peeled for a day or two following prolonged contact with the mixture, but whatever damage it caused was acceptable considering the remarkable cleaning job it did for us. Electricians were the only one's with access to rubber gloves — and their gloves were much too large, too awkward for our use.

When either of the steaming modes were up and running we would rinse the entire engineroom with boiling hot water from the pressurized DA tank. We used a hose attached to the sight-glass blow-down valve to rinse everything, a really effective way of rinsing everything directly into the bilge — but the wasting of feedwater was heavily frowned upon by the Engineer Officer. We were careful to make sure that he never knew of our cleverness, our inventive capabilities. When there were feedwater shortages, it was easy to attribute the problem to system leaks, never to improvised methods of cleaning.

The aluminum deck plates also received greater attention on field day. They looked like new following the thorough wire brushing they received by those of us in pay grades E-4 and below. That took about an hour and a half of strenuous scrubbing while on our hands and knees — but the end result was something we admired and took pride in. All of the brightwork also received an abundance of attention on field day. By the end of each Friday the after engineroom sparkled. Boyd would not have it any other way. We then took extra precautions to make sure it remained inspection perfect until Saturday morning, when it was routinely inspected by the skipper or his representative, an officer or group of officers under his command. There was never any doubt as to whether or not our space would pass inspection. Saturday, liberty commenced immediately following inspection for all hands in the liberty section, for all except those who were assigned to spaces that failed.

It seemed that most "white-hats," which included all grades below chief, had a habit of adorning their working uniforms (dungarees) with one kind of trinket or another. Almost everyone had some sort of chain, or other attachable device, hanging from a belt loop. Usually there were keys, wrenches, or some other gadgets that may just as likely have been useless as they might have been useful. Snipes preferred miniature crescent wrenches or some other miniature tools hanging alongside their keys.

"Short-timer's chains" were highly disapproved of by all of the lifers. Such chains were nothing more than a single strand of one type of chain or another, usually found dangling loosely from a belt loop. The number of balls or links represented the number of days the "adornee" had remaining before being discharged from active duty. Each day another link would be publicly, almost ceremoniously, snipped from the bottom of the chain. The shorter the chain, the more boisterous and obnoxious the short-timer(s) would invariably become. It was a way of flaunting a somewhat questionable tradition and was considered reserved for those with one month or less remaining. The premature wearing of a short-timer's chain drew harsh criticism by those who really were nearing the end of their enlistment. I longed for the time I could wear my own.

Periodically, in port as well as at sea, the doc and his strikers would conduct "short-arm" inspections of all enlisted men below the grade of E-7. Chiefs and officers were above such degradation. Inspections were easily accomplished on payday because of the guaranteed turnout. Right after being paid, prior to leaving the mess deck, we were each required to drop our drawers, skivvies and all, and display our genitals for inspection. One by one we were closely and carefully inspected for crabs and for any other indications that one venereal disease or another might have infected us. Each of us was then required to "milk it down" as the final phase of the inspection. Invariably the doc found one or two individuals with problems that had to be corrected. Corrective action meant medication along with an automatic thirty-day shipboard restriction.

Restriction was tough to take. I had been in a variety of altercations, and the Old Man, Captain Keedy, usually gave me two weeks to a month of on-board restriction. Sometimes I thought the skipper was too lenient with me, but I'm sure he took into consideration my work history along with whatever unfavorable activity it was that had brought me before him. I nearly always walked away from Captain's Mast feeling lucky, but never with the feeling that I had put something over on anyone, or had skillfully pulled off something illegal.

I recall one Captain's Mast in particular. As usual, it came about as the result of my big mouth. I had been fooling around on one of the engine-room sound-powered phone systems and had inadvertently reached one of the snipe-type officers. I said a few cute things and then hung up on him, never expecting him to follow up on the conversation. Within a minute or two the officer was standing right in front of me with a glare I had become a little used to, and he proceeded to give me what I perceived to be an unwarranted tongue-lashing. I was undeserving of the severity with which he executed his verbal reprimand, considering the insignificance of my action. I stood there, taking it like a man, but when he finally wrapped up his well-planned oration and he folded his arms defiantly in front of himself, I looked him straight in the eyes and said, "Sir, you could write me up for what I did, right?"

"That's right, Adkisson," he practically snarled at me.

"But you can't write me up for thinking, can you?" I said through my best challenging smirk.

"That is also correct," he said with absolute conviction.

"Well, Sir, I *think* you are full of shit!"

I had obviously gone beyond the limits. Quite expectedly I was placed on report, and within days I found myself standing in front of the Old Man trying to explain. Another officer later told me that the skipper had a tough time holding back his laughter as I stood before him, rightfully accused of insubordination. The skipper had told the officer, "That kid has guts."

Procedures at Mast were always the same. There could be any number of accused at any given Mast, and they, along with witnesses, were the first to line up in their inspection uniforms. Additional witnesses were sometimes called upon when needed. Division Officers were present, the Chief Master at Arms was there, and usually the Executive Officer was there. There was always a Yeoman on hand to take notes of the entire proceedings.

Once everyone was in place, the Captain was summoned. He then took on the task of judge and jury as he examined the evidence of each case, individually. His first question directed at each of the accused was always the same: "State your name, rate, and service number."

Captain Keedy asked me that first question, but before I could open my mouth in response he continued, "Never mind, Adkisson. I know your name, rate, and service number better than you."

That got my attention. I don't remember what punishment he meted out to me that time, but whatever it was, I'm sure I deserved it.

There were ways to get around restriction, illegal ways that would compound penalties if one managed to get caught. Spare liberty cards were not uncommon. They could be "purchased" at the Ship's Office if the right person was asked. A liberty card could also be borrowed or "rented" from some of the men who didn't mind the risk. The OOD seldom, if ever, actually made a close comparison between the name on a liberty card and the name on the accompanying ID card. As long as one of each was presented simultaneously, and one's uniform was presentable, permission to leave the ship was granted.

When ships were nested, more than one tied up alongside each other, restricted sailors were more likely to jump across from one ship to another, being particularly careful not to be seen by the OOD on either ship. It was easy having a friend occupy the attention of the OOD long enough to make the jump. Anyone on illegal liberty had to watch the clock closely to make sure he was back aboard ship when restricted men were called to muster. Sometimes the mustering petty officer could also be bought; in which case it was not necessary to be so cognizant of the time. There were special precautions and concerns that had to be considered when it came time to return to the ship. Who would have the quarterdeck watch, who would be the OOD, and would they be aware of the restricted status of anyone returning from an unauthorized period of liberty? Would they be able to jump across one or more of the nested ships — unseen? The biggest fear was, had there been any working parties called? If so, all restricted personnel were required to participate, and the failure to show up was evidence enough that they had jumped ship.

On one occasion, when I was ashore after having jumped ship, I captured a small lizard, probably no more than an inch in length. Strange mischievous thoughts have always been known to pass through a young sailor's mind, but at the moment of that lizards' capture I had no specific intentions. I do recall several thoughts coming to mind as I was on my way back to the ship, each well intended on "grossing out" some unsuspecting shipmate(s), but the action I ended up taking was totally spontaneous. Once I was safely back on board and I knew that my period of absence had gone unnoticed, I headed for the berthing compartment — lizard still in hand. Unfortunately for one sleeping shipmate, who had the habit of sleeping flat on his back, I dropped the happy-to-be-released lizard directly into his gaping mouth. Instant response! He never saw me, far too concerned about whatever it was in his mouth or throat that was having difficulty figuring out which way it wanted to go. I don't believe I have ever been witness to a man scrambling out of his bunk with such haste. However, when he began choking, I began to realize just how stupid I had been. Thoughts that my prank might turn into some kind of unintended death scene raced through my mind as I hid near my bunk on the far side of the compartment. Once again, luck was on my side. After several seconds of severe choking the man coughed up the lizard; it, in all probability, was in better condition than the man.

Some months later, for whatever reason sailors do stupid things, I did something of a repeat performance with almost identical results. I was eating peanuts while en route to my locker, and without thinking I dropped a peanut into the open mouth of the very same sleeping sailor. I had instant flashbacks of the lizard incident when I saw the guy leap from his bunk and gag repeatedly before managing to hack up the peanut. I found myself wondering what possessed me to play such games; pranks that went beyond common sense and were dangerous in every sense of the word. I was sorry — but knew better than to identify myself as the culprit in any attempt at expressing remorse.

Frequently Tom Mundy and I enjoyed liberty together, particularly in Yokosuka. We enjoyed barhopping from place to place, and neither of us would ever turn our backs on, or run from, a fight. Our likes and dislikes were very similar, as were our ages and pay grades. Tom was something of an exhibitionist. He would do just about anything to gain the attention of those around him.

Tom and I were together on liberty in Yokosuka, not very far from the White Hat Club, wandering around with our Argus cameras at the ready, when we came across a small indoor/outdoor market. There were huge

166

vegetables of every variety, all much larger than anything grown in the United States. There were some vegetables and other foodstuffs that neither of us could identify. Tom decided to show off his ability to juggle, and he selected eggs as his primary tools with which he would perform. He would miss an egg now and again, only to pick up a replacement from the large, filled-to-capacity box of eggs there on display, and continue with his act. The proprietor became more and more upset at Tom's antics and at the slippery mess he was inadvertently creating. Finally, when the proprietor had contended with enough, he threw his arms upward as if in defeat and walked away. He was only gone an instant when he returned with a local policeman. Tom and I laughed at the scene, pretending it was no problem at all, and paid the few cents we were told the damages would cost us. We went one step farther and bought several of the gigantic carrots that were also there on display. That brought about a big, happy smile to the face of the policeman and proprietor alike. They made it known that we were welcome to return at anytime.

After a full evening of drinking and teasing the local bargirls, Tom and I headed back to the ship. On our way we came across a foreign ship tied up alongside one of the docks. Tom suggested we board it, just to "check her out." It sounded like a good idea to me, and there didn't appear to be anyone around to stop us. We were most interested in the engineering spaces and we toyed with the idea of lighting off the plant, and then getting the vessel underway. We just might have carried out that plan had we been able to illuminate the engineering spaces — fortunately, we couldn't locate the light switches. So, as an alternative, we climbed the ladder up to the top of the smokestack, where, after tossing several carrots inside, we listened intently for the sound as they hit bottom. We were "taking soundings" to determine the depth. *And we were caught!* I do not know to this day what country the ship was from, nor was I able to determine the nationality of the rifle-carrying guard that stopped us. That guy was dead serious; he actually jacked a round into the chamber of his weapon and pointed it at us. We just laughed at him like a couple of fools; we even dared him to "go ahead and shoot." Thank God he took us for what we were, a couple of drunken sailors just being our mischievous selves. He didn't bother to stop us as we walked past him, continuing on our merry way, eventually finding our way home to the *Colahan* without further incident ... *that* night!

The move from anchorage to the shipyard docks went smoothly. As soon as the ship was on shore power we shut down the auxiliary plant. Almost immediately the engineroom temperature lowered to a comfortable level. We could forget about monitoring plant parameters, and we were no longer restricted as to which machinery we could or could not work on.

While we were in Yokosuka Naval Shipyard, most shipboard time was spent performing maintenance and repairs, a routine that was common just about everywhere we went. Keeping up with repairs to steam leaks occupied most of our time, whereas maintenance to major machinery was performed by "yardbirds," a term considered derogatory by the "repair facility workers" but was widely accepted and frequently used by sailors when discussing or identifying them. Japanese yardbirds were fascinating. They were capable of climbing up and over, around and beneath, through and in between machinery and structures that no American would ever so much as consider attempting. The Japanese had a knack for it. Their short, thin bodies easily fit where our larger bodies could not. But there were those crewmen who dared to try.

FN Charlie Mares, or "Moose," as he had become known because of his size and strength, was successful at climbing down under the lower-level deck plate brackets. He was not very successful in his attempt to get out! In order to free him from his temporary but extremely uncomfortable imprisonment, we ended up having to cut the brackets surrounding him with the aid of a cutting torch. Moose just shrugged the matter off and maintained his usual self-composure. His comment upon being released was simple and to the point — it put the whole matter to rest.

"Guess I musta got all swelled up or somethin'."

The Japanese were under contract to perform specific maintenance and repairs; they were not supposed to go beyond the scope of the contracted work. But the Japanese had one particular weakness of which we never hesitated in taking advantage. Sugar! A cup of coffee meant absolutely nothing to them without sugar. I mean *sugar*, lots and lots of sugar, never less than a dozen or so spoonfuls to a cup of coffee. They liked syrup, not coffee. By providing them with all the sugar they wanted, we were able to "buy" additional maintenance services. They would do much of our work for us, and they would do it efficiently. That didn't mean we just stood around and watched; to the contrary, we were able to get caught up in some areas and a little bit ahead in others. The Japanese workers were a happy lot

168

and they seemed to enjoy the work they were doing. They were cheerful, almost ecstatic, whenever they had a cup of coffee syrup in hand.

While in Yokosuka I eventually did take the walk through Souvenir Street and up the alley to Hotel Green Heights. Kimiko was happy to see me and praised me for having been promoted two grades since I had last seen her. She knew precisely what to say in order to please me; however, when she saw the wedding band I was wearing she actually broke down and cried. In the past we had been very close during brief periods of time, but never had I led her to believe there was a future for us. Her very real tears confirmed that she had thought otherwise. That time I didn't stay long, even though I had paid Mama-san for a standard "short-time." I knew that I would return some other time in hopes of recouping the special relationship Kimiko and I had previously cultivated and enjoyed so openly and freely.

"Work hard; play hard," was the rule most of us lived by. If we did the work, we could go ashore. Once in awhile it was necessary to work beyond liberty call, which meant that when the time came and we finally were ashore we had to make up for lost time. Those of us that went ashore latest were almost sure to return to the ship the most inebriated, a phenomenon only a sailor would understand.

Sometimes, in order to facilitate a more rapid means of becoming inebriated, we, usually Tom and I, would smuggle small sample bottles of Lucy ashore, where we would proceed to mix it with beer. The mixture provided for the creation of a powerful boilermaker that was sure to deliver a rapid blow to the brain. It was not only a means of expediting inebriation; it was the cheapest means. We never considered the dangers associated with the consumption of ethyl alcohol.

I became hooked on nightlife in Yokosuka. It was addictive, inebriating with or without benefit of alcohol. I loved the night-lights and I enjoyed constantly being accosted by street vendors selling their wares. It was great, always being surrounded by beautiful ladies of the night. I particularly enjoyed the coziness provided by the small yet accommodating nightclubs and bars, and I was always amazed at the number of remarkably talented musicians who played superb renditions of music previously made popular by Glenn Miller, Perez Prado, Elvis Presley, and others. It was a form of paradise, and it gripped me unlike anything or anyplace I had ever seen, heard of, read about, or ever considered the existence of remotely possible.

When the time came, the middle of May, I did not want to leave Yokosuka. Apparently, a couple of men liked it more than I, since they failed to return to the ship prior to our departure. Missing movement was a serious offense, one that I avoided like a plague. I knew that I would return to Yokosuka from time to time, so there was no sense in suffering severe penalties for intentionally violating a rule that did not need to be violated. I looked upon fighting with a different perspective. I believed that fighting was different, that it required violating the rule. I thought that backing down, showing any form of fear, or being submissive would cause me to once again become labeled, that I would be taken advantage of at every opportunity as I had been as a "boot camper." I later changed my assessment as to the necessity of fighting, although the desire to unleash that ornery part of my inner being was periodically rekindled with the right provocation.

We spent several days at sea before once again dropping anchor, this time off the coast of Nagoya, Japan. It was a short three-day visit, just long enough for all hands to see and experience another Japanese port.

Nagoya was nothing like Yokosuka. It was one of the largest cities in the nation, yet, to my surprise, the lifestyle was far more subdued. Sure, there were girls and there were bars, but it lacked the night-lights and excitement Yokosuka offered. Nagoya was more of a metropolis, not exactly a sailor's paradise, but truly a beautiful place. The people of Nagoya were probably smart in not encouraging visits by the U.S. Navy. They had a lovely city and apparently it was their intention to keep it that way. Through my eyes, I saw a large city surrounded by a significant suburban population — a place one might visit to relax, well away from people and places that cater to the military.

Two weeks later we returned to Yokosuka, my heartfelt adopted home. Why not? I had spent more time there and I knew my way around better there than in any other port outside CONUS. Furthermore, Kimiko was there!

By this time I had established my "bank" and the interest I was collecting supplemented my pay such that I could buy things that would otherwise not have been affordable. I developed a system whereby I could get higher interest than other banks were getting. It was somewhat sneaky and conniving but otherwise quite successful. After all, if other crewmen couldn't handle their funds and they were willing to pay the exorbitant rate for the use of my funds, why shouldn't I take advantage of the situation? I made it a practice to hang around the ship in my liberty uniform for up to an hour after liberty call. The "clients," unable to go ashore for lack of funds, were bound to see me within that hour. When they did see me, usually one at a time, I always used a variation of a rather simple system.

"Hey, Ad, you got any money?"

"Yeah, but I've only got ten bucks to my name and I'm going ashore," was my typical response.

Then came the bickering and bartering. I wanted to go ashore, and so did they. Were they willing to pay enough to get my last ten dollars, thereby keeping me on board and preventing me from enjoying liberty of my own? Of course they were. I usually doubled my money. Sometimes, particularly while in Hong Kong, I could triple it! The system was simple. Once the negotiated figure, the loan, was agreed upon and the funds passed hands, I would immediately go to my locker and get another ten or twenty dollars. I may have had hundreds of dollars stashed away, but my convincing story that I only had five or ten bucks to my name always succeeded in getting the highest return. I used a similar system while I was ashore on liberty, where I was seldom without a few extra tens carefully stashed in different pockets. When I was seen ashore by someone who had exhausted his funds and wanted to borrow money, I'd tell him that I was down to my last ten dollars and I had intentions on using it. After a period of similar bartering, and an agreed upon high "use" fee was negotiated, I'd make the appropriate entry in my little black book, and everyone was happy. Especially me! Did I get rich? Not exactly, but I was able to buy some of the nicer souvenirs — and I was able to provide for my family above the poverty level as a result.

We departed Yokosuka the middle of June and steamed directly toward Sasebo, Japan, where we arrived just two days later. I was excited at the thought of returning to the Jungle Club, and gaining the sexual favors of Takiko, favors that I had missed out on a year earlier. I couldn't shake the picture of her feminine perfection from my mind, even though we had never shared the ultimate of intimacy, or much of a real friendship for that matter. Takiko was not at all like Kimiko, but petite and adorable she most certainly was.

171

Living and working in hot humid spaces had another down side. At one time or another most snipes suffered from a condition known as "the creeping crud," a rash that was further aggravated by heat. Marcel developed a serious case that covered most of his upper body, and he was miserable. The discomfort of having a rash was bad enough, but whatever it was that intensified the condition was immune to medications such as calamine lotion. As the condition worsened, the accompanying itch worsened. Usually, after-shave lotion or other substances that contained an abundance of alcohol, when applied directly to the rash, would burn like the devil but helped to dry it out and clear it up. Marcel's rash was as bad as I had ever seen, and it was getting the best of him. The usual alcohol treatment didn't help. Instead, it seemed to make it worse. Baby powder was another approach that in many cases eased the terrible itching that accompanied the rash, but it did little to reduce Marcel's discomfort. I thought he was very near having some kind of mental breakdown as the "crud" controlled his every move. If he accidentally brushed against something or if someone accidentally touched him, the itching would become so severe that Marcel would begin scratching himself in a frenzy — to the point of drawing blood. There was no cure, other than time, and I was beginning to think Marcel was going to end up in the hospital when his condition finally began to clear up. None of us ever complained again about our rashes, knowing what misery Marcel had managed to contend with.

No amount of itching or pain could keep a sailor from liberty once he had a mind to go ashore. Marcel was such a sailor, and we prepared ourselves for liberty the usual way.

Well-showered and well-shaved, Marcel and I were two of the first to approach the quarterdeck at liberty call.

"Permission granted," the most important words a sailor wanted to hear, were spoken by the OOD, and Marcel and I were on our way. We grabbed the first minicab that came along and directed the driver to take us to the Jungle Club, "Takusan Haiyaku."

As already described, Japanese taxi drivers were undoubtedly a little bit crazy. They must have been kamikaze leftovers, because they exhibited blatant suicidal tendencies; they feared absolutely nothing. With one hand on the horn and the other on the steering wheel, accelerator flattened to the floorboard, they maneuvered through the dense traffic with total disregard to life, limb, or property. Tell them to drive faster and they would! They did exactly as they were told, and they were tipped generously for their obedience and their skills. Rarely were they ever involved in an accident of serious consequence.

"*Hai!*" our driver exclaimed as we came to an abrupt halt at the curb. Marcel and I were bewildered; there was no Jungle Club. In its place was a newly remodeled movie theater. At first we thought we were at the wrong location, so we reminded the driver of our destination. The driver, not at all proficient in English, made it known to us by shaking his head while waving his hand in front of his face, palm toward us, fingers pointing upward, that there was no more Jungle Club! My heart sank; much to my disappointment, I would not see Takiko that day. I would *never* see Takiko again.

Marcel and I, intent on making the best of the situation, decided to go to the Paramount, a nightclub more often frequented by officers than by enlisted men. Shortly after we entered the club, one of the hostesses came running up and threw her arms around me. Marcel stood there, eyes popping out and jaw gapping open. He thought it was Takiko when, in fact, it was Pat from Club Florida in Yokosuka. She had temporarily moved to Sasebo, following the flow of the American dollar — one smart girl. Marcel and I didn't stay there long; too expensive. Besides, it wasn't much fun hanging out where the officers were, most of whom were still willing to exercise their authority but more in terms of control. Control over the women! So rather than cause some ruckus over female "ownership," we elected to take our business elsewhere. Anyway, I had already been saturated with pleasure by Pat, and for free. I was perfectly willing to let Pat make a living off of some officer's salary and keep mine to waste in some other way. Something at which I was quite accomplished.

Our next stop was Hong Kong where we remained for a few days of R and R. It had been a year since I had adorned my arm with what, over the years, has become the now unsightly tattoo of a sea dragon.

Tom, "Jim Dandy," a new member of the electrical gang, and I, the three of us dubbed and known as "the three musketeers," conspired to create a disturbance while on liberty in Hong Kong. Jim was several years older than Tom or I, and he was larger and significantly stronger. Jim could have taken on a full-grown bull with his bare hands and would have come out the winner. He was the right guy to have on our side.

Prior to leaving the ship, we knew that our afternoon or evening of fun would include fighting. Not among ourselves, but likely with anyone or any groups of individuals that did not meet with our approval. In our minds we needed very little justification, since our disapproval rating of others included the vast majority.

June 30, 1956, we had been ashore barhopping for an hour or so, it was early in the afternoon, when the three of us noticed a lot of funny-looking money drifting down the sidewalk. The orange-colored currency was smaller than the Hong Kong dollars that we had been spending, and all of the strange banknotes were of unbelievably large denominations. Each note was imprinted with Chinese characters. Not knowing whether we had become instant lottery winners or had come across a type of play-money, we scooped up what we could catch and stuffed it into our pockets. Shortly thereafter we decided to settle down at the White Horse Bar. There were an abundance of hostesses, always available to relieve clientele of whatever funds they could con them out of, usually by having them buy costly "ladies' drinks," plain tea served in whiskey jiggers, similar to ladies' drinks that were served throughout the Orient. Buying a ladies' drink also bought a lady's attention for as long as the drink lasted. If a hostess enjoyed the company of her client, she would sip her drink for an indefinite period of time. If she was uncomfortable or saw a potentially better client, perhaps one from whom she had previously made money, she would gulp her drink and be on her way. In any event, when their glass was empty, if a refill was not immediately ordered, they would quickly disappear.

We ordered a round of drinks and slapped a couple of the banknote-type bills that we had found on the sidewalk on the table in payment. The girl's eyes bulged and we were immediately, with sincerity, plagued with a barrage of, "Where'd you get this?" along with other variations of the same question. They backed away from our table and excitedly jabbered in their native language. One finally "accused" us of being "alive," to which we quite readily agreed. After some discussion we learned that the paper currency we had found was "money" that was only intended to be used by the dearly departed. The money was strictly for the purpose of buying their way out of hell in the event their spirits went that way. It was a common practice to bury an abundance of such money with the deceased. Why it was drifting down the street and sidewalk was anybody's guess.

After consuming several alcoholic beverages, I made my thoughts known to Tom and Jim.

"I thought we were going to get in some kind of fight."

Tom's reply was to the point. "Oh what the hell, let's get on with it."

Tom got up from the table and entered the double Dutch-style swinging doors leading to the men's head. Jim and I thought he was going to relieve himself prior to taking whatever action he had in mind. After a prolonged period of time, I went to the head to find out what was delaying Tom. There he was, standing in the middle of the spacious rest room, talking to another sailor. I stepped up and asked the "stranger" what ship he was off of, and he replied, "The *Twining*," one of the three sister ships in our squadron.

I said, "I don't like guys off of the *Twining*!"

"I don't either." His rapid reply didn't stop me. I let loose with an un-provoked and totally uncalled-for series of punches, sending him to the floor; blood was flowing freely from his nose and mouth. It was over too quickly; there was little satisfaction in a battle so easily won.

Jim had heard the scuffle and he came running into the head. As he stood there, assessing the obvious, another sailor started to enter the double doors. Jim had not been adequately apprised of what had happened and he didn't want any outsiders around, so he told the intruder to stay out.

"I'm coming in." We all heard the unfamiliar voice.

Jim said, "No you're not."

Yet there was that persistent and demanding voice that insisted; "Oh, yes, I am."

So Jim just grinned, raised his right hand, and motioned with his index finger as he said, "Have it your way; come on in."

No sooner did the stranger pass through the Dutch doors than Jim belted him with a powerful jolt to the chin, knocking him backward with a force that sent him back through the swinging doors and onto an occupied booth. Drinks scattered in all directions and the occupants of the booth were im-mediately provoked. Then, as they say, all hell broke loose. It was fun, but it didn't last long. The three of us settled the situation quickly. There were several bloodied sailors evenly "disbursed", none of whom showed any interest in continuing to fight. Amazing as it may seem, there was no blood on Jim, Tom, or me. We simply strolled back to our table and ordered an-other round.

Within a couple of minutes several Duty Shore Patrol sailors were on the scene. One of the hostesses walked directly to our table with the Shore

Patrol. She spoke with anger as she pointed an accusing finger that encircled the three of us.

"They did it!"

"Well, thanks, bitch." Jim's inappropriate comment was well addressed. We were all apprehended and we were taken directly to Shore Patrol Headquarters, near the Fleet Landing, for questioning.

We were somewhat lucky that afternoon because one of our own officers, Ensign Lull, was on duty with the Shore Patrol.

Mr. Lull always took his job seriously. He was one of the finest ensigns I ever came across. He stood up for his men, a rare trait seldom practiced by the younger inexperienced officers. Unfortunately, on this occasion, Mr. Lull was not really knowledgeable of what had happened. He thought we had been accused of fighting among ourselves instead of with others, and he didn't wait to hear the whole story before coming to our defense. He assured the senior Shore Patrol officer that we had been falsely accused, that we were very good friends, and that no way would we ever strike a blow at each other. And after all, look at us. Did we appear as though we had been fighting? Not at all. The senior officer believed Mr. Lull, however, he felt that Tom was drunk and that his liberty should be canceled for the day. Tom was sent back to the ship whereas Jim and I were released with the strict admonition that we were not to go back to the White Horse Bar. We promised faithfully that we had no intention on going where the possibility of trouble existed.

Once released from Shore Patrol custody, Jim and I stopped at the first bar we came to, had a beer, and decided it would be appropriate for us to at least make a showing at the White Horse Bar. A "let them know we got off the hook, rub it in their nose" kind of infantile posturing. So we did. We walked in, proud as could be, and made certain that our presence was well known. We ordered two cold beers, and after gulping them down we "graciously" departed. The glares we got while we were there were returned with the friendliest smiles we could render. The remainder of the evening we enjoyed nothing beyond good clean fun. It might have been different had Tom been with us.

There were other things to do besides cause or participate in some form of disorder. There were places to go, sights to see, and of course Hong Kong was a shoppers' paradise. There were bargains to be found everywhere, but for the convenience of military service members, nearly every need could be fulfilled at the China Fleet Activities, not far from Fenwich Pier, Fleet Landing. The China Fleet Club, as it was also known, was a BX/PX type facility, and proof of military service (ID card) was required before a purchase could be made. The huge facility was several stories high; each level provided a wide variety of marvels, everything imaginable other than pornographic or illegal contraband (which could always be purchased on the black market). Pots and pans, cooking utensils, clothing, wood carvings, diamonds and jewelry, jade and ivory carvings, paintings, furniture, and on and on. The prices were fixed; they were not negotiable. But they were in line with the best prices in town. Most sailors, officers and enlisted men alike, took advantage of the China Fleet Club. Its convenient location not only made purchasing easy, it made it easy to carry out goods to the Fleet Landing from which waiting water taxis would transport us directly to our ship.

The Peak Tower provided a fantastic panoramic view of Hong Kong and Kowloon Peninsula. Tiger Balm Gardens was of particular interest to photographers as well as sightseers; tourists from all over the world frequented both. I was very fascinated by the gardens. There were acres of brightly colored cement statues, an extensive array of grotesque human and animal forms, the legends and folklore behind them not always explained with understandable detail. And there were beautiful pagodas, temples of traditional Chinese architecture. One could easily spend an entire day marveling at the storybook appearance of their surroundings while at Tiger Balm Gardens.

Aberdeen, the fishing village, was another famous tourist attraction. It became even more famous following the release of the movie *The World of Suzie Wong*. Aberdeen Harbor was filled with too many fishing boats to count. Some boat occupants, although difficult to believe, lived out their entire lives without ever setting foot on land. They lived and died in their own small world, families tightly crammed on board vessels that were barely seaworthy. The boat people accepted disease as one of the necessary aspects of life; consequently lives oftentimes cut short of expectancy. I have often wondered how they felt as they were being observed and photographed like animals by rich and privileged tourists. From all outward appearances they did not seem to mind the gawking to which they were always being subjected.

177

There was also the famous floating restaurant that was, the vast majority of the time, anchored farther out in Aberdeen Harbor. At night it was lit up brighter than a Las Vegas casino, and it also attracted tourists from every part of the world. Any of the boat people would gladly provide transportation to and from the restaurant for a very small sum. Patrons of the restaurant could make a selection from the menu or they could pick their own fish meal from a variety, still alive and swimming in large glass aquariums on board. We were cautioned not to eat there, since most of the fish were taken from the contaminated waters of the harbor. Yes, on one occasion I ate there, and I thoroughly enjoyed my fish meal. Somewhat foolishly, I believed that the restaurant could not have remained in business if many of those who ate there got sick or died, and that if it was all right for other tourists than it was damn well all right for me. A variation of that concept would eventually catch up with me.

Hong Kong police officers were easily recognized by their distinct uniform. Those that could speak English wore red hatbands as a convenience to the predominantly English-speaking tourists. As Hong Kong was a British Crown Colony, the English spoken there carried a strong and distinct British accent and was sometimes difficult for us to understand without asking for further clarification. All in all, most sailors favored Hong Kong. It was a beautiful combination of maximum liberty time ashore coupled with all the wonderful and interesting things that Hong Kong had to offer.

Before returning to the States, we would make two final port calls, Kaohsiung, Taiwan (Formosa), and Yokosuka, Japan. We first patrolled the Taiwan Straits for three weeks, investigating merchant ships and challenging aircraft. There was a lot of time spent at General Quarters, but the time did pass and on July 12, 1956 we entered Kaohsiung Harbor through the narrow, well-protected, channel entrance.

It was my first visit to Taiwan. The ship tied up alongside the pier so we were not inconvenienced by having to wait in lines for liberty boats. We simply walked across the brow and headed toward town.

The Seamen's Club was just a short distance from the pier. Many sailors couldn't wait for that first cold beer, so they stopped there. Some of them never got any farther!

Rickshaws were the primary means of transportation, and at a cost of about twenty-five cents in won, the local currency, we could ride the relatively short distance to town. The strip, a continuation of the dirty, and for the most part unpaved, road leading directly from the pier, was a sailor town of another kind. There were only a dozen or so authorized bars; all were easily identified by the familiar blue class-A signs hanging in their windows or on their doors. The bars were squeezed against each other much the same as they were in Japan, and they lined both sides of the road. As I had become accustomed to seeing, there was an abundance of attractive women standing in front of every bar, all beckoning our attention as we walked past. Only the stronger-willed individuals passed the torment of having to turn down all the beautiful girls along the way. At the end of the strip was the Dragon Club; U.S. military-owned and operated.

As for me, I didn't make it that far. I had been easily convinced by a very young and sensuous Chinese girl named Katie that I should accept her offer of free drinks at the OK Bar — about halfway between the pier and the Dragon Club. That brief stop, my meeting Katie, would become significant much later during my military service.

The Dragon Club was there for the benefit of officers and enlisted men alike, one of the few joint clubs in the world at that time. It was run by men of the military command stationed there and was supplemented with officers and enlisted men from visiting ships. It was a decent club three stories high, the second floor being the primary place of congregation. The breeze was welcomed as it blew through the netting that surrounded the rooftop facility when the weather was hot and humid. The more easily prepared foods, mainly sandwiches and French fries, and the booze of choice, were all offered at very reasonable prices.

The club also had slot machines, a means by which the bargirls, and other ladies of the night, could supplement their income. The girls, whores, hookers, acquaintances, or whatever name they could be categorized under, could not enter the Dragon Club unless they were sponsored and accompanied by a member of the military. The military member need only sign his "lady" in and accept responsibility for her behavior, and as a guest she had access to everything inside. I was Katie's escort and I signed her in later that evening, after my two free drinks and the two drinks for her that I paid for. Once inside, the female guests usually asked their escorts for a roll or two of nickels so that they could play the slot machines. No escort was ever so cheap as to deny his companion the opportunity to play the slots. The girls were usually successful in conning their escorts out of a never-ending supply of nickels, right up to the time they hit a jackpot. The odds were in their favor; sooner or later they were bound to strike it rich. Rich in terms of their for-the-moment lifestyle. However, the girls were not authorized to collect the winnings, not without their escort's signature on the payout log as winner. But guess who got to keep the winnings? The girls of course. And they were not about to share their winnings with their escorts or anyone else! The girls figured they had earned their winnings, so it was theirs. No argument was convincing enough to change their minds. The escorts seldom complained since the whole idea was to keep their ladies happy enough to reciprocate in kind by engaging in as much sexual activity as time allowed before the expiration of Cinderella liberty. Of course the ladies also expected a generous tip after sex. Seldom was either party disappointed, although escorts always ended up either broke or nearly so.

The girls were unbelievably psychic. From the moment we met they knew almost to the penny how much money we had on our person, and they were proficient at achieving their goal of making sure we either spent it on them or we gave it to them. We always made ourselves believe that they were worth it.

I had a great time with Katie. We danced to the music of a small band and we stuffed ourselves with sandwiches and chips. I drank beer while Katie drank wine. I was having so much fun that I didn't realize how quickly the night wound down. I barely had enough time to get back to the ship when I said good night to my "date." It had been an evening of good clean fun, and I really didn't feel that I had missed out on anything. I did manage to see Katie again before the ship got underway a couple of days later. I learned that she was illiterate. She was only able to write her own name, and then only using the alphabet instead of Chinese characters. She had been orphaned at a very early age and had relied on handouts nearly all of her life. I liked Katie and she seemed to like me. All of the girls working at the OK Bar admired Katie, even though they teased her about her being a cherry girl, a virgin. The other girls thought Katie was in safe hands with me, that I wouldn't take advantage of her. The girls were wrong! They were right in that I didn't take advantage of Katie, wrong in their belief that she was a virgin. She had lost her virginity to someone else, some time before meeting me, but she had kept it a secret from her close bar friends. Katie was inexperienced, as I found out, and she swore me to secrecy or else I would never be allowed to touch her again. I kept my promise and Katie was good to me. She never asked for monetary compensation. I really believe that Katie wanted to learn more about how to make a man happy.

That was the profession she had entered, and I had become something of a teacher to her. She trusted me, and that in itself provided me with as much satisfaction as I could have hoped for.

There were any number of things to do and see while in Taiwan, but due to the three-day-in-port time constraint, many of us zeroed in on what we missed most; booze and female companionship. Relatively few sailors ventured outside the immediate confines of Kaohsiung proper.

Souvenirs purchased in Taiwan usually consisted of copycat replicas of American brand-name products. At that time there were no laws or international agreements that prevented the Chinese from violating our copyright or trademark laws. By our own laws, if we purchased any item with a U.S. trademark or logo, we had to either obliterate it or remove it. No one wanted to intentionally remove what made the merchandise appear more appealing or more valuable, so temptation usually triumphed and we concealed (smuggled), some items with their trademarks intact — clearly in violation of U.S. Customs regulations. Books, records, and stereo systems were big items. They were accurate replicas, identical in every detail, perhaps manufactured with a lower-grade material but otherwise every bit as good as those made in the United States — but at a fraction of the cost. There was no way we could pass up some of the bargains available to us. Most of the men, officers and enlisteds, did not particularly like it there, but Kaohsiung was still in its infancy, it was growing, and I could see great potential for the future. I liked it there, but I found the three-day visit far too short for me to learn much about the place. I knew that I was bound to return at some future date, at which time I planned to stray from the beaten path and to learn more about the people and the surrounding area. The U.S. Navy's role in patrolling the Taiwan Straits was a well-established routine and it wasn't about to be curtailed in the foreseeable future.

Our final thirteen days of that deployment were spent in Yokosuka. For those who had not yet done so, it was their final opportunity to buy souvenirs from the Orient at typically low bargain prices. As usual, every barkeeper, every bargirl, and every souvenir shop, regardless of size, knew of our scheduled departure. It was kind of an impasse; they knew it was our last opportunity to buy the same as we knew it. Sometimes it worked as a buyers' market, sometimes as a sellers' market. A lot depended on how near payday was and how many ships were in port. Being told by street vendors, "You no can buy this stateside" was persuasive enough for us to make some purchases, whether they were needed or not.

It was also time for final farewells. Some interesting friendships had developed. I had found that the Japanese were really no different than us. Most of them had been victims of the war and they were struggling desperately to survive by whatever means available. Regardless of their profession, prostitutes had feelings; they had the same needs and desires everyone else had.

Kimiko and I shared some tender parting moments. The tears were evident in my eyes as well as in hers. We knew that we could, and would, always trust in each other, married or not. We had experienced a kind of love few sailors are ever privileged to share, or at least admit to. When we embraced it was not out of lust but out of love and affection; sincere concern for each other's future. We were well aware of each other's feelings, as was obvious when we looked into each other's eyes and said, "Sayonara."

That time I walked instead of taking a taxi back to my ship. I wanted to make sure there was absolutely no evidence of how upsetting it was to me, having to leave such a special friend behind. Within hours, perhaps minutes, I knew that Kimiko would be faking happiness and pleasure with someone else.

For the most part, the trip back across that wide ocean was uneventful. We did suffer one very bad oil spill during an at-sea refueling operation that took place under severe weather conditions. One of the fuel hoses broke and subsequently sprayed black fuel oil all over the ship. All hands E-5 and below were tasked with the cleanup detail, a very dangerous detail at that. Fuel oil and water, either of which is slippery without the other, provided a situation that was more like walking on ice with rubber-soled shoes. But the ship, according to the Exec, had to be washed clean regardless of the weather.

We were provided with buckets of diesel fuel and an ample supply of rags as a first step in diluting the more viscous black fuel oil. The compounds of soapy solutions that followed didn't make matters much worse, but didn't make it any easier either. I remain surprised to this day that no one was washed overboard as the result of the extreme swaying and bobbing of the ship. The men were truly at the mercy of the sea as the ship took on remarkably steep angles caused by the massive swells. I do not think the person or persons responsible for issuing the orders to clean the ship were cognizant of the dangers to which we were subjected. I would hate to think anyone would intentionally place the ship's exterior appearance above that of human life. There was, in my opinion, whether intentional or otherwise, an obvious lack of concern for the safety of the men involved in that detail. Luck was on our side, as we suffered nothing more than a few minor bruises while carrying out our orders.

The remainder of our trip home was a reversal of the trip west six months prior. We stopped at Midway Island long enough to refuel, and we stopped in Pearl Harbor for a very brief two-day visit.

The excitement we all felt at returning home far outweighed all other concerns. The closer we were to CONUS, the more excited we all became. "Channel fever," a condition few could avoid, infected most of the crew. Some suffered the fever several days out, but nearly everyone felt the full impact no later than that last day and night at sea before entering port at San Diego. Channel fever cannot be adequately described. For many it was unavoidable, and the symptoms were unmistakable. Full-fledged insomnia a state of mind that prevented sleep! The excitement was just too much for the body to accept, so many of us substituted other activities for sleep. There were card games, letters being written, and books being read. Sightseers, from the bridge to the fantail, strained their eyes through the darkness of the night for that first glimpse of land. Radios were tuned to local stations, and nearly all hands, willing or not, participated in a kind of "unscheduled alertness" watch. I had suffered different degrees of channel fever at every port in the Orient, but the most severe attack was most obvious the night before returning home.

September 30, 1956, the *Colahan* inched her way into San Diego Harbor. Ships in a squadron entered port in order of command seniority. Unfortunately, our skipper was junior to the others, so we were to be the fourth and last to tie up. We were required to stand at attention at assigned quarters in our finest uniforms, a standard procedure strictly enforced whenever entering port, but adhered to with greater pride upon returning home after having been away for six months. Disregarding our liberty time, we knew of the many challenges with which we had been faced and had overcome, and of our many accomplishments that had contributed significantly to the successful deployment from which we were returning. There was also a special inner feeling that made us want to look more professional and more desirable to our loved ones. As the ship got closer, we could see hundreds of dependents lining the pier. They were boarding each ship as soon as it was tied up and it was safe for them to cross the brow between ships. It was difficult recognizing friends and loved ones from a distance and nearly impossible for them to single out one of us, especially with the near-identical uniforms we were wearing.

The mothers, wives, relatives, and friends of the men of the *Colahan* were sure to notice changes in our habits and our personalities due to the experiences we had shared while deployed. For many of us, a great deal of maturing had occurred after having been separated from our homeland. Some men had become fathers but were unable to be present at that most important time of their lives. We had visited some of the most exotic ports of the Orient and had been fortunate in meeting and mingling with the natives, sometimes making lifelong friends, and in other instances renewing old acquaintances. Many of us had learned a great deal about the customs and traditions of the Orient while we made honest attempts to learn a bit of the local languages. We had shopped at some of the world's most famous bargainers' paradises and we were returning home with some remarkable souvenirs. We had seen and participated in the nightlife; we had witnessed the daytime beauty of Oriental landscapes and had marveled at many architectural wonders. We had talked with street beggars, seen the crippling results of malnutrition in children and adults alike, we had felt the uneasiness of being alone in unfamiliar surroundings while at the same time we had experienced a warm and receptive hospitality by the people of the host countries. We had seen miles and miles of ocean, we had been subjected to severe tropical storms, and we had lived with anxieties that only a sailor truly understands. We had all become a little bit older, some of us a lot wiser. Upon return to the United States we would each relate our experiences in our own way. The trinkets and stories we brought with us were a very real part of our lives, and we looked forward to sharing everything with the most wonderful and cherished people in the world. Our loved ones at home!

And so it went; work routine and liberty routine. Good times, bad times, and in between times, always seeking and usually finding something new and intriguing to occupy my spare time. I never thought possible what the future had in store for me; excitement and danger beyond my wildest

184

dreams, inconceivable within the realm of my imagination, were yet to come.

8

THE END OF AN ERA

I knew that I could never condone the Navy way of life beyond that of my current enlistment. The manner in which I saw men treated and the variations in the application of Navy rules and regulations by different officers and different commands were confusing and terribly unfair. If there were to be rules, I believed that they should be enforced evenly, regardless of who was in command. For example, the growing of beards was allowed on some ships, while on the *Colahan* they were not. Midrations, meals served at midnight to those who were either getting off watch or going on watch, while underway, were served on some ships whereas on the *Colahan* they were not. A complete uniform, skivvy shirt, dungaree shirt, and squared white hat might or might not be required at sea. On board the *Colahan* a complete uniform was required at all times. Tailor-made uniforms were encouraged on some ships, while on others, the *Colahan* included, they were taboo. Hours allocated for liberty was very generous on some ships, while on others they were very restrictive. It was the compilation of many easily recognized, sometimes-menial differences observed on different ships and stations that made the entire system seem unfair. Shipboard life was dependent upon the whim of the Executive Officer and was normally agreed to by the Commanding Officer. Why anyone on board the *Colahan* would consider "shipping over," reenlisting, was beyond my comprehension. The only understandable reason would have been to negotiate a transfer as part of the reenlistment contract. Even then there could be no guarantee that things would be any better at the next base or station. I was determined to do my time, to carry out the terms of my agreement, and to get on with my life as a PFC (proud fuckin' civilian), as those who knew they were getting out called themselves. My decision was firm and had been made well in advance of the expiration of my enlistment. I was sure that nothing would change it. So I conducted my life accordingly, no longer caring about strict adherence to the orders that were issued by my seniors. I wanted an honorable discharge from the Navy — nothing more.

My efforts to correct unnecessary nuisances, sometimes one-man vigilante efforts, whether or not covered under military law, had not gone unnoticed, but the results were not always lasting or absolute. For example, I hated the smell of dirty feet, feet that were not properly cared for. There were some men — thank God there were only a few — who insisted on wearing shoes without benefit of socks. That in itself was an irritant to me, but the smell created by naked sweaty feet inside leather shoes was putrid and disgusting. Socks were washed periodically, but shoes worn without socks seemed to ferment; they became more and more offensive with time. The stench was transferred from the shoes to one's feet, regardless of the degree of cleansing the feet might have undergone. It was a fair assumption that the men who had the problem did not practice good personal hygiene.

When my variety of warnings (threats) to those inconsiderate individuals went unheeded, I sometimes took matters into my own hands, literally. I was determined to eliminate either the smell or the shoes — I couldn't eliminate the feet. Since I had no power over a man's feet, my only alternatives were to deal with the man first, and if that was not effective, deal with his shoes. I would eliminate them.

Of all the unruly things I might have participated in or been accused of, one thing was a certainty; I was not a thief. But if I couldn't control the smell by pouring after-shave lotion or some other perfumed aqueous concentration into the shoes, the shoes just had to go! Everyone had at least two pairs of shoes, one for work and one for inspection or liberty. Denying someone of his only pair of shoes was not my intention. At first I would hide the offensive pair of shoes in the engineroom where the combination of heat and ventilation was near certain to take the smell out. In a week or two, however long it took to complete the airing-out process, I would return the shoes in the same mysterious manner they had disappeared, but with a note conveniently tucked inside each one: "Wear socks," or, "The smell goes or the shoes go." I was always a suspect but I was never caught by anyone who was temporarily inconvenienced by the loss of his work shoes.

I did have an attitude problem, but I did my work professionally, to the best of my ability; not because I was dedicated, rather because of my upbringing. My father, from time to time, had to remind me, and eventually he permanently instilled a concept within me, a way of life that was based on the words he often spoke.

"Once a task is begun, never leave it 'till it's done. Be it labor great or small, do it well or not at all."

During one in-port period of time, while the ship was undergoing routine maintenance, several of us were lounging around on the fantail when we heard the word passed over the 1-MC, "Duty Corpsman [the Doc or one of his strikers], lay to the forward engineroom immediately."

That was not the first time a corpsman had been summoned with urgency, but for whatever reason I blurted out to a shipmate, "Hey, great, let's go see some blood." We walked at a rapid pace to the engineroom scuttle and proceeded to climb down the vertical ladder to the upper-level of that space. I could see some kind of activity on the lower-level and continued climbing to that level. The Chief Corpsman was on his knees, bending over someone who had apparently been hurt. I placed myself in a position where I had an unobstructed view of the injured man, an electrician friend who was about my age. The man was lying on his back, and the Doc had inserted a plastic breathing apparatus into his mouth and down his throat. Doc was making an effort to assist the man in breathing by providing mouth-to-mouth resuscitation. I stood there somewhat mesmerized at the scene, not knowing exactly what had happened but fully cognizant of the possibility my friend might die. I watched as the Doc cut a small slit in the skin of the man's stomach, and I realized that as the skin pulled back there was not the slightest indication of blood or bleeding. At that moment I knew that there was no heartbeat. The man was rolled onto his stomach, and the obvious became more profound. I was shocked when I saw how the blood had drained from the front of his body to the back, his back having taken on the appearance of one massive bruise from the pooling of blood inside his body, noticeably contrasting the ghostly white his stomach had turned. My friend was beyond help. I had never felt quite so paralyzed during my lifetime. There was absolutely nothing I could do except stand there gawking. I was in shock and disbelief as I watched my friend's body, his corpse, as it was being removed from the space with the aid of a wire-mesh body stretcher.

188

Later I learned that my friend had been working on a fire pump, a pump used for providing water pressure to the ship's fire-main system, and that one of the precautionary measures had been inadvertently violated. The man had been electrocuted and had died instantly. I have always felt guilty about my uncalled-for "Let's go see some blood" comment when the corpsman was summoned. From that day forward I took, and I still take, a very strong exception to anyone poking fun at the need for medical attention.

For the next several months, between weekly underway periods, several of us in the engineroom began experimenting with hypnosis. We had accumulated quite a library of books on the subject and we shared a sincere interest. We spent hours discussing the subject and eventually took that daring step; we practiced on one another. Not many crewmen were privileged with the knowledge of our activities, only those of us that were close friends, a small group of E-4s and below. It would not have been wise for us to leak our activities to higher-ups, since the Navy considered hypnosis as taboo, something in line with witchcraft. We confined our activities to the after engineroom. It kept us occupied as we gained proficiency in the "art."

A couple of men among our small group were very receptive to hypnosis, "somnambulists," and they would carry out posthypnotic suggestions with unbelievable clockwork precision. No suggestion was ever implanted that would cause any harm or outlandish embarrassment to anyone. We considered what we were doing as serious business. Our goal was to improve our lives by making our minds more alert to everything around us. We wanted to improve our memories, make learning less of a chore, and we wanted to become better people. Our efforts did have an impact on our lives as we gained a new respect for hypnosis. The knowledge of its workings did not detract from a certain degree of awe; how the suggestions of one person were so easily accepted and carried out by someone else. Some of our "self-help" suggestions included improving our ability to understand, and instilling a genuine motivation toward achieving higher goals. Once we were satisfied that we had gained sufficient confidence in our knowledge and proficiency, we discontinued those activities. We did, however, continue discussing the potential dangers, the possibility of long-lasting psychological damage that could be caused by unintentionally implanting or failing to remove some suggestions from the minds of willing volunteers.

Most important, we learned that the subconscious was not a toy and was therefore not to be played with.

At about this time, we began receiving more recently released movies. It was a tossup whether we would see something in color or in black and white. Wide-screen movies were coming into being but they were still a rarity. Some of the newer releases included: *The Great Locomotive Chase*, an adventure drama staring Fess Parker and Jeff Hunter; *High Society*, a musical starring Bing Crosby and Grace Kelly; *The Swan*, a comedy starring Grace Kelly and Alec Guinness; *Johnny Concho*, a western starring Frank Sinatra and Phyllis Kirk; *The Mole People*, science fiction starring John Agar and Cynthia Patrick; and *The Unguarded Moment*, a drama starring Esther Williams and George Nader.

Also at this time there was a great deal of emphasis on weaponry systems. Some of the headline-makers were:

Sidewinder: A nine-foot-missile that operated on a "heat homing" guidance system.

Bullpup: A new 600-pound air-to-surface missile developed for Navy and Marine aircraft for use in close air support of ground troops.

Sparrow III: An air-to-air supersonic guided missile, which could be fired above or through clouds with complete accuracy — called the most advanced weapon of its time.

Talos: Planned as an addition to the arsenal of the fleet the following year; the Navy's long-range surface-to-air guided missile.

Polaris: This surface-to-surface 1,500-mile range ballistic missile, which was planned on becoming operational within a few years, was the subject of a $10 million contract. The contract called for the design and manufacture of complicated handling and launching systems for the missile and would involve the development of both electrical and mechanical devices for launching. The program involved a series of experimental systems, leading ultimately to surface ship and submarine launching systems.

Hasp: All missiles were not developed to deliver death at the end of the line. Hasp was a high-speed antiaircraft rocket, converted into a collector of weather data for naval shipboard use.

190

All of those systems seem rather primitive in comparison to today's weaponry. It becomes even harder to imagine what weapons of death and destruction will be operational in the future.

Looking back at what a retiring CPO received in retirement pay makes that period of time seem even more primitive. A chief retiring after twenty-two years' service received $175.89 a month! On active duty that same chief received a monthly base pay amounting to $319.80!

That was also at the time an endurance and altitude record was claimed for the "new" high-altitude version of the FIREBEE jet drone target missile. Launched at Holloman Air Development Center, Alamogordo, New Mexico, an XQ-2B experimental FIREBEE soared to 53,000 feet and remained in the air on remote control for one hour and forty-four and one-half minutes before it was recovered by its own parachute release system, which safely lowered it to the desert floor. This operation was believed to have set world records in altitude and duration for drone missiles specifically designed as targets.

An altitude of 198,770 feet — nearly thirty-eight miles — was reached by an Air Force officer in an aeromedical altitude chamber test. At that time it was the highest simulated altitude ever reached by man. It was during a time when many a sailor (and his family) sought overseas shore duty at the largest U.S. Naval base in the West Indies; Guantanamo Bay (Gitmo), Cuba — where the climate was near-perfect (semitropical), Officers' and Enlisted Quarters were fully furnished one-, two-, and three-bedroom apartments and/or houses, U.S. currency was used exclusively, and free bus transportation was provided throughout the seventy miles of passable roads within the naval base. (The actual mileage from one end of the base to the other was nine miles.) Pleasant relief from the heat could be found at the swimming pools and bathing beaches — and of course Havana and Cardenas, as well as the rest of the island, were available to those who wanted to witness some of Cuba's charm.

From December 1956 to February 1957 the *Colahan* underwent a major overhaul at Mare Island Naval Shipyard near Vallejo, California. It seemed like the ship was totally dismantled from stem to stern. All personal belongings, including bunk mattresses, were warehoused at a designated location at the base. Huge gaping holes were cut in the hull and in the main deck to accommodate access to, and the removal of, large machinery and equipment. Standing cold iron watches, usually highly desired by snipes, was miserable in this instance. There was no heat and no ventilation. It was very cold and there was no place to relax in comfort. Being surrounded by the cold and moist iron of the ship made conditions that much worse. The command failed to consider the lack of berthing facilities for the enlisted men having to stand duties on board during that period of time. On duty nights, those sailors that had to remain aboard had to improvise with a great deal of imagination. I was never comfortable during the nights. I scrounged around the ship in search of something flexible and suitable enough to wrap around my cold, shivering, body as I attempted to gain sufficient sleep. It was terribly uncomfortable utilizing cardboard or heavy-duty asbestos permeated canvas as a blanket; however such materials did provide some protection from the cold as they formed a barrier that helped to retain whatever warmth my body generated.

Since shipyard workers were doing most of the work, the lower-graded enlisted men were frequently called upon to stand "fire watches." Whenever there was welding, cutting, or grinding, any activity that might produce sparks or could be considered fire-conducive or a fire hazard, we were called upon to stand nearby with fire extinguishers, fully prepared to take necessary corrective action. It was not at all uncommon for sparks to cause smoldering in anything nearby; paper, rags, or any other combustible materials. Smoldering occasionally ignited when it went unnoticed long enough. Fire watches were an absolute necessity. It was mandatory that they be present before any "hot" work began.

CO_2 fire extinguishers, normally for emergency use only, were always available for fire watches. It was important that each fire watch check to make certain his extinguishers were full. Not only were they frequently used to extinguish fires, they also served another useful purpose. The powered "dry ice" emitted from a CO_2 extinguisher provided an ideal medium for cooling down beer quickly! Two shipboard violations; the unauthorized use of a fire extinguisher and having alcoholic beverages on board. Its consumption would have been a third offense.

Enlisted men did contend with a miserable way of life. There was little solace in the few comforts derived out of violating rules. The violation of some rules was considered, by most enlisted men, a necessary part of shipboard life. Since officers were taught that enlisted men were "sneaky

192

and not to be trusted," we sometimes felt justified, even obligated, to make factual that which they had learned in school and believed to be true.

Enlisteds never ceased playing tricks on one another. Whenever opportunity presented itself, someone was sure to be the brunt of a prank. It helped to pass the time and was a continuing means of amusement. I was surprised at how often I could conceal the hat of any officer foolish enough to hang it on some fixture or lay it on a piece of machinery while he was in the engineroom. It took but a moment to turn the cap device, the officer's insignia, upside down and then return the hat to wherever the officer had left it. It was another short-term means of relief, watching an officer don his hat and proudly strut away, ready to carry on the heavy responsibilities entrusted him, with his cap device upside down! No enlisted man below the grade of chief would tell them, but the chuckles and laughter that went on behind their backs, sometimes to their faces, were good medicine to the enlisted men. Chiefs were no exception, but they were wise to such pranks. They had no doubt participated in similar activities during their earlier years. It was more of a challenge, catching a chief off guard. More than once I heard one chief or another say, "You're fuckin' with the wrong man," or, "How'd you like to spend a few hours in the bilge?"

One evening several of us with the duty were down in the aft engineroom sitting in a semicircle, each of us with a cold beer in hand. We had smuggled a couple of six-packs aboard earlier, and the time had come to enjoy them. We were all sitting on the deck plates in front of the throttle board when someone saw khaki trousers descending the port ladder.

"Christ, it's the chief," I heard my frantic voice as I choked on a gulp of beer not yet swallowed.

"What'll we do?" someone else quickly whispered.

There was not enough time to hide anything. Besides, as soon as the chief reached the bottom of the ladder he would have a nearly unobstructed view of us.

"It's too late; we'll just have to offer him a beer and hope for the best," I said.

The best turned out better than expected. I shall always believe that Chief Rogers saw what we were doing and that he opted to save our butts. When he reached the bottom of the ladder, instead of turning to us, he walked around the base of the ladder and strolled slowly toward the opposite side of the main engine turbines, his line of sight well obstructed by machinery and the throttle board. As quickly as possible we concealed all of the beer, empty cans included, in a spare-parts locker conveniently located under the throttle board. The chief intentionally took his time, eventually emerging at the throttle board where we were gathered.

"So what are you men up to?" he said, as if he didn't know.

"Nothin,' Chief, just shootin' the shit," somebody responded.

Chief Rogers slowly scanned the group of us and as he turned to leave he said, "Well, you men stay out of trouble, Okay?"

"Okay, Chief," several of us responded in unison.

We were all scared. It had been a very close call. There had not been time enough to consider the possibility that the chief had intentionally given us a break. As we talked of the incident, we knew that there were too many unfavorable conditions present and that the chief could not have overlooked them all. Our nervous reaction to his presence, the strong odor of beer around us, and the most likely giveaway — the view he had of us as he descended the ladder. We couldn't say it then, but now, for the entire group, "Thanks, Chief."

During the overhaul, off-duty personnel were berthed ashore. The married men were provided off-base housing whereas those that were not married lived on base in a barracks. The officers, depending on their rank, had better housing that consisted of private or duplex units on base. The policy of absolute separation between officers and enlisteds provided for the distinct difference between the military lifestyles and privileges of the two groups. The separation was of necessity; the military system could not have functioned effectively otherwise. It was based on the belief that familiarity nurtured contempt. Combining the two would have allowed for fraternization; it would have created an organization based on persuasive association, a society that would rely more on friendships than military rule or vested authority. Socializing *was* allowed, however it was normally discouraged. It would have been difficult exercising authority, issuing or accepting unpleasant orders, where close friendships existed. So socializing between grades was done more in secrecy than in public. Somewhat in conflict with the no-fraternizing policy, socializing between grades was encouraged at ship's functions such as "beer ball games," "ship's parties," or other gatherings where all hands' participation was expected.

Seniors learned a great deal from their subordinates at all hands' social functions; tongues loosened up after a few beers. Unfortunately, so did tempers. There could not be a ship's social function without at least one fight. It was an inherent characteristic, a requirement of sort, for an innocent misunderstanding to quickly turn into a brawl between two or more men; never between officers, always between enlisted men. Life at sea, living in close quarters and working or standing watches seven days a week — constantly struggling to maintain one's equilibrium with each shipboard step — not being able to walk around a base or through a town window-shopping — not having the choice of eating out or of drinking a beverage of choice — and, in general, living the life of a prisoner, were all contributing factors that prompted or encouraged men to unleash their frustrations through physical violence. Ship-sponsored functions were a similar continuation of that close quarters prisonlike life; consequently, with the consumption of alcoholic beverages added to the equation, tongues loosened and confrontations occurred.

At those functions, Shore Patrol was provided by "Ship's Company," men from our own ship, but they were inclined to be lenient, not wanting to get involved until it was too late. Breaking up a fight could be dangerous. Shore Patrol or not, those volunteering to break up two or more angry, probably drunk, individuals were bound to suffer a few bruises themselves along with some damage to their uniforms. It was a good bet that there would *always* be at least one fight, probably more!

I did not participate in sports, whether it was baseball, football, or anything else. I did participate in the consumption of free beer even though I was underage. Ship's sponsored recreation was one of the few times and places I could drink in public without fear of being arrested. My problem was that I had not yet acclimated to the influence of booze. At one ball game, after having acquired sufficient alcoholic-induced courage, I decided that there was far too much beer stacked near the ice-packed cooler bins, and that I should hide some of it from the crew. I managed to carry two cases across a field unnoticed and I stashed them inside a stack of baled hay, intent on retrieving them later.

The ball game was enjoyable. The more the participants drank, the more fun it was to watch. Arkie was a bit "rate-happy," and as such, he enjoyed exercising his authority. He was probably more right than wrong when he chose to enforce the rules, but a beer-ball game just wasn't the place to be overly strict. Arkie should not have been so quick to reprimand me for drinking too much, especially since he had sneaked a few beers for himself, a violation for anyone on duty but far more serious when the duty was that of Shore Patrol.

Arkie, feeling superior because of the "police" function with which he was temporarily vested, coupled with the fact that he was a grade senior to me, topped off with his own state of inebriation, approached me the wrong way.

"All right, Ad, you've had too much to drink and you ain't gonna drink no more."

"Says who?" I snapped back.

Arkie's tough-man approach only aggravated me when he menacingly said, "I ain't afraid of you."

Who the hell do you think you are, raced through my mind as I openly stated,

"Well pal, it's time for you to get afraid."

One thing led to another, and I lost my temper. The men around us intervened quickly, however Arkie had already suffered the brunt of my attack. Arkie went his way and I went mine, but I remained quite angry. The fight that ensued could have been averted had Arkie used a little more tact in his approach. He knew from a history of previous performances that I was not one to be intimidated — whether or not I was under the influence of alcohol.

My thoughts quickly returned to the beer I had stashed earlier. I knew that since Tom had "wheels," he would provide transportation to retrieve the beer. The car he had driven to the ball game was not his; it had been entrusted to him for safekeeping while the owner, another shipmate, was off enjoying his thirty-day reenlistment leave. The car, an impressive and reasonably new convertible, had been purchased with the owner's reenlistment bonus. It was supposed to remain parked on the street near Tom's residence during the owner's absence, but since Tom was to "look after it," he was also entrusted with the keys. Tom probably drove that car to the ball game under the pretense, perhaps out of honest concern, that it should not sit idle at curbside for a prolonged period of time.

The ball game was nearing an end when I told Tom about the "extra" beer. The timing was perfect since he was about ready to leave, so he was anxious to accommodate me (and the beer) with transportation. Several shipmates climbed into the convertible, top down, and Tom drove straight to the stack of baled hay. I was reluctant to recover the beer because one of the ship's officers had joined our group. The officer, willingly sworn to secrecy, congratulated me for having "put aside" our share. Tom remained at the car while I tossed six-pack after six-pack to him. I was not totally coordinated and Tom was not 100% alert when one of the misdirected six-packs smashed into the windshield, driver's side, shattering it in all directions. The damage was more than could be ignored although we shrugged it off as one of the hazards of doing business. We were far more interested in getting the beer to our destination where we could continue with our own private party. We did precisely that, without having to worry about rules, regulations, or fights. Strangely, the officer, an ensign, fit right in with the rest of us, and we all partied well into the night. The owner of the convertible never learned how the windshield damages were incurred — but thanks to his foresight he had full insurance coverage, and the windshield was replaced at no cost to him.

During the shipyard overhaul, funds were extremely tight. It was expensive living off of the ship. By that time my daughter was a little over a year old and my wife was pregnant with our second child. Halfway between paydays I found myself broke, truly destitute. There was nothing in the small substandard military apartment for my family to eat. I couldn't take any leftover food from the ship since the galley was being remodeled — the crew was being fed at the mess hall on the base. Until that time I had never submitted a request for special pay; I had never experienced the need. But with things as they were, I submitted my request for special pay through appropriate channels. I very clearly addressed the urgency; the immediate need in order for me to provide for my family. The request was blatantly denied, with unnecessary comments written in the 'REASON FOR DISAPPROVAL' block: "Too near payday. You must learn to handle your finances in a more mature manner."

I don't recall what took priority in the order of my hatred, the Navy as a whole or the Executive Officer alone, for his intentional abuse of authority. He had, as far as I was concerned, gone too far when his denial of my request was to affect my family so directly. What kind of a "man" would allow any family to go without food, especially knowing there was an infant child involved? He had gone too far, but there was little I could do about it. I didn't have sense enough to go over the Exec's head, or maybe I sensed the sort of reciprocal action the Exec might have taken against me had I disregarded his decision and bypassed the chain of command. I never considered asking the Red Cross for assistance.

There was no one other than Tom Mundy to turn to, since my other friends were off to school or at their homes enjoying leave. Tom also had a wife, and a son about the same age as my daughter. Regardless of our friendship, I was very uncomfortable asking for a handout. I was afraid that Tom might think I didn't know how to handle my money, and that I was neglecting my family. In fact, I was surprised to find that Tom was having similar difficulties in making ends meet. It was questionable whether his food supply was sufficient to last until payday, another four days away. Friendships became unusually tight during times of genuine need. Tom showed me the true meaning of friendship when he opened his wallet and showed me his last dollar bill. Without that dollar he would have been as broke as I was. I am not sure whether I would have done for him what he did for me that day, although I'd like to think that I would have. Tom accompanied me to the store where he split that dollar with me. I knew that I would have to make it as best I could, on fifty cents. I don't know what Tom and his family lived on during those four days, but I do know that my family lived on bread and milk, and we were thankful for having that. That experience made me despise the Navy even more, but it also taught me a valuable lesson. I would do whatever I had to do, including loansharking via an illegal "bank." I would never allow myself or my family to go without basic needs again.

By the middle of March we had completed the overhaul and had undergone a severe shakedown cruise to make sure all systems were functioning properly. We returned to our home port and tied up to a buoy in San Diego Harbor. It was late May and it was hot. A small group of us discussed how inviting and refreshing the bay water looked. Tom was sitting on the starboard bulwark. His plan was that he would fake a loss of balance while a second individual, in an effort to "save" Tom, would also be pulled overboard. Tom's final words came as he feigned his loss of balance: "No guts, no glory," and over the side he went — but he was unable to drag his no-longer-willing-to-participate accomplice overboard with him. Tom looked up at us, grinning from ear to ear, and he spoofed us with a very bogus, "Help! Help!" Tom was probably the only enlisted man ever allowed to board the *Colahan* by way of the ladder reserved specifically for officers.

"What do you think you're doing?" the OOD directed his logical question to one very wet sailor as Tom pulled himself up and onto the ladder.

Tom's whimsical, almost believable, reply came as if he were guessing the answer to a difficult test question; "Trying to come aboard, sir? So that I don't drown, sir?"

Two of a kind

As time passed, I became more and more contemptuous with regards to the Navy way, as well as with much of the leadership to whom I was subordinate. I actually began looking for reasons; sometimes intentionally creating situations that would most likely result in causing a fight. Fighting became a way of life for me, a way of proving my ability to rule, if not by authority, by threat or brutality. It made no difference to me how big or how small, what pay grade or what branch of military service my adversary was in. My ability to fight surprised even me. I was seldom hurt, and there was never any doubt as to who had won the battle at hand. I enjoyed being provoked; it gave me the opportunity to vent my frustrations by offensive aggression.

I began to think of my actions as necessary rather than uncalled for. I thought nothing of slapping men around for their failure to change socks frequently, when their feet emitted an unnecessary stench that encircled the berthing compartment. While ashore I "decked" shipmates and non-shipmates alike for little more than their failure to get out of my way. One time ashore, Chief "Motorcycle" saw me "cold cock" (knock out) one of his men. Then, when he questioned me about my conduct, I decked the chief too. In retaliation for something he had done to aggravate me several days prior, I ripped the shirt off of one shipmate while he was lying in his bunk. I tore off chunks, one piece of his shirt at a time, and I called him and his family names no man would normally stand for, yet that man simply cowered next to his bunk and begged me not to hurt him. As the bully I had become, I enjoyed tormenting others to one degree or another. I did not seem to care about the consequences of my actions.

Whenever I was caught fighting by a chief or an officer, I was placed on report and consequently suffered whatever penalties were imposed.. When I was not caught or no one complained, I thought of myself as a big shot, superior. I was quite proud of my ability to stand up and fight; it made no difference to me whether I was in the right or in the wrong. I had achieved what I thought to be a significant goal; I had become known as a "bad ass," *precisely the type of person I had at one time feared and despised.*

One time, while on restriction, I didn't limit my consumption of formidable ethyl alcohol and I became seriously inebriated; really out of hand. Tom knew of my condition and he dared me to "drop" the OOD. As I staggered toward the ladder in response to, and to carry out, his dare, Tom stopped me. Apparently Tom felt there was a need to give me the beating of my life, at a time I was about as incapacitated as I could possibly have been. It was his dare, and my attempt at compliance, that provided Tom with sufficient reason to exercise his absolute control over me. Tom's actions reminded me of some of my own; how I had overwhelmed others when they could easily have been contained without having severely beaten them. I almost lost the vision in one eye after landing, eyeball first, on one of the ladder-well stanchions upon which Tom had thrown me. In all probability, Tom wanted it known, particularly among the engineers, that he was "king of the mountain."

Tom remained my close friend after that incident, but he lost some of the respect he had previously gained. Provoking someone into a fight was not unusual for Tom (or me), but everyone knew that he had gone too far; that the damages he had inflicted were unnecessary, especially to a very close friend. I looked pretty bad during the next couple of weeks. My face and my left eyeball were badly bruised and my upper lip was split, but I wrote the whole incident off as a learning experience. It was my turn, I was long overdue, for a term on the short end of the stick.

The *Colahan* got underway for another WestPac deployment on June 8, 1957. Crossing the ocean had become routine to me. I knew we would stop in Hawaii for a couple of days of Cinderella liberty and that Midway Island would provide the only other break in our underway routine before arriving at Yokosuka, Japan, our first scheduled liberty port in the Orient.

The "buddy system" was always encouraged while on liberty. It was never wise, regardless of the port or country, to be a "loner" while on liberty. Sailors were known to get drunk, and every so often one would be "rolled," robbed. I normally went along with the buddy system, but I did not live by it. Sometimes I would wander off intentionally, just to be alone for awhile.

I didn't visit Kimiko as frequently as in the past, but whenever the ship was in Yokosuka I occasionally dropped by to inquire about her health and well being. She always seemed happy to see me, and we always had ample topics to discuss during our visits. I was still something of a youngster but I was no longer the boot-camper school-kid she had met a couple of years prior. We continued to take walks together, and we shared time sitting on the mountainside overlooking Yokosuka. Those were rare moments of serene pleasure when we were both able to escape from our usual way of life and relax informally, surrounded by peace and quiet. We shared many tender moments together. I treated Kimiko unlike the way she was accustomed to being treated; as a lady, with respect. I did my best to completely disregard her profession. She knew that I was a little "different;" that I had always been quite kind to her, and she made my life much more pleasant as a result of it.

As I became more experienced in the real world, I also became more aware of and alert to some of the tricks bargirls used in accomplishing their goals. A promise to "meet later" meant very little unless the sailor was really a "high roller" and he was willing to spend a great deal of *okane*, money. The girls would promise anyone just about anything, as long as it resulted in the purchase of another "ladies' drink." They would make the same promise to any number of sailors, to meet "out front" or "out back" after closing, then they would slip out the opposite door to meet that one special guy, the one who spent the most *okane* on her. I learned through experience — it was not a proud moment finding oneself waiting outside the bar with several other sailors, all waiting for the same girl! Some bar-girls would give out phony home addresses and then tell their "suitors" they would meet them there after the bar closed, that they could not be seen leaving the bar with anyone. That could be costly. Taxi fare to and from a phony address made for ill feelings; the one duped might take any number of retaliatory measures, all dependent upon how sharp his memory was the following day. The girls gambled that the guys would forget which bar and which girl it was that took advantage of them, and they usually won their bet. The few sailors that could retrace their steps would first attempt recovering their loss, only to be met with a variation of, "You crazy boy-san, I no make promise; what kind girl you think I am?" At that juncture most sailors would accept things as they were, but there were always a few that would go off someplace, fill themselves with liquid courage, and return for their second attempt. They might go so far as to slap the girl around, or break a few things in the bar. Invariably those few rowdy ones ended up spending the night behind bars of a different kind.

I did not believe in that kind of foul play, although I did engage in actions unbecoming a petty officer. While riding in a Japanese minicab with three companions, the driver heard the word "stop" within the content of our conversation. He mistook it to mean stop, literally. The driver jammed on the brakes and brought the cab to an abrupt halt. I explained as best I could that we did not want to stop, that he was to continue on his way. The driver didn't like the confusion, so as he started the cab moving he also started grumbling something that was obviously derogatory. I didn't like his grumbling so I grabbed him around the neck with my forearm, in something of a choke-hold, while I yelled in his ear, "You don't like the way we talk, asshole, then stop your fuckin' cab!" He stopped and within seconds I was chasing him around the cab like a dog chasing its tail. Each time the driver ran past the trunk of the cab, he tried to open it — but Johnson, one of our group, prevented him from getting whatever it was he wanted. Don and Marcel yelled at me, "Knock it off, Paul!" but I had other thoughts as I kept up the chase. A crowd quickly gathered. Crowds always gathered hastily when there was any kind of confrontation involving Americans and Japanese, but that didn't stop me from my pursuit. Too bad for me that I managed to catch up with him, because in an instant that driver flopped

202

me around like a wet rag. He wasted no time in flipping me into the *benjo* ditch that ran alongside the road. I was nowhere near his match — certainly not the badass I thought I was. For the benefit of the uninformed reader, a *benjo* ditch can be an open or closed trench or trough of varying size, constructed for the sole purpose of allowing waste matter to flow from point of origin to larger *benjo* canals or dump sites located some distance away. All *benjo* ditches have a distinct smell about them that clearly identifies them as something no one wants to be near.

The ditch I found myself in was open and large enough to accommodate me. The white uniform I was wearing quickly became camouflaged in appearance, saturated with unsightly, smelly waste, but it didn't end there. Next I was arrested and booked by the Shore Patrol for "assault on a foreign national." I had every reason to believe that Captain Keedy would most certainly make an example out of me; this time for sure.

At Captain's Mast several days later, the skipper was unexpectedly lenient. I guess I had already made enough of an example out of myself. But the skipper's voice was clear, and he meant business, when he went on to tell me, "Adkisson, if I ever see you again, for any offense while under my command, I'll have that crow you're wearing." His words meant that there was a strong probability I would be busted, demoted, and that I would suffer a reduction in pay. As it was, the Captain penalized me with two weeks' restriction. What the skipper didn't know was that there was already another unfavorable report on me, another violation pending. Only one day before, I had also been apprehended as I was about to ride a motorcycle, an activity I did not know was illegal. I knew that I was going to lose a stripe for sure. Within the week I was once again standing in front of the Old Man, listening to my own voice as I acknowledged the offense, and scared to death of the punishment that was about to be imposed upon me.

"Adkisson, had I known about this offense when you were last standing in front of me, I would have stripped you of your crow. But now, considering how minor this offense is, I don't think it would be appropriate. According to Navy law, petty officers cannot be awarded 'extra duty,' but I'll bet you would be willing to volunteer for extra duty instead of losing that crow!" He glared at me. I would have been an absolute fool had I said anything other than the "Yes, sir" I clearly and politely spoke.

I had twenty-eight hours of extra duty to contend with following the two weeks' restriction. But extra duty was not nearly as bad as restriction; I could go on liberty after working two extra hours each day. My extra duty consisted of chipping and painting the ladder-well and the deck outside the Ship's Office, and doing more of the same in one of the forward ventilation blower rooms. The work wasn't difficult, but I hated having to work for a Bos'n Mate with no more stripes than I was wearing. I considered that terribly degrading.

**Without Pride in Uniform
or Appearance**

Raggedy Adkisson

Illegal drugs were a significant shipboard problem, especially overseas. I do not know why I never got involved in drugs when there were so many other sailors that did. I'm sure that being married had a great deal to do with my decision to remain "clean," but in being honest with myself, I know that there were times when I did consider experimenting. Had my close friends been involved with drugs, it would have been far more likely that I would also have gotten involved. As it was, to my knowledge, none of my friends used any illegal substance, marijuana included.

Drugs of all kinds were easily obtainable in the Orient. Heroin (disregarding marijuana) was the most prevalent hard drug sailors (and civilians) most abused during the late fifties, and it was far more dangerous using it overseas than it was in the States. Heroin was produced over there. It had not been cut time and again as it was before reaching the drug market in the States, therefore it was quite pure, and extremely potent.

All hands were well indoctrinated on the penalties as well as the dangers of drug abuse. There was a great deal of emphasis on the dangers of its use while in the Far East. Some men listened, others did not. Some men looked forward to experimenting with stronger and more dangerous drug derivatives — and some men died as a result of overdosing. It was always sad to lose a member of the crew, regardless of the circumstances, but it also provided an excellent warning to those men who might otherwise have taken similar paths toward self-destruction.

Marcel and I frequently enjoyed liberty together at the White Hat Club in Yokosuka. It was a small place and it was conveniently located. There was a wrought-iron winding staircase that led from street level to the second floor, where sailors enjoyed dancing with their favorite bargirl(s). Separated from the dance floor there were also several small booths toward the front. One booth was appropriately located at a large window that provided for a view overlooking the narrow street below.

I was never much of a dancer, but if there was a place to learn it most certainly was the Orient. All Oriental women knew how to dance! They knew the steps to all of the different dances, and they were highly skilled at each.

Whenever Marcel and I were at the White Hat Club we preferred sitting at the upstairs window booth drinking Nippon beer, where we had an unobstructed view of everyone as they walked the street below. Sooner or later we would find ourselves out on the dance floor. There were plenty of chairs surrounding the dance floor, and there was one long couch that was placed against one of the walls. The couch provided the most comfortable place to rest between dances. Behind the couch, out of view, there was a door. Apparently, at some time in the past, the door had provided access to and from the adjoining building, but it had been permanently sealed off with brickwork. Why they left the door there was anyone's guess — but it will come into play shortly.

Sailors usually singled out one favorite girl at each bar and they would rarely *chocho* (butterfly) to another girl at the same location. Connie was "my" girl at the White Hat. I was an awkward student, but Connie was patient and she took the time to make sure I got the dance steps right. Rock and roll was going strong, although the jitterbug also received a fair amount of attention.

One warm evening while Marcel and I were dancing ourselves to exhaustion, I decided to remove my jumper. It was far more comfortable with only the white skivvy-shirt on my upper torso. Since I was not fully clothed, I was "out of uniform" and in violation of regulations, those governing the liberty dress code. I was having fun, so my thoughts were more in tune with a "Who cares?" attitude. The Shore Patrol showed that they cared as they made their rounds through the White Hat Club and they saw me dancing without proper attire. I questioned their reason for demanding that I put my jumper back on.

"This is a public place and you have to be in a complete uniform," one of them explained.

Being my typical argumentative self, I sarcastically spewed out, "Like hell! This is not a public place; only downstairs is public." I knew that my argument was not well founded, but I had formulated a foolish plan.

"This is a whorehouse and you guys don't even know it," I continued.

The two Shore Patrol had been stationed at the base for some time, and they certainly knew the difference between bars and whorehouses. Nonetheless, I continued heckling them with fictitious information that I was in hopes would victimize them; make them look foolish as a result of their own actions.

"You shore pukes don't even know about the secret door, the passageway between the dance floor and the beds," I convincingly continued to mock their apparent ignorance, "and you live here!"

"What secret door, smartass?" the second class petty officer snapped at me.

"The one behind the couch, you stupid fuck!" I could hardly hold back my laughter.

Marcel, slightly grinning, a little puzzled, was half wondering and half knowing what I was up to. We stood there watching as the two Shore Patrolmen pulled the couch away from the wall. They looked at each other and smiled back and forth as if they had discovered the secret of the century. They practically stumbled over each other, each one wanting to be the first to open the door and gain entrance to an unlicensed, illegally run brothel. When they jerked the door open, no longer able to contain myself, I burst out laughing with gusto. Marcel and I both laughed even more raucously as they attempted to push the solid brick wall, thinking or hoping that they might be able to push it aside and gain access to whatever secrets there were behind it.

"Okay, smartass, put your jumper on; we're taking you in." They carried out the only retaliation they could fall back on. Legitimate at that, since I really was out of uniform.

As I was being escorted out, I told Marcel, "Don't worry. These guys don't know what they're up against; I'll be back in a jiff!"

"Oh God, you're not gonna . ." Marcel's voice faded away as he followed the three of us down the winding staircase. Upon reaching the bottom of the stairs, Marcel seemed to be more upset than I was as he vented his anger. He kicked viciously at the bottom step, expecting there was a board below the front of it, and his lower shin smashed into the iron step. Marcel blurted out a few anguished expletives, primarily out of pain but also accusingly at the Shore Patrol — as if it were their actions that had caused him to injure himself.

As soon as we were around the first corner and out of sight from the club, I started wheeling and dealing with my captors. I reminded them that they didn't really want to go through the hassle of having to write me up, and that they probably would prefer not having to document their own embarrassment at having fallen for my trickery, and surely they did not want to go back to the Shore Patrol Headquarters knowing full well it would make for a far more entertaining and enjoyable evening were they to remain on foot patrol in town. They listened to my convincing argument and they let me go, but only after I promised not to remove my jumper in public again — not that night!

No more than ten minutes had passed since I had been escorted off to jail, and there I was back at the White Hat. Marcel looked at me inquisitively, his head cocked, squinting through eyes of suspicion, thinking that I might have played badass and had managed to fight my way free.

"You didn't. You wouldn't," Marcel said.

I grinned and suggested he forget about the patrol — it was party time once again. But Marcel could no longer dance; his leg was painfully bruised and noticeably swollen. He voiced his opinion that there was no fairness in situations where I was involved. I, after having been apprehended for violating the rules, was still having a great time while he, as an innocent bystander, had to sit there in terrible pain and watch me as I continued to enjoy myself; pain-free.

During that deployment the *Colahan* returned to Kaohsuing, Taiwan, and I was able to renew my acquaintance with Katie. We also visited ports I had not been to before. We visited the beautiful honeymooners' resort town of Atami, Japan, with its cobblestonelike streets and community bathhouses; where restaurants and pubs were scaled down in size, miniaturized to accommodate the comfort of the Japanese, sometimes to the discomfort of the typically much larger American. Atami was unsurpassed in its beauty and cleanliness. Marcel was my running mate, my companion, and I actually behaved myself there. We pulled into Naha, Okinawa, only to depart that same day. Kobe, Japan provided us with a week of interesting liberty, and we returned to Nagoya for a two-day stopover. Hong Kong, as always, was greeted by everyone with great anticipation. Hong Kong meant R & R for everyone; that well deserved break that we looked forward to and we thoroughly enjoyed.

While in Hong Kong, Tom succeeded in pulling off one of the most dangerous shipboard pranks possible. Fireworks of all types were frequently displayed and sold on the open market. But like alcohol, fireworks were not allowed on board Navy vessels. Firecrackers could be bought in strings of just about any length, or in rolls varying from five inches up to two feet in diameter. Tom bought, and somehow managed to smuggle several huge rolls of firecrackers aboard, each a foot or more in diameter. His original idea was to return to the States with the fireworks, however his mischievous ways of thinking overruled. It was midnight, or shortly thereafter, when Tom very carefully lowered the hatch to the stairwell leading to the aftermost berthing space, well to the stern of the ship. He quietly and cautiously opened the small scuttle in that hatch, being careful not to wake those men sleeping peacefully below. He then tied one full roll of firecrackers to the inside of the scuttle handle, lighted the fuse, slammed the scuttle shut, and hightailed it to his bunk.

In order to fully comprehend how traumatic it must have been to the men sleeping in that compartment when all hell broke loose, understand that there was also a five-inch gun mount above, and an ordnance magazine within and a part of the berthing space. There could have been no doubt in their minds that the ship was being blown to bits as they were so abruptly awakened by the blinding flashes, accompanying explosions, and the dense smoke.

I had been on Shore Patrol duty that night and had not observed what took place. There was still smoke coming from that compartment when I boarded, and I heard the OOD and the quarterdeck watch discussing the probability that Tom was the perpetrator. I went directly to Tom's bunk, where I found a body tightly wrapped in a blanket, from which strange sounds were emanating. It was Tom, and he was having a hard time keeping his giggles and laughter muffled. I told him that he was the number-one suspect, and he told me to get lost! I did. No one could ever prove Tom's involvement. Whenever the subject came up he would simply laugh it off, neither acknowledging his involvement nor disavowing it.

Yokosuka was the final stop before being detached from our WestPac commitment. We remained there for a week before heading home. I had a little over a year remaining on my enlistment and I did not know whether I would ever again see any of the places I had been so fortunate to visit. I wanted to make the best of that final week, to buy everything I wanted or needed, and I wanted to spend more time with Kimiko, the closest and most understanding friend I had acquired overseas. I considered the possibility that it might also be my last opportunity to enjoy the lifestyle of a sailor, where my behavior, not always acceptable, was more apt to be condoned. So I tried to do it all that final week. It was like shaking off that last bit of adolescence before entering the world of adulthood. It was past time for me to act more like the adult I wanted to be, but I was not quite prepared to let go — not just yet.

With only a couple more liberty days remaining, I had the duty and was catching up on some much-needed sleep. I was awakened by the voices of two snipes arguing. MM3 Henry, nicknamed Happy, an experienced but underweight ruffian from New York and a friend of mine, was about to become overpowered by an angry sailor twice his size. Happy grabbed one of the many available bunk-chains from an unoccupied bunk, wrapped it expertly around his right hand, and he swung it menacingly in circles to his front and side.

I had been in my share of fights, more than my share, but what I was observing scared me. A bunk-chain could easily be used as a deadly weapon, and the harm it could inflict was sure to be severe and permanent.

"Knock if off, Happy; put down the chain," I heard myself say.

"You think I'm crazy?" Happy continued, "No way would I have a chance against that big bastard without this equalizer!"

Happy was right and wrong at the same time. Wrong in provoking the fight but right in that he was way out of his league. The serious look on his face spoke clearly to those of us witnessing the ordeal; no one should consider any attempt to get between them.

The larger of the two made his approach toward Happy, not readily accepting the dangerous situation he was in. Happy, an experienced street fighter, refused to back down. He swung that chain as if he were a martial arts expert. The steel hook at the chain's end repeatedly found its mark on the head and body of his opponent. Blood streamed from the many gashes caused by that hook. Happy kept yelling, "Get this big son-of-a-bitch away from me before I kill him!" Murder was not in Happy's mind, but his appeal, his call for assistance in stopping the fight before his outrage resulted in more serious damage, made good sense. The fight didn't last long, perhaps three or four minutes; bunk-chain-wielding Happy was the undisputed victor. I had heard of bunk-chain fights but I had never actually been witness to one prior to that night. I never wanted to see another one, and I sure as hell never wanted to become involved in one. I never did — and I never was.

The excitement of the evening did not end there, although what followed was as humorous as it was serious. Sometimes men with the duty would ask a shipmate to bring back a hamburger, a pizza, or some other snack when they returned from liberty. It was not much of an inconvenience, and the favor was reciprocal; at another time their roles would be reversed. Earlier that day, Fireman Jim Hedin had asked such a favor of a shipmate.

It's difficult determining what a sailor might do when he is awakened from a deep sleep, but it's almost guaranteed to create an unfriendly atmosphere if the one sleeping is grabbed or shaken. It was always safer standing to the side, behind one of the supporting bunk-chains, and then call the person's name in a low voice. Gently shaking the bunk would be the preferred next step. Jim's friend, a Good Samaritan of sorts, did as he had been asked. He returned to the ship with a decent meal for Jim. I don't know how Jim was awakened, but I do know that he came out of his bunk like an angered lion. He pounced upon his "prey" and proceeded to give him an unexpected and thorough thrashing. The poor guy on the bottom had little luck in his effort to explain who he was and why he had awakened Jim. It took about a minute before Jim became alert enough to realize what he was doing. Of course he was very apologetic, but the recipient of his onslaught made it abundantly clear that he would never make a "home delivery" again.

At the end of our final liberty night in Yokosuka, Tom and I returned to the *Colahan* together, each of us carrying two perfectly round watermelons. We went directly to the 0-1 level and positioned ourselves safely behind the protective plating surrounding Mount 42, where we proceeded to bombard the ship alongside with our well-ripened produce. Tom and I were having what we thought to be good clean fun as we watched each melon explode upon impact. We were not at all concerned about the chunks of rind and the sticky mess someone on our sister ship was going to have to clean up. The knowledge of our activities spread quickly, and within moments we had a full-fledged watermelon rind-flinging contest between several of that crew and the two of us, each side fully intent on making sure every chunk of rind was quickly thrown back on board the ship from where it came. It was always interesting to note how Tom and I retained our good dispositions, smiling or laughing all the while, when our opponents were invariably angered. The *Colahan*'s OOD took it upon himself to investigate, intent on locating the instigators, and to put a stop to it before it spread into some kind of riot. Tom and I must have looked downright foolish as we crouched behind the gun mount, surrounded by chunks of watermelon rind, thinking we were well hidden and wouldn't be found. The OOD walked directly to us. We explained how the watermelon attack had been "launched" intentionally by "them" and that we were rightfully and dutifully bound to "return fire" upon the "enemy." The OOD did not see the humor in our explanation, but he did allow us to "retreat" to our bunks. That was one of the

..s when we were actually caught in the act, but for some unknown ..son we were not placed on report.

On another occasion, Tom and I chose the same gun mount as we proceeded to launch an attack on our own quarterdeck, this time our weapon(s) of choice were small "pop-balls," peanut-sized explosive devices that detonated upon impact or when stepped on. As expected, we were caught that time too, and we were once again unexpectedly forgiven. Sometimes there was strong evidence — times when some officers appeared to be disappointed that they were educated to be officers and gentlemen first, that they could not be willing participants in the foolishness enjoyed by enlisted men. It was expected of us — although it was generally not condoned.

Shortly after returning to the States I was again promoted. That second-class crow felt good, and with it came added responsibilities. I remained assigned to the after engineroom, but my underway watch-station became that of top watch. I became responsible overall for the proper operation of all after engineroom machinery. I also became responsible for the training, the casualty control procedures that were to be followed by all watchstanders in my section, and for making proper decisions in ordering variations of machinery configurations to ensure maximum reliability and efficiency of the plant. I became responsible for the machinery history log, in which I had to maintain accurate and up-to-date entries regarding preventive or corrective maintenance accomplished on all engineroom machinery. That was my first taste of the administrative side of engineering. Somewhat to my surprise, I enjoyed it.

The year that followed, very little changed. The routines that were followed at sea and in port were either repeat performances or variations of things I had experienced in the past. There was very little variation. Toward the end of our six-month Stateside assignment, we went through the rigors of underway training, after which we were once again deployed to the Far East. While en route, somewhere between Midway Island and Japan, the lube-oil purifier failed. That was one piece of machinery that was known to cause problems and therefore needed to be watched continuously. The purifier was in constant use except during brief periods of time when it was being cleaned. It constantly circulated several hundred gallons of oil to and from the sump under the main-engine reduction gears as it removed impurities by centrifugal force as the oil passed between thirty or so cone-shaped discs. Once in awhile, usually as a result of heavy swells, the purifier would lose its "seal." The result, its failure to purify, was usually corrected quickly by priming it with water. The worst result from the loss of its seal was for the purifier to overflow oil directly to the bilge. The worst happened on my watch, and we were not alerted to the problem right away. The ship had been cruising at the same speed for hours. Under such ideal conditions watchstanders were more apt to become less attentive to their responsibilities. Little could go wrong, since steam supply and demand remained fairly constant. All of us on watch had congregated in the vicinity of the throttle board, and we were discussing our upcoming liberty expectations, a subject that easily distracted us from the more important duties at hand. After a prolonged period of time, the messenger reported a very low oil level in the main-engine sump. Sure enough, the level was dangerously low; the unnoticed malfunctioning lube-oil purifier had lost its seal and had pumped nearly all of the oil from the sump directly into the bilge. Under normal conditions, the replenishment of lube-oil was accomplished through the process of "striking down" from fifty-gallon drums up on the main deck. That was usually an in-port function and it was time-consuming. It would have been difficult and dangerous to attempt that procedure while the ship was underway. Besides, if I had to replenish the loss of oil I would have to explain how the loss occurred. My explanation, if I were truthful, would be self-incriminating. Being inattentive to all plant parameters while on watch was inexcusable. My immediate order was to modify the suction piping on the purifier, attach a hose to that piping, and "purify" the oil out of the bilge back into the main-engine sump. It was, as far as I was concerned, an act of genius, and it worked flawlessly. Before the end of our watch the sump oil level was fully restored and no one outside our small group of watchstanders was any the wiser.

At sea we spent ample time preparing and maintaining our best liberty uniforms; making sure they were always in good repair and that they would satisfy the strictest of uniform demands enforced by any OOD. Special attention was also given to the care of our liberty shoes. I was surprised when I learned of the burning method of preparing liberty shoes. They would first be covered with lighter fluid and immediately ignited with a match. The momentary, not-to-be-overdone, burning process hardened the leather and made a more permanent shine possible. When I saw one shipmate overdoing the burning procedure, I openly laughed at him. He was unappreciative of my expression of ridicule and he assured me that he knew precisely what he was doing. He continued spraying the already well-cooked, flaming shoes with additional Zippo lighter fluid. Finally, after blowing out the dying flame, he held one shoe up in front of me and proudly stated, "Now that's absolute perfection!" Then, as he held that shoe by the toe in one hand and by the heel in the other, he flexed the shoe — and it immediately broke in two.

"Yeah, that's perfection all right," I laughingly agreed.

His words, "Well fuck it," did not adequately express his frustration and embarrassment, as he discarded the shoe off to one side.

Another shipmate painted his shoes. The heavy coat of wet black paint was impressive. The shoes reflected remarkably clear images and he was quite proud of their superb gloss. He then took his shoes down into the engineroom and placed them near the incoming draft of a ventilation blower, believing the air would assist the paint in drying. The following day when he retrieved his shoes he was more than disappointed; he was shocked at his "creation." The shoes looked more suede than anything else; they were covered with multicolored particles of dust, lint, and other substances that were always present in the engineroom. His visible disappointment fed our appreciable amusement.

Lighter fluid served another useful purpose. It was also great for cleaning ribbons. Masking tape was used for removing lint from our uniforms, and a toothbrush was great for cleaning the white piping on the sleeves and flaps of our dress jumpers.

At sea we utilized some of our spare time sewing up torn or damaged work uniforms and skivvies. We were proud of our handiwork. The older and more faded the garment, and the more visible the sewing/patchwork, the more proud we were wearing it. My dungarees and my shirts were extremely faded and paper thin, and I never hesitated wearing them. In fact, the more comments I received as to their appearance, the prouder I became. I enjoyed displaying the unprofessional side of my attitude; a bad example to follow, that of not caring and of having very little pride. It was a way of expressing my disliking for Navy ways in general.

There was one guy, some kind of cleanliness freak, who had a heck of a time using the toilet while the ship was underway. He absolutely refused to sit on the seat, no skin-to-toilet contact. It was a joke watching him as he tried to balance, bracing himself between stall partitions while attempting to relieve himself. I once told him that if he ever shit anywhere other than in the toilet bowl I would personally volunteer to clean it up, and I would use him as the cleaning medium.

I had not been back to Subic Bay, Philippines, since that flight from Treasure Island, fresh out of Boot Camp. My memory of Subic Naval Base provided me with no interest in returning there, but since it was on the *Colahan*'s itinerary I knew that I would make some attempt to learn more about the area. I wanted to make the best of my final days in the Far East.

Since I thought of Olongapo as nothing more than a small, filthy town with little to offer, I spent most of my time on base. The EM Club and other recreation facilities provided ample opportunity to participate in a variety of healthy activities. I saw no reason to cross "Shit River," just outside the main gate, and walk the streets of Olongapo. I had a good memory, and I believed the rumors about how dangerous it could be off base, mingling with the locals.

The base was well protected by strictly enforced tight security measures. The black Aeta, an aboriginal pygmy people of the Philippines and descendants of the earliest Negritos, the term by which they were more popularly known, were allowed unrestricted access to the base. Their authorization to enter the base and sell their handmade products had been negotiated as part of the base agreement; a portion of the base was situated on land they owned. The Negritos roamed the base practically naked in their flimsy but colorful native garb. They were always equipped with a good supply of crude but sturdy handmade weapons that they sold as souvenirs. They spoke their own language, and many were unable to converse in Tagalog, the national language of the Philippines. The Negritos were a fascinating people and I wanted very much to learn more about them.

One morning Marcel and I spent an hour or more as we tried to hire a taxi driver that would take us to a mountainous jungle area that was known to conceal a Negrito village. Some drivers were more than reluctant, they appeared to be afraid of approaching or entering the Negritos' domain, an area on which the drivers claimed we had no business trespassing. The more common excuse was that there was a language barrier and it would not be wise to violate the sanctity of the Negritos' privacy without being able to communicate with them; a preconcluded dangerous disadvantage. None of the objections discouraged Marcel or me. We knew what we wanted and we were intent on finding someone willing to assist. Eventually we found that person — a taxi driver of Negrito descent, and one proficient in their language.

Surprisingly, the distance we traveled by taxi was relatively short, but it was quite time-consuming. The road was plagued with hairpin curves. Our safety-conscious driver took his time and exercised good judgment as he carefully negotiated the many sharp turns en route.

As if by instinct, since there were no noticeable landmarks, the driver knew exactly when and where to pull his cab off to the side of the road. He nonchalantly told us that we were there. There was absolutely no evidence of life around us other than the thick tropical jungle on both sides of the road. We were assured that "this is the place" so we got out of the cab, cameras and extra film in hand. We were immediately faced with our first disappointment when the driver insisted there were to be "no cameras!" He explained that there was a superstition within the tribe that prohibited any outsider from taking pictures. We were to consider ourselves lucky just being able to enter an area and to see things, according to the driver, no sailors had ever before experienced.

I felt a strange nervous sensation as we wound our way back through the thick green tropical foliage. Marcel and I shared the same disturbing thoughts; that there was a very real possibility that we had placed ourselves in serious jeopardy, we were entering an area from which we might not exit. We had not disclosed our intentions with other shipmates, which meant no one would ever find our remains if we were to "disappear." Abruptly and unexpectedly, as we walked into something of a clearing, we found ourselves surrounded by a group of "little" dark-skinned people. I can only compare everything that we were surrounded by to images I had seen within the pages of *National Geographic* magazine. My heart jumped up into my throat as I felt a surge of excitement come over me. There were bare-breasted women, naked children of all ages, and the men were wearing nothing more than small flaps over their genitals.

One of the group stepped briskly up to us, and we were greeted. He was elderly and malnourished but someone of apparent distinction within his tribe. His eyes squinted intensely and inquisitively through barely opened eyelids; his face was well weathered, overly wrinkled from years of exposure to the hot sun and the humid Philippine climate. He was the Village Chief. The driver wasted no time in explaining our purpose in being there. The Chief looked almost pleased. He quickly turned to the villagers and issued his instructions. The women disappeared into the surroundings, per-

216

haps having been directed to do so, while the children brought forth a variety of handmade weapons. There were bows and arrows with authentic bird feathers for quills. There were leather quivers made from the hide of wild boars, and there were colorful blowguns of varying lengths with accompanying darts. The aging Village Chief took one of the bows, placed an arrow properly against the string of woven bark, and sent the arrow flying off into the dense jungle. Within moments one of the alert children retrieved the arrow and returned it to the Chief. That display of talent was repeated several times for our benefit.

Marcel and I used our driver frequently to obtain answers to our many questions. We were told that most of the weapons they were showing us would eventually be displayed with other handmade items where everything would be sold as souvenirs to sailors on the base. We questioned the variety of arrowheads and we were fascinated as we were informed of their many uses. One arrow tip consisted of a single square prong surrounded with numerous hand-cut barbs. Its purpose was to shoot fish. Another similar style had three equally spread barbed nails and was used specifically for killing birds. There was a well-flattened single spearhead-shaped tip that was for killing wild pigs. We had picked the right sequence in asking the significance of the different arrowheads. When we asked about the single remaining well-flattened, heavy-duty double-spearheaded tip, the Village Chief grinned from ear to ear and displayed a mouth full of jagged rotting teeth as he answered. The verbatim translation was chilling. "This kind is for killing people!" It was time for us to go! We bought everything the Chief offered for sale and we departed — rather hastily. We failed to ask what kind of people or under what circumstances such an arrow might have been considered necessary. No doubt his answer would have been interesting.

We returned our colorful souvenirs to the ship and stored them in the engineroom. On occasion temptation would get the best of us and we would put to use some of our handmade weapons. PO1 Boyd would have been totally aghast had he caught us target practicing with bows, arrows, and blowguns. Our target? The well-insulated DA tank in "his" engineroom was terribly abused as our convenient but unconventional target.

I had a distinct disliking for Olongapo, but eventually I did venture outside the confines of the base. I felt uncomfortable around Filipinos, probably because I had never associated with people of that race beyond the very few I had met in the Navy. I was, for reasons I can't explain, reluctant to cultivate friendships there. We were informed of the "Benny Boys." They were bisexual or homosexual, and their features along with their attire made them nearly indistinguishable from female hostesses. Benny Boys usually remained within a certain area of town, an area where uninformed sailors were occasionally known to be misled by what they thought were lovely and seductive "ladies."

Prices were cheaper in the Philippines than anywhere else I had been, yet I did very little shopping there. Woodcarvings and shells of all kinds were the predominant souvenirs, but dirt-cheap as they were, I didn't buy any. Instead, I elected to spend the ten-cent jeepney (also known as jitney) fare and go from Olongapo to White Rock Beach, where I could swim in the warm ocean water. One time, when three of us were at White Rock Beach, we met a very young Filipina, probably no more than thirteen or fourteen years of age. She seemed a little shy, and she didn't say much, but she followed us as we walked along the sands of the beach. One of the guys offered her a peso to take him into the bushes and have sex. I was more than surprised when she said, "Okay, but I hope my boyfriend doesn't catch us!" Off into the bushes they went, returning about fifteen minutes later. She looked somewhat disheveled, he looked quite satisfied, and I was concerned about the boyfriend (who never did show up). The actual cost of that brief sexual encounter, at the then-constant conversion rate of 3.8 pesos to the dollar, came to about twenty-six cents; enough money to provide the girl with several decent meals.

Olongapo was also known for the extremely high rate of venereal disease. Gonorrhea (clap), the most likely form of VD contracted there, was curable, but the most active strain had developed an immunity to conventional medication and it was not easily treated. Sailors were reminded time and time again about the hazards of unprotected sex, but they had minds of their own and many took their chances. Some commands, ours included, sanctioned the issuance of condoms and penicillin pills, options available to anyone intent on having sex. Unwittingly, the issuance and use of penicillin pills was one of the primary contributing factors that resulted in the hard-to-kill, highly resistant strains of VD found there.

I continued my studies during periods of time at sea, hoping for another promotion before the end of my enlistment. With my history of Captain's Masts and other infractions, I really don't know why I was recommended

218

for E-6, Machinist's Mate First Class. I took the exam along with other shipmates who, from a disciplinary point of view, were probably far more deserving of advancement than I. I PNA'd (Passed [but] Not Advanced) that exam. It was not uncommon to be PNA'd. In fact, individuals that were trying to advance in fields that were overloaded with competition expected it. It was not as common for those in critical fields such as mine, so I was understandably disappointed with the knowledge that I probably had not done all that well on the test. Anyway, I was getting out of the Navy so I shrugged it off.

Instructor Training? Why Me?

The *Colahan* encountered severe typhoon conditions during that deployment. I had never seen the sea that rough. The skipper passed the word on the 1-MC that there was to be absolutely no foot traffic on the main deck, and anyone finding it necessary to go forward or aft would only do so on the 0-1 level — while wearing a life jacket. During that storm Tom Mundy and I took a lot of footage with our 8mm movie cameras. That was the only way we could capture and provide proof positive that the swells were so gigantic and that the sea could be so dangerous. We took movies of the main deck awash from stem to stern, and the ship as it cut through the ocean more submerged than on the surface. We took ample footage of wave after wave crashing over the sides, completely covering and concealing the ship's fantail from view. We knew that the movies would be amazing, but we wanted our film to be even more spectacular. We wanted to be participants in the conditions we were filming. So we filmed our way aft without benefit of life jackets. They would have been too bulky and would have made it too awkward for us to carry out our intentions. We took turns filming each other as we made our way to the main deck on the fantail. Frequently we swapped cameras to make sure we captured as much activity as possible, and also to make sure that we had backup protection in the event one of our cameras or some film became damaged. So there we were, without life jackets or any other safety device, filming each other as we were literally washed back and forth across the fantail, protected only by the handrail netting — it being totally underwater more often than not. It was the most dangerous thing either of us had ever done. It was dangerous and stupid, yet we thrived on the excitement and somehow managed to come through it unharmed.

Following that deployment, the *Colahan* was selected to attend the Rose Festival in Portland, Oregon, an honor and a privilege granted to very few commands. It was an interesting and enjoyable trip as the *Colahan* made its way up the Columbia River. It was the first time the *Colahan* had been in fresh water. Seldom had I seen so many men topside other than at times they were required to be there — upon entering port. Everyone had their cameras in hand as they roamed the main deck and took pictures of the riverbanks and the terrain on both sides of the river. There were some stretches along the river where the differences between the Washington and the Oregon sides were amazing. The Washington side was much more mountainous and there were dense forests of trees and other greenery, whereas the Oregon side was more sparsely planted with less attractive forests on rolling hills — a more uniform terrain.

We were all surprised and disappointed to find that our Exec would not approve any overnight liberty to the crew while visiting Portland. We probably should have expected it, we being so aware of how the Exec ruled. One crewman was from Portland, his parents still lived there, and yet he too was denied overnight liberty. That sailor did precisely what I would have done — he disregarded the Cinderella liberty policy and elected to suffer whatever the penalty might be. His punishment turned out to be a period of time on restriction, the usual punishment for minor offenses.

In port, regardless of the port, every morning at precisely 0755 hours, all hands were treated with, "Now first call to colors," over the 1-MC. That was the reminder that in exactly five minutes the flag would be hoisted at the fantail. During "colors," the raising of the flag, all hands are called to attention and are required to maintain a smart salute toward the flag up until, "Now carry on," is passed over the 1-MC.

One morning, during our visit to Portland, one of the female visitors (they visited the ship during all daylight hours) was up on the bridge, in the pilothouse, one of several locations where the Duty Bos'n could access the 1-MC public address system. It didn't take a whole lot of encouragement — in fact, the female guest felt privileged when several of us, including the Duty Bos'n, suggested that she issue the "Now first call to colors" order. It was magnificent. Her voice was probably the most welcomed change ever to pass over the *Colahan*'s 1-MC. There were more men standing topside in anticipation of saluting the colors than ever before.

But our little prank did bring about an immediate reaction when the OOD, an ensign, quickly made his way up to the bridge and demanded to know, "Who was responsible for that!"

Three cheers to the girl when she stepped directly in front of the officer, her beautifully endowed chest unmistakably thrust out for his benefit as she snapped her rendition of a salute and exclaimed, "I am, Captain! Am I under arrest?" The red-faced ensign just grumbled something that suggested we better not encourage it again. That insignificant episode probably brought the crew's morale to an instant, all-time (but short-lived) high.

Portland was a beautiful place, and I enjoyed many of the festivities provided by the celebrated Rose Festival. There was an abundance of female companionship, but the girls could not understand the liberty policy any better than we could. It was embarrassing, being treated like youngsters, having a curfew imposed upon us in our own country!

Tom and I spent an evening of liberty at a bar in downtown Portland where we watched a championship fight on TV. While we were there, we met two couples, lawyers and their wives, who treated us with an uncommon respect. They insisted that we accompany them to several other nightspots where they insisted on paying for everything. At the end of the evening they graciously returned us to our ship. Larry Landgraver, one of the lawyers, and if my memory serves me correctly, a contender for the position of District Attorney, was kind enough to invite us to his country estate for dinner the following night. We accepted.

The Landgraver estate was absolutely beautiful. Larry himself had played a significant role in the design and construction of the home. We ate a delicious meal that had been prepared especially in our honor. The Landgravers walked us through their luxurious and spacious home as they pointed out things and areas they had personally designed. I was most impressed with their octagonal breakfast room that extended outward from the main house into their equally impressive backyard. Larry and his gracious wife told us of their many sightings of deer and other wildlife from the vantage provided there. It was a rare experience, meeting and being treated with such kindness by total strangers. That was one of those truly wonderful experiences relatively few sailors are fortunate enough to encounter.

That same year the *Colahan* was also approved for a port call at Vancouver, B.C., Canada. I had been there with my parents as a youngster but I had no recollection of much other than the ferryboat ride between Washington and British Columbia.

That first day in port, Ed, a fellow snipe, and I wasted no time in getting off the ship when liberty call was announced. We spent most of the afternoon just wandering around town window-shopping. The bars were different, something of a disappointment in that all of those we encountered were split three ways. That is, there were three different entrances, each for a specific clientele. The center doorway was for couples, while the doors to the left and right were for singles, ladies to one side and gentlemen to the other. I never learned what purpose was served in having such an arrangement, but whatever it was, it was easily circumvented as introductions took place just outside — after which the new acquaintances were free to enter the couples section.

It was quite late in the afternoon as Ed and I exited the men-only side. We initiated a conversation with Rose, a very attractive Indian girl who was standing outside. She wanted to join us at another place where all three of us could drink together. Unfortunately, Ed and I were short on cash.

"That's Okay," she nonchalantly said. "Just wait for me here on the corner and I'll be back with some money within an hour!"

We had nothing to lose so we decided to wait.

222

Rose walked a short distance down the block, then turned and waved to us as she entered a fairly decent appearing hotel.

About thirty to forty minutes passed before Rose returned as she had promised. She was all smiles as she waved a fistful of Canadian money in front of us.

"Where'd you get all the money?" I asked, even though I really didn't care.

"I'm not a very nice girl!" Her response left little doubt as to what services she had been paid for performing; but she seemed so young. The Orient was more like a different world, where one expected to see, or was more aware of, teen prostitution. Canada was too much like home; it mirrored the United States, where teen prostitution, though not unheard of, was never openly solicited.

Rose suggested we buy a bottle of lime-flavored vodka and that we go to one of the "bottle clubs" where we could relax together as a threesome; a place where we would only be required to buy ice and mix since we would have our own booze. She stuffed her money into my jumper pocket and said, "Here, it's all yours. There's lots more where this came from."

I had never tasted lime-flavored vodka and I was surprised to find that I liked it. Again, at Rose's suggestion, we mixed it with a form of ginger ale — and it was refreshing. We talked about Canada and about the United States and about other countries sailors were known to visit. Rose was excited *and* she was exciting. Ed and I both had thoughts of bedding down with her, but for the moment we did not know which of us would end up the lucky one. A three-way "sandwich job" was not a consideration.

After finishing off the bottle of vodka we continued on into the night walking the streets. It was early morning and all of the stores were closed, but Rose wanted to continue walking. Probably somewhere around 2:00 A.M. one of us suggested that we should get a hotel room for what little time remained of the night. Rose agreed. In fact, she took us to one that wouldn't cost us an arm and a leg.

The three of us got a room that was about twelve stories up. Ed and I were still wondering which of us, if not both of us, was going to make it with Rose. But Rose became something of a different person once we were all in the room. The vodka had caught up with her, and she started feeling sorry for herself. Our efforts to calm her, to stop her from her incessant crying jag, was useless. Ed and I were frustrated — and a bit concerned

223

that someone in the hotel might complain. And what action might be taken against us, two sailors in the room with one, possibly under-aged, girl?

Rose told us she would be all right after she used the bathroom; it being a short distance down the hall and around the corner of the adjacent room to the left.

Ample time passed and Rose did not return. Our first and most logical thought was that she had left us; possibly for "greener pastures." But when we checked and found that the bathroom door was locked, we had good reason to believe she was still there. We knocked on the door but there was no response from within. We then figured that she probably passed out, or she was no longer interested in sharing time with us.

I don't know what caused me to go to the window in our room other than the fact that I knew the bathroom window could be seen from there. There was only one room between the corner and ours — and the bathroom was just around that corner. Maybe I thought she could hear us if we called out the window, but what I saw still brings cold chills to my body. Rose was sitting on the ledge of the window, legs dangling outside. Her head was leaning over her torso, and she was looking down at the cement alleyway that had instantly taken on the appearance of miles, instead of floors, below. Her hands rested on both sides of her, on the windowsill, where she was seated, a place and situation that would offer little resistance if she were to intentionally or unintentionally lean beyond her point of balance.

I frantically called Ed to the window as I waved my pointed finger, "I think we're in bad trouble!"

"Jesus, Ad, how are we gonna explain this if she jumps?"

Our quick assessment of the situation determined the need for immediate action in one form or another. We probably should have alerted the desk clerk — and we should have asked for police assistance — but we elected to do otherwise. Ed would attempt gaining entrance through the bathroom door while I was to make an attempt to reach her from the very narrow eight- or ten-inch ledge that formed a part of the building's architecture. The ledge was in line and level with all of the windowsills on that floor.

I was able to hold on to the brickwork as I inched my way along the ledge, and as I stood just outside of the neighboring window a terrible thought gripped me. *What if the occupant or occupants see a figure outside this window? What action will they be most apt to take?* I never thought about the possibility of the more immediate threat — that of losing my own balance.

I saw Ed's arms scoop around Rose from behind as he pulled her back inside the bathroom out of my view. My relief at her rescue did not abate the fear I had of falling backwards off of the ledge; meeting instant death upon impact so many floors below. My heart pounded as I slowly inched my way back to my window. Once I was safely inside I collapsed into an overstuffed chair, thoroughly exhausted from the overexertion and anxiety I had experienced.

Ed had already returned to the room and he was standing guard over Rose. Once he saw that I was all right he called it quits for the night.

"I've had it! I'm going back to the ship," he said rather angrily.

I should have gone with him, but I was afraid of leaving Rose there alone. I knew that if she were to carry out her suicidal thoughts, if she actually jumped, it would not have been difficult locating the two sailors that had last been seen with her. It would have been difficult, if not impossible, proving where we were when she fell. How could we have proven that she died as a result of her own conduct and not as a result of her having been pushed or thrown from the window.

Rose and I talked for awhile before we finally crawled into bed together. I learned that she was a homeless runaway and that she had to prostitute herself in order to survive. She needed far more help than I was capable of providing, but I was truly concerned and sympathetic about her situation. The only thing I could offer or do for her was to show her the best time possible for as long as I was there.

That morning I took her to the ship and showed her "my" engineroom, where all of my engineering buddies admired my catch. Rose talked to all of us about her dream to move to the United States. She spoke quite seriously of her desire for us to smuggle her to San Diego!

"I'll make you guys happy on the way," Her words left no doubt as to what services she was willing to provide in return for passage as she continued, "Whenever, wherever, and however you want it!" We actually discussed the possibility as we took into consideration all that such an endeavor would entail. We considered the prospect in more favorable terms, the "probability factor" of pulling off such a caper. Food was no problem — we could each take small portions from each meal so that she would always have sufficient food. Concealing her down in the engineroom would be a problem because of the extremes in temperature. She shrugged that off as insignificant when compared to her strong desire to go with us. We jokingly argued about who would be responsible for dumping her own specially assigned "shit can." Regardless how near we came to doing it, we knew that it was far too risky. Keeping a secret of that magnitude just wasn't within the realm of possibility. So we turned Rose down.

When I felt that my remaining Navy days were deserving of advertising, I adorned my dungaree trousers with a short-timer's chain. As it grew shorter with each passing day I became more and more possessed with the idea of getting out of the Navy and earning my way as a "free" civilian. I enjoyed flaunting my short-timer attitude much to the displeasure of the career-minded personnel, the lifers, around me. I would go out of my way to awaken shipmates in the middle of the night, intentionally irritating them with my incessant questions: "Who's short?" or, "Guess how many days I have left?" The more upsetting my attitude was to them, the more I enjoyed flaunting it. But the fact was, I really was nearing the end of my service contract and I could not have been happier about it. I began intentionally irritating the MPA, the Main Propulsion Assistant (assistant directly under the Engineer Officer), with my daily entries to the machinery history log. I concluded each day's entries with a very short one-liner that clearly stated how many days I had remaining in the Navy. I thought it was "cute," constantly reminding one of my officer leaders of my short-timer's attitude. Periodically, whenever the MPA reviewed the log, he would date and initial it thereby certifying his official visit. Once, after he had thoroughly scrutinized my entries to the log and it had been returned to me, I noticed that he had initialed it as usual but he had also written the following note; "No comment on number of days remaining." My attitude, with so very few days remaining on my enlistment, had taken a strong hold and I made another entry directly below the MPA's. "No comment was necessary!"

Everyone departing had their own way of leaving some reminders of their having served on board. M.D. Adams had stamped his initials in the top of the Main-engine lube oil strainer with a steel lettering set, a permanent reminder to all future lower-level watchstanders that at one time someone with the initials *MDA* had been there. I left my own *PLA* permanently stamped very near the bottom of the main condenser, a place only the deepest of "bilge divers" would ever venture; a place that would probably never be seen again. The possibility that someone, by chance or by choice, or as a result of punishment, while cleaning the lowest portion of the bilge would see my initials, made the awkward and strenuous effort to imprint them

seem worthwhile. It was a manner of leaving my mark as o
me, probably in hopes that someday someone would wor
hell *PLA* was, having gone to so much effort in permanent
initials in such a remote location.

During my time aboard the *Colahan* I became known ... ... cartoon
caricatures I drew of fellow shipmates. There was always some sort of resemblance to the person depicted, however, my drawings were quite outlandish. They looked more like creatures from other galaxies, gruesome
and nonsensical. So as the end of my enlistment neared I spent as much
time as I could drawing pictures and drafting short notes — and I hid them
in every possible nook and cranny for future sailors to eventually come
upon. I spent hours hiding my notes and drawings mainly inside things that
I had to dismantle and then reassemble.

"PLA WAS HERE!" "WHAT THE HELL ARE YOU DOING IN
HERE? — PLA," and PLA, GONE BUT NEVER FORGOTTEN," were
my most common notes but the pictures that I painstakingly hid were all
originals. Thinking back, I wish I had kept some of the drawings; they were
truly a part of me.

Happy's enlistment was due to expire during the time the *Colahan* was
scheduled to visit Mazatlan, Mexico. My discharge date was several days
after the *Colahan* was due to return to San Diego, following to the Mazatlan
visit. I wanted desperately to be discharged on the same day with Happy so
that we could celebrate together — so I submitted a special request that I
desired to be transferred to the base (for separation) with him. Apparently
the command was fed up with me, because much to my surprise, my request was approved. That approval was all the authority the base needed in
order to process me out early. Happy and I were both released from active
duty and we were transferred to "Ready Reserve" status as full-fledged
civilians on December 3, 1958. That was two weeks prior to my expiration
of obligated active duty service and a month and a half less than a full four
year enlistment. I silently thanked God that I was no longer under mili
control and that I was free to get on with my life. I fully believ
would never be subjected to military discipline, that I would
associate with so-called lifers again.

9

ANCHORS AND EAGLES

I began attending classes at Bakersfield College shortly after being released from active duty. It wasn't easy keeping up with my studies because I had obligated myself to carry as many courses as were allowed. I not only wanted an education; I needed the supplemental income as guaranteed by the education provisions of the G.I. Bill. After school, I worked full time at a foundry where I was responsible for heat treating castings of a variety of different metals and alloys. I enjoyed working in the laboratory during periods of time the treatment furnaces were in use. There I conducted a variety of stress, ductile, hardness, and other metallurgical tests. The little time remaining in my twenty-four-hour day was carefully rationed between study time and sleep.

I attended three semesters at Bakersfield College studying criminal justice and criminal law. During the first semester I completed U.S. Government, the only course I lacked toward obtaining my high school diploma. I finally received my diploma four years after my high school classmates. In a worldly sense, based on my travels and experiences, I considered myself far more educated than those classmates who had graduated so long before me.

I began thinking about my age, my family status and what I was doing with my life. I was twenty-two years old and I was the father of two beautiful children; a daughter and a son. I lived in an uncomfortable, low-income, housing project and I was ashamed of the comparison between my place of sidence and the more desirable middle- and upper-class homes. I took a ful look around me and I began to realize how difficult it was going to me if I expected to achieve any real degree of success. It would take urthering my education before I could achieve a worthwhile degree

228

in any field of law, and then I would be starting at the bottom, competing in a world about which I knew practically nothing. I wanted to do well, but the competition in the civilian world had begun to overwhelm me. I knew of my potential, particularly in the Navy where I had done quite well, even with my record of violations of military policy. I had been promoted five times within four years, considered a noteworthy achievement and an accomplishment that was not achieved by a majority. It was time to have a serious talk with my family about our future. It didn't take long; the decision came quickly.

I found it strange that I never thought about the bad times I had experienced as a sailor, nor did I think about the multitude of questions I really should have considered. I never thought about how many times I might again be governed by a chain of command consisting of unfair or unqualified officers and senior petty officers; how difficult it might be, accepting or carrying out the orders given to me by such individuals. I didn't think about the life at sea I had already lived, a life of little privacy and chafing confinement, and that I would once again be restricted by a type of segregation — governed by rules that discouraged or prevented the cultivation of friendships where there were differences in grade or rank.

I was still young, but I no longer considered myself an adolescent. I had become a man at a very young age and I knew that I had to accept full responsibility for my actions. I did not allow myself to consider the more discouraging aspects of military life; rather, I thrived on thoughts of future promotions and the privileges that would come with them.

The decision was firm. I would reenlist in the Navy with full intentions on becoming a successful member of the military; thereby providing a better future for my family as well as for myself. That decision became an accomplished fact in 1960 when I reenlisted at the same grade I had previously held: E-5, Machinist's Mate Second Class. The only difference in my uniform was the addition of a single hash mark, which represented four years of military service already served.

It was not until I was actually wearing the uniform that the full impact of my decision began to unfold within my mind. Briefly, while walking across Long Beach Naval Station toward my new duty station, the USS *Cowell* (DD-547), I had uncomfortable second thoughts as to whether I had made the right decision. Was I really prepared to accept a way of life that I had resented and rejected so vehemently? I thought about Commander Keedy and chuckled at the remote possibility our paths might cross, and I wondered how receptive he might be, having me under his command once again. Quite unexpectedly my skin crawled as a vivid recollection of the *Colahan's* Exec and his immature, unacceptable conduct flashed before me. I could only hope that I would never see him or his likes again.

During that walk, I saw things that were familiar to me, but I began thinking of them in a different light. I realized that in the past I should never have taken for granted many of the things I was surrounded by. I began to think in more encompassing terms as I focused on the "big picture."

During my first enlistment I had been reminded frequently that I was not a "wheel," that I was merely an insignificant spoke. I had failed to consider the correlation between the two, that all spokes had to be properly fit and functional for the wheel to run true. The failure of a seemingly insignificant spoke would, in fact, reduce the capacity as it affected the efficiency and the reliability of the wheel; the wheel equating to every piece of machinery, every level of authority, every shop, every office, every ship, and virtually every thing. Without strong spokes, without each one fully supporting the purpose for which it was intended, whether simple or complex, the wheel would not function proficiently. I felt good as I came to the realization that being a spoke was far from being insignificant. I would always be a spoke to one degree or another, but as a petty officer I would also be expected, I would be required, to serve as a wheel. I realized that for me to function professionally I needed the best supporting spokes I could come by and/or mold. From that very moment I knew that I would never maliciously denigrate anyone as a worthless or trivial "spoke." Instead I would make sure that my subordinates were made fully cognizant of the fact they really were a valued, significant, and necessary contribution to the big picture. My thoughts on the subject concluded with, *Without spokes there can be no wheels.*

I continued walking toward Pier 7, where I knew I would find the *Cowell.* I thought about how lucky I was in that the *Cowell* was another destroyer of the same class as the *Colahan* and that I would already be familiar with the ship and its machinery. The only difference would be the unfamiliar faces that I would soon come to know. I also thought it something of a good omen, the hull number being 547, since the reduction of each of the *Colahan's* hull numbers (658) by one digit each resulted in 547. But of more notable coincidence was the fact that both destroyers had been commissioned on the same date; August 23, 1943. I was never superstitious, but I never overlooked things or signs that were extraordinary for one reason or another; things, signs, or other indications that might somehow be to my advantage.

As I walked I found myself in a world surrounded by anchors and eagles of all sizes and shapes. Nearly everything around me had one or the other mounted atop it or beside it, or a likeness permanently etched or carved into it. There were impressive replicas of anchors and eagles positioned at entrances, at exits, and at other locations where the presence of such symbols were deemed appropriate or in some way further enhanced their surroundings. The rating badge I was wearing, as with all Navy rating badges, consisted of an eagle perched with wings expanded, head facing the eagle's right. Undeniably it was not a "crow"; however, the word *crow* was the popularized descriptive term that was totally acceptable Navy-wide in identifying not the eagle on the badge, but rather the entire badge of every petty officer. I thought of the simplicity of an anchor and of the awesome power it had in holding a vessel fast. I thought of the anchor as the "wheel" at the end of a chain of "spokes"; and of how true it was that the chain was only as strong as its weakest link. I thought of the correlation between the strength and dependency of the anchor and its chain with that of the power and the authority and the incontestable responsibilities vested in all Commanding Officers, and the dependency and reliability they must have of their crew. Such thoughts caused an awakening within me, a change that would be of significant importance as I reentered a world for which I had previously held in such contempt. As I crossed the brow and approached the OOD, my orders in hand, my thoughts were clear. I knew how important it was for me to give it my best and to encourage, demand if I must, the absolute best of my subordinates. I had chosen that way of life and I would strive to make it better by virtue of my own hard work and professional attitude — a dramatic change from my past.

The USS *Cowell* carried with it the tradition of four wars; her namesake originated during the War of 1812, when the sloop *Essex* was undergoing heavy bombardment by several British men-of-war. Several officers had been injured, which necessitated the exercise of leadership by junior officers. Midshipman John G. Cowell assumed the position of Acting Lieutenant during the breakthrough. According to the battle report, Midshipman Cowell was mortally wounded; however, he remained at his position and exercised leadership throughout the encounter before he collapsed from loss of blood.

The original *Cowell* was a destroyer that fought in World War I. In 1942 she was given to Great Britain and renamed HMS *Brighton*. The *Cowell* I was reporting to was commissioned on August 23, 1943, at Bethlehem Shipbuilding Corporation, San Pedro, California. Shortly after completing her shakedown cruise, the *Cowell* joined the Pacific Fleet.

The *Cowell's* characteristics included an overall length of 375 feet; extreme beam, 39 feet; full load displacement, 2,900 tons; maximum speed, thirty-five knots; and cruising radius, 4,800 miles.

Engagements with Japanese forces were many, for the *Cowell* participated in every major operation conducted after January 1944. Notable among those were air and surface strikes against the Marianas, New Guinea, the Philippines, and Formosa (Taiwan). Cited for her performance during the Okinawan campaign, the *Cowell* received the Presidential Unit Citation. She destroyed twenty enemy aircraft with her guns.

The *Cowell* remained as a unit of the occupation forces prior to her returning to the United States for inactivation in July 1946. She was recommissioned in July 1951 for service with the Atlantic Fleet and was assigned to DesDiv (Destroyer Division) 282. The *Cowell* completed a six-month assignment during the winter of 1952 with the Seventh Fleet in Korean waters, where operations against enemy troops, ammunition depots, and land communications were conducted.

In January 1955 the *Cowell* changed her home port to Long Beach, California, where she became a unit of DesDiv 192. Since joining the Pacific Fleet, she had, up to the time I reported for duty, completed a tour in the western Pacific every year.

Upon reporting aboard I was immediately assigned to M Division, and therewith came my first disappointment; I was assigned to the forward engineroom. The machinery configuration was different than it was in the after engineroom, but otherwise the plant functioned exactly the same. My second disappointment came when I was placed "in charge" of the lower-level with duties and responsibilities I had exercised as an E-4. It was not easy backsliding (my opinion). It made it easier accepting my assignment when I thought about Machinist's Mate First Class Boyd, and how he had turned an entire engineroom into a showplace, whereas all I had as a primary concern was the lower-level — less than a third of the overall area of the entire space.

Machinist's Mate First Class Herman, a well-qualified MM, was in charge of the forward engineroom. Herman took everything that related to his space seriously and he expected the men under him to do likewise. It took very little time, a month at most, before my efforts were recognized and, I, too, became an example to follow. The lower-level outshined the rest of the engineroom in all respects, and Herman expected similar results from the rest of his men. I appreciated his compliments, they made me feel good, but deep inside I knew that I had actually made myself feel good. I appreciated his recognition when he commended me on the results of my efforts, but it was my own strong drive, my own motivation, and my own desire to do my best, and then seeing the results that truly made me feel good about myself.

January 17, 1961, the *Cowell* prepared to get underway. "Daddy K," as Chief Knadler was frequently referred to, the chief in charge of M-Division, asked me on what underway watch-stations had I previously qualified. I assured him that I was thoroughly qualified on all stations but I was probably most experienced as throttleman.

"Okay, Ad, take 'er out!" The chief's words, his verbal assurance of apparent trust in me, were music to my ears. I stood proudly at the throttle board, carefully scanning all of the numerous gauges and monitoring devices, making sure I was fully cognizant of all plant parameters. I wondered if one of the gang, perhaps the chief himself, might shut the isolation valve to one or more of the gauges as a test of my alertness — the "customary" procedure on board the *Colahan*.

I have neglected to explain an important mechanical feature relevant to the situation I was about to encounter. I had qualified on board the *Colahan*, where I learned all there was to know about the throttle board. Throttle valves were opened and closed by turning the large wheels at the throttle board, they being attached to universal jointed linkages and shafts that led to the steam valves at the main-engine turbines. Each wheel at the throttle board measured one to two feet across, similar in appearance to the helm on a sailing vessel but without handles. The efficient control of steam to the engine turbines required that there be three separate throttle wheels. One of the wheels was used for the sole purpose of allowing the flow of steam to pass through the astern turbines — thereby causing the ship to back down as with reverse in a car. The other two were used for

233

providing steam to the ahead turbines. Each throttle had a feel of its own, a consideration of supreme significance to the throttleman. In an emergency situation the throttle man might be called upon to respond without benefit of monitoring devices by which he could otherwise gauge his actions. I want to emphasize the fact that I had an abundance of experience and I was very proficient, a master on the throttles. I had previously learned exactly how many turns it would take on each of the throttle wheels in order to compensate for whatever speed the bridge demanded. The astern throttle, used primarily for unusual maneuvering such as entering or leaving port or anchorage and for "parking" pier-side or alongside another vessel, was the easiest to open and close. With little more than a flick of the left wrist, arm assisted, the astern throttle wheel would spin open counterclockwise just enough revolutions to provide a strong shot of steam to the astern turbine. In closing the throttle, it spun with even greater ease, thereby assuring that it closed quickly and it sealed tightly.

USS *Cowell* — Fletcher Class Destroyer
December 1960 to September 1961

The *Cowell* was fully prepared to get underway, and I stood at the throttles patiently waiting for that first bell from the bridge. I was prepared to respond quickly, without hesitation, regardless of speed or direction ordered. I was anxious to show the skills I had acquired aboard the *Colahan*. While I was waiting for that first order from the bridge, it was necessary to rotate the main-engine shafts one and a quarter turn every three minutes as a precautionary measure; to prevent damage or distortion to turbine shafts.

"Request permission to spin main engines, Chief?" I said.

"Granted, spin main engines as necessary," Chief Knadler responded.

Understand that the *Cowell* was still snugly in place at Pier 7 with all lines securely tied from ship to shore as I proceeded to spin that astern throttle wheel with the zeal of a true professional. I allowed just enough time for the necessary shot of steam to start the shaft rolling, and immediately spun it shut — just as I had done thousands of times on board *Colahan*. I turned to the chief, who was unusually wide-eyed, and heard him yell directly in my face, "Close the throttle!"

"I did, Chief, I spun it shut." I half-smiled at the chief, thinking he had never seen the skills I had so masterfully exhibited. I should never have taken anything for granted. Had I followed correct procedures, had I looked at the astern turbine pressure gauge instead of assuming I had shut the throttle, I would have known better.

The chief knocked me out of his way and he hastily proceeded to shut the astern throttle. It never entered my mind what I should have instinctively known, that no two throttle valves felt or operated the same. I had simply spun the slack out of the valve mechanism without even beginning to shut off the steam supply to the astern turbine. I was very fortunate in that as the port screw churned and the ship strained to back down, the mooring lines held fast.

"Adkisson, get your ass out of here – you're relieved of throttles!" The chief's words stung; not even a day at sea, and I had already made a fool of myself. There was no excuse for my mistake, and I knew that it was going to take quite some time and a great deal of effort before the chief would again show that he had confidence in me.

I was very surprised to find that during my break in military service, eggs to order had become a daily breakfast routine instead of Sundays only as I vividly recalled. Someone high up had finally realized the importance a sailor placed on his stomach. The meals on the *Cowell* were cooked with taste as well as with nourishment in mind. And "midrats," midnight rations, were prepared and served in much the same manner as any daytime meal. There was actually an ongoing effort throughout the Navy to make life at sea less arduous and more comfortable; a realistic approach for which I was completely unprepared – but I eagerly welcomed.

When there was little else to occupy my time I usually found myself visiting in the after engineroom, where I always felt more comfortable. I missed the after hole; it had been my home for nearly four years while I was stationed on board the *Colahan*.

Pinhead, a nickname similar to his real name Pinnell, was the Machinist's Mate First Class in charge of the aft engineroom, and I wasted no time in developing a friendship with him. Pinhead was right out of a storybook, a sailor's sailor. He was 100 percent "salt" from head to foot. His upper torso and his arms were covered with the fading remains of what once must have been remarkably colorful tattoos. He always wore his own distinctive device, a shark's tooth, dangling from a gold chain around his neck. He also wore a large gold earring in his pierced ear when he was ashore and in civilian attire. Pinhead's sense of humor made up for the lack of it in Herman. They were not rivals, nor were they competitive in their duties. Each was responsible for his own engineroom. Pinhead's ability to grab everyone's attention by telling interesting yarns was a constant irritant to Herman. Pinhead would exaggerate, twist, reverse, condense or expand his stories, all in the interest of maintaining an inquisitive and alert audience. He was a genius at confusing whomever he chose, and I was intrigued by his exceptional ability to do so. I would watch him intently as he talked. His stories always started out with a reasonable description of something totally believable. Then little by little, after drawing the full attention of an entrapped audience, as his stories unfolded they would begin to fall apart and would invariably reveal some nonsensical trap he had success-fully suckered everyone into believing.

MM1 Pinnell was a hardworking sailor, as much or more so than any-one I had ever met. He took his job seriously and he preferred, whenever possible or practical, to accomplish tasks at hand himself rather than assign the work to someone else. He knew it would be done right the first time that way. Pinnell's knowledge of the engineroom and of its machinery was impressive. He knew what had to be done, why it had to be done, and, most importantly, how it was to be done. Pinnell's mind worked much the same as mine had in the past. He exercised his devilish imagination whenever possible while I, with my newfound acceptance of responsibility and devotion to duty, had become more inclined to curtail mine.

On one occasion I entered the berthing compartment and found Pinnell chuckling half to himself and half out loud as he reached well into the depths of Herman's upright locker. I startled him when I approached from his blind side. He immediately pressed his index finger to his lips, indicating that I was someplace I shouldn't be, that he was up to no good, and that I should keep my mouth shut – keep whatever I had seen, a secret.

"What the hell are you up to now?" I asked.

"Jesus, Ad, don't bother me; I'm fixin' to drive Herman crazy!" he answered in a prophetic whisper. Then, not being able to withhold from showing me his latest form of trickery, Pinnell chuckled mischievously as he took the time to demonstrate his handiwork. But first, in order to appreciate that demonstration, it must be realized that whenever Herman was in his bunk, his head rested within inches of his locker. Pinnell reached back into Herman's locker and retrieved a round, approximately four-inch-diameter metal fruitcake container. He removed the lid and proudly showed me the few loose marbles in contained. The idea was that when Herman turned in for the night he would hear the irritating sound created by the balls rolling around inside the round metal canister. The level of noise induced would be directly proportional to the rocking of the ship. It was a brilliant idea and one of which I fully approved. So Pinnell carefully put the lid back on the container. He was trying to conceal it in the farthest, most difficult place to reach; his arm stretched as far into the back of the locker as he could reach, when Herman unexpectedly showed up!

Getting into someone else's locker without his prior consent was never condoned. Thieves were plentiful in the Navy, and lockers were always a prime target. It was very rare that a thief actually got caught in the act of breaking into someone's locker, but in Herman's eyes – he had caught Pinnell red-handed.

"Pinhead, you son of a bitch, I caught you! What the fuck do you think you're doing?"

With the dumbest expression imaginable, Pinnell just looked at Herman and said, "Uh, nothin', pally. Just checkin' to make sure everything's shipshape."

"Well, by God, everything better be shipshape or I'll have your ass!" Herman said dead seriously as he jerked Pinnell away from the locker. Herman then conducted a search of his locker and he quickly found the device. Following a few moments of absolute silence, scowl on his face, he leaned slightly toward Pinnell and said, "You know, Pinhead, one of these days yer gonna go too far!" Herman, tight-jawed, slammed his locker door shut and spoke once again as he turned to leave. "I mean it, goddamn it!"

Pinnell was having a difficult time holding back his laughter. He very sheepishly responded, "Gee, I'm thorry I upthet you, Hermie."

Unimpressed at Pinnell's intentional quip, Herman spun around one final time, but only to glare at Pinnell for another second or two.

It was fun being around Pinnell; his work hard, play hard attitude was right in line with mine, and he didn't exercise his authority unnecessarily, as did other E-6s. He had the loyalty and full backing of his men much the same as M.D. Adams and MM1 Boyd. Pinnell never threatened anyone with anything other than his middle finger, and that finger was used for much more than an obscene gesture. That finger was inflexibly strong and hard as steel. When Pinnell needed to get someone's undivided attention he poked that finger into the chest of inattentive individuals enough times and with sufficient force to cause acute pain – sometimes causing noticeable bruising. It was quite an effective means of grabbing the absolute attention of anyone. No one ever challenged Pinnell's methods. He was too well liked.

On occasion Pinnell shared his liberty time ashore with his men. On one such occasion several snipes, Pinnell the senior member of the group, decided to have an all-night party at Balboa Park. Plans were quickly formulated as we all chipped in for the purchase of two cases of cold beer. We knew that the park would provide us absolute privacy. No one other than occasional transients ever entered or remained in the park overnight. There would be no traffic, no phones, nothing to interfere with our little gathering. There were a total of five of us in the group, and since we couldn't find a cabby that would violate the four-passenger limit we had to hire two cabs to take us to the park. Pinnell, with the two cases of cold beer, rode in the back seat of one of the cabs. We met at the park as planned, watched the cabs disappear into the night, and we began searching for that perfect spot where we could party.

"What the hell, let's have a beer," came the words we all wanted to hear.

"Oops," came Pinnell's single-word response.

"Wha' d'ya mean, 'oops'?" came my words.

So there we were, stuck in the park with several hours of darkness remaining, nowhere to go and nothing to do, with Pinnell's unacceptable explanation that he "forgot" the beer! We probably made some cab driver very happy that night. We also made sure Pinnell never forgot that night and his inattentive performance.

Credit where credit due, Pinnell was also a talented artist. His drawings were somewhat abstract and they usually depicted some supernatural form or being. They were gruesome drawings of bloody skulls, knives, and daggers, each awesomely detailed with unmistakable skill. It was Pinnell's hand, his pencil to paper, that designed the first *Cowell* plaque; voted on and accepted by the entire ship's company.

February 27, 1961, the *Cowell* headed west. It was to be my fifth overseas deployment – two years since my last taste of liberty in the Orient. I no longer entertained thoughts of instigating or participating in undesirable or unacceptable activities, however my sense of humor remained alive and active. Fighting was out of the question, although I knew that there could be circumstances under which I might not have much choice in the matter. I did not wish to take on the appearance of being a coward or of being too meek, nor did I wish to be known as a bad-ass or a bully. I knew there would be judgment calls and that sooner or later I would have to stand up and be counted for as a man fully capable of carrying his weight – but I was no longer interested in encouraging such situations.

As the ship pulled into Yokosuka, our first liberty port, I found myself wondering if Kimiko was still there. She would be first on my list of liberty priorities. I didn't know whether to hope that she was long gone, that she had found happiness away from her profession, or to hope she was still there so that we could renew that special friendship only she and I could fully comprehend and appreciate.

Kimiko was there and I spent a great deal of my liberty time visiting with her during the single week the *Cowell* remained in port. We both thought we would never see each other again, so we took advantage of every moment we could to fully apprise each other of our lives. We were both good talkers as well as good listeners. Questions and answers were always straightforward and honest. At that time I fully believed that Kimiko was the only person in the world with whom I could be totally honest. She understood me and I understood her – there was absolutely no reason to keep secrets from each other, so we entrusted each other with the most intimate details of our lives; things so private that we would never have considered sharing them with anyone else. I always felt comfortable when I was with Kimiko.

The *Cowell* was ordered to patrol the Taiwan Straits for the following three months. We were in and out of Kaohsiung, Taiwan, sporadically – sometimes for a day or more, sometimes only for a matter of hours. Cinderella liberty was the law while in Kaohsiung. Curfew was strictly enforced by the Taiwanese Chinese military police, supplemented with local civilian police. Curfew violators, though few and far between, were subject to severe punishment by the Chinese as well as by the U.S. Military Command. We had to time everything just right to make sure we were back aboard ship prior to midnight. It was also in our best interest to be on good behavior there, where tensions always ran high, and where the local police didn't care to accept our sense of humor – nor did they elect to exercise their own – if they had one.

On my first liberty I found that Katie was still working at the OK Bar and we picked up right where we had left off. I took her everywhere with me. We were inseparable. Shipmates poked fun at me for hanging out with Katie instead of with the guys, but I didn't mind; I enjoyed Katie's company and she enjoyed mine. Katie was always a tremendous help in negotiating the lowest prices on souvenir purchases. By sunset each day Katie and I usually ended up at the far side of town, across a river bridge, in one of the finer hotels.

Katie was much younger than Kimiko and she was far less experienced with life in general. She was fun to be with but not one with whom I cared to share stories of my life as I did with Kimiko. Katie was poor and she relied upon "Ski," the bar owner, for a meager allowance, a place to sleep, and meals. As was the case throughout the Orient, the more income generated by the hostesses, the higher the commission they earned. Hostesses in Taiwan could generate income by the number of ladies' drinks bought for them, the number of drinks clients bought for themselves, or a contract agreement; a fee paid for the "rental" of a hostess. The contract was the only recognized authority that legitimized girls being on the street with their American escorts. It was a violation of law for the girls to be without that document when in the company of any foreigner.

I tried to slip Katie a little extra money from time to time, bι reluctant to take it. She was terribly afraid that Ski would find oι was skimming and that he would then kick her out of the only shelter she knew. It would have been totally acceptable for me to give Ski the extra money and allow him to distribute it. That way he would be able to keep his percentage of "earned income." I was willing to help Katie, but not Ski. I always thought of him as being too greedy, vindictive, and without scruples. Because of her youth and inexperience, Katie was not receiving her fair share from the bar, and she knew it – but again, she feared Ski's retaliation if she were to complain.

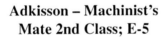

Adkisson – Machinist's Mate 2nd Class; E-5

I spent a lot of time teaching Katie how to read. She knew the alphabet but she needed a great deal of help with phonics. I did the best I could during the brief periods of time I had with her, and I was pleased at her progress. That was my first experience in providing assistance in the form of education/instruction in a foreign country, and I enjoyed my own self-satisfaction as much or more than the satisfaction my student clearly acknowledged. We both realized a certain degree of achievement.

May 17th was my final liberty day with Katie. I gave her my cigarette lighter with the ship's emblem attached, neatly wrapped in a ten-dollar bill, as a farewell gift. I insisted that she keep the ten spot – with or without Ski's approval. I did not want to know if she intended on sharing it with Ski. There were tears in her eyes as we embraced for the last time. I knew that her tears were not solely the result of my kindness or of my parting; they were also caused by her feelings of uncertainty – the many lonely tomorrows with which she would no doubt be faced. Who would be there after I left, to provide some degree of compassion along with that little bit of income necessary for another day's provision of food and shelter? But all bargirls were survivors, and I knew that Katie would manage just as others had for years and years before her time.

The Gold Dust Twins

The day after departing from Taiwan, the *Cowell* pulled into Subic Bay, Philippines, where she remained for several days. I had become a friend of another Paul, a Boiler Technician second class. Besides having the same first name, we shared the same birthday, we were similar in size and shape, and we were both E-5s. We knew that behind our backs we had been dubbed "the gold dust twins" because of our similarities along with the appearance that we were never in need of additional funds. We knew how to budget – and we occasionally made a little extra off of those who borrowed from us.

Paul and I became good friends and liberty partners while the ship was in Taiwan. Our likes and dislikes were also about the same. We were both husky and we were fully capable of taking care of ourselves should the need arise. Both of us had outgrown the desire to intentionally provoke others into any kind of physical confrontation.

Paul had spent a lot more time in Subic Bay than I had, and he knew his way around Olongapo City. I followed his lead and in no time at all I began to realize that liberty there was as good or better than elsewhere. I found that I liked Olongapo and much of what the city had to offer. Air-conditioned bars and nightclubs had become plentiful, and there was an abundance of beautiful women everywhere. Still, most of Olongapo was off-limits; the road leading from the main gate was about the only place a sailor could legitimately go. That road was lined on both sides with souvenir shops, a marketplace, and bars. There were always a wide variety of souvenirs, and the prices were almost too good to be true. The price of a cold beer in a decent place was less than a dime. The girls were free! There were no stringent rules governing them. Most girls worked out of their own club, but they were free to leave at any time with whomever they chose. They earned commissions regardless of their location; as long as drinks were served. The girls got 50 percent of the cost of their own beer and 10 percent of the cost of the guys' beer. They did not drink "ladies' drinks" of watered-down tea as was customary in other countries. The Filipino hostesses drank right along with their sailor companions, sometimes outdrinking them. It was not at all uncommon for the girls to get drunk right alongside their benefactors. Filipino women were really fun to be with. They refused to take life seriously. They lived for that particular day, for the moment, and they refused to worry about the past or the future. Tomorrow wasn't real, whereas the moment at hand was. The bad side was that most Filipinas were insanely jealous and dangerously protective of their turf. Their turf included their men. The information grapevine was flawless. All girls in all bars knew who belonged to whom and who was unattached or available. The determining factor was simple. The girls never asked for monetary compensation, whether their time was spent bar-hopping or in bed with a male suitor. If the guy accepted sexual favors and did not volunteer or offer payment, he automatically became hers! There was seldom any kind of problem as long as voluntary monetary compensation was made. The girls would not only fight among themselves over "ownership" of a man; they wouldn't hesitate to physically abuse any guy dumb enough to ignore their expectation of acceptable behavior. It was always safest to stick with one girl. I would observe some remarkable changes to these policies in years to come.

During that deployment the *Cowell* visited three ports I had not been to before; Buckner Bay and Naha Port in Okinawa, and Beppu. All were Japanese ports. We spent a couple of days in Buckner Bay and several more in Naha Port, where I found my surroundings a little different than I expected to find in Japan. Okinawa, under U.S. control, was more Americanized. Vehicular traffic remained to the right of the road, as in the United States and the Philippines, instead of to the left, as was customary throughout the rest of the Orient. There were several military bases on Okinawa and two major towns that catered primarily to satisfying the off-duty desires of U.S. Forces. Koza was the farthest from Naha Port, and Namanui was nearest. I preferred Namanui not only because of its close proximity to the ship, but also because I could enjoy a decent meal as I watched talented Kabuki dancers perform a variety of skits and plays at the Teahouse August Moon. The teahouse was situated on top of a beautiful knoll, surrounded by botanical gardens, right in the middle of Namanui. It was not the kind of place you would expect to find sailors; however, within a block of the teahouse there began a row of bars and clubs that were there specifically to serve the military.

Not all port calls allowed ample time for exploration. For example, our visit to Beppu, Japan, on July 17, 1961, was only an "overnighter." Many of us in the liberty section did go ashore, but we learned very little about the area except that it was not a port frequented by the Navy.

Over the next couple of months, the remainder of that deployment, we were in and out of Sasebo, Yokosuka, and Subic Bay. Paul and I took the time to visit Nagasaki, where, somewhat to our surprise, we observed a huge community fully recovered from the total destruction it had suffered when on August 9, 1945, the second atomic bomb had been unleashed. Rebuilt to modern specifications, Nagasaki had become the administrative, commercial, and cultural nucleus of the 35,000-square-mile island of Kyushu. In its shipyards some of the world's largest tankers were being constructed. Millions of people who used to fish for a living had converted their lifestyle to that of businesspeople; preferring to work in the offices of this sprawling metropolis.

244

While in Sasebo, Paul and I stopped at one of the many café/restaurants for our "meal of the day." One never knew whether there would be the time or even the consideration for another meal when bar-hopping had a tendency to take priority. We were off of the beaten path, but the place we were standing in front of looked as good as any others we had seen or been in. Two waitresses greeted us and we exchanged the customary polite bows of mutual respect as we entered. We were escorted to a nice but small booth toward the back of the place, right next to an open window. The slight breeze entering through the window felt good. I had never eaten authentic *sukiyaki*, so at Paul's suggestion we ordered enough for two.

Two waitresses scurried around and quickly gathered up all of the ingredients needed for the preparation of our meal. The vegetables were cooked on a small portable gas-fired grill in the middle of our table, and the inviting aroma stimulated our appetites as we toasted each other with beer. Periodically the attending waitresses poured small amounts of soy sauce from a teapot container as they stirred it into the veggies. I was never one to appreciate eggs that were not fully cooked, but at Paul's insistence I agreed to have the fresh-cooked veggies stirred directly into the raw egg in the bowl before me. I was assured that the heat from the vegetables would cook the egg "enough."

Paul and I were doing just fine, and we were working on our second or third helping when we both noticed "something" accompanying the soy sauce as the waitress continued to season more of the cooked vegetables. She quickly scooped whatever it was out of the preparation and tossed it out the window. I looked out the window and instantly recognized the "something" as one very dead carcass of one previously very healthy cockroach. As the waitress tried to grab the soy-sauce container, I intercepted. I looked into the pot and could not believe my eyes. I handed the pot to Paul and said, "You won't believe this!"

The entire surface of the soy sauce was covered with floating dead cockroaches! We had been eating, probably gorging ourselves with, vegetables well marinated in "juice du cockroach."

I think the term *pissed off* was more than appropriate for the occasion. Paul and I didn't create any kind of scene. We just got up and walked out without saying a word. One waitress caught us by surprise as we exited. With her very polite bow she said, "You please to come again, ne?"

245

Paul and I entered the first bar we came to and tossed down several straight shots of whiskey – the idea being that the alcohol would kill whatever disease-bearing bacteria we might have ingested.

Time at sea was usually uneventful except for the occasional extremes in weather conditions to which we were subjected. We had good weather between Japan and Hong Kong, our next eagerly anticipated R and R port.

While the ship was in Hong Kong I read a Navy release that announced the need for engineers in the Navy's rapidly expanding nuclear power program. I remember thinking what an opportunity it would be for me to gain an education in a field shared by the civilian world as much as or even more than within the Navy. I knew that if I was accepted into the nuclear program and successfully graduated therefrom, if I were to change my mind about making the Navy a career, I could easily utilize my nuclear skills in civilian industry. It was an opportunity I could not ignore.

My request to attend nuclear power school was favorably endorsed by the command and was forwarded to the Bureau of Naval Personnel for consideration. Meanwhile, I became subjected to envious ridicule by most of the snipes. I was repeatedly told by those around me that my request didn't have a chance of being approved. I was also told that I didn't have enough "smarts," that if I did attend nuke school I would never be able to keep up the pace – and I would follow in the footsteps of many others who had already tried; I would subsequently fail or drop out. Much to my disappointment, even Chief Knadler snickered at me and voiced a similar opinion instead of offering words of encouragement. *Who the hell are you,* I thought to myself, *thinking you know more about my motivation and capabilities than I?* I believed that given the opportunity I could do anything I set my mind to. With a little outside encouragement I might even surpass my own goals.

Within three weeks I received a favorable response to my request. With the approval came orders directing that I report to the U.S. Naval Nuclear Power School at Vallejo, California, no later than September 28, 1961. I was to become a student in Class 61-4, the last class to convene that calendar year. My shipmates assured me that I would be back on board in no time – after flunking out. I thought otherwise.

Nuclear power school was every bit as difficult as I had been led to believe it would be. Everyone became discouraged at one time or another. One man, I was told, had committed suicide in the very dormitory-style room

246

that I was then occupying. He had hanged himself from the
with his belt. There were stories of others that had failed in sim
to end their lives. I always set aside my frustration and studie
harder when things got tough. All students were required to maintain a 3.2
grade point average or they were dropped from the program. Considering
the courses of instruction, 3.2 was not an easy average to maintain. Within
the first six months we were force-fed courses beginning with basic math
and progressing rapidly through courses in algebra, geometry, calculus,
trigonometry, nuclear theory, physics, nuclear physics, chemistry, thermo-
dynamics, electricity, and electronics. I was no longer in a work hard, play
hard environment; it was all hard work and no time for play.

I did receive one unexpected bonus while attending school; I was promoted to Machinist's Mate first class, E-6, which meant more pay but nothing else in terms of added privileges or responsibilities. Pay grades meant
nothing while attending school. Scholastic standing meant everything.

Upon satisfactory completion of the first six months of training, and
with the recognition of the school command that I had proven myself capable of satisfactorily completing the entire course, I was transferred to
A1W, the fully operational nuclear power plant prototype near Idaho Falls,
Idaho, for the final six months of hands-on-training.

Most A1W students lived in Idaho Falls, the largest nearby city. Others
lived in Blackfoot or Pocatello. The actual site of the prototype was about
fifty miles west of Idaho Falls. We had the option of taking the free bus
or using our own privately owned vehicles to and from the site. The bus
was great for catching a little extra sleep while en route but it was sometimes delayed at one end or the other, an inconvenience with which most
of us preferred not to contend. During the winter months it was far too cold
standing on the corner waiting for the bus.

The learning experience at A1W was not quite as demanding as it was
at Vallejo. At A1W we were allowed periodic breaks of several days off in
a row. There were no military duties required or expected of us during the
final six-month phase. Nor was there any kind of homework. The time we
spent at the prototype made up for the absence of duties elsewhere. It was
mandatory that all school attendees fully qualify on the operation of each
piece of machinery as well as on every component part. We were te⌐
and retested by a number of instructors, each time having to pr⌐
proficiency by physically carrying out operational instruction⌐
of us. It was not a plaything that we were dealing with·   ⊙

ısiness, and any student who took on the appearance of thinking other-wise was immediately removed from the program. The routine was simple, the task at hand difficult. We had to exert our maximum effort in order to qualify in an orderly and timely manner. As soon as we qualified on one station we would begin qualifying on the next. All instructors were highly proficient. They had to be constantly alert to the activities of the trainees; one simple unobserved mistake could result in an emergency situation, something none of us wanted any part in. Safety first was drummed into us over and over. We were to insure that "ZD," zero defects, was a constant regardless of the routine or function being performed. I was taught the dif-ference between a slight "tweak" and a "RCH," a tweak being slight but visible movement whereas a RCH, as the initials implied, was the almost invisible movement, comparable to the thickness of a "red cunt hair." I had already learned how Navy jargon had a way of consistently putting things into simple but understandable perspective with the use of "appropriate" four-letter words. In any event, absolutely nothing took priority over the safe operation of the plant. There were multitudes of safeguards built into the plant that made it virtually impossible to make an irrecoverable mistake that might result in a hazardous situation. That did not mean it couldn't happen under extreme conditions or unusual circumstances. So the training went accordingly; at all times we were to remain fully prepared to respond to any condition, emergency or not, and we were frequently tested on our ability to do so.

About halfway through the final training I submitted another request – this time for submarine duty. Understandably, nuclear-qualified sailors could only be assigned to aircraft carriers and submarines, since there were no other nuclear-powered vessels operational or in commission at that time. Once again the Bureau smiled upon me and approved my request. Upon satisfactory completion of the prototype training I was directed to report to the submarine base at New London, Connecticut.

October 19, 1962, I graduated from nuclear power school and was assigned the Navy Enlisted Classification 3355; Nuclear Power Plant Operator.

Following a brief period of leave, I reported for training at the subma-rine base and was assigned to Class 267. Sub school was easy in compari-
˙on to the year I had just been through. There was ample time to relax and
˙joy myself when I was not attending school. During one of those times,

while I was at the Petty Officers' Club, one of the men sitting at our table was a bit too anxious in his desire to drink the club dry. He and the sailor sitting next to him were celebrating one thing or another, and their alcohol intake was making its effect apparent on both. Their participation in the ongoing conversation, for lack of continuity, was being ignored by the rest of us. One of the two began to take on that easily recognized pale expression of one who was about to throw up. Almost frantically, he grabbed the nearly empty glass of water from in front of his oblivious neighbor and immediately filled it up with an almost-colorless liquid matter. He then very nonchalantly returned the glass to where he had obtained it – directly in front of his inattentive friend. Two of us who had observed what had taken place looked at each other with disgust, but we simply shrugged our shoulders as if to say it wasn't a problem worth raising an issue over. Then, almost immediately, the friend/neighbor reached out and picked up the glass of vomited booze. Even as my friend and I yelled, simultaneously waving our signals to cease and desist, the guy went right ahead and drank the entire contents! When he sat his glass down he asked what was the problem, but all we could do was look at each other in disbelief. What would we have accomplished after the fact?

On another occasion I was at the same club enjoying a few sociable drinks with school chums. I had not yet been indoctrinated as to the importance a sailor placed on being submarine qualified, nor did I understand the significance of the dolphins that were worn by submariners as a testament to having fully qualified. What I did know was that at the booth next to ours there was a group of submarine-qualified sailors who were enjoying their evening too – only they made it a point to boast of their status (qualified) while they ridiculed ours. We being the lowly unqualified or nonqualified "useless surface skimmers"!

It had been a long time since I felt my adrenaline flow in anger. It was beginning to bother the others in my group as much as it irritated me, so I took the initiative and said, "Why don't you guys either shut up or take your party elsewhere!" As one of them began to stand, I scrambled to my feet, anxious to become involved in an activity that I thought I had outgrown. When he once again made comments reflecting our inferiority, followed by the magic words, "I don't see no anchor up your ass," suggesting I was unable to move out of fear. I swung my right fist with all the power I could gather. I wanted to put him down and out with that single power-punch. I swung so hard that when my fist missed him the momentum pulled me right

it – and I landed flat on the floor beside him. I had unintention-
nyself look like a fool, thereby confirming his thoughts while
ine. I stood up and looked directly into his eyes. The fool stood
there with that "I have conquered" smirk on his face as I calculated my aim
with a little more care. My second swing found its mark dead center as
my fist smashed into his nose and mouth. He "hit the deck" hard. I turned,
politely excused myself from both groups, and I walked out of the club. I
knew that if I remained, there would be more trouble, and in all likelihood I
would end up behind bars – possibly suffer the loss of that first-class crow I
had not yet grown used to wearing. I suffered a gash to one of the knuckles
on my right hand, certainly not a significant battle scar, so I went directly
to the barracks where I could enjoy peace and quiet, and sleep.

On Our Way to Becoming Submarine Sailors

When I awakened the following morning I could not ignore the fact that
my entire right hand was swollen up like a balloon so I reported to Sick Bay
for evaluation and treatment. The corpsman sutured the gapping wound to
my knuckle (caused by somebody's teeth) and he gave me a supply of pills
to take. Following two days of medication, with the realization that the pain
had become quite severe and that the swelling had not subsided, I returned
to Sick Bay. Prognosis; blood poisoning. Treatment; massive doses of an-

tibiotics and bed rest. Subsequently I was admitted to the base hospital. I found it almost humorous that my status as victor had flip-flopped. There I was in the hospital whereas my opponent probably suffered nothing more than a sore nose and a fat lip. Unfortunately, as a result of being hospitalized, I was not able to accompany my class during hands-on conventional submarine training at sea. I had been near the top of my class at the time I was hospitalized, so the classes I missed did not lower my grade point average enough to hold me back. On January 18, 1963, I graduated with my class.

During submarine school we were all required to submit updated "dream sheets," a form on which we designated our first, second, and third choices – our preferences as to new duty assignment locations. I selected Hawaii as my first choice, Japan as my second, and I left my third choice up to the Bureau, where the decision would be made anyway. Hawaii was a priority choice for most of the graduates, which made it less likely that I would be one of the few selected to go there. Having two children reduced the odds even more, since funds allocated for "PCS," permanent change of station, moves were always tight. We were each to receive our orders during graduation ceremonies.

With graduation came a feeling of relief. I was happy knowing that my school days had come to an end, and I was equally enthusiastic about what I had learned of the submarine way of life upon which I was embarking. I wondered just how much longer my luck was going to continue when I read my orders. I was to report to the USS *Seadragon* (SSN-584), permanently home-ported at Pearl Harbor, Hawaii! The first choice on my dream sheet had been approved.

February 5, 1963, I reported for duty on board the USS *Seadragon* as directed.

That was the first time that I had ever set foot on a submarine. *Seadragon* was a "fast attack" nuclear submarine and had recently made history after a rendezvous under the polar cap with the USS *Skate*, a sister vessel of the same class. That, in itself, was reason enough for me to be a proud member of the crew. Along with checking in with the various department heads came the realization that my school days were far from over. Someone of a lower rate than I quickly informed me, that I was of little value to the ship or crew until I was fully qualified. I was also told that until such time

251

I should forget my pay grade (except on payday). "Get qualified," became the phrase I heard most frequently, several times a day for months.

USS *Seadragon* (SSN-584) – Fast Attack Nuclear-Powered Submarine – February 1963 to December 1965

March 23, 1963, was a day that provided me with the thrill of a life-time. It was my first experience at sea on board a submarine. I found that unlike surface craft operations, nuclear submarine operations were highly classified, even to the degree that at times the crew did not know or could not depend on advance knowledge of where they were going or when they might return. The day before, I had been told to make sure I had a full sea-bag on board. Whenever I asked how long we might be gone, the typical response was: "Who knows? We might be out for a while or we might not," and "Be prepared for the long haul."

Seadragon got underway that morning on schedule. Shortly after leaving the harbor waters the ever-so distinctive voice of Chief Breault an-

252

nounced the testing of all alarms over the 1MC. Immediately following a variety of dissimilar alarms, each distinct in identifying a different emergency situation, the chief announced, "Now dive! Dive!" Down we went, and my heart pounded with excitement. I had no idea that the *Seadragon* would remain underwater until May 13, some fifty days later! There was ample time to familiarize myself with the "boat" and the crew as I made satisfactory progress in the qualification process. By definition, a submarine is actually a "ship," not a boat. However, to those who serve such a craft, submarines are always referred to as boats. The senior chief on board every submarine is known as the "COB," the Chief of the Boat.

On April 10, 1963, during an otherwise-routine underway day, we received disturbing news that the USS *Thresher* (SSN-593), a different class nuclear-powered submarine, had failed to surface as scheduled. The news that was being released was vague, but we all knew that the *Thresher* and crew had to have been in serious trouble. Many of us knew *Thresher* sailors from nuke school or Sub school, and our concerns for their safety were clearly visible. All submariners are thoroughly trained on survival and rescue techniques, all of which can only be followed if their boat is intact; has not broken up or imploded. Within several hours we received the devastating news that the *Thresher* was at the bottom of the ocean, about eighty-four hundred feet down, and it was unlikely that there were any survivors. Fellow submariners prayed that the news was somehow in error and that there would be survivors. The terrible truth came out quickly, and the world learned that some kind of "mishap" had caused the loss of 129 lives – volunteers for the submarine service, a service only those who lived it truly understand.

All submariners were extremely angered at the wording with which the news media expressed the tragedy. It was insulting and insinuating: "USS *Thresher* is the first nuclear-powered submarine that has failed to surface." Our justifiable anger was based on one word, *first*, which suggested there would be more such incidents. We believed the word *only*, which it was at that time, would have been more appropriate. Unfortunately, some five years later there would be a second similar disaster that took the USS *Scorpion* (SSN-589) and her crew of ninety-nine men about ten thousand feet to the bottom of the ocean. That unfortunate disaster took place some four hundred miles southwest of the Azores in May of 1968 while the *Scorpion* was en route to the United States from the Mediterranean. We grieved with sincere compassion for those who lost their lives, but also with equal or greater compassion for those who lost their loved ones as a result of those two regrettable incidents. Such disasters heightened the awareness of all seagoing men to their surroundings and to their responsibilities, regardless of the type ship on which they were serving. The reality of such losses made it that much more apparent how quickly a situation could turn into a disaster, particularly on board a submarine.

Life on board the *Seadragon* was entirely different from that which I had grown accustomed to while serving on board destroyers. Meals, whether underway or in port, were widely varied and were always of the very best quality. In a word, they were delicious. I was treated to frog legs for the first time in my life while on board the *Seadragon*. I learned that within the Navy supply system, submarines took priority over surface craft. Submarines were provided with a greater "per man" food allowance than that allowed for surface craft. Steaks procured for submariners were not the gristly cheaper cuts that were prepared for surface craft – they were gristle-free, practically fat-free, and as palatable as the finest filet mignon served at the most elite of restaurants. Breakfast consisted of eggs to order, bacon, sausage, grits, pancakes, fruit, bread or toast, and frequently steak. We had our choice of any single item, or we could partake of the entire menu; and there was no limit – we could eat as much as we wanted at each sitting! There was no such thing as food rationing. Not only were meals served every six hours, around-the-clock, we also had the option of cooking our own meals at any in-between times with but one stipulation – that we clean up whatever mess we made in the galley. The food was a gigantic plus above and beyond whatever life aboard a destroyer had to offer. We were also paid hazardous duty pay in addition to our regular pay. There were significant differences between the life of a submariner and the Navy life I had previously experienced. One remarkable difference was that there was absolutely no thievery aboard the *Seadragon*, an expected and ongoing activity aboard the two destroyers on which I had served.

On May 13, 1963, the *Seadragon* pulled into Naha Port, Okinawa, where she remained tied up for a week. I found that Namanui had changed very little, but I was disappointed to find that the Teahouse August Moon had been placed off-limits to the military. I was told that it had lost its Class-A status as a result of drug dealings that had taken place on the premises.

254

There were a number of nightclubs and bars in and around Namanui. I preferred the London Club, a quiet place with barely enough room for a stand-bar, three booths, and a jukebox. Keiko, Miko, Mickey, and Mimiko were the hostesses who worked there. I was immediately attracted to Mimiko, a "cherry girl" who was under the ever-watchful eye of Mama-san. The other girls, much to their delight, were quickly claimed by other shipmates. So London Club became a "CP," command post, for several *Seadragon* sailors. We would first do our sightseeing and our souvenir shopping – then we would relax at London Club.

Mimiko had a sweet innocence about her. She would cuddle up to me as if she were looking for some kind of protective barrier between her and the rest of the world. She absolutely refused to drink anything other than tea, which was all right with me, as long as she remained by my side.

The Okura Hotel was another command post of sort. It was a meeting place of another kind for those crewmen who preferred to remain ashore for the night. The Okura was a nice place and it was only a few short blocks from the bar district. Lining both sides of the halls and stairs, embedded in the floor and covered by heavy-duty clear glass, there were a variety of colored lights. The decorative effect added a touch of elegance to the otherwise clean but simple hotel interior features. Mirrors lined the walls and ceilings of most rooms and provided for the unobstructed view of bedroom activities from a choice of angles. The hotel also provided all guests with kimonos for their added comfort as they relaxed within the confines of the hotel – in or out of their rooms. The cost of an overnight stay was well within one's budget. The price of a room was fixed; it did not change if an individual later brought in a "guest." The hotel was immaculate, and the management/owner always responded quickly to requests for food and beverages. Our privacy was always respected at the Okura Hotel, whether we were alone or in the company of a female companion.

The night prior to the *Seadragon's* departure, three of us decided to steal the courtesy kimonos the hotel had provided us. We made a bet that whoever showed up in the morning without their souvenir kimono would be faced with some agreed upon penalty. When I exited the hotel the next morning I realized that I was the only one there without the garment. Whatever the penalty, no way was I going to face it. So I returned to the hotel, retrieved my kimono, paid management for all three garments, and joined my partners. Even though the hotel had made a bundle off of us during our stay, I could not convince myself that complying with the bet was worth the theft. We had been well cared for and it was important that we would always be welcomed when we returned. The owner would probably have given us the kimonos had we taken the time to ask.

May 20, 1963, we departed from Naha and steamed directly to Pearl Harbor. We arrived June 3. A month later the boat was moved to the Pearl Harbor Naval Shipyard where she remained for nearly a full year while undergoing a major overhaul.

During the overhaul, we worked in eight-hour shifts, twenty-four hours a day. It would be wrong to believe that shipyard workers did all of the work unassisted by the crew. We had to observe and/or participate in every phase of the overhaul. Yardbirds could not so much as open or close a valve without one of us either witnessing it or doing it for them. When work was being performed on any part of the "primary" system, strict adherence to many precautions and safeguards were followed each step of the way. The primary system was any part of the interlinking network of pipes, valves and pumps that carried radioactive matter. The special precautions included the mandatory wearing of uncomfortable head-to-foot protective clothing while observing or participating in work on or near primary components. The heat and the lack of sufficient ventilation, particularly in the reactor compartment, made it necessary for us to work in short shifts, sometimes only minutes at a time. It was also important that we maintained a close watch on our pocket dosimeter to make sure that we remained within – were not exposed to – an excess above specific radiation limits. Pocket dosimeters were about the same size as a large pen or pencil. As the hairline monitor approached the maximum readable figure, we knew that we had received our maximum limit of radiation for a given period of time. Maximum doses could be measured in terms of a day, week, month, year – and lifetime. Some individuals thought very little of going beyond specified limits whereas others lived strictly by the book. One prank, not always taken in jest, was when one individual would grab the dosimeter of a shipmate, quickly insert the eraser end of a pencil into the sensor end of the device, and then hand it back to its rightful owner. The choice of pencil eraser was because it fit perfectly and it caused no damage to the dosimeter. As a result of this prank, the dosimeter was immediately discharged to zero – making it appear that the unit had not been subjected to any harmful radiation. In other words, there was no longer an excuse for not reentering a radiation zone/area. Some individuals, foolish at that, did not take the limitations seriously and intentionally zeroed their own dosimeter "for laughs."

Working on the primary system was tedious and was far more time-consuming than working on the "secondary," the uncontaminated side of the plant. We each took our turn regardless of pay grade or time in service. The workload was distributed as fairly as possible as the engineers willingly rotated between demanding jobs and jobs that required less effort. Eventually everyone participated in the workload to about the same degree.

We knew going into the overhaul that it would be a long time before the *Seadragon* would be seaworthy again. The crew was divided into two groups: the "nose-coners," the non-nuclear-trained, and the "nukes," the nuclear-trained engineers. Everyone was responsible for continuing their training and for maintaining a high degree of proficiency on all of the submarine's systems. We knew that the day would come when the results of our training would be tested to the highest degree – the day we would once again take the *Seadragon* back to sea. Snipes were always known for having a tough life, but the nuclear-trained snipes had it toughest of all. Aside from having to work in the engineering spaces and aside from having to update and maintain their submarine qualification status, they also had to participate in a very comprehensive and vigorous training phase that was designed to ensure the safe and proficient operation of both primary and secondary systems. Most engineers put in a typical twelve-hour-day working and training. There were eight hours of physical work on the plant and eight hours on call. On call meant being prepared to respond immediately, but much of that time was devoted to attending classes, continuous refresher courses in the operation and maintenance of the plant. Chief Burge determined which courses we would be required to attend and which courses we would be required to instruct. Either way, we were sure to become more knowledgeable of all plant parameters and configurations. I preferred being an attendee to that of being the instructor. Teaching required extra research and there could be no doubt that it was the best way to sharpen the instructor's knowledge and skills. Each of us had about the same number of turns instructing as we had attending.

As a "nonqual" I had to squeeze in extra study time whenever and wherever I could in order to keep up with my submarine qualification program. Qualifying while in the shipyard was notably difficult since many shipboard systems were not functional while in port. I knew that my own personal qualification program would need the benefit of additional under-way experience before I could truly consider myself completely qualified. It was a most hectic period of time in my life, but I remained fully intent on keeping up with the pace. Thus far I had always been able to prove that I was one never to be discouraged from achieving every goal that I had established for myself.

Every submarine had a qualification or requalification program tai-lored to the specifics of each individual boat. Both programs required a working knowledge of the entire submarine, stem to stern. Submarine sail-ors, to a far greater extent than surface craft sailors, fully depended upon each other's decisions and actions. One mistake could mean the lives of the crew, an injury to a shipmate, or damage to equipment. In the event of an emergency, it was the responsibility of the senior occupant in the compartment where the emergency occurred to take charge and to direct the recovery process. With that in mind, one can more readily understand why qualification programs were taken very seriously. It would have been difficult sleeping without having complete confidence in the qualification program as a whole, certainly the full confidence in the decisions being made by shipmates on watch – decisions that might be made under severe stress or emergency conditions. A nonqual, a person such as myself, not yet qualified throughout the submarine, was a person not to be relied upon; a category everyone fit into at one time or another, but a category from which everyone wanted to be disassociated as quickly as possible.

Understandably, the more qualified I became, the better I felt about everything and everyone around me. It was a good feeling, knowing the purpose and inner workings of the shipboard equipment by which I was constantly surrounded.

Twin dolphins, the emblem worn by qualified submariners, was the well-earned device that identified individuals as members of an elite and distinct group. There was a fellowship – a strong trusting relationship that surpassed anything I had ever experienced. Submariners did not fight among themselves; they served each other.

November 22, 1963, was a day many people remember as the day Pres. John Fitzgerald Kennedy was assassinated. It was an important day in my life too, although it is certainly not my intention to imply that there was any significant comparison to the murder of a president. Early that morn-ing, I reported to LTjg V. C. Hunsinger, who had been assigned to "take me through the boat," to give me the final examination toward submarine qualification. Some officers were known to conduct lengthy and more complex exams, while others were known to be more lenient. Mr. Hunsinger's methods for testing were not well known, although he himself was known as a straight shooter – a serious but fair, dedicated officer.

The exam consisted of two phases; the verbal question-and-answer phase and the walk-through phase. Questions were totally at the discretion of the examining officer and were designed to test one's depth of knowledge on any shipboard device or system. Most officers were known to ask a significant number of "damage control" and emergency procedure type questions. Mr. Hunsinger was well into the process of conducting a thorough and professional examination when we were advised of the President's assassination. It became as difficult for the examiner as it was for me to keep our thoughts on the test instead of the crime that would, to some degree, affect most of the world. Mr. Hunsinger made the decision to close the exam. He said it was his opinion that enough ground had been covered and he would recommend that I be designated "Qualified in Submarines" effective that date. His recommendation was forwarded and approved by the Executive Officer that same day.

There were several of us that completed our sub quals at about the same time. On the morning of November 23, 1963, while the crew was standing at dockside quarters, our Commanding Officer, CDR D. B. Guthe, complimented our achievement as he addressed the crew. He then personally pinned brand-new silver dolphin devices on each of us. One by one, as he shook our hands in genuine congratulations, he also presented each of us with a submarine qualification certificate that read:

"Having successfully completed the rigorous professional requirements for qualification in submarines, having gained a thorough knowledge of submarine construction and operation, having demonstrated his reliability under stress, and having my full confidence and trust, I hereby certify that he is 'Qualified in Submarines.'"

Our certificates were signed by the skipper, Commander Guthe. With that, my rating became MM1(SS); the "(SS)" designator was authorized and required in identifying submarine-qualified personnel along with their rating.

The ceremony could not have been considered complete without benefit of another customary ritual. One by one we were detained, then escorted to the side of the dock, where, fully clothed, we were thrown into the ocean alongside the boat. But even that didn't finish it. The "shit tanks," the waste holding tanks, were then blown to sea and we were immediately surrounded by "wrinkle-neck trout" floating all around us, feces of all shapes and sizes. There were small pieces of toilet paper and other small (but recognizable) brown particles clinging to our hair and eyebrows as we pulled ourselves from the water. It was a most undesirable situation to be in, but we were unbelievably proud as hell to be there. I have been told that this form of hazing is no longer considered acceptable behavior, although I have an idea the talented and imaginative submarine sailor of today's Navy has improvised effectively.

That same evening the celebration continued at the EM Club. There was one more custom commonly referred to as "drink your dolphins," not necessarily considered a requirement, but usually carried out by the newly qualified as the final step of initiation. The procedure consisted of placing one's newly earned dolphin device into a water glass, then filling the glass with shots of whisky, hot sauce, vodka, gin, scotch, beer, and other "contaminants." The glass was filled all the way to the brim. We then ceremoniously drank our way to the dolphins, preferably without stopping for a breath, and retrieved the dolphins by grasping them with our teeth. It was not an experience anyone enjoyed, but it got the party off and running. Again, I'm told, the drinking of one's dolphins has been outlawed. Accurate sources have informed me that to some degree it is still practiced, however not nearly as blatantly as it was in the past.

10

UNDERWAY ON NUCLEAR POWER - SUBMERGED

May 8, 1964, was a day that would have the *Seadragon's* entire crew alert and performing to the best of their ability. The reactor had been refueled, modifications and upgrades to shipboard systems had been completed, and it was the day to prove everything was as functional at sea as it was during dockside tests.

Early that morning we began preparing in accordance with a variety of checklists. Everything had to be accomplished in compliance with current directives – in specified order, and with absolute precision. The reactor was brought critical, ship's generators were placed on the line, shore power was severed, and the *Seadragon* became fully self-supporting and ready for the strenuous conduct of sea trials that was about to begin.

The thoroughness of "shakedown cruises" and "sea trials" is seldom understood by anyone other than those individuals who have actually participated in them. Equipment failures are somewhat expected, and the crew is relied upon to take immediate corrective action; to take and maintain control of all possible situations. We all knew that the failure to take the right action, on the part of a single individual, could result in irreparable damage or total disaster.

The *Seadragon* slowly made her way out of Pearl Harbor and headed out to sea. The ocean floor off of Oahu Island drops off quickly beyond the reef, so we did not have to wait long before we heard the rasping *oogah* from the klaxon followed by words we had not heard for eleven months: "Dive! Dive!" Ballast tanks were flooded, the *Seadragon* submerged, and the testing of shipboard equipment began immediately. If all went well, testing would continue until every component of every system tested satisfactorily. The thoroughness of each test was shared equally whether the systems being tested had been worked on during the overhaul or they had remained intact and dormant. All systems were pushed to their limits; not just one time, but several times, to ensure their proper operation and reliability. Tests continued until there was no doubt as to the performance of ship and crew – in unison.

We returned to Pearl Harbor late in May and immediately began a three-week upkeep period at the Pearl Harbor Naval Shipyard where calibrations, adjustments, and other modifications were accomplished on those systems and components that had been found to be deficient or had otherwise failed to perform up to standards.

Following the upkeep, during the months of June and July 1964, the *Seadragon* spent some time at Bangor Wharf, Dabob Bay, near Bremerton, Washington. Most "liberty hounds" selected Seattle, Washington, as their home away from home. I took a couple of weeks' leave so that I would not have to commute back and forth to the ship. The time off provided me with an opportunity to continue my studies toward promotion without any interference from shipboard distractions. I found Seattle to be a very friendly place – comparable to Portland, Oregon, in many respects.

There was one particular dance hall in Seattle that *Seadragon* sailors adopted as their hangout. It had a huge dance floor that was surrounded by tables, and it provided the place and the opportunity for people to meet. Singles, particularly the local females, were known to hang out there – and they had a special liking for visiting sailors.

One evening when I arrived at the dance hall I noticed that one of my shipmates, nicknamed "Animal," looked despondent as he sat with several others at one of the tables. Animal was usually the life of the party, full of vim and vigor. He was always fun to be around. On board ship he could be relied upon to lift our spirits when we felt a bit down and out. He had a tremendous imagination and he was known for his ability to play outrageous pranks on others – in which he took great delight. The men sitting with Animal had been unsuccessful in their attempts to bring him back around to being his normal happy-go-lucky self. It was obvious that he did not want to participate in the fun the rest of us were enjoying. After watching Animal for a while, I decided to join him in hopes that I might be able to cheer him up. I sat next to him and with honest and sincere interest I asked what was troubling him. After some coaxing, Animal confided in me that he had taken a strong liking to one of the "lovelies" sitting at the bar.

"God, just look at her; ain't she something? I'm in love with her, Ad."

"Well, why don't you go up to her and introduce yourself?" I suggested.

"Oh, hell, Ad, she's so beautiful I know that she'd turn me down – I wouldn't have a chance."

"What in the hell do you think she's here for if she's not here to meet guys – particularly guys that are interested in her?"

Animal seemed to be quite serious. He glanced up at the girl from time to time, and then he would slowly shake his head as his gaze returned to the table before him. He was completely withdrawn from the rest of us, so I decided it was time to do something about it.

I approached the girl at the bar and introduced myself. "Hi, I'm Paul and I've got something of a problem that you just might be able to help me with."

She looked at me suspiciously and said, "And just what might that be?"

"My buddy sitting over there," I pointed Animal out, "the guy looking so glum, is usually one hell of a happy guy. But right now he's in some kind of shy mood because he finds you so attractive. He says he's in love with you." I spoke somewhat jokingly but tried to sound serious enough so that she would believe in Animal's genuine interest. "Will you join him, even if only for a little while?" I asked.

"No, I don't think so," she told me, "but he's welcome to come over here if he wants to."

With that bit of encouragement I returned to Animal. He repeated his fear of rejection as he told me in absolute terms that he would not, under any condition, walk over to her in front of his friends – only to be humiliated.

I returned to the girl and practically begged her to accompany me to Animal's table so that I could introduce him to her. After several minutes of my near pleading she finally agreed.

Animal was aware that we were nearing the table and he looked up as we approached.

"Animal, I want you to meet Michelle—"

Before I could complete the introduction, Animal looked directly into Michelle's eyes and in a loud, clear voice said, "So what the fuck do you want, bitch?"

My world collapsed. I had been instrumental in accomplishing several unintended things. I had made a fool out of myself by falling victim to the type of prank Animal was known and named for; I had angered one very adorable and accommodating "lovely", and I had provided Animal with a live stage upon which he could perform. Animal knew that what he had done was revolting and offensive. His boisterous laughter only compounded my embarrassment as it bolstered his personal assessment of what he thought to be extremely humorous. The girl was a little bewildered and a lot angered. Since I was within reach, I thought she was going to slap me instead of taking it out on Animal. Her only comment, "I should have known," would have been more appropriate coming from me. I really should have known, whereas she had no idea what Animal was like. Michelle left in a huff and relocated at the farthest end of the bar, her back facing us. She maintained a visual awareness of our activities as she watched our reflection in the mirror behind the bar – probably to make sure she could get away should one of us start to approach her again. Animal, having miraculously recovered from his well-feigned state of depression, partied along with our group the remainder of the evening. I swore that I would never forgive him for having tricked me – but within hours, if not minutes, the whole matter became a bit of humorous, inconsequential history.

There was another nightclub in Seattle where I liked to relax. It was much smaller than the dance hall and it was clean and quiet. Unintentionally, almost by accident, I became a friend with Beth, the rather attractive proprietor of the place. Beth had seen me on several occasions as I sat alone reading Navy study guides and writing letters. She approached me one afternoon during a lull in business, sat in the booth with me, and told me that she found me "interesting" and "different." Her opinion, she said, was based on her observation of me writing letters and studying instead of chasing girls and overindulging as had been her experience with most sailors. Beth suggested we have dinner together after closing, and I accepted. After dinner she took me to her apartment, where one thing led to another and shortly before sunrise we were quite comfortably in each other's arms, between the sheets of her bed.

During her spare time, Beth showed me a great deal of the area in and around Seattle. She was actually attracted to me rather than to my wallet, and she did everything right in making my stay comfortable, enjoyable, and memorable. The morning of *Seadragon*'s departure, Beth chauffeured me all the way back to the boat. I experienced the strangest feeling of guilt, as if I had taken advantage of my time spent with Beth. She had done so much for me, and I had done very little for her. I did let her down in that I failed to keep my promise of corresponding with her. I never saw, or heard from, Beth again.

The boat returned to Pearl Harbor late in July and once again got underway the first week of August. We had a very short R and R visit to Lahaina, Maui, Hawaii, that lasted a single day. We then returned to Pearl Harbor, where we began making preparations for what we believed would be an extended WestPac deployment. In hand with those preparations, a few of us smuggled a variety of booze aboard. I preferred beer but found it to be far too bulky; difficult to conceal in preferred quantities. I did, however, make sure that I had no less than a six-pack in my locker prior to departing. Whiskey was the beverage of choice for most of those who chose to violate Navy law by drinking on board. It lasted much longer, however added precautions had to be taken. The smell, whether on one's breath or from an open container, was very noticeable.

The specifics of submarine operations while at sea were always considered classified. While the submarine was deployed overseas that classification was usually upgraded due to the more sensitive nature of our operations. In general, we were tasked with observing and recording traffic in various shipping lanes while we remained undetected. At times it became a game of cat and mouse, or more adequately described as *Blind Man's Bluff*, the fitting title of a remarkably detailed book [PublicAffairs, 1998] that more thoroughly illustrates American submarine espionage. Most often we followed, although at times we were the ones being tracked by, submarines of other nations. Regardless of our primary mission, we always had many opportunities to put the submarine through a full gambit of exercises that were designed to test ship and crew on their ability to perform up to expectations. It was not only necessary that we exercise our skills to perfection, it was fun as we witnessed our purpose in being there grow from nothing more than a plan to that of "mission accomplished."

Our operations included remaining undetected as we tracked a Soviet submarine from its home port at Vladivostok (at that time part of the USSR) all the way across the ocean to a point near Seattle, Washington. We were successful in confirming that a certain class Soviet submarine was nuclear-powered as we passed its hull close enough to monitor and record emitted radiation levels. We witnessed Soviets target practicing at sea with newly developed and very sophisticated heat-seeking weapons that were fired from both aircraft and ships.

There was an occasion when I was roaming around the boat when the skipper asked me if I wanted to take a look through the periscope. I knew that we were tracking a merchant vessel but I was nonetheless shocked when I saw how close we were to it. Its massive propeller was churning directly in front of my view.

"Impressive, wouldn't you say," the Captain asked me.

"Damned impressive, sir, just how close are we?" I asked in response.

"Just about close enough," was his vague but understandable comment as he regained control of the 'scope. If we had been any closer and the ship had slowed or changed course abruptly, we would have been in danger of suffering some severe damage.

Unlike my experience on destroyers, there was always an excitement, a strong desire to participate in submarine operations. Whenever we returned to port, regardless of the significance or magnitude of the mission in which we had participated, there was always a feeling of accomplishment among the entire crew. Another thing that made a great deal of difference between destroyer duty and submarine duty was the reliability factor. Submarine officers had trust in the capabilities and decisions being made by enlisted men. Submarine officers never neglected the crew. They made themselves available to discuss anything, with anyone, at any time – and it was obvious to us that they truly had our best interests at heart. I was very much aware of how fortunate I was serving as a submariner. Serving with officers and men who looked after each other instead of looking down or with suspicion upon one another was a significant privilege seldom exercised outside the submarine service.

During periods of time while the boat was tied up alongside a pier, topside watches had to remain especially alert. They had to be alert to unauthorized personnel attempting to board, and to unauthorized photographs being taken of the boat when periscopes or other sensitive or highly classified components were extended in full view above the "sail" (the structure above the hull). There was also an ongoing, unauthorized competition of sorts for which topside watches were constantly on the lookout. Submariners enjoyed taking chances, so crewmen of competing submarines, usually under the cover of darkness, would attempt to violate the integrity of sister ships. They would do so by swimming to their target unobserved, and paint a slogan or some other bold mark of distinction on the superstructure while remaining undetected. The Captain (as well as the crew) did not take it lightly when words such as I SANK YOU or BANG - YOU'RE DEAD mysteriously appeared somewhere on the superstructure in large white letters during the time there was supposed to be an alert topside watch on duty. Pranks that they were, they were nonetheless a means of exposing a weakness in security. Such games did no harm; they were an effective and persuasive means of communicating the need to strengthen a first line of defense where it needed it. As for the other side of the coin, it was an honor worthy of special recognition when the topside watch caught the perpetrator(s) in the act.

August 1, 1964, the *Seadragon* deployed west. Little did we know at the time of our departure that the ship and crew were about to make history. While en route to that significant destination I was sleeping soundly in my bunk, above the starboard torpedo-loading ramps, in the stern room (AKA after torpedo room). I was awakened abruptly by a muffled explosion accompanied by a ball of fire and a blast of intense heat directly in my face. My first thought was that there could be no escape; my time had come. I saw another shipmate scrambling around like a caged squirrel in his bunk on the port side. The initial severity of the flames quickly diminished, but the thick smoke that was quickly filling the compartment was equally alarming. Instinctively I knew that I had to act quickly if there was to be a chance of survival. I jumped from my bunk to the deck some six feet below where the bottoms of my bare feet were instantly burned by numerous small smoldering embers that had melted into the fire-resistant tile. Escape was my primary concern, so I ran, my arms and my hands fully extended in front of me in a futile attempt to push the smoke out of my way. As luck would have it, I found that in my haste I had attempted exiting in the wrong direction! In my confusion I had run aft instead of forward and I found myself trapped firmly against the after torpedo tubes. But I was not alone! Bill, the shipmate I had seen scrambling around in his bunk, had also chosen the wrong direction. We looked at each other a bit bewildered – then simultaneously yelled, *Let's get out of here*! As we made our way forward to and through the compartment hatch that led to the safety of the engineroom, we heard the fire alarm accompanied by the words: "Fire in the stern room." I slammed the hatch shut and spun the hand wheel to form an airtight seal, thereby isolating the fire.

As I turned around the skipper immediately confronted me. His words gripped me with a different kind of panic.

"Is everyone out of there? Is anyone hurt?" he asked me.

"Hell, I don't know," was my awkward but truthful response. Without reluctance or hesitation, the Captain yanked open the hatch, entered the compartment, and conducted his own search of the space. I breathed a sigh of relief when I learned that I had been the last man to leave the compartment.

The fire started as the result of one shipmate having put his cigarette out in a trash can not knowing that there was an abundance of cotton infused with highly flammable oxygen-generating dust therein. The cotton ignited instantly and the flames leaped within the narrow walkway between bunks. We were fortunate; it was a very minor fire that had contained itself almost as quickly as it had ignited. But the experience made a believer out of me. I had encountered an unexpected state of confusion, a state of mind I previously thought I could easily handle. I knew that I would have to force myself to think more clearly if I was ever again confronted with a similar or more serious situation.

Extended periods of time at sea were frustrating to one degree or another – regardless of seagoing experience. It did not matter whether ships were floating on top of the ocean or they were submerged well within its depths; shipboard sailors never ceased searching for new ways of eliminating whatever frustration they felt. Sailors needed to be entertained, if not by someone or some other instrument, then at the expense of someone or some thing. All sailors had imaginations that needed to be exercised from time to time. The result could be beneficial or detrimental; there was no guarantee of the outcome even though appropriate precautions were always taken to retain friendships.

The more inventive one was, the more he was apt to share his idea(s). It was unusual for anyone to be creative for no purpose other than his own personal satisfaction, but there were instances when one needed to maintain absolute secrecy. For example, I exercised my own imagination, and I kept it a secret, when I realized that the outlet from one of the air-conditioning ducts on the lower-level of the engineroom could serve me well in a way other than its intended purpose. The cold air provided obvious comfort to the lower-level watch-stander, who would normally station himself in front of, or very near to, the outlet. The outlet was covered by heavy-duty mesh that was held securely in place by three machine screws. By removing two of the screws I could swing the mesh to one side and thereby gain access to the inside of the duct. A perfect place to conceal my last can of beer; as far as I could reach back into the duct – well out of sight – to be recovered and consumed in a day or so. I was pleased with the genius of my idea, knowing that I would be able to enjoy a cold beer instead of one cooled only to the ambient temperature inside my locker. I took pleasure in teasing myself with the knowledge that I knew where there was a cold beer just waiting for my retrieval. I knew that the longer I waited, the more refreshing it would be. While lying in my bunk I chuckled to myself as thoughts of my secret crossed my mind. I knew that I could reward myself at any time with a treat that was properly prepared and ready for consumption.

Three days passed and I felt that I had punished myself enough. Unlike most times, I was anxious to report for duty on the lower-level. My flavor buds were wide-awake, and my mouth was watering with anticipation. After a couple of hours on watch, I began removing the first machine screw that was holding the mesh to the duct, knowing that my hand would soon be wrapped around a very cold can of my favorite beverage. My smile quickly changed to near panic as I reached farther and farther into the duct, my hand grasped nothing other than cold air. *It must have been jostled around during maneuvering – probably just inches out of my reach – maybe stuck on one of the duct joints or seams,* I thought to myself as I shook the duct hoping to free my prize. Still nothing! There was no beer there! The disappearance of the beer remained a mystery to me until a year later when Dick, another shipmate, told a group of friends, me included, about an unusual situation he had experienced at sea. He had been on watch, the boat had taken a hard-down angle, and he had heard a clanking sound coming from the air-conditioning duct. Very much to his delight, Christmas had come early and Santa Clause had delivered a nice cold beer for his personal enjoyment. I laughed along with the others, after which I told them my story and of my disappointment when I found that my beer had mysteriously disappeared.

Time at sea could also be boring if we allowed it. Most of us had our own way or ways of keeping occupied. The qualification process took up a great deal of time, and that was anything other than boring. In between meals the mess hall was used for a wide variety of activities. Card games such as hearts, cribbage, and poker were favorites. Dominoes, chess, checkers, and acey deucy, a variation of backgammon, were also enjoyable time-consumers. Contests were held and appropriate trophies were awarded to the winners. Since I was more talented on the engineroom lathe than I was at contests, I volunteered to manufacture some of the trophies that were to be awarded to the winners. CL, Beetle, Bill, and I played hearts frequently. Three of us always conspired to do whatever we could to drop the "bitch," the queen of spades, on Beetle whenever possible. As an ELT, an Engineering Laboratory Technician, Bill had access to photo-processing equipment. With his technical assistance we were able to reduce the size of a photo of Beetle's face to the exact size of the queen of spade's face. It was then a simple matter of laminating Beetle's face on the card. Bill and I were the only ones aware of the altered face while the cards were being dealt. We knew that we would always know where the

Some Trophies Handmade by Crew Members and Presented to Game Winners (I made the Chess Piece)

queen was by watching facial expressions. CL began choking back his laughter when he looked at the hand he was dealt, a sure giveaway to Bill and me that he had the queen. It then became our goal to maneuver the game in the right direction so that at the appropriate time the "Beetle-faced bitch" could be dumped on Beetle. It worked precisely as planned, and three of the four of us laughed poor Beetle right out of the game. He just didn't see the humor, at least not to the degree the rest of us saw it. That was an ongoing part of life at sea, especially aboard *Seadragon*, where there was a never-ending crusade to catch each other off guard by successfully orchestrating some new gag worthy of boasting about.

Silver nitrate, one of the chemicals used for testing boiler water for salt content, produced a rather startling reaction when skin contaminated with

270

it became exposed to sunlight. The skin would immediately turn black, and no amount of scrubbing would remove it. The backs of hands, forehead, and cheeks were considered fair targets the day before or the day of entering port. The dark splotches would slowly fade over a two- or three-day period, eventually disappearing completely with no permanent harm done. That was considered a one-time-only gag since it cost the victim something in his appearance while ashore on liberty. The idea was never to anger a shipmate, but rather to irritate certain individuals to whatever extent possible without fear of serious repercussion.

Anytime unusual photographs were taken, capturing someone or a group of men in unexpected or awkward poses or situations, there would be photo caption contests. It was difficult determining which of the captions submitted was the funniest. They were all imaginative; each worthy of recognition, but only one per photo was selected as the first-place winner.

At one time or another, newcomers to the submarine service were indoctrinated through initiation into taking special precautions when using the head. The sanitary system, more often referred to as the shit tanks, the tanks into which all drainage from sinks, basins, showers, and toilets drained, had to be emptied whenever they approached capacity. Waste was literally blown overboard by isolating the entire system, pressurizing the sanitary tank(s), and then opening the overboard discharge valves. Pranksters would occasionally bleed a slight pressure into the sanitary tank while some unsuspecting sailor was sitting on the toilet. When it came time for any sailor to drain his waste from the toilet bowl down into the tank, he very carefully and with extreme caution cracked the toilet flapper valve before fully opening it to make sure there was no buildup of pressure. Failure to bleed off any pressure buildup usually meant someone would end up wearing whatever waste he had just deposited in the toilet. No one ever suffered the consequences of his own negligence in that manner more than once.

Being inattentive to sanitary tank levels could also result in other problems. Once I neglected to check the tank level prior to taking a shower and I quickly found myself wading in nasty turds. Then, wrapped only in my towel, I had to suffer the ridicule of the crew as I made my way through the boat from the stern room to the forward torpedo room shower. There was no specific number of tests a sailor had to undergo before he could truly be accepted within the submarine service. A good sense of humor was mandatory.

Sailors, whether nuclear-trained or not, never allowed their minds to remain idle for long. It didn't take much genius for us to devise a way of making booze while at sea. The first concoction I participated in the making of was a mixture of juices, mainly pineapple juice that almost filled a five-gallon glass container. With the addition of some sugar and a little yeast we had all of the ingredients needed. Within several weeks the chemical reaction produced a consumable alcoholic beverage. We achieved similar results with other readily available ingredients such as combinations of fruit, raisins, sugar, and plain water. Ethyl alcohol, as on surface craft, was available for conducting chemical analysis of boiler water, but it lacked flavor, and the punch it packed could have easily resulted in one's unexpected overindulgence. We drank in moderation, never in excess, while at sea. It was never difficult exercising good judgment on a submarine at sea, where we knew how important it was to rely upon each other's ability to perform.

There was a time, during an extended period at sea, when we had a five-gallon container of raisins and a variety of other fruit "cooking off" under the high-pressure air compressor on the engineroom lower-level. Although not a distillery, it did tend to take on a similar appearance. Polyethylene tubing ran from the container, through a cork cap, then wrapped around the container several times thereby providing a path through which gases could escape. Our brew was nearly ripe, and we were looking forward to sampling it, when the Executive Officer paid us an unannounced visit. He had been strolling around the ship and decided to walk through our space, the engineroom – upper and lower levels. He saw the container under the air compressor and jokingly said, "Damn, that looks almost like raisin jack."

The two of us that were on the lower-level chuckled at his "humor" as we simultaneously agreed with something like, "Guess it does at that." We did not expect him to take a big sniff directly out of the jug – but he did!

"My God, it *is* raisin jack!" His accurate assessment of our efforts sounded like bad news. But the XO then did something that took us both by total surprise. He put the cork back in place, slid the container back under the air compressor, and continued on his way! By way of an immediate unanimous vote, those of us who made the stuff decided to dump the entire batch into a sanitary tank. We were never reprimanded by anyone for our irregular and highly illegal activities. The XO played his cards right. He gambled that we would take the initiative, and he was right.

Some of my spare time was utilized writing poetry. I sent most of my poems home to family members, however, there was one place on board the *Seadragon* where I left short four-liners for the crew to "appreciate." My four lines were written to take the place of the four-line captions under each of the twelve monthly Playmates on a *Playboy* calendar. My poems were as obscene as I could make them, so I was always very careful not to be seen when I taped them over the top of the calendar's originals. My work, as with the work of the original poet, described each of the twelve monthly Playmates, but mine was far more graphic. I never told anyone that I was responsible for the unofficial versions – and I enjoyed hearing the encouraging comments made by crewmen who read them. I found it equally humorous listening to those who thought my work was categorically disgusting. The following, as originally written, are examples of what I wrote.

Miss March was illustrated sitting on a wooden chair:

Miss March is always in great fear
Of losing all she holds so dear,
So with crossed legs she sits about
To keep her guts from falling out.

Miss May – taking a shower:

The sweetest thing is Miss May.
Her charm will put you in a trance.
She takes a shower every day
Because she shits her pants.

And Miss July on her hands and knees:

Miss July has but one ambition
For which she's in the right position,
For any man or any critter
To stick his cock into her shitter.

Not exactly award winners, and admittedly uncouth – but at the time it was just another way of humoring myself while entertaining others. What was obscene to relatively few was found to be clever and witty to many others.

On December 18, 1964, I was directed to report to the mess decks, where I was to cut the birthday cake that had been prepared in my honor. Birthdays were always recognized on the *Seadragon*, so I had no reason to suspect mine would be any different than anyone else's. Captain Guthe, his hand extended in congratulations, greeted me as I entered the mess decks. When I looked at the huge cake I could feel the blood rush to my face in humiliation and embarrassment. Right there, in front of everyone, was a beautiful cake with the words: **HAPPY BIRTHDAY, PLAYBOY POET.** I had not realized, until that moment, that I had been seen – that my deeply guarded secret had not gone unnoticed after all, and with that cake it had become instantly and blatantly evident to the entire crew.

I was not the only man aboard that toyed with poetry. The posting of poems on the mess deck's bulletin board was a game of sorts. Participants were always trying to outdo each other, and the crew enjoyed reading and criticizing each new poem as soon as it was posted. Jack, a nose-coner, was a routine participant, but I thought his poems lacked luster. Without considering his feelings, I attached the following poem to one of his:

Jack
There was a "small" child
With initiative – mild
Who attempted to do something new.

He's written his verse,
I suggest he rehearse
Else his work shall be stenciled "P.U."

It's disgustingly sad,
His rhyme's horribly bad,
Evidently he does not know it,

For the poems I've seen
Are really quite green
And the same must hold true for the poet!

I'll not take the time
To write excellent rhyme
Nor shall I attempt at wit.

274

The point I must make
Is for your own sake,
"Give up, sonny, you just ain't got it!"

Jack, perhaps rightfully so, took a very strong exception to that which I thought was clever. He was abrupt when he thoroughly chastised me; I had taken things too seriously and I had been too quick to publicly ridicule him. After some thought, within a couple of hours of our conversation, I decided to take a chance. I wrote and posted the following:

Jack
After our little debate
I must reiterate,
It appears I have caused you great harm.
Now I'm forced to come back
With more poetry, Jack,
Though this time I'll turn on some charm.

Wipe the tear from your eye.
It's not manly to cry.
In the future I'll not be so rank.
I'll make an attempt
To be more of a gent;
The crew knew it was only a prank!

In my calculation
You felt condemnation,
Though my act was overt – agreed?
Now I must repent
And you must relent.
I've learned a great lesson indeed!

If it makes you feel better
And your eyes won't get wetter
I'll rephrase my snide conversation.
Your verses are grand.
You deserve a big hand
For they're written with organization.

They're fetish of sort.
I don't blame your retort.
As I read them I feel quite a spasm.
I chuckle and smile
And in a short while
I generally end in orgasm!

Your poems aren't green
If you know what I mean;
They're honest, straightforward and true.
So instead I must say
That is, — if I may,
They're not green; they're red, white and blue!

I'd have more to say
But it's been a long day;
Next time I ask – don't misconstrue.
But a last word from me,
When I'm in Waikiki,
It's my turn – but the drinks are on you!

I was sitting in the mess hall when Jack entered. He immediately noticed the poem – his name typed boldly at the top – and he grabbed it from the bulletin board. Jack stood there red-faced as he absorbed that which I had written. When he finished reading it his eyes scanned the mess hall and he quickly made eye contact with me. Then, much to my relief, Jack grinned as he gave me a thumbs-up. He had gracefully accepted my taunting. He proved his acceptance by going one step further as he proceeded to put the poem back on the bulletin board. Jack had always been a fine shipmate and a good friend. I never picked on him again.

I wrote one poem for my daughter while I was aboard the *Seadragon*. I am including it here in hopes that when she reads it she will take some time to reflect on that particular time in her life.

A story or two
I'll tell to you
'Bout a baldheaded ant

In the New York Zoo.

His ears were so big
And his feet were so small
That a slight gust of wind
Would cause him to fall.

His right hand was big
But his left hand was bigger.
His nose was so small
That it looked like a chigger.

His eyes, he had six;
They were formed in two rows.
Do you know where they were?
On the tips of his toes!

His legs were too short,
They could hardly be found.
Too short? Yes indeed
His feet couldn't reach ground.

The baldheaded ant
Was growing quite young.
Once a week he would shave
All the hair off his tongue.

One night, in the morning
He looked through his toes
And saw two purple hogs
In the shade of his nose.

He sneezed so hard
That his fingernails curled,
And the purple hogs rolled
And they bounced and they twirled.

Eight monkeys giggled

And fell into a trough.
They laughed and they laughed
Till their elbows dropped off.

The cross-eyed gorilla,
The bow-legged snake,
The skunk and the lizard,
The fish in the lake

All polished their shoes
With sand-flavored jelly
While the baldheaded ant
Started painting his belly.

The baldheaded ant
Planned a party one day
To honor his friend,
The ring-tailed Blue Jay.

The party was held
On the edge of a dime.
Refreshments were served;
Bananas, creamed lime.

As they danced, all the partners
Were something to see.
The elephant's partner,
A green bumblebee.

A turtle – a hippo,
A toad and a goose
Danced circles around
The one-legged moose.

A fox kissed a spider
Upon his big toe
While a horse and a beetle
Held hands with a crow.

A squirrel and a camel,
A giant bullfrog,
Watched a one-eyed mosquito
Bark like a dog.

The three-fingered ape,
The tiger and quail,
The zebra, the gopher,
And polka-dot whale,

A parrot, a wolf,
A giraffe, and a rat
Sang songs with the help
Of a fly and a cat.

The panther, the eagle,
The raccoon and snail,
The leopard and buzzard
All landed in jail.

When the sun started down
All the animals knew
That the party was over
That day at the zoo.

As the rain turns to sugar,
The stars become glue
And the baldheaded ant
Has nothing to do,

He wants to have fun
And make a strange sight;
He's inventing a dark
To turn on in the light.

This ends the story
I wrote just for you,

Now I'm going to bed
And chew on my shoe!

* * *

Submariners worked hard. They took their jobs seriously and they were rewarded accordingly. I attribute the most distinct difference in attitudes between submariners and surface craft sailors to the backgrounds of each. Surface craft sailors were only required to make it through boot camp to show their worthiness to serve. Submarine volunteers were carefully screened following their initial application. It was required that they pass a more detailed physical, they had to satisfactorily complete submarine training, and nearly all snipes on nuke subs had to complete nuclear power training prior to being assigned. By the time all the preparatory legwork was done, most enlisted submariners had already been promoted to E-5 and they had proven their dedication and their motivation. They were, for the most part, far more matured than their surface craft counterparts.

We had been at sea a month when we pulled into Subic Bay, Philippines, for eleven days of upkeep and liberty. The *Seadragon's* three-section liberty routine was implemented differently than that of the destroyer Navy. My experience while on surface craft destroyers, discounting weekends, was a routine workday from 0800 to 1600 hours. It did not matter how hard enlisted men worked while the ship was at sea; the in-port routine remained constant: At 1600 hours two liberty sections were granted liberty while the third, the duty section, remained on board. Liberty sections and duty sections were rotated such that everyone eventually served equally within each category. The *Seadragon* ran things differently. Section leaders, usually E-6s (with oversight approval by their chief), determined the work routine and the liberty schedule. By working hard while underway, we could count on maximum liberty while in port. The duty section was exactly that – the on-board working section. The day before *and* the day following duty days were normally days off, as long as the workload permitted – and it usually did. Two days off out of every three was, as the expression went, "not too shabby." We did have to muster daily, but other than that we were, on liberty days, free to come and go as we pleased. There was always the understanding that should we elect to remain aboard during our off time, we would, on occasion, be called upon to assist in the workload. It was a totally acceptable work routine to all hands, from the seniormost officer to the

280

juniormost enlisted man. As long as there was no slippage in the workload, and there rarely was, the in-port routine remained constant.

The naval base at Subic Bay had changed a great deal for the better since my first visit there. The base offered every kind of facility in support of morale, welfare, and recreation. Sailors no longer had to venture across "Shit River" into the town of Olongapo, but by choice many did. There were several air-conditioned dining facilities on base that provided everything from junk food to fine dining. The gymnasium provided every variety of device with which the health nut could work out. The base theater always had first-rate movies where the cost of admission was a quarter. There were several clubs in which food and beverages were served by very attractive local hostesses. I was one of those who preferred to enjoy the intrigue of off-base liberty where there was never the possibility of boredom.

Olongapo City had become one of a kind. Depending on individual perception, it could have been considered the perfect example of a town where wishes and expectations easily became realities. There was a never-ending source of entertainment there. Interestingly, there was no in-between inasmuch as a person either loved it or hated it there. I was one who first hated it, but in time, after becoming familiar with the area and the people, I realized that it had everything to offer; I enjoyed myself there more than anywhere else I had ever been. Expectedly, the "first-timers" to Olongapo City usually found it difficult acclimating to the kind of life the "old-timers" enjoyed there. Food was plentiful in Olongapo, however eating while in town was not always a safe thing to do. Those who did partake in meals in town were taking a chance on suffering the consequences, usually severe diarrhea or stomach cramps. Filipinos were immune to the bacteria that attacked us. I was never the one to turn down the offer of food, regardless of how disgusting or unpalatable it appeared. I "earned" the right when on occasion I became ill. As a result of eating food that was offered, food that had been prepared by the local nationals, unexpected things happened. I gained a little respect by them and I became a more acceptable foreigner. I learned firsthand what the local cuisine tasted like, and I met people I would never have otherwise been privileged to meet. If I didn't like the taste of the food that was being shared, I did not ask for second helpings. The first time I saw someone eating a *balute* I was sickened. *Balutes* are duck eggs that contain dead embryos at various stages of development. Some had indications of feathers just beginning to grow. They were suitably fermented while in the egg shell, prior to being offered for consumption. Sailor that I was, after having indulged in enough alcoholic beverages, I ate one. At first, with the knowledge that I was eating half egg and half duck, and with the flavor of something between a hard-boiled egg and an oyster, I was more than a bit surprised to find that I actually liked the horrible-looking things. Few Americans ever gained enough courage to eat one, and those who did rarely went back for seconds. I found that many of my American friends were disgusted with me when I joined in and partook of *balutes* right along with the locals. I also ate *aso adobo*, dog stew. That might be looked upon with disgust by more civilized people, however one need only take into consideration the fact that some dogs were raised specifically as a food source, not at all unlike Americans raising other meat products, should make it a little bit more understandable – perhaps no more acceptable, just understandable. Consider how we, as Americans, must be looked upon by those relatively few countries where the cow is considered sacred. Having visited different countries and having seen the differences in living conditions made it easier for me to understand how a people raised to accept certain standards, to include the preparation and consumption of animals we might be more inclined to think of as pets, did so as a matter of routine as well as in order to survive. My favorite Philippine foods, also considered quite palatable to most other Americans, were fried *lumpia*, something similar to Chinese egg rolls but with more meat filling, and Shanghai-style *pancit*, fried noodles with a variety of meat and vegetables mixed in.

It was during that brief eleven-day period of "down time," while the *Seadragon* remained in Subic Bay, that several of us congregated at the Rio, an upstairs combination dance hall and beer garden. We became engaged in a conversation with Hernando Hernandez, a local resident not significantly older than any one of us. We knew absolutely nothing about him, nor did he know anything about us, but we became instant friends. Hernando, or Nando, as we learned to call him, invited us to attend the cockfights with him. He knew that the arena was outside the well-established boundaries, the line beyond which there was no legitimate liberty, but he assured us that we had nothing to worry about. We accepted his invitation and agreed to accompany Nando the following day. Five of us showed up, and Nando was there at the entrance to the arena waiting – all promises had been kept. Our group consisted of CL, Whit, Double L, Ken and me; all *Seadragon* crewmen.

The arena proper was a well-contained wooden structure, octagonal in shape and of questionable structural strength. We saw Nando stop briefly at the pay booth, where he told the attendant we were all his guests. We also noticed that no money exchanged hands! The hospitality was a welcome surprise, as we were escorted past the pay booth and into the bleacher area of the arena. As we entered, we were immediately confronted with the unmistakable squawking and cackling of fighting cocks. They were everywhere. Some of the gamecocks were being held by their owners, some were contained within small cages, and some were tethered by short two to three foot lines, one end tied to the bird's leg with the other end nailed to the ground. Some cocks were being squared off with potential contenders. All of the birds were being carefully evaluated by owners and observers as to their winning potential. Selections were carefully made as to which cocks would fight each other, what the owners were willing to bet, and what the odds might begin at. The odds were dependent upon many variables, primarily a history of wins and the differences in the size of contenders. Sometimes even the color of a bird would change the odds. All of the birds, regardless of size or color, exhibited a 100 percent willingness to fight to the death as they were being matched.

Nando had his own mean rooster, which he kept close by at all times. He was in the process of acclimating his bird to the crowd and to the constant squawking in and around the arena. We were assured that in due time we would see his bird fight – and when that time came we would witness the meanest bird of all times. Nando was very convincing that his bird was fully capable of fighting and killing every opponent with which it came in contact. We were also encouraged to bet a lot of money on his bird when the time came; it couldn't lose! We were anxious to see that bird fight, but Nando knew the skills required of a fighting cock and he wanted to make sure there was no room for error. Nando's mean bird needed more time to further augment its skills and to do whatever else Nando deemed necessary in preparation for battle. Nando walked us around and under the bleacher seats as he explained the do's and don'ts of cock fight strategies. Just prior to the first fight of the afternoon he escorted us directly to front row seats where we had an unobstructed view of the fighting arena. At this point we learned that Nando's father owned the arena, which explained the favorable treatment we had received.

The actual fighting arena, the cock-pit as it was more commonly referred to, was a little smaller than a professional boxing arena. It was surrounded by closely spaced vertical bars to a height of approximately four feet. The floor was compacted dirt. We were seated so that our eye-level was just about three feet above the cock-pit floor.

There were six or seven rows of bleacher bench-type seats. Each row toward the back was sufficiently higher than the row in front of it to allow all spectators a good view of the fights. Hanging across and above the center of the arena, corner to corner, was a tightly strung wire that passed through a single, easily recognizable bead; suspending it above everything, thereby making it highly visible to all spectators. The referee would slide the bead toward the favored bird or position it directly in the middle when the odds were even. Sometimes a hat was used for the same purpose, it being worn by the owner of the favored bird or by the referee when odds were even. Normally, only three people were allowed inside the fighting arena; the referee and the two bird owners. Odds fluctuated as personal bets between bird owners were being funded by sponsors, friends, and other hopeful benefactors. It was difficult for me to completely understand all that went into the system of determining odds, but from what I observed, unsophisticated as it was, it was a system that was totally acceptable to everyone. It was a system in which the referee's guesswork took the place of a calculator and/or computer. At some point the referee locked in on specific odds. The moment the referee signaled the spectators that the odds would no longer change, betting became spontaneous and frenzied. Depending on the history of the two birds fighting, there might be hundreds of spectators, all intermingled without regard to individual bird preference(s). Spectators yelled their bets in all directions; all the way across the arena to the far sides, as well as directly at those seated around them. They flailed their arms to attract the attention of opposing bets, and everyone had a system of sign language betting that was immediately recognized and accepted. I found it virtually impossible to keep up with what I saw as absolute confusion – yet those who were familiar with the game never lost sight of what was taking place or of the bets being placed. The five of us usually bet among ourselves, preferring not to engage in a system we did not thoroughly understand. Once in a while, when the odds were confusing to us, or they appeared to be in conflict, Nando would make our bets for us. At some point in time, after it appeared that all bets were in, the referee would put a stop to all betting.

Usually, each bird had one razor sharp blade attached to one leg just about level with its lowest spur, the blade pointing toward the back of the bird. Blades were about two inches in length and resembled miniature single-edged swords. The bird owners, birds in hand, approached the center of the arena and caused the birds to menacingly intimidate each other. Owners took turns, each holding his own bird while the opponents' bird pecked at its body, then owners would reverse roles so that each bird received a like number of tormenting pecks. The procedure was intended on infuriating each bird into its most ferocious fighting mode. Owners then placed their birds on the dirt floor facing each other – close enough so that they would attack without prodding. The rest was up to the skill and luck of the fighting cocks. Most fights were furious while a few were less than sparring matches. It was disappointing to the spectators, but extremely exciting and welcomed by the owner of the winner, when the first blow struck was a fatal one. The fights that lasted the longest in duration guaranteed that the front-row spectators would become spattered with blood as the two cocks fought ferociously around the cock-pit.

To an outsider, the fighting of cocks might seem a bit cruel. To the owners and spectators it was a sport that also provided a means of legitimizing gambling. It was a favorite pastime, particularly for the men. Many fighting cocks became famous as a result of their ability to conquer and survive. The best cocks were believed to be sure bets, while the challenging bird owner stood to make a lot of money should his bird win.

Most fights were short, seldom lasting more than a minute or two. The longer the fight lasted, the more intense and excited the spectators became. The crowd would roar at each physical encounter; with each clash one or both birds would suffer damaging wounds. A single wound in the right place, the heart, brought the fight to an instant finish. Winner took all. The owner of the winning bird received his monetary reward along with the losing bird; his dinner. Losers always displayed shock and disbelief as they blamed their birds for having failed to fight in the manner they had been trained.

A bird did not have to die to lose. Some cocks simply quit fighting and they would run to the surrounding barrier in a desperate attempt to get away from their opponent. The final determination, as to which bird won, was made by the referee and was approved by the entire crowd. The referee would hold both birds face to face by their back feathers and slowly bring them together. When one bird successfully pecked the other bird three times in succession without the other bird pecking back a single time, the fight was officially over. Then the money started flying in all directions. That was quite a sight in itself. Spectators never lost track of what they had bet, with whom they had bet, and how much they had won or lost. Wads of money were thrown across the arena and in all directions, somehow always managing to reach the hands of the rightful winners. I found it amazing that all bets were nothing more than gentleman's agreements, simple promises, that in most instances were conveyed by gestures instead of verbally. Yet all bets were paid without hesitation. There must have been occasional misunderstandings as to the bet(s) placed, but I never saw an argument that might tend to validate that thought. There were rare instances where American servicemen placed their bets with other than trustworthy acquaintances, oftentimes someone they had just met at the arena. As a result they soon realized that the money they had bet disappeared right along with their newfound "friend."

Nando was an exceptional friend. He extended his hospitality to an even greater degree when he invited several of us to his home; a very small place across the street from the cockfight arena. The living quarters were behind and part of a very small and somewhat congested *Sari-Sari*, convenience store. The home and store were poorly constructed, as were most structures in and around Olongapo. One room didn't even have a roof. Nando's wife, Aurora, was very hospitable, but she showed understandable vexation at Nando's decision to bring foreigners to their home without her prior knowledge or concurrence. It was not only out of character for Nando to bring guests unannounced – their home was also out of bounds to the military. It did not matter to us; we felt privileged having been invited. His real motive was to show us his other fighting cocks and the manner in which he trained them for battle. It was interesting and entertaining as we watched fighting cocks spar with miniature boxing gloves on instead of the deadly battlefield swordlike blades. Nando's mean bird proved to us that it was every bit the fighting cock he had previously assured us it was.

Over the remaining few days of in-port time, the five of us became good friends with the Hernandez family, including their three young sons who ranged from one to ten years of age. Whenever I visited at their home, I made sure that I had several candy bars or chewing gum to share with the children. Aurora nicknamed Whit, the shortest of two, "Little Tom" and Double-L "Big Tom." Little Tom and I probably spent more time visiting at the Hernandez residence than did the others. As a result of their complete hospitality during our visits we began to feel more like family than company. It was not exactly comfortable there, and it was far too crowded for a group to visit inside, so we would usually sit outside – in front of

286

the *Sari-Sari* store. We knew that sitting outside was chance-taking in that the Shore Patrol might see us during their periodic mobile patrol rounds. We knew that being caught would mean immediate detention, possible arrest, and certainly the end of that day's liberty. So we took our chances – and we got caught! In keeping with the more understanding and realistic relationship that existed between officer and enlisted ranks of submarine personnel, we were all back on the beach within minutes of explaining the relative innocence of our illegal/unauthorized behavior to the Executive Officer. He even showed an interest in joining us in such an endeavor at some future time. Had we been destroyer sailors, at the very least it would have meant two weeks of on board restriction, possibly the loss of a stripe or two. *Colahan's* XO would have been more apt to sentence us to time in the brig on bread and water, the loss of two stripes, *and* thirty days of on board restriction.

Considering the exchange rate from pesos to dollars, the $250 per year income earned by the average Filipino, and the truly destitute conditions under which most of them lived, the theft of American property became reasonably understandable. It was not considered a serious offense for a Filipino to steal from an American, but any American caught stealing from a Filipino was in very serious trouble – not just from the perspective of military justice. The offended Filipino would, if possible, take severe measures of retaliation, up to and including maiming and murder.

The rules for carrying money or valuables were consistent throughout the world, but they were followed more closely in the Philippines where survival of the fittest (or fastest) was so apparent. We never carried money where it could be seen or where it could be reached without our knowledge. Stretch wristwatch bands openly invited theft. Flashy jewelry might invite an unwelcome "Mickey Finn," whereby the victim would awaken some time later with little more than his clothing. With the existence of a small middle class and a very large poor class, theft and trickery was an acceptable way of life; a matter of survival for many Filipinos, a game that was won with a great deal of consistency by them – rarely by us.

While in Subic Bay, *Seadragon* sailors had to submit an off-base address with their request for overnight liberty; theoretically the address where they would be staying. My address, 61-A East Eighteenth Street, was used by many of the crew – but to my knowledge I was the only one who actually stayed there. The building at that address was a two-story structure. The upper level had been partitioned off to accommodate the privacy of four tenants. I became a friend with all of the occupants; three were employed as bar hostesses. Mina and Elena worked at the Savory, a small bar at the far end of the main strip, within walking distance of the East Eighteenth Street address. Liberty, the most attractive of the group and proficient in martial art, freelanced as a prostitute. The fourth, Deloras, worked at The Corner, much closer to the base.

The Savory became a meeting place for Whit and me. It did not have the highly desired benefit of air-conditioning, but it did have two large fans that blew the hot, dusty air around sufficiently to create a feeling of coolness as it came in contact with our sweat-drenched clothing. We liked it there because it was quiet; it was never packed to capacity as were most of the air-conditioned places.

Several hostesses worked in the Savory, and Whit and I had our favorites. I was usually in the company of Mina (of the East Eighteenth Street address), although I had my eyes on the younger and more attractive, fun loving Elena (also of the same address). Once in a while I would go to other places nearby only to return to the Savory later. I was known to stray next door to the Hong Kong bar, where Lolita was a most willing and desirable hostess. But I had to exercise extreme caution when I was away from the Savory because Mina was known to be possessive to the point of violence. The Harbor Lights was another spot that I frequented. Nina, appearing young and innocent, received my undivided attention there. Next door, on the other side of the Savory, was the Greenland, where CL and another shipmate could usually be found with their favorite hostesses, Cora and Naomi. Ken and Double-L were more apt to remain on their own; they seldom locked in on any particular location.

The time came, much to Mina's disapproval, when I did make my move on Elena. That night Mina consumed more beer than I thought she was capable of drinking – certainly more than she was accustomed to. Without warning she rushed toward the table where Elena and I were sitting. I thought that she was attacking me, but there could be no doubt as to who the real target was when Elena and Mina began grappling with each other on the floor. I had seen females fight before, but never with such vengeance. Those two were out for blood – and they were very successful in drawing it. The fight lasted longer than most, probably five or six minutes, but the damages inflicted were evident on both of them. Elena, the smaller and less experienced of the two, was the obvious looser. But with her loss she gained the spoils: me! Mina moved out of the East Eighteenth Street apartment shortly thereafter. I always felt sorry for Elena, since in effect she had been victimized by my decision to violate that unwritten rule – never to dump one girl for another, especially when they both worked at the same club. Freedom of choice did not exist there. Once a selection was made, the relationship suggested joint concurrence in a one-sided implied marriage – one in which only the man had to remain true! As a result of that fight, Elena suffered two significant cuts that would scar her for the rest of her life. I sometimes wonder if she remembers the circumstances under which she received them. To the best of my knowledge that was the only time two women considered me a catch worth fighting over.

The Gateway was the first club on the right side of the street as one headed into town from the base – the last club one passed before crossing Shit River on the way "home." Every morning, around 0600, a few sailors suffering from hangovers would start wandering into the Gateway for "sick call," where we could grab the "starter upper" cold beer cure-all for which our throbbing heads and aching bodies felt the need. We would wolf down at least two, sometimes more, depending on our duty status and what we knew of the shipboard workload. We always made our way back to the boat in time for muster. Our mornings at the Gateway were almost ritualistic; we looked forward to swapping horror stories about the night before as we drank the liquid panacea.

The *Seadragon* departed Subic Bay Naval Shipyard on September 21st. The entire crew became much more alert to our status and our mission as the Commanding Officer advised us of the extremely sensitive high-level negotiations that were taking place between our government and that of Japan. The *Seadragon* had not been the first, nor had it been the only nuclear-powered vessel considered for entry into a Japanese port. But it was, at that time, the only nuclear-powered vessel that was being considered *and* was readily available. Every day we received favorable reports that we would be entering port at Sasebo, Japan, within days or even within hours – only to be disappointed when the Japanese government repeatedly squelched the plan. Several times we were given the green light to enter port only to have the approval canceled while we were en route. We were all enthusiastic about the possibility of the *Seadragon* being the first of its kind to break the nuclear barrier and thereby open the door for future nuclear-powered vessels to visit Japanese ports. The Japanese were reluctant to allow any vessel capable of carrying nuclear weapons into their waters or their ports (regardless of whether or not the vessel was nuclear-powered).

Since it was the policy of our government, never to divulge whether we actually had weapons with nuclear warheads on board, it made negotiations difficult. We could only say that which they already knew – that we had the *capability* of carrying and launching such weapons.

As time passed we began to have serious doubts that we would pull into Japan right away. There was still enough time remaining on our six-month scheduled deployment to allow for further negotiations while we visited other ports. So we remained fully prepared to change any itinerary on a moments notice; to discontinue any operations and depart from any location in order to set a course for Japan immediately upon gaining permission. Patience, for a time, became the word by which we lived.

What was so important about the United States pressing for, and Japan eventually agreeing to, visits by U.S. Navy nuclear-powered submarines to Japanese ports in the face of mass leftist agitation against them? As reported by the media, the primary reason was to help gain acceptance of atomic-powered ships in ports around the world in light of the general conviction that the future of both warships and merchant vessels would rely on nuclear energy. Japan, a maritime power, saw the need for removing fears of shipboard nuclear reactors as well as the United States. Tokyo's Nuclear Ship Development Agency had plans for a 6,000-ton atomic-powered oceanographic ship costing $10 million. Another important reason for the willingness of both the United States and Japan to hold fast against demonstrations against the visit of the USS *Seadragon* to Sasebo was the fact that the defense policy of both countries was based on close cooperation. The snake-dancing mobs put into Japanese streets protesting the *Seadragon's* visit were viewed at the Pentagon as motivated by Communist and other far-left agitation against Japanese-American military cooperation rather than fear of nuclear accidents from the sub's reactor. Street mobs were easy to organize in Japan, particularly when there was a nuclear aspect to the protest. At that time, the record of U.S. nuclear ship operations, which included more than 100 visits to foreign ports and many more to U.S. harbors, convinced Navy authorities that such ships were no more dangerous than tankers or ammunition ships.

Under the 1960 U.S. Japanese Security Treaty, the American Seventh Fleet helps defend Japan against attack and has the right to operate from bases in Japan.

American attack submarines, including the *Seadragon*, had a primary function of antisubmarine warfare, in which there was particularly close

Japanese-American cooperation – and it made no sense to Pentagon authorities that some U.S. vessels could put into Japanese bases and others had to go to much more distant ports.

A desire to permit crews of such submarines to have liberty in the more attractive Far East ports was another reason for the Navy's pressing for nuclear ship visits to Japan. Nuclear submarines, until very near that time, were only able to enter Subic Bay in the Philippines during their long deployments.

On October 11, we returned to Subic Bay where we remained for two weeks. Several of us attended the cockfights, and I always made sure that the Hernandez children received their treats. Candy, as well as nearly everything that was sold at the Navy Exchange or the commissary, was highly desirable on the black market. That made it illegal to take anything off-base in quantities that could be considered greater than those amounts needed to satisfy personal needs. One candy bar, one pack of cigarettes, and one bar of soap were but a few of the limits imposed, which made it necessary for some of us to conceal quantities over the allowable limits somewhere on our bodies. We did so even knowing that we would be carefully scrutinized, possibly patted down, as we walked through the single-file personnel exit at the main gate. I was not interested in dealing on the black market, but I was intent on making sure the Hernandez kids were never disappointed whenever I visited them.

The *Seadragon* was not only being considered for entry into Japanese waters; negotiations were also ongoing to consider her entry into Hong Kong Harbor. Much to our surprise and pleasure, negotiations quickly finalized and they were favorable. On October 27, 1964, the *Seadragon* became the first nuclear-powered vessel to enter and anchor within Hong Kong Harbor.

Hong Kong provided for an excellent pre-Japan training location and environment. We anchored in the harbor a long distance out in the event it became necessary to depart in haste – something of an inconvenience for the liberty party but nothing with which we couldn't contend. Instead of the usual three-section liberty, the crew was split in half. Two-section liberty provided ample backup in anticipation of every possible threat or activity aimed at disrupting our stay there. We expected, and were fully prepared, to repel any effort by individuals or anti-American groups that might attempt to board the *Seadragon* or to sabotage her in any way. Fire hoses were strung "at the ready" throughout the boat and topside, to be used as the first line of defense should anyone attempt boarding. Extra lookouts were stationed, and divers with SCUBA gear were available and fully prepared to exercise their skills if necessary. Our visit there was scheduled for three days or less, depending on local acceptance or subversive activities, or our higher-priority visit to Japan was authorized.

Hong Kong never seemed to change. Over the years, since my first visit, I found that the colony had remained much the same. There were more high-rise structures, most of which were condominiums. Patios extending from those apartment residences had garments, rugs, and other fabrics hanging haphazardly on clotheslines and over the guardrails – thereby causing the entire structure to take on the appearance of a giant patchwork quilt. There were many department stores and there seemed to be very little room remaining for additional high-rise structures.

I thought of Tom Mundy as I approached the White Horse bar. Several years had passed since Tom, Jim, and I had instigated a fight there. I found myself wondering if I would recognize the place and if any of the same hostesses were still working there – and I thought about the unlikely but remote possibility I might even be recognized. I thought about how great it would be if the three of us could have revisited not just the White Horse, but all of the countries and places in which we had shared so many memorable experiences. I then thought of the likelihood that we would have become involved in some form of trouble if we were a team of the Three Musketeers again, and I realized that I was probably better off reminiscing by myself.

It was strange, walking the same streets I had walked so many times in the past. I felt a peculiar sensation as I walked alone, lonely for companionship, and I slowed my pace. I wanted to take in all that there was to see as I formed mental comparisons between the past and the present. With wishful thinking I hoped to see the face of a past acquaintance.

I found the White Horse bar unchanged – yet somehow different. I did not spend a great deal of time attempting to differentiate between my recollection of the place and whatever changes it may have undergone. My recall of past experiences at the White Horse had somehow lost the significance I had, at one time, placed on them. So I decided to revisit another place some distance across town.

The Golden Dragon was still there, however the name had been changed to Peter's Bar. It had never been a very active place; too distant for most sailors. For me, it was just another one of those out-of-the-way places I had unintentionally come across at a time I had wandered away from more frequented paths.

As I sat alone at Peter's Bar I thought about my desire to wander without regard to direction and without any specific destination in mind. It had always been a part of my character, seeking places my cohorts had never been, meeting and mingling with the people who lived well away from and outside of the more popular boundaries better known to sailors and tourists. It was a way of life for me regardless of the country I was visiting, and it paid rewarding dividends by many different means. Prices were always better, although the selection was seldom as varied. The scenery was real; it was not constructed or prepared for the purpose of enticing foreigners. Getting away from the well-traveled path always provided unexpected opportunity to observe things as they truly were – in the "raw" – to meet far more interesting people, and to engage in spontaneous activities that were apt to create a more favorable and trusting awareness between two different cultures. My enthusiasm and my natural inquisitiveness were all the encouragement I needed. I was intoxicated by intrigue and infected with excitement and emotional appeal to be a living part of my surroundings. My inquiring nature always outweighed most considerations akin to the existence of, or the incidental exposure to, danger. Luck, when my better judgment failed me, remained my faithful companion throughout my military career.

Following that very short three-day visit, the *Seadragon* took to the sea and continued playing a waiting game – this time in closer proximity to Japan. We were in and out of Naha Port, Okinawa, four times during the next ten days; twice for overnight stays. The negotiations between Japan and the United States were gaining momentum, and with each passing day it appeared more and more likely that the *Seadragon* would be the first.

Naha provided brief but refreshing breaks for the crew, especially in the small community of Namanui, where most of the crew frequented the many stand-bars, nightclubs, restaurants and souvenir shops. Naha had become another of the most favored ports for submariners. Roger, Bill, and I had previously adopted the London Club as our own private haven, and with each *Seadragon* visit we wasted no time getting there. Mama-san and the hostesses, Keiko, Mimiko, Miko, and Mickey were exceptionally nice and they never expected a great deal of monetary compensation from us. They knew we would drink a fair amount of beer and that occasionally we would buy a ladies' drink for them. It was enjoyable and fascinating talking to the girls and listening to their remarkably accurate description of ship and submarine movements in and around the area. We knew that a certain percentage of bar hostesses were out-and-out spies. Attractive girls were frequently recruited for the purpose of gaining valuable information from members of the military service. We were all very much aware of the WWII slogan, "Loose lips sink ships." It was impossible recognizing which ones were really spies, so we treated all of them as if they were. On the other hand, it *was* easy recognizing, being able to distinguish between, phony hostesses and those that were willing to establish more meaningful friendships. Money was usually the key issue. At London Club money did not appear to be a concern. I knew that I would be every bit as welcome there with or without funds. And Mimiko would be right there by my side, perfectly content with nothing more than companionship and conversation. It was another home away from home.

Simultaneously, the *Seadragon* received final clearance to enter port at Sasebo as the Japanese government openly declared its approval of our official visit. The first U.S. nuclear-powered submarine to visit Japan would take place on Thursday, November 12, 1964. Japanese Socialists promptly promised to greet our arrival with a 5,000-man protest demonstration. Immediately the word spread across Japan that the 2,552-ton U.S. Navy submarine *Seadragon* was scheduled to enter Sasebo at 8:00 A.M. that date for a two-day visit. Geographically, Sasebo is but thirty-five miles from Nagasaki, the second target of U.S. atom bombs in August 1945, a place where victims and survivors were known to seek refuge and a place where sentiments in opposition to our visit were strong.

Despite assurances that no radiation danger was involved, leftist protests continued and it developed into a politically explosive situation for newly installed Prime Minister Eisaku Sato. Reports from Sasebo, where 40,000 demonstrators and 500 students had clashed with police the previous Sunday, said news of the *Seadragon's* imminent arrival had sent left-wing organizers into a new flurry of activity. The Sasebo Nuclear Submarine Protest Committee, which included members of the Socialist Party and the giant left-wing labor federation *Sohyo*, promptly dispatched a fleet of loudspeaker trucks through the streets exhorting people to join in the demonstrations. A small group of rightists had a truck of their own telling people to ignore the demonstrations. But most people in the port city of 262,000 appeared to be indifferent. The government, at Washington's request, agreed to the use of Japanese ports by U.S. nuclear-powered submarines under the U.S.-Japanese Security Treaty on condition that they carry no nuclear weapons. Sasebo and Yokosuka (near Tokyo) were designated as the ports to be used. The Japanese government's agreement, announced August 28, came after extensive tests to confirm there would be no radioactive contamination or danger and allay fears among Japan's nuclear-sensitive populace.

Some two thousand determined Japanese students kept alive the demonstrations protesting the *Seadragon's* visit – but did little to interfere with her shore/liberty-minded crew. About one hundred *Zengakuren* students, whose federation had spearheaded the bloody 1960 demonstrations against the United States-Japan Security Treaty and prevented a visit to Tokyo by former President Eisenhower, sat down in front of the Navy base where the *Seadragon* was tied up. A column of Socialists and labor unionists marched around a circular intersection 100 yards from the main gate before being blocked by some two thousand police, all wearing white raincoats. Taxis and other vehicles carried base sailors as well as members of the *Seadragon's* crew off-base where we were subjected to occasional shouts of "Yankee, go home!" Many Sasebo residents countered as they drove among the Socialist ranks in about forty automobiles while flying crossed Japanese and American flags and banners reading: WELCOME SEADRAGON.

Tokyo reported that fifteen policemen were injured when students hurled rocks and attacked them with placards at a rally at Hibiya Park, near the Imperial Palace. Two students were reported arrested. An attempted march on the parliament building was blocked, and a second rally at Hibiya Park, again sponsored by the leftist *Sohyo* Labor Federation, was quickly dispersed.

The *Seadragon* and crew were more prepared than ever to contend with just about anything during the short two-day visit. It was something of a repeat performance, as we had experienced during our visit to Hong Kong. We fully expected subversive activities, especially around the boat. There were only a couple of times when it became necessary to pressurize the fire hoses and shoo away the small handful of banner-waving demonstrators that had approached within close proximity to *Seadragon*.

There was never any reluctance for crewmen to go ashore. There was, however, a great deal of anxiety, especially knowing that we were required to remain in uniform; intentionally and identifiably visible. In a sense we

were required to flaunt our presence among a potentially volatile crowd.
We had our instructions should we become involved in an incident – but
even the instructions went little beyond common sense. We were to exercise caution and we were to behave ourselves; good advice for anyone to
follow regardless of time or location – but at that particular time and place
it was excellent advice that was to be practiced religiously.

**In Recognition of the Occasion – USS *Seadragon* (SSN-584)
The First Nuclear-Powered Vessel to Enter a Japanese Port**

Beetle and I were the first two sailors ashore. As we approached the
main gate leading to town I ran ahead, thereby achieving my pointless goal
– that of being the first nuke-boat sailor to "arrive" at Sasebo. We headed
straight for the bar district. It had been a long time since I had been to
Sasebo, and I was anxious to reacquaint myself with the area. I thought
about the possibility that I might see Takiko, the girl I had met at the Jungle
Club years before, even though I knew how unlikely it would be that I
would recognize her. I did not recognize much of anything; so much had
changed. It was no longer the crowded hustle and bustle of sailors, bars,

hookers and souvenir seekers. Such activities were not nearly as conspicuous although they were still there.

There were an abundance of Japanese television crews strategically located along the roads leading from the base to the bar district. Television crews also covered the downtown area to capture the incidence of our arrival and to provide the world as well as the local populace the opportunity to observe history in the making. That afternoon Beetle and I learned from a shipmate that we had been captured on film as we walked the strip, that we had been identified on local television as the first arrivals. Later in the evening, well after dark, there were more and more snake dances, all for the purpose of protesting our presence. That night Beetle and I were rather concerned as we returned to the boat by taxi. The only route was through an area somewhat congested with protesters. By removing our eye-catching Dixie-cup white hats as we sat low in the back seat, we were successful in not attracting attention. Our stay there was successful; we departed on November 14th knowing that there had been no significant incidents involving *Seadragon* personnel.

On November 18th following a short three-day return visit to Naha the *Seadragon* returned to sea where she remained over Thanksgiving, Christmas and New Years. On Thanksgiving Day, Captain Guthe spoke on the 1-MC, broadcasting words I never dreamed I would hear in any manner other than jokingly. They were words only familiar to seafaring men of bygone years, but words that had a very distinct meaning.

"This is the Captain speaking; now splice the main brace. I repeat; splice the main brace."

To the run-of-the-mill landlubber *splice the main brace* has little or no meaning, and according to directives and regulations in effect at that time, such words were absurd since they clearly meant that it was time for the crew to drink their ration of alcoholic beverage. Immediately following that brief attention-grabbing message a second message was broadcast: "All hands not actually on watch are invited to the mess decks to partake in the rationing of alcoholic beverage in recognition and celebration of Thanksgiving Day."

No one had seen the skipper and/or his accomplices smuggle the case or so of Old Methuselah whiskey on board. Certainly no one expected such a treat. The whiskey was not the best quality, but the spirit and thought behind the Thanksgiving surprise was yet one more plus on the side of submarine service. Those of us who drank gratefully accepted our two-ounce ration and immediately began searching for the nondrinkers. With their co-operation, some of us were successful in obtaining two or more rations. When the time came, the off-going watches also received their ration.

The following Friday night, the skipper arranged and coordinated "Casino Night." He invited all hands to attend in civilian clothes; another unheard-of underway event but very much to the delight of the officers and crew. Captain Guthe showed up dressed to kill in his black bow tie, red cummerbund, and black coat with tails. The mess deck tables were deco-rated with green felt, and each table accommodated a different game of chance; roulette, black jack, poker, or dice. The Captain, in anticipation of the extended period of time at sea, had written to several major casinos in Las Vegas in request of cards, game layouts, dice and anything else the ca-sinos were willing to donate. The items he received were quite impressive and they added significantly to the casino atmosphere. The officers played for the house where all winnings went directly into the ship's recreation fund. Winnings by the crew were theirs to keep. Casino Night became a repeat performance every Friday right up until our next port call.

Christmas Eve there was another attention-grabbing 1-MC broadcast by the skipper. Once again we all heard the unbelievable words: "Now splice the main brace," and another invitation to partake in the rationing of alcohol "in recognition and celebration of Christmas." This time the bever-age was champagne and the ration consisted of about four ounces per man. Once again those who drank quickly claimed the nondrinkers' rations.

On New Year's Eve, at precisely midnight, the almost-familiar words and the very familiar voice, "Now splice the main brace," were again passed over the 1-MC by the skipper. The ration consisted of a can of beer per man. Those were the only times I was fortunate enough to hear those ar-chaic words officially passed and the only three times alcoholic beverages were sanctioned and served by the Commanding Officer himself. Captain Guthe was one hell of a skipper and he always had a full 100 percent back-ing by his officers and crew. He knew that it was not necessary to "buy" or otherwise treat his men with special favors in order to retain their loyalty. What he did, in clear violation of Navy regulations, was completely of his own volition and was done strictly with the idea of pleasing the crew in a profound and unique manner – with total disregard as to the possibility of negative consequences from his superiors.

Within the confines of a submerged submarine recreational choices were limited. On *Seadragon*, "Ooly" contests were a kind of favorite pastime. For the usual brief duration such contests took, participants were able to shift their thoughts from serious to recreational. The loser of an ooly contest was always obligated to foot the bill for five-cent Coca-Colas for the group. To ooly was to participate in a simple game of chance whereby any number of individuals could participate. Oolies were three of anything that could be easily concealed in one's hand; nuts, bolts, coins or the like. Two or more men would stand looking at each other, each trying to psyche out the other(s) with serious stances of superiority and skill. The group would agree beforehand whether the contest was to be left- or right-handed. Participants would then conceal both of their hands behind their backs, carefully maneuvering their own choice of oolies (from zero to three) into the hand that was to be played. Once all players had their tightly clenched ooly-holding "game hand" extended to their front, one by one and in a clockwise direction, as each man guessed the total number of oolies being held, they exposed the number they were holding. Once a number was selected other players could not duplicate it. Each round a single winner dropped out of the game. By the process of elimination, in the end, there remained a single loser. The loser was immediately ridiculed for his lack of proficiency after which he was dispatched to buy and deliver Cokes for the group.

At some time during each annual extended deployment the crew could expect to see some variation of the following **NOTICE TO ALL HANDS** posted:

> Notice is hereby given to all hands of the forthcoming MULLETUS GRANDUS (Big Fish) Oolymanship Contest. The rules and regulations governing this contest are herewith set forth. All hands are directed to read the following with extreme care and take steps to insure there are no misunderstandings. In the past there have been ... uncooperative contestants ... blackmail ... marked oolies ... shifty fingers ... and left-hand fouls. It must be fully understood that in this contest as with all future contests such behavior will not be tolerated. This is an ALL HANDS EVOLUTION, there will be no exceptions.
>
> A. On (date) at 1030, all hands will muster with their respective divisions.
> B. All hands will insure they are equipped with three oolies. Some of the more prominent ooliers on board have had re-

markable luck with hammers, files, locker-doors and shoes though these items are not recommended. Mental oolies are not acceptable.

C. Each division will commence their individual contests when the word is officially passed over the 1-MC

D. Each division, through the process of elimination, shall "elect" its finalist.

E. The divisional finalists shall immediately upon being elected,
   1. Report to Control and announce he is (X) Division Mullet.
   2. Lay to the Crew's Mess and place his (or her) name in the appropriate space (on the CONTEST CHART).

F. All electees shall muster in the Crew's Mess at 1515 (the same day) for the finalist falsetto!

G. The "Hot Line" from the mess to control will remain open to transmit on-the-spot "live" proceedings that will be disseminated promptly over the 1-MC

H. When all is lost – and there remains but one single contestant – the MULLETUS GRANDUS Crowning Ceremony will take place.

I. A person of high authority will preside over the ceremony, and last year's MULLETUS GRANDUS award winner will be on hand to extend his sincere congratulations.

J. Immediately following the brief ceremony, the MULLETUS GRANDUS will personally purchase Cokes for the entire crew and his "aids" (all Divisional Electees) will carry Cokes to each member of his division.

K. The MULLETUS GRANDUS will wear his Mark of Distinction (a fish plaque) hanging around his neck for seven days, ending at 0800, (date). During this time he will accept with humble gratitude all criticisms and suggestions. His reign will continue for approximately one year!

I had the misfortune of representing my division and I came very close to being the final loser that year. The fact that I would have been required to wear the very fish plaque that I had designed and manufactured would have made me something more in line with that of double-loser. On board the *Seadragon* there was no such thing as a 'sore' or a 'poor' loser.

January 6, 1965, the *Seadragon* returned to Naha for a brief stay before returning to sea for another unexpected extension of our deployment. We returned to Naha two more times during the remainder of that deployment.

All Hands, Including the Skipper and the XO

Grand Champion Being Crowned "Ship's Worst Ooly Player"

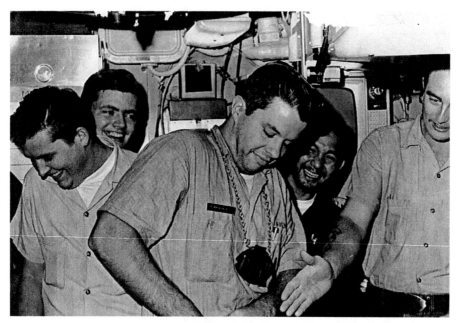

Congratulations Offered by Outgoing Grand Champ

Roger, Bill, and I were always welcomed at the London Club where we had established ourselves. One evening while we were partying, Miko and Mimiko unexpectedly drank an excess of alcoholic beverages. We were truly shocked as we watched them express themselves in a most unusual manner. Apparently they were active lesbians and they appeared to be sincerely in love with each other! Roger thought it was one of the funniest things he had ever seen, especially knowing how I had always been attracted to Mimiko's exceptional beauty and feminine ways. I just couldn't believe what I was witnessing, but I had no choice other than to accept things as they were. For obvious reasons I never thought I would be as cozy or friendly with Mimiko again.

On March 4th we finally returned to Pearl Harbor, thoroughly exhausted but happy to be home.

As a result of personnel transfers, the crew of any ship is continually changing. It was extremely unusual for an entire submarine crew to spend sufficient time intact to become 100 percent qualified on the submarine to which they were assigned. As the *Seadragon* entered the harbor that day she was flying the dolphin pennant signifying the fact that all hands were fully qualified – a sight and condition rarely seen and a proud accomplishment shared by all on board.

The remainder of 1965 the *Seadragon* spent most of her time in and out of Pearl Harbor while conducting hunter/killer exercises with U.S. and other Allied forces. It was arduous training as we sharpened our readiness and preparedness for any event, up to and including nuclear war. Unlike training conducted on surface craft, damage control drills were always an acceptable, almost-welcomed part of training. On submarines, no one ever had to be reminded how important it was to respond without hesitation, without regard to the actual or perceived degree of danger. Depending on any number of parameters, in a matter of minutes a seemingly small compromise to the watertight integrity, a small leak, could result in the loss of ship and crew! I am not suggesting damage control drills and other forms of shipboard training were an unimportant part of life aboard surface craft; I am pointing out a significant difference in what I have already described as the reliability factor. On submarines, every member of the ship's compliment was responsible; each was relied upon to respond quickly and correctly regardless of rank, rating, authority or physical location at the time of any and all malfunctions. That reliability factor, the absolute confidence submariners had in each other, did **not** exist on surface craft. It is very understandable why such a great deal of emphasis was placed on the rapid yet thorough qualification process that was to take place within specific time limitations. Every man, upon reporting for duty, whether previously qualified on another vessel or not, was required to qualify or to requalify on that boat. Failure to qualify in a timely manner was ample justification to transfer individuals out of the submarine service permanently.

Captain Guthe was, by grade, a lieutenant commander, which said a great deal about his selection to command a nuclear-powered submarine. Up until that time, he was probably the most likable, dedicated, and understanding commanding officer I had served under. The entire crew was happy for the skipper when he was selected for promotion to full commander. We were ready and we responded quickly the morning Captain Guthe showed up at Quarters for Muster wearing his brand new hat; gold "scrambled eggs" embossed on the brim. He then boldly challenged us as he said, "I'll bet a beer party for the entire crew that there aren't enough men amongst you to get me wet." Without waiting to be dismissed from Quarters, the entire crew rushed the skipper. He was quickly detained and he was escorted to the edge of the pier where, after being swung back and forth by his hands and feet, he was released on the usual three-count. Captain Guthe's awkward belly flop splash upon hitting the water brought with it a grand round of applause. One of the crew hollered, "Here, you'll need this!" as he tossed the skipper's brand-new hat into the ocean after him.

The pierside party that followed was one never to be forgotten. We knew we had one of the finest skippers in the U.S. Navy and there was nothing any one of us would not have done for the man.

The latter part of May 1965, while operating a little farther from Hawaii, our new skipper, Commander Engle, requested and received permission from the Wake Island command for a Ship's Party on the island. That might sound somewhat routine, not terribly unusual, until the conditions leading up to the request are more closely examined. Sometimes, on rare occasion, the *Seadragon* altered the time. That is, we would conduct operations under the assumption that there was a twelve-hour difference in our time and real time. 12:noon became 12:midnight. Underwater, it made no difference whether the sun was shining or not, but it did make a difference in the conduct of sensitive or unusual operations and the training associated therewith. It must have been a bit unusual for the Wake Island Command, having received our midnight radio message (noon to us) requesting not only permission to have our middle of the night party there, but also for the shore-based command to arrange and provide "Mike" boat round-trip transportation to and from our distant anchorage. Without delay arrangements were made and by 0100 (actual time) the first liberty party was on its way ashore. It was truly remarkable how quickly the skipper's request was processed. I have always suspected that there might have been a friendship between the base skipper and CDR Engle, knowledge of each other at the very least. It came as even more of a surprise when we reached the party site and found charcoal, hot dogs, hamburger patties and buns along with numerous cases of beer and soft drinks already on ice. We pitched horseshoes, engaged in a variety of ball games, observed literally thousands of nesting terns not far from the party site, and we were amazed by the size and numbers of hermit crabs crawling along the beach areas. The party was a great success and it continued up until around 0400 when we were hoarded up and bussed back to awaiting M-boats; our transportation back to the *Seadragon*.

On the bus, I mentioned to the shipmate sitting next to me that I had concealed several cans of beer that I was going to smuggle on board to share with some of the less fortunate shipmates who were unable to attend the party. He confided that he had also concealed several cans for the same purpose. We were pleased at our having considered other shipmates and we were a little loud as we laughed and bragged to each other of our booty when someone sitting directly behind us tapped our shoulders and said, "Be careful not to drop any when you climb down the ladder." While laughing we turned around and found ourselves looking directly into the face of the Executive Officer. The unbelievable part of it was that he meant what he had said! Our conduct could in no way be explained away, as if the previous skipper had established some kind of precedent, that because he had spliced the main brace over the holidays we somehow had the authority to continue drinking alcoholic beverages at sea. Our intentions were clearly a violation, yet the Exec elected to overlook our actions. His words were encouraging; he voiced no fault in our decision to provide a little refreshment to those who were unable to participate in the festivities. Another example of the vast difference between life as it was on surface craft as compared to life aboard submarines; more specifically, life aboard the *Seadragon*.

There were no provisions within Navy regulations for a vessel of the U.S. Navy to carry alcoholic beverages for purposes other than medicinal. The dispensation of such required the Secretary of the Navy's approval. Miniature 2-ounce containers of rum were carried aboard; safely maintained under lock and key by the doc, and were "issued" only under extreme conditions. A prescription, per se, to be consumed by someone retrieved from the ocean after having fallen overboard – or the survivor(s) of a downed aircraft, or equivalent conditions. Being caught with alcoholic beverages on board surface craft, or attempting to take them on board, would have resulted in immediate and severe punishment meted out by the Exec or the Captain. On board the *Seadragon*, we were all treated as adults and with far greater understanding when on occasion we failed to comply definitively with rules, regulations, suggestions or other expectations.

That month, after having my first request for duty in Vietnam denied, I submitted a second request. The Chief of Naval Personnel could find no acceptable reason to approve the transfer of a nuclear-power trained sailor to Vietnam, where his skills in that field could not be utilized. I was twenty-seven years of age, and the disappointment I felt, having had my request denied, enlivened me to resubmit my request; this time with greater emphasis:

I am resubmitting my request for duty in Vietnam because I feel I have an obligation to do so. I am obligated to myself, to my command and to the Navy as a whole. In my initial request I stated, "I have a sincere desire to be transferred to Vietnam," but I now find that I must emphasize my desires and my reasons in greater detail.

In accordance with the U.S. FIGHTING MAN'S CODE, the CODE OF CONDUCT, paramount under *all* conditions and at *all* times it is my duty to defeat any enemy of my country. I am well acquainted with The Code and I make an effort to abide by it. "I am an American Fighting man." But am I? Would it not be more appropriate for The Code to state, "I am *'prepared to be'* an American fighting man?" The fact is, The Code was not prescribed exclusively for those members of the Armed Forces of the United States who were actively participating in combat.

It seems that 'under all conditions' and 'at all times' would erase some of my responsibilities as a NEC 3355 Machinist's Mate, if not completely eradicate them, under the existing conditions in Vietnam. Actually, the Bureau would be making an ideal step forward by authorizing my request for several good reasons. My present enlistment expires before Christmas this year, and if my request is not authorized I will guarantee (my family) that I will be home for Christmas and every day thereafter. The Navy has been my life but this request will no doubt play a significant role as to my entire future.

Might I remind the Bureau that all petty officers are first military men and then technicians, and that military duties are equally as important as technical ones? All of the information I have been able to obtain, considering my NEC, indicates the Bureau is phasing out 3355 E-6s and E-7s. If correct, this is a perfect opportunity to phase me out, to authorize my request by placing me on the front and maintain the career status of this individual.

Touching briefly on a slightly different subject, I would like to mention leadership. The purpose of most leadership books is to encourage each individual to learn all he can about his professional work and about leadership, to encourage him to reason and, when faced with problems, make logical decisions based on his knowledge and experience; to reassure him that he has the authority to act; and to impress on him that he must have the courage to act. "He must have the courage to act," one more simple but important statement which prompted my decision to resubmit my request.

Every man who carries an Armed Forces Liberty Pass and men in possession of nearly every publication prepared by the Bureau of Naval Personnel can read: "The roots of the Navy lie in a strong belief in the future" and I am dedicated enough to believe my presence in Vietnam is needed and necessary to help insure a prosperous and most successful future awaits our nation. Give me the opportunity to help, as one individual, to provide aid in that particular troubled spot immediately. I must emphasize; every man knows his own capabilities and I am certainly aware that I could benefit my country more by displaying those capabilities rather than being forced to keep them concealed.

I am confident in my ability to serve my country. I am asking for position, for the opportunity to meet the challenge in Vietnam. My capabilities, my ability to adapt rapidly to different environments and my determination to serve my Navy and my people make this request most reasonable, advantageous and beneficial to the United States Navy.

My letter of request, somewhat rough around the edges and a bit lengthy, provided the Commanding Officer the basis upon which he processed his own favorable endorsement. I was very pleased:

Forwarded, recommending approval.

ADKISSON's request is quite sincere. Discussions with the Commanding Officer and other officers of this command, explaining the mission of the Navy and of this ship, have failed to change his driving desire "to get to the front." This is not a misguided desire to be a hero, nor does it appear to be a dissatisfaction with his career to date. Rather it stems from a genuine sense of mission, a feeling that he must contribute more directly, and with more immediacy, to the struggle in Viet Nam. His compulsion might be compared to that which prompted Theodore

307

Roosevelt to resign as Assistant Secretary of the Navy in order to see active service in Cuba.

ADKISSON is exceptionally well qualified for the duty he has requested. He is an outstanding machinist and machinery repairman. He has demonstrated a knack for making jerry-rig repairs and for maintaining equipment under adverse conditions as regards repair facilities and logistic support. He is an outstanding senior petty officer, well qualified to lead. His personal appearance and conduct are above reproach. Working with our allies and with other services, he would be an excellent representative of the Navy and of the United States.

His enlistment expires on 17 December 1965. If not offered orders to a tour of duty in Viet Nam as a reenlistment incentive, it is highly probable that he will enlist in another service, provided they will offer him such duty. He is well aware of the financial sacrifice this would entail but he seems prepared to make it to accomplish his primary goal.

Seadragon is presently under allowance in Machinist Mates (335X). If transferred to Viet Nam prior to November 1965 a specific relief will be required, to be on board by 1 August 1965 and at least one month prior to ADKISSON's detachment. If transferred in November or later a contact relief will be satisfactory. ADKISSON is heartily recommended for return to submarine duty upon completion of his tour in Viet Nam.

The present shortage of Machinist Mates (335X) is well known. However, in view of all facets of this request it is considered in the best interests of the Navy to grant it. It is strongly recommended that ADKISSON be offered a tour of duty in Viet Nam as an incentive for a six-year reenlistment and that he be transferred to such duty in November 1965.

* * *

The third week of September 1965, the *Seadragon* was once again deployed for another important but short WestPac cruise. While at sea I received notification that I had been selected for promotion to chief petty officer, E-7. That would be my most significant promotion (up until that time), and I was unimaginably excited. I had dreamed of what it would be like, joining the ranks of other chiefs, discarding my Dixie-cup white hat and the uniforms I had become so accustomed to wearing, and replacing them with a uniform far more personifying respect and authority. And there were an abundance of other privileges that were inherent with the rate. Every chief and officer on board went out of his way to congratulate me on my having been selected. I felt a little strange, as though I had just been accepted as someone special instead of just another sailor doing his job. I was proud as I could be but a little disappointed at the same time. Disappointed in that none of my closest friends had been selected for promotion along with me.

Late in November, following two months of submerged antisubmarine training, we pulled into Sasebo for our second visit. Other nuclear-powered submarines had visited the Japanese port since our initial visit, and the people there had grown more accustomed to such visits. The snake dances, the riots, and other types of demonstrations had all but disappeared.

In practically every liberty port most sailors have their favorite bar in which they prefer to hang out. In Sasebo I favored the New York bar, and it was there that I met Shigeko – just another bar girl but one that showed me yet another side of Japanese hospitality. The *Seadragon* was to remain in port a week during which time I spent all of my liberty time with Shigeko. She showed me the countryside surrounding Sasebo and she introduced me to many of her hardworking farmer friends. I was treated to authentic home-cooked Japanese food at each home we visited. I was surprised to find that everything I tasted – I liked. The more I ate the more my friendly and generous hosts insisted I eat. The language barrier was evident, but through gestures and a variety of finger signs I never found it impossible to communicate. Shigeko intervened whenever the need for a more thorough understanding developed.

I hated leaving Sasebo that time. I felt uncomfortable leaving Shigeko to the only world she knew – that of a bar hostess and plaything to whomever came along with the funds to pay for her company. All barmaids, hostesses, hookers, or businesswomen by any other name had remarkable acting skills. They could easily perform any number of personalities, each fitting in with any given situation. They could laugh or cry in an instant, and they could gain the immediate attention and sympathy of anyone and everyone around them. I was always amazed at how things invariably turned out in their favor or to their benefit. It was easy, perhaps desirable, to believe in everything those extraordinary women said and did. I believed that the tears Shigeko shed during our final moments together were very genuine and that they were an honest expression of her affection for me. I may very well have been wrong, but at that time, in my eyes and in my heart she was her true self, and it was my choice to believe that my kindness to her had encouraged her to think of me as someone special.

While at sea, on the return trip to Honolulu, I received transfer orders. I was filled with exhilaration when I realized that the Bureau had dealt favorably with my second request for duty in Vietnam. Having already been informed of my upcoming promotion, coupled with the knowledge that I would soon be on my way to Vietnam, sparked a new form of enthusiasm within me. I did not sleep comfortably until several days later, after the gravity of it all seemed to become less significant.

During my time aboard the *Seadragon*, I qualified for and carried the titles of Leading Engineman, Engineering Plant Operator, and Machinery Watch Supervisor. I had been responsible for overall plant performance, evaluation of plant parameters, and for recommending more efficient and safer operations. I had been responsible for making workload assignments and for maintaining accurate and up-to-date machinery history records. I had been assigned as Duty Chief on duty days, during which times I had been overall responsible for the entire Engineering Department. Most important, I had satisfied all of the requirements and had gained a thorough knowledge of the entire submarine to the extent that I had become a fully qualified submariner. I was completely satisfied with my accomplishments and with the trust I had gained from all of my shipmates, from the Commanding Officer down to the juniormost enlisted man. It was time for change.

My orders directed me to report for temporary duty at North Island, San Diego, California where I was to attend appropriate preparatory classes. December 12, 1965, immediately upon return to Pearl Harbor, I was placed in a leave status during which time I prepared for the dramatic change that was about to take place in my military career. I would be entering a world totally unfamiliar to me, a gigantic step into a world of unquestionable danger that went far beyond the intrigue and adventure I had, up to that time been familiar with and was, in a sense, addicted to. I was confident that I was prepared for whatever controlling factors awaited me in Vietnam.

USS *Seadragon* **(SSN-584)**
Thanks, Skipper – Your Endorsement Is Appreciated

11

A SAILOR'S VIETNAM

Christmas Eve, 1965, just twelve days after the *Seadragon* returned to Hawaii, my brief period of leave ended and I was officially transferred. My orders directed that I report no later than December 30, 1965, to NAVPHIBASE, Coronado (near San Diego, California), where I was to receive specialized instruction in internal security, counterinsurgency and country orientation, advanced weapons training, survival, evasion, resistance to interrogation, and escape.

The counterinsurgency phase of training was intended to provide attendees with a basic knowledge of how South Vietnam came to be, how it had been at war for one reason or another for hundreds of years, how the Communists had infiltrated and their continuing effort to take over the South as they had done in the North, how the French had failed during their occupation, and how the United States was going to prevent any further communist expansion. This training was a period of force-fed propaganda fully intended to effectively and successfully educate or "brainwash" all U.S. forces with the knowledge that we were about to enter an unfairly embattled country to serve a meritorious purpose, that we would drive the enemy out and we would assist a backward people in building a democratic system of governing. In so doing we would save a people from the terrible onslaught they had suffered as a result of their own inability to do the job without our assistance. The vast majority of us (in the military) believed what we were being told and therefore prepared ourselves accordingly. We became not only willing but also anxious to participate in the imaginary goals that had been established by our government. With public opinion becoming so radically opposed to our part in the Vietnam conflict, the purpose of the counterinsurgency phase of training we were required to go through was readily apparent. We were being "enlightened" as to the "truth," whereas the general public just wasn't as aware and therefore could not be expected to understand our position in sending U.S. troops to war in this faraway place. I was patriotic and believed completely what I was being told. Why shouldn't I? Would the U.S. government have any reason to be anything other than honest with the men it was sending there?

The self-protection phase was actually an advanced weapons training course. We were bussed to Camp Pendleton where we spent several days living as Marines. We were berthed in poorly insulated prefab Quonset huts constructed of corrugated metal and wooden floors. We became familiar with an impressive variety of foreign (particularly Soviet) and American hand-held weapons. Most of our time was spent learning how to field strip them, how to clean them, and how to reassemble them before we went to the range where we fired them. It was interesting, but from a sailor's point of view it was a miserable phase of training. There was never enough time for sufficient sleep, our meals consisted of field rations, it was cold and uncomfortable at night, etc. No wonder Marines were so tough. What we thought was miserable well beyond the uncomfortable stage was little more than an acceptable inconvenience, a way of life, for them.

The SERE (Survival, Evasion, and Rescue) training was the most strenuous training I had ever been through. The group I was with was flown to Whidbey Island, Washington, where we remained for a week. There we were subjected to what I believed to be the most important training any member of the military could experience. We were told from the very beginning that anyone failing to satisfactorily complete SERE training would no longer be considered physically qualified to remain on active duty. Anyone failing the first time through would be given a second chance – but no more! Failing the second time meant a quick return to civilian life, regardless of the number of dedicated years an individual had already devoted toward a military career. In preparation for actual field exercises, classroom training was provided. In class we were taught how to survive alone, primarily in the tropics and in the desert. We found that somewhat humorous, since we knew that our field exercises were to take place in the middle of winter, where we would be surrounded by snow. Not only that, we were destined for Vietnam, longitudinally in line with the Philippine Islands and Guam but nowhere near as hot and humid – and certainly not a desert. We received a brief refresher course on the use of the compass and were reminded several times of our boot camp training and our responsibilities in the event the enemy captured us. We studied the rules as established by the Geneva Convention and became thoroughly familiar with our rights should we suffer the misfortune of becoming prisoners of war. We were reminded that the senior man present, whether enlisted or of officer rank, regardless of education or specialty, was always in charge, and we were also reminded of our duty, our obligation, in the event we were captured by the enemy we were to make every effort to escape.

With full backpacks, we were loaded on a bus and were transported to a "drop point," an isolated heavily wooded place near the ocean where we were told that we had three days to make our way through the "wilderness" to "Freedom Road." We were supposed to make our way without being captured by the "enemy," they being comprised of our instructors. It was midday when we were dropped off and we were all hungry. Intentionally we had been denied any form of nourishment that day. During the field exercise we had just embarked upon we were to exercise all of the skills we were supposed to have learned in the classroom; we were to "survive."

Our first project was to scout for food. The SOP, Senior Officer Present, an ensign (O-1), failed to issue orders directing groups or individuals to share in the search for food, so individually we decided to fend for ourselves. I searched the area for anything green, anything growing through the thin layer of snow that covered most of the surrounding terrain. I found some vegetation that had edible roots about the size of very young carrots, not enough to satisfy a baby's appetite but food nonetheless. The afternoon passed quickly and I realized that my hunger problem needed more attention. I joined several others at the coastline where we all managed to catch a few sand crabs. As darkness approached and the tide was right, we began groping along the rocky beach in hopes of finding some clams. In no time our hands were thoroughly numbed by the freezing ocean water and it became nearly impossible to distinguish between clams and the rocks that were so similar in size and shape. A couple of men did find several clams – I was not so fortunate. That night as I prepared to dine lavishly on my harvest of sand crabs and greens, someone in the group successfully snared a small rabbit. The suggestion was made that we all contribute whatever edibles we had into the makings of a pot of rabbit stew. We all agreed. That single rabbit (with garnishings) made enough stew (broth?) for the lot of us – about twenty in all – a ration of about one cup each. This time I was lucky; my share contained a couple of sand crabs and a rabbit bone!

We all knew that we were subject to "attack" by the enemy at any time during our effort to reach Freedom Road, so we tried to locate areas that might provide some means of concealment as we bedded down for the night. I found a place surrounded by thick brush and crawled into my poncho-style sleeping bag fully clothed, shoes and all, in an effort to retain some body warmth. I don't think anyone got much sleep that night. It was far too cold, and I, as did most others, suffered significantly from "Montezuma's revenge" (diarrhea) during the night.

At the very first signs of light I heard others in the camp starting to move about, so I crawled out of my poncho in anticipation of the day ahead. No sooner did I have my gear stowed when I heard shouts and gunshots coming from a short distance away. The enemy was attacking. Once again I felt that luck was with me as I located a fallen tree, the bottom half well rotted out, and I crawled under it. I heard others nearby as they were being captured and thought to myself how fortunate I had been in locating such an ideal hiding place. *I'm going to make it to Freedom Road with or without the others.* No sooner had that thought crossed my mind when I felt something hitting my leg. I heard the words: "Get on your feet, American capitalist pig." Instantly I knew that another phase of training was about to begin. I had tasted the survival phase, I had not been very proficient at the evasion phase, and I knew that I was about to find myself in captivity, where my next challenge would be that of escaping my enemy.

No one evaded capture! I think we were all too naïve, thinking as we did that there were places to hide where we could not be found. The instructors, the enemy, had already been over every inch of that land, not just once but routinely every week. They knew every rotted-out log, every thicket, every possible place of concealment, and they wasted no time in locating each of us – to the man. We were a cold and hungry, ragged-looking bunch. We did not know it at the time, but we were probably more on the comfortable side in comparison to the treatment and experiences we would soon be required to endure.

The compound we were taken to, heavily guarded and fenced, was realistic in all aspects; a very real POW camp. One by one we were interrogated, sometimes by two men at a time. We were repeatedly tricked into doing or saying things that were violations of the training we had undergone. For example, when we demanded certain treatment as guaranteed by the Geneva Convention, we had to prove such guarantees by pointing out where it was written within those rules. Then, very much to our surprise, when we were shown copies of the convention rules we found that our demands were out of order; we were wrong! We found out later during our out-processing critique that the rules we had been shown while being held captive had been intentionally modified; a very effective means of causing confusion among us. We should never have backed down from our demands; we had been absolutely right all along. Similarly, we were each asked questions that went beyond the: "Name, rate, and service number," to which we were allowed to respond; simple questions that few of the group felt guilty about answering. Then later, when tape recordings were played at the final critique, the questions and answers were out of context, having become taped confessions of serious crimes by us or by our government. Photographs taken by covert cameras clearly depicting individuals signing "confessions" had been taken of men who had been doing nothing more than writing down their name, rate and service number – or simply doodling while they were being questioned. We learned never to hold a pen or pencil while being interrogated, especially if there happened to be a sheet of paper within close proximity.

The first two days of captivity were pure hell. Our demands for food and water (again, Geneva Convention rules) were not met, and we were harassed incessantly. Sleeping was forbidden unless there was some kind of agreement reached – any agreement that would, to some degree, acquiesce to our captor's demands. We were required to do many demeaning things for which we suffered ridicule and embarrassment. Clothing was stripped from our bodies, and we were compelled to crawl on hands and knees through the snow slush, body against body, the nose of one captor against the crack of the butt of the man in front of him. We were all forced, totally naked, into one small room; our clothing and boots were haphazardly thrown in behind us, and we were expected to find our own garments in almost-total darkness. Some time later, when we were allowed to exit from that structure, I realized that my shoes were on the wrong feet! My feet, being so numb from the cold, plus having to dress without benefit of sufficient light, were significant factors that contributed to my mistake. I had to scramble in order to reverse my shoes without attracting attention. Luckily, I had not yet laced them, which made the switch a little easier. Had I been seen, I would most assuredly have become the target of severe ridicule – an E-6 too stupid to know my right shoe/foot from my left. I later learned that there had been others who had made the same mistake; it was an expected blunder!

We were forced to crouch on our hands and knees in customized wooden containers, each fully adjustable to hold a man of any size tightly inside. The lids were closed against our backs and were then securely latched on the outside. We remained in that awkward and uncomfortable position long enough to lose the circulation and the sensations in our lower bodies. I could hear others around me as they were being released, and I wondered why I was caused to remain confined longer. When the lid of my containment was opened I found that everyone was being released at the same time. Our captors had tricked us into thinking that some of the group had been released sooner. We had been fooled into believing what we could hear but could not see; all of it very effectively staged for our benefit. Only a few of our group were able to walk immediately. Most of us suffered from severe numbness to our lower bodies such that our legs would not cooperate or even acknowledge the demands being made by our brains to "get up and walk." So we were forced to crawl, dragging our limp legs, to a nearby fence where we were made to grasp the linkage and pull ourselves to upright standing positions. The loss of sensation slowly receded as we were forced to move about.

Frequently, in their never-ending pursuit of causing discord among our group, minorities were reminded how they were referred to as "niggers," "spics," and "greasers" by a prejudiced white race. Every effort was made to make sure we were never comfortable and that we remained thoroughly confused. We had no control over anything. Our trust in one another began to vanish as a result of well-orchestrated psychological abuse. It became more and more difficult trusting our own leader, the one we were required by military law to follow.

The ensign in charge of our group was just a youngster himself. Beyond his officer training he probably had very little leadership experience. Our well-trained captors did an excellent job of making him look like a fool. They poked at him with sticks and they tickled him, always pointing out to the rest of us how childish our great leader appeared. They questioned why we accepted the orders of a child when there were others among us with far more experience. At one point the ensign was forced to stand naked in a drum of ice water. He was weak and he showed it when within moments, when he thought that he could take no more, he began to whimper and cry! Our captors then referred to him as nothing more than a crybaby. The ensign was released from the drum of water and was allowed to dress and warm himself. But within an hour, the enemy Compound Commander came out, walked directly up to the ensign, and in a voice heard by all clearly stated, "I think we all want to see you cry again; take off your clothes and get back into that drum!"

We had all been taught prior to the field exercises that in the event of our capture we should never immediately follow any malicious orders issued by our captors – that we should harass them, play dumb, and intentionally make mistakes. We were also taught that we should be particularly alert to the attitudes of our captors in an effort to recognize when we were about to cross that thin line between what we could get away with and what might result in severe punishment. I believe we were all quite effective at following those instructions, some of us more than others, but the hunger we were all suffering had begun to play a significant role in our abilities to cope.

The ensign argued profusely at the manner in which the Compound Commander was treating him. He reminded the Commander that he was an officer in the U.S. Navy and that he was to be treated as such. The poking and shoving was no longer an effective tool; the ensign stood his ground well. But when the Commander told the entire group that there would be no food for us unless our glorious leader followed the orders, the ensign immediately removed his clothing and climbed back into the drum of ice-cold water. Once again he was taunted by our captors' sarcastic jeers. But this time the ensign maintained his composure well. With a rather stern look on his face he stood tall. No tears! We applauded our leader for having complied on our behalf and for having gathered and exhibited the additional strength he truly needed. He was quickly released, this time having passed the agonizing test with honors.

We had been in captivity for almost two days, we had suffered numerous methods of humiliation, and our demands for food had not yet been met. Our tempers were being tested along with other physical and mental limitations. It was late in the afternoon on that second day when one of our captors told us we could start a fire to keep warm by as we cooked food. We were provided a large cauldron and were told to start boiling water – that they would bring us meat and vegetables with which we could make stew. With what we had already been through there was no reason for us to believe what we were being told, yet we knew that sooner or later they would have to feed us. So we started the fire and watched as the water began to boil. Even if the promise of food was to be denied, we had the warmth of the fire as temporary relief from the bitter cold. Much to our surprise, large chunks of meat and a variety of vegetables were delivered as promised. We were even provided salt and pepper. Everything immediately went directly into the pot. Our attitudes began to change, as we became jovial with the knowledge that we would soon be able to satisfy our hunger. The aroma grew more and more inviting as the stew cooked. We huddled near to the fire and we talked about the meal we were about to eat. Our hunger did not interfere with our better judgment; we did want the food fully cooked. The large chunks of meat needed extra time to melt away the fat and to cook properly.

The stew had been cooking just about an hour when the Compound Commander, accompanied by several of his sidekicks, came storming out onto the compound in our direction, screaming insults of every nature, then, "Who in the hell authorized this? You people will be punished severely." And with that he intentionally kicked the cauldron over. Eyes wide, aghast in absolute disbelief, we watched as the stew mixed in with the well-trampled muddy slush. Before we had time to gather our thoughts of whatever retaliation we might have considered, the Commander followed up with: "Gentlemen, this concludes your POW phase of training. You will now be escorted to a classroom for debriefing, after which you will be bussed to the cafeteria where you will be fed steak, eggs, and a wide variety of nutritious food. You will not be limited to the quantity of any particular food item, nor will you be limited to the number of helpings you might be in want or need of." His words were sincere and we knew that our training was about to conclude.

Debriefing was more of a critique, and even though our stomachs were howling for food, it was a worthwhile part of the training. We learned of our mistakes and of our strengths. We learned why certain things were done as they were, and I believe we were all satisfied with the manner in which the entire exercise had been presented. We learned that what we experienced was nothing compared to the actual agonies American POWs suffered at the hands of North Vietnamese captors. I became an immediate believer in that I felt every member of the armed forces should be required to successfully complete such training as a part of boot camp. I was, and remain, in complete agreement that individuals incapable of passing such training, regardless of gender, should not be allowed to serve within any branch of military service. The survival phase was an invaluable source of information that everyone could benefit by, particularly individuals who enjoy hiking, backpacking, or traveling to remote or scarcely populated areas.

Immediately upon completion of SERE training I was flown from Whidbey Island to Saigon, Vietnam. En Route there were brief stopovers at Treasure Island, California, Tokyo, Japan, and Clark Air Base, Philippines. I remained at Camp Alpha, somewhere on the outskirts of Saigon, for a little over a day.

Camp Alpha, a U.S. Army camp, was the pits (in my opinion). Of course I was biased by the sharp contrast between the Navy way of life with which I was far more familiar and the Army way of life by which I was then "challenged." The entire camp was dirt. There were no walkways, just plain dirt everywhere. Everything was covered with dust, and the extremely hot and humid weather made matters worse. We stood out like a bunch of sore thumbs, as we truly were sailors completely out of our environment.

Shortly after our arrival we were briefed as to the manner in which we would conduct ourselves as long as we were there. We were told to salute every officer we came in contact with, at each meeting, regardless of the number of times our paths crossed during a twenty-four-hour day. As was required of the soldiers camped there, we were to remain on our feet during the normal eight-hour duty day. We were to show no signs of boredom, fatigue, exhaustion, or laziness. We were to walk briskly and stand straight, and we were never to lean or prop ourselves against anything. We were, in a sense, back in boot camp where we were to remain 100% military at all times! Yet, even with the strict rules in effect, we were given something in line with preferential treatment. The soldiers, most of whom were combat-experienced, many suffering combat injuries, were required to spend the workday policing the area. That is, picking up cigarette butts and other small particles of trash – anything that could be identified as other than dirt.

I was pleased when one of our group told me that standard green fatigues were available for issue at Camp Alpha, that I need only go to the place of issue and ask for a set. I was more than anxious to get out of my whites and into something that would allow me to blend in more reasonably with my surroundings, so I went directly to the supply building.

Up to this point in my military career, I, for whatever reasons, thought that the rules of military etiquette were the same in all branches of the armed forces. I "knew," for example, that one normally removes his hat when inside a building and that in the Navy salutes are not rendered when one is uncovered (unless failure to do so would create embarrassment or misunderstanding—a judgment call). Apparently, what I "knew" held true for sailors did not hold true within other branches of military service.

I removed my hat as I entered the supply building and walked directly to the First Lieutenant (0-2), who was sitting behind the only desk in sight. He was talking to an enlisted man who had enough stripes on his sleeve to clearly identify him as one of a senior grade. I had enough sense not to interrupt; I did not need any military training or special instructions on how to be courteous. So I stood there, somewhat relaxed – certainly not at attention – and I waited to be "recognized." The 0-2 looked up at me with something of a disgusted scowl, which I took as having been recognized, and I started to ask, "Is this where . . ." only to be abruptly cut off by the officer's sharp and immediate response.

"Is this how you normally conduct yourself?" Without waiting for my reply, he continued. "Have you ever approached an officer before?"

Perhaps I wasn't the brightest of my pay grade, but it did not take a whole lot of imagination for me to realize the officer wanted to be recognized with a salute even though we were indoors, so I promptly accommodated him. I then asked if I was in the right place to receive an issue of fatigues.

"Have you ever approached an officer before?" I heard him repeat his question.

"Yes, sir," I answered.

"And this is how you normally conduct yourself?"

I thought to myself, *What the hell is this idiot after?* I had saluted him while uncovered and I was not being rude, so I simply answered his question.

"Yes, sir, I'm just trying to obtain a set of fatigues and was told this was the place to make my request."

The senior enlisted man was sitting back in his chair next to the 0-2 enjoying my lack of compliance to their way of military discipline, certainly the lack of "etiquette" I was apparently displaying. I felt terribly awkward and stood there dumbfounded, not knowing just what I was doing wrong and not knowing what I should do to make it right. For the moment, I was surrounded by deafening silence.

The 0-2's words cut deeply when he questioned, "Just what kind of military man are you?"

No doubt my face was beet-red when I made the decision to forget about the fatigues.

"Sorry to have interrupted," I said as I turned to leave.

"Is that the way you excuse yourself?" I heard coming from behind me.

"You got that straight," I blurted out. My embarrassment had turned to anger, and I continued walking, at a faster pace, toward the door. My abrupt response apparently caught the 0-2 off guard, because I was not intercepted as I exited the building. I fully expected someone to come after me, and that as a result of my insubordination I would likely suffer some form of punishment. There could have been no misunderstanding my intentional disrespect. The senior enlisted man who was sitting there probably intervened. Perhaps he advised the 0-2 that they had merely observed a perfect example of just another dumb sailor, that there would be no sense in punishing someone for conducting himself in a manner precisely in line with that which should be expected of him.

I, along with most of the rest of the group of sailors temporarily confined to Camp Alpha, quickly developed an attitude. We could not, for example, understand why combat soldiers should be required to pick up cigarette butts when they were probably far more deserving of rest, recuperation, or recreation. We decided that we should be ourselves, that regardless of Camp Alpha rules, we should be what we had enlisted to be: sailors. With that, we went to our tentlike barracks and relaxed in the comfort of assigned bunks. Those "Doggies" that saw us through the dusty window netting must have thought we were all crazy. What we were defiantly doing, intentionally disregarding the rules, was unthinkable in their eyes. And we did so without worrying about having to explain our actions.

As one soldier was picking up butts near our barracks, he somewhat frantically told us, "Man, you guys are out of your minds laying around like that."

Someone spoke for all of us when he answered, "So what are they gonna do to us, send us to Vietnam?"

A murmur of agreement came from the group. All warnings went totally unheeded, and we were allowed to have it our way.

The following day, February 12, we were flown to the Air Force Base at DaNang (frequently spelled Danang, Da Nang and Da-Nang), where we were furnished with additional transportation by military bus. The bus provided me with a more immediate firsthand realization that I really was in a war zone. All of the windows and doors had been reinforced with heavy-duty wire mesh, a deliberate precaution that was intended to prevent objects – including hand grenades – from being thrown on board. As the bus exited the Air Force base, I got my first glimpse of civilian life as lived by the local residents. The small, dirty community of ramshackle structures that we passed through was known as "Dog Patch" and was the nearest liberty village available to the Air Force. I was amazed at the amount of concertina and other types of barbed wire and fencing that surrounded nearly every structure. Private residences quite similar to many poorly constructed homes I had observed in the Philippines, were reinforced with sheets of corrugated metal among other scraps of usable materials, most of which was probably stolen or obtained by way of the black market. There were children everywhere. Most were clothed, but some ran around naked; all of them proudly displayed the **V** sign with their fingers as they ran alongside the bus. The children's arms and hands were outstretched toward us as they begged for money, candy, and cigarettes. Two different types of law enforcement agencies, the CS or Canh Sat, representing the local police, and the QC or the Hien Binh, representing the RVN (Republic of Vietnam) Military Police, were in groups of three or four at every intersection, always at the ready with their weapons fully loaded.

The bus dropped most of us off at the "White Elephant": headquarters for Naval Support Activity (NSA) DaNang, neighboring the Han River on Bach-Dang Street. I entered the compound and found my way to the personnel office, where I reported for duty. My state of confusion was seriously aggravated when I was further directed to find my way and report for duty at LCM6-10, a small Mike boat that was located at a place called Tien Sha Ramp.

"How am I supposed to find my way?" I asked the officer who had checked me in.

He routinely told me to "Catch a boat or take the barge across the river, then take a left at the dirt road and hitchhike the remaining four miles or so to the ramp." I was assured that the drivers of all vehicles heading in that direction would know where I wanted to go and would assist me in getting there.

So there I was, in a foreign country, surrounded by and probably mingling with an enemy I could not identify. I did not know north from south, and there was a war going on all around me. I was supposed to find my own way to some place called Tien Sha Ramp several miles away, on the other side of a major river, with only the hope and prayer that someone would pick me up as I hitchhiked my way into the unknown! I do not think I ever felt more helpless – at the total mercy of whoever happened to pick me up and whatever additional directions I might be given. But I did as directed.

The walk to the river's edge took no more than several minutes from the White Elephant. Then, as if I was once again in boot camp as an R and O, I had to ask where the transportation was that would take me across the river. I needn't have asked; the obvious was within sight. U.S. forces shuttled a large floating barge back and forth across the river all day, and it was easily seen as it beached very nearby.

The uneventful crossing of the river took fifteen to twenty minutes, but as I disembarked I could not help but wonder whether or not I would find the rest of my way safely, without some unexpected complication. I walked to the narrow, unpaved, dusty road, crossed it, and stood there wondering what kind of vehicle would stop to pick me up. Within minutes a large stake truck pulled over and the driver told me to hop in the back with several other hitchhikers. Once I was safely seated and the truck was on its way, I began asking directions to Tien Sha Ramp. One by one the other passengers told me they had never heard of it, that I was probably mixed up and that more than likely I meant Camp Tien Sha – an old French Army camp at the foot of Monkey Mountain that was being rejuvenated by the U.S. Navy. I readily agreed that I was thoroughly mixed up but that I was sure of my orders.

Several miles down the bumpy road the truck made a right turn. We were at the gate to Camp Tien Sha, and most of the riders hopped off. The driver suggested that I accompany him down the road another mile to Son Cha Village, where we could have a couple of cold beers at one of the small bars while seeking directions from the sailors that hung out there. *Sure, why not?* I thought to myself. I was more than willing to take a break. After all, no one at the ramp was expecting me.

Before I had time to finish my first Vietnamese brew, *Bia Ba Muoi Ba*, Beer 33, I met a sailor who lived at Tien Sha Ramp. He suggested I hang out with him and that shortly he would accompany me the rest of the way. That seemed to me the best advice I had been given since my arrival in Vietnam, and I willingly complied!

The first day on my own, in that small uncomfortable bar, completely lost and confused beyond description, I met Kiem, a beautiful Vietnamese bar girl who caused me to forget my immediate problems and brought a smile to my otherwise-bewildered face. Kiem was another acquaintance that wanted only to survive in a way that she knew would provide for her.

324

She could not speak a word of English, and I knew nothing of her language. With the aid of her dictionary we had fun putting our thoughts into simple, easily translated words. When my newfound Navy friend was ready to go, I said god-bye to Kiem with my promise to return when opportunity allowed. Within twenty minutes I was at Tien Sha Ramp reporting to the Chief in Charge.

The ramp was actually a pier extending from shore into the Han River near the point where the river flowed into the ocean. There were several small craft, primarily Mike-6 and Mike-8 boats, tied up alongside. Tien Sha Ramp was a satellite facility; the beginning of what would eventually become a full-fledged repair facility. The boats and boat crews assigned to the ramp were periodically dispatched up and down the river to assist wherever they were needed. Mike-6, #10, the craft I was assigned to, was the boat most fully equipped to make repairs and was therefore dispatched more frequently than the others. Such trips were dangerous and frequently drew small-arms fire from a well-concealed, "invisible" enemy. Regardless of the conditions, the men seemed to enjoy their work. I was eager to become one of them. I felt that I was fully prepared to accept any assignment as well as the consequential results. The chief could see that I was anxious to get involved – perhaps too anxious.

A small group of five or six men lived at the ramp in a well-constructed but uncomfortably compact structure. The only major inconvenience was the lack of inside plumbing; no toilet facilities. It was dubbed the Playboy Club and had the Playboy logo, the bunny, painted proudly at the entrance. Some hundred feet or so from the quarters there was an outside head that consisted of nothing more than a large open pit surrounded with mosquito netting. It was an outhouse that lacked walls. Without regard to that inconvenience, I was anxious to become a member of this select group and looked forward to roughing it with them. I liked the idea of living in a remote location, a place that was off-limits to outsiders – and was not under close scrutiny by anyone other than the senior occupant living there. The chief seemed perfectly happy with things the way they were although he preferred berthing at the CPO barracks at Camp Tien Sha. I was also entrusted with a tightly controlled secret, that there were times when some of the local "ladies" not only visited – they sometimes remained overnight at the Playboy Club. I was next in line due to my seniority in pay grade; it was simply a matter of time before one of the occupants would be transferred.

I spent my first five days in-country berthed on board the USS *Magoffin* (APA-199), anchored in the Han River. I hated hitchhiking by boat and by vehicle to and from the ramp every day, but I knew that sooner or later I'd be billeted closer – at Camp Tien Sha or preferably at the Playboy Club.

Within those first few days after reporting for duty at the ramp, I was advised that the Planning, Estimating, and Production Officer for the Repair Department, a lieutenant, had committed suicide with a .45-caliber pistol. I was not privileged to inside information as to what led up to the lieutenant's decision to end his life. Much to my surprise, I was temporarily assigned to fill his position pending the reassignment of a qualified officer. It was a job of significant importance whereby I became responsible for estimating damages to everything from broken bicycles up to and including an eighty-foot Coast Guard cutter that had been seriously damaged while mistakenly under attack by friendly forces. I was also responsible for planning the most feasible approach to making repairs as well as the assignment of repair teams in an effort to ensure repairs were accomplished expediently.

The predominant mode of transportation for local residents in and around DaNang was by bicycle, usually ridden by two individuals at a time. There were also a lot of Vespa motorscooters, remnants of the French occupation. And there were taxis, but they were rare. The more affluent Vietnamese and government officials were most likely to take a taxi or drive their own car. All others opted to walk or take a *siclo*, a three-wheeler that was probably a takeoff from or a modification to the Chinese rickshaw of past. Instead of pulling a two-man carriage on foot, the driver of a *siclo* pedaled his bicycle with its passenger carriage in front. Two could fit comfortably in the carriage however it was common to see entire families – six or more – all sitting on top of one another, all tightly crammed into a single carriage. At times, when the load was too heavy for the drivers, they would push their *siclo* while walking alongside instead of pedaling. *Siclo* drivers worked desperately in their attempt to accommodate any request to transport heavy loads of people or property. Oftentimes motorcycles (usually after having been involved in an accident) were transported by *siclo*, one piled on top of another. I frequently utilized the *siclo* mode of transportation while in town; it was cheap and reliable.

To my benefit, on February 17, 1966, I was reassigned to berthing in the first-class barracks at Camp Tien Sha – much closer in proximity to the ramp and one step closer to the Playboy Club. Living on base had many

326

benefits the men in remote locations did without. Having access to modern facilities was a big plus. For example, the Mess Hall, the Movie Theater and the "BX," the Base Exchange, among other things. Movie stars and other well-known celebrities visited the bases. In fact, within a few days of my moving on-base, movie star and well known celebrity Robert Mitchum paid the first-class barracks an unexpected visit. He fit right in with the rest of us. Bob, as we all called him, was as much or more of a beer drinker than the best of us. He was probably well ahead of us when he arrived, and he never slowed his pace during the three hours he remained. It was great hearing someone from home, especially someone as well known as Robert Mitchum, telling us how great we were doing and that he personally backed our contribution to the war effort 100 percent. Bob never hesitated to auto-graph anything placed in front of him, Vietnamese currency most often. He expressed his views openly, clearly demonstrating that he had a mind of his own. Bob was something of an irritant to the Special Services Officer who was responsible for escorting him. Over and over the officer kept telling Bob that he had to move on, that he couldn't remain there any longer, etc. Good old Bob boldly and bluntly told his escort to kiss off – that he (Bob), did not *have* to do a damn thing – that he was a civilian and as such he was not subject to the same military discipline to which his escort was subject. It was a rare pleasure seeing Mr. Mitchum as himself, without script to fol-low and not part of a cast. Just a regular guy sharing time with a group of total strangers – men he would probably never see again – while, without the slightest reluctance, he expressed his sometimes-unorthodox but wel-comed views in support of U.S. troops in Vietnam. When Bob left, there was no doubt that he, as with the rest of us, had his fill of beer. Even with the usual background noises of sporadic small-arms fire and other explo-sions that had a tendency to keep me awake at night, that night I slept well. One might say that I had arrived.

U.S. Naval Support Activity, DaNang, the command to which I was attached, was established on October 15, 1965, just four months prior to my arrival. Its mission was to provide logistical support for the more than 85,000 Free World Forces in the I-Corps Tactical Zone from Quang Ngai in the South to the Demilitarized Zone in the North. When commis-sioned, NSA, DaNang started with 1,412 officers and enlisted men. Little did I know that I would be there to observe and participate in its quick and steady growth from its beginning, as not much more than an anchor-age, to a bustling deep-draft seaport, to the Navy's largest overseas shore command with the largest public works department in the world; the third largest Navy supply depot after Norfolk, Virginia, and Oakland, California; the largest combat casualty hospital in Vietnam; a fleet of 225 lighterage and service craft; a small-craft repair facility with two floating drydocks capable of handling vessels up to the size of a destroyer escort, a full-scale communications-electronics department with its own repair facilities; an enlisted personnel command with responsibility for nearly 10,000 men; billeting facilities for over 6,000 men at Camp Tien Sha; a 1,600-man security force; and a 100-man full-time civic action program in the villages around DaNang.

The workday averaged about twelve hours, and the workweek was always a full seven days. There were periods of time when the easily identifiable sporadic popping of small-arms fire could be heard, more so during the night but also during the hours of daylight. Occasionally there would be rocket explosions within sight but nothing that seemed to be dangerously near me or that targeted the ramp.

During my few off-time hours I spent as much time as I could with Kiem at the bar in Son Cha Village. The back room of the bar consisted of a large space with sheets hanging from the ceiling to partition off individual beds. The first time I "bought" Kiem, she smiled and enthusiastically showed me the way to her bed. After making sure we were surrounded on all four sides by sheets, she began to remove her clothes. I immediately stopped her and motioned for her to sit beside me on the bed. I told her, "No boom boom," which she had no difficulty understanding. "Boom boom," an expression of unknown origin, very closely, if not precisely, meant "to fuck." Kiem did not want to accept payment for services not rendered. She broke down and cried as I explained, with the aid of her dictionary, that all I wanted was her company and her friendship – that I had no other choice but to pay mama-san for her "services." I suggested that Mama-san should be allowed to believe whatever she wanted to believe, that Kiem should not feel guilty, and that she should always accept her share of income willingly. I was satisfied with this agreement, whereas Kiem felt differently. She felt that I was being cheated out of my money. There was no getting around the fact that she, like many other girls I had met, was a prostitute. All prostitutes were unique in their own way, but Kiem was truly different. She was very much ashamed of her predicament and felt particularly humble whenever I paid the bar madam, the Mama-san, to take her in the back room. I convinced

Kiem that the payment was for her assistance in teaching me some of her language – that was semi-acceptable. It became fun for both of us as we learned a little more of each other's language at each meeting.

One night, while I was visiting with Kiem at the bar, the sounds of war, small-arms fire, and occasional mortar explosions became more pronounced, closer than usual. I was not yet totally accustomed to my surroundings and therefore made the calculated decision to remain at the bar overnight. All of the beds in the back room had been taken, which left me one option, that of sleeping on the compacted dirt floor. Kiem somehow managed to convince Mama-san that she should be by my side that night instead of in bed with a paying customer. I suspect she paid Mama-san for that "privilege."

When the bar closed and the lights were turned off, Kiem and I tried to find reasonably comfortable positions on the floor. I knew that by remaining in the bar I was somewhat protected from the hostile activities that were occurring in the village and the adjacent fields. That night Kiem and I were as close to each other as we had ever been when we finally fell asleep in each other's arms.

At some time during the night I was awakened abruptly by a tickling sensation around my face, particularly my nose. I brushed my face with one of my hands as I attempted to wipe away the unknown nuisance, the thing that in total darkness I was unable to see. I could hear faint sounds and sensed the movement of something nearby, so I reached into my pocket for my faithful Zippo cigarette lighter. As usual, it lit on the first strike of the flint, and I was instantly overwhelmed by my surroundings. The floor was literally teaming with huge rats, all of them scurrying to escape the provoking light cast from the flame of my Zippo. My uncontrollable gasp, immediately followed up with, "Holy Christ," and a few pointed expletives, awakened Kiem. Surprisingly Kiem was quite comfortable with our surroundings, and through gestures she let me know that the rats were insignificant, that I should not be concerned. It was the activities outside that I should be concerned with – and that we should try to get more sleep. Yeah, sure, like I was going to sleep among a hoard of rats! After some coaxing I followed Kiem's advice and covered my face with my hands and arms. Just as she had assured me, I was no longer bothered by the rats. I did, however, remain semi-alert to my surroundings; the sleep I managed to get was anything other than the nourishing sleep I would have preferred. It was a restless sleep, and I was happy when the first signs of morning light began to make an appearance. The rats had disappeared for the time being – probably to return again that night and every night thereafter.

I had no more than gained confidence in my ability to get around on my own, and had barely begun to grasp the significance of my job, when on February 25, I, along with eight others, unexpectedly received TAD (Temporary Additional Duty) orders. In part the orders read: "You are directed to proceed on or about 27 February 1966 to 15th Aerial Terminal, DaNang Air Base, DaNang, Vietnam for onward transportation to Subic Bay, Philippines. Upon arrival, you will report to LT TAYLOR, Officer-in-Charge, AFDL-23 at the Ship Repair Facility, Subic Bay, Philippines for temporary additional duty for a period of about THIRTY (30) days in connection with the activating of the YR-70."

Until that time, I did not know what an AFDL or a YR was. I learned that the AFDL was a 288-foot-long floating drydock and that the YR was, or would become as a result of our efforts, a fully equipped repair craft. Neither vessel was capable of self-propulsion. Most individuals would have been happy receiving such orders, whereas I, having set my mind as I had, was disappointed. I wanted nothing more, nothing less, than what I had worked so hard to obtain; a tour of duty within Vietnam. I expressed my reluctance to go, however I had second thoughts after being reminded that there were many different ways of assisting in the war effort. The vessels whose refurbishing we were to be responsible for were very much in demand in Vietnam, and it was of extreme importance that they become part of the NSA Repair Facility without delay. I also knew that I had the added benefit of having friends in the Philippines and I did look forward to seeing them again.

As I prepared myself for the temporary assignment I thought of Kiem and how she was going to get along during my absence. I decided to make one last trip into Son Cha and tell her of my orders.

Kiem, as usual, was all smiles as I entered the bar. She was sitting in someone's lap, but quickly leaped to her feet when she saw me enter the door. Her potential customer grumbled to her, loud enough for me to hear, "Jesus, you got a boyfriend?"

Kiem didn't answer; she just ran to me and embraced me. After paying Mama-san, Kiem and I once again headed for the privacy of the hanging sheets in the back room. Kiem was disappointed with the news that I would be gone for about a month, but she was pleased with my promise to return to her as soon as I got back. I tried to provide her with a little extra money, but she flatly refused to accept it. She gave me a photo of herself and insisted that I take it with me.

February 27, 1966, just two weeks after reporting for duty at NSA, DaNang, I was flown to Clark Air Base in the Philippines, from which further transportation by bus took eight of us to the Subic Bay repair facility. Upon reporting for duty that same day, I was assigned to the YR-70, where I became responsible for ensuring that all mechanical functions of the craft were fully operable; capable of continued operation under heavy workload conditions. In other words, the complete upgrade/outfitting and overhaul of the craft. On board the YR berthing was uncomfortable and cramped, but those of us assigned to the craft were required to berth aboard it. I was one of two E-6s on board; both of us were snipes. Snuffy, appropriately nicknamed because of his addiction or habit of always having a noticeable quantity of snuff tucked behind his lower lip, was a first class Boiler Technician. The complement of lower-rated men was sufficient to do most of the hands-on work. Snuffy and I, working directly under Chief Rickabaugh, the senior member of the crew, were supervisors.

Snuffy, a husky macho type, was about as sincere an individual as I had ever met. He was an interesting person, knowledgeable in many areas outside his own rating, and he was easy to get along with. Chief Rickabaugh made my suggestion a reality when he officially made Snuffy the Chief Master at Arms, the on-board police force as it was. I became responsible for monitoring the progress of all work.

The chief, a slim-framed, stern-faced individual, was intent on making sure we all did our jobs to perfection. He was proficient at giving orders and he fully expected them to be followed. Chief Rickabaugh had been awarded the Bronze Star for heroism while under enemy attack during the Korean War but preferred not to discuss the actual conditions under which he had miraculously survived. He was seldom seen during the workday – very soon after issuing orders at 0800 he would disappear. Late afternoon he could be counted on to return with alcohol-laden breath to check on us. The chief liked being referred as the "Officer in Charge," "Skipper," or "Captain." As the senior man on board he was allowed, if not legitimately entitled to, such recognition.

"Rick," as I was allowed to call the chief, knew that I had been selected for promotion and he was happy that he would no longer be the only CPO on board. We got along well together even though I sensed that Rick would probably spend more time away from the YR-70 as soon as there was another chief on board; me!

On one occasion when he had overspent his earnings, Rick asked me to loan him fifty dollars. For collateral he placed a beautiful pocketwatch in my hand. The watch had the name CHESTER WOOLWORTH engraved on the inside. It was a very old and very heavy "keywinder" manufactured by the New York Watch Company. Its case was coin silver, and most of the works were gold. The watch kept perfect time. I knew Rick and his spending habits and I had no reason to think that he would ever come up with fifty dollars to spare, but seeing there was some value in the watch, I staked him the fifty. The watch comes back into play later.

I wasted no time in making contact with the Hernandez family. They had moved into another home a little higher up on the side of the mountain; still within close proximity to their original home. With each meeting I grew to love and admire the entire family a little more. I knew that I had become an accepted foreigner at their home, and I acknowledged that acceptance and their kindness by providing them with small trinkets from time to time – gifts of little intrinsic value but meaningful enough to bring big smiles to the faces of adults and children alike.

I also made contact with Elena (of East Eighteenth Street), who, with no reluctance whatever, invited me to move in with her. I accepted. Overnight liberty was privileged and I knew that I would have to request it on a daily basis in hopes that it would always be approved. As long as the work progressed satisfactorily I could count on permanent overnight liberty.

At some point the overhaul of a third vessel became another of our responsibilities; YD-195, a floating crane. All three vessels were destined for DaNang. Lieutenant Taylor, a mustang officer with prior enlisted service, was the OinC, the Officer in Charge, of all three. He not only had the appearance of being in charge, he made damn sure that his authority left no doubt in anyone's mind. More than once Rick felt the brunt of Taylor's anger, usually for being hard to locate. The lieutenant made his point to Rick via the harsh message that Rick's "hat" was at stake if he didn't take his job more seriously. The threat of losing one's hat was the threat of being busted back to white-hat status, from pay grade E-7 to E-6. On one occasion I was shocked when I watched Rick, frustrated and angered, intentionally throw his hat at Taylor – and with equally harsh words clearly and distinctly growled, "You want my fuckin' hat, well, take the fuckin' thing!" I think that was the only time I ever observed Taylor's lips curl into the slight resemblance of a smile. He had finally pressed Rick's button hard enough to get a response well outside the usual self-imposed subservient boundaries, beyond his usual and expected "yes, sir" or "no, sir." Taylor enjoyed toying with Rick; he never spoke to him without accusing him of either failing to do enough or failing to do anything at all. Taylor knew full well that the work was being done and that ongoing tests proved that it was being accomplished proficiently. He enjoyed prodding Rick to see what kind of response he would get. Rick just never caught on to what I believed to be the lieutenant's sense of responsibility as exercised in hand with his unique but easily misunderstood sense of humor. I favored LT Taylor's methods and admired him for the manner in which he accepted responsibility just as he demanded others to accept responsibility. As the final authority for any special requests, including overnight liberty, he was *not* the one to lock horns with!

Working hours remained fairly constant, 0800 until 1600 daily. Sometimes because of some glitch, some problem that had to be resolved, our working hours were extended. Even then, complaints were few and far between. Most of the men were happy to be in the Philippines, working under less stressful conditions with more lenient liberty than they had in Vietnam.

My work routine became more and more awkward as Rick took me under his wing and made me accompany him whenever he felt like disappearing. In his mind he was preparing me for the gigantic step from "white hat" to "chief." In my mind I was shirking my duties and I was privileged with far too much free time.

March 15, 1966, Rick handed me a very official-looking set of orders. I was directed to report for duty the following morning, the 16th, in unusual fashion; khakis turned inside out and worn backward. I was disappointed that since I was the only E-6 on the base being promoted to E-7 that date, Rick had not been successful in gathering enough support for a full-fledged initiation at the Chief's Club. It was not practical to set up the club for the purpose of initiating a single candidate. Taylor, who had at one time also been a chief, and Rick, got their heads together and made their own private arrangements to make sure that I was, perhaps not as thoroughly but no less memorably, initiated into the world of CPOs. March 16th was the most significant and memorable day of my military career up to that time. After having been duly initiated by and in the presence of a small handful of officers and chiefs, I became an extremely proud chief petty officer. I looked at the eagles on the captain's collar devices as he pinned my collar devices on, and I thought to myself how my devices, furled anchors, would always be the most significant reminder of the anchors and eagles I had chosen to be associated with throughout my career.

The following charge, as originally written by Captain Charles G. Strum, USN, was presented to me immediately following my initiation:

During the course of this day you have been caused to suffer indignities, to experience humiliations. This you have accomplished with rare good grace, and therefore, we now believe it fitting to explain to you why this was done. There was no intent, no desire, to insult you, to demean you. Pointless as it may have seemed to you, there was a valid, time-honored reason behind every single deed, behind each pointed barb.

By experience, by performance, and by testing, you have been this day advanced to chief petty officer. You have one more hurdle to overcome. In the United States Navy, and only in the United States Navy, E-7 carries unique responsibilities. No other armed force throughout the world carries the responsibilities nor grants the privileges to its enlisted personnel comparable to the privileges and responsibilities you are now bound to observe and are expected to fulfill.

Your entire way of life has now been changed. More will be expected of you, more will be demanded of you. Not because you are E-7, but because you are now a chief petty officer. You have not merely been promoted one pay grade – you have joined an exclusive fraternity, and as in all fraternities you have a special responsibility to your brothers, even as they have a special responsibility to you.

Always bear in mind that no other armed force has rate or rank equivalent to that of the United States Navy. Granted that all armed forces have two classes of service, enlisted and commissioned, however, the United States Navy has the distinction of having four, i.e., enlisted, Bureau-appointed CPO, Bureau-appointed warrant, and commissioned. This is why we in the United States Navy may maintain with pride our feelings of superiority once we have attained the position of E-7.

These privileges, those responsibilities, do not appear in print. They have no official standing, they cannot be referred to by name, number or file. They exist because for nearly 200 years chiefs before you have freely accepted responsibility beyond the call of printed assignment; their actions and their performance demanded the respect of their seniors as well as their juniors.

It is now required that you be the fountain of wisdom, the ambassador of goodwill, the authority in personnel relations as well as technical applications. "Ask the chief" is a household word in and out of the Navy. You are now the "Chief."

The exalted position you have now received, and I use the word "exalted" advisedly, exists because of the attitude and the performance of the chiefs before you. It shall exist only so long as you and your compatriots maintain these standards.

So this then is why you were caused to experience these things. You were subjected to humiliations to prove to you that humility is a good, a great, a necessary change which cannot mar you – which, in fact, strengthens you, and in your future as a chief petty officer you will be caused to suffer indignities, to experience humiliations far beyond those imposed upon you today. Bear them with the dignity, with the same good grace with which you bore these today.

It is our intention that you will never forget this day. It is our intention to test you – to try you – to accept you. Your performance has assured us that you will wear your hat with the aplomb brothers in arms have before you.

I take a deep sincere pleasure in clasping your hand and accepting you into our midst.

I felt the tears welling in my eyes as I listened to and absorbed each word as the charge was read. I silently prayed that with God's help and guidance I would fill the shoes of a CPO in a manner well beyond that expected of me. I would strive to become the example of what being a "chief" was all about.

The TAD orders that had taken me to the Philippines were approximate in terms of duration. The estimated thirty days passed quickly. The next

ss was that in all probability we would press on for at least another
thirty days. There was a great deal of pressure from a higher command that
we complete our restoration/refurbishing projects ASAP. The repair facility at DaNang was in dire need of the added support, so we voluntarily increased our working hours to twelve-hour workdays and pushed on toward
completion.

Adkisson – Newly Appointed and a Very Proud Chief Petty Officer

Taylor, tough as he was, made up for the added efforts required by
the handful of senior petty officers, E-6 and above. He requested and the
Harbor-Master authorized the use of a motor whaleboat to take eight occupants, girlfriends included, out of the harbor for recreational purposes.
Taylor declared that day to be an unscheduled holiday for the liberty sections so that the hardworking lower-rated men could also enjoy some additional free time.

Our journey began shortly after sunrise, the Whaleboat ride was slow and consumed a good portion of the early-morning hours. We had all prepared properly and our provisions included plenty of beer, soft drinks and hard liquor. We also had an excess of all the makings for one grand barbecue: steaks, hot dogs and potato salad.

We beached the boat on one of the many surrounding uninhabited islands, where the beauty and serenity of the beach and tropical greenery were remarkable, and it was party time. It was the very best, by far the most enjoyable, party I had ever attended. We danced, sang, and we chased our girlfriends through the vegetation in hopes of getting lost in the botanical-like surroundings for a "shorttime." We were probably all successful in that endeavor since we were out of sight from one another for periods of time that would have allowed for such activities.

We also had ample time to anchor out a short ways from our party site while we enjoyed SCUBA diving and snorkeling. The water surrounding "our" island was crystal clear, and we marveled at the abundance of sea-life that seemingly was intended for the sole benefit of our small group. I located several large sea snails, live crustaceans that contained eatable animals inside; beautiful shells that I brought up to the surface for others to see. Had there been more time I would have cooked them, but as it was I stashed them on the boat with intentions of cleaning them later. They were beautiful reminders of a beautiful day – souvenirs that would last forever.

While we were at anchor one of the E-6s picked up Elena's squirming body, paid no attention to her panicky screams that she could not swim, and he threw her overboard. It was sheer luck that I came to the surface for air having exhausted my lung capacity searching the ocean's floor for additional shells. Elena was thrashing around frantically and she was swallowing seawater as she struggled to remain afloat. Once again I was lucky. Elena recognized who it was that had responded to her sincere cries for help, she did not struggle or fight me off. Instead she did precisely that which every swimming lifesaver prays for. She followed my instructions to relax as I helped her back to and on board the boat. Had it not been for her total trust in me, Elena might very well have drowned – possibly taking me with her!

Once back on board Elena was one sick gal. She gagged and vomited, and vomited and gagged. But she was alive and her full recovery did not take long. I was quite angry at the E-6; first for having thrown Elena overboard but more so for not having taken immediate action when he could see that she was in serious trouble. All he could say was, "Jesus Ad, I thought she was just foolin' around."

Over the remaining years that we were able to keep in touch, at each and every meeting Elena thanked me over and over for having saved her life. I always thanked her for having cooperated at that crucial time. It would have been difficult explaining the how and why of her death had she not survived what began as a simple prank.

I, as the only other chief aboard the YR, assumed the title and the responsibilities of Executive Officer while Rick retained his honorary title; Captain. Under Rick's direction, as the XO, I should not be diving in, dirtying my hands, actively participating in machinery maintenance. I was to align my thoughts, my abilities, and my efforts toward the accomplishment of administrative functions and leave the physical work to the fully capable crewmen that had been purposefully selected to do precisely that. I did the best I could to satisfy Rick while he was on board, but when he was out of sight, which was a good portion of the time, I kept him out of mind as I rolled my sleeves up and worked anywhere I thought my assistance was needed. Even though Rick and I were the only ones that did not stand any watches during liberty hours, I never felt guilty at the end of the workday when I put on my civvies and headed for town. Rick, as likable as he could be, made himself more and more scarce as the work progressed. He began drinking more heavily and he was usually in a state of near-stupor. During the course of any given day he was often inebriated or severely hungover. Seldom, if ever, was he totally sober. Rick depended on me to carry out his responsibilities along with my own, and I did the best I could to cover for him. Taylor, far more alert than many gave him credit for, could see what was going on, but he chose to overlook it as long as I wasn't complaining and satisfactory progress was evident.

Elena and I were best friends as well as lovers. We remained together most of my off-duty time, and we never argued. It was a new experience for her, living with a steady boyfriend and not having to prostitute herself. I was her provider, but I never reminded her of that fact; I didn't have to. Elena was well aware that her "vacation," her hiatus, was anything other than permanent.

Elena was good as gold to me. She did her very best to make me happy, and I tried in many ways to show her my appreciation. Very much to her surprise and satisfaction, I painted the inside of her apartment for her. I later learned that while I was at work (aboard the YR) she was proudly showing off her apartment to numerous friends and neighbors, not necessarily for the purpose of showing the fresh paint, more so for the purpose of showing what her boyfriend had done for her. Boyfriends just didn't do such acts of kindness. It was very unusual for a boyfriend to provide anything beyond a few pesos from time to time, and it was understood, whether spoken or not, that a gift of money was nothing more than payment for sex. I do not mean to infer that there was never such a thing as true love between American servicemen and their Filipino girlfriends. Some of those marriages tended to prove quite the contrary. However, accurate statistics that were maintained on American/Filipino marriages did not speak well for the retention rate. At that time, approximately 5 percent of such marriages were what could be considered successful. Even with a great deal of marriage counseling, coupled with the knowledge that such marriages were practically guaranteed to fail, American servicemen elected to ignore the warnings and they got married anyway. Most marriages were based on something other than love. The majority of the brides-to-be, understandably so, wanted a life far better than the one they knew. Many wanted security, whereas others only wanted a ticket to the United States. The servicemen, on the other hand, were many times victims of their own greed. They fell in love with beauty instead of the person. Nowhere in the world could there have been a greater or more dense population of beautiful, anatomically perfect women. Such love was not restricted to or reserved for the inexperienced younger serviceman; it applied equally to the older, more experienced, and theoretically wiser serviceman. It was an expected phenomenon easily comparable to a virus that would sooner or later infect almost every serviceman visiting or stationed in the Philippines and was primarily the result of loneliness.

I took pleasure in the manner in which I chose to assist Elena. Once I gave her a *komik* (comic) book in which I had hidden peso notes of varying denominations between the pages. She literally squealed with delight when she realized there was more to her book than the stories it contained. Elena, in her continuous efforts to please me, was eager to teach me Tagalog, the national language. I was equally anxious to learn. There was really no need to learn or to speak Tagalog, since all Filipinos were very proficient in English, but it provided me with an edge, an opportunity to show my willingness and my strong desire to be more readily accepted. I would also then have the advantage of understanding some of what was being said when the natives decided to converse in Tagalog. I found the language fairly easy to learn. There were a lot of similarities between Tagalog and Spanish, and I was surprised at how quickly I picked it up.

I had not realized that Elena had a sense of humor to which I could relate until one evening when she came up with what we both agreed on as a great idea. She suggested that we go barhopping and that as we go from one place to another we feign anger, we argue in front of whoever happened to be witness to our intentional diversion. I had become proficient in all the bad words and I knew how to piece them together effectively, so I willingly agreed. That was to be our evening's entertainment.

Elena and I headed for the strip with plans of attracting and deceiving a crowd, inevitably becoming the center of attraction. Our intention, her idea, was simple enough – we were going to cuss each other out in public and in Tagalog. The plan was to first fool everyone around us and then, once we had their undivided attention, divulge our act of deceit and laugh along with whatever audience we had attracted. The idea was to go from place to place as we put on repeat performances. It sounded like fun to me, so we decided that Pauline's, a split-level club near the main gate, was a good place to begin.

Pauline's was one of the nicer places where a serviceman could relax. The air-conditioning provided there was reason enough to attract plenty of customers. Many bars along the strip did not have that luxury. One of the unusual attractions at Pauline's was the penned-in area at the entrance to the place where two alligators lived in a small pond. There were always a couple of street vendors close by selling baby chicks and ducklings to those who wanted to feed the 'gators. It might seem to be a little gross, but everyone had to make a living one way or another. The chicks served two purposes; they provided the vendors with a source of income and they provided nourishment to the hungry 'gators. The sideshow effectively stopped nearly everyone who passed by, a sure way to attract additional customers into Pauline's. The "show," for the most part, was imaginative, effective and lucrative.

The floor at street-level inside Pauline's was well equipped with tables and chairs. I always preferred sitting upstairs, where the upper deck surrounded and overlooked everything below. It was also much safer upstairs because whenever a fight broke out the patrons upstairs were known to throw beer bottles at those fighting below. There were other occasions when for no apparent reason someone would intentionally drop a bottle on some unsuspecting customer below. The hostesses were no exceptions; when they were provoked they could be extremely accurate, hitting their targets with ashtrays, bottles, and their shoes. The bottle-throwing episodes were just as effective breaking up fights as they were initiating them.

As soon as Elena and I were settled at Pauline's our Tagalog "game" began. Elena started out by telling me I was ugly, and I told her she smelled bad. She told me she hated me and I called her a useless whore. And so it went, with believable sincerity, until I told her that her face looked like money, a pointed insult that meant she would do *anything* for money. As soon as the words passed my lips, Elena threw her purse at me with tempestuous hatred in her glaring eyes. The purse glanced off the side of my head, slid across the floor, and slammed into the far wall. I was bewildered as I recognized her unmistakable anger, and I quickly asked her what the hell was her problem. Her response, as she reverted to perfect English, told me that our little plan had somehow gone awry and the game was instantly terminated; "You son of a bitch, you didn't have to say that." I reminded Elena that it was her plan to do precisely what we had done, but in her mind I had gone beyond the limits of parameters I did not know she had imposed. The small audience we had been so successful in attracting could never have been convinced that our argument was intentional, that it all began as a practical joke that was supposed to culminate in laughter. Well, the joke was on me, and I was anything other than appreciative, especially when Elena refused to talk to me the rest of the night. Nor did she ever apologize for her part in ruining what I thought was an Academy Award-winning performance.

My work routine and liberty routine remained uncomplicated and fairly constant. Rick and I knew that soon we would be returning to Vietnam with the YR-70 under tow. We devised what we thought was a thorough checklist, intended to make sure all equipment was functioning properly and that the vessel was 100 percent seaworthy. One slight problem we had not considered was the fact that we, the entire crew, were all snipes. We were hands-on maintenance types, engineers. The powers above, those responsible for handpicking us for the refurbishing projects, had not considered the need for a cook. At the time it probably didn't seem necessary, since we all had access to the base Mess Hall. But things were different now that we were preparing to cross a rather wide body of water. Not surprisingly, we found that Snuffy had another talent. Not only could he cook; he enjoyed doing so. So Snuffy unexpectedly, yet enthusiastically, took on the added responsibility of making sure all galley equipment was fully functional.

A couple of days prior to our expected departure, Snuffy went shopping at the Commissary. Lieutenant Taylor did not burden Snuffy by any budgetary funding or quantity limitations. The Lieutenant knew that it was not going to be easy crossing the South China Sea under tow, and he wanted to make sure that we were not deprived of anything that might make our time at sea more comfortable. In this instance that meant unlimited food of choice.

Snuffy returned from his shopping spree grinning from ear to ear, and his first remark was an accurate indication of what he had done: "We're gonna eat better than the officers at Annapolis as long as I'm the chef on board this craft." Without limitations or restrictive guidelines to follow or abide by, Snuffy had taken his task to heart. He bought provisions that were fit for royalty and in quantities that far exceeded our needs for the four-to-five-day tow across the ocean.

Without my knowledge, Lieutenant Taylor had terminated liberty on the YD-195 and the YR-70 at 2400 hours, midnight, on April 14th. He had arranged for a YTD, a very large seagoing tug, to initiate the tow at 0500 the following morning, almost three hours before I thought liberty expired. The morning of April 15th I considered myself extremely lucky when I awakened quite early and decided to go to work earlier than usual. I boarded not more than ten minutes before the gangway was removed as the final step in preparation for departing under tow. Rick, not knowing how to locate me, was in a state of panic thinking I would miss embarkation. He was also concerned because he knew that it would have been his fault, his failure to tell me about the change in liberty hours. I laughed the matter off, even though inside I was somewhat angered. Had I missed movement, regardless of whether or not I shared the blame, there would have been a strong likelihood that I would be reassigned or relocated somewhere else.

It must have been a strange sight to see from the air: two vessels under tow, one trailing behind another. The YD was first behind the tug, and the YR trailed farthest behind. The AFDL was not ready at the time our tow was initiated so, for the time being, it remained in Subic Bay. The tow cable between vessels was lengthy and at times, due to weather or heavy swells, it was difficult to see either the YD or the tug from the YR. We had failed miserably in providing appropriate contingency plans in the event of an emergency. We were derelict in our responsibility to ensure that all considerations for the safety of the crew (as well as the vessel) had been properly initiated or otherwise enforced. We did not have radio contact with either of the other vessels, but we did have a "very pistol," a gun that was capable of shooting different-colored flares. We had made prior arrangements to ensure that designated individuals on the other vessels would be alert at 0800 each morning to observe our simple and easily understood signals. A green flare would be our assurance that everything was fine, whereas a red flare was to indicate we had a very serious problem that needed immediate attention; it meant, "help!" Under no circumstances would we fire the red flare without the presence of significant urgency. We had failed to consider our direction of travel, among other things! At 0800 each morning when we fired a flare, the glare of the rising sun directly behind us blinded anyone in front, seriously impeding their view. Distinguishing its color was quite impossible. The skipper of the tug either didn't consider it a problem or didn't care – he could easily have changed course each morning shortly before the designated time of our signal flare, thereby eliminating the glare of the sun as a disabling factor. Of equal or greater concern to those of us on the YR was that we did not have an operable bilge pump – nor did we have any other type submersible pump that could have been utilized in the event of flooding, an oversight unheard of on any seaworthy vessel.

We were well aware of our mistakes and of the potential for disaster should an emergency situation arise. But our concerns were offset to some degree by the quality and quantity of food Snuffy so professionally prepared. Since the crew consisted of such a small handful of men, we had the favorable consolation of being able to order meals tailored to individual likes. Snuffy had no difficulty in satisfying everyone. We had eggs to order, the finest cuts of steak, shrimp galore, every fresh vegetable imaginable, chicken, French fries, and on and on! And there was no waste! We snacked on leftovers at all hours of the day and night and we knew that there was plenty more where that came from. Snuffy became known as the Master Chef, a most appropriate title for one heck of an accommodating cook. That was the first time I had ever been to sea without having to stand watches or worry about the proper operation of main propulsion machinery or auxiliaries. As long as the generator kept generating, we had little to do except relax, observe the sky and the water around us; and eat.

We successfully crossed the South China Sea without incident, and Vietnam was within sight. The date was April 19, 1966, and anxieties were running high. General Quarters was called, which meant little more than

343

being alert and not being conspicuous as the tug slowly made her way up the Han River, YD-195 and YR-70 following under tow. No one knew what to expect from the unseen and unpredictable enemy who was, no doubt, alert and watching our approach. Two individuals were stationed on top of the YR, manning *nonfunctional* gun mounts. The idea was to take on the appearance that we were capable of responding should we come under attack. We somewhat expected incoming rounds of small-arms fire, and it was an uncomfortable feeling knowing that we would not be able to respond in kind; we had no weapons of our own. From the first day out I had taken a very strong exception to the policy that we were not allowed to have weapons of any kind, we were completely at the mercy of the enemy should we become their target. The two individuals manning the topside gun mounts were sitting ducks – decoys, in a sense. They knew better than anyone that the gun mounts were nothing more than props and that they would be the first targets in the sights of any weapon trained on or fired at us. I knew that it would have done no good to complain after the fact, assuming we came through unscathed. The powers above us would have taken a stand of logic that since nothing happened we were not in danger, and therefore we were not in need of weapons. Had we been fired upon, had we suffered casualties, or had our vessel been sunk, I'm equally sure that the powers above us would never have allowed the facts of our ill-equipped and helpless situation to be known. We were all enlisted men on board that YR, and never before had I been exposed to a more perfect example of just how expendable, just how insignificant, we really were. We had been sent to the Philippines to carry out a very responsible mission. Once that mission was completed, our worth diminished proportionally. We had been flown to the Philippines and could just as easily have been flown back to Vietnam instead of by means of the cheapest possible transportation - on a vessel incapable of self-propulsion, under tow, entering hazardous (war zone) waters without any means of protecting ourselves. The YR could just as easily have been towed with fewer men on board, without placing the entire group at risk. That was the way we all felt.

The trip up the Han River was a little nerve-wracking but otherwise un-eventful. We anchored the YR out near the middle of the river, a couple of miles from Tien Sha Ramp. The YD was "parked" several miles away along-side the deepwater pier. That week, YR-70 and YD-195 became the first major fully functional elements of the NSA DaNang Repair Department. The Playboy Club at Tien Sha Ramp could no longer be considered appro-

344

priate berthing for me. There were no chiefs berthed there. It was a place occupied by individuals who preferred staying away from CPOs, especially during their off-time. Likewise, it would not have been right for me, as a chief, to consider myself properly berthed among white hats, sailors of pay grades below that of E-7. Granted, I was a chief, but I needed a great deal more exposure to other chiefs as a part of my learning process. CPOs were, or at least had been for quite some time, people I chose not to associate with; they were the enemy of another kind. They enforced the rules that I often chose to ignore. They were feared far more than they were admired by the majority of lower-graded enlisted men. I felt a very strong obligation to myself and to the Navy that I should make every attempt to bridge those feelings of the past. It would be another of my goals - that I would strive to be the exception to the rule and would earn acceptance by the lower-graded men, not out of fear, but out of trust and respect. But first I had to be accepted within the ranks of CPO's; then I would mold myself into an individual that would be fully accepted by superiors, by equals, and by those subordinate to me. Those were my thoughts, and that was my plan.

As a temporary measure, Rick and I were assigned berthing in the CPO quarters on the APL-27, another vessel anchored in the Han River that was utilized for the sole purpose of providing food and berthing for the overflow of personnel assigned to NSA, DaNang. I hated living on the APL. The berthing quarters were overcrowded, and it was a nuisance finding water transportation to and from the YR.

I retained the title Planning, Estimating, and Production Officer, though my duties changed somewhat. I became responsible for receiving work requests, screening them, and coordinating job assignments. I spent a great deal of time traveling up and down the river keeping tabs on all repairs being accomplished by the Repair Department.

I wasted no time in my quest to be berthed at the CPO quarters at Camp Tien Sha. The relocation would compound some inconveniences that I was already experiencing in that I would not only have to hitchhike from the base to Tien Sha Ramp, but I would still have to worry about water transportation from the ramp on out to the YR – and vice versa. I could accept that aggravation knowing that I would have access to the exchange and the clubs; I would be able to walk around without having to contend with crowded shipboard conditions. I was placed on one more of the numerous waiting lists I would find myself on during my tour of duty within the Republic of Vietnam.

Somehow the tightly concealed secrets of the Playboy Club leaked, and at a most inconvenient time that nice little private club was raided. It was late that night, and most of the occupants had their girlfriends with them. The OinC of ramp activities frowned heavily on such activities – so the very next day the Playboy Club became history. It was totally dismantled and became nothing more than a fond memory for those privileged few that had lived and "played" there. The girlfriends suffered the most. Some of them had relied heavily on their boyfriends, only to be told that they would have to find housing elsewhere. The men who had lived there took the stand that in causing the girls to become homeless the command had hurt Vietnamese-American relations. There might have been something to that train of thought.

Rick, some time earlier but similarly to me, had also been assigned to the repair facility at NSA prior to his stint in the Philippines. He had thoroughly briefed me on all he knew about NSA, DaNang and he looked forward to showing off the club that he insisted he had been responsible for constructing and furnishing: the CPO Club. Rick bragged incessantly about how he had managed to "cumshaw" this and that, how he had begged, borrowed, and stolen whatever was needed in order to provide the chiefs with their own club. He was also anxious to introduce me to his girlfriend, ostensibly employed by the club as a waitress.

Rick was outraged when he took me to the base that first time and found the Chiefs' Club was still under construction. Even the nearest re-stroom facility was still several blocks away, unless one elected to use the outdoor urinal, a large four or five-inch pipe that protruded from the ground at an angle to a height of about three feet, intentionally placed right next to the Club to serve that specific purpose. During club hours there was usually a line of GIs waiting their turn at that urinal pipe. There was no privacy curtain or wall of any kind; the pipe was totally out in the open. Whenever Vietnamese men or women walked by, they ignored what to them was apparently an acceptable practice. Off-base it was very common for Vietnamese women and men of all ages to squat alongside the road in plain view of pedestrian and vehicular traffic, without the slightest sense of modesty or humiliation, as they publicly relieved themselves.

Rick was even more enraged at what I thought was quite humorous when he found his girlfriend had not waited for him; she had been unfaithful. In his opinion, the worst part of it all was that she had chosen an African-American chief to take his place! She was no longer the sweet Vietnamese girl that Rick had previously described to me – the one he had been so anxious to introduce me to. From that day on, Rick always referred to her as "that cock-suckin' nigger-lovin' bitch."

While I was in the Philippines all liberty in the DaNang area had been canceled. Even the small village of Son Cha, where Kiem lived, was off-limits. That came as a really big disappointment. I wanted to get the word to Kiem that I was back but didn't know how to go about it. I knew that any "extracurricular" activities had to be done illegally, on the sly. I figured that in due time, given ample opportunity, I would find a way to see or to get a message to her.

Somehow, by questionable means I'm sure, Rick managed to acquire a civilian jeep. He stuck to his story that some important Vietnamese woman known as Madam Nu had loaned it to him for as long as he was in the country. Rick never admitted to having done a thing in return for this rare privilege. Anyway, I no longer had to rely on hitchhiking as a means of getting around. We then had an added benefit; we were able to traverse areas that would otherwise have been out of the question. On one such occasion we showed a young Navy ensign some of the back roads. He was assigned to what was known as the LARC Base near DaNang Airport and was responsible and subordinate to the NSA Repair Department. He had seen very little of the area other than the direct route to and from the LARC Base so Rick and I decided to enlighten him. As we were driving along the beach route, a route the ensign did not know existed, our wide-eyed passenger told us that he had been in-country for several months but he didn't feel as though he was in a war zone because he had never fired his .45. I said "Well, why don't you fire the damn thing?" To show him I was sincere I yanked my weapon from its holster as Rick pulled the jeep to an abrupt stop. I "aimed" at the ocean and quickly squeezed off two rounds. The ensign looked thrilled at my encouragement, at my having blessed him with the authority to do as I had done. He carefully removed his .45 from its holster, took attentive aim at some distant piece of the ocean, and he squeezed the trigger.

"Why don't you try jacking a shell into the chamber?" Rick mockingly suggested. The ensign looked embarrassed as he followed Rick's advice. The three of us heard the click of the hammer as it fell, an apparent misfire.

Rick jammed the gearshift into low and as the jeep lurched forward he proceeded to scold the ensign.

"Jesus Christ, we've got us a goddamned academy man, a friggin' war hero who can't even fire his gun."

I followed up with my two cents' worth: "You had your chance, now put your toy away like a good little boy."

It was not often that opportunity knocked loud enough for an enlisted man, regardless of grade, to address an officer in that manner. We all had a good laugh and felt better for it. I do not know if the ensign ever tried to fire his weapon again.

The question of "Why Vietnam?" was being asked more and more frequently by members of the military. I still believed in what we were doing there, particularly when the only official propaganda at my disposal was of U.S. government origin. The following is a duplicate of an article published in the August 1966 issue of the *Information Bulletin*, also known as the *ComServPac* (Commander Service Force, Pacific Fleet) *Information Bulletin*, a Navy release:

History Does Not Repeat Itself!
Contrary to common belief, history is an everchanging pattern. Vietnam is proving that. What is obvious is that change is a must in our current situation. The policies we used in Korea do not necessarily apply in Southeast Asia although the enemy is the same. The "dollar-diplomacy" used for the Dominican Republic in 1916 bears no [more] resemblance to present-day relations with that nation than does Teddy Roosevelt's "big-stick" theory. What is important is the fact that we learn from history, remain flexible in face of its lessons and apply what we learn with as much wisdom as we can.

With this in mind, we can ask the following:

What exactly is our foreign policy with Vietnam?

Why did we send troops into the Dominican Republic?

These questions and their answers go to the very nature of a diplomacy continually fanned by the winds of change. They show the increasing complexity of foreign policy between nations whose oceans are no longer walls between them.

SHIFT IN WORLD POWER

Under Secretary of State George W. Ball faced the problem squarely when he stated: " ... events of epic dimensions, crowded into less than two decades – a mere moment in time – have produced massive shifts in the world power balance. They have revolutionized not merely the practice, but the substance of diplomacy."

Now, two powerful systems face each other. One is based on free choice and the other on the sacrifice of the individuals for what their rulers consider to be for the good of the state. No more are there great colonial empires. Now there are new struggling nations, each trying to stand on its own feet.

Today the United States is the world's richest and most powerful nation and has assumed the responsibilities that go along with this power – the protection of the interests and security of free people around the globe.

DIPLOMACY AND VIETNAM

How has this change in diplomatic philosophy affected our current policy in Vietnam? To answer this let us go back to the early 1950s and the lessons of Korea.

The enemy is the same: Communist ambition. However, the methods are far different from those used in Korea. Before, the Communists operated in a traditional manner. They moved large bodies of organized troops into non-Communist areas. We and the other United Nations countries acted and they were thrown back. Now the Communists have ambitions in Vietnam – but their tactics are much more subtle. They work through the villages and hamlets, terrorizing selected sections of the population, destroying organized government by killing off its leaders and replacing them with their own group of propagandists. For over ten years, the government and most of the people of South Vietnam have fought this invasion. We have assisted them with advisers and equipment, and now we have stepped up this assistance and will continue to do so until the security of South Vietnam is once again insured. [Oh, yeah?]

MORAL DIPLOMACY

Again in the Dominican Republic, we played a far different role than we ever had before.

In 1916, we poured men and material into that nation, controlled the economy, influenced the government and – although not admirable – it was our idea of diplomacy. They called it "dollar diplomacy," and that is exactly what it was. Now, in 1965, we are involved in "moral diplomacy." [Double oh, yeah?]

During the first days of the rebellion in the Dominican Republic, our embassy was engaged in evacuating citizens of both the United States and other countries who desired to leave the island. All at once, machine-gun fire blazed in an evacuee assembly area. President Johnson immediately gave the order to send the danger zone an emergency force of U.S. Marines, which had been pre-positioned for just such a contingency to protect U.S. citizens and interests. At the same time he called for an emergency meeting of the Organization of American States. This was no "colonial adventure" of the 1900s. Rather, it was a mature attempt to protect lives, property and the security of our inter-American agreements and relationships. As soon as the OAS was ready, we turned over our responsibilities to them.

What does this show?

Simply that we have turned to "moral diplomacy" both in Vietnam and Latin America. It shows that we must be open to change – for the world is an ever-changing spectrum of international colors. It shows that intricate, delicate problems need open minds and a willingness to change.

John Donne once said, " ... no man is an island. Ask not for whom the bell tolls – it tolls for thee." In this world, it rings louder and more truly than ever before.

This concludes the article as it was originally published. I include it as a small example of the information with which we were constantly supplied. It always reinforced my belief that what we were doing was right – and that we could not help but come out on top. After all, didn't right always win over wrong? The answer, in my mind, was that right *did* overcome wrong. The more appropriate question eventually became ... *who* was right?

It was not long before I lost my impressive title, Planning, Estimating, and Production Officer, to Lieutenant Randall, a fine mustang officer who had an acute sense of pride and duty. I became his immediate assistant, with a new title, Assistant Planning Officer; however, my duties remained much the same as they had been prior to his arrival. The YR-70 became the un-contested hardest workhorse in the area and was known as the Small Craft

Repair Facility. The title was fair; however, the work orders we processed provided far more than support for small craft. We, the YR-70 personnel, provided well-balanced support for all branches of the military, including foreign allied forces, and we were occasionally called upon to provide assistance to nonmilitary or civilian projects. Lieutenant Randall, as the only officer on board, held the title Officer in Charge, YR-70.

LT Randall, "Randy" to his officer friends, insisted on a full day's work, never less than twelve hours and frequently up to sixteen or more, seven days a week. It was a guaranteed 365-workday per year for everyone assigned to the YR. But the Lieutenant was also a steamer. His *modus operandi* and mine went hand in hand, so we got along well. He did have a tendency to pick on Rick occasionally, but that was more of necessity than as the result of malevolence. Rick was easily sidetracked when he was away from the YR. Sometimes he would stop off at the CPO Club and, appropriately, Randall would have to admonish him. It was not easy keeping Rick away from booze – but during periods of relative sobriety he produced double the work otherwise required.

LT Randall preferred the CPO Club to either of the two "O" (Officers') Clubs. One, the I-Corps Officers Mess, later renamed the "Stone Elephant," was located at the far north end of DaNang, which meant several miles of water transportation from the YR to the White Elephant dock via the river, and then another mile or so down Bach-Dang Street to the Club. Not only was it too far; it was too stuffy inside. The other "O" Club, the "Little Elephant," was located not too far from the Chiefs' Club at Camp Tien Sha, but it did not provide the right atmosphere. Officers (and gentlemen) did not, or were not allowed by protocol to, enjoy themselves – at least not to the degree to which Chiefs were known. Activities at the CPO Club fell somewhere between those of the Enlisted Men's Club and those of the Officers' Club. Rules of the CPO Club were specific in that only enlisted grades E-7 and above were allowed inside. Officers were allowed but only if they were accompanied by and the guest of a chief. Those rules held true at all CPO Clubs worldwide. Randy had Rick or me to rely upon for access to "our" club, and we never let him down.

The work routine, except for the long hours, was simple and somewhat monotonous. I worked hard from the early hours of each morning until late afternoon every day. At the end of each workday I headed for the Chiefs' Club, where I knew that I could relax in comfort and flirt with my favorite Vietnamese hostesses.

Water transportation back to the YR was very much dependent upon what time we left the Club. One particular night, quite late, Rick and I found ourselves stranded. There were no Mike boats running, our river mode of hitchhiking, and the U-boats (Utility boats) were only authorized to take on and discharge passengers at specific locations. The YR, for reasons I'll never know or understand, was not considered an authorized stop. We tried using our authority as chiefs – to no avail. Finally I told Rick that I would get us on board by any means; by trickery and/or by treachery!

There was a dump site within a short walking distance from Tien Sha Ramp where I could reasonably assume I would find a piece of unrecognizable trash, something I could use as an instrument of persuasion in gaining our much-needed transportation. At the dump I found several strange-looking, twisted "widgets," things I had never seen before but things that, appearance-wise, were very useable.

"Come on Rick; I've got our tickets to the YR in hand."

"What in the hell are you gonna do with them things?" Rick asked as he looked at me with curious doubt.

"Just watch, listen, and learn as you play along!"

It wasn't long before the next U-boat came along. As usual, I first asked for transportation to the YR, and as usual I was told, "Sorry, Chief, no can do."

"What the hell do you mean, 'no can do'?" I demanded.

He went on to tell me that which I already knew. I pretended to be confused and furious. "Look, pal, we were dispatched from Hue because of that damned YR. They have an emergency need for these *fillyosicrofoliums*. We've been through a living hell getting here, damn lucky to be alive, and you say 'no can do'? I think you better reconsider your orders or face some rather serious consequences!"

"What'd you say those things are?"

Fillyosicrofoliums, goddamnit; now we're coming aboard."

"Sure, Chief. You guys hop on board and I'll get you there pronto."

The coxswain pulled away and gunned it flank speed straight to the YR-70. Rick never forgave me for what I did once we were safely at our destination, on board the YR. I looked at Rick and said, "Guess we don't need these things anymore," and I tossed them overboard – right in front of the U-boat coxswain!

Hell, Ad, you didn't have to do that. That guy will never give us another ride," Rick scolded me.

"So we'll just have to commandeer his boat then, won't we!" I said.

"Damn, Ad, you're gonna be a fine chief."

I liked it when Rick spoke to me in that manner. I knew that he was joking – but the inference that I had what it took, CPO qualities, was encouraging.

Club hostesses, as with all foreign nationals applying for employment, regardless of the position, were carefully screened prior to being hired. There were probably as many Communist sympathizers and/or full-fledged Viet Cong as there were pro-democracy/pro-Americans working on base. The girls were screened not only for their beliefs, but also for their beauty. None of them spoke fluent English, which made it that much more fun for me. I learned and used basic words and simple phrases in Vietnamese as frequently as I could, and I gained respect (a little favoritism) from the hostesses as a result. "Mai," not nearly as attractive as others working at the Club, was my favorite. She was freckle-faced as could be, extremely shy, and she was never without her impressive and vibrant smile. I enjoyed teasing Linda, the very capable bartender but little more than a youngster – and "Le," one of the two more attractive club sweethearts; "Lee-Lee" the other. And there was "Smiley," dubbed so by Randall. Smiley had eyes for the Lieutenant, and he enjoyed all of the attention she gave him. Randall also enjoyed teasing Smiley. Even though she understood very little of what he was saying, she always grinned from ear to ear as she listened intently to whatever double-talking nonsense he said to her.

Hostesses doubled for waitresses whenever needed. They were there to help create a favorable and friendly atmosphere where chiefs could congregate and enjoy the company of other chiefs as well as that of female employees. The hostesses were required to move from table to table every fifteen minutes to prevent them from becoming too attached to their favorites. That policy also prevented CPOs from holding claim to those they favored for lengthy time periods. Club policy included a well enforced "hands-off" that demanded absolute respect for female employees. Physical contact between customers and employees was strictly forbidden. Flirting was fine, but nothing more while on duty or on the premises. I was never naïve enough to think that none of the chiefs were gaining sexual favors;

I just couldn't figure out how I might become one of the lucky ones. I did, after quite some time, gain the trust of Mai to the point that she allowed me to provide her with transportation (Rick's jeep) to her home a couple of miles away. She lived in My Khe Village, several blocks from China Beach. This was a gigantic step in the right direction, not for any special favors, but toward fostering a meaningful friendship with Mai, her parents, her sisters, and her brother. There were no "on-limits" places in or around DaNang, and Mai's home was no exception.

Rick and I were together the first time I visited Mai at her home. The main route from Camp Tien Sha to her home was via Cach-Mang Street, also known as Highway 13, the same rugged road that I had hitchhiked when I first arrived in-country. It remained the same rough, narrow, dusty, chuckhole-filled, well-traveled road. By day, there was always an abundance of traffic. Pedestrians were always the majority; bicycles took a very close second, followed by motor scooters and military vehicles. There were no shopping areas along that road, very little of anything other than the steady coming and going of local residents, most of whom were poor peasants. Some sort of heavy load invariably burdened everyone walking. The Vietnamese were a thin-to-the-bone people, by appearance half-starved, both male and female destined to carry heavy loads on their backs or hanging from both ends of a well-balanced pole on their shoulders and loads of "whatever" in their arms. They skillfully maneuvered pushcarts and pullcarts, usually overloaded with bags of rice, through a variety of hazardous traffic conditions. The much narrower side-road that crossed the peninsula from Highway 13 passed through My Khe Village and ended abruptly on a sandy South China Sea beach, provided for the hustle and bustle of far more crowded pedestrian conditions. That road, barely wide enough to accommodate vehicular traffic, had a scattering of small shanty-type road stands where vendors made a paltry profit selling and trading a variety of food and household products.

Mai's house, not far off that narrower road and within short walking distance of the beach, could only be approached by foot down a heavily trodden path through brush. Most of the homes, as well as other structures in My Khe Village, were haphazardly constructed of bamboo reed or of some other strong plant fiber. Roofs were thatch or corrugated metal, and most had open doorways without doors. Animals – ducks, chickens and the like, were free to roam and were as welcome inside the homes as they were outside. Her home, also that of her parents and siblings, was very small but of better construction than other homes nearby. Mai contributed most of her earnings toward upgrading their home, thereby making living conditions better for her family and herself. There were only two rooms in their home – practically no privacy. Yet the entire family lived there in reasonable and affordable comfort. The beds were small, barely of length and width to accommodate the occupants. They were of wooden construction and served their purpose without benefit of mattresses.

Rick and I were greeted by the family and were made to feel welcome. Mai appeared to be proud that I had shown enough interest in her to visit her home.

That first visit we partied. Rick and I bought an abundance of Beer 33, and we remained well into the night. We were offered food (of unknown origin and preparation) which we politely accepted, taking only enough to show our respect – and to get an idea of how palatable it was. Flies were a major problem. It was difficult seeing them on some of the food items; however, they were quite distinguishable when the background was white rice. It was impossible keeping the flies off the food. We followed our host's lead and realized that any flies clinging to the food or to the chopsticks carrying it would invariably take to the air prior to entering one's mouth. Some of the nearby neighbors joined in, and songs were sung to the tune of crude, primitive-appearing, handmade musical instruments. Mai's father was exceptionally talented on an instrument similar to a banjo, but with only one string. The bridge for the string rested on snakeskin that had been stretched tightly over a coconut "canister." I had never seen or heard of such an instrument and became so intrigued by it, and the sounds it produced, that I ended up buying it before the night ended. The old man did not want to sell, but when he realized that my offer, having been increased several times, was sufficient to replace the instrument while providing him with an impressive profit – he agreed.

Rick and I did not get much sleep that night, but the experience and the knowledge I had gained was invaluable – a truly worthwhile adventure few sailors would ever encounter. The experience would, not of choice, remain an ongoing thing for a couple of weeks as a result of the severe stomach cramps that accompanied the dysentery I subsequently suffered. I thought the periodic quinine pills we were all required to take were a pain in the ass, but the pain in the ass (quite literally) caused by dysentery was far too real. It was necessary that I continue taking the dysentery medication for several weeks before I returned to normalcy. Did I go back to Mai's home for seconds? Absolutely! I had hopes that my stomach had acquired immunity to the bacteria – and, even more hopeful, that the food was prepared under more sanitary conditions.

Whenever I visited with Mai or her family at their home, I did so at some risk. I totally disregarded any possibility that I might not return alive, that I might be captured or killed by an elusive enemy. I was more concerned that I might be caught by the Military Police and suffer some form of punishment having intentionally violated the off-limits policy.

Rick fell in love with Diep, another club waitress/hostess. He was quite a bit older than she was, and she always tried to discourage him from making advances. Anyone could easily have fallen love with Diep; she was as sweet and shy as she could be, and it did not appear feigned. Plus, she was beautiful to boot. Rick bought her gifts from the PX, which was also very illegal since most gifts eventually found their way to the black market for resale. Rick was very sincere about Diep and he went the distance; he proposed marriage. Much to his disappointment, he was turned down! He was "too old" for her. Rick did not give up easily; he continued with his offers of marriage right up until the time he was transferred. She, likewise, continued telling him – he was too old!

The "Take Ten," located a couple of blocks west of Bach-Dang Street at the far south end of DaNang, was a U.S. military club that catered to members only. In order to gain membership one first had to be in possession of an "I-Corps" card to prove his or her legitimacy within the area. Since the club imposed a strict limit on the number of memberships it could issue, one could expect to remain on a waiting list four months or more. First come, first served – those who signed up first were the first to fill vacancies as they occurred. Guests, never more than one at a time, were allowed. Rick had a Take Ten membership, so I had access as his guest while I waited for my name to reach the top of the waiting list. My first visit to the Take Ten provided me with a very rude awakening to the realities of war.

During that first visit, Rick and I were inside the club, well to the back, quite some distance from the door that led from the vestibule into the club.

We were taking a break from whatever activity we might otherwise have been involved – enjoying American beer instead of the local brew – when all hell broke loose. There were two "healthy," almost simultaneous explosions that within a second or two were followed by a third. The accompanying concussion was severe throughout the Club, and the place immediately filled with a combination of dust and smoke. Glass and other debris flew all over the place. GIs tried to calm their female guests and the panicked club hostesses as everyone scrambled for some means of protective cover. The sounds of screaming were evident but were muffled by a temporary loss of normal hearing. Rick and I were both on the floor seeking refuge from the chaos, not knowing whether to run, hide, or remain where we were. It was a terrible scene to witness. Several senior NCOs, well-seasoned field soldiers, immediately took charge and directed perimeter coverage. A thorough search of the immediate area around the Club was conducted, but nothing out of the ordinary was found. Once we were given the OK, everyone was ushered out of the building. The Club was immediately closed until further notice – and we were directed to return to our respective commands.

Briefly, what had happened could probably have been prevented. One individual, no doubt Viet Cong, had ridden his bicycle past the gate guard straight to the front entrance of the Club, where he threw (to my understanding) a string of hand grenades through the wide-open double doors. The string had been cleverly attached so as to pull the already partially removed pins, thereby releasing the spoons from each of five grenades. Result; immediate detonation! The pins jammed in one or two – otherwise the damage would have been more severe. From what I saw, I believe there were three killed in that incident. One girl and one GI, probably in the company of each other, were in the vestibule where the grenades exploded. From the appearance of their bodies I am sure they must have been killed instantly. All of the windows between the vestibule and the game room had been blown out, subsequently everyone playing slots at the time suffered minor to severe wounds. I believe there was one person killed in that room. There may have been other casualties, although I am not aware of any. I do know that the sounds and sights I experienced impressed upon me the fact that I was, without any doubt, in a war zone! To the best of my knowledge the perpetrator(s) of that deed was/were never found. Measures were immediately taken to prevent such a thing from happening again. Within days a steel-gated, totally contained extended walkway of heavy-duty chain link was constructed as a caged pre-entry approach to the Club. Members then had to pass through the containment barrier before entering the double doors to the Club. Similar measures had already been taken but became more commonplace at the entrances to most downtown bars and shops. All repairs to the Take Ten were accomplished quickly, and the Club was again open for business within a couple of weeks.

Mai also worked at the Take Ten for a brief period of time. Rick always allowed me the use of his jeep so that I could provide her with transportation home at the end of her shift. One night, just after she was seated in the jeep, two noticeably drunken Green Beret soldiers approached the jeep and asked me where I was going. Without thinking, I answered honestly and told them I was taking Mai home. They turned to Mai and began questioning her as to whether she had a sister or if there were other girls living with or nearby her. Mai pretended not to understand. The two soldiers boasted of their time out in the field and that they were determined to get laid that night. They became more and more persistent, and before I could drive away they forced their way into the backseat of the jeep. Their demand was simple; I was to take them with us. I could see the handwriting on the wall and knew that there was reason to fear for Mai's well-being. Chances were that if she refused to accommodate them willingly she would be raped. As for me, I knew that I was in the awkward and potentially dangerous position of having to protect Mai, and that in all probability I was about to have the living hell beaten out of me. Those guys were dead serious, and Mai and I both knew it.

There were two routes to Mai's home. I could easily have taken the normal route across the peninsula on the road, or I could take another road to the beach and approach Mai's home from the back. My brain raced as I decided to take the back route and I began to formulate a clever plan of deceit. As soon as we reached the beach I asked the two intruders if they had heard of the famous beachfront whorehouse, the one that we were approaching. They, of course, had not. I explained that it was without doubt the finest "house" with the most beautiful women in the world, and all of the girls were closely monitored to make sure they did not have any kind of VD. I told the soldiers that the house was on the U.S. payroll, that it was there for the specific purpose of satisfying GIs. Our new found "friends" were pleased with the information I had provided, and their excitement peaked as I pointed out the not-too-distant reflections of lights that supposedly identified the house and the party that was always going on there. The lights became more evident as we drove parallel to them, although the house itself was not visible. Almost simultaneously both of our uninvited passengers hollered for me to stop the jeep; they wanted to go where the action was! I congratulated them on their decision and told them to follow the lights, that within a few minutes they would be satisfied beyond their wildest imagination. With that, weapons in hand and lust in mind, they jumped from the jeep and began jogging toward whatever dream their imaginations had concocted. Mai and I looked at each other and simultaneously burst out laughing as we drove off. As I gained some distance I knew that my plan had worked flawlessly. I was only sorry that I could not have been there to see the expressions on their faces when they realized that their anticipated destination, the famous beachfront whorehouse, the lights they had so willingly and anxiously followed was actually the perimeter lighting at the headquarters of Lt. Gen. Lewis W. Walt, Commanding General III MAF!

One night Rick's jeep broke down about halfway between Camp Tien Sha and Tien Sha Ramp. I was alone and it was too late for me to walk the remaining distance to the ramp with any expectation of catching water transportation back to the YR. As I didn't want to make myself a target by remaining in the jeep out in the open, I decided to make my way inland on foot, away from the river, and hopefully find a reasonably safe place to sleep the remaining hours of darkness.

I was in luck, at least to my way of thinking. I walked directly into a graveyard, a place the extremely superstitious Vietnamese people never ventured after dark. Club hostesses had told me of their numerous ghost sightings, particularly in and around graveyards. I chuckled to myself as I wondered whether I would be a welcome guest or would I be haunted, injured, or killed by the deceased instead of by the living enemy. Such thoughts did not last long. I had grown accustomed to hearing the sporadic small-arms fire accompanied by other explosions and within moments I was asleep.

I awakened startled by Vietnamese voices and realized that I had overslept; the sun, shining in my eyes, was already well into the sky. I jerked myself into a sitting position and saw that I was the subject of the conversation. Several Vietnamese had gathered nearby and were no doubt confirming their suspicions that Americans truly were a strange bunch. The "bed" I had slept on was one of the aboveground cement tombs; the elevated cross that extended a couple of inches above the top of the tomb had been my pillow. It had been an uncomfortable bed but it served my purpose well. My embarrassment at having been seen sleeping there was outweighed by my thought of having missed morning muster, so I hopped to my feet, gave a cheerful morning greeting to my observers, *Chao cac ong*, and hastily made my way to the road. As usual, luck was my companion; I not only caught a ride with the first vehicle to pass, I also learned that there had been no boat runs that morning. I was in the company of others who had also been stranded for the night. There would be no reprimand for my late return to the YR.

Rick was waiting impatiently for me; probably more worried about his jeep than of me. He insisted that we immediately return to the jeep and make repairs, or arrange to have it towed. We both knew that any jeep left unattended very long was sure to be stolen.

We got the jeep running after performing some relatively simple maintenance and returned to the YR where we then had to explain our period of absence to Mr. Randall. Where the jeep was concerned, his as well as our transportation to and from the Club, our time away from the YR was quickly overlooked.

Teasing the girls that worked at the club(s) was fair game. We all did that, and sometimes the girls reciprocated, teasing back. One time, as Rick and I entered the heavily guarded gate at Camp Tien Sha, we saw Le walking. We politely offered her a ride to the CPO Club where she worked. Le climbed into the jeep and we headed toward the Club, but instead of stopping we drove past. Our intentions were good, we just wanted to have a little fun with Le, but she panicked. Quickly her short utterances of surprise became more threatening screams for help. Even after we stopped the jeep we refused to let our little toy out. Her alarm was unnecessary since we had done nothing to cause her such panic. She should have known that we certainly weren't going to harm her right there in the middle of a base, in the middle of the day, with Americans and Vietnamese walking the street on both sides of us. Apparently she thought otherwise.

A stocky, balding American in civilian clothes stepped up to the jeep and demanded to know what we were doing.

Rick, just as abruptly said, "Well, just who the fuck are you, and what the fuck business is it of yours?" I was impressed with Rick's ability to stand up to that uninvited nuisance – after all, just what business was it of his that our temporary, somewhat meaningless, amusement should be questioned.

"I am Captain Mays, Commanding Officer over Camp Tien Sha! Give me your names, rates, and service numbers!" His words stung and will forever ring in my ears.

With some reluctance, we provided the Captain with our names, etc., and we tried to explain the little prank we had played on Le. Captain Mays was not the slightest bit impressed. So Le was freed and Rick and I were allowed to go about our business. About a month later, while Rick and I were at the Chiefs' Club, a chief walked in escorting a guest known to us – Captain Mays. The Captain stopped briefly at our table, looked first at Rick, then at me, and with a broad smile said, "Well, Chief Rickabaugh and Chief Adkisson, have you two been behaving yourselves?" The man had a sense of humor along with a remarkable memory for names.

That same evening, as Rick and I departed from Camp Tien Sha, we picked up a couple of GI hitchhikers that were also en route to Tien Sha Ramp. On the way, for whatever reason, both of the passengers began ridiculing us. Their innuendos were always in the context that all chiefs were stupid. I suggested they keep their thoughts to themselves, which only confirmed that they had been successful in irritating me. So they continued making similar remarks. I knew that what I was contemplating was wrong, but those two needed to be taught a lesson. The moment Rick parked at the ramp, I jumped out, grabbed the guy nearest me by his shirt, and literally jerked him out of the jeep. He was not prepared for the thorough thrashing I gave him. I vented whatever frustrations I had, all that had been building within me for a long time, on the effort I put into slamming one fist after the other into his face and body. With each blow I urged him never to underestimate the strength, speed, or wisdom of a CPO – me in particular. When I realized the degree of injuries I had inflicted, I stopped, turned – and to my surprise the other guy was still sitting in the jeep. I wasted no time in delivering a second assault on him. My second victim did an excellent job of dodging my punches. I quickly realized that my knuckles were bruised and bleeding, having struck parts of the jeep as often as I had struck him. Rick, as surprised as our passengers were at my anger, made it clear that I had done enough damage. He pulled at the back of my shirt as he yelled at me to, "Knock it off, Ad!" The fight was over as quickly as it had started. The two GIs had been sufficiently roughed up; the blood on their faces confirmed that they would probably suffer some noticeable, if not painful bruises. My fists suffered likewise.

Within two weeks of that incident, again at night, I was at the ramp waiting for water transportation to the APL. There were only three or four of us in need of transportation, and one of the LCM-6 coxswains volunteered to give us a lift. I had not noticed at the time, but the Coxswain was one of the two men I had roughed up two weeks prior. Since the group of us was so few, the Coxswain allowed us to remain standing beside the pilothouse instead of down in the well deck. I began to sense the need to repeat that performance of two weeks past when one of the other passengers started insulting me as well as the CPO insignias I was wearing. One thing led to another, and I decided to make a believer out of another "uneducated" sailor. When I suggested that my tormentor accompany me to the well deck, where we could easily settle our differences, I was surprised to hear the Coxswain, whom I had not recognized until that moment, warn my opponent that I was no one to mess with. Besides, the third-class petty officer that was doing all the insulting was just a little guy and would be no match for me. The Coxswain assured him that it would be no contest, that he himself (the Coxswain) had learned the hard way that I was not the Chief to be "fucked" with. The third-class electrician was a feisty little guy and insisted that he would do just fine against "this stupid chief." With that, we climbed down into the well deck and prepared for battle. My opponent demanded that I remove my .45 pistol before we pursued the matter further. I did so, and the battle erupted.

Never in my life, until that moment, was I subjected to such a thorough thrashing! The "little" guy was proficient well beyond my expectation. Every swing he took was dead on target, and each of his punches was immediately followed up with several more – each one landing hard on one part of my face or another. I could taste the blood coming from my mouth, and I knew that my upper and lower lips had both been split. I felt the blood gushing from my nose; it having been well flattened by a series of properly placed blows. For a moment the fight ceased. I had been beaten beyond anyone's doubt, and the electrician asked me if I had had enough. Instant anger – I came back swinging with rage; no way was I going to allow that little know-it-all to come out the uncontested winner. The second performance was a very near repeat of what I had just been through, one that had I exercised better judgment I would not have had to suffer. Yes, I *had* had enough and I admitted it. I had been beaten severely by someone, I later

362

learned, who had been a well-trained boxer. He knew precisely what he was doing, and he went about it with a great deal of skill. What I did not know but was later told by the chief he worked for was that I had gained a great deal of respect, not just for myself, but for having stuck up for the CPO community as a whole. I took the time, after having healed sufficiently, to pay my young friend, the (little) third-class petty officer, a deserving visit. I congratulated him on his pugilistic abilities. It was then that I was enlightened, but not surprised, about his training and experience in the ring.

Bruised and Beaten - Fair and Square

Letters from home were always appreciated. On rare occasions I received short letters from ex-shipmates. One letter in particular stirred my interest in an all-but-forgotten recreational pastime. Some crewmen of the *Seadragon* had come to realize that the Playboy Poet was no longer there to "secretly" post his works. That letter, from a *Seadragon* pal, requested a specific type of poem – one that would describe my surroundings humorously, "if possible." The following poem was the result of that request, and I wasted no time in sending it to the *Seadragon* for "appropriate" display.

Your courteous request for poems "By Paul"
is accepted industriously,
but your wishes require humorous dire,
which affects me most nauseously.

What I reveal is the way that I feel

363

toward the horrible facts around me.
I feel my harangue should be based on DaNang
and the problem of insurgency.

So I will discuss miscellaneous
items without hesitation.
First on the list, now don't get pissed,
is the lack of fornication!

The policy known as "don't bury your bone"
presently promulgated,
makes relations "unsat" when you realize that
here sex is simulated.

The gals on the street all walk on bare feet
wearing scabs instead of fine leather.
The scabs, I suppose, are from sucking their toes;
I'm in love – I'm in love, altogether!

All joking aside, with you I'll confide,
the females should all be arrested.
They're so debonair as they squat anywhere
and drop everything they've digested.

Where do I go to see a good show
on a cool, quiet tropical night?
To the cemetery, where it's customary
to scream "KILL, KILL, KILL!" with delight.

To the barbecue when there's nothing to do
where I can see at the "games,"
the hilarity of a real fricassee
as a Buddhist goes up in flames.

Have I one friend, on whom I can depend,
since I'm not the one to beg,
who'll not write a letter – but do something better;
won't someone just send me some leg!

It never ceased to amaze me how Vietnamese, at least those I personally observed, took their baths. First, it should be explained that running water was a rarity. Most water was obtained from wells. Those who could afford electricity could pump the water from their wells up into holding tanks, to be gravity-fed as needed. But that was a luxury most villagers could not afford. Bathing was a matter of stripping down to the least amount of clothing possible without being totally naked, and then dowsing one's self with buckets of water dipped from a well. They soaped themselves under their clothing and rinsed in the same manner. They took, in the strongest sense of the word, "public" baths, with a side benefit having washed their undergarments at the same time.

Another interesting observance, very foreign to me, was that Vietnamese soldiers made it a practice to hold hands with other soldiers as they walked around in public. It was more unusual to see two men walking together that were *not* holding hands! In or out of uniform, men holding hands in public was totally acceptable. The opposite held true for men in the company of women. In public the slightest show of affection between members of the opposite sex was taboo. Dancing, publicly or privately, was also frowned upon. To dance was to show signs of happiness, and one was not supposed to be happy while at war. Some readers, those of you who were there, will disagree with me – because you did dance (as did I) and it was, to some extent, in public. Yes, it did occur, but only with a great deal of discretion and caution. It was done as the result of Western influence; always to accommodate some form of moneymaking interests.

Funeral processions took place daily, sometimes several in a single day. The Viet Cong were vicious killers; they had no respect whatever for human life. The VC were known to kill sporadically, needless killings that not only served to create fear among villagers – but killings that always served their purpose for the VC. Such killings were an effective means of coercing those individuals who were not harmed into assisting the VC. VC recruitment figures increased significantly in and around villages that suffered the loss of loved ones at the hands of their own race, their own people.

One of the girls that had at one time worked at the Chiefs' Club had become pregnant by an American chief. She was murdered as a result. The VC learned of her condition and paid her a midnight visit – only to slice open her bulging stomach and to kill the unborn child as well as the mother. Their bodies were left in the middle of Son Cha Village as a cruel warning to others. Understandably, activities such as that were taken seriously by other girls that worked on base. Many quit out of fear while others, those on the VC payroll, continued working on the base as they gathered bits and pieces of intelligence. Their job, easy but costly, was to report everything they saw or heard – and to turn over most of their earnings to the VC; proof positive of their sincerity in providing everything they possibly could in support of the Communist cause.

Late one afternoon I was dispatched to the White Elephant to assist in coordinating repairs needed at one of the construction battalion camps in the area. It was approaching dusk when the Mike boat in which I was a passenger beached near the White Elephant. I instructed the Coxswain to wait for me, as the duties I was to perform would not require that I be away for long. A couple of hours passed before I returned to the Mike boat. The Coxswain was noticeably irritated at the delay, but he did his best to act otherwise. Working hours were long enough without having to sit around after-hours while waiting to provide transportation for someone. It was well into a very dark night as we made our way back down the Han River and we could hear the usual background sounds of mortars exploding and the popping of small-arms fire. The sky and the surrounding terrain were lit up by luminous flares as they drifted downward on miniature parachutes that effectively slowed their descent. That night was no different than many others before it. About halfway back to the ramp we very unexpectedly became targets for some well-concealed sniper(s). The Coxswain was protected on three sides by the metal pilothouse as he maneuvered the boat. I jumped into the well deck, where I knew that I would be well protected from anything less than armor-piercing projectiles. We had no problem recognizing that we were the targets as several rounds of red-orange tracers streaked nearby. We discussed the possibility of returning fire but knew that it would do no good; the enemy was totally concealed by darkness and was firing from a known populated area. Besides, our firepower was limited to my .45 pistol and the Coxswain's M-16 rifle. The Coxswain took evasive action by maneuvering quick turns as he crisscrossed an imaginary path at high speed. The attack on us did not last over a minute or two, barely enough to get a pronounced flow of adrenaline. Fortunately, whoever it was that had done the shooting was not a proficient marksman. Not a single round touched our fifty-foot landing craft.

Five days of R and R, Rest and Recuperation (sometimes referred to as Rest and Recreation), was a benefit to which everyone stationed in Vietnam looked forward. Two such periods of R and R were authorized during each one-year tour in the country. During the early days of U.S. presence the only R and R locations that were available outside Vietnam were Japan, the Philippines, and Thailand. Eventually Hawaii was added to the list, which made it particularly nice for those who lived or had family there. China Beach also provided for short-term R and R visits, seldom more than a day or two of refuge from the field. With the many restrictions that were constantly imposed on members of the military it was understandable why China Beach was not the greatest R and R location in which one chose to "rest" and "recuperate." Surprisingly, there were always an abundance of men taking their breaks there, where they did not have to worry about lengthy flights to and from another country.

My first request for R and R was approved. I decided on a place that was relatively inexpensive; a place where I had friends. On June 21st, 1966, I once again left the war zone and headed for Japan. The route was well traveled; a quick stop at Taipei, Taiwan, and on to Tachikawa Air Base where a bus provided the final leg of transportation to Camp Zama, an R and R base in and of itself – a place where many men preferred to remain during their entire five-day R and R period. I suspected that they were probably reluctant to step out into unfamiliar territory, foreign soil with which I had long before become acquainted. I, unlike those who elected to remain at Camp Zama, wanted nothing less than to remain on some military installation, whether or not it had an abundance of recreation facilities. Besides, I had made prior arrangements by letter to spend my time off with Shigeko, the girl from Sasebo who had long before shown me the countryside and had introduced me to so many of her friends. As soon as I was in civvies I hailed a taxi and headed for Tokyo. I met Shigeko at Tokyo Station, the main train depot, and the two of us immediately began touring Tokyo. We spent the first two days sightseeing as we enjoyed the night lights and the many nightclubs that Tokyo had to offer. Our activities were far more strenuous than they were relaxing, but one heck of a lot more enjoyable than the alternative – Vietnam. It was a great reunion, time spent with Shigeko, and there was little doubt that she was equally pleased at my having invited her to join me during my brief stay. The following two days we toured Yokohama, about thirty minutes by taxi from our Tokyo hotel. The morning of the fifth day we took a taxi to the town just outside Camp Zama where

367

we spent that final day and night relaxing in our hotel room, reminiscing about places we had been and things we had done. We also talked about Sasebo and the times we had shared there; and we talked of the possibility that we would see each other again at some future time. It seemed likely that we would.

Within a month of my return to Vietnam, Rick received "PCS," Permanent Change of Station, orders to the Philippines. That had been his first choice on his "dream sheet," his official request to the Bureau of Naval Personnel, for his next duty station. I had always known that he would be leaving Vietnam before me, but once he had orders in hand I knew how much I would miss his companionship. Diep, the girl Rick wanted to marry, invited the two of us to attend a small party at her home in Son Cha Village as a farewell gesture in Rick's honor. We knew that it was off-limits, out-of-bounds, potentially unsafe, etc., but having taken into consideration the chance Diep would be taking – having two American GIs at her home, there was no way either of us would consider turning her down.

Diep's home was a short walk from the road, down one of the many narrow paths that were plentiful and so typical of all villages in the area. Rick and I arrived at dusk and Diep accompanied by several of her neighbor friends greeted us. Diep had not known whether or not to believe our promises that we would show up, so she had intentionally delayed the preparation of food until we arrived. Her home was small and from the outside it appeared to have no more than a couple of rooms. Neither Rick nor I entered the structure, not even for a quick inquisitive peek. The walls were of scrap wood and corrugated metal, and a shabby thatch roof that showed signs of severe deterioration covered it.

Diep and her friends began to rush around excitedly as they gathered all the makings of the feast in which Rick and I would soon partake. We watched as two healthy geese hung by their feet and had their throats cut. Great care was taken to catch every drop of blood as it drained into a carefully placed bowl below. The blood was then whipped into something of a frothy mixture before it was offered as a drink to everyone present. Rick's eyes met mine, as we instinctively knew that our thoughts could only have been one and the same: *What have we gotten ourselves into and how can we, without insulting anyone, get out of it?* I, always the bolder, took what appeared to be a very small sip, but what was really nothing more than a gesture. I barely wet my lips, nothing more. Rick, believing I had done the unthinkable, followed suit – and had to swallow more than once to keep it down. Neither of us accepted a follow-up offer of what they assured us was delicious and nutritious refreshment. To us it was what it was; coagulated blood! The geese were then well cooked on an outdoor barbecue as Diep's friends brought in numerous other dishes of home-cooked delicacies. Rick and I were treated to a feast fit for royalty, and neither of us held back our ravenous appetites. Everything was delicious. Diep and her friends were happy that Rick and I ate what they had gone to such extremes to prepare. They watched intently as we took each bite – and they grinned at each other; pleased that Rick and I apparently found their meal as tasty as it was to them. We left shortly after completing our meal – we did not want to overextend our welcome. It would not have been wise for two Americans to remain too long after dark, nor would it have been in our hostess's best interest, having us there beyond what some neighbors might have considered a reasonable period of time. That was one of the most memorable nights I was privileged to enjoy during that tour of duty in Vietnam.

Things were never quite the same after Rick left. I continued to frequent the Chiefs' Club, many times with Lieutenant Randall as my guest, but "Mr. Randall," as I never failed to properly address him, was not the partner or friend that Rick had always been. There was always that aura of seniority present, of my being subordinate, which interfered with whatever friendship we might otherwise have developed. Not to slight him, Randall was a man to be admired, but he was always an officer first. His individuality was of a lesser priority, and his personality suffered as a result.

Rick's jeep was also sorely missed, and hitchhiking once again became my only mode of transportation. It was more difficult getting to and from Mai's home, since very few military vehicles traveled that road. But that didn't matter, since her home was not a place I visited frequently.

I tried to improve my Vietnamese vocabulary on a daily basis, and at every opportunity I used the language. My ability to communicate in the language contributed immeasurably toward my acceptance in what might otherwise have been a very dangerous situation. It was during one of my infrequent visits to Mai's home that I experienced one of the most remarkable events of my life. I went to her home immediately after I got off duty, somewhere around 1800 hours, and remained there well into the night. We were sitting around visiting, Mai, her brother, her younger sister, and I. Tom, Mai's younger brother, was always very accommodating when he anxiously volunteered to go out into the village to buy beer and soft drinks for everyone. I always provided the funds for such purchases. It would never have been appropriate for me to allow a family living in poverty to spend their meager income on things that were so unnecessary. There was no reason for me to think that particular night would differ from any other night – but I sensed things were "different" when another visitor joined us. Those around me, all Vietnamese, seemed a little uneasy at the newcomer's presence and I observed an abundance of quick, nervous glances by my hosts, back and forth between the newcomer and me. My first thought was that Mai was married and that it was her husband who just happened to pop in. He refused the first beer I offered him. When I made the same offer in Vietnamese, almost to the point of insisting that he join the rest of us, he reluctantly accepted. One beer followed another, and before long, as the man became more relaxed, everyone began to show signs of relief. I do not know why I had not seen or had not paid attention to the rifle he had with him. I was startled when I first saw the banana "clip," the magazine that was so easily recognized and identified as belonging to the Soviet AK-47 assault rifle. The weapon was carefully propped up against the table very near to him. As I focused on the rifle, I began to suspect that I had placed myself in a very awkward situation, that of being in the company of the enemy. What I didn't know was that he had always thought that I knew he was VC. During the course of our conversation the truth came out. He knew very little English, whereas I had learned enough Vietnamese to make myself understood. When I thought the time was right, I openly asked him, almost jokingly, if he was Viet Cong. I had not realized the gravity of my question until I heard his honest reply. While he looked me straight in the eyes, almost daringly and without the slightest reluctance, he quite proudly acknowledged that he was very much VC; he was as much my enemy as I was his! The man followed with an awkward explanation that he was willing to take time out from the fighting and killing to talk to me one-on-one about Vietnam and about our personal beliefs.

Mai did not know whether to be happy or concerned as she watched the two of us; him with his rifle and me with my holstered .45. Mai served as translator whenever the need became apparent.

"Charlie," the name by which GIs most commonly referred the Viet Cong, is most appropriate in identifying my most recent acquaintance. Charlie was not at all happy with American presence in Vietnam. I was uncomfortable with many of his questions about U.S. policy as demonstrated

370

by our involvement in the war. My answers seldom, if ever, satisfied him. I was uncomfortable with many of the answers that I was giving – the very same answers I had previously thought would be easily understood and acceptable – but suddenly and unexpectedly I began to see the questions and the answers in a different light. For example, I did not really know why I was in Vietnam other than the fact that I had volunteered to be there. I could not accurately respond to the root of the reasons behind the United States being so firmly committed there. He made me acutely aware that the Vietnamese people just wanted to be left alone, that if all foreigners would leave the country there would be no war; that Americans had absolutely no idea of the dedication and strength behind their (the VC) effort. He bluntly told me that Americans were stupid and that the only reason the Vietnamese had developed anything resembling a friendship with us was for their personal gain, not ours. He readily admitted that the broadest smile was always there for whoever gave the biggest handout. He explained in terms of rice; that their smiles would be for Communist sources if they provided two bags of rice instead of the single bag provided by other sources – including the United States, and the opposite would hold true if the United States provided the biggest handout. His honesty surprised me. My honesty made me appear more ignorant. I did not know much about anything other than that my government was the force behind the when and where our military might was to be exercised and that such decisions were based on the need for American presence in certain regions of the world. I explained that as members of the military, we did not normally question the wisdom behind such decisions. He asked me if that was the type of democracy America wanted the world to "enjoy." He suggested that if what I was telling him was true, then a dictatorship ruled my life more than his. The two of us never argued, and we kept our voices low. Occasionally we were able to turn our nervous smiles into brief sessions of chuckles that sometimes approached open laughter. Charlie assured me that he would never again share time or fraternize with those that he believed to be the enemies of his people. He could not give me a reason for having spent so much time with me other than that our meeting had been a very unusual by chance situation. He had been encouraged to continue the visit only after he heard me speak a few words in his own language. We both came out of our "by chance" meeting a little more enlightened by each other's honest replies to the variety of questions asked. He, on the other hand, was probably sorry for having shown a momentary weakness. Could I have killed him? Absolutely not! That is, not

371

unless my own life had been in imminent danger as a result of his threat. I liked Charlie, the "Communist aggressor," whose name I never learned. Our conversation continued until around 0300, at which time he departed just as quickly as he had arrived. I spent the remainder of the night sleeping on the floor beside Mai's small wooden bed.

There was another instance where I knew that I had, to the extreme outer limits of good judgment, overstepped the boundaries of common sense and acceptable reasoning. It was during one of the few times that I walked the pathway into Son Cha Village to pay Diep and Smiley a visit. They were perfect hosts, as they always tried to have food and drink available during my unannounced infrequent visits. It was a great feeling, that of being fully accepted in an environment so filled with distrust, confusion, and fear. I felt safe while I was in the company of either; as though they provided a safety barrier all around me, thereby protecting me from whatever dangers there might have been lurking about.

Thoughts of the various rules and regulations that I was violating crossed my mind as I left Smiley's home and began walking the path that would lead me back to the dirt road on which I would hitchhike "home."

American servicemen could get away with violating curfew as long as they could convince whoever caught them that they were coming from one legitimate location and were on their way to another. Since I was not coming from a legitimate location, I was subject to arrest. I was always prepared with a believable story in the event I was caught. All Vietnamese were issued ID cards that identified the bearer by name and by home address. They had no acceptable excuse for being out after curfew. All Vietnamese were required to be at their own residence during the hours of curfew; being found elsewhere was a serious offense – possible conviction of being VC, or otherwise involved in assisting the Communist insurgency in some other illegal after-hours project. I had been told of many instances where men and women suspects were tortured when they were discovered after curfew away from their legally registered residence. Similarly, GIs caught within the city or within surrounding villages after curfew were usually turned over to U.S. authorities, who then made the determination as to whether or not they would be punished under UCMJ. I was always aware of the chance(s) I was taking when I strayed into areas, according to the rules I was supposed to abide by, had no business being in or near. I thought other-

372

wise. I held to the theory that it would have been a waste, spending a year of my life in a foreign country without taking the time or exerting any effort to learn as much as I could about the people, their customs and traditions, and the area in general. I also believed it to be significantly important that I know my way around in the event I had to escape some kind of ambush or attack on an area where I might have legitimately been. I wanted to know where all the pathways and roads led, and during my brief tour of duty in the country, by one means or another, I had acquired a fair knowledge of nearly all of them on the peninsula.

I was careful to stay on the path with which I was most familiar as I made my way from Smiley's home. I tried to be quiet so as not to disturb sleeping villagers or attract unnecessary attention by my questionable presence. I froze in my footsteps when I heard the low-keyed voices of people approaching and very quickly I hid in a thick growth of plant life. Very slowly I slipped my .45 out of its holster and released the safety. One round was already chambered. I knew that whoever they were, they were just as much in violation of curfew as I was – and chances were they were people with whom I did not want to deal. I could see a half-dozen or so black-paja-maed, heavily armed, Vietnamese men as they approached. They were half crouching as they hurried past me, each of them passing within a yard or so of me as they followed the same path by which I had come. RVN troops always wore plain or camouflaged green fatigues whereas the Viet Cong were known to wear the simple lightweight black pajamas. There was no doubt in my mind as to which that small band of black-pajamaed individuals represented. My body was shaking, not entirely from fear, but certainly from a combination of emotions that told me how very stupid I had been in allowing myself to stray so far outside the area of safety and good judgment. I had a very strong desire to explore, to gain knowledge, and the information I wanted could sometimes most easily be obtained in the manner I chose. Unfortunately, that sometimes meant without regard for my own best interests, self-preservation being but one. In retrospect I showed a great deal of immature behavior, that of someone lacking the maturity commensurate with his age. I did not take my life nearly as seriously as I took my job. For a while I considered remaining right there for the entire night, safely concealed in the thick bushes. I probably would have, except I was afraid that if I fell asleep my snoring would attract attention. So I remained concealed until I was absolutely positive no one was nearby. For the rest of the trek to the road I remained particularly alert to my surroundings and I took every possible precaution not to be seen or heard. Once I reached the dirt road I walked to the main gate at Camp Tien Sha where I was picked up and given a ride to the ramp.

Life aboard YR-70 became more and more routine. It had taken months of trial and effort before we really knew what our limitations were as a repair facility. It was our policy never to turn down a work request; one way or another we would accomplish the work ourselves or we would as-sist in its accomplishment. Vietnamese civilians were hired in order to as-sist them in providing for a better standard of living for themselves while helping us to some degree. Supposedly they were carefully screened prior to being issued an official pass, their authorization to work on board. The majority of the work performed by Vietnamese was menial – tasks such as chipping and painting, sweeping, or other cleanup-type chores. They were provided Mike-boat transportation to and from shore and they reported for work daily at 0800. All Vietnamese were frisked as they boarded the YR, a precaution known to be necessary as the result of the planting of bombs at other U.S. facilities. Those who did the frisking took their jobs serious-ly, as they patted down each man thoroughly upon boarding. Those being frisked let it be known that they did not like being searched, but that was one of the agreements that accompanied employment. No frisk, no job! Unintentionally the workers did not make it easy for us, considering all the different types of food containers they brought with them. Containers were usually stacked three or four high, and each had to be opened and inspected at the time of boarding. To the best of my knowledge, we never found any contraband that might have been a threat to ship or crew, but that was only because we never lowered our guard. We always insisted that preventative measures were, without exception, strictly enforced.

One time, as it neared 1600, the end of the workday for civilian work-ers, one of the crew mistakenly left his watch beside a washbasin in the head. He realized his mistake within a minute, so he rushed back to re-trieve his watch. As he entered the head one Vietnamese worker was exit-ing; and the watch was no longer where he had left it. Since there had been such a short lapse in time there was good reason to believe there had been no other individuals in the head other than the one that was seen leaving. Immediately we established a very tight system of surveillance by placing crewmen at unobstructed locations, and we made sure the Vietnamese sus-pect remained in sight at all times. All of us on surveillance saw what we believed to be the worker's intentional concealment of an unrecognizable item, possibly the watch, inside one of his food containers. The man who had lost the watch wanted to take immediate action, but he was told that the search would have to take place in the normal manner; when the suspect left the craft for the day. We knew how sensitive a search could be, so the decision was made to continue our surveillance and, in compliance with current policy, conduct thorough random searches as the workers prepared to board their water transportation. When that time came, we zeroed in on the suspect and searched his stack of food containers. We found nothing! We had him turn all of his pockets inside out. Again nothing! The sailor whose watch we were trying to recover was adamant; he was sure the worker had it and insisted that we continue our search. The worker showed signs of anger and reluctance when he was told to remove his shoes and trousers, but with some "encouragement" he complied. Like a streak of lightning the sailor grabbed one of the worker's ankles and physically turned him upside down as he yelled; "Here it is, you goddamn thief." Somehow, our uninterrupted, well-monitored, "sophisticated" surveillance system had failed. Our team had vigilantly observed the suspect and all of his activities while, without being seen, he had managed to remove one shoe and sock, slip his naked foot inside the watchband, and put his sock and shoe back on. A very good job of concealment, but not quite good enough. The watch was retrieved, and the worker lost his job. The incident reconfirmed that our practice of taking whatever steps we deemed necessary was appropriate where theft was suspected.

The only other incident that occurred on the YR, not exactly spectacular but nonetheless unusual, was when one of the crew was in the process of separating several sheets of four-by-eight-foot heavy-gauge sheet metal. In order to save space and to facilitate easier separation, the sheets were stacked upright, on edge, instead of lying flat on the deck. While he had his arm inside the "V" that had been formed by the two separated stacks, the YR rocked and the two separated stacks came together. I heard a distinct *crack* that sounded much like the breaking of a healthy tree branch. The man's grimace as he struggled to free his tightly pinned arm confirmed what I suspected; his arm was broken. I pried the two stacks apart so that he could free his newly disfigured forearm from the grip in which it had been entrapped. I grabbed the nearest thing I could find, a brand-new *Playboy* magazine, to use as an immobilizing splint on his arm. As I tied the magazine securely around his arm, I jokingly suggested that he might enjoy reading the magazine at the hospital. He, of course, was in no mood for humor, but he did acknowledge his gratitude for my assistance. I immediately made arrangements to provide emergency transportation to the hospital at China Beach, where he could be properly treated.

Several hours later the man returned, his arm in a cast but in much better spirits than he was when he departed. He told me that through some quirk, likely assisted by my quick action and *Playboy* magazine, hospital X-rays had confirmed the break, but the bone had "reset itself" in perfect alignment! There had been no need for further professional assistance other than the application of a cast! That was the good news. The bad news was that he had lost the *Playboy* magazine while he was at the hospital.

When I became eligible for my second R and R trip Okinawa was my destination. I asked my closest friend, Don, if he would accompany me.

Don was an impressive E-6, and we had a lot in common. He, too, worked hard and played hard. His features mirrored those of Nat "King" Cole, and his ability to imitate Cole's voice was uncanny. Don was reluctant to spend his R and R time in Okinawa because there were rumors that the Japanese (particularly the women) discriminated against Negroes. I had never seen such discrimination and therefore assured Don that he would be treated well, particularly if he remained close to me and didn't stray off into out-of-bounds or other undesirable areas. Don accepted and within a few days we were en route to Naha, Okinawa.

I thought of Don as my brother as we made our way from the Okinawa landing strip to the nearest taxi stand. It was an entirely new world to Don while it was more like returning home for me. In no time at all Don and I were at the London Club where we were both greeted enthusiastically. Mimiko was as sweet as ever and seemed thrilled to see me. Flashbacks came to my mind as I vividly recalled the lesbian affection Mimiko and Miko had at one time expressed for each other. Immediate relief came over Don's face as he realized that I had not exaggerated – he was among friends.

Don relaxed a little too much that first night and the heavy intake of alcoholic beverages took effect. Instead of remaining with me, he decided to go exploring on his own. He returned to the London Club several times that night, each time more inebriated than before, and each time he overwhelmed me with his gratitude for having asked him to accompany me to Okinawa. Much to the pleasure of the hostesses, Don sang Nat "King" Cole songs flawlessly, never forgetting the lyrics and always with extraordinary similarity to the professional stature of Cole himself. There came a time when Don failed to return after singing his way out the door. I was of the opinion that he had probably made an abundance of friends up and down the strip with his charm and his engaging King Cole impersonation. There was no reason for me to be concerned over his extended absence. Rather, I turned to thoughts of my own and made a play for Mimiko! The challenge of making it with a lesbian excited me.

Mimiko had always been special to me, disregarding the Miko—Mimiko incident, even though she was quite untouchable by males (to my knowledge). She had always been Mama-san's baby and she was never known to leave the club with a man. But that night Mama-san gave Mimiko and me her blessings as she allowed that sweet, young, and beautiful (lesbian?) girl to accompany me out into the night. Mimiko, very nervous and uncomfortable at the experience she was expecting to take place, accompanied me to the Okura Hotel. I felt somewhat honored, being trusted by Mama-san (and Mimiko) that way. I believed that Mama-san intentionally sent Mimiko with me for the purpose of finding happiness with a male instead of continuing along a lesbian path. I did not accommodate Mama-san in that sense. Instead, I comforted Mimiko as best I could and we simply lay there in bed together, awake most of the night. Any thoughts of the challenge I had previously considered became thoughts that any kind of lovemaking with a nervous lesbian, or with anyone reluctant to participate, would have been too closely akin to rape.

The following morning, one very hungover "King" Cole look-alike showed up at the London Club. Apparently he, probably an easy target, had been rolled the previous night and all of his funds had been stolen. Luckily, I had an excess of funds that I willingly shared with Don the remainder of the five-day vacation. Neither of us was ready when the time came to return to Vietnam – but we knew better than to miss our flight.

I either experienced or witnessed many strange things during that tour of duty in Vietnam. One incident in particular stands out above most of the others. One evening, while I was indulging in alcoholic beverages at the CPO Club, a new arrival entered. That chief had been through the hitchhike routine, as many of us had previously experienced, and he had managed to find his way to the club. He was, just as the rest of us had been, thoroughly confused.

His words sounded all too familiar. "God, it's great to be among fellow chiefs. Maybe you guys can tell me where the hell I am and where the hell I am supposed to go from here,"

One of the more seasoned chiefs welcomed him to Vietnam and to the CPO Club in particular. We ordered a beer for him and suggested that he join us while we would do our best to answer all of his questions. When he sat down he appeared a bit exhausted but otherwise happy to be associating with fellow chiefs, that tight fraternity with which he was most familiar and comfortable. I recall thinking to myself, as he lifted that can of cold beer to his lips for that first sip, *You'll feel so much better after you quench your thirst.* The very moment the beer can touched his lips he slumped over to the right side of his chair – and he died on the spot. Death had been instant; there had been no sign of pain, only slight fatigue and confusion, the very things we had all experienced and expected of others. When the responding medics arrived, one of the chiefs commented, "Ain't that a bitch; he came all the way to Vietnam to die, and he won't even get a Purple Heart!"

December 24, 1966, with PCS orders in hand, I boarded a military aircraft at DaNang Air Base for the long, tedious trip home. I did not sleep a bit; my mind was much too preoccupied with thoughts of all that I had done and seen during that past year.

No one was there to meet me when I arrived at Travis Air Force Base, California. Returning Vietnam veterans were never greeted with much enthusiasm; that fact is a matter of history. Suffice to say I was extremely upset that no one thought of me as being important enough to welcome me home. The person who was supposed to meet me [my not-very concerned spouse] had been there earlier that day but had not waited long enough for me to get from the airplane to the waiting room before leaving! The loneliness I felt standing alone in that terminal remains one of the most haunting and heart-breaking memories of my life. I am unable to express or explain the emotions I felt other than to relate that experience, that particular incident, as a significant contributing factor that encouraged a serious drinking habit I was in the process of developing. My family life, the life I am not writing about, was destroyed not as a result of my drinking, but rather as a result of those things that gave me excuses to drink.

I am not proud of the way I conducted a good portion of my Navy life while away from my family, although I am not entirely ashamed of it either. There was no excuse other than my own desire to be wanted, to be loved.

It was unfortunate that I felt as I did, needed and loved to a greater extent far away from my family than when I was with them. They did not know of my behavior while I was away, and I always did my best to provide for them the best I knew how when I was home, but separations that are caused as a result of the needs of the military all too often contributed to family problems. I was a prime example.

Following a brief period of leave, I went through a one-week "debriefing" at Coronado where I was enlightened with the truth; more specifically, reminders as to my immediate conduct. I would not discuss things (keep my mouth shut) that civilians did not understand (did not know about), and I was to disregard the misleading and/or misrepresented (factual) feelings of a very small percentage (growing majority) of public opinion that was in opposition to our role in Vietnam. I accepted that which I was told and looked forward to moving on with my military career.

Upon completion of the debriefing I was directed to report to Commanding Officer, Commander Submarine Squadron (ComSubRon) 15 Rep., Pearl Harbor, for further transfer to the USS *Tecumseh* (SSBN-628), a nuclear-powered FBM (Fleet Ballistic Missile) submarine, my new permanent duty station.

12

BACK TO REALITY

Following a much-needed rest and the usual period of leave, I reported for duty at ComSubRon 15 Rep. as directed. The USS *Tecumseh* (SSBN-628) was at sea at the time, so my orders were temporarily modified. As an interim duty station I was assigned to the "Blue Crew" (to be explained later), on the USS *Stonewall Jackson* (SSBN-634). On April 1, 1967, after attending a variety of technical refresher courses, I reported for duty at my final destination, the USS *Tecumseh*. I immediately accepted the title of Chief Petty Officer in Charge of the Engine Room and Associated Reactor Plant Components, and I became responsible for proper planning and coordination of many engineering functions.

The Tecumseh, named after the Shawnee Chief and said to mean "Crouching Panther" or meteor, which was called by the Indians the Panther of the Sky, was one of seven SSBNs assigned to Pacific patrol. The following is a brief history of Tecumseh.

When Tecumseh was approaching manhood, he went off into the forest alone to endure hardship and fasting, in order to prove himself worthy of becoming a "brave." After days of hunger and roaming in the deep forests, he threw himself exhausted at the side of a brook, where he fell asleep and dreamed of a cluster of stars out of which there shot one brighter than the rest and with a shining tail. This flaming meteor, which resembled a crouching panther ready to spring, appeared a number of times, and Tecumseh accepted this as his symbol, "The Radiant Guardian of Destiny."

Tecumseh, the great Shawnee Indian Chief, was born in 1768 in the area of Piqua, Ohio. In his youth, Daniel Boone became Tecumseh's foster brother, living for a time with his family after being captured by the Shawnees. While yet a young man, Tecumseh distinguished himself as a warrior in the border wars, yet even among his enemies he achieved a reputation for mercy and fair dealing, particularly in putting a stop to the torturing of prisoners. He was described as "a man of great courage and conduct, perfectly fearless, who inspired his companions with confidence." As he saw the lands of the Indians being swallowed up in the advance of the white settlers, with the destruction or dispersal of tribe after tribe, Tecumseh conceived the idea of uniting all western and southern Indian tribes into a great confederation, with the purpose of holding the Ohio River as the permanent boundary between the two races. He denied the right of the U.S. government to make land purchases from any single tribe, on the grounds that the territory belonged to all the tribes in common. Pursuing this objective, Tecumseh visited and spoke eloquently to the Indian tribes from the head of the Missouri River to Florida. He had a great gift of oratory and was compared to Henry Clay in this ability. Tecumseh spoke vehemently and movingly and could sway his listeners even when they lacked full understanding of his language. While he gained much support, the old tribal rivalries prevailed, and the Indians never made a united stand. During his absence on a journey to organize the tribes of the South, his plans were thwarted by the Battle of Tippecanoe on November 7, 1811. With the start of the War of 1812, Tecumseh led his forces to the support of the British, with some 2000 warriors of the allied tribes under his command. He was killed in a bloody battle on the Thames River near Chatham, Ontario, on October 5, 1813, while covering the retreat of the British after Commodore Perry's victory on Lake Erie. From all that is said of Tecumseh in contemporary records, there is no reason to doubt the judgment of Trumbull, an historian of Indian Wars, who in 1850 declared Tecumseh "the most extraordinary Indian in American history."

Other significant descriptions that have been written of Tecumseh include:

He was called a greater military leader than McDowell (1818-35, general in the Union Army – fought in the First and Second Battle of Bull Run), Rosecrans (1819-98, American general, in command of the Department of the Cumberland and in the battle at Stone River, minister to Mexico, member of Congress and registrar of the United States treasury), Sheridan (1831-88, Union Army general, commander of cavalry, appointed Commander in Chief of the United States Army), Custer (1839-76, defeated and killed in the Battle of Little Big Horn) or William H. Harrison (soldier and states-man, ninth President of the United States and son of Benjamin Harrison, a signer of the Declaration of Independence).

Devotion to justice was so firmly a part of Tecumseh's nature that it stood always as the primary force, even above his Indian Confederation.

Even William H. Harrison is credited with having said, "Tecumseh was one of those uncommon geniuses, which spring up occasionally to produce revolutions and overturn the establishment order of things. If it were not for the proximity of the United States, he would perhaps be the founder of an Empire that would rival in glory that of Mexico or Peru."

U.S.S TECUMSEH

USS *Tecumseh* (SSBN-628) – Ballistic Missile Carrying Nuclear-Powered Submarine – May 1967 to January 1968

The USS *Tecumseh* (SSBN-628) was a beautiful and powerful ves-sel and was rightfully named for such a remarkable Indian warrior. The *Tecumseh* was the eleventh of the Lafayette-class FBM submarines and the second warship to bear the name of the great Shawnee Indian Chief. The first *Tecumseh*, a single-turret monitor, was launched September 12, 1863, and was lost on August 5, 1864, to a Confederate torpedo in the Battle of Mobile Bay. The USS *Tecumseh* (SSBN-628) was launched at Groton, Connecticut, on June 22, 1963, and she was commissioned at the Electric Boat Division of General Dynamics on May 29, 1964. During extended underwater voyages, she stood ready to fire any of her sixteen Polaris A-3 missiles if directed to do so by the President. Her all-volunteer crew consisted of twelve officers and 124 enlisted men, all highly skilled professionals in their respective fields. Nowhere else in the armed forces were servicemen required to perform their duties under such unusual conditions, completely submerged for periods of sixty days or more.

The *Tecumseh's* FBM weapon system, better known by the name of its missile, Polaris (named for the North Star), had a 2,500-nautical-mile A-3 (third generation) operational capability. Each missile was about thirty-two feet in length, and about four and a half feet in diameter and weighed about thirty-five thousand pounds. Destructive power: unimaginable, more than all of the explosive power used by all sides during World War II, and all carried on board a single submarine.

Life aboard the sleek and powerful-looking nuclear-powered vessel was quite different than that aboard any other type naval ship. Officers and crew were fully prepared for the tasks demanded of them by weeks of intensive schooling and training. In between watches, normally manned on a "six on – twelve off" basis, the undersea sailors had a variety of activities with which they could occupy their time. The crew's library, maintained on an honor system, contained best-sellers as well as several private collections that were brought aboard by members of the crew to be shared by all. Movies were shown twice each evening, and pinochle, acey-deucy, and other tournaments were held regularly. There were many similarities in life on board all submarines, regardless of size or class. "Open galley," one of the most active and appreciated privileges, allowed the men to "raid the icebox" at any time of the day or night. The ship's entertainment system provided a wide variety of music.

During patrol, the *Tecumseh* maintained radio silence. However, since communication was the vital authority link that could order missiles launched, the radiomen kept a vigil around-the-clock. Besides the possibility of receiving the order to fire, should it be sent, the radiomen provided the only contact with the outside world. Daily news broadcasts by the Armed Forces Radio service were picked up for general information, but the crew considered "familygrams" most important. Crewmen received brief personal messages from relatives and friends letting us know how things were going at home. Each man was allowed four fifteen-word familygrams per patrol. "Babygrams," stating pertinent facts of new arrivals, were sent/received when someone became a father.

At the end of each two-month submerged patrol, the men were relieved by another crew [the two crews were termed Blue and Gold] and were flown by chartered airline from Guam, the submarine's home port, back to their home base in Hawaii. There, after one month of R and R, they received further training as they attended special schools to sharpen their knowledge in respective fields. Extensive refresher training was normally pursued at the Fleet Submarine Training Facility in Pearl Harbor.

Following approximately three months ashore the crew was returned to the *Tecumseh*, again by chartered commercial airline, to prepare for another patrol. Each man located his counterpart, and a thorough transfer of pertinent information was passed from the off-going crew to the oncoming crew. A brief change-of-command ceremony took place, and the fresh crew accepted total responsibility for the craft. Within a month, after the officers and crew thoroughly checked out the submarine, another two-month underwater patrol would begin.

At about the time I reported for duty on board the *Tecumseh*, several interesting things were taking place within the military services: An anti-tank weapon that hurled guided missiles and was fired from an infantry-man's shoulder was being developed for the Army. The weapon was called the Dragon. It was the Army's first guided missile system portable enough to be used by a single infantryman against such targets as tanks and bunkers. Because it weighted only twenty-seven pounds, it was also well suited for airborne and airmobile operations. After nearly 177 years as a member of the U.S. Treasury Department, the Coast Guard joined the newly formed Department of Transportation, and a tiny two-way radio for use in rescue and survival operations was about to be tested by the Air Force. The experimental radio – called a transceiver because it transmitted and received voice and tone signals – resembled a pocket-sized transistor radio. Interesting developments at the time – now, for the most part, historical museum relics.

When I first set foot aboard *Tecumseh* she was in port undergoing her upkeep and maintenance period inside Apra Harbor at Polaris Point, Guam. I found that the comforts provided on the *Tecumseh* were much better than those I had experienced on the *Seadragon*. The *Tecumseh* was much the larger of the two vessels, and there seemed to be more methods of entertaining oneself during periods of relaxation. The Chiefs' Quarters were exceptionally comfortable, something of a new experience for me. It was a world some men loved because of the many actual, as well as perceived, benefits it had to offer. Every man on board knew exactly when he would be home and when he would be away. It was a very dependable cycle of which spouses were equally aware. Submarine pay (hazardous duty pay) was attractive by itself; especially knowing everyone drew it whether they were attached to the off-duty crew or the on-duty crew. There was a full month of R and R that followed each period of patrol time that was in addition to the month of annual leave everyone also accrued. And time at sea was quiet, a slow and steady patrol within a designated area without ever having to worry or wonder about where or when the submarine might surface again.

I had a different concept of desirable duty. I found myself back in a world of nuclear power, a world that required continuous studies, never-ending refresher courses on a multitude of subjects, many of which I had little memory or had completely forgotten. I had to learn about all of the changes that had come about during my year away from the nuclear power program, and there were new and demanding courses I had to take that were full of upgraded information. On top of that, I was once again a "non-qual," and therefore had to spend most of my off-duty time qualifying on a class of submarine about which I knew practically nothing. The strain I was under, coupled with the knowledge that I would no longer be returning to the foreign ports I had grown to love; that I would not be renewing the many friendships I had acquired in those ports, made it difficult for me to concentrate on my responsibilities. I was far too adventurous, apparently spoiled by the freedom from studies I had enjoyed during the previous year. I found myself thinking it strange that I had been so much more relaxed and under far less strain while serving in a war zone, where I had been subjected to constant danger, where I had been targeted and shot at by the enemy, and where the daily routine included nearby intermittent small-arms fire and sporadic explosions of deadly rockets and mortars. I knew that I had to make one of the biggest decisions of my life. Would I allow myself to be "tortured" by the stress I felt and continue to do that which I was under orders to do, or would I speak out as a man and attempt to break free from a Navy of which I no longer cared to be a part; the nuclear powered Navy? I would give the question serious thought before making my final decision.

Guam, one of the Pacific Mariana Islands and located in an area frequently referred to as Micronesia, was something of a cross between Hawaii and the Philippines. It was always hot and extremely humid – and was known for the many war relics scattered about the island. There were

385

tanks and personnel carriers that for one reason or another remained behind at the war's end; all were rusting away on unattended, out-of-the-way hills and fields. One could expect to find live ammunition, unexploded missiles, and other types of military ordnance while exploring secluded sites. The rule was "hands off" for obvious reasons, but that didn't seem to discourage individuals from keeping finds of live small-arms ammunition. No one was discouraged from visiting those sites where the remnants of war were so prevalent; however, one needed to obtain a "Boonie Pass," written permission to depart from the main road and from well-beaten paths. That way the command would know where to start searching in the event someone got lost or suffered some sort of immobilizing injury that would prevent him from returning to the boat on time.

I became good friends with two other chiefs; Julius, an electronics technician, and "Doc," the hospitalman. I spent nearly all of my time ashore palling around with one or the other – or both. On one occasion while Doc and I were sitting at a bar in the town of Agat, I overheard two Guamanians not only conversing in Chamorro, their native dialect, but periodically speaking short sentences or phrases in English and Vietnamese. I threw in my two cents' worth by introducing myself in Vietnamese, knowing there was always a certain bond that existed between most individuals who had served in Vietnam. Recognizing the common ground we had at one time shared, we began swapping stories about our memories of Vietnam. Within a very short period of time we established a trusting friendship. Before the "bull session" broke up, we all agreed to meet the following day, at which time our new friends, Al (Alejandro) and Joe (Joseph), promised to show us around the island and guide us to some very remote places where they had recovered evidence proving the Japanese had remained hidden there long after the war's end.

The following morning Doc and I, dressed in working khakis, were picked up on schedule by Al and Joe. They laughed at us when we expressed our doubts that they would really show up. First, they took us to Al's home; remotely located outside the town of Barrigada, where we were shown an impressive display of war souvenirs – all Japanese relics that consisted of swords, belt buckles, knives, wristwatches, currency, and a variety of other interesting trophies. Al had found them while exploring several hidden caves that he had come across over the years. Just looking at the display created that much more curiosity about the adventure in which we were about to take part.

We were being treated with a hospitality we did not know existed in Guam, and quite the contrary to the rumors more familiar to us – that Guamanians liked to roll GIs and take their money. There was that traditional and familiar story about how Guamanians always carried a two-by-four in their car for the purpose of cracking American GIs in the back of their heads as they walked along the side of the road. I had shared that story with Al and Joe at the bar the previous evening at which time they had laughingly admitted that they never traveled the streets and roads of Guam without certain "building materials." At Al's home we transferred to the back of a pickup truck to accompany them into the "boonies" where they intended on cutting several coconut trees that were to be utilized in the construction of a home. There was no road to follow as we drove the truck cross-country, in between a variety of tropical trees that flourished there. We drove through gigantic spiderwebs that were strung between the trees; most of which contained huge yellow-and-black spiders suspended in the middle – the largest spiders I had ever seen. I have always had a fear of spiders and would never have gone on that adventure had I been aware of their presence and size. There was no way of avoiding the webs, and those of us in the back of the pickup were kept busy brushing spiders off one another. Our local friends just laughed at our concern (my horror) and told us not to worry, that the spiders were harmless. *Like hell*, I thought to myself. We also saw a few coconut crabs, land-dwelling crabs that had small bodies in comparison to their huge claws, which they used to crack open coconuts. Apparently they fed on coconut meat and were themselves later fed upon by the locals.

After delivering the freshly cut trees we again changed vehicles to one of comfortable size and one in which we were protected by sides, windows, and a top. We headed off in another direction down what must have at one time been a trail but showed no signs of recent vehicular traffic. Once parked, Doc and I were told that we had to hike the remaining mile or so farther into the boonies, the wilderness. Fortunately, we had been forewarned that the hike would be strenuous and that if we were at all out of shape or reluctant we should not go. But Doc and I were both in excellent physical condition, and we were not the least bit discouraged.

While hiking that final distance we saw one large iguana sitting proudly on top of a pile of rocks. Joe had a rifle with him but couldn't squeeze off a shot before it scurried for cover. We had been told of the abundant fruit bat population and of the remarkable size to which they grew. We were also told that fruit bats and iguanas were edible, especially when prepared *kelaguen* style. *Kelaguen* was a term that described one method of preparing any kind of raw meat. The meat, whether bat, iguana, beef, chicken, or anything else was cut up into bite size strips and mixed with salt, vinegar, and tiny but blistering red-hot chili peppers. Theoretically, or probably factually, the vinegar and chili cooked the meat without any other source of heat.

Within an hour or so of strenuous climbing down the side of the mountain, we approached a partially concealed rocky opening; the mouth of a cave. Inside the opening there was an immediate and sheer drop-off to another level some twenty or more feet below. Interestingly, as if more than by chance, there was a single tuber that had grown from a well-established tree directly above the opening; the root was the size of a ship's mooring line and hung straight down to within a foot or so of the cave's floor. One by one we jumped from the lip of the opening to the root and eased our way down into the dark and moist cavern below, never once worrying or considering how we might struggle to get back out – with or without benefit of that root. We had been assured that our efforts would be more than adequately rewarded.

Joe and Al had flashlights, hardware that Doc and I had failed to consider the need to carry. Al took the lead; I was second, followed closely by Joe and Doc. In that manner we had sufficient light to see as we began our way into the depths of the mountain. The caverns that we passed through varied in size and consisted primarily of moist limestone. The path we followed took us from one cavity to another, separated sometimes by openings barely large enough to squeeze or crawl through. As promised, when we entered one of the larger cavities there were many indications that Japanese survivors had indeed made that their hideaway for a considerable period of time. There were remnants of clothing, pieces of handmade sandals, deteriorated metal cans long since devoid of descriptive labels, and there were hieroglyphic-type markings in Japanese katakana, hiragana, and kanji characters inscribed in the walls. There were also skeleton parts that were unmistakably of human origin and could reasonably be assumed to be the remains of Japanese soldiers too proud to surrender and/or ignorant of the fact that the war had come to an end. I was fascinated by what I saw and I

388

felt a bit awkward as we moved about, unintentionally desecrating the final resting place of an unknown number of onetime proud fighting men. I was not disappointed when we reached the point where the passage had filled in over time, too narrow to pass through. We did not have the tools to scrape or widen the opening, so our search and discovery ended there. Al and Joe both remarked on how the last time they were there the gap had been large enough to squeeze through and how disappointed they were in not being able to recover the relics they had previously left beyond that point. I thought of myself as not just at a grave site, but actually within the grave, that it might be better to leave things as they were, at peace, and leave the area as we found it. I was not squeamish per se, but I was sensitive to my surroundings and was not enthusiastic about altering or desecrating an area that could in any way be construed as "sacred ground."

We made our way back out of the caverns as we had made our way in, stopping momentarily to review the things that had attracted our attention on the way in, back to the dangling root by which we had gained entry into the secluded caverns. I was a bit overwhelmed by what I had experienced, and I was grateful that Joe and Al had shared their secret – their knowledge of the caverns with us.

As I looked up that root I thought to myself, *I wonder how many times Japanese soldiers climbed up or down this tuber – to gather food, enjoy a brief period of sunlight, a breath of fresh air, or more likely to escape and hide.*

We exited as we had entered, Al first, me second, Joe third, and Doc last. Once outside, we all smiled at each other, but any open discussion regarding our observations was noticeably lacking. For the moment, our thoughts and feelings remained concealed within our hearts and minds.

The return hike up the side of the mountain, as difficult as it was, was accomplished without a hitch and without complaint. I think we were all somewhat preoccupied with our own thoughts, and the trek was more in silence than in the company of conversation. We drove back to Al's home where an abundance of food and drink was prepared. The food, beef *kelaguen,* was delicious. At the time I thought it was the best-tasting food I had ever eaten, considering everything we had seen and done as well as our lack of food intake that particular day. Our friends returned us to the boat safe and sound late that evening.

Julius and I made it a point to visit the class-six (liquor) store at the nearest military installation, where we bought enough booze to last the upcoming two-month period of patrol at sea. It was more convenient to buy the small boxes of twenty-four two-ounce miniatures instead of taking a chance on boarding with larger and more conspicuous quart-size containers.

The *Tecumseh* got underway for patrol that same month, and I was immediately tasked with the never-ending responsibility of requalification. During that time underway, Julius and I made it a practice to periodically meet in the CPO Quarters before turning in for a period of sleep – the purpose being to share in a moment of peace as each of us indulged in two ounces of our own beverage of choice. It was almost ritualistic as each of us poured a self-imposed daily limit of the contents of one two-ounce miniature bottle over ice, then toasted each other for one reason or another. It was nice, sharing those moments of privacy, although one time it came very near backfiring. The Chief Engineer violated the sanctity of the CPO quarters by not knocking on the door before he opened it. Julius and I were the only chiefs sitting at the table, and each of us had a pale yellow/orange colored iced drink sitting on the table directly in front of him. We both noticed the chief snipe glance back and forth between our faces and the drinks, but neither of us showed the least sign of panic or concern. We could not have been more nonchalant, which must have given the appearance that we were drinking iced tea or apple cider. Either that or the Chief Engineer chose not to challenge us, to overlook the apparent violation of Navy regulations. In either case, he asked his question and immediately departed, closing the door behind him. Simultaneously, without any further delay, Julius and I immediately grabbed our "highballs" and downed them without regard to taste or effect. We then had a good laugh and turned in for the night.

I spent about half of that first patrol thinking about my predicament, weighing the pros and cons carefully, but the result was invariably the same. My decision was not only in the best interest of myself; it was also in the best interest of the Navy, the nuclear submarine Navy in particular. Once my decision was final, I knew that I would have to stand by it, even under severe criticism. I also knew that the probability of my being favorably considered for future promotion would, understandably, diminish accordingly. My decision had not been as difficult as I had thought it might be.

Within days after the *Tecumseh* returned to port and I was back in Hawaii, I notified the XO in writing, via chain of command, that I was no longer a volunteer for submarine service!

Within moments of the XO having received my written notification I was directed to report to him. At first he appeared concerned for me as he asked me a number of questions about my reasons for wanting out of the submarine service. It was not easy for me to explain my reasons for rejecting that life, at least not in acceptable terms. The harder I tried to get my point(s) across, the more difficult it became for me. I knew of the severe headaches and the lack of sleep I had been suffering as a direct result of my inability to cope with or otherwise accept the never-ending study routine. I knew what the surface-craft Navy was all about; that it, too, had its up side and its down side; that it did not provide an atmosphere of continuous threat or any other means of undue stress. The "pro pay," proficiency pay for enlisted men in critical ratings, and the submarine pay had ceased to exist as attractive bargaining tools.

I no longer cared about the extra money nearly as much as I cared about my mental health and my happiness, something the XO found hard to accept. He made it very clear when he said, "Chief, you can volunteer for submarine service but you cannot un-volunteer. The needs of the Navy determine where you serve."

"Sir, regardless what the Navy needs, I will not be on board the *Tecumseh* the next time she gets underway."

My words were not at all what he wanted to hear, and he immediately, a bit menacingly, responded; "Chief, that sounds like you are threatening me."

"No, sir, I am not threatening you. I am telling you that if you want an Engineering Department chief on board when the *Tecumseh* gets underway you should start making arrangements immediately, because I will never again go to sea on board a submarine – not the *Tecumseh* or any other." I also made it clear that I wanted my 3355 NEC removed, that I was no longer able to function adequately within the nuclear power program. I told the XO that I would willingly volunteer to remain with the Gold Crew up until the time the *Tecumseh* got underway, thereby assuring him that I would assist in whatever upkeep the Engineering Department might be faced with when the time came to relieve the Blue Crew. The XO didn't like being told by a chief what that chief would or would not do. He was the one who was in charge, not I.

The Exec wasted no time in having me replaced. On January 3, 1968, just two weeks after *Tecumseh* docked at Polaris Point, Guam, I was issued a set of orders directing that I report to ComSubRon 15 Rep. for temporary duty while awaiting reassignment. I felt exuberant in that I had been officially transferred without having had to place myself in violation of Navy regulations, that of missing ship's movement – a court-martial offense. Had it been necessary, I most assuredly would have missed movement and then would have had to plead my case in court.

Upon reporting for duty at ComSubRon 15, I was assigned as Chief Master at Arms for Security, responsible for ensuring that tight security measures were enforced throughout the Fleet Submarine Training Facility. It was a routine assignment, that of checking personnel for proper access badges, issuing badges to authorized personnel, and investigating various alarms throughout the facility whenever they were activated – usually as a result of accidental unauthorized entry into restricted areas. I learned to recognize a broad variety of identification papers and armed forces identification cards of foreigners who were allowed to share our facilities, including civilian dignitaries. It was a relatively simple assignment but carried a heavy load of responsibilities. I enjoyed the work. It was as though I was on display, a martyr of sort, as I checked the access badges of many nuclear-trained sailors with whom I had previously served. I was one of a very small handful of individuals that were known to have "escaped" the nuclear program successfully, without having violated rules or regulations. I never met a nuclear-trained snipe that did not want out of the program. I also never met one that was so set on getting out that he was willing to risk his career as I had. I was thought of as something of a fool, yet I was admired for having had the courage to proceed.

The Personnel Officer at ComSubRon 15 Rep. was not at all sympathetic toward my attitude or me. At our very first meeting he questioned why I was not wearing my dolphins. I told him that I was a "nonvol" and that I no longer considered myself a submarine sailor. He told me that I had not been disqualified and as long as I was designated "SS" I would be required to wear the dolphin device. I very politely told him that I refused to wear it. I shall never forget how he, a full lieutenant but a man who had advanced through the enlisted ranks before having become an officer, tried to contain his anger. He invited me into his office, where, through semiclenched teeth, he very calmly said things to me that I would never forget.

"Chief, your previous command recommended you for participation in the upcoming E-8 exam. Well, it just doesn't go hand in hand, quitting submarines and promotion, so here is what I am going to do. I am *not* going to pull that recommendation – but I *am* going to lose your test. I am also going to make sure you are never promoted again and that you never get a decent set of orders again!"

I wanted more than anything to say, "Fuck you, asshole," but instead I looked him straight in the eye, forced a smile on my face that in itself irritated him, and said, "My goal was to become a chief in this man's Navy, and by God I did it. You might think you can hurt me or my career, but you, sir, are what you are; dead wrong!"

His simple, "We'll see," probably provided the first spark in lighting a motivation within me that I would continue to fuel throughout my remaining military career.

Prior to leaving the *Tecumseh* I had, through appropriate channels, requested transfer out of the submarine service and out of the nuclear power program. I had also written a strong letter expressing my desire to return to Vietnam. My letter was direct and to the point. In part, it read:

> There is no doubt in my mind. I know I can serve my country much more effectively and perform more efficiently if I am reassigned to a shore facility in Vietnam. The experience I have already acquired allows me to make this request knowing the consequences involved. I have lived among the Vietnamese people and have shared their poor standards. I have adjusted to the extreme climatic conditions and have a good knowledge of the Vietnamese people. I have a limited knowledge of the language, which I could improve through a proper language school or through self-study, and I have already satisfactorily completed survival (SERE) training, counterinsurgency schooling, and advanced weapons training.

I was surprised and pleased with the Commanding Officer's favorable endorsement, which read in part:

> Chief ADKISSON has demonstrated exceptional adaptability, management, and leadership qualities while supervising his division in the course of a complex Polaris submarine refit and

patrol. His technical ability with machinery and the quality of his leadership coupled with his experience from previous service in Vietnam make him an outstanding volunteer for a return to such duty. Chief ADKISSON's dedication to his country and his personal conviction is thrilling and inspirational. He is most sincere in his determination to serve again in Vietnam where he is certain he serves best. Without doubt he will perform superbly in whatever duties assigned in Vietnam.

Every day ComSubRon 15 Rep.'s Personnel Officer went out of his way to make sure I saw him. He always had a slight evil grin, which was, I suppose, to remind me of his threats, that he had ruined my career and that, as a result of his power of persuasion, I would never receive another set of orders to my liking. I always waved at him and grinned back, hoping he might think that I knew something he didn't.

I disregarded the Personnel Officer's uncalled-for remarks and did the best job I could while waiting for the Bureau's answer to my request(s). It was very unlikely that everything would result in my favor, but I refused to give up hope.

It was also unlikely that the Bureau would waste a whole lot of time determining what to do with me, but I was in no hurry. In fact, I was beginning not to care. The job of Chief Master at Arms met with my total approval. I had more liberty than I had ever had – and there was no requirement that I remain on duty overnight. At about 1600 every weekday I was relieved by one of the duty chiefs and I was free until 0800 the following morning. I was off every weekend. It was probably the best duty to which I had ever been assigned since having joined the Navy.

It could not last forever. March 25, 1968, while on duty at the Chief Master at Arms desk, I received a phone call from the Personnel Officer. I knew by the tone of his voice that the news he was about to give me was not going to be pleasant. He did not want to discuss anything over the phone and he directed that I report to his office immediately. I didn't know whether he had figured out a way to hang me for something I might have unwittingly done, if he was transferring me somewhere else where I might not have it so good, or if my orders had come in and they were so pleasing to him that he wanted to see my face when he delivered them to me.

"Well, Chief, your orders came in and I wanted to give them to you personally." He did not look at all pleased.

I stood there, fully prepared to congratulate him on his success in getting the Bureau to screw me, and he handed me the official orders. I skipped over the "Intermediate Station" block and focused directly on the "Ultimate Destination" block. I found it impossible to withhold my yelp of glee that seemingly ricocheted around his office when I realized that I had been ordered to return to NSA, DaNang, for a second tour of duty in Vietnam, precisely what I had asked for. The Personnel Officer just looked at me and muttered something to the effect that I should get out of his office, gather up my things, and be on my way. I looked him straight on and grinned as I first thanked him for his role in getting me "such a lousy set of orders," then went on to tell him, somewhat sarcastically, that I looked forward to seeing him again somewhere down the road. I purposely chuckled out loud as I exited his office. As far as I was concerned, the news was good as gold, almost too good to be true. I believed that the additional year away from the nuclear power program would very nearly guarantee that my 3355 Job Code would be dropped. For the time being, that had become of lessor importance. I only wanted to pack up and move on.

13

VIETNAM – FROM ANOTHER PERSPECTIVE

My orders directed that I report to NAVPHIBASE Coronado for approximately four weeks in connection with the Counterinsurgency Orientation and Naval Internal Security Course of Instruction as an intermediate duty station. I had already attended the counterinsurgency course; better yet, I had already served a year in Vietnam and had firsthand knowledge in addition to that training – so my plan was to swap that course for the condensed Vietnamese language "crash" course.

April 24, 1968, I checked in at Coronado and immediately requested permission to speak with the Command Executive Officer.

I have neglected to explain an interesting phenomenon that became readily apparent when I advanced from the white-hat ranks, E-6 and below, to that of chief. Sailors, the usual term reserved for naval personnel, but more readily associated with those wearing a white hat, were not easily recognized by people unfamiliar with the differences in uniforms between all branches of the military. The khaki uniform worn by naval officers was not at all unlike the khaki uniform worn by CPOs and was similar in many respects to the uniform worn by Marines and Army personnel. I was called "soldier" on many occasions when I was away from the high concentration of Navy personnel that was always present around a naval facility or base; most frequently when I was on leave or en route from one duty station to another. The phenomenon to which I refer was an immediate transition that took place, within the officer ranks in particular – to a lesser degree within the lower grades. Prior to wearing the CPO uniform, as a white-hat (other than within the submarine service) there was an obvious distrust and very little noticeable respect. What an amazing difference a uniform made! Immediately when one donned the CPO uniform that distinguished E-7s and above from E-6s and below, instant trust and respect were miraculously bestowed upon us. Every chief I ever approached on this subject agreed with me in this observation. I recalled being taught in boot camp that one was required to respect the position, the devices one wore – not necessarily the person. Hence enlisted men were required to salute all officers, out of respect for their rank, regardless whether the officer was admired or hated. It was a great feeling, being treated almost as an equal, sometimes with more respect than some officers were. It was a type of treatment that should not have been based solely on the uniform one wore. I would have preferred appropriate recognition, trust, etc., based on my own particular talents and performance rather than having had something analogous to a magic wand waved over me that somehow made me better than the white-hat I used to be. Not all chiefs felt quite as I did. Many of them felt they deserved, and they expected, the more favorable treatment they received. Some fully believed that they really were better than the white-hats below them. Better? Not at all. More authority? Absolutely! Arguing the difference between the two was not always an easy task; totally dependent upon the individual to whom I was explaining the disparity.

Keeping in mind the above, it might be easier to understand why the XO, upon being informed of my request to speak with him, immediately invited me into his office. I'm not saying he would not have done the same for any enlisted man, regardless of his grade, but I know that my own personal experience led me to believe I had a distinct edge as a direct result of my pay grade. The polite words the XO spoke, "What can I do for you, Chief?" were a far cry from the more blunt "What is it you want?" expected to be directed at a white-hat.

I chose my words carefully and knew that I had to express my request with dignity and brevity, using words that could not be misunderstood. In no way could I appear to be begging. My words flowed smoothly as I addressed the issue. The explanation I gave was straightforward and made good sense. The XO was in complete agreement with me, and he made immediate arrangements through the Personnel Officer to modify my orders. I was no longer required to repeat SERE or counterinsurgency training. Instead I was offered my choice of several other courses, from which I selected the Vietnamese Language School. The internal security course, also to my liking and certainly to my benefit, remained part of my scheduled training. The odds were in my favor that upon completion of that course my primary and secondary job codes would be changed. If that happened, I would never again have to worry about duty on any nuclear-powered vessel – at least not in the sense that I would remain an integral part of the nuclear program.

I thoroughly enjoyed the short Vietnamese language course. Classes consisted of individualized training, usually five or six men to a group with one "homeroom" instructor who remained with the group most of the time. Instructors were rotated periodically to make sure we had the benefit of men as well as women instructors; there was a distinct difference between the way women talked and the way men talked. Had women only taught us, we would have sounded like women when we used the language. We were taught the North Vietnamese dialect, which differed noticeably from the dialect of the South. I found that it was not all that difficult to convert back and forth between the two.

The group I was with had the prettiest little Vietnamese homeroom instructor there. She was the wife of a U.S. Navy lieutenant and she spoke excellent English. Other than that, we learned very little about her. She did have a tendency to flirt, and we all loved it. We knew that she intentionally wore short skirts and when she sat on her high stool we all admired her panties. She wore a different color panty each day, and we made bets as to what color she might adorn herself with the following day. I had an advantage over the rest of my group; what they thought to be a strange and difficult language I was already somewhat familiar with. At the end of each day we were required to converse with the instructor in complete sentences, each day using more words as our vocabularies developed. That period was my favorite because I always tossed in a few extra words that had not been taught in class. That was my way of flirting with our little darling of an instructor – and she loved it. Once, after I told her in her native language that she needed to know me better, she quickly responded with a flurry of words while she maintained a sly little smile on her lovely lips. Just as quickly, as if her response to my flirtation had been a bit too spontaneous, she reverted to English, openly stating, "I better watch out; this is getting a little dangerous." I do not know what it was that she said. However, if in her opinion it was getting dangerous, I suspect that she had openly agreed that the opportunity to know each other better was not entirely out of the question. I was inclined to pursue that possibility – however, I never acted on it. Her quick but easily recognizable teasing eye contact, coupled with an occasional flirtatious innuendo, was gratification enough. I liked being liked.

During my first tour in Vietnam I learned that handguns were scarce. It had taken me a great deal of finagling and a little bit of diplomacy before I managed to acquire the .45 that became my daily companion. My current PCS orders had been issued without the usual PERSONAL WEAPONS UNAUTHORIZED stamped thereon. With the knowledge I had of the scarcity of weapons and how individualized the policy was that governed the issuance, I decided to pack my own brand-new Remington model M1911A1 .45-caliber pistol along with my personal belongings and shipped it to Vietnam.

June 18, 1968, I returned to DaNang, but this time I skipped the preliminaries of checking in at the White Elephant. I knew that nearly all arrivals were thoroughly confused and that they seldom reported to their job site expeditiously, so I went directly to the Chiefs' Club at Camp Tien Sha.

The club had undergone some remarkable changes since my last visit. It was still the same structure; however, on the inside it had an entirely new appearance. It had been transformed into a place to be admired by chiefs and their guests, completely modernized from top to bottom. It had new ceilings with beautiful light fixtures, walls that were beautifully paneled and appropriately decorated in nautical motif, and newly carpeted floors. The bar was in the same place, beginning to the right of the club entrance and extending about twenty feet along the wall into the club. Much to the convenience of all chiefs, it also boasted a brand new barbershop where it cost 25¢ for a decent haircut. The menu was as impressive as the surrounding décor. It provided a decent variety of meals and snacks varying in price from a high of $1.50 (complete dinners) to a low of 25¢ (a variety of soups and sandwiches). Smiley and Le were still there, and when they saw me they ran over to welcome my return. They told me that Mai had been transferred and that she was working at the 'O' Club, the Little Elephant, there at Camp Tien Sha and that she was temporarily on some kind of leave of absence. I looked forward to seeing her again. My biggest surprise was to see I.P., a Chief Yeoman who had also served on board the YR-70 with me, sitting at one of the tables with another chief. I.P.'s eyes opened wide with a pleased expression of surprise as I approached their table. Almost in unison we both asked the same thing; "What in the hell are you doing here?"

I.P. intended on remaining in Vietnam forever – as long as his requests for extensions continued to be approved. He had found a home to his liking, a rare situation for most individuals serving in Vietnam; probably a condition most difficult to comprehend by those who never served there – impossible for the vast majority of those who had. I was one of those who preferred such duty, war zone or not. For me, it was a whole lot better than living at sea or working on nuclear power components.

Following a couple of cold beers and after briefly reminiscing with I.P. about numerous things that had occurred during our tours on the YR, "Gib," the other chief at the table, began telling me about the Foreign Claims Office where they were both assigned. The more Gib talked, the more intrigued I became. The duty he described was as close to what I had always wanted as I could ever have dreamed existed.

Simply put, the U.S. Naval Foreign Claims Office was within the jurisdiction of the JAG, the Judge Advocate General, an office located at the White Elephant that was composed of law specialists who were graduate lawyers specially certified for legal duties within the naval establishment. The Foreign Claims Office was located at 17 Yen Bay, only two blocks west of the White Elephant. Personnel assigned to the Foreign Claims Office investigated claims against the U.S. Government and U.S. military personnel. They collected evidence and other data for use in determining liability when any person of foreign nationality filed a claim for injury or for some other wrong that was caused by an agency or element of the U.S. Government.

Gib, the Chief Investigator, had overall responsibility for the office. I.P., senior to Gib in longevity, typed and assisted in the processing of claim documents after the investigative process ended. There were three sailors, E-6 and below, that were members of an immediate response team. Whenever there was a radio or messenger notification of an accident, regardless of the severity, the response team was dispatched to the scene, where they usually met and coordinated their investigative effort with U.S. and RVN Military Police. The local police were seldom enthusiastic about assisting; expectedly more "cooperative" in leaving the details up to others. There were also two Vietnamese women typists, one male Vietnamese lawyer, and two Vietnamese men that translated, interpreted, and assisted in determining legal decisions relating to Vietnamese law.

Within two hours of having learned the details of the Foreign Claims Office I was at the White Elephant in search of the JAG's office. A personable lieutenant commander at the front desk very politely asked me what assistance he could provide. He was wearing dolphins and I immediately realized that my chances of having my request favorably honored had died an instant death. After all, I was a "quitter" in the eyes of those who were not aware of, or did not understand, my reasons for getting out of the submarine service. I handed him my service record and asked if he could modify my orders so that I could work out of the Foreign Claims Office instead of Compound Security, where I had been ordered. The Lieutenant Commander looked at the jacket covering my records and noticed the very bold **QUALIFIED IN SUBMARINES** clearly stamped on it. That was all it took; he did not check the contents of my record, but instead he welcomed me as a fellow submariner and told me he would take care of my request personally and immediately. Within five minutes my orders were changed and I became a full-fledged Foreign Claims Investigator, the Assistant Chief Investigator.

Working out of the claims office had its distinct advantages. We lived and berthed downtown DaNang instead of on the base, a privilege in itself. We were a unique group, completely independent of everyone else. I was issued official credentials, properly endorsed by the Provost Marshal and the Staff Legal Officer that read in English on one side and Vietnamese on the other:

> The person whose signature and photograph appear hereon is a FOREIGN CLAIMS INVESTIGATOR for the Foreign Claims Office, United States Naval Support Activity. He is authorized to visit Vietnamese establishments, public or private, on official business.

I was also issued another form of credential, a certified permit that read:

> This is to certify that the bearer of this permit is authorized to transport Vietnamese Nationals and other Foreign Nationals with him in U.S. Government vehicles.

Such credentials could easily have been misused or abused. It was a good feeling, knowing that I was a member of such a unique team of trusted men.

Shortly after my arrival in-country my personal belongings were delivered. Much to my satisfaction and relief my .45 arrived intact, although I had no way of knowing that I would have absolutely no use for it. As it was, I had been issued a .45 immediately upon reporting for duty and it remained in my possession throughout my tour of duty. Since I did not need my own pistol I advised JAG of the weapon I had shipped into the country. He did not see a problem but suggested that I turn it in to the armory at Camp Tien Sha for safekeeping. I did just that.

The Billeting Office assigned me to a downtown hotel that had been converted into military "housing" where some 40 enlisted men lived. "Tortilla Flats," as it had been dubbed by one of its occupants, was located at 4B Nguyen Tri Phuong, near the corner of Phan Dinh Phung and Duy Tan, about a block and a half farther into town than was the claims office. All but one of the rooms were multiple-occupancy with a single shared bathroom and shower between rooms. The only room that provided absolute privacy, ample room, overhead fans, and its own private bathroom and shower, was reserved for the senior occupant – I.P at that time. I moved in with Gib and immediately began making suggestions for improving our standard of living.

Gib was a very likable young chief who seemed to take his job quite seriously. He was to be commended for the responsibilities he willingly discharged. It must have been a little awkward for him, being in charge of an office where there were two other chiefs, both senior to him. I admired him for his patience and his willingness to listen when I.P. or I made suggestions. He would carefully evaluate what we said, come to his own conclusions, and then make his decisions. I can't think of a single situation when Gib decided against whatever we recommended, and that's not to say he was a "yes-man." The things we pointed out were never construed as insignificant. In other words, Gib was the guy in charge, but we all shared in his responsibilities. It made life a whole lot easier knowing there was by no means any conflict among us.

Promotions for those serving in Vietnam, commonly referred to as "field advancements," were based on a variation of the system that was in place for other Navy personnel. Enlisted men could be recommended for advancement in instances when, due to operating conditions, they were unable to prepare adequately for the Navy-wide examinations. Commanding officers and officers in charge of units in Vietnam could waive the examination, including E-4/E-5 military leadership exams, for any rate within established quotas as administered by Commander U.S. Naval Forces, Vietnam. Individuals not eligible for field advancement had to compete under the normal advancement system. To be eligible for field advancement, one had to meet all the requirements for advancement except they did not have to take the exam. They had to be serving in Vietnam on the examination date. Field advancements were authorized for pay grade E-4 through pay grade E-7. In the case of E-7, however, the individual must have previously passed the CPO examination within the past three years. In 1966, as a result of the first field advancements of the Vietnam conflict, 240 men were advanced to CPO, 967 to E-5 and 897 to E-4. Unfortunately, the system of field advancement that allowed many men to be advanced to petty officer grades was also a disservice to the men and to the Navy when the service member reported to his next duty station. Many field "promotees" knew practically nothing about the rating, the specialty field, in which they had been advanced.

The field promotion system was a bit of an irritant to those of us who had been promoted the normal way, but it did not take away any of the respect due the grade to which they had been promoted. Chiefs who had been advanced based on having been PNAd were affectionately referred to as "Ho Chi Minh" chiefs. They, on the other hand, took strong exception to being cataloged in that manner.

Gib was a Ho Chi Minh chief, which might have had some bearing on the cooperative attitude he regularly exercised when dealing with I.P. and/ or me. I believe he was doing precisely what I would have done had I been in his shoes; he listened intently to those chiefs around him, and he learned all he could from them. Gib was in the process of growing into the uniform and pay grade gradually instead of exhibiting the know-it-all attitude that some Ho Chi Minh chiefs had a tendency to demonstrate.

As Assistant Chief Investigator of the Foreign Claims Office, I was charged with the responsibility of investigating cases involving personnel attached to NSA, DaNang; cases that might have given rise to claims against the U.S. Government by inhabitants of the Republic of Vietnam for personal injury, death, and/or property damage. I collected and preserved all available evidence and factual data that was considered useful in determining liability and I submitted written reports that included recommendations on action to be taken. I worked hard to show the others working for the claims office that I was intent on doing the job thoroughly and efficiently.

There were three vehicles assigned to the Foreign Claims Office: one one-ton truck, one half-ton truck, and one small Bronco. Each vehicle was equipped with two-way radio communication between vehicles, with our base station at the office, and with the U.S. Military Police. Our base call sign was "Johnny Dollar," and the vehicles were "Johnny Dollar One," "Johnny Dollar Two," and "Johnny Dollar Three." The Bronco was used primarily by the reaction team, those that responded with immediacy to accidents that had just occurred. The two trucks were available for investigating claims. All three vehicles were in terrible shape and could be described as undependable at best. I was told that the office would have to do the best it could with the only vehicles that were authorized and available.

Gib could not possibly have selected a more challenging claim for me to investigate and process as my very first assignment. It provided me with a nearly impossible task, that of investigating a graveyard that had been inadvertently dug up by a construction battalion unit and the remains of an unknown number of decedents scattered as fill where some sort of construction was taking place. It was not just a single claim; rather, it was a stack of claims that continued to build on a daily basis. Individuals, as soon as they found that the remains of their beloved ones were no longer at their intended final resting place(s), were directed to file their claims with our office. Determining which claims were valid was a challenge in itself. Burial records were not always maintained, and those that were available were sometimes vague or misleading. And just how does one place a value on remains that have been disturbed or, in this case, misplaced? The identification of bone relics, the determination of which belonged to whom, was an impossible task in satisfying such claims. So Gib, perhaps intentionally so as to test my ability, laid a heavy load on me with that first assignment. He could then determine whether or not I was really capable of conducting investigations. What he did, knowingly or not, was provide me with an excellent opportunity to prove myself – and I became even more enthusiastic. During the conduct of that first investigation I always had one of the Vietnamese interpreters with me. He was very knowledgeable of the area, had a good personality, and he translated with ease and understanding. Together we visited the more remote villages and we traveled over the worst roads I had ever experienced. He assisted me as I rummaged through virtually impossible to understand official records. I saw firsthand the sometimes-gory evidence of the war that was going on all around, and I became more at ease with my surroundings as each day passed. My interpreter was also quite sincere and cooperative in pointing out areas that were known as heavily populated with VC. He cautioned me never to go into those areas alone.

My first assignment never really ended, although I did manage to close the original case file. Stragglers, some probably with valid claims and others with fraudulent claims, continued showing up at the office for a long time. The original claims were probably valid, and for the most part I disregarded "burden of proof" and substituted "preponderance of evidence" as my guide. Once it became obvious that some individuals were trying to take advantage of the unfortunate situation we became hard and fast in requiring absolute proof. Related claims then quickly discontinued.

After I had completed processing a reasonable number of claims, I was evaluated by the JAG and was pleased to learn that I was considered an outstanding investigator in all respects. The evaluation described me as having "an excellent understanding of the legal principles involved and the techniques of writing concise, logical reports," that my motivation was demonstrated by my continuing efforts to improve and expand my Vietnamese vocabulary, and that as a result I was able to obtain far more information out of claimants and witnesses than the average investigator. It also read:

> In all aspects of his naval career he continually seeks new challenges and masters them with great skill. He has demonstrated exceptional adaptability, leadership, and managerial skills in the performance of his duties. He relates well to his superiors and always obtains the best that his subordinates have to offer. He always displays great imagination in completing his assigned tasks and can be relied on for constructive suggestions that are continually improving and upgrading the performance of the Foreign Claims Office. His military and personal behavior is exemplary. His military appearance is impeccable. Chief ADKISSON is a truly exceptional Chief in all respects.

I was proud and could not possibly have been more pleased, knowing that I was thought of so highly. I always had the utmost confidence in my abilities, however, the realization that my efforts and accomplishments had not gone unnoticed, well beyond the self-satisfaction I personally felt, boosted my motivation and charged me with even greater enthusiasm.

The claims office was responsible for conducting investigations that took in nearly a fifteen-mile radius. Most of our efforts were within five miles which was still well into hostile areas. There was no way of predetermining just what we might be confronted with once we left the office. The more distance, the farther out in the field, the more cautious we had to be. If we had been ambushed there would have been very little we could have done in our own defense with our peashooter .45s. Occasionally the interpreter and I would purposely take side roads when we were returning to the office. I always preferred the change in scenery, the opportunity to see other places and things. It also provided me with a better knowledge of the area, should I find myself in the awkward situation of being alone and in need. Sometimes the interpreter would threaten to no longer accompany me when I was too insistent on taking certain roads. Beyond any doubt he knew something that I did not, and I never challenged him.

Gib, I.P, and I were the only claims personnel living at Tortilla Flats. The other men lived in the back of the claims office, where suitable berthing for several men had been constructed. Gib and I discussed several possibilities – things we could do to upgrade the office as well as our billet. First we had a sheet metal stand manufactured for our billet at Tortilla Flats, to safely contain our double-coil electric hot plate. This gave us the ability to heat up some snacks whenever we wanted. We always had a variety of packaged dried Ramen-type noodles that we bought on the open market near to the office. Preparing Ramen noodles meant nothing more than boiling water, a talent in which Gib and I became quite proficient. We then processed a request for an air conditioner for the office, something we desperately needed during the hot months. Gib was a little reluctant to transfer the television from the berthing area behind the office to our room – but I convinced him that it was only right that we share it. The men living at the office were noticeably disgruntled being temporarily inconvenienced by the loss of the only entertainment they had. But we convinced them that we also deserved some entertainment. It was not a case of rate having its privileges, but a reasonable and fair system. Every two weeks we rotated the TV between Tortilla Flats and the office.

Probably the only appreciable disadvantage, living at the converted hotel, was having to share the rest room and shower among four or more occupants. Even at that it was better than having to live the far more restrictive military lifestyle of those billeted on base.

The Admiral's "Chase Team" was also billeted at Tortilla Flats. The team consisted of a group of four or five handpicked well-armed sailors that followed the Admiral around in a "Chase Jeep," a team of bodyguards – his protectors. The Chase Team was privileged with a telephone in their room, a luxury most difficult to obtain, but in their case it was considered a necessity. The Chase Team was required to respond on a moment's notice, day or night. I felt that Gib and I, as Chief and Assistant Chief Investigator of the Claims Office, should also have telephone communication. Since the switchboard for the NSA consisted of an antiquated operator-assist system, it made it easy to tap into another phone line. I advised the Chase Team that we would be using their phone number, Motley 113, but that callers wishing to contact Gib or me would advise the operator of our "two short-rings" code as opposed to the "one long-ring" that would be for them.

Getting another telephone and splicing into the line was a simple procedure. Within hours of making the decision Gib and I had telephone communication throughout NSA. It took very little time before Gib's eyes were opened to the "fringe" benefits that came with having me around. I not only had some beneficial ideas, I was not reluctant to put them into practice.

The Army Foreign Claims Office was located directly behind our office, at the same address. The Army was responsible for payment of all foreign claims, whether they had been processed by the Navy or by their own staff. Directly below our office was the Office of Civic Action. They were primarily responsible for assisting villagers in the building and/or rebuilding of homes, churches, schools, and other structures. There was nothing strategic about our location other than the fact that it made it easier, more convenient, for claimants to file. If our office had been on base, claimants would have had an abundance of paperwork to process just to gain permission to pass through the main gate. The intent, for public relations purposes, was to make it as easy as possible for any foreign national who had been wronged to file their claim(s) without any unnecessary hassle. The Army and Navy claims offices were totally unprotected from attack or from access by the enemy – and we all knew that we had probably been visited by the VC occasionally. There were probably as many VC as there were "good guys" that had claims processed in their favor. There was no way to distinguish the difference, certainly not by appearance. The Navy Foreign Claims Office blended right in with the multitude of other shops in the downtown area. Our office was upstairs where we had a perfect view overlooking Yen Bay Street, where, during daytime hours, there was always a continuous flow of traffic. It was interesting watching pedestrians as well as vehicles as they made their way around the barbed and concertina wire barricades. All such obstructions were strategically placed so that they protruded a little over halfway across the streets; some left to right, others right to left, all for the purpose of slowing traffic and/or stopping it entirely. Checkpoints were established every few blocks at which time and place all vehicles were stopped and thoroughly searched. U.S. military vehicles were no exception; however, they were not searched quite as diligently. During the night, no one, Vietnamese or any other nationality, passed a checkpoint without being thoroughly scrutinized.

I was beginning to make a more noticeable impression on Gib with my ideas and my unshakable intentions on making things better. Once he thought I was absolutely nuts, when a Vietnamese delivery driver came into our office and asked if he was at "the investigation place." As Gib scanned the shipping documents, I looked out on the street where the driver had parked his flatbed truck. Loaded on the back were two large boarded-up crates, their contents well concealed. Gib told me the delivery was not for us, that it was for CID (Criminal Investigation Division), and I immediately reminded him of the question the driver had asked.

I then took the clipboard in hand and confirmed that yes, we were "the investigation place," and I signed as recipient for the unidentifiable delivery.

Gib asked me if I knew what I was doing, and I assured him that I did. He was very concerned about what I may have signed for. My response was that I really didn't care – that I would have signed for two Sherman tanks just as quickly had the same question been asked. So Gib and I pried open the crates and found two beautiful hand-carved wooden swivel-type desk chairs as our newly acquired property. Sometimes I wondered about Gib's mental normalcy when he asked questions like the one he then asked.

"What are you going to do with them?"

"Well, Gib, I intend on using this one right here behind my desk – and I suggest you use the other one behind your desk," accompanied by something of a 'duh' look.

Nervous as he was about the whole incident, Gib decided he would follow my lead.

About a month later we were paid a surprise visit by an officer and several of his sidekicks, all properly identified as badge-totin' members of the much dreaded, usually feared, and nearly always hated CID. They had done their homework and they were prepared (probably anxious) to take prisoners, a real macho group of enforcers – jerks in the eyes of many. The officer thrust the receiving document into my face and demanded to know whose signature was at the bottom.

I casually looked at it and very politely said, "That's my signature; is something wrong?" I was then asked by what authority had I signed – to which I immediately responded, "By the authority vested in me as Assistant Chief Investigator of the Navy Foreign Claims Office." I then very calmly explained that the documentation was somewhat misleading and that since the delivery driver had been so insistent that we were "investigations," which we in fact were, I had signed and accepted the delivery. We sure as hell couldn't leave the crates out on the street, so we opened them and removed the contents.

"So where are the two chairs?" the officer demanded, Gestapo-like.

Again, very politely, I simply pointed to my desk and told him that I had been using one and that the other was behind Gib's desk. I pretended to be relieved that the rightful owners had finally shown up to claim the misdirected delivery. I also volunteered our assistance if they needed any help in hauling the chairs downstairs – or, for that matter, all the way to their proper destination. CID was happy to get what they had ordered and could find no intend to defraud anyone out of anything. Gib and I willingly and cooperatively gave up "our" chairs without a contest and all ended well. Gib told me that he thought I was the luckiest SOB in the world. I laughed as I told him that I wasn't lucky – just smart! At that moment he thought of me more as a smartass.

Vietnamese people were not greedy; they were poor and they wanted anything of value that they could get their hands on. It would have been the exception for an American truckload of goods, regardless of contents, eatable or otherwise, to arrive at its destination fully loaded after passing through any populated area. That is, unless someone was riding shotgun in the back of the truck along with the cargo. Children and adults alike were skilled at jumping on board passing vehicles and then tossing everything they could over the side, where other locals scrambled to retrieve them. The Vietnamese made no distinction between high- and low-value cargo. Their goal was simple, to get and keep (or resell) anything and everything.

On several occasions I witnessed a very dangerous method of theft accomplished by motorcyclists. This method was more common when cargo-carrying trucks were traveling at higher rates of speed, faster than those on foot were capable of running. The motorcycle driver balanced his accomplice precariously on the handlebars while he approached the back of a moving truck. When the front wheel of the motorcycle was within inches of making contact with the truck, or in some cases actually under the back of the truck bed, the accomplice would leap to the truck and immediately begin off-loading as much as possible as the truck continued down the road. Rarely did any carrier recover his stolen cargo. It disappeared as quickly as it was thrown overboard. The raiders were smart enough to pick their targets where side-of-the-road congestion of one type or another guaranteed a reasonably secure escape route. The thieves were seldom caught.

During Red Alerts, when one of the bases or the city of DaNang was under enemy attack, Americans responsible for guarding or protecting supplies, whether the supplies were en route or warehoused, were directed *not* to take physical action against anyone that was seen stealing! Under no circumstances were they to fire on them. There were to be no so-called international incidents of that nature. With the risk factor very near the non-existent level, theft became a practical endeavor that was practiced brazenly by the Vietnamese whenever opportunity knocked. Our policy of not taking more severe action against the perpetrators tended to legitimize theft. We held no animosity toward these clever, in many instances brave thieves, as a poverty-stricken people will do what they must to survive.

Twice during my second year in 'Nam, the major ammunition dump near the air base suffered direct hits by the VC. In both instances it took nearly three days and a tremendous effort by every firefighting unit in the area to suppress and eventually contain the fires and explosions. It was very similar to a gigantic Fourth of July fireworks display. The skies were lit up spectacularly, and the continuous deafening explosions prevented anyone within miles from getting any meaningful sleep. It was quite an impressive sight to see, but the resultant damages that were incurred by all of the nearby villages were devastating. Gib and I scouted the area within a couple of days and took some amazing photographs of things and situations we never imagined possible. The absolute and total destruction of homes, businesses, and other structures was caused as much by concussion as it was by the ordnance. More amazing yet were the cheerful smiles present on the faces of the children in that area, definite confirmation as to just how acclimated they were to the horrible conditions with which they were constantly confronted.

There were several means by which current local and worldwide news was made available to us. "A-farts," AFRTS, Armed Forces Radio and Television service, provided constant coverage of the news as well as other recreational programming. Short serial segments of *Chicken Man*, the never-ending "drama" (comedy) of the "worlds greatest hero," were broadcast via radio several times daily. Everyone serving in Vietnam that had access to a radio probably had the opening of *Chicken Man* memorized: "It's Chicken Man – he's everywhere; he's everywhere!" followed by the ridiculous mimicked clucking of a chicken. We also tuned in on "Hanoi Hanna," the counterpart to Tokyo Rose of World War II fame. Little did Hanna or her listening audience know how much truth she was spreading within her propaganda broadcasts. We were constantly told that we had no business there and that we would be run out of the country. At that time we considered her airtime as our entertainment time. Her "lies" were always scoffed at, and we considered her just as much of a joke as that of the propaganda she broadcast. Time would tell, as it most assuredly did, that Hanoi Hanna was proven to be more right with her predictions than she was wrong.

Typical Scenes Following Incoming Mortar Attacks

We were also provided free issues of *Stars and Stripes*, the daily newspaper written by and for members of the military worldwide. And there were the *Army Times*, the *Air Force Times*, and the *Navy times*, weekly military newspapers with worldwide distribution that were edited and tailored in the best interests of each respective branch. All issues of the *Times*, regardless of the branch of service for which intended, provided an abundance of interesting news. The *White Elephant News*, a four-to-six-page mini newspaper with a circulation of about nine thousand, provided local news of NSA activities. The Public Affairs Office, NSA, DaNang pub-

412

lished it twice monthly. Statements, views, and opinions appearing therein did not necessarily reflect the policy of the U.S. Navy. There were other means of releasing news briefs tailored to specific units or detachments. One with which I became most familiar, since the claims office was in such close proximity to theirs, was the *Naval Support Activity Civic Action Newsletter*. It was usually four to eight pages of news describing significant accomplishments by Civic Action teams and by individuals assigned to Civic Action projects.

Happy Faces without Regard for the War

But I've once again gotten ahead of myself. Mai, not to be forgotten, was notified almost immediately of my return to Vietnam. I found out that she had been on a leave of absence because she was nearing her time to give birth. On my second visit to the Chiefs' Club, probably the second or third day following my return to Vietnam, Diep ran to my table and excitedly told me that Mai was outside waiting to see me. I excused myself from the table and headed for the door. Mai, with her beautiful hair longer than ever and combed straight back, draped partially over one shoulder but otherwise hanging well below the bench upon which she was seated, greeted me with the happiest smile I had ever seen on her face. She was all giggly and didn't know what to say; my return was a genuine surprise to her. We did not talk long, that first get-reacquainted session. Mai knew that she was not supposed to be on the base without having official business there. Being employed provided an official reason, however, Mai was not there to work;

she was there to see me. I shooed her on her way home and promised faith-fully that I would soon visit her.

Soon stretched into about two weeks. I needed the time to get settled into my new job and my new home. I was at the CPO Club when I was again approached by Diep, this time more excited than ever. She told me that Mai had given birth to a daughter that very day. One of the chiefs offered to give me a ride into Mai's village, and I accepted. He also offered to return and pick me up two hours after "drop off." There had been no changes in the off-limits/out-of-bounds rules since I left Vietnam, and liberty had not been reinstated. In other words, other than traversing from one military installa-tion to another, everything and everywhere was off-limits! With that, I was very appreciative of the chief's offer to provide me with transportation into My Khe Village. On the other hand, I had legitimate credentials that autho-rized me to "visit Vietnamese establishments, public and private, on official business." I convinced myself that my visit would be official.

Mai's home had been remodeled and it stood out as one of the model homes in the village. It was a sturdy structure that had been rebuilt to last and had been enlarged to include two more rooms. Mai's entire family, her mother, father, brother, and two sisters, greeted me. They welcomed me back and escorted me into their home. Mai was in a room to herself and she looked terribly uncomfortable. She was covered with perspiration and in a great deal of pain, but she was alive and so was her child. In Vietnam it was almost expected, given the lack of proper medications and facilities, for the mother or the child – sometimes both – to die during childbirth. Mai was caught completely off-guard by my visit, but she was nonethe-less pleased to see me. Only her immediate family had been there. Her husband, an RVN soldier, had not yet seen his newborn daughter. Mai sat upright and grinned like a child with a new toy. It was not a grin of pride or of accomplishment; it was a grin welcoming me. The matter of her having just given birth appeared to be of lesser concern than that of my visit. I felt honored, but I showed concern for the baby too. Mai's family trusted me, and they thought nothing of me remaining alone in the room with Mai as I sat on the bed by her side, holding her hand. I was once again being treated as a family member. I surprised Mai even more when I exercised my ability to speak Vietnamese with greater fluency. After visiting for a few minutes I slowly but deliberately leaned over to her face and very gently kissed her on her lips. That was, though there had been other opportunities, the first time I had ever kissed Mai. She, equally deliberate and with a tenderness I had not previously known, placed her arms around me and returned my kiss. I had intentionally crossed the line and was a little frightened by it. I had always thought Mai was the sweetest thing around – something special, but it had never been my intention to encourage anything beyond that. However at that particular moment I felt an emotion, something of an obligation to Mai. I did not fully comprehend the potential consequences of the apparent signals we were sending each other.

Within three weeks Mai was back on the job at the Little Elephant.

It was a tiring workday, one that had taken me farther away from the office than usual, and my interpreter and I were on the return trip from one of my investigations when I was flagged down by an American Marine. He explained to me how he had accidentally struck a cow with his jeep and he did not know what to do. He was concerned about the small crowd of Vietnamese peasants that had gathered at the scene. The cow was unable to get up, and it was bleeding from its mouth. Its chance of survival did not look very promising, so I thought the only humane thing for me to do was to kill it. I had proper identification and I assumed that my interpreter would inform the animal's owner of the claims process. As I removed my .45 from its holster, fully intent on putting a single bullet right between the animal's eyes, I heard a distinct increase in the pitch of surrounding voices – and my interpreter stopped me cold.

I had forgotten what I had been taught; in Vietnam the cow was considered sacred. The animal had to be left alone to die its own slow, possibly torturous death; I could not "murder" it. I tried to explain that I only wanted to put it out of its misery and that my intention was not exactly analogous with murder. No way was I going to be allowed to take the cow's life. I suffered a bit of culture shock.

The best advice I had to offer the GI was to suggest that he get in his jeep and high-tail it out of there before the cow died. My Vietnamese interpreter could not predict what action the farmers and peasants (many of whom were probably VC) might take once the cow died. For the moment, there was a very slim possibility that the animal would survive, which in turn would exonerate the Marine from any wrongdoing. I took my own advice and wasted no time in carrying it out. I wished the GI good luck as we headed on down the road.

It became increasingly apparent to me that my mode of transportation during field investigations was unsatisfactory. The Bronco was in dire need of overhaul and it could not be trusted to get from one location to another. The one-ton truck was too large to traverse most of the back roads. The need for a four-wheel-drive jeep was very apparent, so the first week of August 1968, I initiated an official request to procure two. The request is duplicated below to provide a more accurate description of conditions as they were:

6 August 1968
From: MMC Paul L. Adkisson
To: Chief of Staff, U.S. Naval Support Activity, DaNang
Via: (1) Foreign Claims Officer
(2) Staff Judge Advocate
(3) Transportation Officer
(4) Public Works Officer

Subj: Jeeps for the Foreign Claims Office, request for

1.   As a Foreign Claims Investigator I spend a great deal of time traveling in the DaNang area. A day does not pass that does not necessitate driving either to a claimant's residence or to a witness's residence. During these travels certain things have occurred which I feel are important and require immediate action.

2.   The Foreign Claims Office has three vehicles assigned. A 1-ton pickup, USN #94-66506; a ½-ton pickup, USN #94-73918; and a Bronco, USN #94-68533. The Bronco is used exclusively for traffic investigations when it is operable. This vehicle has been plagued with problems (steering, brakes, & engine) since it was first assigned to this office. Claims investigators use either the 1-ton or the ½-ton pickup as their means of transportation during investigations. Neither of these vehicles is suitable for investigations for several reasons.

a.   Practically all contacts or investigations require driving through extremely narrow alleys, some of which are not much more than cow trails.

b. In some cases it is impossible to drive either the 1-ton or the ½-ton because these particular vehicles are unable to turn the sharp corners found in many alleys.

416

c. In all areas the number of children is extremely high. It is required that the investigator drive slowly due to heavy pedestrian traffic, condition of alleys, and the closeness of private property to the alley. Children climb either over the side of the truck(s) or over the tailgate for a ride. Sometimes they hang on the tailgate in hopes they won't be seen – there are probably times that they are not seen. The investigator must stop his vehicle under these conditions and attempt chasing the children away. Sometimes this subjects the investigator to ridicule and often small objects such as rocks or cans are thrown. By the time the investigator gets back in the truck the little darlings (the children) are regrouping and have formed another plan of "attack." It cannot be overemphasized how difficult it is trying to watch for children while at the same time drive in a safe manner down these winding narrow roads.

d. We cannot leave our vehicle(s) parked and walk very far to the residence as the possibility of explosive devices being planted in the vehicle is not out of the question, or the vehicle could be stolen. It is not a good idea to travel by foot in some of these areas. Also the children like to get into the vehicle(s) and twist knobs, etc., and could easily injure themselves.

e. It is difficult to determine quickly just what has been thrown into the bed of a truck when you are the driver. On one particular occasion while driving the 1-ton through an unfamiliar area it was noted there was a lack of children. The usual friendly expressions were lacking on the faces of the villagers which put the investigator on guard. He saw an object hurled through the air and land in the bed of the truck. A quick decision was made that the device might be an explosive so the driver slammed on the brakes and jumped out – seeking shelter in front of the truck. The object thrown was a rock! The investigator would take the same steps were the situation to repeat itself; however, it does no good to our image when an American fighting man dives for cover because a rock is thrown in his direction. This investigator returned to the office thoroughly shaken and quite angry.

3. The Foreign Claims Office is desperately in need of two jeeps. This has been mentioned on many occasions and our need has not diminished. We have no need for either of our pickup trucks. We do not haul anything. The most passengers in the investigator's vehicle at any one time are three;

417

the investigator, the interpreter, and possibly the claimant. The only type vehicle appropriate for this type job is a 4-wheel drive jeep.

Very respectfully,
Paul L. Adkisson

My request, written unprofessionally but with the right intent and adequate justification, was favorably endorsed by the Foreign Claims Officer as follows:

11 August 1968

FIRST ENDORSEMENT on ltr of MMC Paul L. ADKISSON, USN, of 6 August 1968

From: Foreign Claims Officer
To: Assistant Chief of Staff for Administration
Via: Staff Judge Advocate

Subject: Jeeps for the Foreign Claims Office, request for

1. Readdressed and forwarded.
2. The basic correspondence is concurred in and approval is strongly recommended.
3. It is noted that a Foreign Claims Investigator is expected to be a paragon of safe driving practices, since their duties involve the compensation of victims of our negligence. This goal may best be achieved by providing our investigators with a vehicle best suited for driving in difficult areas. Obviously a jeep may be maneuvered with greater safety through narrow, crowded alleys than a ½ ton truck.
4. Of primary importance is the personal safety of the investigator, who is daily called upon to venture into insecure areas to aid us in fulfilling our obligations to injured Vietnamese. Certainly our investigators deserve and need every measure of support that we can afford them, and this support should not fall short of providing them with vehicles that may prevent their own or a Vietnamese civilian's injury.

For the foregoing reasons it is strongly and urgently recommended that the vehicles presently being used for Foreign Claims Investigations be exchanged for jeeps.

Very Respectfully,

P.A. Clark

Not surprisingly, almost expectedly, the request was flatly denied with the explanation that there could only be one jeep allocated to NSA, DaNang. That single jeep was assigned as the Admiral's chase jeep. What made it even more of an irritant was that the Admiral's chase jeep had reserved parking at Tortilla Flats, where the Chase Team (lower-rated enlisted men) resided, an eyesore and constant reminder that the efforts of the foreign claims investigators were not considered important enough to spend a few dollars in support.

Chief Adkisson – out of Bounds?

Ho Cong Lo, Mr. Lo to most of us, was the Navy Foreign Claims Office Attorney. He was the ideal choice for the job, not only because of his education in law, but also because he spoke fluent English, Chinese, French, and Vietnamese, all of the predominant languages known to the area. I never saw Mr. Lo lose his temper or get noticeably upset about anything. He showed up at work, did his job professionally, and departed with a smile at the end of each workday. I liked Mr. Lo and I knew that he was the one to go

419

to whenever a question was raised to which only an educated person would know the correct answer, legal or otherwise. Mr. Lo also spent a great deal of his spare time assisting me with my Vietnamese language course(s). He was extraordinarily patient with me. Working with him paid big dividends in my ability to speak and understand a higher level of the language.

Mr. Lo was quite well known within the community, and when he decided to get married we suspected that it was going to be quite a festive occasion. It was an honor for anyone to receive an invitation. Gib and I were so honored, and we attended. It was an interesting afternoon that took Gib and me away from our usual activities; however, it was not any more spectacular or unusual than American wedding ceremonies or the receptions that followed. The food was the only noticeable difference – and the accompanying smell of *nuoc mam*, a salty fish sauce that was always available where Vietnamese food was prepared and/or served.

I was intent on doing more than my job while serving in Vietnam. I wanted to assist in any way possible and so I asked Mr. Lo where I might expend some of my energy to the benefit of the Vietnamese people. He suggested that I teach English at the Vietnamese American Association during some of my off-duty time. I asked him if there was an orphanage in the area that might be in need of assistance, where I could spend additional off-duty time. Mr. Lo suggested that we check with the director of China Beach Orphanage located in My Khe Village. *My Khe*? That quickly perked me up; that was the village where Mai lived! Mr. Lo was just as anxious as I was when I suggested we not wait, that we visit the orphanage that very day. He agreed.

Mr. Lo was a bit surprised at my knowledge of the area as I drove directly to My Khe Village. As we neared the trail that led off to Mai's home, Mr. Lo provided me with the final directions. I was pleasantly surprised to find that the orphanage was located about a block from Mai's home.

Mr. Lo located the director, Mr. Vuy, and we had a brief conversation. Mr. Vuy was pleased with my offer to spend time with the children. He commended me on my interest in teaching them English and assured me they would be willing students. I promised that as long as my military duties allowed I would conduct one-hour conversational English classes three evenings a week. We shook hands in agreement, after which Mr. Lo and I departed.

420

Our next stop was at the Vietnamese American Association at Phan Thanh GIAN School (within walking distance of Tortilla Flats), where Mr. Lo assisted me in making arrangements to teach an adult class of conversational English another three nights a week. Accordingly, I was issued a letter of authorization from the Foreign Claims Officer that authorized me to travel to and from both locations "in connection with teaching."

I then suggested a change to Gib's and my seven-day workweek routine. Gib was reluctant to follow suit, but I convinced him that we should at least have the option of having weekends off – at our discretion. My suggested routine became commonplace: I worked eight to twelve hour days Monday through Friday in my military role as a claims investigator. After work on Mondays, Wednesdays, and Fridays I drove to China Beach Orphanage and conducted English classes. After work on Tuesdays, Thursdays, and Saturdays I either walked or drove to Phan Thanh GIAN School to conduct classes there. Following the teaching sessions, whether to adult associates of the Vietnamese American Association or to the children of China Beach Orphanage, I usually headed for the Chiefs' Club, where I was sure to find camaraderie alive and at its best.

Gib followed my lead and organized his own class of English students at the orphanage. It was a lot more fun and certainly more challenging as we instructed two separate groups of kids and held contests between groups to judge the progress of each. Gib truly had a knack for teaching, and his kids absorbed everything he taught them. My kids were no dummies, but my class usually lost when it came to contests. I never considered teaching the children as a task. It was much too enjoyable. Sometimes I'd hang around the orphanage and encourage the kids to show me relatively insignificant things that were important to them: little trinkets of one kind or another, shells they found while walking along the beach, toys made of tree bark, and anything else they were proud of. Periodically, as an unexpected bonus, Gib and I took small groups of five or six orphans to the Chief's Club where we treated them with their favorite meal; fried chicken. They were kids! They were not at all different from kids anywhere else in the world except for the fact that they had lost their parents as a result of a war they had no part in creating.

Entrance to China Beach Orphanage

Gib and I were recognized twice in articles published in the White Elephant Newspaper. One article was based on our having made arrangements and taken a group of forty children from the orphanage for a visit to the USS *Eldorado*, an amphibious force flagship, temporarily at anchor, that had been operating in the waters off South Vietnam. It not only provided the children with an opportunity to get away from the orphanage, it gave them a chance to converse in English with total strangers. The kids had a great time, especially at the end of their tour when they were unexpectedly treated to ice cream and cake in the mess hall.

The second article in which Gib and I were recognized was a half-page story describing the English Language School we had established at the orphanage. It was a thorough and well-written article that detailed student enthusiasm and participation within the class. It acknowledged things Gib and I had tended to take for granted – such as the children standing outside the classroom that lined up along the open windows, too shy or for some other reason unwilling to sit with the class. They too, had pencils and pads,

422

and they listened intently and took notes of their own as we conducted our classes. That article also pointed out that we had spent much of our own money to obtain materials for the orphanage and that we had done other things for them that were unrelated to our teaching efforts. Gib and I had not expected such recognition. What we had accomplished was brought about only because we shared an honest interest in the children's welfare; it came from our hearts and we never expected anything other than the smiles we helped to create on the faces of those beautiful but unfortunate children.

A Special Treat – Orphans Tour the USS *Eldorado*, Amphibious Force Flagship

423

**Orphans Patiently Waiting for Instructions
While Touring the USS *Eldorado***

Departing USS *Eldorado*

424

As a result of one or the other of the articles, perhaps both, finding their way to "the world" (the United States), Gib and I began receiving pen-pal mail from interested strangers. The majority of those who wrote wanted additional information about the orphanage and about the specific needs of the children living there. We began receiving items of clothing and toys, much of which were donated anonymously. Some people who sent items did want recognition, but only in the sense that their gifts were to be delivered along with their best wishes and prayers. Mr. Vuy was always appreciative when Gib or I arrived at the orphanage with a box or two of clothing, blankets, toys and/or a variety of other items. We seldom delivered anything immediately upon our receipt. It was better that we accumulate enough so that when we made a delivery it was more like Christmas for everyone instead of for a pointed few. Gib and I felt great when we were able to make things a little bit better there, but we never lost sight of the fact that it was the unsolicited donations provided by total strangers that made much of it possible.

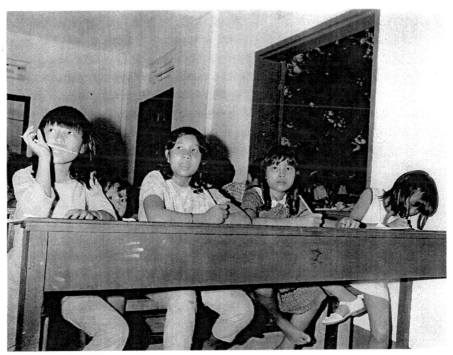

Vietnamese Orphans Attending English Classes

I.P. decided to move to the Claims Office because he didn't like the short walk to and from Tortilla Flats. That move made me senior occupant at the Flats, great news for me because it meant I could immediately move into the most desirable room there: a private room with a balcony, far more comfortable and with maximum privacy. It became official on April 5 when I received instructions appointing me Senior Occupant of 4 Nguyen Tri Phuong, aka Tortilla Flats. On July 31 I received additional orders designating me Compound Defense Officer of the same billet. The internal security course I had attended at Coronado paid off as I used the knowledge gained there to piece together a workable battle plan. I devised and implemented a complete plan for the entire billet in the event of attack and I promulgated and distributed standing orders that included individual responsibilities required of all residents. When it came time to fill sandbags some distance from the compound, the Chase Team "skated." That is, they enjoyed themselves by doing as they pleased, relaxing in their bunks. They were the untouchables and had to remain at their billet in the event they were called upon by the Admiral. That small group was frequently referred to as a bunch of "gold bricks" because of their "you can't touch me," lay around, do nothing attitudes. However, when it came time to haul the filled sandbags up onto the roof of the compound, and to other locations, and to stack them in semicircular protective bunkers, I demanded that they assist. They were disgruntled about my insistence on their participation, but they had no basis for argument when I allowed one of the team to remain in their room by the phone. I took my job as Compound Defense Officer seriously, as was subsequently recognized when I was next evaluated by JAG:

> In addition to his primary duties as an investigator, Chief ADKISSON is the Compound Defense Officer of his billet which houses approximately 40 people. These duties require a continual updating of plans and procedures and demand a high state of preparedness at all times. Chief ADKISSON has carried out these duties with enthusiasm and ingenuity, efficiently planning all aspects of defense including procurement of emergency rations and ammunition and assignment of personnel. These tasks require the expenditure of many off duty hours and carry a grave responsibility which Chief ADKISSON has eagerly assumed.

I was pleased when I saw that the evaluation had gone farther and had also recognized and commended me for my outside volunteer interests:

On his remaining off duty hours Chief ADKISSON has contributed immeasurably to Vietnamese American relations by personally organizing and teaching two conversational English classes at China Beach Orphanage. Chief ADKISSON unselfishly sacrificed much time and personal expense for materials in this project, receiving no compensation other than the happiness he brought to the lives of the children at the Orphanage. Throughout his tour of duty at U.S. Naval Support Activity, DaNang, Chief ADKISSON has demonstrated exceptional professional accomplishment, initiative and enthusiasm for his many tasks. His imagination and determination have continually inspired those with whom he served and have earned him the respect and praise of all who know him, both American and Vietnamese.

I began thinking that if I continued receiving write-ups such as that, *how can I not be considered for future promotions?* I gained a little more confidence in the system and began to realize that my prospects for promotion would be considered the same as anyone else's. At least, I had higher hopes.

One of my responsibilities as Senior Occupant at the Flats was to make sure that all of the residents complied with curfew. It was dangerous after dark, and U.S. personnel were subject to arrest, the same as the local nationals, if they ignored curfew. There were places, not too distant, where female companionship was available. The "OK Hotel" was known for its attractive prostitutes, and it was only a block away. So there was a strong temptation for the men who were supposedly under my control to violate curfew. But life at Tortilla Flats had another fringe benefit in that living right next door was a very attractive Vietnamese known to accept money for sexual favors. Lan lived in a very small shanty-type structure immediately adjacent to but separated from Tortilla Flats by a coil of stretched concertina wire. The only source of water available to Lan and the other residents that lived within that group of small residential units was a well to the front of the property and was used more for washing clothing than anything else.

Lan was a prostitute in every sense of the word; however, I reluctantly label her as such because I only knew her as a person. I did not question her reason(s) for living the life she led. It was a war zone – it was danger-ous living close to Americans – and the American dollar was oftentimes valued higher than self-esteem. The occupants of Tortilla Flats knew that I was willing to close my eyes, to ignore their after-curfew activities, as long as they wandered no farther than next door, where I could reason-ably believe that they were in safe company with Lan. The men who felt the need to satisfy their sexual desires could do so without having to place their lives on the line by sneaking off into the boonies where the VC were always more active after-hours. Not only were the local brothels off-lim-its; getting to them usually meant violating curfew. Lan never knew what a favor she was doing for me as well as for my men. Without her I would have had more problems than I could have controlled. With her, not only was she providing somewhat of a needed service; in doing so she was able to provide a better life for herself and for her half-American baby boy.

Every day Lan walked the street in front and to the side of Tortilla Flats, totally unashamed as she proudly displayed her beautiful son she carried protectively in her arms. Lan was very personable, she never pre-tended to be anything other than herself, and I found her easy and enjoy-able to talk to. Her ability to converse in English was very good, and she always had a beautiful smile and a pleasant word for everyone around her. Whenever I saw Lan and her baby I offered the child a small piece of candy. Lan, after accepting for the child, always followed up with: "What about me?" or, "Where's mine?" Her sweet tooth, along with those of most of the neighborhood children, was always satisfied whenever I had the resources.

In Vietnam, as in many other places in the Orient, some vitamins were taken by injections instead of being ingested as pills or capsules. Lan trust-ed me not as a "client" but as a friend and one evening while I was visiting with her she asked me if I would give her a shot. After she assured me that the shot was vitamins I agreed. I was "tickled" to find where I was to give the injection. I had never "bought" my way into Lan's home and I had never seen her naked bottom – even though I had always admired her shapely fully clothed butt whenever she walked by the Flats. When she lowered her

428

pants for me to give her that first shot I couldn't help but think about how good it must have felt to those men who had paid to go all the way with her.

I became Lan's *bac-si*, her doctor, and I was frequently called upon to give her injections of the vitamins she was so insistent on taking. I was probably one of a select few who was privileged with seeing the fully exposed skin on her butt without having to pay. I thoroughly enjoyed my brief visits to Lan's home; not only when I gave her a vitamin shot, but also during the times when we just sat and talked. During one of those visits Lan told me that there were times when her light switch would not work. She asked me if I could fix it. It was a simple matter, removing the outer cover and then tightening up some loose screws. When I finished, the light switch worked perfectly and Lan was impressed and happy. There was no need for the manner in which she elected to show her appreciation; however, I willingly followed her as she tugged at me, somewhat playfully, and guided me to her bed. Neither of us wasted any time as we assisted each other in disrobing. The sex that followed was great – but what made the entire episode more rewarding was that it had taken place spontaneously, without promise or guarantee of anything. I had received a "freebie," and I was of the opinion that somehow we had both benefited from it. What happened that evening made no difference in our attitudes toward each other. Lan remained a very good friend, nothing more, nothing less, and the incident was quickly ignored – as if it had never happened.

There was another incident involving Lan in which I took a very special interest. I took such an interest that I went with my conscience instead of policy; I did what I believed to be in the best interest of all parties concerned. As Lan walked by the Flats with her baby, I noticed that she was making an attempt at hiding her mouth from view. I could see that she was bruised, but I could not tell to what extent. I approached her and asked what had happened. Lan uncovered her mouth and revealed her severely bruised lips and the fact that her front teeth were "missing." Very reluctantly, probably out of fear, she told me how an American Military Policeman had been in her home the previous evening. He had been drinking heavily and he wanted to have sex with her. Lan believed that she was very near the point of being raped, but she refused his demands. The result of her failing to comply was having her teeth knocked out with the butt of his pistol! Coward that he was, he then ran from her home and disappeared into the night.

It was not a function of the claims office to advertise the availability of U.S. funds for the purpose of making payment for wrongs that had been committed against inhabitants of Vietnam by representatives of the U.S. Government, members of the military in particular. I compromised policy by giving her advice – to the point that I urged her to submit a claim for damages. Then, after I provided her with the appropriate forms, I assisted her in filling them out. She did have a valid claim; it was not as if we were somehow in collusion to commit fraud. One of the questions that had to be answered was what amount Lan considered fair as full compensation for her injuries. I had seen my share of inflated claims and had grown to expect them, so I asked Lan to be honest with me and tell me how much she thought it would cost to have her teeth repaired. Even though I expected her to be honest, I was surprised when she was; her estimate of $200 seemed low to me. I did not argue with that figure, but I did suggest that she ask for $300, which would cover pain and suffering along with any unexpected related costs. She was thankful for my suggestion, and her claim was submitted with the $300 figure in place. I handled Lan's claim a little differently than any other that had ever been (or ever would be) processed through my hands. I hand carried it directly to the Army Foreign Claims Office and "presented" it to a good friend of mine. I briefed him on the situation and asked that he expedite the processing and adjudication as soon as possible. Lan could not make a living (prostitution) as it was, and the men billeted at Tortilla Flats were sure to seek their pleasures elsewhere without her. So Lan's claim was immediately processed, and she received an appropriate settlement. In fact, she received a little bit more than she had asked for, compliments of my friend at the Army claims office. It was only a matter of a few days before Lan came to see me. She greeted me with her usual radiant smile and as she proudly displayed her new teeth she thanked me for having assisted her. Conscience clear, free of guilt, I felt equally happy having done so.

Lan eventually got herself a steady boyfriend, Fred, an older American who worked out of the Civic Action Office. He spent a great deal of time out in the field as a member of a "VAT," Vietnamese Assistant Team, which meant there were periods of time when Lan was alone. During Fred's absence Lan would sometimes have "guests," a means by which she could supplement whatever income Fred provided.

It was nearing Christmas, 1968, and I had been celebrating alone. After having had a bit too much to drink, I decided to pay Lan a visit. I arrived drunk and Lan was not at all happy seeing me in such a state. She knew, first and foremost, that I was not a paying customer. Rarely did I go to her home uninvited, but when I did, it was to converse, to practice my Vietnamese language, or just to get away from my otherwise-drab surroundings. That particular night, drunk as I was, I was unintentionally interfering with whatever other plans she had. Lan was upset with me and told me flat out to "go home." I wasn't happy about being sent away, but I didn't argue. I was better off home in bed anyway.

The next day Fred, an E-6, paid me a visit. He was polite when he spoke to me.

"Chief, Lan asked me to talk to you. She said last night you were at her place drunk and she doesn't want you to go there again." With that, Fred had delivered Lan's entire message.

I immediately felt a sensation of anger, particularly with the knowledge that so many other GIs had frequented Lan's place. I also thought, *How many times have I assisted Lan? What gives you the right to place her home off-limits to me?* But I suppressed my thoughts and my feelings, as I valued Lan's friendship. I had been wrong the night before, and I knew it.

"Sure, I'll stay away from her place. Tell Lan I'm sorry about last night, I just got carried away – it won't happen again."

"Thanks, Chief, I'll tell her," Fred said as he turned to leave.

But that didn't end it! It began to eat at me. I had been more than a friend to Lan and I did not like being considered some kind of outlaw cowboy. I had enjoyed her friendship and her company and I was frustrated by her rejection of me. So Christmas Eve I wrapped up several toys in colorful paper, beautiful ribbons and all, and I paid Lan a visit. She responded quickly to the knock on her door. At first she looked a bit disturbed by my presence, but her eyes quickly darted to the colorful parcels I was carrying and her expression of concern immediately turned to that of delight. I thanked her when she eagerly but politely invited me into her somewhat-cramped quarters. Lan was truly shocked at the small stack of gifts I had delivered, and she thanked me over and over. I told her that all of the gifts were for her son, that I had nothing for her except a message.

"Lan, I understand that you do not want me to come over here anymore. That is what your boyfriend told me, so I won't come back." I stood and began walking toward the door. I stopped after opening the door, turned and looked directly into Lan's wide eyes, and said, "But I want you to know that every time I see a GI visit your place I am going to tell Fred all about it!"

Lan saw red! She yelled, "I don't want this stuff!" and she began to throw the parcels at me.

"No, Lan, the gifts are for your son; they are not for you, so you cannot give them back."

I quickly closed the door behind me and made my way back to Tortilla Flats. When I got back to my pad I was pleased with my act of petty revenge – but within minutes I realized how very wrong I had been. I allowed a couple of days to pass before making amends. Lan quickly accepted my apology, almost as though she had been as hopeful to regain my friendship as I had been not to lose hers. We remained very good friends right up to the time of my transfer some months later.

Mama-san and Bruno, our two mixed-breed German shepherd mascots also entertained those of us living at the Flats. The dogs were friendly to all occupants and to the adjacent neighbors but showed distrust for everyone else. Bruno claimed Mama-san as his own but was not always alert to her "extracurricular" activities. Occupants of the Flats watched as Mama-san, absolute slut that she was, sneaked out of the compound and allowed every dog around to climb aboard her. She seemed to be perpetually in heat. It was comical watching as Mama-san kept looking toward the Flats for her "mate" as she was being screwed by every passing stranger. Then one day, as Mama-san was being intensely humped, several of us called Bruno to the front. We wanted to see Bruno's reaction. Bruno broke into a gallop, half growling, half-barking, straight at the engaged couple. Mama-san's suitor dismounted and turned to run, but as it turned out they were tightly, butt to butt, locked up. Bruno attacked viciously as the other male dog tried desperately to escape; Mama-san unwillingly being dragged along behind him. Once freed the outsider high-tailed it down the road while Bruno escorted Mama-san back to the compound. That bit of entertainment might seem to have been a little cruel, but there was really no harm done. Bruno was true to Mama-san, and we thought it was time for her to be equally true to him. But was she? Absolutely not!

New Year's Eve was a night somewhat different than most others. I was at the house of an American civilian friend as the roar of weapons being discharged reached a crescendo. The sky was aglow with a most remarkable and indescribable latticework of crisscrossing tracer bullets and flares, everything other than the kind of fireworks with which most people would be familiar. GIs released a lot of their anxieties as they celebrated the coming of a new year by firing their weapons into the air. The distinct sounds of live ammunition going off all around were exhilarating, and no one seemed too concerned about the accompanying dangers. I pulled my .45 from its holster, jacked a round into the chamber, and fired at one of the ceramic electric wire insulators on a pole nearby. As the bullet hit the insulator it severed the wire. Immediately the lights went out in most of the houses around me. I came very near losing some of my civilian friends, as they had to go without electricity for the next several days. I had not considered that my part in the celebration would cause so many residents to go without heating, cooking, refrigerators and other electrical appliances. From then on, any time I was in the area, I was reminded to "keep your weapon holstered!"

As a teacher at the Vietnamese American Association, I was provided with some unexpected benefits. Periodically I received complimentary tickets to attend variety shows and other functions. The Brass Ensemble of the 226th U.S. Army Band put on many concerts. I rarely attended, due to my self-imposed busy schedule, but it was an honor being invited. There were other American instructors who taught at the Vietnamese American Association, and I learned from them that I was the only teacher who taught voluntarily – without monetary compensation. There was a time when I did consider accepting payment; however, my conscience could not or would not provide justification in doing so. It wouldn't have been right, charging for having established such a trusting and dependable interface between my students and me.

On one very special occasion Gib and I were invited to attend a luncheon that was given in honor of the Mayor of DaNang. It was held on one of the craft owned by Alaska Barge and Transport, Inc., an American company doing business in Vietnam. The greatest thing about JAG granting us permission to attend the function was the unheard-of authority we were also granted; that of wearing appropriate civilian attire. As it turned out, the only person in attendance that wore a uniform was the Mayor himself. Everyone that attended looked magnificent. Following introductory remarks by several guest speakers, the Mayor spoke. Most of his remarks were in gratitude for the American presence in the DaNang area and for all of the unsolicited assistance we were always so willing to support and/or provide. When the Mayor finished his speech, all attendees were

Attending a Vietnamese Function

**A Rare Occasion When Military and Civilians Honored
The Mayor of DaNang**

treated to a barbecue cookout that had been planned and prepared by employees from Alaska Barge and Transport. Some of the Vietnamese that were in attendance seemed embarrassed at the quantity and quality of the food. To the people so used to conserving everything, such an abundance meant that some would have to overindulge or there would be waste – a no-win situation. Drinks of choice were also provided. It was one of those very rare instances where I forgot the war effort and instead thoroughly enjoyed mingling with some rather important people, some of whom were elected government officials.

I reserved Sundays for a break in my routine. Usually I just sat out on my front balcony, the veranda that overlooked Phan Dinh Phung Street and the intersection at Duy Tan Street. Accidents of one kind or another were frequent, and I always had my camera in hand to capture on film whatever I could. Bicyclists were a clumsy bunch. They could not seem to maintain their balance for any prolonged period of time. Bicycles and motorcycles were most frequently involved whenever an accident occurred. Sometimes, for no apparent reason, bicycle riders lost control and ended up sprawled out with their bicycles riding them. Drivers and passengers of motor scooters and tricycles (also called *siclos*), similar to the hand-pulled rickshaws of Hong Kong only powered by pedal, probably tied for second in poor driving or riding skills. Privately owned automobiles were scarce, and they were usually used by few other than the wealthy. Military vehicles were more commonplace and were probably involved in the majority of all accidents. Drivers used their vehicles' horns as means of advising everyone around of their right of way. Whoever honked first was assumed to have notified all within hearing distance that someone, driving something, was executing his or her right to pass through without interruption. The system failed as often as it was successful, as was confirmed time and time again as I watched from my balcony. Amazingly, seldom did anyone suffer serious injuries, although tempers did flare. More amazing yet were the number of and manner in which damaged bicycles were stacked on tricycles to be hauled away. From outward appearance, one would think the *siclo*-tricycles were manufactured in a manner and of materials that failed to consider strength, stability, or safety factors – yet they withstood tremendous loads of people and cargo. Stacking up three or four motorcycles on a single tricycle was one good example.

Nearly every evening, usually right after holding classes and when we were both at the Flats, Gib and I would meet for cocktails on my balcony and watch the variety of activities within our view. We counted on seeing B.T., one irrefutably vivacious Vietnamese woman, at about the same time daily. We had nicknamed her B.T. because she was much more noticeably endowed than typical Vietnamese girls were. B.T. was simply our abbreviated form of identifying her as "Big Tits." Neither Gib nor I ever spoke to her; we just sat there like a couple of vultures with our eyes on our prey whenever she walked by. She knew we were there, watching her – but she never cast so much as the slightest glance in our direction. Acknowledging our presence would have been an invitation that she did not want to imply. Our conversation prior to her arrival was centered on what color her *ao dai* would be, how her hair would be combed, whether or not she would look our way or smile for our benefit. It was as if our day could not be considered complete without watching our favorite soap opera – in this case, B.T..

Adkisson's Billet
Overlooking the Street – What War?

Our need for more reliable transportation never diminished – it continued to get worse. Some investigations could not be properly conducted because of the distance or poor road conditions. Somewhat by chance I learned of an Army jeep that had been abandoned and had subsequently been confiscated by the local police. Gib and I (we went practically everywhere together) had Mr. Lo accompany us to the police station in hopes that with our credentials and our attorney's power of persuasion we could gain custody of the vehicle. After an hour of negotiations it was agreed that we had the authority to take charge of the jeep. The next step was to figure out a way that we could use it without fear of having to relinquish it back to the Army. Our honesty in bringing it to the Claims Officer's attention was not rewarded quite as we had hoped. He was concerned at the manner in which we had claimed title, so he directed that before we could use it officially we would have to check with all of the Army units within our area to see if we could determine where it belonged. We were to provide him with a report of our efforts – to include a list of all Army units we had visited. It was a pain in the butt, having to do the research, but otherwise I did not see it as a problem we couldn't overcome. Gib, usually thinking of the negative aspects instead of the positive, was sure that we would find its rightful place and then lose custody of it. I had a greater imagination than Gib and explained to him that if during the course of our search we were able to determine where the jeep belonged, such a finding would work to our benefit! At that point we could terminate our real investigation and utilize our imagination in the fabrication of our finalized official report. In simpler terms we could identify every Army unit in the area (all but one) as *not* having that particular jeep within its inventory *without lifting another investigative finger*. That is, we could submit a lengthy investigative report in which we could *not* determine the unit to which the jeep was assigned *by leaving that unit out of the report*! So Gib and I set out to conduct a fictitious investigation into a "hit-and-run" accident in which one Army jeep, serial number so and so, had been positively identified. We visited one Army post after another; we checked in with every Transportation Officer and at all Public Works Units. We always had our credentials in hand and we were always on official business as we "investigated" the artificial matter. We never did find where the jeep belonged, so the report we eventually submitted was absolutely accurate and complete. Nothing had been fabricated and nothing was intentionally left out. As a result of our efforts we got to keep the jeep! The Foreign Claims Officer presented the JAG with an official letter of authorization for his signature, a letter that specifically designated the Foreign Claims Office responsible for the use and maintenance of the jeep until such time as the unit to which it rightfully belonged came forth and claimed it. The letter clearly identified the vehicle as having been abandoned prior to our accepting responsibility for it. It was a well-written official letter, and it was the legal tool that was needed to keep us all out of trouble if and when the Army came around to reclaim the jeep.

Our new jeep was in excellent condition. It had a few scratches but no dents. First I made arrangements to have it painted. I made sure that the same Army identification numbers were repainted on each side of the hood; however, I allowed my imagination to assist in that matter. In large, bold capital letters, directly above the very small Army identification numbers, I had the single word **INVESTIGATIONS** painted in the same yellow color as the ID numbers. I knew that no one would ever read the numbers! Next I had a siren and red lights installed. The only thing that would catch the eye of even the most alert individual was sure to be the red lights and the word **INVESTIGATIONS**. Then came the final touch, the installation of a two-way radio so that we would have full communications between all vehicles and the base station – and "Johnny Dollar Four" became a full-fledged member of the Foreign Claims fleet of vehicles. The jeep became an overnight success in helping us conduct our investigations. Its use was very much in demand, however I was the primary driver since I was out in the field more than Gib. It also became our private mode of transportation to and from the Club as well as anywhere else we decided to go. I became Mai's personal chauffeur in that whenever I was available I provided her with transportation from her job at the Little Elephant to her home in My Khe Village.

Within a couple of months, I began to sense that Gib was envious of my having all but taken over the jeep. I knew that Gib, as Chief Investigator, should have a jeep of his own. In a matter of days I learned of another jeep that had been questionably "requisitioned." More aptly put, it had been wrongfully appropriated; it was stolen. It was a jeep that had been claimed by a Navy officer as his personal property, and he used it only for the purpose of providing himself transportation to and from one or another of the "O" Clubs. He was afraid to use it officially for fear of being caught in possession of stolen property. Unfortunately, that officer bragged of his acquisition to the wrong people: those officers and enlisted men he thought he could trust, and the secret was subsequently leaked. I knew, as I have already written, that NSA allocated only one jeep, the Admiral's chase jeep. Therefore, the Navy officer would not be able to complain of its theft – were it to disappear. I convinced Gib that the Foreign Claims Office was more in need of a jeep than some low-ranking officer that used such transportation for no more than frequenting an "O" Club. He agreed. So one evening, Gib and I paid a visit to the facility where the officer was known to park his jeep, his place of work. The jeep was parked behind one of the Quonset-type structures and stood out like a sore thumb. The steering wheel was secured with a padlocked chain, something we had not counted on. But again, with a reasonable amount of imagination, we easily overcame the problem. I casually walked into the front of the facility and asked if there was a bolt cutter available that I could borrow for a few minutes. I was quickly and politely obliged. End of story! Jeep *and* bolt cutter quickly disappeared into the night. Gib and I wasted no time in outfitting his jeep in the same manner as mine; fresh paint, red lights, siren, two-way radio, and **INVESTIGATIONS** painted above small serial numbers. The Claims Officer winced when we told him that we had another jeep at our disposal. I told him not to be concerned, that I would process appropriate paperwork similar to that which allowed us to use the first jeep, that it was not necessary for him to get involved at all. Gib was no longer envious, as his vehicle became "Johnny Dollar One" and mine slipped into the "Two" slot. The other vehicles took on the numbers that we vacated.

Chief Adkisson, Foreign Claims Assistant Chief Investigator

Red Alert, called whenever there was an apparent attack on or near the city of DaNang, was not exactly a frequent occurrence – but it was not all that infrequent either. Attacks were most likely to occur late in the evening or during the night when I was in bed – somewhat protected by the safety of my surroundings. There were three major rocket/mortar attacks on the city of DaNang between September 1968 and May 1969. During one of those attacks, accompanied by an abundance of incoming small-arms fire, I was on the roof of Tortilla Flats. During the attack I directed all personnel on the roof to go below and to prepare their weapons in the event the assault on the city became a more direct assault on our compound. I remained on the roof to observe as much as possible, to better prepare me in making decisions regarding the safety of the occupants and the billet for which I was primarily responsible. Mortars landed on all sides of the Flats; four exploded within two blocks. There did not appear to be enough shrapnel or debris to cause me major concern, although I admit that it was not in my own personal best interest to remain on the roof. My obligation and objective was to remain totally aware of all activities taking place within my range of sight.

I was truly fortunate in that the only wound I suffered was very minor. I was struck on the front of my left lower leg by a short metal rod that had been wrapped with concertina wire. After seeing the small tear to my trousers and feeling only minor discomfort, I was relatively unconcerned as to the severity of the wound. I do not recall how long the attack on the city continued, however, I do know that as the "incoming" subsided I became aware of my blood-soaked trousers. I went to my room, where upon removing my trousers I was surprised to see that I had suffered a deep, somewhat jagged eight-inch-long wound centered between my left foot and knee. There was little I could do other than clean the wound and plan on seeing the Doc at the White Elephant as soon as time and conditions permitted. The following day I saw the Doc. He scrubbed the wound, applied medication and a sterile dressing, and advised me that even though the wound was minor, certainly not life threatening, I would live with the scar the rest of my life. He also told me that I was eligible for the Purple Heart if I wanted one. At that time I did not feel the wound was significant enough to expect an award as meaningful as the Purple Heart. Since that time, over the years, I've met many Purple Heart recipients and have been amazed at the wide spectrum of relatively minor wounds quite a few had suffered, yet they were nonetheless eligible for such recognition. More recently, as I was writing this book, one individual laughingly admitted to me that the wound he had suffered was probably less severe than a common hangnail! With that in mind, I wrote to the Bureau of Naval Personnel and requested appropriate recognition for the wound I had received, based on the eligibility criteria in effect at that time. After a lengthy period of waiting, I received a response: my medical records could not be located – no proof, no recognition!

On the occasion of another major attack on the city, Gib and I were tape recording the action. The idea was to send the tape home, to "impress" our loved ones with how real the sounds of war were. A day or so later, we reviewed the tape for clarity and ended up having quite a laugh. The tape had captured the sounds of everything with astounding clarity. There were rockets exploding one after another and there were the continuous popping sounds of small-arms fire. One could hear the unmistakable roar of several tanks as they passed directly by our compound. Then, right in the middle of the tape, with all the sounds of war going on in the background, Gib's distinct voice clearly said, "Hey, Paul, d'ya want some Jell-O?" Who would have believed that the city was virtually surrounded and under heavy attack with the offer of Jell-O at hand?

Another time Gib and I were standing up on the roof of the Flats, each of us relaxing with a cold beer in hand, when we both heard the distinct pop from a weapon being discharged nearby. There was never immediate concern when we heard such sounds; they were fairly common and our systems had grown a bit immune, somewhat contemptuous. We also heard the spent round as it whizzed nearby.

"Boy, that was a wild shot," I said.

We continued drinking our beer, perfectly silhouetted against the sky, when we heard the second crack of gunfire; a second bullet whizzed by, and instantly we both knew that the first shot, as well as the second, were anything other than wild. I don't know which of us hit the deck first, but it had to be a near tie. Our bodies were flattened against the roof, faces toward each other as we both acknowledged, "The son of a bitch is shooting at us." I'm sure Gib has, as have I many times over the years, wondered which one of us was the intended target, which of us was actually in the sniper's sights as he or she squeezed off those two rounds.

Concertina wire and razor wire was hard to come by. It was everywhere, but it was always in use. Tortilla Flats was not completely surrounded by an adequate means of repelling outsiders. The compound was badly in need of additional concertina wire, but I was unable to locate a source. Gib and I were on our way to the Chiefs' Club when I noticed two or three rolls of concertina wire rolled up and neatly stacked right next to the guardhouse at the gate to one of the many military compounds in the area. I half hollered at Gib to stop the jeep and turn around, that I had seen the wire and that we were going to get it. Gib, as usual, thought I was a bit crazy, but he also knew that I was usually successful in getting things accomplished one way or another. He said, "This is all your doing," meaning he wanted no part of whatever I had in mind, but he obliged me as he made a quick U-turn and pulled right up to the guardhouse. I jumped out of the jeep and imitated anger and disgust as I demanded, "Just who in the hell is responsible for leaving these rolls of concertina wire laying here?" The guard, probably new in-country, looked dumbfounded and could not immediately find his voice. I stepped a little closer to him and became more domineering.

"Do you hear me, mister?" My voice thundered as I growled, "Do you know how scarce this shit is?"

The guard assured me that he knew nothing about the wire, that he had not been instructed as to how scarce it was, and that he did not know what to do with it. I could feel my face getting red as I began to experience the anger I was supposedly acting out.

"Jesus Christ, man, I don't know how in the hell we're supposed to win this war with uninformed boot campers like you around. Get your ass over there and load that wire in the back of this jeep now!"

The very cooperative guard complied with an obedience that Gib and I admired. Tortilla Flats had a new look within a couple of days.

One day, without any advance notice, a member of the *Hien Binh* came into the Claims Office and arrested the interpreter that usually accompanied me, the one who was so knowledgeable and informative about the areas known or suspected to be more heavily populated with VC. We learned within a day that he was VC and that quite an armory of weapons had been located under his home. Mr. Lo invited me to witness the execution of our previous employee, by firing squad, but I turned him down.

I did however, on other occasions, observe methods of interrogation that were guaranteed to bring about confessions whether or not the person being questioned was actually guilty. I was at one of the police stations where I witnessed one Vietnamese lady, probably in her late twenties or early thirties. Her hands were tied to a ceiling pole above her and her legs and feet were tied to chairs that had been intentionally placed some distance apart. The girl was naked and several QC were taunting her. They "knew" that she was VC and they would not be content until she admitted her guilt. I watched as they spit at her and yelled obscenities. I was disgusted, without regard to whose side the girl was on, as one of the QC slowly dragged a beer bottle between the girl's legs, against her bottom, threatening to penetrate her most private parts if she did not confess. The hysterical girl swore over and over again that she didn't know what she was suspected of nor did

442

she know what they expected her to confess to. Without further warning, the QC plunged the neck of the bottle as far as it would go, alternating between her vagina and her rectum as the girl screamed. There was as much fear as there was pain in her voice. Never before had I felt the desire to kill another human being until that moment. As far as I was concerned, that piece of human garbage, that particular policeman, had no right to live. He enjoyed what he was doing, but he began to grow angry when he did not get results with the immediacy he demanded. I watched as the QC angrily swung the bottle against a table, thereby breaking off the neck and leaving only the base of the bottle with sharp, jagged edges remaining. He then held the bottle in both hands, jagged edges upward between the girl's legs, and swore that he would thrust the bottle upward and make both holes one and the same if she failed to confess. She cooperated, having no other reasonable choice. I believed the girl was innocent – and the QC, the Vietnamese Military Police, did not really care.

I was witness to another means of torturing a confession out of a suspect. First, I must describe the very small chili peppers that grow so well in Vietnam. They are tiny red peppers that never grow larger than a little fingernail, and they are the hottest things I have ever tasted. Such peppers were frequently used in soup, but they could also be found in a lot of other locally prepared foods. I watched as the QC crushed a bowl of those peppers into a salsa-type mixture. I was told that some victims of the torture I am about to describe died as a result of it. The suspected male VC that was tied to a chair was no less emphatic about his nonparticipation in subversive activities than the girl I previously described. One QC walked behind the suspect, grabbed a handful of hair, and jerked his head as far back as possible. Another QC quickly, again without warning, rushed over and poured some of the chili mixture directly down (up) the victim's nostrils, momentarily squeezing both nostrils to force the mixture as far back into his nose as possible – followed immediately by holding the man's mouth shut! The only way he could breathe was through his nose, and it shouldn't take a whole lot of imagination to realize what happened when that man gasped for air through the only passageway available. I cannot imagine the pain he must have suffered, but I did see the results of it. I will not describe the horrible scene other than to say the man passed out. He may have died; I did not stick around to witness anything else. I knew then, as I know now, that our so-called allies were not worthy of the many sacrifices our troops made on their behalf.

Gib was responsible for interviewing applicants to replace the interpreter we lost. One applicant, "Co Tiep," a very sweet and petite darling of a girl who was very fluent in English, was my first choice. I was impressed with her attitude and her mannerisms as well as her ability to translate. Her innocent appearance and attractiveness were secondary attributes, but they did not go unrecognized. Gib asked my opinion of those he had interviewed, and I zeroed in on Co Tiep. I.P. carried the motion as a third member in favor of Tiep – and she was hired on the spot.

Co Tiep, *Co* being the Vietnamese equivalent of "miss," was impressive in all respects, and I frequently chose her as my primary interpreter/translator to accompany me in the field during my investigations. She was really a delightful girl, and it didn't take any time at all before she became completely comfortable around the entire office staff. Co Tiep's sense of humor was right in line with mine, a bonus to our already-excellent working relationship. Soon I was able to drop the "Co" and I spoke to her on a friendlier basis, as Tiep. She enjoyed playing a variation of Tic Tac Toe with me during breaks, and her laughter and smile always contributed significantly to elevating office morale. The office had been a bit drab prior to her coming on board.

While en route to and from field investigations, Tiep and I talked incessantly about everything in general. We questioned each other about past experiences and our expectations of what the future held in store for us. Politics were never discussed, although religion did enter the conversation periodically. Tiep probably never knew that I placed the same value on her friendship, her companionship, that I placed on her professional assistance. She, by her presence alone, contributed immeasurably toward making my job more enjoyable. But Tiep had a down side, too. Her feelings were easily hurt, and when she was upset everyone in the office was uncomfortable. At first we figured "to hell with her"; however, after we realized how easily her persuasive moods rubbed off on the rest of us, we took a closer look at what we were doing to upset her. We valued Tiep's presence since far more often than not she made the office a more cheerful workplace. We learned that it was nothing more than the inflection in our voices that bothered her. Sometimes she thought we were angry with her when we were, in her opinion, too abrupt. Once we became aware of the problem, we corrected it. We probably had been too abrupt occasionally.

Once, at a hospital, when Tiep was assisting me in the investigation of a claimant who had allegedly been struck by a U.S. military vehicle, I asked her to tell the attending physician I needed to see certain medical records; including any X-rays that had been taken. She did so. Tiep knew from our many conversations that although I was not fluent in her language, I had gained a decent level of proficiency in it. I listened intently when Tiep translated for me and I could generally understand enough of what she said to confirm the accuracy of the translation. The physician asked Tiep why I wanted to see the records and the X-rays. Tiep turned to me and translated his question. I said, "Please remind the doctor that I am a Foreign Claims Investigator and that the claim I am investigating was submitted by the individual whose records I have asked to see. Tell the doctor that without proper confirmation that injuries were sustained, the injured man will have his claim denied. Make sure he understands; it is imperative that I see the documents so that the claim can be processed without delay."

After Tiep assured me that she understood what I had said, what she was to convey, she turned to the doctor and in Vietnamese that I clearly understood, she said, "Chief Adkisson wants to see the records because he does not believe you!"

I was stunned by what I heard. Immediately, before the doctor could respond, I angrily told Tiep to tell the doctor precisely what I had said and to never improvise or alter the meaning behind my words again. Tiep had, for the moment, forgotten about my ability to speak and understand the language. She was embarrassed and upset, but she complied.

For a couple of days following that incident Tiep did not want to accompany me in the field. I, on the other hand, began to see some humor in what she had done at the hospital. She had not intended to call the doctor a liar; far from it. She thought she could expedite the investigation by making things easier; get to the facts by being more blunt; save time, help me, etc. Americans have a tendency to beat around the bush before zeroing in on the meat of the subject, whereas Vietnamese (and many other Orientals) skip over all of what they consider unnecessary dialect and get right to the point. Skipping over what we consider necessary preliminaries leaves room for error – which we try to eliminate. After I had explained that to Tiep, she no longer tried to shortcut translations.

I had heard a lot about Marble Mountain and the stone carvers that made a living sculpting marble statues, but I had never been there. I asked

Tiep to accompany me to the famous landmark so that I could purchase several souvenirs. Specifically, I wanted a lion, the typical roaring lion standing with one foot on a round object, sculpted out of marble. The other sculptures I was in hopes of buying were those of an old man standing and an elephant. I had pictures of each, and Tiep assured me that I would have no problem having the statues chiseled to exact specifications – but that it would cost me a lot of money. I knew that I would be overcharged; that was expected in all parts of the Orient, where Westerners were considered rich and it was believed that we could afford to pay more. But I also hoped that Tiep would assist me in my efforts to barter.

Marble Mountain, aptly named for its seemingly endless supply of marble, was also a major U.S. military base. Many years later, well after the end of U.S. involvement in Vietnam's affairs, the world learned that directly underneath our military installation was an equally impressive, even larger, underground VC base! But that is another well-documented story.

Tiep and I did not have to enter the military compound to locate several of the local artists. I showed an aging gentleman my magazine pictures, and Tiep explained the sizes that I wanted the finished figures to be. The man and I haggled back and forth a few minutes, long enough for both of us to feign being taken advantage of, before we agreed on a firm price. After I left him with a substantial deposit, Tiep and I departed. Tiep told me that we were to return in two weeks, at which time my marble sculptures would be finished.

Tiep and I returned to the mountain a couple of times during the two-week period to monitor the progress. I was more than impressed. The work was right on schedule, and the old man had proven that he truly was an artist. When Tiep and I showed up on the fourteenth day, the old man was still working on my lion – even though it was completed. He wanted absolute perfection and would have continued babying the project(s) additional days had we been late. I paid the agreed-upon price (plus a totally unexpected but clearly appreciated tip) and took my prize possessions directly to the office, where each sculpture passed inspection by everyone there. I was as proud as I could possibly be with the knowledge that the day would come when I could return to the States with my newly acquired treasures, my most prized possessions from the Far East. To this day I continue to marvel at the intricate and proportionate details on my lion sculpture.

Tiep was something of a flirt, and I loved every bit of attention she gave me. She knew that she was the office favorite and sometimes she would intentionally take advantage of our tolerance. She never did anything outlandish or anything that might have jeopardized her job, but she did have a way of saying things that would have been considered out of line had someone else said them. She was allowed more than generally accepted customary fringe benefits, more independence than other Vietnamese employees. We all knew that it wasn't fair – but Tiep was like a small puppy that needed a little more personal attention. Sometimes she would do a little shopping during working hours. No one ever complained. Tiep never overly exercised the few extras she was allowed. We could have put an immediate stop to it, but we chose to keep Tiep happy. That way, as previously explained, everyone in the office remained happy.

Tiep and I became very special friends. Fun friends – by no means lovers! She could come to me with her problems. I was not only a good listener, I tried to give her good advice. She hated it when Gib came to work a little hungover, or whenever the effects of alcohol were evident. She would scramble into my small office cubical and squeeze between the wall and me – a safe haven where Gib would never follow. Tiep did not realize that Gib was actually at his peak, in his friendliest mood, when he had a little alcohol in his blood. He was a family man, and I never knew him to cross the line, to do anything outside the boundaries of the marriage to which he was so committed. Gib, like the rest of us, liked Tiep. His problem was that he was rarely complimentary, unless he had that little bit of supplementary audacity, the kind that came in a bottle.

Sometimes Tiep would show her affection for me in a very daring way; a way that she would always deny as credible evidence that there was anything serious between us. She enjoyed pretending to kiss me as she slipped a piece of ice from her mouth into mine. Co Lan, a typist, always appeared shocked beyond belief when she saw Tiep's lips touch mine, an extremely bold in-public display by Vietnamese standards. I never complained. As far as I was concerned, it was nothing more than a genuine kiss of friendship, and I appreciated knowing that Tiep was that comfortable with me. Besides, being in public view we could not have been safer. I would never have allowed it to go any further. It would have been far too dangerous developing any kind of romantic relationship within a working environment. She knew

447

that I thought a great deal of her, and I knew that she thought highly of me. That was good enough for me – and it seemed to do for her.

Much to my chagrin, there was a day when Mai showed up at the office to show off her new permanent. I was quite angry, but I tried not to show it. I was upset that she had cut her beautiful long hair and I was furious that she had come to the office. In her attempt to please me she had tried to Westernize her looks by having her hair cut and curled up in a permanent. I told her how nice she looked, but the truth was I thought she looked terrible. I loved her long, dark, flowing hair, and I knew that it would take years for her to reacquire it. Her visit to the office also tended to authenticate what everyone already suspected – that I had a girlfriend!

From the time of Mai's visit, Tiep began showing signs of jealousy, particularly whenever the name Mai was mentioned. I thought of it more as a joke until one day when Tiep and I had just completed an official investigation and I told her that I was going to pick Mai up at the base and provide her with transportation to her home. That alone did not set well with Tiep, but when we got to the base and I told Tiep to ride in the back seat of the jeep, I could see tears forming in her eyes. I knew immediately that I should never have asked that of her. I tried to make her believe that I was only joking, that she was my partner and that she would always have front seat priority – but Tiep was deeply hurt and she scrambled into the back seat where she sulked. Even after I dropped Mai off at her home Tiep refused to get back up in the front seat! I began to feel a little angry even though I knew that I had been wrong. So I parked the jeep alongside the road and told Tiep that I would take her home too, as soon as she returned to the seat by my side.

The little tiffs Tiep and I began having were a bit of a confirmation of the growing affection we were unintentionally fostering toward each other. I knew that the affection Tiep and I had for each other was platonic and that it could never go beyond that. Mixing business and pleasure had its limits, and the one hard and fast rule that I never compromised was; *no intradepartmental relationships/affairs.* I would never engage in a close relationship with anyone within my organization or under my control. That held true for those senior as well as those subordinate to me. Tiep and I conducted nothing more than a flirtatious relationship. We were both active participants, but we had an unspoken understanding that it would never go beyond that stage.

Mai, on the other hand, was fair game. Fair in that her marriage had been forced upon her, an arranged marriage agreed upon by her parents and the parents of her husband – but a marriage that Mai had never willingly entered into. So Mai and I also had a flirtatious relationship, but there was always the possibility that it might go further. And so it did, but the occasion was unexpected. Mai showed up at Tortilla Flats one day and I introduced her to my neighbor Lan – who invited both of us to her home, where the three of us visited like old friends. Unbeknownst to me, Mai asked Lan if we could use the privacy of a side room and Lan agreed. Up until that time I had held hands with Mai and I had kissed her – nothing more. It was Mai's call and I willingly went along with it. The side room had a high and very narrow bed alongside one wall. There were the makings of a thin mattress on top. Mai and I went through the preliminaries as we hugged and kissed, touched and squeezed, and I made a move to remove her garments. I had experienced the unhooking of bras and the unbuttoning of clothing, but I was faced with something entirely new to me. The outer garment, the *ao dai* (ow-yai), or long shirt, was easily removed; however the undergarment was incomprehensible. I fumbled around searching for anything that resembled a zipper, button, or latch, but I felt nothing recognizable and nothing where I expected something. Mai was beginning to giggle as I groped my way; totally inexperienced in disrobing a person who was adorned by a garment that had some secret combination required to unlock it. The humor she saw did not help me any. In fact, it almost deflated a very important part of my anatomy right along with my ego. Not being one to give up easily, I found the well-concealed latch on the side of the garment. Once I figured out how to release it we were free to go the distance; there were no more obstacles between us. So it happened; Mai and I had our first sexual encounter. We finally consummated a fantasy that both of us had considered for a very long time.

Several days later I found out that Lan was in trouble with her landlady. The landlady had seen Mai and me enter Lan's home and she knew that we had remained inside for about an hour. The landlady had accused Lan of pimping, of making extra money on the side by renting the bed in her home as short-time space – like a mini hotel where couples could copulate to their hearts' desire for an hour at a time. Lan was not able to convince her landlady that Mai and I were friends and that we had only stopped by to visit. I suspect the landlady probably peeked through some small crack in the wall and was able to observe what had occurred, but she did not know that Lan had cooperated with us in friendship – certainly not to make money. Lan's rent was increased as a result of that misunderstanding.

There were many American civilians working in DaNang during my time there. Some were civil service employees while others were there for the big bucks that were being paid by large corporations. The latter were the lucky ones, not just because of the high salaries they were paid, but also because they were not governed by U.S. military rules. They were able to roam around the business district and shop wherever they wanted, and they could enjoy the drinks of their choice at any of the many bars without having to worry about paying a penalty for being out-of-bounds or off-limits. They also lived in comfortable homes of their choice, usually in neighborhoods where the more prominent Vietnamese lived, well distanced from military installations. I was fortunate because I had become a good friend with a group of three civilians; all tenants in the same house. One had his live-in girlfriend, and the other two lived as bachelors. Their home became my most favored place of recluse. It also became the place where Mai and I spent many Friday or Saturday nights. Chris, the oldest of the three tenants, was particularly understanding as he went out of his way to make Mai and me feel welcome and as comfortable as possible. I tried very hard not to abuse a good thing, but it was difficult not taking advantage of the uncommon hospitality Chris so willingly made available to us. He encouraged me to spend as much time there as I wanted, so whenever Mai and I could get away for one or two weekend nights we knew that we had a safe and secluded place to stay.

My pad at Tortilla Flats had many advantages, too. Perhaps the most significant, it provided me with absolute privacy. My balcony adjoined that of the house next door. Bert and Paul, the two American civilian tenants there, were also very hospitable. Gib and I were routinely invited to their patio where they shared chicken and steak that they had grilled on their outdoor barbecue. Their home cooking was a far cry better than the rations we were accustomed to eating. Another privilege I had, a luxury no other tenant of Tortilla Flats had, was that I had my neighbors' permission to use their front entrance as my own entrance. In that manner I did not have to pass either of the RVN guards that were stationed at the front and side gates at the Flats. My situation was as near that of a civilian as could have been possible. I entered my neighbors' home at street-level, walked up a single flight of stairs, and stepped from the adjoining balcony on to mine. Having that alternate entrance provided Mai as well as myself with easy access and egress to and from my apartment without anyone being the wiser. Female guests were not allowed inside the Tortilla Flats compound. Had I been caught during any of the times Mai visited there, sometimes overnight, there was the strong probability that I would have lost my senior occupant status and would have been relocated to Camp Tien Sha.

There had already been one occasion when Mai and I did get caught. It was during an afternoon several days before I moved into the single-occupancy pad. I had escorted Mai by the Vietnamese guard after advising him that she was a co-worker, and we proceeded upstairs to the room that Gib and I normally shared. Gib was away and I knew that Mai and I would be uninterrupted for a couple of hours or more. In Vietnam, time could be very precious and it was seldom wasted; within seconds Mai and I were making love on my small bunk.

The head, as previously described, was available for the occupants of two adjoining rooms. What Mai and I did not know was that we were putting on quite an exhibition for the dozen or so maids that serviced the entire compound! One maid had entered the restroom, probably overheard some 'unusual' sounds, and had peeked through the rather large, antiquated, skeleton-key type keyhole, through which she had an unobstructed view of our activities. She then wasted no time in telling the others about her observation. One by one they had taken their turns at the keyhole until all were totally appeased by the live porno show in which Mai and I had unknowingly participated.

Mai and I had been doing our thing off and on for over an hour when someone knocked on the entrance door. I figured it was Gib, so I was not reluctant to open it. But it wasn't my roommate. Instead it was a representative from the Billeting Office; an E-6.

"What's up?" I asked, probably a bit sheepishly.

"Chief, do you have some women in there?"

"I wish! No, my secretary is in here. Why? What's the problem?"

"The problem is that all of the maids have taken a turn watching you through the keyhole in the door to the head – and one of them reported you to the office. You better get her out of there!" He made his point and I didn't argue.

"Not a problem; we'll be out of here in no time."

I found out some time later that the only reason one of the maids had turned me in was because she had been prostituting herself to some of the occupants and she did not like the idea of competition. Anyway, I was lucky that the Billeting Officer never learned of the incident, or perhaps he decided not to make it a legal issue. The offense was not a major one but could have resulted in a significant reduction in my freedoms.

Another luxury I inherited when I moved into the single-occupancy pad was that my civilian neighbor, Bert, was a high-level boss for the American organization for which he worked. He had a wide range of authority, and sometimes he exercised it on my behalf. Whenever my jeep started running a little rough, Bert would take it to his company's nearby vehicle repair shop and have it tuned up for me. Bert never passed on whatever expenses there might have been. It was the same as if the work had been done at one of the military facilities – but far more convenient. Bert provided me with official credentials that identified me as a civilian electrician; employed by the company he represented. With those credentials I was able to wear civilian clothing and I could barhop along with them, or alone if I preferred. I rarely did either, but just knowing that I could was satisfaction in itself. Eventually, to some degree, I was able to reciprocate and show my appreciation for all that he had done for me.

My own personal maid was an unattractive girl around 17 or 18 years of age. She spoke absolutely no English, and it was rare that we required the assistance of one of the other maids when we conversed. No doubt everyone who ever gained a reasonable amount of proficiency in a second or third language found themselves awkwardly embarrassed at some misuse or misunderstanding while using their newly acquired language. In my case, it became more than apparent that I was not quite as proficient as I had thought. But this story begins at a time when I found a baby bird that had fallen from its nest. I took it to my pad and fed it with nourishment that consisted of ground-up bugs and worms. My maid was fascinated at my apparent tender side when she saw the care I was providing the poor little creature. I, on the other hand, saw what I thought to be her not-so-innocent side at about the same time. She caught me totally off guard when I returned home one day. Her words were quite clear and I understood them explicitly, although I was quite set back upon hearing them.

"Show me your penis," she said in concise Vietnamese.

"I'm sorry; I did not understand you. Please repeat what you said," I said in my best Vietnamese.

452

"Please show me your penis," she repeated.

"Why do you want to see my penis?"

Her words certainly left no doubt as to her request as she told me, "I want to see how big it is – and I want to hold it."

I tried one more time to make sure there could be no mistake. "You want to see my penis because you want to see how big it is and you want to hold it?"

She looked almost frustrated as she assured me that was exactly what she wanted. So I thought to myself, *What the hell, you've probably never seen an American's cock – so here, enjoy it,"* and I proceeded to unbutton my fly. You'd have thought she had come face to face with a murderous enemy as she screamed in anger. Instantly I realized what I had unintentionally done, but there was no way I could expunge or otherwise remedy the rather traumatic insult I had delivered. The word *penis* in Vietnamese is *cu* (or *con-cu*), a word also used as a term of affection when speaking to or of a baby boy. Its context would normally define its use. *Cu*, or *con-cu*, unfortunately for me, also means, "bird." She was no longer interested in either seeing my bird or holding it.

I enjoyed what little free time I had. I considered my travel time while en route to and from different locations as free time. I enjoyed driving down the sandy beach route along the oceanfront, where there were always an abundance of fishermen making repairs to their fish nets and their boats. It was interesting watching as small groups of fishermen worked their boats back and forth to free them from the sand where they had previously beached at high tide. Eventually they worked their unseaworthy-appearing vessels far enough into the water to gain the buoyancy needed to float. When fishermen returned from sea they would again exercise their strength and their skill as they maneuvered their vessels ashore, always working in harmony and unison with each other while they made certain their vessels were beached in the higher sand, well above high tide. I never saw any large fish brought in, but I did see an abundance of small sardine-like silver fish that were quickly spread out on the sand to dry. Depending on the size of the catch, the area required to dry the fish ranged from a few to several hundred square yards. There was a time when I was on my way from Camp Tien Sha to the orphanage, not paying a whole lot of attention to anything other than the numerous children that were always playing along the waterfront, when I heard a very angry Vietnamese man yelling frantically at me. I realized that I had driven right into a rather large area of drying fish. I jammed on my brakes only to find that I had stopped right in the middle; I was completely surrounded by small silver fish. I saw the man running towards me as he waved his arms in all directions, a definite indication that I had done a terrible thing. I felt bad but my decision was instinctive. I knew that it made no difference whether I backed out or continued dead ahead, the damage had already been done. So I said, "Ong, xin loi!" (Sir, I'm sorry) accompanied by the *I didn't see it* shrug of my shoulders, and I continued on my way. I recall having thought to myself, *No wonder "Yankee, go home" slogans exist.*

Attacks on the city of DaNang were frequent, but the magnitude varied widely. There were flurries of small-arms fire that may or may not have been directed at live targets, and there were from one to several dozen rockets or mortars fired into the city during a single night. To some degree my inquisitive nature had rubbed off on Gib, and he was almost as interested as I was in driving through areas that were known to have been under recent bombardment. Opportunity knocked when Gib and I learned that the previous night one of the nearby villages had been attacked by friendly forces, our own and allied. We had witnessed the strafing and the bombing that had taken place from our strategic balcony perch: the roof of Tortilla Flats. So we decided to conduct an unofficial investigation of our own in that area, primarily to take pictures of the damage. We left the office without telling anyone of our plans. I don't recall the name of the village we went to; however, I will never forget what we saw. There were bodies scattered all through the village; many had been dragged out onto the road where they were already well bloated, accelerated by the terrible heat. Most of the villagers had their faces covered with any kind of available cloth in their somewhat futile attempt to filter out the overwhelming stench of decaying flesh. There were unattached body parts scattered about; there were burned bodies, bodies with no legs, and bodies without recognizable faces. It was a horrible sight and an uncomfortable position for us, but we did what we had planned to do, although I'm sure to the Vietnamese we were not popular for doing it. We took pictures. We were just about to leave when we heard the roar of tanks approaching. There was no reason for us to be concerned since "Charlie" (VC) would not be active during daylight, so we watched the tanks as they approached. Neither Gib nor I could determine the color of the single bar the Officer in Charge wore on each of his collars, those of

454

either a first or second lieutenant, but we did understand the hysterical and aggressive words spewing from his mouth as he sat atop the lead tank.

"What in the hell are you two doing here? This area is not secure; it is still under attack."

He must have been quite shocked at our lack of concern as he continued; almost in a frenzy, "You men are now my responsibility and under my command. Pull your jeep in behind this tank and follow!"

His orders were clear and concise. Gib looked at me in disbelief. I looked at the officer and in a very loud voice, with equal clarity said, "Like hell! Why don't you follow us instead?" I then turned to Gib and said, "Let's get the fuck out of here!" We promptly drove away in the direction of our choice, leaving behind one clearly ruffled, probably more confused than ever, officer of the United States Army.

War Casualties

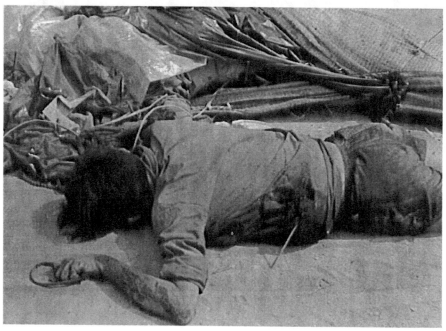

For a brief period of time I had a very unique responsibility. One of my civilian friends returned to the "world" (the United States) for a two-week vacation, and I volunteered to baby-sit his pet monkey. It was great fun at first. I took the rascal everywhere with me, always tethered to his leash. At the Claims Office, I released him from the leash, only to wish I had not done so very shortly thereafter. He was everywhere at once as he pounced from desk to desk and grabbed every item of food he came across. Some of the employees made it a practice to bring fruit to the office so that there was always a variety to select from. Bananas were the most favored and therefore the most plentiful. I never knew a small creature could fit so much food in its mouth. What that monkey could not swallow he stuffed in his cheeks. Watching him go crazy as he scooped up all the food was the fun part of having released him, and we all laughed as he rambunctiously ransacked every container he could get his hands on, purses included. It was only after the monkey calmed down that we all became more concerned. The little "monster" began losing control of his bowels and wasted no time in messing from one end of the office to the other. Likewise, he urinated, making sure all waste matter was evenly distributed. It took the combined effort of the entire office staff to corner and capture the little devil, and it was made known to me by all present that I had better not bring him back. Bring him back? I was ready to fry him! But I had promised to take good care of him, so I did. I enjoyed his company during the evenings as I sat out on my balcony. He seemed to enjoy watching the people below as much as I did. Within several days, after we were accustomed to each other, I thought that I could trust my little friend enough that he would remain by me without the leash. For the second time I unhooked him, and he sat contentedly on the balcony table where he had been previously tethered, a place with which he was most familiar. The moment he realized he was free from his line he leaped from the table and began playing hard to get. He made his way up onto the roof, where I knew I would never be able to retrieve him. My pesky companion was having the time of his life as it became more apparent that he was not willing to return to captivity. I tried desperately to coax him back, but he had ideas of his own. About the time I was ready to give up I remembered that I had one banana remaining in my room. Banana in hand, I returned to my patio with little hope of finding the monkey. But there he was, on another roof two apartments away. I managed to attract his attention, and the instant he saw the banana he pounced his way right back into my hands – back into captivity. I rewarded him with the banana as I breathed a heavy sigh of relief. I was relieved knowing that I would not have to tell my civilian friend how I had lost his pet. When the time came, I was just as happy returning the monkey as the owner was having it back.

Disregarding the war and the atrocities associated with it, perhaps one of the most disturbing things I was witness to in Vietnam was totally unintentional. Movies were shown every night up on the roof of the Flats, weather permitting. During the hot weather it would have been too uncomfortable seating the men inside without having the benefit of air-conditioning. On the roof we could usually depend on a warm evening breeze that cooled us as it came in contact with the ever-present perspiration our bodies so willingly released.

One evening I wandered up on the roof to see what was showing. I learned that one of the men had obtained some pornographic movies from a nearby construction battalion base, and everyone was concerned that I might put thumbs down on allowing them to be shown. I assured the men that I was no virgin, that I had seen my share of porn, and that I had no intention on interfering in their evening of entertainment. After I watched for a few minutes, I was disturbed at the content of the film. Not because it was pornographic, but because it went well beyond the limits of what might be described as decent or acceptable porn. The movie was of foreign origin;

it had no plot to it and was made up of numerous short scenes of every conceivable act of sex between animals and human beings. Disgusting as it was, the men laughed at the acts being performed. As repulsive and offensive as some scenes were, they could also be described as quite remarkable. Had I not seen the film I would never have believed that some of the "feats" were possible. I just happened to turn around and was momentarily petrified with a different kind of shock. The roof of the building across the street was literally jam-packed with "unauthorized," certainly unwanted observers. The unfortunate truth was that those observers were all wide-eyed children, probably none of whom had reached their teens. I immediately pulled the plug! The dissent among the men was obvious. Some did not share in my concern; they lacked the decency to care that youngsters had been watching. I made it absolutely clear that if the men wanted to see those particular films they would have to observe them within the confines of one of their rooms. I was surprised when they decided against watching a decent movie on the roof and instead opted to retreat below to the intolerable heat of a stuffy room – just to watch the rest of what I would now call believe-it-or-not porn. I still feel terrible that those children were exposed to such trash. At the time, those poor kids probably thought those movies depicted normal American activities. Again, signs displaying *Yankee, go home* came to mind.

The rainy season, more appropriately the monsoon season, was unreal. I never knew so much water could fall from the sky. It rained nonstop day and night, and the water was not readily absorbed into the ground. What didn't run off into the river or the ocean took on the appearance of swampland. It became impossible to travel many of the roads. Useable roads were dangerous because it was impossible to distinguish the road from the shoulder through the muddy water. There were a few times, of necessity, when I had to take my chances on the flooded streets. I had to aim my jeep toward known landmarks and then drive through the flooded areas with nothing more than the hope that I would safely cross the deepest parts. More than once I found the depth of water to be greater than I had thought, well above the floor of the jeep, during which times I found my feet underwater. Fortunately, my jeep was properly fitted, which made it difficult to flood the engine. Numerous vehicles were abandoned in the high waters. There were buses that had to be pushed in waist-high water by the passengers they were supposed to be carrying, and there were dead animals that had exhausted themselves while attempting to swim to safety. Disease was one of the unfortunate yet expected results of the monsoon season. The sicknesses that were spread were far more predominant among the Vietnamese, most of whom were undernourished, had never been vaccinated, and had little resistance to contagious diseases and bacteria. Americans were practically immune, as long as they practiced good hygiene and took whatever medications they were prescribed. Hospitals were always filled to capacity with individuals suffering from war-related wounds, but during the wet season hospitals were lined wall to wall with people suffering from everything imaginable. Conducting investigations that required visiting hospitals during that time was not only difficult and dangerous; it was hazardous to one's health. For the most part there were no isolation wards for those suspected of, or actually inflicted with, communicable or contagious diseases. Whenever I could accomplish my investigations without having to enter a hospital, I did so; however, there were occasions that required on-site hospital interviews or the review of pertinent hospital documents.

Monsoon Rains – Roads Replaced with Flood Waters

Monsoon Weather

The Rain Kept on Coming

I had completed numerous investigations and felt relatively comfortable with my job when another of those unexpected things happened, something that awakened me to the realization that I would probably never be fully prepared for whatever might confront me next. It was one of those times

461

that of necessity I had to conduct a portion of my investigation inside a hospital. Tiep obtained directions, and we were escorted into a waiting area where we found ourselves crowded by several occupied gurneys. The one nearest to us immediately caught my eye. There was a brave young girl, no more than ten years of age, laying there in terrible pain, but she was able to contain herself as she struggled to withhold her tears. A younger friend, possibly her little sister, was standing beside her with a small hand-held fan, shooing the flies away from the open wound that had accompanied the badly broken leg the youngster had suffered. The compound fracture had occurred near the ankle, and her foot was twisted in an awkward position, almost at a ninety-degree angle out of alignment. It was an offensive sight; her leg bone protruded grotesquely beyond the open wound. The sight alone was enough to turn my stomach, but what followed was more than I could bear to witness. A doctor approached the young girl, hacksaw in hand, and without the slightest hesitation began amputating the leg just below the knee. I turned to Tiep and told her that I could not remain within sight of the procedure that was taking place. The fact that Tiep did not understand why I was upset was beyond my comprehension. To her, things like that were commonplace – they were to be expected. To me it was barbaric. I felt ill and I told Tiep we would continue that investigation some other day.

There were far too many things that happened during my second year in Vietnam to include in this book. Many things that might seem to have been of little or no significance to the reader were rationalized differently, given the circumstances at the time and place of occurrence. For example, I built an "ant farm" out of scrap Plexiglas and placed it on my desk. Within a couple of days I had placed a sufficient quantity of ants in their new home. As each day passed and the ants continued their tunneling activities, the Vietnamese staff became more dumbfounded. They accused me of sneaking back into the office every night and dismantling the contraption – of somehow carving the tunnels and then reassembling the thing. They had never heard of such an interesting cage, and it took no less than a full week, and constant vigilance on their part, before they became believers in what their eyes had been telling them all along. Only after they came to realize that the ants had done all of the work themselves did the Vietnamese become truly fascinated as they observed the ants' never-ending toil.

Whenever I ate at the Chiefs' Club I was intrigued by the way Vietnamese doctored their French-fried potatoes. In the States I had seen, and tried, just about everything to further enhance their flavor. I had used ketchup, the most common dip, and I had used mayonnaise, a little less common. I had dipped fries in steak juices and steak sauces as well as a wide variety of salad dressings, and I found that everything I tried further enhanced their palatability. But the Vietnamese had their own idea and one that I could never bring myself to try. They covered their fries with an abundance of sugar and claimed that to be the most appropriate method of preparation. They thought of us as a bit strange when we added salt or dipped our French fries in ketchup.

Trung Thu Chi, the Vietnamese autumn festival, was an annual celebration, one in which I was witness and participant. On the fifth day of the eighth month on the Lunar Calendar, which corresponds with the fifth, sixth, and seventh of October, falls the *Trung Thu* autumn festival. The festival originated in the North many centuries ago from China's Celestial Empire. Called the Chung Chau Chi in Chinese, the *Trung Thu* was planned to fall on the most beautiful moonlit night of the year. A night filled with bouncing lanterns, swirling dragons, and children's antics. Although originally a festival for children, the celebration gradually changed to encompass everyone.

Parents prepared a party for their children. Children in turn invited their friends to partake in delicate dishes of fish, meat, and candy. There was also dancing in the gaily decorated, lantern-lit gardens. Also, special small round cakes, *Banh Trung Thu*, were prepared. There were two types, the first a golden yellow cake of fried white flour and the second a white cake made from glutinous rice. Both were filled with candied fruits and nuts. Adults often ordered a large *Banh Trung Thu* to give as special gifts to old and dear friends or greatly admired people.

There was a professional side to *Trung Thu* as well. Two days before the feast, drums and tambourines could be heard in town alleyways where people practiced for the big event. Professional children schooled in the performance of the Dragon Dance went to each house to wish the owner well with dancing. One of the dancers wore the mask of *Ong Dia*, or the God of Earth. He had a smiling face and was robust and satiated with good things. The remainder of the troupe was arrayed as *Mua Lan*, a unicorn with the face of a lion and the body of a dragon. They performed the Dragon Dance for *Ong Dia*. The most professional and adept dancers were found among the Chinese. (There was a large concentration of Chinese in Vietnam – in fact, the Vietnamese race originated in China before migrating to the area they now occupy.) The troupe combined complicated dance steps with skilled and clever gymnastics to the deep-toned beat of tin tambourines. If *Ong Dia* is pleased with the performance he shows his appreciation, enjoyment, and pleasure by extending his finger in his large dimple and blows on his fan with contentment. Then the unicorn performed with his greatest acrobatic skill. The owner of the house placed money for the troupe high up in the outside corner of his house. The dancers formed a pyramid higher and higher, finally gaining their prize.

Truly a festive occasion and one that, for the moment, disregarded the surrounding conflict.

Gib and I had strong feelings about the differences between serving offshore on board ship and serving on land in Vietnam. We decided to submit our proposal for a new Service Medal through appropriate channels via the Commander, U.S. NSA, DaNang. Our proposal was valid and was submitted in hopes of providing appropriate recognition for those serving, or who had served, within the geographical boundaries of Vietnam. Our letter of proposal clearly identified the need to distinguish those individuals who were constantly subjected to enemy harassment such as small-arms fire and rocket or mortar attacks while they provided valiant, strenuous, and other necessary support to all combat operations. The proposal was not intended on making heroes out of anyone; it could easily have been considered similar to other occupation medals that had been issued in recognition of U.S. forces serving on foreign soil. Even those who served a year at the polar cap received a medal for doing so, certainly without threat of hostile fire, although terribly isolated. Quite simply, Gib and I believed our proposed service medal would be an appropriate means of distinguishing those individuals who spent an extraordinarily arduous tour of duty within the Republic of Vietnam.

We were pleased when the Commander, U.S. NSA, DaNang, favorably endorsed our recommendation. That endorsement read in part:

> At present, it is not possible to distinguish the individual who earned his Vietnam Service Medal while serving in a ship operating off shore in the contiguous waters away from the threat of enemy attack from the individual whose service was ashore in an operational or support capacity who is frequently under en-

emy attack, but not necessarily assigned a position from which he could take offensive or retaliatory action qualifying him for the Combat Action Ribbon. It is apparent that there is a decided category separate from overall eligibility for the award of the Vietnam Service Medal and the qualification for the Combat Action Ribbon for which tangible recognition is appropriate. Accordingly, the recommendation has merit and consideration is recommended.

Gib and I gained additional confidence when we learned that the second endorsement to our proposal, provided by Vice Adm. E. R. Zumwalt, at that time Commander, U.S. Naval Forces, Vietnam, was even more favorable. It read in part:

Military decorations and awards are for the purpose of publicly recognizing and rewarding extraordinary, exceptionally meritorious or conspicuously outstanding acts of heroism or service which are above and beyond that normally expected. The Vietnam Service Medal provides recognition to all personnel who have served the United States in aiding the Republic of Vietnam. The recent addition of the Combat Action Ribbon has filled a previous void and gives recognition to naval personnel who actually engage the enemy in combat. There still exists a need to give recognition to those personnel in-country who are daily exposed to the mortar, rocket and random terrorist attacks prevalent throughout the Republic of Vietnam while serving in the vital support role so essential to operations in-country. Commander U.S. Naval Forces, Vietnam notes with pleasure the interest and initiative of [Gib and Adkisson]. The spirit and intent of their recommendation clearly demonstrates the desire of U.S. Navy personnel in Vietnam to be associated with the conflict and typifies the vigor with which Navy personnel pursue their assigned tasks.

Our bubble burst and our hopes went right down the drain when the third endorsement by John J. Hyland, at that time Commander in Chief, U.S. Pacific Fleet, was unfavorable. It read in part:

465

It is considered that an award such as the proposed one is not appropriate and if adopted would, among other things, tend to degrade the prestige of the Combat Action Ribbon. In those relatively few cases where personnel are genuinely exposed to repeated enemy attacks, it would be appropriate for them to be armed and engage in retaliatory actions and in so doing to qualify for the Combat Action Ribbon. Aside from these few occasions on which a sailor ashore assigned to a support, vice a combat function, may be exposed to danger more than his seagoing counterpart, it is not considered in the best interests of the Navy to attempt to single out one or the other as relatively doing more or less for the overall cause. Each has its relatively hard and relatively easy characteristics. Accordingly, the Commander in Chief U.S. Pacific Fleet recommends disapproval of the recommendation.

How about that! "Degrade the prestige of the Combat Action Ribbon"? Every ship in the fleet that was shot at from shore and returned fire, so much as a single shot, automatically qualified every sailor on board for the Combat Action Ribbon. Yet most individuals who served in Vietnam under the constant threat of hostile action and who, knowingly or not, were shot at by rockets or mortars aimed at areas in general, as opposed to individuals, did *not* qualify for the Combat Action Ribbon! Only those individuals who fired back were eligible, and I can assure the reader that many could have and would have fired back had they been equipped with the weapon to do so. "In those relatively few cases where personnel are genuinely exposed to repeated enemy attacks . . ." I took a very strong exception to Mr. Hyland's insinuation that, first, there were "relatively few cases" (small arms fire was a daily routine that everyone stationed in Vietnam was aware of and constantly exposed to) and, second, the insulting insinuation that exposure to repeated enemy attacks could be considered anything other than "genuine."

Expectedly, based on that third endorsement, Adm. B. A. Clarey, at that time Chief of Naval Operations, concurred in Hyland's recommendation and disapproved our proposal. Unquestionably, those with firsthand knowledge and adequate time and experience as related to shore facilities and activities within the Republic of Vietnam recognized the value of the proposal and endorsed it accordingly.

When the time came for advancement considerations I received an extremely impressive recommendation for advancement to Senior Chief (E-8) along with an equivalent evaluation of my performance. I began to think very positively about my chances for further advancement. I feel awkward when I include excerpts from some of the more profound things written about me, as I was perceived and/or personified by others, but if this book is to include how I was looked upon by others as well as how I thought of myself, I must do so. A portion of that recommendation follows:

> Chief ADKISSON has adapted extremely well to the position of a Foreign Claims Investigator, which requires, among other qualities, initiative, perseverance and great attention to detail. He has demonstrated these qualities continuously through his logical, thorough and well written investigative reports. He constantly strives to improve the functions of his office, utilizing great originality in his efforts to obtain efficiency. He improves his Vietnamese vocabulary daily to enable himself better access to information and factual data for his investigative reports. There is no doubt that Chief ADKISSON possesses the ability to meet any situation and make the right decision, as is shown by his general attitude and motivation. He exercises his natural leadership ability whenever and wherever he can, always taking the initiative and seeking new challenges. He is ambitious, capable, and does not shrink from responsibility.

At that time, all personnel that were recommended for either of the top two enlisted grades, E-8 and E-9, were required to undergo the scrutiny of a team of three officers, none of whom had ever met the candidates before. Candidates were interrogated on any subject matter the officers elected to reflect on. Again, I was pleased with the results of my interview. Each of the three officers graded me "Outstanding" in all areas, and each included a short summary statement of their overall evaluation. Without favorable statements, chances of promotion were zero. Two lieutenants and a lieutenant commander evaluated me. Their brief statements follow:

An outstanding candidate. Extremely conversant and interesting. Expresses his ideas very well and with confidence. An impressive man.

* * *

Chief ADKISSON presents the appearance of being an all around outstanding individual who is highly motivated to assume additional duty of great responsibility, in or out of his rate. He is considered an outstanding candidate for advancement to E-8.

* * *

One of the most impressive candidates interviewed. Appears motivated towards a 30-year career. Should perform in an outstanding manner as a Senior Chief Petty Officer.

* * *

I remember thinking to myself, *With evaluations like these, all I need to do is continue to exercise my abilities, pass the written exam, and I'm in.* Optimistic as I was, I became what I.P. thought of as "arrogant." When there was spare time at the office I.P. always had his nose buried in Navy self-study courses. At every opportunity he would suggest, "Hey Ad, you better hit the books; the E-8 exam is coming up." Unbeknownst to him, I studied diligently when I was alone, never while within sight of others. So when he reminded me that I should be studying I usually irritated him with something like, "Study what? I already know everything!" Of course it was always in jest, but with reasonable conviction. I.P. thought otherwise. He was very wrong in thinking that I didn't care about being promoted. I was fully prepared and I looked forward to taking the upcoming exam.

As my tour of duty neared an end, Gib decided to terminate his English class at the same time I ended mine. The staff and the children of China Beach Orphanage honored us both on our final day there. They had practiced several skits for some time in anticipation of our final visit and they performed beautifully for us. They were so sweet as they sang songs and acted out short skits. Mr. Lo told me that I was expected to make a short speech following their presentation, so I cleared my throat and began thanking them for having allowed Gib and me into their hearts. While I was searching for appropriate words I realized that my only thoughts were of the uncertain future in store for all of the children I had grown to know and love. I knew that I would not be able to express my true feelings. Some of the older kids probably understood when I broke down and cried right in front of the entire group. I tried hiding my face, a little ashamed that I was not able to control myself, and Mr. Lo delivered whatever it was that was

468

expected of me. Gib and I were then informed that on another day there would be additional festivities that included a luncheon, and we were expected to attend. Since it was to take place prior to my scheduled departure date, we accepted.

The luncheon was impressive. Gib and I were both hungry when we arrived, and the incredible and extravagant assortment of food that covered several picnic-bench-type tables was awesome. There were numerous guests, most of whom neither of us had ever met but who knew of us and were there to thank us for our work at the orphanage and to bid me farewell. The flies were worse than ever, far more than all of us there could collectively keep shooed away.

Just as we were about to be seated, Mr. Vuy slowly made his way around the entire circumference of the adjoining tables, politely excusing himself as he leaned in front of us one by one, and sprayed GI-issue bug repellent directly over all of the food. Not just a slight film, a heavy coating that not only glistened in the sunlight, but also filled our nostrils with its unmistakable odor. The flies that didn't die from the dousing remained airborne, a nuisance of another kind, but flies that were no longer interested in sampling the food. Neither was I, but since others around me were loading up their plates I decided to join in. The first bite was strongly flavored by the spray, but I managed to chew and swallow. The second bite I had to swallow twice, and even then I came very near losing it.

At this point it is important to understand that the Vietnamese culture does not readily accept a straightforward refusal to attend or partake of an invitation. In America, when offered food, one can accept or say, "No thank you." In Vietnam, "No thank you" is no different than bluntly saying, "No." Not that "thank you" isn't translatable; it is just as polite when translated as it is in English. That might seem a bit contradictory, but what I mean is, that it is unacceptable and not considered polite to turn anything down, with or without the thank-you trailer. It is, however, perfectly acceptable to give excuses in not accepting an invitation. For example, when one is made an offer of food it would be acceptable to say, "I'm sorry; I just finished eating," or, "I have an upset stomach and I should not eat anything right away," or the most common response, "Not now, perhaps a little later."

With that, you can see the predicament that I was faced with. I was familiar with Vietnamese customs and I certainly did not want to insult anyone on my last day, a day on which I was being complimented and thanked. Everyone knew that I had come to eat and that I was hungry when

I arrived. That, plus having already taken a bite, made for a lack of accept-able excuses. One more bite and I knew that I would have ruined it for more than just me. The only thing I could think of, and the thing that I used as my excuse, was that I had an appointment elsewhere, official business that I had no choice other than to attend. I explained that I had not allowed sufficient time between appointments. Gib picked right up on my excuse, and we very politely excused ourselves from the table. After making sure everyone there knew of our appreciation, we departed. We both wondered if we would ever be able to eliminate the taste of bug spray.

Certificate of Appreciation

Several days prior to my scheduled departure the entire staff of the Claims Office also threw a farewell party for me. Chris, my civilian friend, provided his home as the party site. It was unbelievable, the effort every-one took to make the occasion memorable. I was presented with gift after gift, each accompanied by short speeches of appreciation, and each not-ing something special for which they recognized me. They remembered little insignificant things I had done that had sentimental meaning to them, things I had forgotten or considered inconsequential. And once again I broke down, unable to cope with all the attention I was receiving. It was a marvelous experience, and as soon as I regained my self-composure I partied right along with everyone.

As curfew approached the crowd began to disperse – it was time for everyone, the Vietnamese in particular, to return to their homes. I had planned on remaining all night, so I continued to party. It was well after curfew when Tiep came to me and very nervously asked what was she to do. I suggested that she sleep in the spare bed in the bedroom with me. She asked me if I would leave her alone, and I assured her that I would. When the time came we turned in as planned, she in her bed and I in mine. She wore my shirt as her nightgown and she looked absolutely adorable. Within minutes I suggested that she join me in my bed. It took a little coaxing, but within a few more minutes little Tiep was lying beside me. She was cuddly and she felt good as we lay there together. Regardless of the desire either or both of us might have had, I maintained my self-imposed restraining order and refused to fraternize beyond the "touchy feely" stage. We slept together, nothing more!

The following morning I took Tiep directly to the office, dropped her off, and proceeded to the flats to shower, shave, and change into a fresh uniform. I asked Tiep to make sure Gib knew that I would be there shortly.

Within 30 minutes I walked into the office and immediately noticed some unusual, almost uncomfortable expressions around me.

Gib came straight to me and said, "You did it, didn't you!"

I assured Gib that I was in no mood for games. "What do you mean, I did it?" I asked.

"You won't believe what Co Tiep did."

"Okay sonny, I give up, so what did Tiep do?" I was suffering from a hangover and I spoke with the distinct inference that my patience was wearing thin. Gib went on to tell me that no sooner had Tiep entered the office than she loudly and clearly announced to the entire staff, "I slept with Chief Adkisson last night!" Tiep had successfully conveyed the strongest and most believable insinuation that we had done more than sleep. I called Tiep over to my desk and asked why she had told everyone that. Her answer: "Because you were going to tell them anyway." She knew that she had not used good judgment when I made her realize that I had no intention

471

on telling anyone a damn thing. What would I have gained? In fact, I would have lost a great deal of respect, and as a result of her outlandish insinuation I probably did anyway. Tiep felt bad and she tried very hard to change her story into a near-truth; that she had slept in the same room but in a different bed. The more she tried to make things right, the more convinced everyone was that something extraordinary had happened between Tiep and me. They were right – but their suspicions were wrong.

Mai knew that my days in Vietnam were nearing an end, too. Mai and I had been through a lot together, and there could be no doubt that we had an honest affection for one another. She had been my friend, my mentor, my companion, and my lover. She had provided me with a kind of affection I had never before experienced, quite literally an affair that could have meant the death of either, or both, of us. Mai had her own idea on how we should part. She implored me to accommodate her in fulfilling her wish, that of going to bed one final time with her, but instead of making love we were to place a hand grenade between us and hold each other in one final embrace as our lives came to an end simultaneously. We would then be together forever. Once she told me of her wish I became very concerned for my well being. I began to think about how she might pull it off with or without my consent. I reminded Mai that I had returned to Vietnam once before and promised faithfully, with all the sincerity I could muster, I would return again – and that she had every reason to believe me. She accepted me at my word – and I never saw Mai again.

It had been some time since I turned my .45 in to the armory for safekeeping. I retrieved the weapon, still unused since the day I originally purchased it, and tried to make arrangements to ship it to my next duty station. I was told that I could not ship it with my personal effects, that I should not have brought it into the country in the first place, and that I could not handcarry it out of the country with me. The pilots of departing aircraft would not allow personal weapons on board, even if they were turned over to the pilots themselves. I had a document properly signed by the Armory Officer accurately identifying my weapon by type, manufacturer, and serial number as privately owned; a legal document that authorized its shipment as part of my belongings to my next duty station. The document, referencing COMNAVSUPPACTDNG Instruction 8370.1A and MACV Directive 210-5 of 25 January 1967, was not worth the paper it was written on, it seemed, since those responsible for making my transportation arrangements refused

472

to acknowledge its purpose. So I decided to give my weapon to Bert, my civilian neighbor friend, in thanks for his friendship and for all the things he had done for me. He was pleased with my gift since his own weapon had been confiscated by the local police during a search of his premises a couple of months prior. Bert promised to return it to me someday, but I knew better than to expect we would ever cross paths again.

Periodically, for the purpose of describing me or my activities as seen through the eyes of others, I will continue to include excerpts from documents of one kind or another. What follows is a portion of an award recommendation submitted near the end of my tour of duty in Vietnam:

Chief ADKISSON reported for duty at the U.S. Naval Support Activity, DaNang in June 1968 and was assigned to the Navy Foreign Claims Office as an investigator, with duties of investigating and reporting on any incident which may give rise to a foreign claim. Although having no prior training in this field, Chief ADKISSON quickly mastered the intricate techniques of claims investigation, which require attention to detail and an understanding of legal principles. He has since completed over seventy lengthy, complex investigative reports of exceptional quality. Chief ADKISSON consistently displayed great resourcefulness and ingenuity in the performance of his duties, continually suggesting new procedures and methods that have increased the efficiency of the Foreign Claims Office. His recommendations have always embodied the principles of fundamental fairness coupled with a zealous guarding of the interests of the Navy. His tireless efforts have saved the Navy thousands of dollars in the administration of the claims program. Prior to his arrival in Vietnam, Chief ADKISSON completed a course in the Vietnamese language at Coronado language school, achieving the highest final grade ever scored at the school. Although there is no language requirement for his present position, he has made a continuing effort to add to his value as a claims investigator by daily improving his language ability through self study and has thus contributed markedly to his effectiveness at the Claims Office. In addition to his primary duties as an investigator, Chief ADKISSON is the Compound Defense Officer and Security Officer of his billet which houses approximately forty people. As such he has devised and implemented a complete battle plan for the billet in the event of attack, and has promulgated standing orders for all hands. Chief ADKISSON has carried out these duties with enthusiasm and ingenuity, efficiently planning all aspects of defense including procurement of emergency rations and ammunition and assignment of personnel. These tasks require the expenditure of many off duty hours and carry a grave responsibility which Chief ADKISSON has eagerly assumed. On his remaining off duty hours Chief ADKISSON has contributed immeasurably to Vietnamese American relations by personally organizing and teaching two conversational English classes at China Beach Orphanage. The classes began on July 16, 1968 and are held three evenings per week, for one hour each. Chief ADKISSON unselfishly sacrificed much time and personal expense for materials in this project. Chief ADKISSON's investigations have frequently led him to remote and hostile areas of I Corps, where he has been subject to enemy small arms fire. In addition he was present in the City of DaNang during the offensive on the city in the last week of August 1968, and the rocket attacks of late September 1968, November 16, 1968 and April 16, 1969

* * *

June 18, the day prior to my scheduled departure from Vietnam, I visited Tiep at her home to thank her for her support within the Foreign Claims Office and for the personal friendship we had developed. I had my short say, wished her a healthy and prosperous future, fired up my jeep, and headed back toward the office. I no longer considered the familiar sounds of small-arms fire and occasional explosions a threat, even though they were present as I was driving. Then, about halfway back to the office, the most unexpected and extraordinary thing happened. A Military Police jeep, red lights flashing and siren sounding, rapidly approached me from behind! Thinking they probably needed my assistance in some manner, I brought my jeep to a quick stop. I remained seated as the MP driver walked toward me with an overemphasized macho strut, his head cocked to one side, looking seriously foolish. His words left nothing to my imagination and caught me totally in disbelief.

"Hey, man, you were speeding."

My answer was not quick enough or harsh enough, but I did manage to respond with my own, "Well, hey, man, you mean to tell me there's a goddamn speed limit in the middle of a fuckin' war?"

"You bet, pal, and I'm gonna issue you a citation!" And he did just that!

"So what happens now pal?" I continued, "Do I go to jail without passing 'Go' or do I suffer some other kind of horrendous punishment?"

I laughed in his face when he said, "You'll be notified through your command when your court date is set!"

I knew that I was leaving the country the following day, so I blasted him with, "You stupid fuck! You probably think I'll be there don't you?"

His acknowledgment, "Oh, you'll be there all right!" would be proven wrong.

I again laughed heartily in his face, put my jeep in gear, and intentionally spun the wheels, thereby leaving him in a cloud of dirt and dust. Did I slow my pace? Not at all. I drove faster than before in hopes that I would get a second opportunity to express my opinion – with greater emphasis on detail. That speeding ticket remains one of my most treasured war souvenirs. Without it, no one would ever believe that it really happened.

I departed DaNang as scheduled the following day, June 19, and arrived at *Tan Son Nhut* Airport in Saigon shortly thereafter. That night I felt that off-limits no longer applied to me. I had served my time in 'Nam and I was going home! After a final barhopping run down the strip in Saigon, I slept comfortably at the Annapolis Hotel. The following day, June 20, during a prolonged wait for homeward-bound transportation, I spent my time inside *Tan Son Nhut* Airport Terminal feeding a stray goat cigarettes. I departed from Vietnam with a very sincere hope that I might someday return, not to serve in a military capacity, but as a tourist.

**Through the Eyes of an
Orphaned Child**

14

SHORE DUTY

My PCS orders were clear and upon receipt of them I relaxed in a way that I had not been capable of for years. The Bureau of Naval Personnel had finally taken the official action I had longed for – it had changed my Primary Navy Job Code from 3355 (nuclear-trained) to 0000 (no specialty) and my secondary job code from 0000 to 9545 (security). I had been successfully terminated from any responsibilities associated with nuclear power and could not possibly have been happier. My orders directed that I return to Hawaii and report to the Commanding Officer, USS ARD-30, "FORDU(SHOR)," for shore duty.

ARD-30 was a Class "C" floating drydock and was launched July 26, 1944. It was commissioned and accepted by the U.S. Navy on June 24, 1945, however, its status was changed to "in service" on September 13, 1946. It was different from other ships of the line, in that it had no propulsion units and had to be towed to wherever its services were required. ARD-30 served at Agana Harbor, Guam, Mariana Islands, during World War II and provided services in preparing reserve units of the Pacific Reserve Fleet for reactivation during the Korean War. Her status was again changed in 1948 to that of "in service – out of commission," to be returned to her "in service" status in December 1958 when it was moved to Pearl Harbor, Hawaii. Since that time ARD-30 remained at Pearl Harbor under Commander Service Force, U.S. Pacific Fleet, for administrative command while concurrently she reported to Commander Submarine Force, U.S. Pacific Fleet, for operational command. Her primary mission was to the submarine forces of the Pacific Fleet.

The life of a sailor is dictated by the needs of the Navy. That has always been an accepted fact, but to many persons uneducated in the ways of the Navy, a brief explanation regarding such needs must be addressed. The different classifications and ratings (specialty fields) varied widely and were broken down into eleven distinct groups. Those groups, in order from I to XI, were identified as: I. Deck; II. Ordnance; III. Electronics; IV. Precision Equipment; V. Administrative and Clerical; VI. Miscellaneous; VII. Engineering and Hull; VIII. Construction; IX. Aviation; X. Medical; and XI. Dental. Each of those groups was broken down further into subgroups, known as ratings. My rating, Machinist's Mate, fell within Group VII. Other ratings in that group were those of Engineman, Machinery Repairman, Boiler Technician, Molder, Electrician's Mate, Gas Turbine System Technician, Interior Communications Electrician, Boilermaker, and Hull Maintenance Technician. Similarly, other groups consisted of different ratings; some entailed a greater number of ratings than others. Ratings determined not only the area of specialty one worked within; they were of primary significance in determining shore as well as sea duty assignments. That made those ratings within the Administrative and Clerical Group in greater demand ashore, and such men were therefore ordered to shore duty with far greater frequency than those within the Engineering and Hull group. For example, since there were few steam-generating plants and no main propulsion plants ashore, sailors within the Machinist's Mate rating could plan on spending a great deal more time at sea, where their skills could be utilized to a greater extent. Similarly, since there were more boilers on ships than ashore, sailors within the Boiler Technician rating would find themselves primarily at sea. Generally I am referring to career people, not single-term enlistees who, unfair as it might seem to the careerist, might spend their entire enlistment ashore. There was a greater number of shore billets available for lower-rated men as opposed to a significant lack of billets available for the more senior grades. No one could possibly be satisfied 100 percent of the time but "lifers," the somewhat-derogatory term non-career personnel used for identifying careerists, were more apt to understand and accept undesirable assignments having the confidence that things would get better in time. At that time there were no special considerations or monetary benefits generated by sea time longevity. It was a simple truth and an accepted way of doing business that some sailors were, because of their rate and rating, eligible for more shore duty than others were. The benefits associated with shore duty, whether on foreign soil or on the home front, could be counted on offsetting the tedious years of sea duty. At sea, most sailors could expect to be on duty four out of every twelve hours. In port, they stood three-section duty; one 24-hour duty day aboard ship and two eight-hour workdays with liberty after working hours. Shore duty was something to look forward to. It was usually that period of time when one could expect between six and twelve section liberty and would only be part of the duty section once or twice every two weeks. It was also that period of time when one was off duty he was really off duty; he was not restricted to the confines of the ship while surrounded by miles and miles of ocean. Shore duty meant that when one was off duty he was able to sleep in the comfort of his own bed, at home. And seldom, if ever, was one called upon in the middle of the night to affect necessary repairs to some component of the ship. It meant walking without having to contend with the never-ending swaying and jerking motions of the ship as dictated by the severity of the ocean's currents and the magnitude of its waves. It was a time one could choose what and where he wanted to eat and/or drink. It was meant to be that period of time best remembered for having been the most enjoyable while serving with the Navy. It was supposed to be all of that and more, and it usually was.

All duty assignments that were designated "arduous," such as serving on ships that spent considerable periods at sea away from their home port during local operations and which when deployed overseas operated at sea extensively, were seldom considered desirable. Most duty outside the continental United States and Hawaii, where accompanied tours were less than thirty-six months, counted as sea duty – which made them highly desirable to most sailors. Unfortunately for me, there were very few overseas billets that were available for Chief Machinist's Mates. There was a far greater number of shore billets, stateside as well as overseas, that could only be filled by ratings other than mine. I knew prior to receiving orders to ARD-30 that I would serve a single tour of shore duty during my entire career. I found it almost comical that in a career spanning twenty years, I would be assigned to shore duty on board a floating dry dock! I would, because of my rating, remain at sea or floating on it. (Vietnam counted as sea duty since it was, as much in fact as it was designated, arduous.)

On June 29, 1968, I reported for duty at ARD-30, the only floating drydock in Pearl Harbor, disappointed in my assignment but happy to be there nonetheless.

U.S.S. ARD - 30

ARD-30 — Class "C" Floating Dry Dock
June 1969 to July 1972

My disappointment increased when by the direction of "Big Mike," the OinC, I was not assigned engineering responsibilities. Rather, I was appointed First Division Officer! Not only had I been assigned to the Deck Department, the opposition in a manner of speaking; I had become overall responsible for it. Immediately the other chiefs dubbed me "Boats," the most common shortened version of "Boatswain," and never used in reference to anyone outside of the Boatswain's Mate rating. That is, never until then. I disliked Big Mike, a mustang lieutenant commander, partly because he put me in the Deck Force but also because of the distinct impression I had that he had forgotten what it was like to be enlisted; that being enlisted was in no way a means of measuring a sailor's intelligence or his ability to reason sensibly. He had done his time as an enlisted man and had no doubt earned his promotion to commissioned officer status. But he was never without his *I'm a little bit better than you* attitude about him. Was he senior? Absolute! But better? Not by the farthest stretch of anyone's imagination; quite the contrary. In fact, without regard to the significance, the seriousness, or the degree of danger involved, had I been in need of assistance I would have preferred any man on board before I would have considered Big Mike. It did not matter to Mike how hard or how many hours the crew worked; he demanded more from them. He never uttered words of encouragement or praise for or to the crew (not until the time came for a change of command, when, in traditional form, he included some complimentary remarks in his farewell address). I had never seen a harder-working group of men, and when I brought it to the attention of the skipper, Big Mike, he brushed it aside and scoffed at me. He reminded me (as if I didn't know it) that I was no longer on submarines and that he was "sorry" (sarcastic sorry) that I was being subjected to such a change, a change that required work! Whatever Machinist's Mate or chief's blood he at one time had in him must have been displaced by a transfusion of questionable origin.

For whatever reason(s), Mike exhibited a peculiar animosity toward enlisted men. He exercised his disliking for me in a way that not only angered the crew, it turned the crew against me. I can chuckle today at the memory I have of that particular occasion and at the planning Mike must have put into it. I've got to give credit where credit was most assuredly due. Mike did it right and I salute him for it. He could not have been hated more as a result, and he took me along for the ride. Mike gave notice to the crew that there would be a dress parade for the purpose of presenting awards. All hands were required to participate, and they were instructed to be in their very finest dress whites with ribbons. That might not sound too unusual, but consider the date with the occasion; December 24, 1969, Christmas Eve! Add to that the fact that it was raining as all hands assembled on the dock alongside the ARD. Top that off with the award ceremony itself and realize just how ornery that man was. The sole purpose of calling the crew in from their Christmas holidays in their finest white uniforms was to stand at attention in the rain while *I* was presented with the Navy Achievement

**Christmas Eve Standing at Attention in the Rain;
Award Ceremony or Vengeance?**

480

**Foul Weather Ignored, the Award Ceremony Took Place
December 24, 1969 [Eye contact said it all]**

Medal and the Combat Action Ribbon! There were no other award recipients. I was embarrassed and angry, certainly not proud as I had every right to be.

I don't know who the crew disliked more, the "Old Man" or me. He was proficient, far more than successful, at causing dissent among the hardworking crew. Their hatred for him became acutely evident one afternoon as he was leaving.

First, I must describe one bit of Navy custom that is practiced by all commands; that of notifying the crew of the arrival and/or departure of the commanding officer. That is easily accomplished by the call on a Boatswain's Pipe, the ringing of bells, or the sounding of some other distinct device followed immediately over the 1-MC with the words: "[Ship's name] arriving [or departing as the case may be]." A distinct pennant flying also signifies the absence of the commanding officer.

I was privileged to be there on Friday afternoon as the skipper crossed the quarterdeck and started across the gangway leading to the dock. The words, "ARD 30 departing," were heard by all hands, and with a spontaneity that could not have been more perfectly planned the crew let loose with hoorays and cheers that reverberated from ship to shore. Mike stopped halfway across the gangway, paused as he slowly turned facing the quarterdeck, obviously disturbed by what he had heard but unable to take immediate decisive action, then proceeded ashore and drove away. A copy of the letter that was distributed to all hands as a result of that incident follows. It says a lot about Mike; it says it all:

FROM: Officer In Charge, ARD-30
TO: All Hands, ARD-30
SUBJ: Custom and Tradition

On Friday, 9 January, 1970, upon the departure of the OinC, a spontaneous and loud cheer was heard by all those in the vicinity of ARD-30 as well as the OinC, for whom it was apparently intended. This resounding display of vocal power, though meaningful and heartfelt, is not in keeping with the U.S. Navy customs and traditions.

Certain customs and traditions have come into being over the years that *are* meaningful and have their place in the scheme of things. These include: piping over the side, wetting down parties, passing out cigars, initiations, etc., however, the U.S. Navy does not as yet have a custom wherein a man is given a rousing cheer when departing. By way of information, the British Navy does have a custom of this nature, however it is reserved for special occasions and is led by the senior person present. In essence, it is the old "Three cheers for — Hip-Hip-Hooray." Recalling your efforts of the past Friday, while the desire was apparently there, the format for doing the thing properly was lacking. [My opinion: It could not have possibly been more meaningfully executed.]

In as much as Navy customs and traditions have taken on added and serious meaning over the years, it would not behoove us to utilize them lightly nor improperly. Therefore, in the interest of maintaining the highest "esprit-de-corps" I strongly request that further boisterous sendoffs be curtailed. Your spectacular efforts in this area, though much appreciated, are not in keeping with naval decorum, nor do they enhance the image of ARD-30, which each of us, individually, should do our utmost to project the best way possible.

With his fancy words Mike probably thought that he did a good job of turning the incident around in his favor. All he was really successful at accomplishing was that of providing the crew with a good laugh. If he was to remind us of customs and traditions that made our Navy so great, he should have made himself a better example of one who believed in that by which he thought we should abide.

It would not have been proper for me to congratulate the crew on their success. But I was part of that crew and I admired their action, whether it was appropriate or not. They got their point across with distinction and perfection. It might be a little late, but I now give the crew a most deserving, "Well done."

ARD-30 was a workhorse. As a submersible/floating drydock, it was counted on to receive crafts of all sizes and shapes, not only conventional submarines, but also surface craft up to and including destroyer escorts. As First Division Officer, I had to research U.S. Navy regulations and ARD-30 instructions as contained within the *Organization and Regulations Manual.* I saw nothing significantly difficult about carrying out my responsibilities other than the fact that most were new to me. Exercising my leadership skills was something of an inherent characteristic and came naturally; however, I had not considered many other aspects of deck force duties or responsibilities since boot camp. Big Mike enjoyed the discomfort I expressed at having been removed from the world of engineering. It was required that I sign an official document acknowledging my acceptance and assumption of the duties of First Division Officer; that I had conducted a thorough inspection of the assigned spaces; that I considered the personnel condition of the division satisfactory; that I considered the material condition of the division satisfactory; that the Cleaning Bill and Equipment Responsibility Bills were up-to-date; that I had a list of uncompleted repairs and authorized alterations available to me and on file; that I had conducted an inventory of equipage and that all was accounted for; that all logbooks, journals, and all other records and papers as required had been turned over to me; and that I had accepted custody of and/or responsibility for all unexecuted orders, all

483

regulations and orders in force, all official correspondence and information concerning the division and personnel, and all documents required by Navy regulations.

Was all that I signed for the truth? Not at all, but I perceived things as already being bad enough, so why should I make things worse by contesting anything. I knew that I could make whatever corrections there were that needed attention, even though in my eyes the entire deck force was a total disaster. So I set about making sure all conditions were as I had acknowledged them to be, and I became the hardened Bos'n's Mate Big Mike wanted. Even that seemed to be a thorn in his side. He never thought that a Chief Machinist's Mate was capable of near-overnight conversion to Chief Boatswain's Mate.

I performed to the best of my ability but was totally disheartened having to fake it, having to pretend I was something other than the Machinist's Mate I set out to be. I was particularly upset on one occasion when we were in the process of bringing a Coast Guard cutter into the flooded basin. Most vessels followed the same procedure as they entered the stern of the drydock under their own power. Once their bow crossed the sill and they were far enough inside to be maneuvered by mooring lines, they shut down their main engines. A minimum of five lines were passed from vessel to drydock. First the bow line, then two to port and two to starboard, and the vessel was pulled in assisted by winches and manpower. I was all the way aft on the port wingwall and was responsible for instructing men on the handling of line four. The skipper, Big Mike, was on the bridge, just forward and outside of the Control Panel Station, shouting his orders over the public address system. His orders were simple and impossible to misunderstand. He would order line number so-and-so held, or taken in, or let out. With submarines his line of sight to all line handlers was unobstructed, however, when handling larger surface craft the superstructure of the vessel being hauled in often obstructed his line of sight. Sometimes the wind made it much more difficult for the crew, which was the case on that day. The wind was forcing the vessel to port, toward me, and line four was hanging near the water, well slackened. But the skipper, with all his wisdom, experience, and sense of superiority, blind to the reality of the situation, repeatedly ordered line four to be let out. Each time he ordered it, I directed the men handling the line to slacken it more. They looked at me with bewilderment, but I reminded them that we were there to follow orders. The skipper, nearly hysterical, practically screamed the orders, "Chief, don't you know what *slacken* means?"

I was furious when I pressed the small toggle switch on the side of a nearby speaker, thereby allowing me to transmit my message back to him: "Line four has always been slackened to the water's edge. Do you want me to cast the bitter end overboard, sir?" In landlubber's terms, I had advised the skipper that in order to follow his orders I would have to throw the line overboard – thereby having no control whatever. The skipper did not respond, although I'm sure he looked into the matter later. That incident caused me to reevaluate my desire to remain on shore duty.

I was also assigned the responsibilities of Chief Master at Arms and was directed in writing, signed by the skipper, to "be guided in the performance of [my] assigned duties by pertinent regulations as may be promulgated by competent authority." Interesting term: *competent*. I recall wondering by whose judgment the term might best be interpreted. I felt very competent

ARD-30 Bringing a Destroyer Escort on Board

about myself. So I adorned my uniform with the shiny brass badge that I had known many a Chief Bos'n to proudly wear, and I became the ARD's one-man police force – another out-of-rating assignment that consisted of duties far removed from those expected of a Machinist's Mate.

August of that year, just two months after reporting for duty at ARD-30, I submitted a two-page typewritten letter to the Bureau of Naval Personnel, to the attention of Senior Chief Machinist's Mate Royce, Assistant Rating controller at that time. Therein I expressed my desire to serve within the Office of Naval Intelligence. It was a sincere request, something I had always wanted but had never pursued, and I had what I thought to be good justification for immediate and favorable consideration. Significant points that I included in that letter follow:
1. I had been selected for promotion to E-8, MMCS
2. There was no billet on ARD-30 for a MMCS
3. There was only one billet on ARD-30 for a MMC and it was filled by a MMCS (another Senior Chief Machinist's Mate)
4. A third MMC was en route to ARD-30, meaning that in November of that year there would be two MMCS's (including me) and one MMC, well over allowance.

USS *O'bannon* (DDE-450) - Docked on Board ARD-30

I explained the unusual situation I was in, that of filling a Chief Boatswain's billet. I knew that Senior Chief Royce would more likely be sympathetic knowing that. I also emphasized my previous experience and success as an investigator. In closing I tried to convey my true feelings as I wrote: "My record speaks for itself. My potential is limited only by the realm of possibility. My adaptability to fill positions not necessarily within my rating comes naturally and my personality is such that I fit in with all types of people. I have the ability, the motivation, and I realize the responsibility which I am eager to assume in putting forth maximum effort toward contributing to the lessening, and perhaps eventual elimination, of the most corrupt activities within the military."

I did not expect, nor did I get, a favorable recommendation from Big Mike. In the final analysis it would not have made any difference, except that his concurrence would have provided a slight boost to my rapidly deteriorating morale. My request was denied with the explanation that Naval Intelligence was in the process of conversion; that it would soon become a civilian organization with relatively few officer billets. Two strikes and I was out.

I turned to the duties expected of me and qualified quickly as Control Panel Operator. With that experience and the proficiency I acquired, I became primarily responsible for controlling the flooding and pumping of ballast necessary in maintaining list and trim within critical limits while lowering and/or raising the dry-dock.

On all ships and commands it was customary for their Captain and/or Officer in Charge to acknowledge promotions of the men under them to some degree. With smaller commands such as the ARD, the skipper was expected to call the crew together and present new collar devices along with his congratulations to those being promoted. I took exception to the allusion I was being promoted by Big Mike. The real promoter, the one whose signature empowered my appointment to the grade senior chief petty officer, was that of the Chief of Naval Personnel, Vice Admiral Duncan at that time. I did not need nor did I want any recognition by Mike or by anyone like him. Intentionally flaunting my feelings along with my knowledge of the system, on October 16, 1969, I boarded ARD-30 with my new E-8 collar devices proudly in place. As expected, the crew was called together and Mike called each promotee forward to be recognized and congratulated. When it came my turn, Mike took one look at my devices and said, "Oh,

I see you have already promoted yourself." I got a little tight-jawed but maintained my composure with a very distinct and overly polite response – hopefully within hearing distance of the crew: "No, sir, I did not promote myself. I was appointed to my grade by Admiral Duncan, Chief of Naval Personnel." I was pleased as Mike's face flushed a brilliant red.

At some point in time Mike began to see potential in me. That became apparent when he sat down with me and discussed my annual evaluation. I had been graded in the upper 10 percent to 50 percent of those within my pay grade, not all that impressive, but the marks accompanied by his written comments did make a difference. It was nice knowing that he was *pleased* to have me under his command. He could have *preferred not* having me, or he could have *particularly desired* having me. Knowing he was pleased was a gigantic step in the right direction for me. Nonetheless, I did not budge in my desire to serve elsewhere – I never gave up hope.

I learned that there was a billet under CINCPACFLT (Commander In Charge, Pacific Fleet) Flag Administrative Unit, that was to be vacated soon; the billet of Fleet Retention Officer's Assistant/Enlisted Retention. I initiated another request in hopes I might be favorably considered for that billet. My request was similar in nature to the one previously submitted; however, it included further justification. After pointing out the excess number of Chief Machinist's Mates on board, and my assignment as First Division Officer, I made my request a little more personal:

I realize personnel are assigned according to the needs of the Navy, however this is one example of dissatisfaction as well as a waste of talent. It is well known that the Navy needs well trained, reliable, efficient senior petty officers who are continuously motivated toward bettering existing conditions. There can be nothing more discouraging or more demeaning than to be assigned to a position where an individual's potential has little opportunity for exercise. I believe I know my own potential and have every desire to perform according to my capability.

Apparently the OinC was intent on keeping me. His endorsement, not all bad but not favorable either, said among other things:

Essentially, the working hours and the type of work which is now his lot have disillusioned Adkisson whereby since he has no immediate control over these matters, he has become dissatisfied with this shore duty billet and feels that his present assignment is not in keeping with his level of experience. Conceivably, the "position" to which he is requesting assignment will be more in keeping with his personal appraisal of his own capabilities.

Thanks, Boss! Of course I apprised my capabilities and myself highly. I did not *feel* that my assignment was not in keeping with my level of experience; I *knew* it! The working hours and type of work, though undesirable, were peanuts compared to conditions at every command under which I had previously served. So Mike's comments, somewhat derogatory, were not all that far from the truth. My request was denied by the Bureau of Naval Personnel along with a clear reminder that I could terminate my shore duty and return to sea if I wanted to. A like-it-or-lump-it situation.

The chiefs were beginning to show a distinct animosity toward me. One of the reasons, my having been promoted to E-8, while they considered me wet behind the ears as an E-7. I couldn't expect them to think otherwise, since they knew very little of my background; I really had paid my dues. I never felt that I was prematurely promoted even though I knew there were others within my field who were equally or even significantly more talented, more knowledgeable, and probably more deserving. The fact they had difficulty passing the fleetwide examination was the only obstacle they could not overcome. My situation, that of being disliked by the skipper, the crew, and my fellow chiefs, made working conditions uncomfortable at best. This was not shore duty as I had been led to believe it would be. Had I known in advance, I would have tried to postpone my shore duty until I had more of a selection from which to choose.

There was always some good to be derived from the bad. I found the good to be in the newly assigned XO, a truly admirable warrant officer who seemingly always had the crew's best interests in mind while at the same time ensured the overall goals of the ARD were satisfied. The XO had a great sense of humor along with a remarkable knack for pacifying people senior as well as junior to himself. He could normally be counted on to listen first, evaluate second, and take action accordingly – based on reasonable judgment. He was solely responsible for a dramatic change that quickly took place in the attitudes and morale of the crew.

With a Change of Command came an even better world. The new OinC had little going for him other than his officer status. He also had previous enlisted service but he was a lieutenant, a grade below Mike. Our new skipper was perfectly content walking the decks playing Captain while the XO exercised the real command authority. All of us knew that things could only get better.

During my time on board ARD-30 I held various titles, most of them simultaneously. It was difficult keeping up with all that had to be done in order to effectively carry out the responsibilities associated with each title, but I tried very hard to do so. I was, among other things, assigned to the Habitability Board, the Planning Board for Training, the Advisory Board, and the Drug Search and Seizure Team. I became the Control Panel Operator Instructor, I was a member of the Recreation Council, and I was appointed senior member of the Welfare and Recreation Fund Audit Board. As if I didn't have enough to keep me busy, I also volunteered to solicit information for the ship's weekly newspaper, the *Moku Nuhou* (Hawaiian for "Ship's News"); plus I edited, typed and printed the same on an antiquated mimeograph duplicator. Each issue was known as a "Docking," the first issue being the first docking and subsequent issues following in numerical sequence. Somehow I escaped distribution responsibilities. I do not recall ever complaining about my duties; I was not the only one bearing the burden of many titles. I was, however, the one assigned with the most.

Piecing together the *Moku Nuhou* was one of the more enjoyable volunteer functions I had undertaken. I tried to publish something of which the crew would enjoy participating in the making. I used my imagination as best I could and put together something I thought would be useful and entertaining. With my recommendation and the XO's approval I ran simple contests; winners and runners-up were eligible for special liberty or something else meaningful. That encouraged greater participation. The name *Moku Nuhou* was the result of one of those contests. I tried to select special titles for weekly columns that would relate to dry-docking functions or some other aspect of the vessel's nomenclature. The "Stern Gate" was a column provided for confidential input on legitimate gripes as well as for the response from appropriate source(s). "How It Ought To Be" was there for the submission of nonsensical suggestions for inclusion in the UCMJ. There was a "Welcome Aboard" and a "Bon Voyage" column, a "Congratulations" column, and there were columns for general information. One space titled, "The 'Old Man' Sez" was there for the skipper to put in his own special message – and "Khaki Korner" was there for CPO input, individually or collectively. I included current recreational events, general news of interest, and without exception each issue included humor; mainly in the form of jokes. There was also "The Left Foot" column; not intended to ridicule anyone but rather to poke a little fun at accidental or unexpected situations or activities that happened on board. The *Moku Nuhou* included classified ads that were restricted to input by ship's company. There was nothing commercial about the paper; it was strictly an in-house publication. I knew it was successful the first time someone asked me if there were any more copies available – distribution had been depleted.

It had always been my desire to work with the Office of Naval Intelligence, even before I had any real investigative qualifications, but time and again I was dissuaded by one means or another. I never gave up, and in 1970 I submitted my heartfelt request to attend the criminal investigation school in Augusta, Georgia. I also included within that request my desire to remain on so-called shore duty for a one-year extension if my request for the school was denied. The OinC's endorsement to my request endorsement (probably written by the XO) was impressive; it gave me hope:

> Senior Chief Petty Officer ADKISSON reported for duty on ARD-30 July 1969. At that time First Division was lacking a person with his leadership qualifications. Though not enthused with this assignment he stepped in, assumed the responsibility, and proceeded in accomplishing requirements which were previously unknown to him. He displayed initiative in achieving goals which prior to his arrival remained stagnate. He learned his newly acquired tasks rapidly and through his efforts succeeded in establishing a training program for his men thereby ensuring a more efficient Deck Department operation. He maintained his unfaltering and proper attitude of continuously upgrading Deck Department procedures materially and administratively throughout his 10 months tour as First Division Officer.
>
> Senior Chief Petty Officer ADKISSON possesses rare qualities which he continuously exhibits in satisfactorily accomplishing his duties. He has proven his capabilities time and again through conscientious and commendable efforts. He is known

for his attitude of getting the job done rapidly and efficiently, he sets his goals and reaches them.

While attached to ARD-30 Senior Chief Petty Officer ADKISSON has held titles of Career Counselor, Project Transition Advisor, Public Affairs Officer, Benefits & Insurance Adviser, Division Officer, Chief Master-at-Arms, and Senior Enlisted Advisor. He qualified as Control Panel Operator rapidly and proficiently and gained the added responsibility of training and qualifying officers and chief petty officers in proper pumping procedures, a task which requires among other things patience, a thorough understanding of vessel stability, and a thorough knowledge of all major docking evolutions. He has made himself available to personally instruct any crew member desiring to learn the control Panel operation. Through this unselfish attitude and determination he has helped numerous individuals become knowledgeable in pumping operations thereby contributing greatly to the state of readiness ARD-30 has achieved.

Prior to Senior Chief Petty Officer ADKISSON's arrival, ARD-30 had no career counseling program. Through long hours of research and much self training, he successfully established a most effective counseling program. Through personal interviews and proper counseling, he is providing an increased dissemination of information the men need and want, thereby gaining a noticeable respect for the Navy by the men of ARD-30.

Senior Chief Petty Officer ADKISSON had indicated great interest in Officer programs but is no longer qualified due to age limitations. He possesses those qualities which are desirable in Officer candidates and would be highly recommended for acceptance into such a program were there no age limitations.

It would be desirable to maintain Senior Chief Petty Officer ADKISSON on board ARD-30 for a one year extension. There is no doubt ADKISSON possesses the ability to cope with any given situation and is therefore highly recommended for the type assignment he has requested.

My request for the school was denied, however I was granted the one-year extension.

492

In April of 1970 a Chief Boatswain's Mate reported for duty on the ARD. I volunteered to pick him up at the International Airport in Honolulu and assisted him in every way possible in an effort to expedite my release from the deck force and the responsibilities of First Division Officer. May 4, after a reasonable period of break-in time, I was properly relieved and the ARD had a real Chief Bos'n for the first time in quite a while. The problem was that the BMC was anything other than an administrator. He was great at walking the decks and enforcing rules and regulations, but when it came time to do paperwork, he called upon me for assistance. I didn't mind; in fact I enjoyed it. I looked at it as an opportunity to keep abreast of areas to which I might someday, once again of necessity, find myself assigned.

E-9, the highest enlisted grade (other than that of the single individual that holds title to "Master Chief Petty Officer of the Navy") was a goal attained by a mere one-percent of all enlisted personnel. I had my sights set on that goal the moment I was appointed as E-8, Senior Chief. It was, however, always in the back of my mind, how the Personnel Officer at the Submarine Training Facility had threatened me with lousy duty and no hope for future promotions beyond E-7, my rate at that time. I fully believed myself capable of overcoming the obstacles I had created for myself in opting out of the submarine service and being redesignated out of the nuclear program, but that shadow of doubt created by the Personnel Officer's threat still existed. I was pleased when I was advised by my command that I had been recommended for promotion to E-9 but concerned about the interview process that was to take place. I could expect being subjected to an interview by a board of officers similar to the one I had been quite successful with when I was being considered for promotion to E-8. All it would take was for one single member of the board to find fault with me, a single negative opinion, and I could kiss E-9 goodbye.

On February 18, 1971, I sat before the group of three officers who, to a major extent, would decide whether or not I would be selected for E-9. All three were ComServRon (Commander Service Squadron) Five Staff Officers. There was one 0-5 (commander), one 0-4 (lieutenant commander), and one 0-3 (lieutenant). For reasons I could not understand, I was unusually comfortable and profoundly confident. Not cocky confident, but sensibly and rationally confident. Following my interview, I returned to ARD-30 with a sealed envelope that contained the written evaluations of each board member.

XO and I had been friends, and we were capable of setting aside our senior and subordinate positions when it was appropriate to do so. I trusted his judgment and he trusted mine. He knew how anxious I was to find out how I had been evaluated by the board, and he wasted no time in calling me into his stateroom so that I could review the appraisals. First he sat me down and very seriously cautioned me that I should not get my hopes up. He, in an effort to prepare me for the worst, went on to tell me that he was a little disappointed in the board's comments, but that they would have to stand as written. I felt my hopes dwindling as I looked at the appraisal sheets XO was holding; I was no longer interested in hearing what he had to say. Very slowly, ostensibly in anticipation of disappointing me, I was handed the appraisals. Much to my surprise, after having been intentionally misled into preparing for the worst, I had been highly graded along with the following comments:

First:
Chief ADKISSON was most impressive during his interview displaying the characteristics of enthusiasm for change and humanitarian concern now of timely interest in the Navy. He had an aura of competence extending from propulsion and machinery technology through concepts of leadership. This was reinforced by his varied background. He can speak and communicate well. Young and clean-cut in appearance, well motivated in attitude, he appears to have considerable potential for future contributions. Recommended for promotion.

Second:
Senior Chief ADKISSON is a well spoken, well versed Navyman. He is able to express himself in a most intelligent manner. Knowledge, conviction and forthrightness are attributes which were apparent during the interview. Chief ADKISSON is considered qualified for advancement to MMCM.

And last:
Chief ADKISSON was very impressive, presented a physically-fit appearance, exhibited an outstanding military appearance. He fielded all questions intelligently on various topics. Candidate appeared very favorably impressed with recent changes by CNO. He exudes the young-thinking type of leader-

494

ship that is required in the changing modern Navy. An outstanding candidate for E-9.

But the XO managed to outdo those evaluations when he wrote the ARD Command's recommendation:

Senior Chief Petty Officer ADKISSON is one of the most intelligent and well versed enlisted men in the Navy. His range of knowledge and practical experience is broad and deep. He thrives on administrative duties and is extremely articulate and persuasive in his presentation either with pen or word of mouth. He is very dignified in appearance and takes meticulous care of himself and his wardrobe. He is truly concerned with the welfare of the men in the command and has been an invaluable asset as career counselor and public affairs officer. A completely well rounded and competent E-8 and in all respects is qualified, capable and recommended for E-9.

The three appraisals as written by total strangers, after having spent no more than thirty minutes with me, gave me a special feeling of pride. First impressions really did tend to have lasting effects. XO's comments on behalf of the command to which I was attached were about as meaningful to me as they could possibly be. He assured me that he had pulled no punches, that my work there had been recognized, and that his recommendation contained a truthful evaluation, nothing more, nothing less, and he wished me good luck! I shook his hand with a grip of friendship but also one of appreciation.

Acey-Deucey, a game requiring a pair of dice and similar to backgammon, was a simple game most sailors understood and enjoyed. It was a game I had only a passing interest in because I had never learned how to play! Thinking back, I recall how dumb I felt knowing that everyone around me seemed to understand what I found by observation to be the most confusing game I had ever witnessed. A roll of the dice and confusing moves with checker-type chips were made without hesitation, moves that were never duplicated even though the same numbers showed up on the dice! I was embarrassed by my ignorance of the game. Having been recommended to the highest enlisted pay grade made me that much more uncomfortable – so

I finally gained enough courage to tell another chief. The Chief Bos'n, the one that had relieved me of deck force duties quickly volunteered to teach me the game. It did not take long, not more than a few minutes, before I had gained a good understanding of that very old seafaring game. I was surprised to learn of its simplicity; that anyone capable of counting to twelve was sufficiently educated to play. I found it to be exactly as it had first been described to me: "a simple game of dice played by sailors."

The Chief Bos'n was the most inquisitive and opinionated person I had ever known. Everyone is curious to one degree or another and we all have our own opinions, but the Bos'n wanted more immediate answers to anything and everything that was going on. He was never reluctant to provide his own suggestions, whether or not they were remotely relevant. The XO could expect a bright and early visit every morning at his stateroom by the Bos'n – coffee in hand. The interrogation began immediately, XO providing the Bos'n with answers to similar questions day after day, most of which related to what was in store for that particular day or what events had occurred that might cause changes in the planned routine. The XO then listened patiently as the Chief Bos'n provided his own speculation and estimation on everything in general. The Bos'n probably deserved applause for his efforts to remain knowledgeable of everything going on, but instead his incessant questioning and opinionated assessments began to gnaw at those of us being approached, the XO in particular. Exercising due restraint along with his sense of humor, the XO initiated some phony "official orders," thereby appointing the Bos'n with unique responsibilities. The obvious purpose of the orders was to poke fun by directing the chief to do more than the impossible, yet always in line with precisely that which he had been doing all along. The orders were written with imagination:

From: Officer in Charge, ARD-30
To: Chief Bos'n

Subj: ARD-30, integrated work load scheduler and job sequence and priority planner; appointment as

Ref: (a) ARD-30 Data Book
(b) BUPEWRS Report 1080-14
(c) ARD-30 Instructions
(d) NAVSHIPS Technical Manual

(e) Consolidated Shipboard Allowance List

(f) CINCPACFLT 5100.1 (Series)

1. Effective this date, you are hereby appointed ARD-30 Integrated work load scheduler, and job sequence and priority planner.
2. In order to properly prepare yourself for this very demanding position, it is mandatory that you become thoroughly familiar with the contents of references (a) through (f).
3. For planning purposes you will have at your disposal the manpower, reference (b), to be used in conjunction with equipment available, references (a) and (e), except as modified by reference (c), and various publications and notices. All work scheduled will be completed in strict adherence in accordance with the applicable portions of references (d) and (f).
4. On the day following receipt of scheduled docking confirmation you will submit a tentative schedule, that will allow for the timely completion of all work, both known and unknown, to be accomplished, by persons known and unknown, to the docking officer.
5. This in addition to such other duties as may have been assigned you and terminates upon your detachment from this command, or by other official notification.

[signed]

The orders had little impact, and the Bos'n maintained his own way of doing things. He and I seemed to get along quite well, and we quickly became good friends. Unfortunately, that friendship was damaged as a result of a series of personal matters; family problems that were not military-related. Eventually the friendship was totally destroyed by unnecessary and strongly opinionated inferences that were based solely on hearsay, openly discussed by ARD-30's chiefs and officers – none of whom had actually been witness to the root of the problem(s); problems that should never have been subject to their scrutiny. The only reason I include this paragraph is to point out how personal situations, totally unrelated to military duties, can have a direct impact on the working relationships between shipmates.

The XO enjoyed rewarding the crew when they were known to have exceeded that which was normally expected of them. It was not uncommon to have the men work around the clock in shifts, in order to accomplish necessary work and repairs expeditiously. ARD's goal was always the same: to get all docked vessels back out to the fleet, where they could meet their commitments, without unnecessary delay. When shift work was not necessary, but the men worked well beyond liberty hours and into the night, they could nearly depend on the XO showing up with a couple of cases of cold beer and soda. It definitely made a difference, the understanding and fair shakes the men were given by the XO, as opposed to the Big Mike treatment of "quit your complaining and get back to work." ARD-30's XO could count on the 100-percent backing of the entire crew; he never for a moment forgot what it was to be enlisted or how it felt being treated as something inferior or unworthy of praise.

Eligibility requirements for officer programs changed periodically, and in August of 1971 I was advised of my own eligibility. Since I had already been notified of my selection for promotion to master chief, E-9, I was not enthusiastic about applying for the Warrant Officer Program. After all, I knew that I would soon be at the highest level of the enlisted scale and that acceptance as a warrant officer would place me at the very bottom of the officer scale. My preference was to be at the top of any scale rather than at the bottom of another. But the XO was persistent and he convinced me that all officers were better off than enlisted men, regardless of pay grade. Hence he persuaded me to participate in the program even though I disagreed with his assessment. I fully believed it when I told the XO that if I were selected for promotion to warrant officer status I would most likely turn it down,

Typical Beer Ball Game

498

that I preferred to remain at the top of the enlisted structure for the remainder of my military career.

Subsequently I was interviewed by a panel of two officers, one commander and one lieutenant commander. As a result of the interview, the commander described me as

"enthusiastic," "sincere," "clean-cut," "concerned," "with a smart appearance," and "lucid." He summarized his evaluation of me as follows:

> Chief ADKISSON created a positive impression as a high quality and well-motivated Warrant Officer candidate. He conveyed an attitude of enthusiasm. Pleasant and clear-spoken, he appeared to have a natural bent for working through stimulating motivation of others rather than through the application of personal technical knowledge and efforts. His diverse background, vigor, leadership, personality and team characteristics would support capabilities to carry forth on Warrant Officer assignments. Forthright, direct and honest, he displayed fine ability to communicate. Young, fit, well-groomed, his appearance was very creditable. Recommend for advancement to Warrant Officer.

The lieutenant commander described me as "clean-cut," "forthright," "relaxed," "mature," "impressive," and "sincere." He summarized his evaluation of me in the following manner:

> MMCS ADKISSON impressed this interviewer as one who is well qualified in his professional field. He conveyed an ability to approach technical problems with confidence and skill. He appears to have an understanding of personal problems in today's Navy and displays competence in relating well both to subordinates and superiors. Highly recommended for the Warrant Officer Program.

Hard-Working ARD-30 Sailors at Rest

My own command's endorsement read in part:

Forwarded, highly recommended for approval. The applicant is eligible in all respects.

Senior Chief Petty Officer ADKISSON is a truly competent engineer and administrator. His ability to control his resources, whether men or material, is extremely effective. His ability as an administrator is far beyond that normally found in the enlisted ranks of today's Navy. His performance as 1st Division Officer, Chief Master-at-Arms, Career Counselor, Public Affairs Officer, 2nd Division Officer and Assistant Engineer Officer at this command have all been handled, not only effectively, but with imagination and an obvious desire to do the job better. His supervisory abilities are well demonstrated on a daily basis and he is always eager to accept further responsibilities. He is the man the crew looks to for guidance and assistance in matters of concern to them, either professionally or personal. Whether it be information on a simple request or how to get the most from a reenlistment, the crew know Chief ADKISSON is the man with the answers.

Senior Chief ADKISSON would be a "Natural" as a Warrant Officer. He is looked up to and respected as a senior enlisted man and would continue to hold this position of respect and leadership as a Warrant Officer. His knowledge and use of the English language make his addition to any conversation or discussion welcome and informative. He is a warm, friendly person and will be a welcome addition to any wardroom in the United States Navy.

Senior Chief ADKISSON's academic ability has been proven by the consistently high marks he has obtained in the many Navy schools he has attended and correspondence courses he has completed. A further attestment to his knowledge and intellect is his being selected for E-9 on his first try at advancement to that level.

Senior Chief ADKISSON's attitude toward the Navy is one of a person who belongs and feels the career he has selected for himself is correct and he constantly displays this attitude by being able to adjust and accept our changing Navy. He is highly motivated and is constantly trying to get ahead and do more than the next man. His motivation is a constant inspiration for the men who come in contact with him and infects them with the desire to do a little better and go a little further than they would have without his inspiration.

All in all Senior Chief ADKISSON is a well rounded Navy man with a self composure that is rare in all respects, and an ideal individual for promotion to Warrant Officer.

I was beginning to feel like I walked on water. Unfortunately, between the time of those positive recommendations, and the time the selection process was completed – I managed to step on some well-deserving but nonetheless influential toes. I would have no way of proving my suspicions, but simple reasoning makes it understandable how it would have taken some doing to undo the exceptionally favorable endorsements that accompanied my warrant officer application. Consequently, I was not selected for the program. Strangely, I was happy not having to deal with the decision of acceptance or refusal. I remained totally satisfied with my undocumented as well as my documented accomplishments to date; my goals remained unchanged and I simply "pressed on."

In early September, 1971, the XO and I were issued joint NO COST TAD (Temporary Additional Duty) orders to report to Commanding Officer, Ship Repair Facility, Subic Bay, Republic of the Philippines, for an estimated period of about three weeks "in connection with dockings." NO COST made it possible for us, it gave us the authority, to fly "space available" on either a commercial or government hop that would land us in the Philippines. Having orders also qualified us to enter the country at either a civilian airport or at a military installation. We checked out from ARD-30 on September 3, and within a couple of hours we were airborne on a commercial aircraft that took us directly to Clark Air Base, Philippines. We were lucky again, and without delay we boarded US Air Force ground transportation that took us the remaining sixty or so miles to Subic Bay. We reported for duty at the Repair Facility on September 4 and immediately began the chore of observing, documenting and taking pictures of the mechanics and inner workings of the floating drydocks that were stationed there. There was absolutely nothing difficult about our assignment, and we added nothing to it that might make it so. Daily, by early afternoon and sometimes well into the night, we were usually on the strip enjoying the local entertainment. The XO and I rented adjoining houses off-base, not far from the main gate.

My first liberty priority was to visit with the Hernandez family. I was thrilled to learn that there had been another addition to the family. Their two-year-old baby girl had been born on June 5, 1969, and both Aurora and 'Nando were ecstatic in that they could finally boast of their success in having a daughter – particularly after having produced three healthy sons. Lea was precious and I was immediately drawn to her as if she were my own child. By self-proclamation I became her godfather. I visited with the Hernandez family frequently during my off-duty time, and 'Nando accompanied me to whichever cockfight arena was open, where my bets were frequently in favor of the winning rooster.

I learned that Rick, my Vietnam buddy and fellow chief, had married a Filipina and had established a monkeypod furniture store on the outskirts of Olongapo. Monkeypod is an excellent-quality dark hardwood with a beautiful grain. The tree grows best where the climate is tropical. It did not take me long to find his place, and I was truly surprised at what he and his wife,

502

Ludy, had accomplished. In addition to their furniture business they also had a bar – hostesses and all. Rick and I celebrated over a few beers as we reminisced. He asked about his old pocketwatch, and I promised that someday I would return it to him – gratis. He called me a "son-of-a-bitchin' liar," and we left it at that. In my heart it was my intention to keep my promise and return the watch on my next trip to the Philippines.

Disaster, to my way of thinking, struck (in more ways than one) on September 17, permanently disrupting my TAD status as well as my daily diversion toward entertainment. While crossing Raymundo Street on the base at Subic Naval Station, walking within the limits of the clearly marked crosswalks, I was struck by a Blaylock taxi. Two sailors waving the 'V' sign with their fingers had captured the taxi driver's attention at a critical moment. While the driver was returning the sign, he was also picking up speed. I was a bit slower than the other pedestrians crossing the street, and even though I could hear the approaching vehicle I did not look up. Estimated speed at impact was twenty miles per hour. The vehicle struck me on my right hand, right hip, and left calf, and I was knocked over the hood and right fender into the windshield; landing on the pavement on my right shoulder and right temple. The folded umbrella I was carrying in my right hand was badly bent and the pointed end had been driven into the muscle mass of my left posterior. Impact by the vehicle's bumper caused a significant hematoma of the muscle mass of my left calf, the most noticeable and painful of my injuries. There were numerous other abrasions and contusions to various parts of my body but most were insignificant and caused very little permanent damage. I was taken for emergency consultation, to Naval Hospital, Cubi Point, where all of my injuries were evaluated and treated. Since I was in extreme pain, unable to walk unassisted, and the expected period of disability was diagnosed at about four weeks, there was nothing more I could accomplish in the Philippines. My nightlife activities came to an abrupt halt! As soon as I was capable of getting around with the aid of a cane, the XO began making arrangements for both of us to return to Hawaii. On September 22nd we were back on board ARD-30, where in addition to carrying out my normal duties, I initiated a claim for damages against Blaylock Transportation Service.

There were three distinct times during my military service when I felt particularly proud. First, my promotion to E-4, petty officer status, when for the first time I received a significant official document bearing the seal of the Department of the Navy. The wording meant a great deal to me, and I posted it on the inside of my locker door where it would serve as a constant reminder that I had become a little more responsible. It read:

> To all who shall see these presents, greeting: Know Ye that reposing special trust and confidence in the fidelity and abilities of PAUL L. ADKISSON, I do appoint him MACHINIST'S MATE THIRD CLASS in the United States Navy to rank as such from the sixteenth day of April, nineteen hundred and fifty-six.
>
> This appointee will therefore carefully and diligently discharge the duties of the grade to which appointed by doing and performing all manner of things there-unto pertaining. And I do strictly charge and require all personnel of lesser grade to render obedience to appropriate orders. And this appointee is to observe and follow such orders and directions as may be given from time to time by Superiors acting according to the rules and articles governing the discipline of the Armed Forces of the United States of America.

Second, my promotion to E-7, chief petty officer, was perhaps the most significant because with that promotion came a change in uniform along with a sense of belonging to an elite group known throughout the Navy as Chiefs. Once again I was presented with a certificate bearing the seal of the U.S. Navy, but the "Permanent Appointment" was worded slightly different:

> To all who shall see these presents, greeting: Know Ye, that reposing special trust and confidence in the patriotism, valor, fidelity and abilities of PAUL L. ADKISSON I do hereby appoint you a Permanent CHIEF MACHINIST'S MATE (SS) in the United States Navy to rank as such from the 16th day of March, nineteen hundred and sixty-six.
>
> Your appointment carries with it the obligation that you exercise additional authority and willingly accept greater responsibility. Your every action must be governed by a strong sense of personal moral and responsibility and leadership. You will observe and follow such orders as may be given by superiors acting according to the rules, articles and provisions of the United

States Navy Regulations, General Orders, Uniform Code of Military Justice, and supporting orders and directives.

Reaching the top in any field or endeavor must be particularly exhilarating to anyone fortunate enough to have experienced such. I achieved that goal which at one time I thought to be impossible, partly because so few individuals ever got there, but also because it had been clearly implanted in my mind when I abandoned submarine service that I would never be promoted again. But I did manage to join that one-percent truly elite group at the very top of the enlisted ranks on October 1st, 1971, when I received my final appointment, promotion to the grade E-9, Master Chief Machinist's Mate, that third distinct time when I felt exceptional pride. Saying I was proud just doesn't do justice to my true feelings.

The OinC called the crew to the foc'sle and made two presentations. The first was in recognition of one man for his first promotion to petty officer status. His comments were a little out of character but appropriate to the occasion as he addressed the crew:

"This is a unique occasion because we are able to honor two men at opposite ends of the promotion spectrum. One for having stepped onto the bottom rung of the ladder as he accepts added responsibilities expected and demanded of the petty officer grade he now holds, and one for having reached the apex of that ladder. Perhaps [name of PO3], as you take this first step, you might establish as your goal that which Master Chief Adkisson has proven to be within the reach of those who are willing to strive for that extraordinary and conclusive pinnacle of achievement."

Being a master chief also had its problems – some preventable, others difficult to escape. There were, and probably always will be, those E-7s and E-8s, as well as E-9s, who preferred not to distinguish one grade of chief from another. I believed otherwise as I insisted that in accordance with military etiquette, everyone, whether officer or enlisted, would address E-7s and above by their correct titles, not all-inclusively as "Chief." E-7s were to be addressed as "Chief," E-8s were to be addressed as "Senior Chief," and E-9s were to be addressed as "Master Chief." Their correct titles were always to be used when they were in public. Within the CPO quarters, between chiefs, titles were no longer of concern and I encouraged the use of first names, last names, and nicknames. As the senior (in grade) chief, whether it was desirable or not, the grade in itself made me responsible for maintaining discipline within the chiefs' quarters. Not that chiefs were incapable of good discipline or of solving their problems without intervention; they usually were. Only on very rare occasion was a voice of greater authority considered necessary in putting things back into proper perspective. As I was only thirty-three, quite young as a master chief and younger than a significant percentage of lower-graded chiefs, it took the combination of strength, courage, skill, and persuasion when it became necessary for me to use my pay grade as leverage in laying down the law. I took my job seriously and like it or not, all enlisted personnel, chiefs junior to me included, had to accept the fact that the devices I wore demanded recognition and respect, whether or not they particularly liked the person wearing them. I was the Master Chief of the Command (AKA Command Master Chief) and as the senior enlisted member on board I had added responsibilities beyond those demanded by my rating. In that capacity I exercised my authority to the best of my ability. At first, I did not fit the shoes of a master chief and I had to feel my way, almost by trial and error, a method to which I didn't profess and one that did not earn me many "points." I had only served with one master chief during my entire career, and therefore I had no role model to emulate. I relied heavily on my own experience in passing judgment and in making decisions; spontaneity was sometimes required for lack of time to adequately calculate the probable outcome. Primarily it was the favorable results of those spontaneous decisions that reinforced and intensified the self-confidence I needed to nourish and sustain my drive. There can be no doubt as to how much I enjoyed the duties and responsibilities of all that came with seniority. Regardless of the confidence I developed, I was never above calling upon one or more of the other CPOs for their opinions and advice. When I needed such assistance I usually called a meeting where, as a group, we could brainstorm ideas and better evaluate the differences of opinion that inevitably surfaced. There were rare occasions, when for reasons that seemed appropriate, it became necessary to meet one on one without regard to rank or rate, in absolute privacy when and where we could express our honest opinions and occasionally vent our frustrations to the point of a physical altercation with neither party having to lose face or suffer a penalty as the result. I was firmly opposed to the concept of winners or losers inside or outside the CPO quarters. I did whatever I believed necessary and in the best interests of the service as

506

well as that of the group as a whole, even if my action or decision did not necessarily guarantee satisfaction to the majority. If I had always allowed the majority to rule, military discipline and Navy regulations would have rapidly become meaningless, difficult if not impossible to enforce. As Command Master Chief I bent the rules on occasion, but never in a direction that would or could have been harmful or dangerous to man, vessel, or the environment. I have already elaborated on some intentional variations of interpretation that "allowed" for slackening of the rules when it was deemed appropriate or necessary for reasons considered valid at the time.

Master Chief Adkisson

I continued submitting requests to the Bureau of Naval Personnel in hopes that eventually my desire to serve within any investigative department, agency, or element of the Navy would be authorized. I volunteered for a third tour in Vietnam with the Office of the Command Judge Advocate, DaNang, only to be advised that the DaNang office was being scaled down and would probably close in the near future. My request was forwarded to the Staff Judge Advocate in Saigon for consideration; again turned down but with a very small degree of hope. The commander who responded to my request included one paragraph with which I was particularly pleased:

Were I to be one of the two officers assigned to the Navy's legal office in July 1972 I would be delighted to have a man with your experience and qualifications. In fact, you would probably run the claims section if one was to be maintained. My guess, and that is all it is at this time, is that the Army will take over the area claims settlement authority needs as they have in the DaNang area.

Because of my Machinist's Mate rating, I was not only prevented from serving more than a single tour of shore duty; the tour I had been selected for on board ARD-30 was only a two-year stint instead of the usual and expected three years authorized at most shore duty billets. At first I was very pleased with the one-year extension, but well before that year neared an end I grew tired of the monotony of ARD services and eagerly looked forward to another assignment, *any* other assignment!

I continued my pursuit for consideration and requested a change of rating to that of Master at Arms. All such requests were denied, and I remained a Machinist's Mate, doing a Machinist's Mate job, for the rest of my military career. The disapproval of those requests was the determining factor in my decision not to remain on active duty beyond the twenty-year point. Had any of my requests for transfer into some type of investigative field been acted favorably upon, I would have put in a full thirty years – probably more.

I made it a point to maintain contact with my "Detailer" at the Bureau of Naval Personnel, the MMCM who was responsible for "detailing" or assigning Master Chief Machinist's Mates to sea and shore billets. It was his job to satisfy personal requests wherever the needs of the Navy and personal desires were in line with one another. Since only 1 percent of the entire Navy enlisted population was comprised of master chiefs and just a fraction of that percentage were Machinist's Mates, billets to select from dwindled proportionately. My desire to remain home-ported in Hawaii made the availability of MM billets even more remote. My Detailer, armed with the knowledge that there was a billet available, tried to convince me that "oiler" duty was not all that bad, and that he would work with me if I would verbally acknowledge acceptance of such an assignment. He identified the Pearl Harbor-based oiler USS *Chipola* (AO-63) and he urged me to check it out.

My first impressions of the *Chipola* were mixed. I had many opportunities to observe oilers and I knew that their responsibilities to the fleet could only be satisfied at sea. An oiler's primary purpose was to refuel ships at sea. They were known for the minimum turn-around time they spent in port, usually just long enough to refuel their holding tanks and immediately return to sea, where their commitment(s) to the fleet would be satisfied. Oiler crews were invariably a motley-looking bunch, and I knew that their engineering spaces were hot, unsightly, and difficult to maintain. Slick, a knowledgeable and personable Chief Machinist's Mate stationed on the *Chipola*, convinced me that oiler duty was "the only way to fly" and that I should look no further for my next home. I was convinced by Slick's influence and wasted no time in giving my Detailer the go-ahead. Quite unexpectedly I became enthusiastic about accepting a challenge of another kind, once again something new and unfamiliar to me, as I had high hopes of returning to sea on board the USS *Chipola*.

May 23, 1972 I was temporarily transferred from ARD-30 under TAD orders directing that I report to "ComServRon FIVE as Assistance to Maintenance Officer" and return to ARD-30 on June 30; accurately calculated to coincide with my permanent transfer date. The reason for my TAD assignment was based on the XO's opinion that I should be removed from the continuing family-related controversy to which he unwittingly became a party. What began as wardroom gossip between chiefs and officers had leaked to and was believed by the crew as common knowledge. Unfortunately it was an inaccurate and deplorable assessment of my family life. It was no longer true that I was having family problems, in fact my home life could not have been better. Nevertheless, it was the XO's opinion that not only were my off-duty activities affecting my military duties, but that the gossip circulating was also having a negative effect on the crew. In his opinion I was the cause of a growing cancer – and I had to be removed. In my opinion, *he* was the major contributing cause – but my opinion didn't matter.

The five weeks I was attached to ComServRon Five I proved beyond any possible doubt that I was capable of accepting menial orders far inferior to anything remotely in line with acceptable expectations or capabilities of any master chief. I could easily have challenged the orders had I taken the matter to higher authority; however, I made the decision to use a little imagination and make the task at hand enjoyable; to laugh off the humiliation. My job, a job that should have been assigned to someone fresh out of boot camp, certainly not to anyone having advanced above the pay grade E-4, was to conduct an inventory of junk that had been accumulating inside a huge warehouse since "the beginning of time," something of a hiding place for literally thousands of items, most of which should have been turned in to Salvage or discarded long before. There was very little of significant value or of current use stored there. The warehouse was filthy and everything inside was covered with a thick layer of dust, a strong indication of just how important everything stored there was. I had a forklift, a clipboard, and several pads of lined paper at my disposal, nothing more.

After the initial shock of what I was faced with diminished, I convinced myself that I would not allow anyone, certainly not those who had been responsible for putting me in such a position, to dissuade me into thinking I was anything less worthy of the grade to which I had been appointed. Instead, I looked upon those responsible for my assignment as having displayed exceptionally poor leadership, appreciable lack of integrity, and questionable moral turpitude. I had seen men convicted of court-martial offenses that had been treated with more respect than that to which I then found myself intentionally subjected. But I did the job and I did it well, wondering all the while whether ARD-30s XO would have transferred me there had he known what duties were in store for me. Not only did I conduct a thorough inventory; I rearranged everything in a reasonable semblance of order. And when I was through, the warehouse was clean to boot! I doubt seriously that anyone truly expected me to carry out the unappealing orders, but I came out the better man having done so without complaining. The experience I gained as a result of such mistreatment remained with me throughout my military career, and whenever I saw any act of intentional humiliation, whether initiated by someone senior or subordinate to me, I was never reluctant to step in and question the purpose.

Apparently, whatever actual or perceived problems I had at one time been accused of were overlooked when I returned to ARD-30 for my final evaluation along with my PCS orders. I was pleased to read, "Overall; Chief ADKISSON's potential and ability to function as a Navy man are boundless." However some time later, after rereading those words, I began to see what I first thought to be a flattering statement as one containing an unflattering innuendo; that my potential and ability to function was limited to that of a Navy man. Was I considered incapable of functioning effectively as a civilian?

On June 30, 1972, with properly endorsed orders in hand, I departed ARD-30 for the last time, anxious to locate and report to my new duty station, the USS *Chipola*. I knew the ship was somewhere in the Far East and I had hopes that I might catch up with it in the Philippines.

15

USS CHIPOLA

I departed Hawaii from Hickum Air Force Base on a military hop that began on August 8, 1972 and ended on August 9, with one brief refueling stop at Anderson Air Base, Guam, before reaching Clark Air Base, Philippines. Another hop took me to Cubi Point. Ground transportation was provided on to Subic Bay where the Chipola was scheduled to dock within two weeks. It had always been my preference to live off-base whenever possible, so after coordinating with the Billeting Office I made my way to the nearest Marmont Hotel, a little over a mile from the base.

At one time there had been four Marmont Hotels in or near Olongapo City; subsequently numbered "Marmont Number One," "Marmont Number Two," and so on. The Marmont Resort Hotel, the largest and without question the most luxurious of the four, was located several miles from the base, a couple of miles beyond the Hernandez home. Besides the inconvenience of travel time, it was too expensive to remain there for more than a day or so. It was known as "the Home of Filipino Hospitality," and its distinctive features included individually designed rooms built to fit the personalities and moods of guests. At ground-level there was a beautiful swimming pool. The backdrop of the hotel provided several stairways that led up the mountainside through beautiful botanical gardens where the "Honeymoon Suite" nestled in perfectly; an impressive two-story unit that overlooked the gardens and grounds below. I enjoyed staying there on occasion, whenever I wanted to get well away from it all and enjoy the absolute peace and quiet it provided. It was also the place where officers and senior enlisted men would most likely take their Filipina girlfriends; a place where their privacy was well assured.

Since the *Chipola* was not in port, I wasted no time in contacting the Assistant Staff Judge Advocate, Claims Adjudicating Officer, at Subic Bay Naval Base for the purpose of obtaining legal advice on how I might best pursue my claim for damages against Blaylock Transportation Service. After he reviewed all related correspondence, he suggested that I allow myself to be placed on "IH," International Hold, until an acceptable resolution could be effected, a situation that did not always work in the best interests of American GIs. Philippine law was not only corrupt; it frequently varied widely from American law. American GIs were easily convicted of slander even though they never said the things of which they were accused. The Filipino attorneys and the judges knew that finding American service members guilty would provide everyone on their side with large amounts of money. While we were in their country, whether we were represented or not, we could usually count on being convicted. My situation was a bit reversed; contrary to the reasons most military members found themselves on IH. Whenever allegations of wrongdoing were levied against a GI, it was common for Philippine law to require the U.S. government (the military service) to guarantee that the accused would remain in the country until the problem was resolved to the satisfaction of the Philippine court system. That meant being placed on IH, thereby guaranteeing the Philippine legal authorities that the accused would not leave the country. There were cases that remained unresolved for years, a terrible inconvenience for the accused. Some individuals had to remain in the country well beyond their enlistment – at their own expense – unless they elected to reenlist, which some did because of financial necessity. It was not a fair system, in the eyes of those familiar with the U.S. legal system, but it was the Philippine system and it worked well in their favor. It was the opinion of many, including me, that as usual our government allowed its servicemen to be screwed by foreign governments, a system whereby the most powerful nation on earth kissed the ass of the weakest! There was an alternative to being placed on IH, but not too many individuals found it acceptable: buying one's way out of trouble. A certain amount of corruption exists within any government, but it was rampant and totally acceptable at all levels of Philippine government. Enough money could buy *anything*. A cash settlement, usually an exorbitant sum, was always acceptable to the accuser and his or her attorney. In my case, I knew that I would be taking a chance, because Filipino lawyers had a way of manipulating the law in their favor and I could very

513

easily have found myself being sued for an imaginary violation of law. The accusation alone would have been sufficient reason to reverse the IH from a voluntary status, a suit levied against them by me, to an involuntary status, whereby I would become the defendant instead of the accuser. In that event, I might have been on permanent shore duty for the rest of my military career, something many sailors would have willingly accepted regardless of the crime of which they were suspected or of which they had been accused. I just wanted a fair shake. I preferred to remain free of any kind of hold and pursue the matter through the Naval Command and Blaylock and/or its insurance carrier.

The JAG did all he could do, which was not all that much, but he did manage to have me remain attached to the Naval Base until September 3rd while I made every effort to perfect my claim.

I boarded the *Chipola* when she entered port and advised the skipper of the reasons behind my delay in reporting for duty. He was not happy about it, but knowing it would only be a two-week delay, he wished me a successful culmination of my claim.

During the pursuit of that claim I wrote several letters to officers and other individuals who were in positions to assist me, and I obtained legal advice from military as well as civilian attorneys. I spoke with Mr. Jacobo B. Abrajano (manager of Blaylock Transportation Service) but was invariably intercepted or warded off whenever I tried to contact Mrs. Blaylock (owner of Blaylock Taxi Company). The procedure I had to follow in order to process a valid claim required, among other things, that I obtain police reports, medical records, statements by witnesses and by the attending physician, and a statement by the OOD on duty the day of the accident. I received written assurance from Mr. Abrajano that my claim had been received, it had been processed, and that I should make myself available to the Blaylock downtown office for final adjudication/payment. I followed the advice right down the line only to be told by the Blaylock representative at the downtown Olongapo office that he knew nothing about me or about my claim! So typical of Philippine underhanded manipulative tactics.

I pursued that claim for over a year after I reported for duty on board USS *Chipola*, up until the time I learned that Blaylock's contract had been canceled. They had been barred from the base *for failure to process or pay claims*. At that time I had no alternative other than to write the whole thing off as a bad experience. I knew it was not fair, particularly without backing by the U.S. government. Our government allowed, and probably still does, host countries far too much control over our military personnel – especially knowing that we are usually there to protect their collective butts.

I visited with Rick and Ludy several times during my two-week claim pursuit. They had closed their bar and had enlarged their monkeypod furniture factory since my previous visit. Their factory, *Monkeypod Infanta*, was named after the place where they had established their residence: Infanta, Pangasinan, quite some distance away. The furniture Rick manufactured was all special-order. Nothing was mass-produced; everything was built by hand to absolute perfection – the result of Rick's strict quality control program. Monkeypod Infanta had become a name easily recognized by base personnel, and Rick always had an abundance of orders. His furniture, while made in the Philippines, was manufactured to American high standards. Rick could be depended on to provide his clientele with the very best quality – at a reasonable price. I was proud, even a bit jealous, of what Rick had accomplished and found myself wishing that I could be a part of his success. Rick was equally jealous of my E-9 pay-grade. He always thought of me as the guy he taught how to be a chief; not as someone who had been promoted two grades higher than he.

I had forgotten to pack Rick's old pocketwatch with my things when I left Hawaii, so Rick once again accused me of being a liar. He *knew* that he would never see his watch again. I assured him that he would.

September 3, 1972, I reported aboard the *Chipola* for duty and was immediately assigned primary responsibilities as Master Chief in Charge of the Main and Auxiliary Engine Rooms, Senior Enlisted Adviser, and Master Chief of the Command.

USS *Chipola* (AO-63) was a full-service fleet oiler with a length of 553 feet, a beam of 75 feet, and a maximum effective speed of eighteen knots. She was named after a river flowing through Georgia and Florida and had a long career since her launching at Sparrows Point, Maryland, on October 21, 1944. She was commissioned on November 30, 1944, and saw her share of action in the Pacific Theater of World War II. The *Chipola* received three battle stars for her refueling of combat operations against Japan and was on hand for that historic moment when the instrument of surrender ending WW II was signed aboard the USS *Missouri* in Tokyo Bay.

The *Chipola* served with the Seventh Fleet during the Korean War, where she earned the Korean Service Medal and the UN Service Medal.

There were two brief periods of time between August 1955 and September 1960 during which the *Chipola* was mothballed, in an out-of-commission status, but for the most part she served as a commissioned MSTS tanker. The *Chipola* also completed numerous Western Pacific cruises, during which she was awarded many medals and commendations as a result of her support to the Seventh Fleet off Vietnam.

Chipola's mission as a fleet oiler was to deliver fuel to ships underway at sea. In this task, her support multiplied the combat capabilities of the fleet. For example, if the Navy did not have fleet oilers and ammunition ships, about three times as many aircraft carriers, cruisers, and destroyers would have been required to maintain the level of combat action in the Tongkin Gulf as was actually used. This was because men-of-war would have had to return to port to replenish fuel and munitions about once a week. This would have been a waste of time in transit to and from port, severely limiting the amount of time each ship could have spent on station. Thus it can be seen that the *Chipola*'s real role was to multiply the combat capacity of the fleet.

USS *Chipola* (AO-63) — Full Service Fleet Oiler — September 1972 to August 1973

In addition to supplying ship and aircraft with fuel at sea, the *Chipola* performed several less obvious services for the fleet. While transferring

516

fuel to her customers, the *Chipola* also supplied fresh produce, repair parts, pressurized gases, movies, and mail. She transported personnel, medical care, duty station changes, and leave for men of the fleet. In that way, the *Chipola* not only served material needs, but also enhanced the morale of fleet customers.

In her efforts to maximize fleet effectiveness through imaginative and responsive support, the *Chipola* performed many unusual tasks, including such unorthodox services as carrying a large gunnery target sled on deck that could be towed in order to offer surface gunnery practice opportunities to combatant ships before or after refueling them.

I wasted no time in calling a meeting of all CPOs for the purpose of introducing myself. The meeting went well as I let it be known that I had but two demands as far as my position of seniority among them was concerned. I made it very clear that I would be addressed by my correct title, Master Chief, at all times *outside* the quarters whenever I was in the company of or within hearing distance of an officer or crew member; otherwise they could call me by whatever name they chose. I let them know that I preferred a more relaxed form of military courtesy; that I elected *not* to have a seating arrangement within the mess during meals as required by chiefs' quarters regulations, but I did expect the courtesy of always having my own seat during meals. I also assured them that my seat was not to be considered reserved during any time other than during meals and that in the event I failed to be there on time for a meal the seat was to be considered open and available. This courtesy might sound a little trivial; however, its purpose served as a constant reminder within the quarters that I was the Command Master Chief and the senior enlisted member on board.

One of the unwritten laws of all enlisted quarters was the acceptance of RHIP, that berthing assignments were more by demand, in recognition of seniority and longevity than by personal desire. Naval tradition and/or custom, over a long period of time, became accepted as law. It was, therefore, accepted policy that a senior man could bump anyone junior to him from a bunk and claim it as his own. It was expected to see men exercise the privilege of upgrading oneself to a more desirable location – usually a bunk that provided more convenience or more comfort. Keep in mind that what one person might consider more desirable another might find inconvenient. Things always had a way of working out when there was some kind of RHIP dispute.

During that first meeting, one of the more junior chiefs, I'll call him Garth, suggested that I take his center bunk while he would take the more inconvenient and less desirable unoccupied bunk. I replied that I did not want to inconvenience anyone, that I would take the available bottom bunk – for the time being. I readily admit that I should have taken his bunk when he offered it. My decision not to take it would later come back to haunt me.

September 7, 1972, the USS *Chipola* got underway, and once again I found myself in an environment with which I was not sufficiently familiar. There were distinct differences between being refueled at sea and being responsible for providing the fuel; the transferring of fuel *to* a ship and the receiving of fuel from a ship. The procedures for each varied widely.

One of my first observations on the *Chipola* was the more appropriate and realistic view that was shared by the officers and men with regard to military appearance. At first sight one would think that the men were shoddy and unkempt. Their uniforms were noticeably soiled. The wearing of anything similar would never have been tolerated at any base or station where I had previously served. It was quickly brought to my attention by a fellow chief that serving on an oiler guaranteed one thing and one thing only – that sooner or later everyone, up to and including the skipper, would acquire stains to their uniforms from the thick black fuel oil that the ship carried. At first it was difficult overlooking the ragamuffin appearance of the crew, but within a reasonable period of time they began to look every bit as good as any crew with whom I had ever served – with or without the stains on their uniforms. Upon close observation I had to agree that the uniforms the men wore were being maintained as well as could be expected. The dark stains were indelible and were sure to remain deeply infused in the uniforms for as long as they were wearable. In a very short period of time I realized that my own uniforms had also accumulated recognizable stains.

It seemed that for the first time I truly realized what being promoted to the top of the enlisted ranks was all about. I was the only master chief aboard, and I had not, up until that time, truly exercised my authority as MCPOC, Master Chief Petty Officer of the Command; at that time most frequently referred to as "Master Chief of the Command." I had read all there was to read about serving as mess president and about maintaining order within the chiefs' mess, but the time had come for me to perform, without benefit of prior meaningful experience. I was obviously a young master chief, and the majority of chiefs aboard were older, many with a great deal of experience. My experience as a master chief was 99 percent book reading, but I was determined to take charge and carry out my responsibilities as I believed they should be carried out.

My duties as SEA were clearly spelled out in BUPERSINST (Bureau of Personnel Instruction) 5400.58, along with the USS *Chipola*'s own version, Instruction 5400.2. Among other things, I was required to keep the command apprised of existing or potential situations, procedures, and practices that adversely affected the welfare, morale, or well-being of enlisted personnel and to recommend actions to eliminate such conditions and further enhance the attractiveness of the naval service. I was required to meet periodically with all *Chipola* enlisted personnel to exchange ideas and disseminate information and instructions that affected the enlisted community both aboard ship and ashore. As SEA I had direct access to the Commanding Officer and all other persons attached to the command and was guaranteed, in that capacity, absolute confidentiality as to sources of information, whether favorable or unfavorable. Complaints made by crewmembers were not to be discouraged, and I was to bring such problem areas before the Human Relations Council (of which I was also a member). The entire crew had unrestricted access to me without consideration of the chain of command. They also had the guarantee of absolute confidentiality of their discussions with me.

It was a bit disturbing, being the senior enlisted snipe while having little or no knowledge of many of the components within the engineering plant that I had become responsible for maintaining. I willingly advised the Engineer Officer of my lack of experience on *Chipola*'s engineering plant.

"I've served on several different ships, including submarines, but I want you to know that I have never had a bit of experience with an engineering plant like this one," I told him.

The chief snipe smiled at me and said, "Well Master Chief, neither have I."

I felt surge of relief and apprehension at the same time. It was sure to make my job easier knowing that I could honestly, and without reluctance, answer my bosses' technical questions with, "I don't know – but I'll find out." It was also disturbing knowing that the senior officer in engineering as well as I, the senior enlisted engineer, were both somewhat oblivious to the plant for which we were responsible. It was time to hit the books once again.

Within a few days of my boarding, the XO called me to his stateroom, where we discussed my military background and my responsibilities to the crew. He advised me that as Master Chief of the Command I would have no in-port duties, that I would have "open gangway" privileges to the same extent as the Commanding Officer. In simple terms, I was told that as long as I carried out my responsibilities in the manner that my prior evaluations indicated I had, I would not be restricted with regard to liberty hours while in port. I would be restricted only to the extent that I issue appropriate orders to my men at morning quarters to ensure the workload was distributed and carried out. I was to make sure that the ship's engineering plant was always capable of providing whatever power requirements were needed to meet in-port and underway commitments. In other words, I had open gangway privileges, but I had better make damn sure I am never ashore when my guidance or leadership is needed aboard ship! I always enjoyed sufficient time on liberty without ever having to abuse open gangway privileges. To the contrary, I *never* left the ship during working hours unless it was to coordinate repairs or activities that were *Chipola* related.

September 9, we arrived in Hong Kong, where the ship remained for just under a week. As has been described before, R and R was the routine with the *Chipola* as it was with all Navy ships visiting there; it was vacation time. Liberty was normally called away (announced) shortly after morning quarters. The duty section performed minor maintenance and kept the spaces clean while the liberty sections were ashore. It was also a time to have the ship painted inside and out by Mary Soo's Side Cleaners. Years ago, prior to my first visit to Hong Kong, Mary Soo had established herself and her all-female crew as hard-working and trustworthy. All Navy ships were quickly approached by Mary Soo and her crew shortly after their arrival. It was a sure bet that the command(s) would, for a reasonable price, allow them to wash the sides of the ship. Over the years Mary Soo's Side Cleaners expanded their operation to include cleaning and painting berthing compartments and other areas aboard ship.

The chief's berthing space needed painting and in preparation it had to be stripped of all mattresses, linens, and belongings that were not inside personal lockers. Garth, the chief who had previously offered me his bunk, had taken leave and was not expected to return for several days; so I took it upon myself to strip his bunk and safeguard the personal belongings he had stashed under his mattress. I also made the decision that since he had already offered me the bunk it would no longer pose an inconvenience to either of us, that when the painting was completed I would go ahead and swap bunks.

Garth burned out while on leave. That is, he had overindulged in every-thing Hong Kong had to offer and had therefor decided to return to the ship to rejuvenate. It was typical for many men on local leave to return to the ship. Sometimes there was a need for more personality (additional funds), clean clothes, a more nourishing meal, or to catch up on some much-needed sleep. It was probably a combination of all of the above that caused Garth to return to the ship.

I was sitting in the CPO mess when Chief Adkins, another dependable, more conscientious and respected chief, approached me. With a sly grin that reflected his amusement, he said, "Hey, *Nine*, guess what's new in the berthing compartment?"

Slick had dubbed me Nine from the day I reported aboard. It wasn't long before I was known as Nine to nearly all of the chiefs. It did not matter where I was, aboard ship or ashore; I always recognized Slick's unmistak-able voice whenever he gained my attention with a loud and clear, "Hey, Nine." Disrespect? Not at all. I enjoyed the nickname as much as I enjoyed hearing my correct title when being addressed by officers or chiefs.

I was not in the mood for guessing games, but I admired Chief Adkins and it was unlikely that he was trying to irritate me. He was, however, pleased that he knew something that in all probability I was not going to be happy to learn.

"So what's the news?" I asked.

"Well, guess who's sleeping in your tree?"

"I give up, sonny; who's enjoying the comforts of my home?" I asked.

Chief Adkins could hardly wait to answer, very intent on seeing how I would respond when he said, "Garth!"

I didn't know that Garth had returned to the ship, but I did know that I had an unnecessary problem that I had to deal with immediately. I went to my bunk, and sure enough, there he was, halfway into the depths of full sleep.

I said, "Chief Garth, we have a problem here."

Garth, hungover and in need of sleep, already sufficiently provoked, grumbled his sentiments. "Don't fuck with me; this is my bunk and you got no right to move it!"

He continued with a totally uncalled for, "In my younger days I would'a stuck you with my knife for less."

Prudence dictated that I back off for the moment. There would be ample time to resolve the matter later. I was confident that the unwritten laws of seniority would prevail; that once I was dealing with a sober, well-rested fellow chief, all would fall into place without a hitch. I was very wrong. Garth was intent on retaining the bunk as his own regardless of my approach. Within a day I tried to explain to him how I had protected his valuables while the compartment was being painted and that it was he who had first offered his bunk to me at a time when I did not want to inconvenience anyone. But Garth remained adamant and firm, and he made clear threats of violence should I take it upon myself to move his bunk again. He had no way of knowing that I thoroughly enjoyed a good fight and that I had come out the conclusive victor in most of my altercations. I had always been confident in my ability to "kick ass," and the "rush" was there; I wanted nothing more than to jerk Garth out of "my" bunk and give him a thorough thrashing. And I wanted to do so within sight and sound of the entire CPO quarters, thereby making sure that everyone could bear witness to a side of me that they were previously unaware of. But I elected to follow a more favorable course. As Master Chief of the Command I had to conduct myself with respect and dignity – above reproach! The matter seemed so trivial – yet one that was clearly testing my seniority, my authority, and my ability to maintain control within the mess. I was faced with a situation that had every chief wondering just how I would handle it. RHIP, coupled with my power of verbal persuasion, was not working.

It was time to call a meeting of all CPOs, a meeting that should never have been considered necessary, but a meeting that would ensure Garth was aware that all chiefs had at one time or another accepted that unwritten rule of bunk bumping based on seniority, and that it was not in his best interest or in the best interest of the CPO quarters as a whole for him to dispute that well established tradition.

Garth was extremely hardheaded and he stood his ground. He had made something of a fool of himself and was causing me to do the same. He had challenged me, my authority, and the entire CPO quarters – and up to that point in time he had proven that he was not about to comply with a damn thing. I pitched my final curve when I reminded everyone present that our problems should never be taken outside the quarters, that we must always resolve them among ourselves regardless how significant or insignificant they might be, but that executive channels was an alternative that I was not willing to rule out. I would elevate the dispute if it could not be resolved at that meeting. If Garth absolutely refused to comply with what had become the will of the entire quarters, I would take the matter up with the Executive Officer. I hated hearing myself say that. To me, and probably to others as well, it sounded like; "If you don't do it my way I'll go crying to my mommy!" The well seasoned Senior Chief Bos'n took a particularly hard stand as he tried to convince Garth that he was wrong. In any event, I knew that I could not afford to lose face. I would not allow myself or my authority to become anything resembling a whipping board. I knew that if the XO chose to have me resolve the matter without his intervention, I would have no choice other than to turn to violence. I was not looking forward to that course of action, but I was prepared if it became necessary.

When Garth absolutely refused to cooperate, I paid the XO a visit. A visit I was very uneasy about. I told the XO how my authority had been challenged and that regardless how trivial the matter might appear to an outsider, it was a significant matter within the CPO quarters where I was supposed to have absolute control. The XO assured me that the problem would be resolved with no difficulty, that I had his unequivocal backing and that he would intervene immediately. He also told me that he would have been disappointed in me had I allowed the situation to remain status quo or if I had turned to violence as a means of resolution. He confirmed my own thoughts in that had I allowed my authority to be challenged without reacting, I was "done for" as far as exercising any future authority over any of the chiefs.

I'm sure every chief on board knew what was happening when the word was passed over the 1-MC, "Chief Garth, report to the Executive Officer's stateroom immediately." I felt sick, truly nauseated about having to take the steps I had taken, even though the XO's words of encouragement had provided me with some relief.

I would have given a great deal had I had the opportunity to be present or to listen in on the conversation that ensued between Chief Garth and the XO. It was short and to the point; within ten minutes Garth was back in the berthing compartment switching bunks. He was, to say the least, really tight-jawed. Garth lost a great deal of respect from the other chiefs as a result of his inappropriate actions. I continued to treat him as a full-fledged member of the CPO quarters; however, I never again considered him deserving of the hat that he wore. There were others who felt the same.

Since I was much the loner while on liberty, I spent most of my time ashore revisiting places I had frequented during previous WesPac deployments, only to find that most of them had changed or were no longer there. Acquaintances of the past were long gone, their whereabouts unknown to the new owners and to nearby merchants. It was saddening not being able to relive the fun and games of my younger days with those who might have remembered me; so unlike the days when I steamed with one or more of my shipmates.

There were no rules of military etiquette that would have prevented me from socializing with other *Chipola* chiefs, but I had not grown to know them as individuals and therefor preferred to allow more time before taking on the appearance of anything other than that of responsibility and authority. I had learned long before, by observation and experience, that it was far better to start out as a strict, rule-enforcing, respect-demanding leader, and then later gain appreciation and admiration as the person others could turn to for guidance and understanding – the leadership they could always depend on as fair. Starting out as the nice guy, friend, companion, and liberty mate, then later trying to enforce the rules or take charge as a superior, their boss, very rarely produced favorable results.

I never learned how or why Slick came by his nickname, but he and I quickly became great friends. He was the first chief I served with who looked at his Navy career as well as life in general much the same as I did. He was an exceptionally knowledgeable and hardworking MM and he had the admiration of officers and enlisted men alike. Slick had the ability to look anyone directly in his eyes, senior or junior to him, and tell him, "You're all fucked up," when he knew the man was wrong in whatever he was doing or saying; and he would get away with it. He did so knowing that whoever he was talking to would accept it as legitimate criticism.

Most sailors enjoyed playing Acey-Deucy during their off time. Chiefs were guilty of playing the game before, sometimes during, and after working hours. Excessive time spent playing the game during working hours, though it was difficult to draw a line of distinction, was an abuse of position. It was a privilege living within the privacy of the CPO quarters, a privilege that in itself could easily be abused. It was a clear violation of those regulations governing the quarters to engage in game playing of any nature during working hours. As president of the mess I was not only responsible for maintaining order; I was expected to set the example, to be the paragon of CPO's. There was no room for interpretation when it came to understanding well-written regulations; however, there were some rules that had to be stretched, sometimes overlooked or disregarded in their entirety, when unusual circumstances warranted. Such judgments were necessary in order to maintain loyalty, respect, trust, and discipline. The game of Acey-Deucy was one of the exceptions I not only allowed, I was a participant. All other recreational games were strictly prohibited during working hours. There were several officers, particularly those who had served as enlisted men prior to gaining their commission, who left the private and protective environment of Officers' Country to venture into the chiefs' domain where they were willing participants in a game or two of Acey-Deucy. It was a momentary means of escape from the real world and provided me, as I'm sure it did others; a period of time to shake off pressing issues and enjoy a bit of recreation. Chiefs, in particular, were called upon at all times of the day and night to provide guidance, oversee activities, and perform any number of other duties. Knowing that, most officers and men overlooked it when they happened to enter the chiefs' quarters and found an ongoing game of Acey-Deucy. Sometimes they would stand there and watch the game proceed, waiting patiently for the end of the game before discussing business matters.

I was commonly referred to as a lucky bastard when I played Acey-Deucy. It was luck indeed when I rolled the dice and frequently the exact numbers I called upon came up. I had a tendency to gloat whenever luck paid me a visit. I would scoff at my opponents, always putting on the most obnoxious act of skill possible; always assuring those playing as well as those watching that there was no competition available that could compete with my shrewd game-playing genius. I did my best to annoy my opponents into making mistakes as they played. Never would I admit to a lucky toss of the dice, instead I remained adamant that it was my skill that caused the right numbers to come up.

Slick and I conspired to create interest within the CPO mess by feigning one hell of an argument as to which of us was the better Acey-Deucy player. Slick was a great player and he shared as much luck with the dice as I did. One day when there were an abundance of witnesses within the quarters, enough that we could count on them spreading the word, Slick and I argued and boasted about which of us was the better player. We made, what to the onlooker appeared to be, a very serious monetary wager on the outcome of a single, sudden-death, winner-take-all, payday stakes bet!

Payday was about a week away, which allowed Slick and me ample time to publicly ridicule each other's lack of ability to play the game, always in jest but also always making sure that we took on the appearance of extreme rivalry. We made it known that our high-stakes game would take place in the CPO mess immediately following the upcoming payout.

The day came, all the chiefs were paid, and Slick and I sat in the mess glaring at each other as we waited for a decent crowd of fellow chiefs to gather. We were both antagonistic (always in jest), and in unison we slapped our payday funds in a single pile beside the Acey-Deucy board. Slick and I were the only ones who knew that following the game we would laugh it off in private, where the winner would reimburse the loser.

The game began and I took an immediate lead. I laughed boisterously at each roll of the dice, always ridiculing Slick's apparent lack of skill. Well past the halfway point, probably three-quarters of the way through the game, Slick rolled a few significant numbers and took an immediate lead. A hush came over those watching. There were no side bets (to our knowledge), no rooting sections, nor were there outward individual comments as to which player was favored. There was, however, an intense interest in the game. I laughed at Slick's lead as I assured him that he did not have a chance, that in the end he would come out looking the fool, and I went on and on. Slick played his role to the hilt, always coming back with similar comments, laughing loudly as he said things like, "Big-shot E-9, but don't know shit about Acey-Deucy," and, "I'm gonna love spending your so-called hard-earned money."

The game was nearing an end and it was becoming a sure bet that Slick was about to become the undisputed winner – although I maintained my boastful mannerisms in hopes of a lucky break. Slick had the game in the bag as he stood up and grinned from ear to ear, the sure winner in mind but not quite in fact. He knew that following my toss of the dice all he had to do was roll them one final time and the game was his – regardless of the numbers he rolled. I, on the other hand, knew that the only way I could win the game was to come up with a "1," an ace on one dice and a "2," a deuce on the other; the odds were astronomically unfavorable. I sat back, dice in hand, and I stared directly into Slick's eyes.

"You actually think I can't do it," I said – and I slammed the dice through the opening at the top of the Plexiglass mixing device. The first die rolled out, hit the backboard, and stopped: two black dots face up. The second immediately followed: the ace face up. I had won! The crowd roared as I scooped up the stack of bills on the table.

I couldn't stop myself from once more ridiculing Slick as I stared into his bewildered eyes. "You easy schmuck," I said.

"You unbelievably lucky sonofabitch!" Slick fumed as I walked out of the quarters clutching a wad of money in my hands, laughing loudly as I exited. But then I did something that Slick had not counted on. Instead of meeting later to return Slick's money, I immediately returned to the quarters and threw his money on the table in front of him.

"Here, Easy; I can win it back at any time." My words hit him right between the eyes when he realized that no matter what he wanted to tell others about our plot, they would find it hard to believe we had staged the bet.

The *Chipola* departed Hong Kong on September 15. Spirits were always higher than usual just prior to visiting Hong Kong, during and for several days following the visit. The officers and men were always anxious to share their stories of the many interesting and exciting things they experienced there. The attitudes and morale of the crew could normally be very predictable. There was an expected and proportionate ratio between upcoming port calls and the general mood throughout the ship. Unintentionally, but with expected results, the old-timers created the basis for interest among the newcomers with their extraordinarily captivating stories about the port we would visit next. Those most experienced, such as myself, who had been there many times prior, always shared our best memories. Whatever bad times we may have had were of little significance when there were so many interesting and thoroughly enjoyable experiences we could talk about. Whenever I heard, observed, or had reason to believe that the morale of the crew was low, I blamed myself along with all of the other more senior enlisted men, chiefs in particular. We had the ability, if we chose to exercise it, to encourage and control the morale of our men. It was not always easy, especially when our duties as required by ship's commitments were abruptly modified, or periods of time at sea were extended for unknown reasons. I took a strong exception to those few chiefs who should have known better but openly and intentionally grumbled outside the quarters in front of the younger men when they were dissatisfied with the ship's operational schedule or shipboard conditions. They were unwittingly and unnecessarily creating a morale problem that could easily have been avoided. Within the quarters I never had a problem with legitimate grumbling. I did not encourage it, but I did not discourage it either. The CPO quarters was the place to vent many of our frustrations – *never* in front of the crew! It was uncomfortable having to remind fellow chiefs of their obligations, but I never shirked my responsibility in doing so, much to the displeasure of whomever I had to remind.

Some chiefs, a small handful but far too many from my point of view, thought they knew everything. They tried to take on the appearance of having some kind of omnipotent knowledge. Some conducted themselves in that manner based on their absurd conviction that when they attained the pay grade E-7 and donned a new style of uniform, they were instantly endowed with all-encompassing mystical powers, an automatic evolution that materialized at the moment of promotion. I took special precautions to make sure that my modus operandi as a master chief never took on that appearance – although it probably did on occasion. I knew that loyalty and respect were not God-given virtues, nor were they realistically within the scope of demand. Rather, they were qualities earned, the fruit reaped as a result of genuine effort, ability, and other professional traits. I was honest with my men. If I knew the answers to questions asked, I immediately responded. In instances where I did not know the answer, and certainly depending on the magnitude or significance of the question, I might have admitted my lack of knowledge or I might have pretended that I had more pressing duties at that moment, with the guarantee that I would get back to him or them with the answer later. I would then do my homework, the necessary research, before I would return to my usual duties. Again, depending on the urgency, I might go directly to the person or persons who had asked the question and provide the correct answer, or I might intentionally forget to return, knowing full well that sooner or later our paths would cross and the same question would again surface. The second time around, after apologizing for not having followed up in a timely manner, regardless how busy I might have been, I provided an accurate and dependable answer. Over the years I became an exceptional source of reliable information to the officers and crew alike, regardless of the subject matter, within or outside the scope of knowledge expected of an engineer. At times I surprised myself when I realized I was knowledgeable of and could respond with reasonable accuracy to some rather remarkable questions.

Delivering Fuel to the Fleet

On September 23, following a week at sea, the *Chipola* pulled in to Subic Bay where she was to remain for a week. Liberty was plentiful as long as required maintenance and other shipboard commitments were met. Fuel tanks had to be refilled, and the never-ending search for and repair of steam and water leaks continued. Electronics and fire control systems had to be recalibrated. There was the task of scraping and repainting where there was any evidence of rust formation. There were tasks required of every division; of each and every officer and crewmember.

Prior to entering any port there was always an exerted effort to accomplish as much maintenance as possible, the smaller tasks that would otherwise take up valuable liberty time. The men were impressive as they "turned to" with exuberance unequaled at other times. Unfortunately, I could never convince my men that greater emphasis on daily underway efforts would eliminate the need to push with such diligence just prior to entering port.

I visited with Rick and Ludy a couple more times where, as expected, I always enjoyed myself. Rick never failed to remind me of his pocketwatch and how he figured I had already sold it for twice what he got from me. Sometimes I would laugh and say, "I didn't double my money, Rick; I tripled it!"

I also made it a point to stop by for short visits with the Hernandez family. I was always concerned about their health and welfare; unnecessarily so, since they had become quite self-sufficient. They were well known and admired by the entire community. I considered them my own family and had grown to love them in a way that it would be most difficult to explain. The entire family had moved higher up the side of the mountain into a more spacious home, one far more comfortable and much more adapted to their needs. Little Lea, age three and the youngest of the Hernandez children, had begun to develop her own personality. She had a mind of her own, but when she pouted she was every bit as adorable and sweet as when she was in her happiest of moods. I became Uncle Paul to her as I was to her older brothers.

The *Chipola* was in and out of Subic a couple of times up until October 19, when we departed the area. Our next destination was Kaohsiung, Taiwan, the place where I believed the women were more beautiful than anywhere I had ever been. The Taiwanese people were of Chinese origin, but most appeared uniquely different. I thought they looked like Egyptian goddesses with an Oriental twist. Their eyelids were not the usual or stereotyped squinted slits through which it was sometimes difficult to determine whether they were open or closed. They had lovely oval eyes, the corners turned slightly upward, their smiles and their cheeks were proportionately perfect, each complimenting the other with a grace and beauty I failed to see in other foreign countries.

I headed straight to the OK Bar, where I was in hopes of finding Katie, the girl I had met in 1956, fifteen years earlier. Having known the Hernandez family for such a long time provided that little bit of hope that with each return to any port I might run into an old friend. Such was not to be the case this time. The OK Bar had been replaced some years back with a small variety-type department store. I wandered around town and eventually found refuge in a restaurant-bar. After taking my order, the mama-san came to my table and asked if I had ever visited Kaohsiung before. I explained that I had, and that I always enjoyed my time there. She sat across from me and appeared to have a genuine interest in the fact that I had been there during a period of time that she, too, recalled quite vividly. As our conversation continued, I mentioned the OK Bar and her eyes lit up. She was very familiar with the place; she had worked there way back when. I mentioned Katie and Mama-san perked up even more. She told me that she knew a Katie but did not know if it was the same person. When I told Mama-san that Katie's Chinese name was Anauana and that she could neither read nor write, Mama-san squealed with delight and confirmed that indeed it was the same girl. I was absolutely astounded when Mama-san sat back, looked straight at me, and asked, "Are you Paul?"

Katie had long since married an American GI, a member of the Air Force, and she and her husband had moved to San Francisco, California, where Katie attended school and had learned to read and write. Mama-san was one of Katie's best friends, and they frequently communicated through the mail. Mama-san first learned of me when she was shown a small glass display case/container that Katie always kept on a nightstand in her room above the OK Bar. Inside there was a Zippo cigarette lighter resting on top of a piece of paper that contained a handwritten note describing Paul as a very decent American guy that had promised to return some day. It had been written by Ski, the bar owner. Katie had spoken of me many times prior to her marriage, and Mama-san shared some of those conversations with me. Katie really wanted me to return. Not for monetary gain, but because she appreciated the manner in which I had treated her. I had always asked her to accompany me as I enjoyed the sights in and around the area, and she had been more of a friend and companion than a sex object for which most sailors used her. Mama-san told me that when Katie wrote, rarely did she neglect to ask if I was known to have returned and, if so, had I made an effort to locate her. I could sense tears accumulating in my eyes as my sentimental side stepped in. It was a good feeling, knowing Katie thought of me as having been such a significant figure in her life, yet I was also sad that she probably never realized the fond memories she had also provided me with. Mama-san assured me that she would, in her next correspondence, tell Katie that I had kept my promise and had finally returned.

October 26, 1972, the *Chipola* returned to sea for extended operations without our knowing when or where we might touch land again. It was one of those unusual times when the ship's itinerary had to be modified to accommodate the unanticipated needs of the Seventh Fleet. It was also one of those times when the men of the *Chipola* had thought they were heading home, to Hawaii. But refueling ships was our primary function, and the needs of the fleet had to come first.

The officers as well as the crew were getting a little bit antsy toward the end of the fueling operations, even more so when the skipper announced that he had two options; charting a course for Hawaii, or heading in the opposite direction for port calls in New Zealand. The reactions were mixed. Generally, the younger married men were more anxious to return to their families while the older men and the single men were anxious to visit another foreign port. And there was another factor to be considered. A visit to New Zealand meant that the ship would cross the equator en route!

It is the dream of most sailors to cross the equator, the invisible line that circles the earth at 00'00" latitude and is at any given longitudinal point equally distant from the North and South Poles. Those who had never crossed, commonly known as Pollywogs, were jokingly ridiculed as being an unworthy group of sailors, inexperienced in the realms of Davey Jones and Neptunus Rex, the "real" denizens of the deep. On the other hand, Shellbacks, those who had already crossed the equator, openly bragged about their position of prominence, their so-called nobility, their rule over certain sea travelers such as all "low-life slime," otherwise known as Pollywogs. Contrary to what many landlubbers might think, not all ships cross that line. Most old-timers, those considered real "salts," had crossed at least once or twice, sometimes several times. They had experienced the initiation process and had, or would as full-fledged Shellbacks, properly initiate all who crossed with them thereafter. The *Chipola* had two prominent Pollywogs; the senior officer on board, the Captain, and the senior enlisted man, me!

The skipper did the democratic thing and had the officers and crew vote on whether they wanted to visit New Zealand or head straight home.

Commanding officers don't normally do that. They are totally responsible for command and usually exercise their absolute authority to make command decisions.

Our skipper was not well liked by the officers or the crew. That is not to suggest that he was anything other than a thoroughly competent commanding officer. It was my opinion and the opinion of many others that he was more of a demanding dictator than a responsible leader. The scowl on his face rarely changed, and no one dared to test his sense of humor. The ongoing train of thought on board *Chipola* was that his face might be permanently damaged, it might crack or break, if he ever smiled. I gave the man credit for getting the job done; however, I did not give him high marks for the manner in which he commanded.

Very much to the displeasure of the Captain, when the final tally came, the vote was in favor of returning home; New Zealand had been unmistakably, very intentionally, voted out. But the Captain heard rumors, probably fantasized to some degree, that some of the crew had been pressured into voting in opposition to their preference. He suggested that out of fear of some kind of retaliatory action, many of the lower-graded men had voted in the manner in which they had been coerced. So, after advising the crew that they had nothing to fear in voting their own minds, the skipper once again did the democratic thing and insisted that a second vote take place, the assumption being that the second time around would determine the honest wishes of the officers and crew. The result was surprising because it became even more lopsided in favor of returning home. The skipper was absolutely furious, so he did the autocratic thing and decided that we would go to New Zealand!

Every ship I had served on, and probably all other ships as well, made it a practice to have at least two full-fledged ship's parties every year, with any number of beer ball games in between. The larger parties would usually take place one in the States and one in some foreign port well away from home. Sometimes the crew would be allowed to vote (legitimately) on the country and even have a say on the location within that country. Safe places such as the EM Club (Enlisted Men's Club) were encouraged; however, it was more common for the Recreation Committee to rent a downtown bar and close it to the public for a full day. Parties helped reduce shipboard tensions and allowed officers and crew to fraternize without having to worry about violating rules or tradition otherwise prohibiting it. The food and drink, of which there was always an abundance, was all paid for out of MWR (Morale Welfare and Recreation) funds. Officers remained officers and gentlemen, while enlisted men, the lower-graded in particular, overindulged. Fights were expected and were usually between two individuals; they rarely escalated among observers and they were usually stopped quickly. The rowdy ones were immediately escorted back to the ship by Ship's Company Shore Patrol. Sailors, under the influence of alcoholic beverages, were inclined to speak their minds and openly discuss shipboard problems with their superiors while on liberty. Likewise, they could be counted on speaking their minds at a ship's party. It was a self-proclaimed sign of being macho when one friend would tell another, "I'm gonna go tell so and so that I think he's a... ." More often than not, it was to tell so and so what an asshole he was thought to be. As a younger sailor I had my say more than once at ship's parties, but as I matured I had a tendency to sit in some remote corner and watch activities as they developed. Sitting in a corner provided me with an unobstructed view of the area all around me while keeping me well protected from being attacked from behind. I had been sucker-punched more than once and knew that there were ways to greatly reduce the opportunity that any would-be assailants were invariably alert to.

Whenever a ship was required to anchor out in a harbor instead of having the good fortune of being tied up at a repair facility or pierside, liberty parties were provided with shuttle boat transportation. There were always too many sailors on the last shuttle boat. Liberty ashore was a precious thing, and most sailors wanted to make it last as long as possible. Put together all the factors: too many sailors in a confined space, most having overindulged, some having been taken advantage of in one manner or anther, and all very tired – more than enough elements present to provide for a very explosive mixture, and it didn't take much to set it off. Someone accidentally bumping into another, unintentionally stepping on the shoe of another, crowding someone, or even making eye contact for too long were sufficient justification to fuel tempers. Also, there were those who enjoyed sucker-punching some innocent passenger for no reason whatever. Sometimes quiet observers would get caught up in the excitement and join in. There were times when the fights became more riotlike and sailors were knocked or thrown overboard. I never knew of anyone drowning as a result of falling, being pushed, or intentionally diving from a liberty boat, but that does not mean it didn't happen. It did, but not in my presence.

Chipola's Engineering Department threw a party in Kaohsiung, Taiwan, prior to the infamous democratic vote on our next destination. It started out as all parties did, everybody mingling, everything copesetic, and everyone intent on having a good time. I knew that one of my men, a Machinist's Mate third class named Jack, was prone to getting involved whether or not he thought circumstances warranted it. He was far more likely to fight while under the influence of alcohol. Jack was a husky type and was never known to lose a fight. He always took the stand that someone else had started it, but shipmates knew better. Jack was far too inclined to seek situations that he thought needed his attention. It did not come as a surprise when Jack began to get rowdy. I saw several of my men trying to control him, but that moose of a man was not one to be restrained easily. I tried to talk him into using his better judgment, his ability to reason, more appropriately. His attitude immediately changed and he assured me that he would behave, that he did not want to make a scene, and that he would make sure there would be no continuance of his disruptive activities. I was satisfied and returned to my corner seat. Within five minutes Jack was giving someone a thorough pounding; probably unprovoked. Jack was detained by the Shore Patrol and was taken back to the ship, where he was immediately restricted pending Captain's Mast.

Captain's Mast was more than familiar to me. I had stood before the Old Man enough times, and I knew that the punishment did not always fit the crime. I knew that the times I stood before one commanding officer or another they had been quite understanding and lenient with me, based on how my supervisors evaluated me. The tables were reversed, and it was my turn to go to bat for Jack, one of my men whom I knew to be much like I had been at one time: immature, hardworking, hard-playing, and known for his fighting capabilities and for the pleasure he gained while exercising them. I remember thinking to myself; *What a show the two of us could have put on during my younger days – I might not do all that bad now.* I had been known to come out well ahead with so-called tough guys, but times had changed and I could no longer exercise that talent even though I never completely lost the desire.

I assured the Captain that Jack was salvageable, that he was one of my harder-working snipes. Other than his apparent drinking problem, he was a reliable individual. When it came to military duties he was always dependable. The Captain listened intently, obviously not happy with what I was saying, probably wishing the contrary was true. The Old Man sentenced

535

Jack to thirty days' restriction to the confines of the ship and "busted" (demoted) him from MM3 (E-4) to MMFN (E-3) with a probational stipulation that at the end of thirty days he would regain his MM3 crow if I personally recommended it. The skipper repeated his decision so that there was no misunderstanding: "All you need to recover your petty officer grade is the Master Chief's recommendation!"

At the end of the thirty-day period, Jack submitted a special request chit wherein he requested that he be reinstated to petty officer third class. Jack had been an outstanding example of what a petty officer should be, and without any reluctance I approved his request and forwarded it through the chain of command. The Division Officer approved it, the Executive Officer approved it, and the Old Man disapproved it! Jack brought the disapproval to me and asked me how it was that he had carried out his end of the deal, and I had approved the reinstatement, yet the Captain had turned him down.

Rarely did I exhibit the degree to which I may have been upset, but this time I was very angry. The skipper had, within the eyes and ears of witnesses, guaranteed Jack something that supposedly I had control over – and he then overruled me! It was no longer Jack's request that had been denied; it was my approval that had been denied! I was something compatible with an angered bull as I made my way the length of the ship and climbed the ladder to the bridge. I went directly to the Captain and abruptly, impolitely, thrust the request in front of his face as I demanded; "Just what the hell is this?" My ability to communicate with respect went right down the drain. The Captain told me that he had seen Jack throw a paint can over the side of the ship instead of over the fantail and that such conduct was not that of a petty officer.

"I don't give a damn what the man did," I continued, "You gave your word at mast that all it would take was my recommendation and the man would get his crow back." The Captain said his disapproval was firm and he ordered me off the bridge. I was fuming!

The XO had observed our confrontation from a short distance away but he did not know what it concerned. He followed me down to the cargo deck, where he questioned me as to what was going on. I explained. The Exec told me that I should not have taken the matter directly to the Captain, that I should have gone to him, the XO. I disagreed, as I explained that I had handled the matter as the Master Chief of the Command and as the Senior Enlisted Advisor – both titles assured me direct access to the Captain in all

536

matters that demanded immediate attention. The XO agreed and disagreed at the same time, but he also asked that I leave the matter in his hands. I assured the XO that if the matter was not resolved to my satisfaction, I would not hesitate in elevating it to higher authority; the Admiral. The XO very politely asked me for twenty-four hours, to which I willingly agreed.

A couple of hours passed and I was sitting in the Log Room when the phone buzzed. The man answering it said, "Master Chief, it's for you."

"Master Chief Adkisson," I said in my sternest voice.

"Master Chief, this is the Captain speaking. There is an error on that special request."

My anger had been somewhat replaced with my ornery side as I responded with, "What request, Sir?"

His voice quivered. "You know damn good'n well what request."

"What was the mistake on that request, Sir?"

His emotion was unmistakable. "I marked the wrong block, Master Chief."

I couldn't stop myself; I was on a roll. "And which block was that, Sir?"

"The request is approved!" And I heard the clatter as the Captain slammed his phone into its receptacle.

Immediately the phone rang again. It was the Executive Officer suggesting I pick up the approved request from him in his stateroom. I very politely thanked him for his involvement.

Jack became an MM3 without further delay. Word quickly traveled to the entire crew, and I became an instant hero for doing nothing more than my job. The crew already trusted in me, but knowing how I had insisted that the skipper keep his word was significant in their eyes. Following that incident I could sense the crew's greater admiration as I walked the decks. Officers and crew alike went out of their way just to greet me with a "Good morning," or "How's it going, Master Chief?" Sometimes there would be a simple head nod accompanied by a grin, another means of acknowledging their approval.

Having completed specific requirements, satisfactorily passing an oral exam and having demonstrated my ability to control engineering plant casualties, I gained the title EOOW, Engineer Officer Of the Watch. That meant I was to execute my duties directly responsible to the Officer of the Deck for speed control, main engines, and operation of auxiliary equipment necessary for the ship to function in its assigned mission. I became responsible to the Engineer Officer for the safe and proper operation of the engineering plant underway. I was eager to accept whatever accountability I was charged with.

I was disturbed with the knowledge that I would be participating in the crossing-of-the-equator initiation ceremonies. I felt that as SEA, the prestige of my position would be humiliated, but refusal to participate would have been radically unfavorable. The word was out, and there was no doubt as to the truth in it, that those who refused to participate in the initiation would be known by a variety of offensive synonyms. They would be sissies, the timid, the spineless, and the gutless. They would be cowardly and weak – outcasts, undeserving of recognition regardless of accomplishment; absolute jerks by any standards. Since I had proven myself as quite the opposite, I had no intention on lowering myself to such levels. I knew that I had to disregard (to a reasonable degree) all military rules, regulations, and etiquette for a matter of several hours, after which I would regain my self-composure and conduct myself much the same as before; with a little more pride having been duly initiated.

Slick, friend that he was, was intent on making me suffer the equator-crossing initiation totally mortified. He had already crossed the equator several times and was instrumental in the preparations for the upcoming ritual. It was Slick who made sure I would represent the Chiefs' quarters in the beauty contest. It was also Slick who made it a point to gather up some very special garments during our recent visit in Kaohsiung. The garments consisted of two wigs, a cheap bra, bikini panties, a miniskirt, and a sweater – all of which had been well used by some street hooker and all of which were badly in need of cleaning. I was expected to adorn my body with those intimate items while attempting to express myself in a manner appropriate to the occasion of the beauty contest. I actually became nauseated whenever I thought about what I was going to do, but I never admitted to just how opposed I was to such humiliation.

October 31, 1972, the Plan of the Day was published and distributed as it was every day, but with a distinct variation in theme:

> Those personnel who do not wish to participate in the initiation ceremonies must turn their name in to the Ship's Office

538

prior to 1000 hours today. An appropriate entry will be made on page 13 in their service record, it will state to the effect that subject man crossed the equator, however, did not become a TRUSTY AND LOYAL SHELLBACK due to his declining to participate in the ceremonies.

It continued:

Today at 1300: All Pollywogs shift into the prescribed uniform.
1400: Station the Special Pollywog Watch.
1530: Beauty Queen contest: Pollywogs, with the exception of those participating in the contest, will be in prescribed uniform:

Pollywog UNIFORM: The following is the prescribed uniform for all Pollywogs and will be worn from 1300 today until after the initiation tomorrow. The only exception to this will be for those personnel standing regular watches wherein a mode of dress would possibly interfere with duties or be hazardous, those personnel choosing not to participate, those Pollywogs participating in the Beauty Queen Contest, and those Pollywogs standing "Special Pollywog Watches" where special uniforms are prescribed.

OFFICERS/CPOs:

KHAKI TROUSERS WORN BACKWARDS
KHAKI SHIRTS WORN BACKWARDS
FRAMES WITHOUT CAP COVERS
LEFT WHITE SHOE WORN ON RIGHT FOOT WITH BLACK SOCK
RIGHT BLACK SHOE WORN ON LEFT FOOT WITH KHAKI SOCK
TIE WILL BE WORN AS A BELT
BELT WILL BE WORN AS A TIE
WHITE SOCKS WILL BE WORN AS GLOVES.

ENLISTED E-6 & BELOW:

SKIVVY SHIRT WORN LIKE SHORTS WITH POLLYWOG PRINTED ON BACK
WATCH CAP
DUNGAREE PANTS WORN BACKWARDS
DUNGAREE SHIRT WORN BACKWARDS
RIGHT BLACK SHOE WORN ON LEFT FOOT
SHOWER SHOE WORN ON RIGHT FOOT
RIGHT PANT LEG ROLLED UP TO THE KNEE
LEFT PANT LEG TUCKED IN GQ STYLE
NECKERCHIEF REVERSED AND WORN BACKWARDS

BEAUTY QUEEN CONTEST: This afternoon at 1530 on the Cargo Deck there will be a Beauty Queen Contest prior to our crossing the equator tomorrow morning. The queen will become a part of the Royal Court upon "her" selection. Each division is expected to have a beauty contestant, the selection will be made by the vote of the crew. Beauty being only skin deep, qualifications will be considered during the voting, such as poise, ability to dance or sing, etc... .

The special Chief Petty Officer Pollywog Watch Bill attached to the POD (names excluded) read:

QMC "B" WILL POST HIMSELF CARRYING A PAIR OF UNDERSHORTS FLYING HIGH IN THE AIR CONTINUOUSLY SINGING OUT IN A LOUD CLEAR TONE OF VOICE AUDIBLE AT LEAST 20 FEET AWAY "MY FOOT LOCKER ARRIVED WITH MY SHARKSKINS."
SKC "N" WILL POST HIMSELF IN THE CENTER OF THE CARGO DECK WITH A BANDING TOOL AND STRAP IN HAND SINGING OUT AT LEAST ONCE EVERY THREE (3) MINUTES IN A LOUD CLEAR TONE OF VOICE AUDIBLE FOR AT LEAST 20 FEET "BANDING MY FELLOW POLLYWOGS' HEADACHES."
HTC "A" WILL POST HIMSELF WALKING AROUND OVER THE ENTIRE SHIP CARRYING A LARGE CARDBOARD SIGN DRAPED AROUND HIS NECK DESIGNED IN THE SHAPE OF A HEART AND

LETTERED "VOTE FOR OUR QUEEN" SINGING OUT IN A LOUD CLEAR TONE OF VOICE AUDIBLE AT LEAST 20 FEET "VOTE FOR OUR SWEETHEART." THIS STATEMENT MUST BE MADE CONTINUOUSLY AND IN A SWEET APPEALING VOICE.

HMC "T" WILL WALK HIS POST AROUND THE ENTIRE SHIP IN A MILITARY MANNER CARRYING A FIRST AID BAG AND A LARGE CARDBOARD SIGN DRAPED AROUND HIS NECK READING "SANITATION INSPECTOR" IN LARGE LETTERS. AS HE WALKS HIS POST HE SHALL CONTINUOUSLY SING OUT IN A LOUD CLEAR TONE OF VOICE AUDIBLE AT LEAST 20 FEET "HAVE NO FEAR THE SANITATION DEPARTMENT IS HERE."

MMCM ADKISSON, DA-NINE REPRESENTING THE ABOVE SCURVY, SLIMY WOGS IN DA BEAUTY QUEEN CONTEST AS THEIR LOVELY CONTESTANT.

The morning of October 31 showed no signs of being any different than any other morning. But precisely at 1300 hours, over the 1-MC in a voice far more distinct than I had ever heard before, came the words: "Now all Pollywogs shift into the prescribed uniforms." I was on watch in the engineroom and I felt the blood rush to my head as I broke out in a different kind of nervous sweat. There was that remote idea toying around within my mind that since I was on watch I might get out of the beauty queen part. I could easily accept whatever other punishment the Shellbacks were capable of dispensing, but it would be very difficult for me to cross-dress, regardless of the occasion.

1400 hours.

"Now station the Pollywog Watch," again from the 1-MC

I ignored the words, but my body responded with that noxious feeling I associated with something between reluctance and fear. What an act I must have put on, attending to my duties as EOOW, making sure the men and machinery were working in harmony and that I was not bothered by outside interference or influenced by the realities that were taking place outside the engineering space.

1530 hours.

"Now all beauty queen contestants assemble on the cargo deck."

I wanted to vomit! Within moments one of the Shellback snipe-type chiefs relieved me from my watch-standing duties. I was directed to prepare myself for the much anticipated beauty contest and to report to the cargo deck.

With far more reluctance than I had ever previously experienced, I made my way to the CPO berthing area, where Slick had neatly and conveniently placed my "costume" on my bunk. There was no getting out of it, I had no choice in the matter, so I made up my mind to play my role the best I could and to get it over with ASAP. Shellback chiefs were unmerciful as they gathered around and watched me disrobe from my dignified E-9 attire and squeeze my lanky body into the repulsive female garments. Their hearty laughter at my obvious embarrassment, coupled with their jovial harassing remarks at my beauty, charm and femininity, made me self-conscious. But I commend myself for not showing the exasperation I felt as it was fueled by their annoying but well-aimed ridicule. I tried desperately to make myself accept the truth in the matter; that it was all in fun.

As I emerged from the semi-sanctity of the CPO quarters and joined with the other contestants, I immediately lost much of my embarrassment. Most of the others had gone all the way toward presenting themselves as womanly as they possibly could. I could no longer recognize one of my competitors. A couple of them were very near the gorgeous stage, absolutely unrecognizable as men. I thought that their female impersonations were a little too realistic, that they were being exercised with more effect and enjoyment than I thought of as normal. They were anything other than the same group of men I had known just hours before.

One by one the senior chief Bos'n called the beauty queen contestants up onstage, the bed of the ship's pickup truck that was anchored securely in the middle of the cargo deck. The stage provided an outstanding view for all observers – a place where the "pageant" could most easily be observed by all hands. There were twelve contestants: six nonrated men, one third-class petty officer, two first-class petty officers, one ensign, and me. One by one each took *her* turn and did *her* thing; they danced and sang, they recited poems, and they played musical instruments. Then came my turn! I looked absolutely disgusting – much like an overworked, undernourished, homeless hooker. I tried my luck at humor by telling a few short jokes that were intended to make a mockery of the skipper and Slick. Any pun aimed at the skipper brought an immediate round of applause; the other jokes brought little more than a murmur. I sang "Please Do To Me What You Did To Marie," while I danced awkwardly around the bed of the truck. When I finished my skit, repulsive as it must have been, it was acknowledged with an ovation that rings in my ears to this day. I did not know whether to be pleased by the crew's reaction or to be mortified by it. When the contest ended and the final vote was in, the Court of Neptunus Rex had a brand-new Royal Queen. The third-class petty officer took first place – and rightfully so! *She* appeared to be feminine from head to toe and *she* carried *herself* with absolute grace; a little bit too feminine! Much to my surprise and a little bewildering, I came in third!

The remainder of that day was challenging to everyone, even the Shellbacks. Pollywogs did everything we could to foul up whatever plans the Shellbacks had made, but we were rarely successful. Shellbacks were dressed impressively in pirate garb; their pants were raggedly cut off between the ankles and the knees, many had cut their shirtsleeves off, and most of them wore striped T-shirts that had been hand-painted only a few days before. Head bandannas were common and added to the authenticity of the conquering pirates, the Shellbacks.

Pollywogs, each of us having been tried and found guilty, by the Royal Court, of crimes against Shellbacks and the sea, took our turns as we were pushed around and swatted with handmade shillelaghs: pieces of fire hose fabric conveniently cut into short paddle-length weapons that caused some noticeable welting and bruises to our backs and butts. Interestingly, those who suffered the greatest pummeling just happened to be the least liked, or should I say, most deserving? During the course of the initiation we all had eggs smashed on our heads and we had grease and grinding compound rubbed into our hair. From the hose of a douche bag we drank some liquid concoction that was made up of hot sauce and a mixture of other horrible-tasting liquids, and we had to kiss the well-greased naked belly of the Royal Baby; the fattest Shellback on board. At an appropriate time and much to the surprise of the Queen (who had been comfortably seated among the Royal Court and had laughed at everything we were subjected to), *she* was grabbed and subdued by arresting authorities. Subsequently *she* was caused to go through the same initiation process the rest of us had undergone.

The skipper, not much the one for games, probably did his best to participate, but only to the extent that he wore his uniform in the manner prescribed. He, by virtue of his position as Commanding Officer, refused to go beyond that point. I could have done the same, but that would have put me in a category I preferred not to be associated with.

The initiation went exceptionally well. There were no serious injuries reported, and there were no hard feelings. Cleaning up was a significant problem for the newly initiated. Fortunately, the old hands knew about the cleanup process and had prepared accordingly. About a half-dozen saltwater showers had been installed on the cargo deck. Freshwater showers were out of the question. We had to use sand soap, soap that was similar to Lava but more in line with course sandpaper. Sand soap had a tendency to take one's hide off along with the greasy compounds that were so difficult to remove. All in all it was a festive experience and I remain proud that I was able to participate. My only regret is that I never again crossed the equator; I was never on the other side, a participant as a giver instead of a receiver.

All new Shellbacks were issued impressive wallet-size cards acknowledging when and where we crossed. Each of us also had permanent entries made to our service records that read:

USS CHIPOLA (AO-63) BOUND FOR NEW ZEALAND FOR REST AND RECREATION AND AN OPERATIONAL COMMITMENT FOLLOWING A TOUR OF DUTY IN SUPPORT OF UNITED STATES OPERATIONS IN VIETNAM CROSSED THE EQUATOR ON THIS 1ST DAY OF NOVEMBER 1972, AT LATTITUDE 00' 00" AND LONGITUDE 147' 30", THEREFORE, BE IT REMEMBERED THAT THE SAID VESSEL AND OFFICERS AND CREW THEREOF HAVE BEEN INSPECTED AND PASSED ON BY HIS IMPERIAL MAJESTY, NEPTUNUS REX, AND HIS ROYAL STAFF AND EACH FOUND WORTHY TO BE NUMBERED AS A TRUSTY SHELLBACK AND HAVE BEEN DULY INITIATED INTO THE SOLEMN MYSTERIES OF THE ANCIENT ORDER OF THE DEEP.

The entry was signed by "His Majesty's Scribe, Davey Jones," and by "Ruler of the Raging Main, Neptunus Rex." This entry was further endorsed by the XO, thereby certifying its accuracy and authenticity.

Following a brief four-day visit at Auckland, New Zealand, the ship made its way to Wellington. I found the country beautiful and the people very hospitable. The money, the coins in particular, was very difficult to convert in my mind. I had never dealt with shillings (twelve pence or one-twentieth of a pound each), florins (two shillings each), or farthings (one-quarter of a penny each). Compounding my confusion was the fact that there were also several different-sized coins within each denomination. Whether one was a tourist or a native of the country, it was necessary to scrutinize all coins in order to determine their value. Even the New Zealanders that I talked with agreed that their monetary system was confusing.

Pollywogs at the Mercy of Shellbacks

Typical Shellback

Initiation in Full Swing

Crossing the Equator "Ceremonies"

Beauty Queen Contestants

Beauty Queen Contestants

Newly Elected Beauty Queen

Our overnight stay in Wellington did not provide enough time to see much more than the inner city, but we did return to Auckland for another four-day visit. For some reason I suffered from a distinct lack of interest there, a sensation new to me. I made little more than a passing effort to mingle with the natives. I was disappointed, having traveled so far, knowing the circumstances that got us there, that we couldn't spend a little more time, see more of the country, and cultivate additional friendships. Since I was neither impressed nor disappointed with New Zealand, I was ready to head home on November 28 when the ship once again got underway.

There was a loud roar as the crew acknowledged how elated they were upon hearing the much anticipated words: "Now set the Special Sea Detail; all hands prepare to get underway for Honolulu, Hawaii."

I enjoyed serving aboard the *Chipola*. It provided me with an excellent opportunity to exercise my ability and authority as a Master Chief. I did not always follow the book, sometimes preferring to follow my instincts when there were extenuating factors to be considered. My instincts paid off and were recognized when I was evaluated by the command. I received two sets of marks (evaluations) during my tour on the *Chipola*. Both sets were high and the comments were inspiring. The first set included the following comments:

RATEE PERFORMS ALL TASKS ASSIGNED AT A VERY HIGH LEVEL OF EFFICIENCY. HIS INNOVATIVE PROCEDURES HAVE DONE MUCH IN RAISING THE MATERIAL CONDITION OF THE SPACES ASSIGNED TO HIM. HIS WILLINGNESS TO WORK LONG HARD HOURS, HIS GENUINE ATTEMPT TO INSTILL PERSONAL PRIDE OF WORKMANSHIP IN HIS SUBORDINATES HAVE BEEN VERY NOTICEABLE AND HAVE STARTED TO PRODUCE RESULTS. HIS ABILITY TO MAKE REPAIRS AND KEEP THE MACHINERY RUNNING DESPITE POOR PARTS SUPPORT AND LACK OF FULLY TRAINED PERSONNEL HAS BEEN A VERY STRONG CONTRIBUTING FACTOR IN ALLOWING CHIPOLA TO MEET EVERY COMMITMENT DURING THIS LONG AND ARDUOUS DEPLOYMENT. RATEE HAS SPENT MANY LONG AND TIRING HOURS IN HIS SPACES IN AN ATTEMPT TO TRAIN HIS SUBORDINATES AND ENSURE THE WORK WAS DONE IN A TIMELY AND COMPLETE MANNER. HIS COOPERATION WITH HIS OFFICERS IS OF THE MOST OUTSTANDING NATURE. HE

WILLINGLY SUPPORTS NEW PROGRAMS AND BECOMES VERY PERSONALLY INVOLVED IN ALL PROCEDURAL DECISIONS MADE BY HIS SUPERIORS; CONTRIBUTING FROM EXPERIENCE AND HIS WELL ROUNDED KNOWLEDGE OF THE VARIOUS TECHNICAL PUBLICATIONS. HIS INITIATIVE AND DRIVE IN SETTING UP NEW TRAINING PROGRAMS HAS LED TO A MUCH MORE CAPABLE CREW. HE PERSONALLY LEADS DISCUSSIONS, AT QUARTERS, OF THE VARIOUS SYSTEMS AND CRITIQUES PROBLEMS THAT HAVE SURFACED. MUCH HAS BEEN LEARNED BY HIS MEN FROM THE TALKS. HIS RESOURCEFULNESS IN OBTAINING SPARE PARTS OR MANUFACTURING THEM HAS BEEN A DIRECT CONTRIBUTION TO THE ABILITY OF THE USS CHIPOLA TO MEET ALL COMMITMENTS. THE FACT THAT 95% OF ALL MACHINERY OR SYSTEM CASUALTIES HAVE BEEN REMEDIED IN 24 HOURS OR LESS IS A DIRECT RESULT OF HIS RESOURCEFULNESS. HIS CONDUCT IS ABOVE REPROACH AND IS ALWAYS IN KEEPING WITH THE VERY BEST TRADITIONS OF THE NAVY. HE TREATS HIS SUBORDINATES AS MEN UNTIL THEY PROVE OTHERWISE AND DEMANDS THAT HIS PETTY OFFICERS DO LIKEWISE. HIS DEALINGS WITH HIS SUPERVISORS ARE ALWAYS HELD IN AN ATMOSPHERE OF MUTUAL RESPECT. HIS PERSONAL APPEARANCE IS SUCH THAT THE EXAMPLE HE SETS IS ALWAYS THE VERY BEST. HIS RELIABILITY AS AN INDIVIDUAL IS ABOVE REPROACH. MMCM ADKISSON HAS REPEATEDLY SHOWN THAT HE CAN STEP INTO A NEW SITUATION AND HANDLE IT WITH THE FINESSE AND SURENESS OF A DIPLOMAT. IT IS FELT THAT HE CAN HANDLE ANY POSITION TO WHICH HE MAY BE ASSIGNED. TRULY AN OUTSTANDING MASTER CHIEF PETTY OFFICER

In June 1973, I was surprised to learn that I had been recommended and prescreened as a nominee for the position of Master Chief of the Command, Service Force, U.S. Pacific Fleet. Having been nominated identified me as one of a very exclusive group of master chiefs considered qualified and capable of carrying out the responsibilities associated with such a prestigious position. If selected, I would become the senior master chief, the spokesperson and liaison between enlisted men and the senior admiral over the entire Service Force, United States Pacific Fleet.

On June 25, 1973, after the process of elimination singled out the two most qualified master chiefs, I was issued TEMADD orders that released me from my current command and directed that I report for duty at COMSERVPAC "To be interviewed for the billet of MCPOC [Master Chief Petty Officer of the Command]. The duration of that transfer was limited to two days, during which time the two finalists would experience extensive scrutiny by several staff officers, up to and including the admiral himself.

That nomination was perhaps the most significant recognition I ever received during my military service. Having been one of the two finalists was an amazing experience and one that gave me cause to pursue the remainder of my career with even greater zeal than prior to that point in time, even though I had not been appointed to the position for which I had been recommended.

I remained with the *Chipola* up until the day of her decommissioning, August 14, 1973. For a relatively short period of time, prior to her decommissioning, she operated in and out of Pearl Harbor in support of local operations. The final couple of months were tough on the entire crew. Everyone was tasked with the removal of equipment, but it took tremendous effort on the part of the engineers. They had to provide technical and physical support in permanently sealing all the main and auxiliary machinery. There was a deadline that had to be met, which meant longer workdays. The work was accomplished on schedule, but with very little time to spare.

The Ship's Post Office closed several days prior to decommissioning. Since I was a stamp collector, a dabbling philatelist, I asked the Postal Clerk a special favor. I asked that he cancel several stamps for me, airmail and first-class, that were on unaddressed envelopes. More specifically, I asked that the stamps be canceled with the actual decommissioning date. He was more than obliging when he canceled some stamps with the original *Chipola* cancellation cachet and others with the current cachet. I was thrilled knowing that I had, and still have, the only envelopes in the world bearing stamps that were officially canceled with the USS *Chipola* cachet and are dated August 14, 1973, her final day in commission; her day of decommissioning.

Decommissioning ceremonies were held on the cargo deck, where chairs were arranged to accommodate former commanding officers, witnessing officials, family members, and friends. A stage had also been constructed to accommodate the Captain, the Executive Officer, and several guest speakers.

As the senior enlisted member of the crew I was also seated on the stage. At an appropriate time, following one of the more senior speakers, I took my turn behind the podium and expressed "my honor and privilege to present [the Captain] with a few mementos from the ship along with the commission pennant." My words were brief and to the point. I wanted to get my part over with as quickly as possible so that we could all shake hands, wish each other well, and get on our way to wherever our new orders directed.

Immediately following the ceremony all hands stood fast and waited impatiently to receive their official orders. Everyone already knew where they were being reassigned, but the orders could not be issued until the *Chipola* was no longer in commission. Names were read, official orders were issued, and the men filed one by one off the ship for the final time.

Decommissioning of a ship is a sad occasion. It is similar to the death of a very close friend that served long and well. One could observe some sailors, particularly the older salts, as they became caught up in sentiment. The sadness very quickly turned more jubilant as the men departed, sea-bags and other belongings in tow, anxious to take some time off between duty stations.

Presentation of Commission Pennant

With my orders I received my second and final set of marks, every bit as inspiring as the first. That evaluation included the following, more condensed comments:

MMCM ADKISSON CONTINUES TO EXEMPLIFY ALL THE OUTSTANDING TRAITS EXPECTED OF A MASTER CHIEF PETTY OFFICER. HE IS WILLING TO WORK THE VERY LONG, HARD HOURS NECESSARY TO MAINTAIN CHIPOLA AT THE PEAK OF ENGINEERING READINESS DESPITE THE FACT THAT CHIPOLA IS TO BE DECOMMISSIONED. HIS PERSONAL CONCERN FOR THE MEN WORKING FOR HIM HAS PAID HANDSOME REWARDS IN THEIR MANNER OF UNSELFISH DEVOTION TO DUTY AND ATTENTION TO DETAIL IN ALL TASKS PERFORMED. MMCM ADKISSON TAKES A VERY PERSONAL INTEREST IN THE MAINTENANCE OF HIS MACHINERY AND THE WELFARE OF HIS MEN. HIS "CAN DO" ATTITUDE COUPLED WITH HIS DESIRE TO MAINTAIN CHIPOLA'S OUTSTANDING RECORD OF READINESS HAS KEPT A VERY OLD SHIP SEAWORTHY AND READY TO RESPOND AT ALL TIMES. IN HIS CAPACITY AS SENIOR ENLISTED ADVISOR HE HAS DONE MUCH TO FACILITATE COMMUNICATION BOTH UP AND DOWN THE CHAIN OF COMMAND. HE IS FORTHRIGHT YET COMPLETELY RESPECTFUL IN KEEPING THE COMMAND INFORMED OF THE FEELINGS OF THE CREW. HIS ABILITY TO EXPRESS HIMSELF BOTH ORALLY AND IN WRITING HAS DONE MUCH TO DEEPEN THE UNDERSTANDING OF THE VARIOUS PROBLEMS THAT CAN PLAGUE ANY LARGE GROUP OF MEN.

With that, I departed the USS *Chipola* with orders to the USS *Preble* (DLG-15).

16

USS PREBLE

There were many expressions used by Navy men, but perhaps the most common was when recalling or describing the best or worst ship or station to which a sailor was assigned. There were two and only two best or worst assignments, and depending on who was doing the talking, they were both one and the same! The previous duty station, the one a sailor was coming from, was the worst, while the duty station a sailor was en route to was the best. A sailor's sentiments were predictable and were expected to be expressed in one of the following manners: "I'll be so glad to get away from this stinkin' place"; "I'll be so happy when I get to my next duty station"; or, "You better hope you never get stationed where I just came from." Sailors were known to argue vehemently about one or the other's merits or lack thereof. It was interesting listening to two sailors, one coming from the same place the other was going to; one arguing in favor of the caliber of that ship while the other argued to the contrary with equal enthusiasm and intensity. Sometimes such arguments erupted into physical confrontations. I learned never to argue over such things. There was no argument – I knew that the best duty station was a figment of everyone's imagination; it was a ship or station otherwise known as Utopia and it did not exist!

Over the years I learned to control the aggressive reaction I had to the flow of adrenaline that had been so prevalent during my earlier days in the Navy. I knew what it felt like to be challenged, and I knew how difficult it was, turning the other cheek. Whenever I came across two shipmates that were about to come to blows – or had completed the preliminaries and were already fighting – I was understanding and lenient as to the action I took. With the right approach such skirmishes could usually be broken

553

up without damaging either man's service record, reputation, or feelings. When attempts at reasoning were not effective and stronger measures were needed in order to bring about a more immediate conclusion, I was one master chief known to jump right in the middle, sometimes getting in a lick or two of my own to gain their attention. That action, not necessarily condoned by higher authority, was always effective. As Master Chief of the Command I was supposed to maintain discipline, not participate in such unruly activities, but I found that there were occasions when my physical involvement was more influential than when I exercised my vocal chords in some authoritative cease-and-desist effort. As the men became more familiar with me, my voice carried far greater weight and physical confrontations became a thing of the past.

The Navy had been good to me and good for me. I rarely counted the years remaining before I would be eligible for retirement pay. I was happy with my job and I did the best I could on a daily basis. I was acutely aware of how fortunate I was, having attained the highest enlisted grade early in my career. Those relatively few individuals close to me, those that I considered real friends, always told me how lucky I was, and I had a tendency to agree with them. But the truth was that I was not lucky at all. What I achieved was no more nor no less than any other highly motivated and dedicated enlisted man could have accomplished, given a mind to do so. I had made the decision to do my best when I first reenlisted – and I never started any kind of a countdown toward a retirement date. I was doing what I enjoyed, and whenever one enlistment neared expiration I reenlisted without ever giving thought to returning to civilian life. The Navy was my home.

There were rapid changes taking place within the Navy, many as a direct result of Admiral Zumwalt, the Chief of Naval Operations at that time. The Admiral preferred his hair longer, more in style with that of civilians, so sailors followed suit. In a short time the rules governing hair length and style changed. The younger men loved the changes, while the older men found them difficult to cope with. Having civilian clothing on board, and being allowed to wear it to and from the ship while on liberty, was a privilege previously earned by virtue of being an officer or by enlisted men in pay grades E-7 and above. It was a tremendous blow to the senior men when the Chief of Naval Operations extended that privilege to all hands. Chiefs and officers were excluded from having to carry "liberty cards" when they were on liberty, while those in pay grades E-6 and below were issued the cards only on liberty days. Liberty cards also became a thing of the past, and the honor system was extended to all hands, another below-the-belt blow to the senior men. It seemed that those of us in senior pay grades were losing privileges instead of the more appropriate milestone, that of the lower graded men gaining privileges. Most senior enlisted men knew that they had earned the privileges that became gratis – thanks to Admiral "Z."

Perhaps the biggest blow of all came when the "Seaman to Admiral" uniform concept was fully implemented. To the CPO population, it was terribly degrading. Earning "the hat" was significant to those being promoted to chief petty officer. When all hands became eligible to wear the very same style hat and uniform that chiefs and officers wore, there became a distinct morale problem that drove a large number of excellent CPOs and first-class petty officers out of the Navy. Many E-6s, that were borderline as to whether or not they would reenlist, made the decision to get out when they saw all the privileges of promotion (other than pay increases) being haphazardly granted across-the-board to all grades. Locker space was an after-the-fact consideration. The "real" sailor uniform, the one with back flap and white piping around the sleeves, was easily turned inside out, folded or rolled up, and stowed in a tight space – never showed a wrinkle because of its design and material. One needed only to remove it from a footlocker or seabag, shake it out, turn it right side out, and wear it! But the CPO/officer style uniform was made of a different material and needed to be hung on hangers in more spacious upright lockers to prevent the formation of unsightly wrinkles and out-of-line creases. Some of the men looked more like Raggedy Andy dolls in their "spiffy" new uniforms, and the OODs allowed them to go ashore in that manner. It would have been difficult blaming the enlisted man who had no place to hang his uniform but elected to wear it on liberty. Chiefs saw it as an absolute disgrace to the uniform in part and to the Navy as a whole. The privilege and honor chiefs and officers had of wearing brown shoes with their khaki uniforms was also taken away, the black shoe became the only color needed to satisfy uniform requirements, regardless of the color of the uniform or the pay grade of the man wearing it.

I was disappointed in many of the changes that were taking place, so for the first time in my naval service I looked carefully at the calendar as I considered my earliest possible retirement date.

Living conditions were continually being upgraded, nevertheless the younger men complained. They were, as I had been at one time, tired of hearing: "You should have seen what it was like back when I ... ," and, "It wasn't like this in the old Navy." I was no longer listening to stories about the old Navy, I found myself describing it! The Navy I had grown up in really was a tougher Navy; there could be no argument about that. The rules *were* stricter, rate *did* have its privileges, seniority *did* mean something, orders by superiors were *never* challenged, and habitability, as bad as it was, was *never* a complaint worthy of consideration. But conditions were changing and the "new Navy" was becoming a far more lenient one. It was rapidly becoming a Navy where sailors were, in effect, encouraged to question the orders of their superiors, a Navy where explanations were necessary before orders were carried out. There was little good that came from the changes that were rapidly taking place. The only good, as I saw it, was the dramatic steps taking place to upgrade and correct living conditions on board ships and at shore facilities. Privacy curtains were installed around individual bunks, and each bunk had its own night-light. The Northampton-style bunks became *the* style and were soon to take the place of all older-style bunks. That in itself was one of the best improvements an enlisted man could have asked for. The Northampton bunk was not only a bed; it was a large storage compartment that was conveniently accessed by simply opening the bunk top. The hinged top provided access to the spacious partitioned locker beneath. The prior problem of insufficient locker space for lower-graded enlisted men was being minimized by the installation of the new bunks. It was believed that within a reasonable period of time all hands would also have upright lockers in which they could properly stow their CPO/officer-style uniforms. Insufficient personal storage areas would become a thing of the past.

August 30, 1973, I reported for duty aboard the USS *Preble* (DLG-15). I was immediately assigned as Assistant "MPA," Main Propulsion Assistant, Departmental Training Officer/Coordinator, and President of the CPO Mess. The *Preble* was the most modern surface ship on which I had ever set foot. She had quite a history:

Five of our nation's ships had been named Preble in honor of Commodore Edward Preble, which perpetuated the name of one of the founders of the strength, tradition, esprit de corps, morale, and discipline of the (at that time) modern Navy. Edward Preble was born at Falmouth, now Portland,

Main, on the fifteenth of August 1761. At the age of sixteen he ran away to sea on a privateer sloop, and two years later he received an appointment in the Massachusetts State Marine. There he attained the position of midshipman on the twenty-six-gun ship *Protector* of the Massachusetts Navy. The ship fought two severe engagements with British men-of-war, before being captured in 1781, when Preble was taken prisoner and confined for a time on the prison ship *New Jersey*. During the next year, Preble became First Lieutenant on the Massachusetts cruiser *Winthrop* and gained a reputation of undaunted courage and great presence of mind in the boarding and capture of a British brig as it lay at anchor under the cover of British guns at Castine, Maine.

After the Revolutionary War, Preble spent about fifteen years in the merchant service. Upon the opening of hostilities with France in 1798, he was appointed a lieutenant in the newly recognized U.S. Navy and assumed command of the fourteen-gun brig *Pickering*. With the squadron of Commodore Barry, the *Pickering* succeeded in protecting American commerce against armed French privateers in the West Indies. One year later, at the age of thirty-eight, Preble was commissioned as a captain and assumed command of the frigate *Essex*. Sailing from New York in 1800, the *Essex* became the first American warship to show the flag beyond the Cape of Good Hope. While in the Straits of Sundra, the *Essex* afforded protection for American merchant ships engaged in trade with China.

The naval war with France was scarcely brought to a close before the war with Tripoli began in 1803. Preble was given command of the Third Squadron to be sent to the Mediterranean, with the *Constitution* as his flagship. He established a treaty of peace with the Emperor of Morocco late in 1803 and, while sailing back to New York to rendezvous with additions to his squadron, learned of the capture of the frigate *Philadelphia* by the Tripolitans. He immediately effected a blockade of the harbor of Tripoli and commenced operations toward the destruction of the captured vessel in that harbor. Stephen Decatur led the daring feat of destroying the *Philadelphia*, while Commodore Preble directed the first assault on the city of Tripoli. On August 3, 1804, in a series of daring raids, Preble's 1,060 men inflicted severe damage on that fortified city of 25,000 strong, a direct result of strenuous training and bold thinking.

Soon after this, a larger and more powerful squadron appeared under the command of Commodore Samuel Barron, and Preble returned home. Preble and his Tripolian campaign became one of the focal points for the development of the fighting traditions of the U.S. Navy. After his arrival home, Commodore Preble engaged in the building of gunboats for the Navy at Portland, Maine. During the next three years his health declined steadily until, on August 25, 1807, he died at the age of forty-six.

Impartial in his judgment and free from prejudice, Edward Preble justly earned the respect and admiration of his officers. His discipline was severe and was imposed on himself as well as those under his command. He made a place for himself among those officers who laid the foundation of discipline and training for the modern Navy. His squadron in the Mediterranean was a forerunner of the modern Sixth Fleet and a training school for young officers who later distinguished themselves during the War of 1812. William Bainbridge, Stephen Decatur, Charles Stewart, Isaac Hull, David Porter, and many of the still younger officers were worthy pupils of this great officer and teacher.

The first ship to bear the name *Preble*, a sloop of eighty tons, sometimes called *Commodore Preble*, was on Lake Champlain in 1813, armed with seven nine-pound cannons, and had a complement of thirty men. The *Preble* was in the squadron of Commodore Thomas MacDonough on Lake Champlain and took part in the decisive Battle of Lake Champlain, September 11, 1814. She was laid up after the battle until July 1815, when she was sold at Whitehall, New York.

The second *Preble*, a sloop-of-war, was built by the Navy Yard in Portsmouth, New Hampshire and was launched June 13, 1839. Her length was 117 feet, beam 32 feet, depth of hold 15 feet, and tonnage 566. This *Preble* was armed with sixteen cannons, each capable of firing thirty-two-pound projectiles. She made a cruise to the Mediterranean (1841 – 43) and was attached to the African Squadron (1844 – 45). The *Preble* again sailed from New York on September 26, 1846, and joined the Pacific Squadron on the West Coast, taking part in the Mexican War. In the summer of 1848 she sailed for the East Indies. She arrived in Nagasaki, Japan, on April 18, 1849, under Captain James Glynn to negotiate for the release of sixteen shipwrecked seamen from the American whaling ship *Lagoda* being held as prisoners in that country. She then sailed for the East Coast of the United States about November 1, 1850, and arrived on January 2, 1851, at New York, where she served as practice ship for midshipmen until 1857. The *Preble* was ordered to the Gulf Blockading Squadron in July 1861 and was engaged in the blockade of the Mississippi River. She suffered a tragic end on April 27, 1863, when she was destroyed by fire in Pensacola Harbor.

The third *Preble*, torpedo boat number 12, was built by the Union Iron Works of San Francisco, California. Her keel was laid April 21, 1899, and she was launched March 2, 1901, under the sponsorship of Miss Ethel Preble. The ship had an overall length of 146 feet, extreme beam of 15 feet, normal displacement of 154.6 tons, and a designed complement of three officers and twenty-one men. Her original armament was three one-pounders and three eighteen-inch triple torpedo tubes. Her design speed was 22.5 knots. This *Preble* was placed in commission December 14, 1903, and was assigned to the Pacific Fleet, operating with the Second and Fourth Torpedo Flotillas, which cruised off the western seaboard from Washington to the Panama Canal Zone. She engaged in that duty from the time of her first commission until late 1908, when she made a cruise to Hawaii and Samoa. She arrived at Mare Island, California, in February 1909 and was placed in reserve.

The fourth *Preble* (DD-345), was built by the Bath Iron Works of Bath, Maine. Her keel was laid April 12, 1919, and she was launched on March 8, 1920, at the Boston Navy Yard, where Commander H. A. Baldridge assumed command. She departed Boston on March 28 to receive torpedoes and equipment at Newport and on April 3 sailed for her shakedown cruise and maneuvers with the Atlantic Fleet in Cuban waters. She returned to Newport on May 17, having sailed via New York.

Assigned special duty in Mexican waters, the *Preble* departed from Newport in June 1920 and arrived in Vera Cruz, making three voyages to Galveston, Texas, to obtain serum and medical supplies to fight bubonic plague in Mexico. She then cruised with the fleet on the eastern seaboard of the United States, and to waters off Cuba and the Panama Canal. Early in 1921 the Atlantic and Pacific Fleets joined in the Canal Zone and cruised to the west coast of South America, engaging in battle practice and combined fleet maneuvers en route. From 1921 to 1937 the *Preble* operated in three fleets, Atlantic, Pacific, and Asiatic.

In 1937 the *Preble* was transferred from Destroyers, Battle Force, to duty with Minecraft, Battle Force, and was converted to light minelayer at Pearl Harbor. Her hull classification and number were changed to DM-20, effective June 30, 1937. She remained in the Hawaiian area until the outbreak of World War II, engaging in mining exercises, maneuvers, and tactics with various units of the fleet and conducting reconnaissance of Midway, Palmyra, and Johnston Islands. On November 21, 1941, she entered the Pearl Harbor Navy Yard for overhaul, and she was in that status on

December 7, 1941, when the Japanese forces launched their attack. Her fire and enginerooms had been secured, and she was unable to get underway. Necessary guns and munitions were not aboard, but two of her crew assisted in manning guns of the USS *Cummins* until that ship got underway. A large number of the *Preble*'s crew fought fires and assisted in the care of the wounded on board the battleship *Pennsylvania*. On January 30, 1942, the *Preble* completed her yard overhaul and, after trial runs, joined the patrol operation just off the Pearl Harbor entrance. The *Preble* participated in numerous operations in the Pacific as a minelayer and swept channels for the larger combatant ships. During the next two years, her mine-laying operations near Japanese combat lanes resulted in the sinking of many enemy destroyers and escort ships.

During World War II the *Preble* served the entire war operating in the Pacific and earned eight battle stars for operations listed below:

1 Star Pearl Harbor – Midway:
December 7, 1941
1 Star Capture and Defense of Guadalcanal:
January 3 – February 2, 1943
1 Star Consolidation of Solomon Islands:
May 6 – 13, 1943
1 Star New Georgia Group Operation:
June 29 – 30, 1943
1 Star Marshall Islands Operations:
January 29 – February 8, 1944
1 Star Western Caroline Islands Operations:
September 6 – October 14, 1944
1 Star Leyte Landings:
October 12 – 20, 1944
1 Star Luzon Operations:
January 4 – 18, 1945

She arrived at San Diego in late 1945 and departed that port for the East Coast. She arrived at Norfolk Virginia, November 20, 1945. After off-loading her ammunition and fuel, she entered the Norfolk Naval Shipyard where she was placed out of commission on December 7, 1945. The *Preble*'s name was stricken from the Navy list on January 3, 1946.

The fifth *Preble* (DLG-15), my most recent duty station, was a leader in the modern Navy, one of the first ships built from keel up to fire the Terrier Guided Missile. Like her predecessor, DLG-15 was built by the Bath Iron Works Corporation in Bath, Maine; she was commissioned on May 9, 1960, at the naval shipyard in Boston, Massachusetts.

In February 1961, the *Preble* had completed testing and training and was assigned to operations in the western Pacific until September of that year. During 1961, she earned the Battle Efficiency Award, Departmental Excellence Awards in engineering and missilery, and the NEY Award for being the ship serving the best meals in the fleet.

After a short Far East cruise and extensive training in 1964, the *Preble* deployed with the Seventh Fleet off the coast of Vietnam in 1965. It was during this operation that the *Preble* conducted shore bombardments south of DaNang and thus became the first of her class ever to fire any weapon at a hostile force. In September of 1965, the *Preble* participated in the first overland rescue of a downed aviator from a sea-based helicopter in the Vietnam War. She returned to her home port of San Diego in December of that year.

The *Preble* was deployed in the Far East from October 1966 until April 1967 and again from January 1968 until July, when she took part in anti-air and search-and-rescue operations. While the ship was assigned to search-and-rescue duty the *Preble*'s helicopter attachment made the first overland rescue in North Vietnam, picking up the pilot and radar intercept officer from a downed carrier-based aircraft despite intense enemy opposition. Late in 1968, the *Preble* returned to the East Coast of the United States, where she was decommissioned at Philadelphia Naval Shipyard. From January 1969 until June 1970, the *Preble* underwent anti-air warfare modernization. New radar and communications equipment was installed, and the weapons system was modified to permit firing of the Standard Missile. The Navy Tactical Data System was installed also, enabling the *Preble* to process by digital computer the information from its sensors and exchange this information by computer-to-computer radio links with similarly equipped ships and aircraft. She was recommissioned in Philadelphia on May 23, 1970. DLG-15 then departed the East Coast on July 11, passed through the Panama Canal, and arrived at Pearl Harbor, Hawaii, August 22, 1970. The *Preble* was the first ship capable of firing Terrier Missiles to be based there. During operations off Hawaii late in 1970, the ship earned Departmental

Excellence Awards in missilery, ASW (Anti-submarine Warfare), and gunnery.

The *Preble*'s mission was to operate independently or with strike, anti-submarine, or amphibious forces, against submarine, air, and surface threats. The ship's "Main Battery" was its missile system, which used Terrier and Extended-Range Standard Missiles to engage surface targets, supersonic aircraft, and missiles. To counter the enemy beneath the seas, the *Preble* was equipped with anti-submarine rocket-thrown torpedoes and depth charges (ASROC) and torpedoes fired from two triple-tube mounts. A five-inch, fifty-four Cal. gun system provided anti-air and anti-surface firepower. Those weapons were supported by a PIRAZ-capable communications suite and updated sensor systems, including surface search radar and air search radar, three-dimensional air tracking radar, and sonar. The *Preble* was powered by four 1,200-pound high-pressure boilers that drove twin screws producing a top speed in excess of thirty knots. She had been converted to use the Navy's antipollution distillate fuel. Her length was 512 feet, beam 53 feet, draft 25 feet, and full load displacement 5,800 tons. Her complement included twenty-two officers and 356 enlisted men.

The *Preble* was capable of self-sustained operations for many weeks at a time. Speed and weather conditions were major contributing factors that determined how frequently she might need to refuel at sea. Sustained operations and maintenance of the ship's complete systems depended upon years of training and experience of her sailors and on the spirit of teamwork, which had become more and more important. Her actions during the 1971 deployment were reflected in the nomination as Ship of the Year by Destroyer Flotilla Five. The USS *Preble* (DLG-15) had earned, at the time of my boarding, the National Defense Medal, Vietnam Service Medal, Vietnam Campaign Medal (five campaigns), and Armed Forces Expeditionary Medal for operations in the Sea of Japan near Korea. Beyond being one of the finest-equipped vessels in the fleet, she had an exceptional record, and I was immediately proud to be a member of her crew.

At that time in my career it was reasonable to assume the *Preble* would most likely be my final duty station. I was beginning to feel a bit disenchanted with a rapidly changing Navy and began to take notice of how many other senior enlisted men had similar feelings. The thirty-year career that many men had intended on serving became twenty-year careers as they elected to take early retirement options and return to civilian life. The

USS Preble (DLG-15) – August 1973 - July 1975

major difference between the twenty-year and thirty-year career was the difference in the monthly pension one would receive. At twenty years, the pension amounted to 50 percent of base pay and was calculated at 2.5 percent per year of military service. Every year served beyond twenty continued to increase the amount by 2.5 percent up to the thirty-year mark, at which time it stopped. The maximum amount one could draw was equal to thirty years times 2.5 percent – 75 percent of base pay. With all of the changes that were taking place, many "lifers" were not looking at the 75 percent figure as a viable alternative. They considered themselves working for half-pay by remaining beyond the twenty-year mark since they knew that they would receive half their base pay at that time. As career counselor I was cognizant of active duty benefits that were lost when individuals got out, but whatever benefits there were, in many instances they were outweighed by a very attractive second civilian career at a fairly young age. A second career while drawing Navy retirement pay was an attractive proposition few failed to recognize and take advantage of. It was not really "retirement" pay when one elected to get out after twenty years. It was "retainer" pay. Retirement from the military was based on a full thirty years, some of which could be, and most often was, Reserve time. Without going into reams of details, the following summary explains: Upon completion of twenty years, most sailors elected to get out and become a part of the "Fleet

Reserve," subject to recall in the event of some kind of extreme disaster or international crisis. These people received retainer pay, since they were considered "retained" by the Navy. Their titles/ratings included the "USN-FR" designation. At the end of thirty years (ten years into Fleet Reserve time), they were transferred/redesignated as "retired," and their titles were changed to reflect their newly acquired status; "USN-RET." There was very little other distinction; they were still subject to recall, but our nation would have to be at war and all other sources would have to have been exhausted before retirees would be recalled. It was extremely unlikely that anyone in full retirement would ever be recalled to active duty.

I began to pay more and more attention to the reasons many chiefs were getting out. Some, particularly those in highly skilled fields such as electronics, knew they could make a great deal more money as civilians and they would no longer be governed by "the needs of the service." There would be no long periods of separation from family and loved ones, no uniforms to maintain, no long periods of time isolated at sea, and no more military discipline that at times required the enforcement of unpopular rules and activities. Other ratings, such as mine, were less apt to find desirable jobs "on the outside." There were, for example, no steam propulsion plants on dry land. Any desire I may have at one time had, to continue working on any kind of steam-generating plant as a civilian, no longer existed. In a sense, I would have to start over, and I was not too attracted to the prospect of starting at the bottom once again. But there was still ample time before I would make the decision on whether or not I would remain beyond the twenty-year point. Besides, I was not anxious to make such a significant decision.

The *Preble* had the largest officer/crew complement of any ship on which I had previously served, and I knew that it would be difficult maintaining the close relationship with officers and crew that existed where I had previously served. I was immediately faced with several CPO related problems that needed my attention if I expected to be readily accepted into their midst. One of those problems was that there were so many chiefs some had to sleep in substandard berthing – in a cramped compartment that lacked the upgrades common to most CPO berthing spaces. There was one CPO berthing compartment at the aft of the ship, one just forward and below the CPO mess, and a third, "affectionately" referred to as the "over-flow," a compartment below the CPO mess that was little better than the one I berthed in while serving as a mess cook many years prior. CPOs, as with officers, were guaranteed better living conditions than E-6s and below. Some larger ships provided special berthing spaces for first class petty officers, others provided for specific petty officer grades. High on my list of priorities was to make the overflow compartment more habitable for chief petty officers, something they should have done of their own initiative long before.

I was surprised to learn that the senior enlisted man, an E-8, was not interested in his responsibility as mess president and had waived his right to that position to another E-8. That gave me the impression different CPO pay grades were not considered relevant by *Preble* chiefs. I felt obligated to change that. Also, there were not enough CPO mess cooks to provide adequate coverage over the areas that required their attention. As insignificant as that may sound, it was a major problem. I had never served at a command where chiefs had to fill in where there was a lack of mess cooks.

The mess cook situation was the problem with which I had the most difficulty. On November 17, three months after I reported aboard, the following hand-written "directive" was delivered to me in a sealed envelope by a very low-rated enlisted man. It read:

FROM: Supply Officer
TO: Master Chief Atkinson[sic]
SUBJECT: Conditions of CPO Passageways

ENCL: (1) Copy of my inspection of these psgys at 1530, 17 Nov 73

1. Since relieving as Supply Officer on 1 June 1973 the worst passageways in the Supply Department have continually been the three CPO PSGYS 2-53-01-L, 1-59-1-L, and 1-66-0-L. Copies of the CO's passageway policy have been given to involved CPO's and the CPO Mess Cooks personally by myself. Numerous discussions have been held regarding care of these areas. The results of these efforts have been nil (see encl [1]). It is obvious to me that the Commanding Officer's policy is not being followed in these areas. There has been a steady and consistent lack of supervision by involved CPO's, namely the Mess President and Mess Caterer, to insist that these duties are properly performed.

2. The CO's policy regarding passageways will be complied with in all respects. The following action will commence as of Monday 19 Nov 73.

A. Each Mess Cook will have a copy of the CO's psgy policy on his person during working hours.

B. Mess Cooks will spend from 0830 – 0930 in his passageway every day – no exceptions – except Sat & Sun as noted in the CO's policy.

C. Between 0930 and 1000 the psgy will be inspected by the Mess President or Mess Caterer.

D. The Supply Officer will then be notified that the psgy is ready for inspection.

3. I simply will not tolerate the continued unsatisfactory condition of these spaces.

Respectfully,
[Signature]
LCDR SC, USN

Enclosure (1) was an itemized list of the lieutenant commander's discrepancies –totally exaggerated, or more appropriately, absolutely preposterous. It made the passageways analogous to conditions found at a garbage dump. The list was lengthy and included things such as "Dirt in corner," "Back of ladder filthy," "Trash laying around," "Black gunk oozing through tile," and "Greasy hand prints," His expected overall evaluation was "Unsat."

An already bad situation immediately became worse, and I was named as having shirked my duties. I was furious because of the lieutenant commander's ignorance – he was apparently oblivious to the unsuitable conditions with which all CPOs were having to contend. Had he been the leader he was trying so desperately to impersonate, he would have taken the time to properly evaluate the reason(s) behind the lack of spit-polished passageways. With that knowledge he would have been provided with an alternative - the opportunity to assist his objectionable subordinates, the CPO community.

I wasted no time in writing the following rebuttal, which I sealed in an envelope and did as the Supply Officer had done; I had the lowest rated mess cook hand-carry it to him.

FROM: CPO Mess President
TO: Supply Officer
SUBJ: CPO Mess areas of responsibility

CPO mess cooks and compartment cleaners have been thoroughly instructed in their duties and responsibilities. They are aware of trouble areas and are striving to improve.

It is apparent to me that little action was taken in the past to provide adequate supervision and guidance for the mess cooks/compartment cleaners. I have taken steps to insure all areas assigned under the responsibility of the CPO mess receive greater attention.

To be assigned as a CPO mess cook is usually recognized as a most desired position. Having occupied a CPO mess for some time, and believing myself to be thoroughly knowledgeable of the duties normally assigned to a CPO mess cook, it is obvious to me [as it should be to you] why USS PREBLE does not have many individuals anxious to serve in this capacity. PREBLE is not constructed nor prepared to carry 29 CPOs. Obviously our overcrowded situation creates a problem in itself. Crowded conditions always cause more clean-up and more personal attention on the part of the CPO mess cook(s). I believe traffic in and out of the CPO Mess is greater than anywhere on the ship. "Go ask the Chief" seems to be much more of a standard than – go ask anyone else. Everyone knows, or can be reasonably sure, where to find "the Chief" if he is not actually on the job. Our mess is frequented by white-hats seeking guidance, officers seeking assistance – and sometimes "refuge," meetings of all types take place there, and one should never forget its intended function; that of providing a lounge area for CPOs.

During other than meal hours a single mess cook is tasked with maintaining the CPO mess – and he does a good job of it when the overall picture is truly taken into consideration. Most CPOs are conscientious about assisting in maintaining the area clean but with the number of CPOs we have and the constant traffic it is a never ending job for the mess cook(s). Our seating arrangement for meals provides nine seats that can only be utilized one at a time. This means added efforts are required to insure all CPOs are fed properly, i.e., additional place settings, insuring serving bowls are adequately filled in accordance with the menu, keeping up with the inflow of dirty dishes/utensils in the scullery/pantry – while at the same time assisting in maintaining the lounge area somewhat orderly.

Navy Regulations addresses consideration for all messes. We are authorized one mess cook for each 15 men, or portion thereof. With only two more CPOs assigned to PREBLE we would be authorized 3 mess cooks.

We are also required to utilize our mess cooks as compartment cleaners due to what has been described as a shortage of manpower. This has been a burden to all of us. We have accepted this – but we are nonetheless concerned about it.

In today's Navy a lot of emphasis is being placed on understanding situations and individuals prior to issuing orders – and not expecting individuals to perform miracle functions of accomplishment when such things as personnel allowed as compared to personnel assigned – man-hours required as compared to man-hours available are not taken into full consideration. Insisting or demanding can certainly be required in many instances, however demands to accomplish some functions which would cause other functions of equal or greater importance to go unaccomplished are not in the best interest of anything.

I must balance the work load between all areas of responsibility – placing emphasis where needed the most. I can not require outstanding results in all areas of responsibility without having the necessary tools with which to work. I most certainly can require all areas of responsibility to receive attention – but not the attention they need without the necessary tools.

Passageways are under constant scrutiny. I receive reminders from various sources that more attention is required. There are other areas of concern that are not under constant surveillance but are of equal importance. Specifically, berthing spaces and heads.

Consider the time involved in breaking out cleaning gear or maintenance gear – in changing back and forth from working uniform to meal serving uniform – in restowing cleaning gear and maintenance gear – and in cleaning up (personal hygiene) prior to serving meals. Consider my responsibilities to the Command, to Engineering and to all CPOs along with my responsibilities to you; that is, primary as well as secondary. The same consideration is due the mess caterer – who is not, and should not be, considered a mess decks MAA.

Perhaps we are not doing our very best, but with all respect I challenge anyone who doubts we are not exerting honest efforts at upgrading all areas of responsibility. (At a CPO meeting held November 10, the Commanding Officer commented on our progress.)

If you assign one additional man to the CPO mess we will have no more – no less than is needed and an immediate reorganization will bring about the results you expect. If we can't perform in an outstanding manner with the necessary tools our competence would then become questionable.

Very respectfully,
MMCM P.L. ADKISSON
CPO Mess President

Immediately I informed the skipper of my letter. I had, to some degree, placed myself in a position of disobeying an order and wanted to make sure the Captain was aware of my reasons. Contrary to what many civilians as well as military men might believe, there is *nothing* wrong with disobeying orders! It is, however, very wrong to disobey *lawful* orders. Since the Supply Officer's orders were beyond the scope of that which could have been either efficiently or effectively accomplished, I considered them something less than lawful. Fortunately, the Captain was already cognizant of the problem and he therefore appraised the situation in favor of CPO needs rather than the Supply Officer's nefarious demands.

My letter, and a timely visit to the Captain, paid off, and promptly the Supply Officer provided the CPO mess with one additional mess cook. I had overplayed my hand when I said we would have sufficient mess cook manpower with the addition of one man. I failed to place enough emphasis on the fact that compartment cleaners were supposed to be a separate entity, that where we could get by with two mess cooks, assuming their duties were confined to those of mess cooking, we desperately needed additional assistance in maintaining the CPO berthing spaces. Since I had placed my competence on the line I had no alternative other than to make the best of what we had. The Supply Officer never spoke to me again – which did not hurt my feelings one bit. I was probably the first enlisted man of any grade that not only challenged his orders, I did so in writing.

The *Preble* was a beautiful ship. It was better-equipped and more modern than anything I had served aboard, and it had a crew that consisted of an exceptionally high number of well-educated petty officers, all of whom were highly skilled and confident in their respective fields. Even with that, it was not long before I began to take on a distinct aversion for both ship and crew. I found that the bigger the size and the larger the complement, the greater the dissent. That is, everything that could be considered adverse appeared to compound proportionately; with greater size and higher numbers, the more portentous conditions or impressions became.

Preble's Executive Officer, a lieutenant commander, was an articulate individual who radiated with intelligence. He was well educated, had a great deal of naval experience, was fully capable of his position, and he utilized good common sense while carrying out his responsibilities. The XO did have one noticeable and irritating quirk; not properly recognizing different CPO pay grades. We were all "Chief" to him. On several occasions I politely brought our correct titles to his attention, citing Navy regulations as the law that dictated correct titles be used when addressing E-7s, E-8s, and E-9s. I reminded him of the pride that comes with promotions; that it was not only required we be addressed correctly, the distinction between grades needed to be recognized. I reminded him that within officer ranks similar distinctions had to be made in respect of the insignia they wore. I also reminded him of the confusion that existed when young, inexperienced sailors and members of other military branches tried to grasp the reasoning behind some Navy officer's titles. For example, at the very bottom of the officer ranks was the 0-1, the ensign, who was addressed as either "Mister" or "Ensign." Ensigns hated being referred to as Ensign. Promotion meant they could be called "Lieutenant," a significantly different title that seemed to carry greater authority with or without added responsibilities. The next higher grade, that of 0-2, (lieutenant junior grade), was preferably addressed "Lieutenant," the same as 0-3s, but they accepted the "Mister" title reluctantly. It did not seem to make a lot of sense, but it was customary and it did shorten some otherwise lengthy titles. Similarly, the officer grade 0-4 (lieutenant commander) was addressed as "Commander," the same as 0-5. Then there was the title "Captain," which was reserved not only for 0-6s but also for any individual regardless of rank or pay grade who had the responsibility of commanding a vessel. Confusing? It seemed so during my younger days, but eventually titles fell into place along with everything else Navy related.

Every time the XO addressed me as Chief I would take the time to remind him that I was not "Chief," I was a "Master Chief" and I took exception to being addressed as anything less. With each reminder I became a little more outspoken, and each time the lieutenant commander grinned when he provided me with a superficial apology. I finally had my fill and was beginning to think the XO was "yanking my chain" by intentionally calling me by the wrong title. It had become an uncalled-for repeated mistake, and I had no intention on allowing it to continue without taking some unusual steps to stop it.

That time came one day as I was walking through the crew's mess. The timing could not have been better – the mess was jammed full. I was a little over halfway through the compartment when I heard the XO's distinct voice call out, "Hey, Chief."

I spun around and in a louder voice than usual I responded with, "Yes, *Mister*, you were referring to me?"

The Commander's face turned a most crimson red and the thought raced through my mind that I had probably gone beyond the limits of good judgment, certainly beyond the limits prescribed by Navy regulations. The "observers," the many enlisted men within sight and sound of my response, didn't know how to react. Some tried to hold back but burst out laughing; there were a variety of chuckles and then dead silence. The crew, those present, sat motionless, all eyes darted back and forth between the XO and me, all were wondering, with the same anticipation I was feeling, what would happen next. I knew that the color of my face probably mirrored the XO's, because I was not only angered by his insistence on calling me Chief; I had also embarrassed myself by the manner in which I had displayed my resentment.

The Commander gained a very high degree of respect in everyone's eyes when he turned away from me and addressed the crew. "The Master Chief has made his point abundantly clear, and it is my responsibility, as it should always have been, to make sure that not only I, but the entire crew recognize and acknowledge the difference between pay grades and that we all use correct titles when addressing one another." He continued, "Master Chief, you have corrected me for the last time." (I saw a slight grin and the hint of a wink.) "I will give it my best effort to address you correctly in the future." Then, as normal flesh color returned to his face, I saw a broad smile that assured me everything was okay, further reinforced with his final words: "Please don't call me Mister again."

I answered through an equally broad smile; "You have my word sir; now what was it you needed?"

The crew roared with laughter when he said, "It couldn't have been important; seems I've forgotten."

The *Preble* was much like the nuclear Navy in that the qualification process was very similar. One of my jobs was to make sure all engineering personnel took seriously their responsibility to put forth maximum effort toward the timely completion of the qualification program they were assigned. Where the nuclear Navy had what was less than affectionately known as "Rickover's Hatchet Team," the *Preble*'s Engineering Department would be subjected to a thorough examination by the "PEB," the Propulsion Examining Board. Members of the board were responsible for determining whether or not the "PQS," Personal Qualification Standards, program was effective to the degree that the ship was seaworthy, engineering-wise. Another part of the process, the "LOE," or Light Off Examination, was also witnessed by highly qualified engineers and was the final step in the qualification process. PEB was a new concept that was being phased in. Once it was fully implemented throughout the fleet, engineers on all U.S. man-of-war fighting ships would be subjected to the testing process. The *Preble* was scheduled for a WestPac deployment prior to the PEB, which would provide some time for the engineers to prepare. But the brunt of the training would take place following that deployment – upon our return to Hawaii.

On September 24, 1973, just under a month after I reported for duty, the *Preble* departed Pearl Harbor and headed west toward the Orient.

I knew my way around the ship, but I also knew that I would have to "burn some midnight oil" in order to more thoroughly familiarize myself with the engineering plant. My own PQS program took up most of my waking moments. As the senior enlisted member of the Engineering Department I was not only expected to maintain the proper qualification profile; I had a very strong self-desire to make sure that I was more qualified, more knowledgeable of all engineering plant parameters, than anyone else. My past experiences on different plant configurations made training easier for me than for most first-timers. I had, as a matter of preparing for advancement exams, learned a great deal about a variety of engineering technology, much of which I had never seen and probably never would see. I lacked valuable "hands on" experience that *Preble* would provide in abundance.

Following the routine refueling stop at Midway Island, we steamed on to Guam, where the *Preble* remained for five days.

I wanted to surprise Al and Joe, the two Guamanian friends that had taken the time to show Doc and me around the island about six years prior. I had only visited Al's home on one occasion and my memory of the exact location was vague, but I did remember that his place was not far from Agana, the capital of Guam, near the town of Barrigada. I rented a Special Services vehicle and relied on instinct as much as memory as I began my search. Locating Barrigada was not at all difficult. After taking several different rural roads off in the general direction of what I could recall, I saw a place that resembled Al's home. I was confused by an abundance of other homes in the area that had been built in the intervening years. Al answered my knock at the door.

Al had changed; he seemed very reserved and not the happy-go-lucky person I recalled. Several times I asked about Joe, but Al had a way of ignoring my queries, preferring to talk of other things. Once Al was completely comfortable with the friendship we had reestablished, he opened up to me. Joe had been a passenger in Al's car, and there had been a terrible accident. Joe was killed in that accident and Al had spent some time in prison as a result of his negligence. I was quite set back at this news because I knew firsthand of the close friendship Al and Joe had shared. Losing a best friend would be hard enough to take, but carrying the responsibility of having caused or been a party to that death could only make it calamitous. Al suffered what must have been agonizing and constant reminders of that tragedy every time he looked in the mirror and saw the noticeable physical scars on his face, scars acquired from injuries he had suffered at the time of the mishap.

Our reunion was not all that which either of us would have preferred, but we made the best of what little time we were able to share. We talked of many things but primarily of the rapid growth in the tourist industry and of the possibilities in making a lot of money in real estate. I did not have the foresight that Al had and I couldn't imagine any real growth potential on such a small, terribly humid tropical island; an island that had practically no nightlife, narrow roads, a maximum speed limit of thirty-five miles per hour, and an island where nearly all structures were plagued by mildew caused by heavy rainfall and very humid conditions. Al could not have realized the magnitude of his prediction, as history would confirm. Guam did grow and it became another beautiful tourist paradise, frequented by travelers from around the world; particularly by the Japanese.

As I was driving along the road on my way back to the ship I thought about the reasoning behind the thirty-five-mile-per-hour maximum speed limit. Most of the more heavily traveled roads were made of crushed coral and cement. At the time the roads were being constructed no one took into consideration what coral consisted of and what the consequences would be by using that medium in the pavement. Coral is a living organism; it is alive and it grows. Without going any further into the process by which it grows, suffice it to say that it can easily be compared to any form of crustacean. The road was made up of something very similar to crushed snails – quite safe when dry but extremely slippery when wet. Since the island receives rain nearly every day, year-round, one can easily recognize the dangers associated with driving too fast. It was annoying having to drive at such a slow pace; difficult for those who were accustomed to driving at much higher speeds, but certainly in our best interest to do so.

The *Preble* was the melting pot of boards, committees, and councils. Anything worthy of being considered was immediately referred to one of them. There were seminars of all kinds, "UPWARD" being one that in my opinion created more problems than it prevented. *UPWARD* stood for "Understanding Personal Worth and Racial Dignity," and its purpose was to bring together racial harmony by openly discussing our "differences." The theory was that by expressing our opinions openly and in front of each other, regardless how derogatory, by name calling as it was, we could learn to get along better. I have always thought of UPWARD seminars as nothing more than just plain bullshit, but I played along with the program. Racial tensions were *not* improved as a result of UPWARD. Exactly the opposite took place. And why not? After all, weren't we being encouraged to tell each other face to face just exactly what it was that we disliked about each other? Instead of maintaining our prejudice to ourselves, we became openly prejudiced. Participation in UPWARD was mandatory. I find it hard to believe, even after all these years, that someone really thought that anything good would come from attending sessions during which we made it abundantly clear the things we disliked about each other. The bottom line

574

never changed; it only made each race that much more insistent on retaining their/our own beliefs and customs. It encouraged individuals, intentionally or otherwise, to flaunt that which they knew irritated those of another race. It caused more distrust between races as highly opinionated feelings became widely known. Blacks knew precisely what it was that whites did not like about them, and they didn't like it; and vice versa – whites did not like being told of things that blacks did not like about them. Was anyone going to make an effort at changing those things? To the counselors at those seminars the answer was a resounding "Yes," but between attendees the answer was a definite; "Hell, no!" UPWARD, as it was at that time, was an absolute failure, a joke that quite expectedly backfired. Many friendships that crossed racial lines were clearly destroyed as a result. A perfect example of good intentions gone bad.

The *Preble* also had habitability boards and various committees. She had a Recreation Council and a Safety Council. There were Commanding Officer meetings, Minority Affairs meetings, and a Planning Board for Training. There were qualification boards and there were meetings to create meetings! Then, there were assignments whereby attendees were individually tasked with carrying out the dictates of the senior members. There was not much time to spare for those who were required to attend. As SEA I was not only an attendee; I was expected to provide meaningful input, always with the crew's best interests in mind. I was growing tired of the whole hypocritical mess; especially knowing that a good portion of my time in attendance was just plain wasted!

I often thought that spare time could be better utilized in matters other than standing personnel inspections. I understood the need for periodic inspections; however, I questioned (in my mind) why the Commanding Officer required that so many had to be conducted while at sea, topside and in foul weather! On one such occasion the skipper called for an "All Hands Personnel Inspection" and everyone fell in at divisional quarters. Engineers were the last to be inspected for reasons I never accepted, presumably because of their location – the last place the inspecting party passed. The inspecting party could just as easily have started their inspection tour with the engineers as ending it there. As the last to be inspected, engineers were required to remain standing the longest. That day it was raining lightly and the sea was fairly calm. The skipper enjoyed taking his time since he had a remarkable propensity for nitpicking. I was furious by the time the Captain finally arrived; more so when he found fault with so many of us. We had been standing out in the rain in our finest white uniforms only to find ourselves looking like a bunch of soggy animals by the time he got there. I recall his hateful stare as he glared at each of us, then picked out insignificant, barely visible faults that he would have us believe might cause the ship to sink or somehow bring about an abrupt end to the world. He spent an inordinate amount of time scrutinizing every inch of my uniform.

"Master Chief, the tip of your belt buckle is showing and I won't have my chiefs dressed so shoddily!" he snarled at me. I was embarrassed the following day when I, along with numerous others who had been identified along with their deficiencies, was identified in the POD as being in need of a complete new uniform. The write-up would lead one to believe that I was anything other than a good example for the crew to follow. I thought of it as poor judgment for the skipper to categorize my uniform as something other than appropriate. Soon I realized that that miserable individual had an outlandish superiority complex. He enjoyed his habit of exaggerating negatives and imagining nonexistent problems, things that were not at all in need of attention. It was his way of showing the officers and crew that he was so superior he had the power to alter reality. My opinion, of course!

The CO was welcome to attend CPO meetings, and he was usually alerted to them in advance. That is, unless we chose not to share our order of business with him. At those meetings he seldom had much to say, but he did offer to answer any questions we might have. At one such meeting one of the chiefs asked a question that we all had a stake in, a real concern for, but most of us were reluctant to ask. We knew that most whites resisted placing blacks on report because of their predictable attitude in claiming such action as being entirely discriminatory. In some instances violations by blacks were overlooked rather than having to face charges of bigotry or some other form of racism. Even with that, there were disproportionate numbers of blacks being written up for breaking the rules. The chief chose his words carefully.

"Captain, why is the ratio of blacks attending Mast higher than that of whites yet the punishment you give blacks is more lenient?"

The Captain was red-faced as he blurted out, "That is a racist statement and I will not respond to it." He then excused himself, probably expecting a barrage of similar questions since the chief had clearly opened the door to Pandora's box. That CO and the USS *Colahan*'s Executive Officer must have attended the same school of thought. They were a great deal alike, although I was far more comfortable serving under the CO. More likely, I had learned to cope.

Strong suspicion led me to believe, although I have no way of knowing for certain, that most chief petty officers who drank ashore probably possessed booze of one kind or another while at sea. It was not something CPOs openly discussed, though, I'm sure, as was the case with Julius and me aboard the USS *Tecumseh*, there were guarded times of absolute privacy when friends shared an after-hours drink. I can honestly say that from the time I was promoted to CPO up to this point in time I had never been offered a drink by a fellow chief while at sea. Not by another chief, not by a lower-rated man, and certainly not by an officer. But somewhere around the middle of October 1973, while we were en route from Guam to the Philippines, Doc, a fellow chief, asked me if I'd care to join him for a drink. I was a little shocked at his offer of "hospitality," surprised at his trust, but I accepted his invitation.

Doc escorted me to the Sick Bay where, once inside, he locked the door behind us. He went directly to his safe where prescription drugs were normally stored. Slowly and methodically Doc twisted the combination knob, and within seconds the door was open. Doc reached inside and retrieved a fifth of very fine whiskey, which he held up to the light in a dignified gesture. Doc and I formed a bond on that occasion. He had trusted me and I had no reason to distrust him. We soon became liberty mates; both of us having earned positions that allowed us the privilege of open gangway liberty.

On every ship I served, I never failed to recognize how the Doc, whoever he was and of whatever pay grade, was always one to envy. In some areas his authority surpassed that of the CO. In the military, a doctor, or in the absence of a doctor his representative (normally a CPO), can countermand a superior's order if he feels the health of a person or persons are endangered. The ship's Doc had amenities and conveniences that were not available to officers or to enlisted men. Not only did he enjoy open gangway liberty while the ship was in port; he stood no duties while the ship was underway. He had access and the authority to dispense medications and was the right person to know when one needed the cure for something he did not want publicized. And the Doc had his own world, Sick Bay, where behind locked doors he could escape all that surrounded him.

577

Preble's Doc was older and more mature than other chief hospitalmen with whom I had served. He was stricter with the younger men as he made it clear to them how wrong they were when they were out of line. Up to the time Doc reported for duty on board the *Preble*, he had served with the Marine Corps. Apparently a great deal of Marine-type rugged individualism had rubbed off on him, and I admired him for it. Too many chiefs were reluctant to take charge. Many preferred to leave well enough alone and to not "rock the boat" while they allowed someone else of authority to take the initiative. Not so with *Preble*'s Doc. He not only took on the appearance of fearing nothing; I believe he welcomed the opportunity to exercise his authority along with his ability. I admired Doc in many ways.

October 14 we pulled into Subic Bay, Philippines, the place I was probably most familiar with; where I always enjoyed myself. The town of Olongapo had changed, much for the better; more noticeably so at night. It had taken on the appearance of a small Las Vegas; a miniaturized clone with its wide and impressive variety of brightly-lighted neon lights. The streets were filled with sailors, but with the change of times it was rare to see anyone in uniform. The choice of bars had become far more varied and the availability of female companionship had multiplied exponentially. There were very few unattractive girls; the competition was congested with multitudes of beautiful and shapely women from which to select. The grapevine of information that had been so flawless back in the late fifties and early sixties no longer existed, and as a result men were far more apt to have several favorites or, worse yet, never go back to the same girl twice. The expected effect of such promiscuity was the creation of new strains of VD that had become resistant to treatment. VD was running rampant, and those who dared to "dip their wicks" without taking extreme precautions were as good as guaranteed an infection of one kind or another.

My first stop was the Hernandez place. Their home was en route to Rick's monkeypod business, which was to be my second stop, and this time I had Rick's beautiful sliver-and-gold pocket watch with me. The Hernandez family had remained in the same home since my last visit, but they had plans on constructing what was going to be one of the most beautiful homes in the area. I was greeted by the entire family with the same hospitality I had grown to expect. Little Lea, age four, clung to me as any child would, knowing I always had some treats with me. It was very unlikely that I would ever show up without balloons, gum, or candy.

Knowing that our stay was only going to be a day or two, I cut my visit short. I enjoyed the Hernandez hospitality, but I also enjoyed the night-life. That afternoon I postponed the trip out to Rick's place knowing there would be other, longer periods of time in port when I could spend more time reminiscing with him and his wife. I was always cautious never to overextend my visits and not to stop in too frequently. I had no desire to wear out my welcome by becoming a nuisance to anyone.

Between October 14 and October 19, 1973, the *Preble* was in Subic Bay a total of three days, barely enough time for the crew, the men who had never been there in particular, to enjoy the nightlife as much as they would have desired. During one of those days, by chance I came across another old friend, Mina, the one who had fought so viciously with Elena for my attention nearly ten years before. It was something of a shock to both of us, bumping into each other in an out-of-the-way nightclub where she still hustled drinks and guys. I know that I must have aged over the years, but Mina had become a very old woman, little more than skin and bones. Her face was wrinkled well beyond her years, and she was no longer the attractive person she had been at one time. We recognized each other, and it was a pleasant but short reunion. We danced and we talked of "the good old days" knowing that they, as we had known them, were gone forever. It was enjoyable talking with Mina but a little uncomfortable – too much water under the bridge. I had outgrown the desire to participate in the antics I previously enjoyed.

Men had many different opinions of the "bar girls," or "barmaids," as they were most frequently referred to, and most were unavoidably based on personal experiences. The girls preferred to be known as hostesses, which made them feel more dignified. I never made an attempt to change any man's mind, whether his opinion was favorable or unfavorable, nor did any opinion change my mind. Over the years I had learned that bar girls were people with feelings and desires, not at all unlike most girls in other professions. Of course there were those that were greedy or who overstepped the bounds of fair play, but they were in the minority. The bar girls could get just as hungry and had the same basic needs that I had, but I was far more fortunate. It was tough in the Philippines, where the girls' earnings (when there *were* earnings) were barely enough to sustain life. That is why there was always such an abundance of beautiful females in and around military

579

installations; that's where the money was. The prettier they were, the more money they could make. They struggled with the competition to make a living and, for the most part, did it honestly. There were always stories of how so-and-so got rolled, or how some "broad" stole someone's money or something else of value, but I had a tendency to believe those individuals unwittingly invited or placed themselves in bad situations that were more conducive to foul play. I enjoyed the company of bar girls and found them to be exceptionally informative, interesting, and knowledgeable. Most of them enjoyed an enviable sense of humor. Without the bar girls, what kind of life would it have been for the typical seagoing sailor? The girls all had a way of making a sailor feel comfortable; more at home. I respected them and their decision to do what they felt necessary in order to survive. There were alternatives, but to the traveler who has visited any country so plagued with poverty and has mingled with such a destitute people, the girls' choice was really not at all as bad as some might think. More than once during my career I was protected or assisted by female acquaintances. I had been put up for the night after curfew, had torn clothing repaired and washed, had been hidden or removed from harm's way, and I had been comforted in some other manner by bar girls. I thank them for having been a very real part of my military career. When no one else was there, no mail from friends or relatives back home, and I felt forgotten or alone and in need of special companionship or friendship, they were there for me and the comfort they provided was appreciated.

There were live shows for the adventurous – those who were more interested in Olongapo's "far out" world of entertainment. Some nightclub acts included audience participation, although getting caught meant serious trouble for the military member. What I am about to describe might not be entirely believable to the average inexperienced individual, but it is 100 percent factual. *Boomba* shows could be seen on television, in nightclubs, or privately in one's place of choice. They went well beyond the boundaries of acted-out triple-X-rated pornographic movies. Boomba shows included "acts" where several attractive female strippers lured members of the audience up onstage. After a certain amount of teasing the girls stripped themselves along with their willing participants; gave them "head," and the live scene quickly evolved into every possible variety of group sex. Doing "69" was as common as "sandwich jobs," one girl between two men. Making a girl "airtight" was another spectacle the audience responded to wildly

580

– a three-on-one situation where every bodily orifice of the female was "plugged" by male audience volunteers. Regardless of how lewd the show was, people returned time and again, because nothing was rehearsed – it was strictly spontaneous. Volunteers from the audience were discouraged from returning to the stage on different nights because management wanted a variety that was more apt to spark continued interest. No one really knew just what would take place next, but it was bound to include sex. Contrary to what I have already written, the unattractive, the truly ugly in every sense of the word, also had ways of making money. For those in the audience who became horny, receptive, and willing to pay for the "service," they too could have fellatio performed on them by anxious and "talented" under-the-table performers. Olongapo should have been known as "Sex City," because that would most accurately describe the prevailing function that took place there. There were no holds barred when it came to putting on live shows of any nature – whatever GIs were willing to pay to see.

There was a nightly live performance at a place called Jolos where less attractive girls provided a different kind of live show. All were acts of sexual intercourse, but the girls each had their own specialty. Each encouraged, assisted, and allowed the animal of her choice – pig, dog, or pony – to repeatedly and visibly penetrate her. Jolo's was best known for the variety of bizarre sex acts performed onstage. If it was not onstage, one needed only to tell some street vendor that which he wanted to see or do and, if a price could be agreed upon, it was quickly arranged.

Out-of-the-way establishments, small hole-in-the-wall places, were also known for spontaneous lewd acts performed by bar girls and clientele. One could almost expect to see sailors or Marines taking turns having oral sex, performing cunnilingus, with strippers right on their table or up on the bar. These were not pay-to-see activities, since they could occur at any time. GIs and their willing female acquaintances were known to have sex in bar booths, on pool tables, and on the floor. Surprisingly, most of those present simply went about their business while relatively few made it a point to watch closely. Those that did watch rendered their applause during and after such acts; the magnitude of the applause was normally a good representation of how well the audience accepted the performance.

Many bars and nightclubs constructed their inside bar counters circular or horseshoe shaped, with a raised dance floor in the middle where girls could dance and strip for the pleasure of those wishing to watch. And there were always strippers willing to squat down and pick up unbelievably tall stacks of large peso coins with their vaginas! They were "gifted" with the ability to count the coins as they were being inserted, without touching them with any other part of their body, and then take (and win) bets on the number they had "engulfed." Similarly, they could make bottles and drinking glasses "disappear." There were girls proud of the fact that they could smoke a cigarette with the same part of their anatomy, actually suck in smoke and blow perfectly formed smoke rings at the nearest patron without removing the cigarette from its "holder." As was done in Hong Kong, some women inserted hard-boiled eggs in that same cavity, and then "shoot" or "pop" them like a cork from a champagne bottle into the hands of a spectator. Onlookers were known to eat those eggs, much to the delight of the girls. I need not explain which jobs or acts the unattractive women performed. What was it that caused so many GIs to go out of their way to seek such bizarre forms of diversion? It was more than curiosity; it was verification, proof positive that such things actually took place.

It was most common, and not considered vulgar or indecent, to find beautiful dancers scantily clad in bathing suits or other Frederick's of Hollywood-type undergarments, dancing erotically for the pleasure of anyone in the club. There was no such thing as a cover charge, and the price of drinks remained constant whether there was entertainment on the premises or not. A cold San Miguel beer, the best beer in the world to many a sailor, cost the equivalent of about a dime. Mixed drinks were a little higher but still dirt-cheap in comparison to the prices paid in the United States. It took a little effort finding a place that did not have one type of entertainment or another. Somewhat surprisingly, places of peace and quiet where one could go for the sole purpose of relaxation over a beverage of choice, did exist. Such places were located not far off the main strip or, for the more adventurous, farther out of town toward or at many of the nearby beaches.

When *curfew* and *out-of-bounds* became terms of the past, conditions that were no longer mandated by law or ordinance, servicemen were granted far greater latitude with respect to their more adventurous desires and activities. Without the fear of getting picked up by the Military Police or the Shore Patrol, servicemen could become more openly brazen and they would exercise their newfound freedoms without fear of being admonished. It was great taking advantage of the opportunity to see what the country was really like without having to skirt previously established borders in defiance of law or other restrictions. Without being bound by such stringent regulations, the Philippines became "that port," the most desirable liberty port in all of the Far East. It provided all that any other place had plus more, and at prices affordable to the lowest-paid enlisted man. But there were some sailors who never ventured beyond the main gate, off base. Perhaps they were a bit fearful of the unknown or unwilling to take a chance on placing themselves in the same or similar category as those who were known to indulge in questionable or immoral activities. Those servicemen who never exited military boundaries, the safety provided by the main gate, missed out on some of the greatest adventures they could ever want to observe or participate in. The Philippines had a distinct "personality," an unequaled beauty all of its own. The mountainous terrain, particularly around Baguio, was inspiring. The terraced rice paddies were extraordinary, and many of the magnificent churches and cathedrals were, incredibly, constructed lifetimes past. The people, the real natives, as I have repeatedly and affectionately referred to them, had a tough life. Many practiced survival on a daily basis as squatters; those who usually lived in grass-covered bamboo *nipa*-huts or shanties without benefit of running water, electricity, or a sewage system – many without means of support other than their daily efforts to find something edible or of value as they grappled through rubbish previously discarded by individuals not much better off than themselves. Unlike the people one sees while going through the pages of *National Geographic* or any other magazine depicting exploration, they were real – not pictures! Seeing such things firsthand made me that much more of a man, far more capable of coping with whatever disadvantages or disappointments I would be faced with during my lifetime. There can be absolutely no comparison, regardless how diminutive or trivial, between reading about these things and actually participating in or being present at the time of their occurrence. It was during this time that the Marcos family was living like Oriental potentates while many of their people starved!

Over the years the population of American military retirees, predominantly Navy men, grew impressively. Many of them settled in or near Olongapo City and either owned or were the financial backbone behind most of the local businesses. They invested in anything that was known to make money; small bars as well as more impressive, beautifully decorated nightclubs that were always filled to capacity and included an abundance of beautiful hostesses. Retirees owned small stores that lacked variety and they owned large souvenir shops that were filled with a wide selection that included monkeypod woodcarvings, jade sculptures, and seashell ornaments of unimaginable variety. And they owned many of the restaurants.

There was no need for retirees to supplement their retirement income, but many bought businesses to provide them with a hobby. They seldom played much of an active role in the hands-on management of those businesses, usually preferring or insisting that their Filipina wives or girlfriends carry out those responsibilities while they themselves drank or played away much of the business profit. Owners and operators knew that most shoppers preferred haggling with locals and that the profit margin would be greater when Caucasian owners remained hidden – out of sight, out of mind. The girls, regardless of the legitimacy of their relationship with the owners, were very willing to carry out managerial responsibilities; it gave them more than ample opportunity to embezzle whatever share of the profits they felt they could get away with or, more accurately, money they believed they deserved. It was an accepted and commonplace way of doing business.

Australians were also finding there was money to be made in the Philippines and they were beginning to buy businesses of their own; not only around Olongapo City, also around Angeles City, the other equally notorious "sex city" just outside Clark Air Base about an hour's drive away. Olongapo and Angeles were identical in most ways. There was no need to travel from one to the other in search of anything. What one had the other had, and the prices, negotiable as they were, were analogous at both locations.

I finally did make the trip out to see Rick and Ludy. I was anxious to see the expression on Rick's face when I returned his pocketwatch – still in excellent condition, still keeping perfect time. I was disappointed to find that Monkeypod Infanta, their handmade-furniture store and their adjacent bar, were no longer in business. I knew that Rick was well known not only at the Chiefs' Club on base, but also out where many other Navy retirees had made their homes.

Directly across from where Rick and Ludy had previously had their business there was another American-owned bar. There I was given the information I needed but did not want to believe. Rick was dead – and Ludy, after closing the monkeypod factory, had returned to the home Rick built in Infanta, Pangasinan, several hours' drive to the north.

One of the youngsters hanging around the bar knew where Ludy lived and volunteered to deliver a message for me. I wanted her to know that I was aware of Rick's death and that I had the pocketwatch if she was interested in receiving it on his behalf.

Within two days Ludy showed up at the Chiefs' Club, one of the places she knew she could find me. We went to Rick's grave where we shared a moment of grief together. Ludy told me how Rick's addiction to rum and Coke had destroyed his health. After showing Ludy the pocketwatch, we came to a mutual agreement that I should keep it. I was more than grateful, even though I had paid for it years prior.

During one of my visits to the CPO Club at Subic Bay, I met Briney, the manager of one of the larger clubs on the base. Briney was also a retired chief and he was well known in the area. He and Elsa, his Filipina spouse, also owned and operated an impressive club several miles out of town at Balloy Beach, a recreational area frequented primarily by military personnel. Their facility, aptly named "Briney and Elsa's," boasted hostesses, food, drink, and pool tables – and it was large enough to accommodate a good-sized crowd. Many retirees made that place their hangout, which made it that much more profitable for Briney and Elsa. Briney, his wife, and I became good friends, and at each visit I found myself being treated with a family-like hospitality. I knew that Briney was one of those accepted American retirees living in the area and that he was considered by the Filipinos as one of them. There was an invisible umbrella of protection against elements of crime that extended, covered, and provided well for all of Briney's friends. Not that such protection was absolutely necessary, but it was always better to have that little bit of an edge than to be without it.

I was on my way to Briney's place in a jitney one evening when a young attractive female sitting beside me struck up a conversation. Since I was no newcomer to the area I logically assumed that she was just another pretty face trying to make a living off guys like me. But her conversation was noticeably different. She seemed genuinely interested in where I was from and what was my impression of the Philippines. I enjoyed the conversation and was disappointed when she told me that her destination was well beyond Balloy Beach. The girl's ability to communicate, her polite mannerisms, and her character in general began to make me feel very fortunate having made her brief acquaintance. She told me about the college she had attended in Manila, the degree she had earned, and her future plans. I was intrigued; I wanted to spend more time with her, learn more about her. The more we talked, the faster I talked, because I knew that within minutes I would be getting off the jitney and would be walking the mile or so down the irregular road to Briney and Elsa's place. I found myself groping for words that should have come more easily for me. I did not know how to convince her to take a break from her trip and join me at Balloy, where we could continue the conversation that had been going so well. She turned me down when I finally made the suggestion. Had I not recognized just a slight pause of consideration before she said no, the story of this unusual and unplanned experience would have ended then and there.

The side road to Balloy Beach was all but in sight and I wanted to enjoy more of the "fresh air" the girl had been providing me with, so I pressed on with my attempt to persuade her. She had never been to Balloy Beach so I told her about all it had to offer, including the benefit of my having friends who lived there, and that she would not have to worry about expenses since I would be her benefactor during the time we were together. Beyond that, I promised nothing. I found my hands gently tugging at hers and I heard myself nearly begging that she accompany me as we approached the cutoff to Balloy. But her mind had been made up, and again she politely turned me down. As I stepped down from the jitney, I thanked her for having been such an interesting conversationalist and I wished her well on her continued journey. I turned away from the jitney and I heard the familiar sound of its engine as it pulled away. Disappointed but intent on reaching my destination, I headed toward the familiar dirt road I had "navigated" many times before.

I did not hear the jitney stop a short distance down the road, my mind having shifted into other thoughts, but I did recognize her voice when I heard her shout for me to wait for her. Lita, as I soon found her name to be, had changed her mind. I was quite pleased, especially knowing that the girl trusted me enough to accompany me through a rather formidable-appearing area as we walked through the noticeably congested plant growth down the dirt road toward the beach.

The sun had already set when Lita and I approached Briney's place. There were no phones, and therefore all visits to Balloy Beach were, for the most part, unannounced. I was a little disappointed when we arrived and found that Briney and Elsa were busy entertaining another retired couple. The four of them were sitting at their picnic table not far from the ocean's edge and they were barbecuing steaks on an outdoor grill. I felt a bit clumsy because I had prepared Lita for an evening of sharing with friends and it appeared that my promise was about to turn sour. I introduced Lita, and the two of us tried to fit into the conversation. As we were unknown to Briney's guests, our presence and our input to the ongoing conversation were being either ignored or overridden by their own preferred topic(s) of discussion. Things were not going well, so I suggested that Lita and I go swimming while Briney and company enjoyed their time together without our interference.

"What will I wear?" she asked.

"It's dark. Why worry?" I responded.

Lita looked directly into my eyes, and dark as it was, her eyes sparkled with imagination and excitement. "You mean, no clothes, naked?"

I assured her that was exactly what I meant. After all, I didn't have a swimming suit either. Briney pointed out a large inner tube and suggested that it was there for just such occasions; that it was not only a good flotation device, it could also be "worn" as a garment to and from the beach.

So Lita and I, like two excited kids, disrobed at the side of Briney's home and made our way to the warm water of the South China Sea some thirty or so feet away. Once in the water we were like two very close friends and there were no holds barred. She was as receptive as I was encouraging, and we soon found ourselves intimately involved with each other. It was an unplanned, unexpected, exhilarating experience that we were both completely enthralled by, and both of us enthusiastically relished within our newfound lust. We remained in the ocean for some time, both of us totally desirous of continuing our antics for as long as we were physically able. When we returned to the house to dry and clothe ourselves, we learned that Briney's friends had departed, having taken a strong exception to our antics. They had, in Briney's words, been a bit insulted by it. Briney, on the other hand, had told them that if they didn't like what they saw or what they were aware of, they could leave just as easily and as quickly as they had arrived. The remainder of the evening, well into the early hours of the following morning, Briney, Elsa, Lita, and I talked and partied. Lita and I enjoyed the steaks that had been intended for someone else. That morning I walked with Lita back up the dirt road to the place our adventure had begun. We talked briefly as we waited for the next jitney. We knew that regardless of which direction it was going, one of us would be departing. It seemed to be more than coincidence when two jitneys approached from both directions at the same time. Lita thanked me for what she described as a wonderful time and I thanked her for having made her acquaintance and for having shared in a rather remarkable adventure. We both knew that our paths would never cross again and that what we had done had already become that which it would always be, nothing more than a memory. No one could have aptly interpreted the broad smiles on our faces as we waved from our respective jitneys, each heading off on the same road but in opposite directions.

October 19, 1973, the *Preble* returned to sea, where she remained on special operations for two months. Upon departing the Philippines she headed toward and through the South China Sea, close to Vietnam, and then toward Singapore. She passed through the Malacca Straits (by Singapore) and crossed the Bay of Bengal via the Indian Ocean, passing close to Colombo, Ceylon (Republic of Sri Lanka). *Preble* then made her way up the coast of India, past Karachi, West Pakistan, to the mouth of the Persian Gulf off Iran. She continued on down the coast by Oman and the Gulf of Adan between South Yemen, Saudi Arabia, and Somalia, Africa.

While operating about sixty miles off the coast of Saudi Arabia, in the Gulf of Oman, I observed a sea remarkably different than anything I had ever seen. I never thought the sea could take on such an appearance, nor did I dream possible I would ever experience dust and sand so far away from land. The sea was still and there was no wind other than the slight breeze caused by the ship's forward motion. Visibility was severely limited by what appeared to be moderately dense fog where in fact it was fine sand that had been blown out to sea. It was difficult to determine just where the drifting sand and the sea met, as the sand formed a thin, buoyant blanket on the ocean's surface. I was disturbed when I began to realize the seriousness of our operations under such conditions. Sand was everywhere. Ventilation filters that covered all of the intake ducts were doubled, sometimes tripled, in an attempt to keep the dust from being distributed throughout the ship. But even with all the precautions that had been taken, the silky film managed to find its way everywhere. Of major concern was the potential for sand causing interference with electronic components, including navigational and weapons systems. Brushing the sand from one's bunk only added dust to the already-hazy conditions within the berthing compartments. Food was not immune to the condition and the minute but noticeable and irritating grit we experienced while chewing was another reminder of the unusual sandstorm through which we were passing. Everyone and everything was affected to some degree, and we were constantly reminded that we all had to participate in a genuine effort to prevent, or at least reduce, the amount of sand allowed to penetrate to the ship's interior. The sandy conditions only lasted a couple of days, but it caused havoc. The recalibration of sensitive equipment and the cleanup process continued for months.

The *Preble* returned to the mouth of the Persian Gulf, where it engaged in operations until December 18, when it returned to Subic Bay. This time we would only remain in port a matter of hours, just long enough to refuel, before returning to sea for another month.

Christmas at sea aboard *Preble* was nothing in comparison to that which I had experienced aboard *Seadragon*. There was an attempt at making the occasion warm and festive; however, the officers and crew just didn't have their hearts in it. It was difficult, almost impossible for us to understand why the *Preble* could not take a break from patrol duties for at least one port call as other U.S. warships had done at Djibouti, Malaysia, and Iran. Most of us believed that it was the skipper's intentional doings that caused us to remain at sea, his way of gaining recognition points, thereby increasing his promotional prospects toward attaining the stripe that would make him an 0-6, a captain. It was believably rumored that skippers who volunteered to remain at sea, subjecting their men to and proving them capable of withstanding the rigors of extended arduous duties, were sometimes recognized as having greater skills; superior or preferred ability to control – traits that were sure to gain more favorable promotional consideration.

After two and a half months at sea, the arduous demands expected and required of *Preble*'s crew began to take effect. "Give me liberty or give me death," though not literally, began to make a great deal of sense as it took on a more personal analogue. The bad news, that we would remain at sea over Christmas and New Year's, was somewhat offset by the good news that our next port call would be Hong Kong.

January 19, 1974, the *Preble* entered Hong Kong Harbor, where the customary authorization of allowing, even encouraging, maximum liberty for all hands, was granted. We were all anxious to get our feet on stationary dry land. The "Walla Walla" water taxis quickly carried liberty parties to Fenwick Pier, where U.S. currency could be exchanged for Hong Kong currency. Greenbacks could also be exchanged or used as legal tender almost everywhere on the island.

Little had changed since my last visit to Hong Kong. Its skyscraper department stores offered every conceivable kind of merchandise, and the side streets were virtually a souvenir shopper's paradise. Gifts from all corners of the globe could be found in the shopping districts. The colony was well known for its custom-made clothing. It was not always as simple as walking into a shop and picking out a shirt or trousers from a shelf. Instead, tourists were measured for the garment of their choice, and it was then quickly sewn to precise measurements. The finished products could be picked up within a day or two. The China Fleet Club always offered its quality services; where items that could not be located or were not afford-able in other countries could be purchased at substantial discounts. Tours around the island were also a favorite pastime for many sailors. The float-ing restaurant at Aberdeen was no longer considered out-of-bounds and many sailors experienced authentic Chinese food such as shark fin soup and Peking duck there. Photographers invariably found the view from Victoria Peak well worth the trip there. From that vantage point one could survey the entire island or watch the ships unload their cargoes in what had become the busiest harbor in Asia. Those individuals not so inclined to take designated tours could ride rickshaws or double-decker buses around the city, or they could walk, as I preferred. The nightlife in the Wanchai District always remained active well into the night. Hong Kong's mean temperature year around is seventy-eight degrees Fahrenheit, making it a perfect climate for swimming and sunbathing. Hong Kong was and probably remains, as it has been most aptly referred, "The Pearl of the Orient."

Upon departure from Hong Kong, the *Preble* visited Kaohsiung, Taiwan, for a brief three days, after which we returned to Subic Bay for a single night before steaming on to Manila Harbor.

The bar district in Manila, the strip, was not nearly as congested as it was in Olongapo, but it provided much the same in entertainment. One ma-jor difference there, the fact that officers and enlisted men were often seen in the same establishments. Not fraternizing per se, just mingling in a man-ner that would not be misinterpreted as socializing beyond that invisible no-no boundary line. That was probably because most of the nightclubs were built with higher standards in mind. After all, Manila was a major shipping port – not only frequented by the U.S. Navy but also by a continu-ous turnover of ships from many other nations. It was also a major tourist port; the nearby Manila Airport supported a heavy flow of international arrivals and departures.

During one of my routine shore liberties I came across the XO, a cou-ple of other officers, and several chiefs at one of the nightclubs. We took advantage of the opportunity to relax while in the company of each other, something of a rarity. Since I was more interested in relaxing with a drink – without female companionship – whereas the others were enjoying female partners on the dance floor, the XO dubbed me "Straight Arrow." I accepted that title graciously and without objection, since it was in no way a derogatory reflection on my lifestyle or of my military title, the one with which the XO had previously had such difficulty. As it grew later into the night I found a fairly decent place where a couple of American civilians had already established themselves. I bought them a customary round in a gesture of friendship, thereby also ensuring my acceptance.

From as far back as I can recall, I always enjoyed sitting back and observing the variety of activities that took place wherever alcoholic beverages were consumed. People, I being no exception, did strange things while under the influence of booze, and it was entertaining for me just sitting back watching. It would be quite impossible for me to count all of the fights and brawls I observed, let alone those in which I had been an active participant. I found the most interesting aspect of my observations to be the bar girls and the numerous modus operandi by which they manipulated their clients. That evening I watched intently as one particular girl performed. She (I called her Charmer) not only exploited the newcomers and single patrons, she brazenly approached some of those who were already taken, those who were already in the company of females. Charmer was, without any stretch of the imagination, a seductive and provocative little wench in all respects. She was as cute as she could be, and everyone was willing to buy her ladies' drinks (tea) just to have her by their side for a few passing moments. She was raking in big bucks in her commissions and there was no need for her to go beyond the limits of good customer relations, but she did. I watched as Charmer flirted at each table, maneuvering her more sensual body parts to intentionally divert the attention of those nearest while at least one of her hands quickly snatched coins and currency right out from under their noses. There were certain times when I knew it best to mind my own business, and I thought it best to do so on this occasion. However, the more I watched, the more intrigued I became. The little thief became my own target, and it didn't take long before I formulated my own special plan. I would attempt to do something I had never done before. It became my goal to turn the tables, to manipulate Charmer instead of being manipulated by her. It was ironic in that I became her target at about that same time. The other patrons had grown tired of her persistence and had found her to be less desirable, more of a nuisance, each time she approached. So she turned

591

to me, the one who had reluctantly bought her a single drink earlier in the evening.

Charmer snuggled up to me as she asked me to buy her another drink. I told her that she could make a lot more money by not asking me to buy drinks. I reminded her that her commission was only 50 percent of the cost of the drink and that if she wanted the full 100 percent she could have that instead. But there was a catch. I told her that she had to remain with me and that the longer she remained, the more money she could make. My promise went beyond bar time. I also assured her that she would be well compensated for the pleasure of her company throughout the night. Charmer was pleased at the thought of making the additional money and she willingly remained close by my side. I knew her for what she really was, a thief, and I knew that if I didn't confront her with my observations I, too, would remain a potential target. When I first mentioned the theft of money, she immediately took a firm stand of denial. I half-jokingly described exactly how she had gone about it; from whom, and what, she had stolen. She gave me a sheepish look and she snuggled close as she promised that no such thing would happen to me. I chuckled to myself as my plan began to unfold.

It was dangerous taking advantage of a local, male or female, regardless of the country one was in. Military members and tourists were fair game to the locals, but stealing from or hurting a local could easily result in the perpetrator suffering serious wounds or ending up in a foreign jail. The locals were professionals and they were totally alert and in tune with their surroundings, whereas tourists were, for the most part, ignorant of the local ways and means.

I knew that what I was doing was not considered fair play, and I realized that being alone, I was particularly vulnerable. I had to carry out my scheme without flaw, with a skill I had never honed, let alone practiced, and hopefully come out of it intact.

When the bar closed, Charmer and I left together. We caught a taxi, and within three or four minutes we were in her single-room studio apartment. Charmer was all smiles and completely confident in me. She had, in her eyes, a real catch that would provide for her in a manner to which she was not accustomed. I pulled her into my arms and reassured her that she would not be disappointed in the morning. That was my direct hint that her earnings would be disbursed after the fact, not before.

There can be no doubt that I had shared beds with many girls over the years. Most sailors, though not all, have had their share of women. Sailors never had to go looking for intimacy, as they were constantly (while ashore) surrounded by it. Girls, whether working or not and for whatever reasons, liked sailors. It was a near certainty that a sailor in uniform could depend on being approached by good as well as by "bad" girls. Sometimes it was hard to tell what type one was being "sought" by. But that night I knew what kind of girl I was dealing with and I knew that I had better watch out when it came time for the showdown.

Strangely, I actually liked the girl. Charmer was a ball of fire in bed, well versed on all of my expectations, uninhibited with regard to sensual or sexual possibilities, and untiring in her efforts to please. There was no time for sleep. Even if there had been, I would have forced myself to maintain vigilance over my wallet. I had to consider her promises even less valid than mine, since her way of life was really based on shrewd, carefully orchestrated opportunity.

At first light I raised my thoroughly exhausted yet incredibly satisfied body from the bed and I told my acquaintance that it was time for me to go. We both dressed quickly, she in anticipation of her promised reward and I with trepidation, wishing that I was already safely aboard the *Preble*. I will never forget the astonished look on her face when I handed her forty pesos, the equivalent (at that time) of about two dollars; her absolute disbelief turned to outrage as she threw the twenty-peso notes back at me.

"You promised! You promised!" she repeatedly yelled in my face.

"You are a thief; be grateful you're getting this much."

My indifference kindled her indisputable exasperation. She fumed, spouting off with a combination of Tagalog and English as she grappled with my arm in an attempt to keep me from leaving her apartment. I, in turn, having retained all the insulting phrases in Tagalog that Elena of Olongapo had taught me years prior, took pleasure in letting Charmer know that I was neither new to the area nor the fool that she had taken so many others for. She continued tugging at my shirt as I made my way from the apartment. I began swinging my arms in hopes of attracting one of the nearby taxi drivers. I knew that I was in need of a timely rescue. One of the taxis pulled up, and I jumped in. I had not planned on Charmer accompanying me, I had hoped that she would accept her own vulnerability, but she managed to squeeze into the cab before I could slam the door. She continued venting her frustration in Tagalog but diverted it to the driver in hopes of gaining support in her attempt to enforce "justice." I interrupted, giving the driver instructions as to my destination. The girl began giving the driver her own instructions, some of which I understood as an alternate route, an intermediate stop prior to delivering me at my destination. I interrupted, advising the driver that as long as I was paying there would be no stops between our current location and my destination. I had been lucky up to that point and had no intention on placing myself in harms way. There was no telling what misfortune might have befallen me had I allowed the diversion. I breathed a sigh of relief as the driver ignored the girl, followed my directions, and delivered me at the pierside gate. After paying the driver I tried once again to give the girl the forty pesos, but she adamantly refused. She followed with a very cold, calculated, and deliberate: "Thank you very much, you are a good teacher, I have learned my lesson well. This will *never* happen to me again!" I'll bet it never did!

Channel fever, insomnia caused by the excitement of returning home after a six-month WestPac cruise, was also a problem for many men when the next port call was a place they had never visited before. I thought that I had outgrown or had become immune to the fever until February 11, 1974, the day before we were to enter the port of Singapore.

Singapore, the name alone carried with it a degree of intrigue. Sailors from time immemorial had left their marks there. Movies were made there. It was one of those ports that welcomed visitors from all countries, a Free Port similar to Hong Kong and a place that I had never been. Channel fever grabbed hold of me, and I spent the entire night playing cards and Acey-Deucy with other chiefs who were suffering similarly.

We observed numerous ships at anchor, far too many to count, as we entered the harbor. Maneuvering the *Preble* between them must have been a challenge for the skipper and/or the pilot.

In shipping, *pilot* is the title given to someone totally cognizant of specific channels, harbors, and any unusual currents or obstacles, who is paid to accept the responsibility of directing a ship to its assigned berth. Piloting is actually the oldest method of navigation, used before men ventured out of sight of land and across the sea. It is a method of directing the movements of a ship by referring to landmarks, navigational aids such as lighthouses or light ships, or soundings. Piloting is generally used when entering or leaving port and in navigating along the coast. Simple as it may sound, it takes one of extraordinary navigational knowledge and carries with it much-appreciated responsibilities. Navigational aids used in piloting include the compass, to determine the ship's heading; the bearing circle, to determine direction of objects on land, buoys, ships, etc.; charts, which depict the outlines of the shore, as well as the positions of land and seamarks and the standard depths of water at many locations; buoys; navigational lights; the echo sounder or Fathometer, which determines the depth of water under the ship's keel by measuring the time it takes a sound signal to reach the bottom and return to the ship; and the lead line, which determines the depth of the water by actual measurement. Tide tables are also necessary to predict the times and heights of the tide, and current tables predict the times, direction of flow, and velocity of tidal currents in harbors, bays, and inlets. Put all that together and that is what a hired pilot does and the tools he uses when requested by the ship's Captain or by the local harbormaster.

Once the ship was tied up I immediately disembarked. Weather and climatic conditions were near perfect and I wanted to stretch my legs on a solid foundation. I was wearing my khaki uniform, since I had not planned on off-base liberty at that time. But as it was, I wandered beyond the limitations of the port, not realizing that it was something other than a military base. It was a shipping port and it lacked the gates expected at the entrance/exit of practically all military installations. Without giving it any thought I had unintentionally violated well-founded rules when I wandered beyond a certain point. I'll call that point the boundaries of the nonexistent base – the port perimeter. I was somewhat surprised when I was apprehended by some kind of police organization. They immediately got me off of the sidewalk and into their vehicle and they advised me that I was in violation of such and such rule/regulation because I was in uniform. If any information had been disseminated regarding the uniform policy at Singapore, it somehow eluded me. The reason for the no-uniform policy was understandable. Since there were ships from such a variety of nations, warships and cargo ships from Communist countries among them, uniformed personnel could have created an uneasy atmosphere in town. Knowingly mingling with the "enemy," particularly in bars, while showing one's colors by virtue of the uniform one was wearing, would not have been wise. Singapore boasted far more Russians than visitors from other nations. As Master Chief of the Command I should have been more knowledgeable, I should have made it a point to learn of peculiarities known to the area. At the very least I should have noticed a distinct lack of uniformed personnel. At the time, I was not concerned about the uniform I was wearing. I was simply stretching my legs and had wandered a bit too far.

The policing agency was not upset at my ignorance. They were very polite and quite helpful – even understanding. I was returned to the port confines, the area I had previously thought had no recognizable boundary, but then found that there was perimeter fencing; I had not paid sufficient attention earlier. It had been a long time since I had been apprehended, arrested, or by any other name detained, and I was a bit embarrassed. It came as a pleasant surprise when I was released on my own recognizance. I had not been arrested; instead I had been provided with courtesy transportation back to the ship. That in itself was a new experience for me, since never before had a police agency picked me up without booking me for having committed an offense.

I boarded the *Preble* and donned my civvies in anticipation of venturing much further into a world I knew practically nothing about, anxious to participate in a new adventure and experience all that I could in the short two-day period of time we were scheduled to remain there. This time I would not only pay attention to everything around me, I would also use the buddy system.

I had been ashore with Bob before and I knew him as one who enjoyed his liberty much the same as I. We shared interests in most respects, and I was confident that our time ashore would be more enjoyable by hanging out together. Bob did have a one-track mind that dictated certain business matters be taken care of before other pleasures. His unusual personality, very likable but different, either caused or encouraged him to do things one would not expect of a normal person.. In Guam, for example, Bob caught a lizard and played geek when he promptly bit off its head. As if that wasn't gross enough, he then proceeded to swallow it. He was much like my *Seadragon* buddy Animal. Bob's unpredictable antics could be just as entertaining as they could be primitive. The more he drank, the more brusque he became.

Prior to entering any port, sometimes more than a day out, Bob would stand face into the wind at the bulwark or the lifelines and he would say things like, "Damn, that pussy sure does smell good." As we shortened the distance between ship and land, Bob would comment on how much stronger that scent was becoming. He was known to brag that if he ever fell overboard he would be able to swim to the nearest woman-inhabited land by simply following his nose.

Bob's first order, business matters, meant sex – so we caught a taxi and gave the driver instructions. I was fascinated as we drove toward the

596

brothel district. Singapore was without doubt one of the most beautiful places I had ever been. Everything was absolutely spotless; and there were strict laws designed to keep it that way. Laws against spitting in public, tossing cigarette butts into the gutter or stomping them out on the sidewalk, or doing anything else that might cause an unsightly condition. I was also surprised that in a place where pornography to any degree was strictly outlawed, brothels were perfectly legal. Being caught with a nudie magazine, such as *Playboy*, was a sure way to get arrested – and the penalties were rather harsh. I insisted that the driver take some side roads, as I was always prone to do in places I had never been. As long as we were paying for the ride, I wanted to see as much as possible en route. I was very impressed by the temples and the beautiful gardens we passed. The driver told us that the real Singapore, the tourist Singapore, was farther down the coast, well away from the town area where we were heading. Not only was it too far, it would have been expensive to go there by cab. So Bob and I stuck to our plan. First he would get "serviced," and then we would spend some time walking along the waterfront business district where we could do some souvenir shopping and observe whatever activities took place there.

The cabby escorted Bob and me into what looked like a private residence but was really a licensed brothel. We were seated in an entry foyer, an antechamber that was not only beautifully decorated but quite comfortably and somewhat lavishly furnished, and we were treated with snacks and beverages. I felt out of place asking for a beer when the surroundings called for champagne by candlelight. Next, in came the "ladies." Equally surprised was I at the apparel they were wearing. There were four girls and they were all centerfold material, yet they were not dressed at all provocatively. They were very well clothed in a manner that would never have identified them with their profession. They were, by all outward appearances, the kind of women one would be proud being seen with, proud to take home and introduce to Mom and Dad. Their femininity was unmistakable, and they carried themselves with grace, never overdoing their role in soliciting our attention. I was not there for the same purpose Bob was, but had I been, I would have found it difficult making a selection. They were all equally desirable.

Bob made his selection and off they went to "lust land." The other girls were disappointed that I was not there to engage in sexual activities (spend money), but they showed no anger. To the contrary, they remained in the foyer with me and entertained me with conversation instead – gratis.

Brothels, regardless of the country, had almost predictable operations. They lived by the same rules and used many of the same expressions. Only the prices varied, as did the physical construction and the inner configuration of their places of business. Singapore was no doubt top of the line. The Philippines, on the other hand, was at the bottom of the spectrum. Horny sailors did not seem to care; they blamed their sexual desires and activities on the premise that "a stiff cock has no conscience." Considering the expectation that brothels normally provided a group to select from, there were relatively few brothels in the Philippines. One need only walk through town (not just any town, but certainly those adjacent to the military bases) and make a selection from nearly anyone they pass. The chance of walking past a woman who was not available was slim indeed. Poverty was so prevalent that at night there were literally hundreds from which to choose. One could be equally sure that all the girls inside any of the bars were also available. The "selector" never knew what to expect upon reaching the "selectee's" residence and/or place of business; the house or structure where sexual gratification was to take place. Some places were fairly clean, decently decorated, and even boasted one or more type of appliance, such as a small fan or a refrigerator. One could also expect to find another person living there. Sometimes there would be one or more "working" friends, a child or two of mixed blood, or even an aging or sickly parent. The bed might have a mattress, or it might be nothing more than a sheet of plywood on a dirt floor. Running water and bathroom facilities were luxuries that only those who were better off could afford. Far more frequently there were community bathrooms, most of which were very unsanitary by any standards; many consisted of nothing more than open pits. Water was usually available; but the walk to obtain it was not always convenient. Hot water was only available in better hotels, and then only during certain hours of the day.

But I've slipped off-track a bit. Many similarities, regardless of the country, were striking and conspicuous. Singapore's "district" shared many of those similarities. The process of negotiating finances was practically identical. "One time," as the phrase implied, meant precisely that. A "short-time" meant an hour or two of whatever activity a person was capable of performing – three or four times for the younger sailor, once or twice for the older ones. And there was the "all night," which, as the term implied, meant remaining with a woman until sunup or shortly thereafter.

Bob had contracted for a short-time, and the hour he had negotiated passed quickly. I had remained with entertaining company and had enjoyed the question-and-answer session the girls had shared with me. When Bob returned he was sporting a broad smile, a sure sign that he had been well satisfied.

Business had been taken care of and it was time to check out the area, time to appreciate other Singapore activities. Our taxi driver had waited patiently outside the brothel and provided us with transportation to the waterfront.

As we walked along the waterfront we looked over the selection of souvenirs the many shops had on display. Hong Kong provided most of the same kind of trinkets and carvings. We saw a couple of snake charmers along the walkway, and they immediately recognized us as tourists. The music they made with their flutelike apparatus was interesting, although they carried little in terms of a recognizable tune. One man was able to coax his live cobra out of its basket, in hopes we would show our appreciation in recognition of his ability, skill, and bravery. We dropped a few coins in his "bank," probably an insufficient amount, but the old man smiled anyway as he thanked us for not ignoring his talent. The second snake charmer, even though he was unsuccessful in proving he so much as had a snake, held out his hand anyway in hopes we might also supplement his meager income. We probably should have, but we chose not to.

At about the time the sun was disappearing for the day, Bob and I chanced upon a decent bar and we agreed that it was time for a liberal intake of liquid refreshment. We started with Tiger Beer to quench our thirst, then switched over to hard liquor – a way known by all sailors to bring about a quick high. As the evening progressed, we were joined by a couple of Soviets who surprised us with their limited but impressive ability to speak English. Bob and I challenged them to a game of darts. We all agreed that the penalty for losing would be that of buying the winners their drink of choice. It became something other than a friendly game; more of a mini-war between the United States of America and the USSR! Bob and I, influenced by the intake of alcohol, made fun of our opponents. We ridiculed them in every possible way in our attempt to distract them from a game at which Soviets were known to be good. It was our day. Our impulsive carefree attitudes bolstered our spirits as our skills surpassed those of our Soviet acquaintances. Bob captured their immediate attention when he suggested that the Soviet military didn't have a chance against us (America) if they fought like they played darts! Bob went even further when he bragged, almost seriously, that he could beat them blindfolded! Without giving them an opportunity to respond to that foolish challenge, Bob turned his back to the dartboard and laughed as he said, "Just watch this, you inadequate Ruskie bastards," and he threw a dart over his shoulder toward the board. A perfect bull's-eye! We all laughed at what we knew was nothing more than a ridiculous and lucky toss – but Bob's ostentatious attitude brought about an immediate end to the game. Games of another kind quickly followed. We won chugalug contests with beer; however, the Russians took first place when it came to tossing down shots of vodka. Before long we were attempting to drown each other out by singing songs of national origin and representation – including our own respective national anthems. I recall thinking to myself how different it might have been had we all been in uniform. As it was, we were all having the time of our lives. Bob finally took top honors when he made it abundantly clear that he thought all Soviets were nothing but a bunch of "sissy candy asses." He even made sure they understood his comment by painstakingly explaining it to them in baby talk, thereby also suggesting that babies would more easily understand. The smiles disappeared from their faces and Bob knew he had been successful in accomplishing his goal; he had finally crossed the line. Bob then held up his hands jokingly, in something of a semi-defensive posture, and asked that they follow his lead in what he was about to do; otherwise they would have to accept what Bob already knew; that they were in fact candy asses. I was as shocked as the Soviets were when Bob picked up a shot-glass from in front of one of the Russians, slowly brought it to his lips, taking on the appearance of draining it of any residual, then broke off a piece of it with his teeth! Bob proceeded to *chew and swallow* the glass.

"You're crazy!" I heard myself shout, and Bob took another bite out of the glass before I could knock it from his hand. Bob was laughing as he swallowed. There was a small trickle of blood coming from his mouth, evidence that there had been no trickery involved. With that, the Soviets decided it was time for them to leave. Bob followed them to the door and repeatedly taunted them with, "You sissy fucks; who's the candy asses? Who's the goddamned sissy fuckin' candy asses?" They left shaking their heads in disgust and disbelief.

Bob wanted trouble. I did not. It was time for me to get Bob out of there before the Soviets decided to return with reinforcements. Besides, I was not too happy with the knowledge that Bob might suffer from some serious internal injuries as a result of the broken glass he had ingested. We paid our bar bill and headed for home. It had been a night of fun that could easily have escalated into an international incident.

Bob swore me to absolute secrecy regarding his glass-eating episode. He had a few years remaining before he would become eligible for retirement and he was afraid the Navy might put him out early as a "basket case." I assured him that there was no doubt in my mind – he *was* a basket case – but I would maintain his secret in confidence. The following day Bob told me that he had chewed and swallowed glass on other occasions and that the only problems he had suffered as a result were cuts to his tongue and the roof of his mouth as well as some rather deep cuts to his "asshole" when he eventually eliminated the sharp undigestible pieces of glass.

I never ventured ashore with Bob again. He had a great personality but he was an extreme exhibitionist who would stop at nothing to gain an audience. I knew that he could be a dangerous person to himself and to others around him when he was drinking. I no longer cared to play or to be a participant in his lunacy.

We returned to sea on the seventh, two days after our arrival at Singapore. Most crewmen were anxious to return to the Philippines, our next scheduled stop, where they knew their way around and where they could enjoy more affordable liberty.

Following a five-day period at sea we once again entered Subic Bay, where we remained for a three-week upkeep period. On March 9, 1974, an anxious crew expressed their feelings when they heard the word passed: "Now set the special sea detail. All hands prepare for sea, our next destination: Pearl Harbor, Hawaii!" It was refreshing, hearing their merriment, their expressions of jubilance, as the background filled with shouts of "All right," "Hooray," and a lot of other incomprehensible hollering. We were all anxious to return to our homeland and our loved ones, equally anxious to leave behind those things that allowed or encouraged our deviance from more acceptable moral standards, in hopes that the knowledge of our promiscuity, in many cases the failure to abide by marriage vows, would remain deeply guarded secrets or would somehow become expunged as the ship took an easterly bearing – homeward bound!

17

TRAINING, TESTING, AND MANIPULATING

USS Preble arrived at Pearl Harbor on March 22, 1974. The base band played as the ship approached the pier, and there was a festive mood among the gathering crowd. The crew was greeted by the cheers, tears, and the waiting arms of their loved ones. It was a time to forget whatever bad experiences we might have endured during our absence from home and a time to share those experiences by which we had benefited. We had some rather wild stories to tell about the places we had been, and most of us were more than anxious to tell them. We placed equal importance on the gifts we had accumulated. With each souvenir came memories of places, faces, and experiences. It was a good time, a time that reinforced that six-month period of separation as having been entirely worthwhile.

Regardless of the arduous duties associated with the six-month WestPac trip, the *Preble* still had commitments. It was only a matter of a few days before we found ourselves back at sea conducting local operations off the coast of Hawaii. But those operations were short-lived because the *Preble* was slated to undergo a complex overhaul that would not only tax the crew from a workload standpoint, but the exhausting training program that was designed specifically for engineers made things even more demanding of them.

The training program was designed to accomplish several goals, all of which were intended on making sure that the engineers were not only fully knowledgeable of their responsibilities, but that they were equally capable of carrying them out safely. The ship would not be permitted to get underway until all phases of training were completed satisfactorily.

All engineers, regardless of their pay grade or officer/enlisted status, would, upon completion of the overhaul, be tested by the PEB, the Propulsion Examining Board. Board members consisted of between four and six very knowledgeable Engineer Officers. There would be two phases to the examination: the question-and-answer portion and the LOE, the Light Off Examination – the observed, hands-on-portion. Only after satisfactory completion of both phases would the ship be considered fully seaworthy, and then only for the purpose of conducting sea trials, the rigorous to-the-limits testing of all engineering plant machinery and related components. Then, in preparation for another WestPac tour, REFTRA, Refresher Training was a must.

I was responsible for making sure the enlisted members of the Engineering Department were actively participating and satisfactorily progressing in the PQS, Personal Qualification Standards program. I established specific goals for the men based on their known capabilities and their previous watch station qualifications. It was my decision, my orders that established the level of qualification each engineer would be required to achieve prior to PEB. I was equally responsible for monitoring their progress and appropriately recognizing those who showed exceptional motivation and progress while admonishing those who were dragging their feet. Liberty was sometimes at stake for the stragglers. All engineers were penalized to some degree, since they were required to remain on board during some of their liberty hours to attend training sessions. The training was comparable to a combination of submarine qualification and nuclear power training. One noticeable difference was that submarine qualification was based on an operational knowledge of the entire vessel, stem to stern, whereas PEB was confined to engineering – as it was with nuclear power training, however PQS was every bit as exhausting. We had time constraints and I had to make sure that when the time came we would have enough fully qualified engineers to man a three-section underway watch bill: four hours on duty, eight hours off. That was going to take a great deal of effort on the part of everyone.

During the extensive overhaul process, engineers spend a lot of time assigned as fire watches, making sure any sparks or small fires resulting from welding or cutting were quickly extinguished. They were also required to observe and approve (or disapprove) hydrostatic tests that were conducted on valves and systems as they were being repaired and/or installed. They also had their own areas of responsibility that included carrying out preventative maintenance requirements to equipment and some minor repair work while at the same time maintaining their cleaning assignments up to par. There can be no doubt that engineers were, and probably always will be, the hardest-working – almost to the point of abuse – of seagoing sailors. They were truly a hardy group, most taking their workload seriously, without complaints, while a few spent more time complaining than working. My efforts to maintain appropriate standards among all engineers were recognized when I received my evaluation marks covering a period of time that ended November 30, 1974. The marks were perfect, scoring me in the highest bracket, the top 1-percent of all areas of evaluation. Those areas were: "Performance," "Appearance," "Cooperativeness," "Reliability," "Initiative," "Conduct," "Resourcefulness," "Potential," "Directing," "Counseling," and "Writing." The following comments reinforced the marks and confirmed that my efforts were definitely worthwhile, particularly beneficial to Engineering Department goals and to the needs of the crew:

Master Chief Adkisson has demonstrated an aggressive, professional attitude in preparing PREBLE for the Light-Off Examination portion of the 1200-PSI Propulsion Examining Board. He has consistently performed all duties in an outstanding manner. His foresightedness and attention to detail, coupled with his ability to keep the big picture, have been a tremendous asset to the Department and the ship.

He is an excellent leader. He has the full support of his personnel despite having to simultaneously demand long working hours and Personal Qualification Standards training requirements. He is knowledgeable about each individual's talents, and uses each man to his best capacity.

Master Chief Adkisson has demonstrated administrative ability. He has almost single-handedly implemented the Personnel Qualification Standards Program for M and B Divisions, and has spent many long hours developing lesson plans and guidelines for the administration of the Engineering Department Training Program. He has personally interviewed each man in M and B Divisions and set individual watch station and advancement in-rate goals. He weekly reviews the progress of each man and prepares a summary of progress for the Commanding Officer.

He is the major influence in developing the M and B Division Quarterly Training Schedule and off ship school quotas.

Master Chief Adkisson helped develop a system of charts to plot actual overhaul progress versus time to better monitor the progress of valve maintenance, gauge calibration, bilge preservation, etc., thereby enabling the Engineer, Executive Officer, and Commanding Officer to make policy decisions in a timely fashion.

He has demonstrated outstanding ability in writing instructions, in preparation for the Light Off Examination. His ability to express himself, oral or written, is outstanding.

Although Master Chief Adkisson was directed to devote his full effort to the administration and training of the Engineering Department in preparation for the Propulsion Examining Board, he has made himself available to counsel individuals after hours and has demonstrated strong personal interest, and professional excellence, in insuring that the Commanding Officer is advised of problems affecting the crew.

All that, despite what the Supply Officer thought of me! Recall his letter reprimanding me for having not required the mess cooks to do more – dirty passageways, etc.

I was not exempt from my own PQS package, the difference being that I was required to qualify from cover to cover on all engineering plant operations and all watch stations. It was no doubt easier for me than most of the men, since the basics of all steam-powered engineering plants were similar. However, I was given no preferential treatment or any degree of reprieve when it came to obtaining the signatures that would acknowledge my progress. Depending on the phase of qualification, I had to prove my ability and knowledge by hands-on operations and oral examinations. There were only two individuals who were considered qualified and eligible to sign me off: the Engineer Officer and the MPA. The PEB would test all engineering personnel, including the Captain, not just the enlisted men. The ship's engineering officers were also challenged by their own training programs. It was a gratifying process for those who wanted to meet the challenge. My training on board submarines and my education in nuclear power provided me with better study habits, a better knowledge of how to go about qualifying and how to help others do the same. I hated the training, but I enjoyed the testing process that I was subjected to by my two immediate superiors. I thought nothing about challenging their knowledge at the same time they tested mine – and it was appreciated. It was an excellent means by which their knowledge and skills were sharpened at the same time mine were being tested. On January 18, 1975, the following administrative remarks were entered in my Service Record:

> **MMCM ADKISSON** has satisfactorily completed the requirements of the qualification standards and has demonstrated to his superiors by oral or written examination and by performance on watchstations the knowledge and abilities to properly execute assigned duties. He is designated as qualified for the following watchstation: ENGINEERING OFFICER OF THE WATCH (EOOW).

That entry certified markedly few individuals as being fully qualified throughout engineering. It also validated the responsibility of those designated to test and qualify others on all engineering watch stations. Finding the time was not an easy task but I insisted on making myself available to all Engineering Department personnel before, during, and after normal working hours for the purpose of testing individuals and groups.

As the oral part of the PEB Examination neared, the training push became more exhausting. There was, in most snipes' eyes, nothing fair about being singled out as the only shipboard department that had to spend an enormous amount of liberty time studying and qualifying while the rest of the crew had no such obligation. It was particularly tough when, at liberty call, snipes were excluded! It was more than apparent that the rest of the crew was thankful they were not engineers.

On one occasion I overheard one of the crew poking fun at several of my men, ridiculing the engineers for having to remain on board while he, the non-engineer, was about to have a cold beer ashore. I advised the liberty-minded man that he was sadly mistaken, that he, too, was going to remain on board until the last of the engineers were equally free to go ashore. I also told the man that I was going to hold him personally and equally responsible for any future mockery or taunting by any other crew member(s)! I urged him to make sure he got the word out that engineers were not to be harassed, *period*! After that, there were relatively few similar incidents.

Shipboard drills were frequent. At the time they were called away they seemed like a pain in the side, but such training was necessary. Fire drills were most common on surface craft vessels, whereas flooding drills were most frequent on submarines. When drills were announced over the 1-MC they were always preceded with, "Now this is a drill . . ." That preface was not intended on slowing down the crew's reaction, although without it one could count on a more expeditious response. There was at least one fire on every ship I ever served, and the well-trained damage control teams never failed to do their jobs efficiently. We never suffered any serious damage as a direct result of their rapid response and the effective utilization of their skills. Only once did I hear the words, *This is not a drill,* preceded and followed by *Flooding . . .*

I was sitting at a table in the CPO Mess when I heard the word passed: "Flooding in Main Control; flooding in Main Control; this is *not* a drill; flooding in Main Control." Even though the ship was securely tied up pier-side at the naval base in Pearl Harbor, Hawaii, it made the words no less demanding of instant response. I *flew* to the upper level control booth, where I found a first class machinist's mate standing in a state of shock – a totally blank look across his face. J.C., the MPA, arrived almost simultaneously, and neither of us could believe our eyes as they followed the E-6's pointing finger. The ship really was flooding! Water was gushing in through the approximately two-foot-in-diameter open manhole to the main condenser. Thousands of gallons of seawater had already poured into the space as J.C. and I scrambled to the lower level of the Main Control engineroom. We immediately found ourselves waist-deep in seawater as we proceeded to isolate the main condenser. Neither of us gave any thought to the potential for electric shock even though there was an abundance of electric-powered equipment and panels around us; all fully energized. Our only thought was that of isolating the condenser as quickly as possible to prevent further damage to equipment; primarily to prevent the ship from sinking right there alongside the pier! We were faced with a very real emergency, and the MPA and I did our part as we took immediate corrective action – commendable action. It was after the condenser was fully isolated and the inflow of water was stopped before either of us took into consideration how the situation came about.

The main condenser, as the name implies, provided that element within the steam cycle that cooled and condensed steam back into water for reuse. Seawater was the cooling medium that flowed through thousands of tubes while steam passed over them. Uncontrolled flooding through an open main-condenser manhole was a sure way to sink a ship. In fact, there was a procedure for flooding and sinking a ship by precisely that means if, during wartime, a ship and/or crew was under eminent danger of being captured by the enemy.

At the inlet and outlet sides of the condenser were manhole covers; normally both were tightly secured by numerous studs and bolts. The manholes were there to provide access to inlet and outlet chambers, each chamber large enough to accommodate a full-sized man. Periodically, as part of the PMS (Preventative Maintenance Schedule), condensers were isolated from the sea by securing the huge inlet and outlet valves. Zinc plates, bolted to the inside of each access cover, deteriorated as the result of electrolysis, thereby preventing the deterioration of condenser components. Periodically, zinc plates had to be replaced. The E-6 MM on the scene, at the time of the incident, was supposed to be replacing old zinc plates with new.

I had, as an E-2 right out of boot camp, accomplished exactly that which any E-6 should have been fully capable of accomplishing safely. When I did that job there were no written procedures; everything was done as ordered, by word of mouth. But times had changed over the years, and the room for error had been all but eliminated with the implementation of a more thorough system. All maintenance procedures were fully documented on 3- X 5-inch cards. One need only pull the appropriate card and follow its written instructions. There was *no* room for error, or so one would be led to believe.

The first-class petty officer had recklessly failed to follow the simplest of precautionary measures when he neglected to close the injection (inlet) and overboard (outlet) valves prior to unscrewing the nuts on a manhole cover. Somehow he had managed to unscrew all the nuts without breaking the gasket seal between the manhole and its cover. Without any warning the cover had blown free, thereby allowing the unrestricted flow of seawater directly into the engineroom. When J.C. and I arrived on the scene the water level was already above our waists as we stood on the lower-level deck plates. It was well above many of the electric pumps and nearly up to our shoulders by the time we fully isolated the condenser. The seriousness of the situation was further compounded by our close proximity to the base headquarters. In no time at all a response team, including the Base Commander, was on board demanding an immediate preliminary explanation, soon thereafter followed up with a full-fledged investigation. I had always known, but had never paid much attention to, how quickly a military career could be destroyed as the result of negligence. I found myself once again thinking, more seriously that ever, about the time I had remaining before I would be eligible for retirement benefits.

Those of us who were directly involved, or could in any way be considered responsible for the flooding situation, up to and including the *Preble's* skipper, were, in a matter of hours, interviewed by an investigating team from the base. The skipper could be, and normally was, held overall responsible for the ship of which he was in command. The Engineer Officer was sure to be held responsible for the engineering plant. The MPA, not only by virtue of his position in the engineering chain of command but also because of his participation in taking remedial casualty control action, would be of particular interest to the investigating board. And I, as Assistant MPA and as the senior enlisted engineer, having also taken part in restoring the emergency condition to a controlled situation, would also be thoroughly interrogated by the board.

I had no problem with the investigation at hand. To me it was an open and closed case of negligence on the part of one individual: the E-6 Machinist's Mate. However, knowing the history of similar investigative boards, I knew that there would be an attempt to spread the blame well beyond that of a single individual. Everyone questioned was required to put their remarks, their explanations, on paper and sign their testimony. When the senior investigating officer, an admiral, questioned me about how this very unfortunate situation came about, I willingly answered with absolute candor. I wanted only to get the investigation over with and get on with restoring the plant to an operational state of readiness. The admiral directed that I, too, sign a written statement. One that he had prepared; presumably based on my responses to his questions. I flatly refused as I politely but firmly told the admiral that since he was responsible for the preparation of the statement then he could also sign it. He was shocked at my refusal to carry out that which was as much an order as it was a request, and his anger clearly showed in his eyes and in his voice when he said, "Do you mean to tell me, Master Chief Adkisson, that you are refusing to sign this statement?"

"Yes sir, that's precisely what I am telling you!"

"Am I to take your refusal as an indication that you have not been totally honest with me?"

"Sir, I have been absolutely honest with you, but you and the rest of your board are going to come to your own conclusions with or without that written statement, so I will stand by my decision not to sign anything. The MPA and I prevented this ship from sinking by taking immediate and decisive corrective action. That is my verbal statement and that has been proven beyond anyone's doubt. With that, sir, I wish to be excused from further questioning so that I can return to my duties."

The admiral appeared to be very displeased, but he released me without pressuring me further.

As a result of the investigation, and as expected, the board found the CO responsible overall. An entry reflecting some degree of neglect was placed in the Chief Engineer's personnel file as well as in the MPA's. Such entries in officers' records were considered quite damaging and were known to play a significant role when it came time for promotional consideration. I found that to be disheartening, since I knew the chief snipe and the MPA to be the hardest-working, most knowledgeable, and by far the most admired individuals I had ever known to have served in those positions. In my opinion the blame should not have gone beyond the E-6 who was subsequently "busted," reduced by one pay grade to that of E-5, as punishment for his role in the incident. That same individual was forced into retirement soon thereafter when he was found at the base cafeteria when he was supposed to be aboard ship – on watch!

I spent more and more time thinking about what it would be like returning to a civilian world. I had heard any number of stories by fellow chiefs prior to their discharge from active service, each story a little different. All chiefs had their own ideas as to what retirement meant. Some had invested in U.S. Government Savings Bonds for a good portion of their military time so that they would not have to rely totally on their retirement pay. Some had managed to save enough to purchase a retirement home, while others were able to boast of their already-paid-in-full mortgage. Some had no savings whatever, having spent their entire income as quickly as it was earned. Those with usable skills, such as electronics, electricity, air-conditioning, etc., were more than anxious to exercise them in a civilian world, where monetary compensation would be more proportionate to the job they performed. I did not have any specific plans, but I had absolute confidence that someone would surely hire me, based on my military record and my sincere interest in starting a new career. Since I could show where I had stuck with one "company" for twenty years, why shouldn't another company consider me as an asset worth betting on?

April 1, 1975, a date I intentionally chose, I submitted my official request for transfer to the Fleet Reserve to become effective precisely one year hence, April 1, 1976. In effect my discharge from active military service would lead me to a second career, and I would always be able to say, "April Fool," whenever the subject of my military retirement date surfaced. *Retirement* to the majority of enlisted men was misleading, since retainer or retirement pay was rarely enough to live on in comfort. On the other hand, for those who had planned and invested wisely, those who had a source of supplemental income, military retirement income could provide for a fairly comfortable life. The main difference between the "haves" and the "have-nots" was a combination of the number of years served and their pay grade at the time of retirement. At that time – bear in mind it was long ago – I was planning on living on a retirement income of less than six hundred dollars a month, an amount that was considered sufficient! My request for transfer to the Fleet Reserve was favorably endorsed by the command and was forwarded to the Bureau of Naval Personnel for consideration.

Meanwhile the extensive training continued. I learned that the USS *Ponchatoula* (AO-148), another oiler, was in need of an E-9 Machinist's Mate and that it would soon be departing for WestPac. I thought about how much quicker my remaining time on active duty would pass if I were in the Far East enjoying liberty instead of spending long exhaustive hours in a steadfast training mode. So I placed a few phone calls to my detailer, the Master Chief Machinist's Mate at the Bureau of Naval Personnel who was responsible for my permanent duty station assignments, and I discussed the possibility of my immediate transfer. I had never met my detailer, but considering the many phone conversations we had shared, he had become as much a friend as he was a detailer. He was more than cognizant of my reasons for wanting a transfer, and he promised that he would do what he could to assist me. In the interim I introduced myself to the *Ponchatoula* skipper and asked that he "work it" from his position of authority while I worked it through my own command. Unfortunately, my request for transfer was flatly denied with the explanation that my presence aboard the *Preble* was mandatory until after the successful completion of PEB testing. The *Preble* skipper had the strongest voice in the matter, since I was already attached to his command, so my request was, for the time being, DIW, Dead In the Water. Meanwhile, after researching my background, the *Ponchatoula* CO began putting pressure on the Bureau. I learned through my detailer that he had not only elevated the issue that he was badly in need of an E-9; he had also made it abundantly clear that I, by name, was *the* E-9 he wanted! Nonetheless I had to accept the likeliness that I would not be transferred until PEB was history or I was retired, whichever came first.

I thought of how lucky I was that over time the system of enlisted distribution had changed as it had. In 1967 the system of communicating one's desires went little beyond that which was known as a "Rotation Data Card," more commonly referred to as one's "dream sheet." The information on this card was sent to the rating control desk in the Bureau of Personnel. Thus, when it became one's turn to be transferred the rating control petty officer had some semblance of information with regards to qualifications and desires. He would, for instance, have my four duty choices in the order of their desirability. He would know my length of obligated service and he would be aware of any special qualifications. He would be cognizant of unusual situations that might affect one's transfer – an expected addition to a family, a child needing special care, and one's views in regard to areas in which he or she did not wish to serve. The old system allowed a ration of one distributor for each 30,000 men in the Navy. The newer rating control system operated with one distributor for each 5,000 men. That was supposed to be about as efficient as the system was considered capable of being. Having access to detailers by phone, the most innovative and by far the most preferred system, made it possible to discuss preferences one-on-one directly with one's detailer.

Unexpectedly, on April 16, 1975, the Bureau issued orders directing that I report for duty on board the USS *Ponchatoula* no later than September 20th. Interestingly, the orders contained a brief comment to the effect that the orders had been issued in accordance with my preference as discussed on the telephone March 6th, one month prior. The only thing that could have pleased me more would have been an earlier report date.

Just a slight departure from the somewhat confusing series of events I am in the process of describing was an interesting change that took place in the designation and the hull number of the USS *Preble*, and the reasoning behind it. Since the Navy was in need of a greater number of DDG-class vessels and it could do with a lesser number of the DLG class, it "proclaimed" the change, and made it official. Nothing else changed – not the size, shape, armament, or complement. Other than her designation, everything remained unaltered. On July 1, 1975, the USS *Preble* (DLG-15) was recommissioned as DDG-46. Quite unexpectedly, as the result of an unplanned commitment, the *Preble* went to sea with "15" painted on one side of her hull and "46" painted on the other! That must have been a first for any naval vessel, certainly a distinct peculiarity. Those of us on board the day the deceptive conversion from DLG to DDG became effective were instant "plank owners," the term used to distinguish original crewmembers of any class ship. The plank owner recognition might have been a little misleading in this instance.

July 11th, I was officially notified by naval Speedletter that my request for transfer to the Fleet Reserve (retirement) had been favorably endorsed and that "by separate action, a Fleet Reserve Transfer Authorization (NAVPERS 1830/2) [was] being issued to be effective on April 1, 1976." Also, within the content, my orders to the *Ponchatoula* were canceled. I was more than disappointed at the thought that I would have to remain assigned to the *Preble* right up until my separation from military service, so I took the only action I could think of that might sway the Bureau into reinstating my orders to the *Ponchatoula*. On July 18th I initiated correspondence advising the Bureau that I preferred orders to the USS *Ponchatoula* and that in acceptance of those orders I would agree to withdraw my Fleet Reserve (retirement) request. Note: The official NAVPERS 1830/2 had been authorized and was issued July 15th but it had not yet arrived. The dates are significant since my correspondence suggested that I would withdraw my "request"; it said nothing about canceling the document that authorized my transfer to the Fleet Reserve. A play on words? Of course it was manipulative; it provided significant leverage in the decision process that followed.

July 24th, the Bureau issued a modification to the original orders, the orders assigning me to the *Ponchatoula*, without realizing that those orders had been canceled two weeks prior – also without the Bureau's knowledge of my more recent correspondence. Timing was absolutely perfect as messages passed each other in the process of distribution. The modified orders directed that I report for duty aboard the *Ponchatoula* no later than August 11 – while my retirement authority remained unchanged!

Preble's skipper required that I remain on board a few more days, right up to the last of the month. He insisted on utilizing me to whatever limits the Bureau allowed, even though I had requested a longer period of leave between duty stations, an expected privilege that was nearly always granted. The pressure the *Ponchatoula*'s Captain imposed on the Bureau, to have me transferred ASAP, along with the Bureau's knowledge of the

Ponchatoula's scheduled WestPac deployment, carried the weight necessary in bringing about my expeditious transfer.

Once the appropriate offices within the Bureau got their heads together and realized what had transpired and how it had all taken place, an immediate effort was taken to rectify everything via the issuance of another official message. It was dated August 4, 1975, two days *prior* to the date I had reported for duty at the *Ponchatoula* and was received by the *Ponchatoula* August 8th,, eight days *after* I had been officially transferred from the *Preble*. It made for interesting reading, since it was issued, and received, after the fact. In part it read:

> Contingent upon MMCM ADKISSON's immediately incurring sufficient obligated service to remain on active duty at least until April 1978, and signing the following service record entry, authority is hereby granted to return NAVPERS 1830/2 [my retirement authority] for cancellation:
>
> IN CONSIDERATION OF CANCELLATION OF MY FLEET RESERVE TRANSFER AUTHORIZATION, I AGREE TO REMAIN ON ACTIVE DUTY FOR A MINIMUM PERIOD OF 24 MONTHS FROM APRIL 1976 AND UNDERSTAND THAT APPROVAL OF ANY FUTURE REQUEST FOR TRANSFER TO THE FLEET RESERVE WILL BE CONTINGENT UPON MY MEETING ALL REQUIREMENTS IN EFFECT AT THE TIME OF MY APPLICATION.

It went on to read:

> Advise this Bureau by Speedletter of MMCM ADKISSON's decision within 5 days of receipt of this Speedletter. If he accepts the above conditions, forward [the NAVPERS 1830/2] and certified copies of acknowledgments as enclosures. Otherwise, effect his transfer to the Fleet Reserve on April 1, 1976 as presently authorized. For planning purposes, in the event MMCM ADKISSON accepts the above retention conditions, it is anticipated that he will be ordered to the USS PONCHATOULA for duty in accordance with MMCM ADKISSON's request.

A bit confusing, since I had already been transferred, even though I had not yet reported for duty at the *Ponchatoula*. On August 10th, when I reported for duty, *Ponchatoula*'s Executive Officer presented me with the above document.

I had quite a discussion with the XO. We talked of the legality of the letter as we took into full consideration the series of events that led up to the ultimatum I faced. The command of *Ponchatoula* had the responsibility to take action in accordance with the letter. In view of my acceptance of orders to the *Ponchatoula*, I had the option of either carrying out the requirements as set forth in the letter, or of ignoring the demands of the Bureau and retiring on April 1, 1976, as had already been approved. It would have been difficult, though not impossible, for the Bureau to require me to do something after the fact, something I might not have otherwise done. It would have been even more difficult transferring me back to the *Preble* since the *Ponchatoula* had already deployed for WestPac August 11th – with me on board. I intentionally took the full five days as authorized before making my decision known to the Bureau. My message was to the point. It read:

IN RESPONSE TO REF A SNM DESIRES TO EFFECT REF B TO REF A AND TRANSFER TO FLTRES EFFECTIVE 1 APR 1976.

In plain English that translates to my decision to ignore the two-year extension provision (since the transfer had already taken place) and that I accepted the already officially endorsed transfer to the Fleet Reserve as issued, approved! I felt very much like a winner where winners were seldom anything more or anyone other than the Bureau and its in-house personnel.

As for my transfer evaluation, my marks were every bit as impressive as the previous set, but this time it was the *Preble*'s skipper who wrote and issued them:

Master Chief Adkisson is a dynamic positive leader whose influence has been felt in all aspects of Engineering Department functions. His most significant influence has been in the PQS Program. He has spent many long hours developing lesson plans and gathering technical data in order that the material might be presented to his men in a logical manner and in a

615

form that would not require each man to complete the same research effort. His technical expertise has made him a valuable asset as an instructor and advisor. He has a solid background in Engineering Administration and technical publications and has made a significant influence on the Department and in the development of petty officers. Master Chief Adkisson has taken the load in developing the PQS Program on PREBLE. His positive approach to the program has been a key factor in the program being favorably accepted on board. His personal influence has created enthusiasm in PQS point accomplishment. During this reporting period PREBLE implemented the "ECCET," Engineering Casualty Control Evaluation Team, concept to train the ship's watch sections. This program first required the development of a complete set of cards specifically spelling out the action of each member of a watch section during an engineering casualty. This required a major effort resulting in the proofing and typing of several hundred cards. Master Chief Adkisson coordinated this effort in an excellent manner. His contribution to the Chief Petty Officer Mess has had a strong positive effect on the entire ship. There has never been any question about Master Chief Adkisson's role as the Senior Chief Petty Officer on PREBLE, and he has never hesitated to provide guidance to junior chief petty officers in improving their management and leadership abilities. This is one of the most significant roles for a Master Chief and he has executed this role magnificently. Master Chief Adkisson has aggressively pursued every facet of his responsibilities in the Engineering Department while also filling his role as the Senior Chief Petty Officer on board and President of the Chief Petty Officer's Mess in an outstanding manner. His administrative and leadership abilities clearly identify him as one of the most outstanding chief petty officers with whom I have had the pleasure of working.

18

USS PONCHATOULA

USS Ponchatoula (AO-148) was commissioned the twelfth day of January 1956 at the Philadelphia Naval Yard. It was the second Navy ship to bear the name Ponchatoula and was named after a river, as were all U.S. Navy oilers. The Ponchatoula River flows through Tongipahoa Parish, Louisiana.

Upon completion of acceptance trials and a shakedown cruise, the *Ponchatoula* sailed for her new home-port, Long Beach, California, via the Panama Canal in March 1956. The *Ponchatoula* wasted no time in embarking on a long career of service. In September 1956, the *Ponchatoula* rescued the floundering Panamanian ship SS *Venus* off the coast of Japan by taking the ship in tow and clearing oncoming Typhoon Ivy. In early 1958, the *Ponchatoula*'s home-port was changed to Pearl Harbor.

The *Ponchatoula* had participated in the Quemoy-Matsu Crisis (1958), operated in support of the Operation Dominic nuclear tests in the Christmas Islands (1962), supported Seventh Fleet units in the South China Sea off the coast of Vietnam, and served as a space capsule recovery ship for projects Mercury, Gemini, and Apollo.

In November 1965, the ship spent ten days on a goodwill visit to Sydney, Australia, where she participated in "Exercise Warrior" along with ships of the British, Australian and New Zealand Navies.

The *Ponchatoula* returned to Pearl Harbor in April 1967 from an eight-month deployment to Southeast Asia, where she again engaged in direct support of Seventh Fleet combat operations off the coast of Vietnam and in the Gulf of Tongkin. The ship set a new Pacific Fleet record by bringing 503 ships alongside and refueling 464 of them. Over 50 million gallons of fuel and many tons of cargo were transferred to combatant ships operating far from their bases.

On her November 1967 to June 1968 deployment, the *Ponchatoula* established another new record for volume of petroleum products delivered to customer ships, pumping over 74 million gallons of fuel through her replenishment hoses. She then underwent a five-month $3 million overhaul.

An April visit to Kobe, Japan, and Expo '70 highlighted the *Ponchatoula*'s 1970 deployment. The ship operated out of Sasebo conducting replenishments in the Sea of Japan for nearly half of her seven months in WestPac.

In February 1971, the *Ponchatoula* served as secondary recovery ship for the Apollo 14 space mission and following a two-day stop-over in Pago Pago, American Samoa, returned to Pearl Harbor Naval Shipyard, where she was converted to burn and carry Navy distillate fuel.

In July 1971, the *Ponchatoula* departed on another WestPac deployment. After her return to Pearl Harbor, she participated in the recovery of the Apollo 16 spacecraft, during which she carried NASA scientists and equipment for studying the capsule's reentry. In April 1972, she participated in the multi-nation anti-submarine warfare exercise RIMPAC 72, during which she operated with ships of the Australian, New Zealand, and Canadian Navies.

Her 1972-73 deployment spanned more than seven months. The *Ponchatoula* supported Seventh Fleet operations during the final months of the Vietnam War and during the mine-sweeping operations that followed.

In 1974, the *Ponchatoula* visited Guam for a six-month $4.5 million overhaul.

In March 1975, the *Ponchatoula* participated in another RIMPAC exercise, again with ships of the Australian, New Zealand, and Canadian Navies.

Since her commissioning the *Ponchatoula* had proven herself to be reliable and efficient. She had been awarded the Square Knot Award for Deck Seamanship for 1973 and 1975 and the Service Force "E" for Battle Efficiency for 1968, 1973, and 1975.

The *Ponchatoula* and I had something in common from the start: we became a part of the U.S. Navy at about the same time. I was immediately proud to be a member of her crew.

My duties were made clear from the start. As anticipated, I was to carry several titles and I was equally responsible to the command for each. My most immediate titles, Master Chief of the Command, Administrative Assistant to the Executive Officer, and Adviser to the Commanding Officer on matters pertaining to the safety, comfort, and welfare of the crew, were not new to me, and I looked forward to the close and constant awareness of crew activities as charged. I would ensure that articulate and accurate information on the needs and desires of the crew were passed on to the command and that explanations as related to command decision and policy were fully disseminated to the crew. Equally and for the most part indistinguishably, I was responsible for providing the necessary interface to maintain open channels of communication between command and crew. The

USS *Ponchatoula* (AO-148 – Fleet Oiler – August 1975 to March 1976

Ponchatoula would be my final duty station, and it was my intention to dedicate my remaining time on active duty toward the continued perseverance of anything and everything that needed my attention, whether such was directive in nature or of my own initiative. It was my character to remain totally involved, and I had no thoughts of slackening off toward the end. I had tasted the fruits of success early in my military career and wanted nothing more than to continue on the same path right up to the time of my separation from military service.

The *Ponchatoula*'s skipper, Captain Furlong, was one of the most admired COs I had ever served. His impressive background included flying aircraft from the carriers USS *Shangri-la*, USS *Hancock*, and USS *Constellation*. He had served as Commander of Attack Carrier Air Wing Fourteen, USS *Enterprise*, and was credited with over two hundred combat missions in Southeast Asia. Captain Furlong was a man to be admired by all who knew him. He was another confirmation of what I had recognized a long time prior, that there were distinct differences between individuals, regardless of rank or rate, who had specialized or unique skills and those who did not. For example, those who wore devices in recognition of special qualifications such as Parachutist, Diving Officer, Submarine Service, and Naval Aviator (plus others that I apologize for not including) were the cream of the crop. There are any number of adjectives I could use to compare these individuals, most of which would be synonymous. The vast majority of those wearing specialty devices, those individuals who went beyond that which might have otherwise been expected or required of them, volunteers for special and unusually hazardous duty, were beyond the reliable and responsible stage. They went beyond being credible and trustworthy. They were compassionate and understanding individuals who were not only interested in their own well being; they were equally interested in the well being of those with whom they served. Captain Furlong fit the mold perfectly, and I was extremely pleased knowing I would complete my military service under his command.

Shortly after reporting for duty I advised the command of my rehabilitation initiative for the CPO mess in the form of a memorandum to the Executive Officer. It was dated August 13, 1975, and read:

I am in the process of initiating the development of an incrementally stepped plan at improving the habitability and social environment of the Chief Petty Officer messing and berthing spaces aboard PONCHATOULA. A definite step in that direction is (already) obvious, however, my intention is to pursue these goals until total accomplishment is achieved. My ultimate objective of habitability improvement is to make PONCHATOULA CPO Mess the unquestioned best for AO's [Fleet Oilers] in either fleet. We of course are limited by space and funds, however, both of these impediments can largely be overcome by ingenuity and careful planning. Presently my plans are to develop a more active and honest interest on the part of all PONCHATOULA CPOs as a first step in establishing logical phases toward the accomplishment of these goals.

Since the CPO Mess is not directly represented in the ship's budgeting councils, habitability projects must be generated by the CPOs with recommendations to the Commanding Officer via you.

Another step toward the accomplishment of these goals is the implementation of a proper set of rules and regulations for the CPO Mess which are current with the ship's policy.

Attached is a copy of the recommended Chief Petty Officer Mess Regulations which was discussed and approved by all Mess Members at our past General Meeting [12 August 1975]. It is requested the final draft be incorporated in the SORM [Ship's Organization and Regulation Manual] as written.

Note: A "bill" is written to cover a certain emergency or job. It describes the duties involved and stations to be manned and it lists the rates required to perform the duties and to man the stations. The ship's SORM describes administrative bills, operational bills, and emergency bills.

Within my first three days I had gained the attention of all members of the CPO Mess and had reinforced the command's confidence that my past performance was not the only indication of what could be expected of me.

August 25, 1975, the *Ponchatoula* arrived at Subic Bay, Philippines. It had been over a year since I last saw the Hernandez family, and I was once again accepted into their home with the same warm hospitality to which I had grown accustomed. The entire family looked great – and for the first time I realized that they always looked great. By that I mean that not a single member of the family ever appeared sick or despondent. They were truly a remarkable family. All members shared in whatever task(s) were in need of attention in and around their home; always while bearing broad smiles. I never heard a single complaint during any of my many visits. There was a sadness that accompanied this particular visit since there was good reason to believe that there would be few visits to follow.

The ship got underway for local operations a couple of days later and it was immediately apparent that the ship's generators were not functioning properly. The need for reliable electrical power was mandatory during refueling operations, so when it became apparent that the power requirements were questionable the Captain made the right decision to return to port where troubleshooting and repairs could be accomplished at the Subic Bay repair facility.

On September 3, 1975, we tied up alongside the dock at the Naval Base where the ship remained for an unprecedented, certainly unplanned, two-month in-port period while extensive work was being accomplished on the entire electrical generating system.

It must have been terribly uncomfortable for the CO, having to sit in port with the knowledge that there were needs for our services at sea. On more than one occasion he called me to his stateroom and asked my opinion as to the progress being made, and whether or not I thought the engineering plant as a whole was reliable enough to return to sea. The generators were the major problem, and the dependability of the entire ship relied on their sound performance. I could not, in good conscience, recommend returning to sea until all electrical problems were fully resolved. The Captain concurred – and the ship remained in port.

The crew loved the thought of living on a "broken" ship. Liberty was great and there was plenty of time for the crew to go outside the immediate area where they could see and do many things for which there had not previously been sufficient time. Some crewmen went to Manila, while others spent time at Baguio where they could enjoy the much cooler, less humid climate.

Since it was a certainty we were faced with an extended in-port stay, I approached the Captain with the proposal that we, in the name of the ship, volunteer for a public relations or community affairs project. The possibility that our assistance might improve living conditions or upgrade some other substandard situation within the local community seemed appropriate. Besides, there were men on board who needed some other outlet to turn to instead of continually participating in the monotonous barhopping routine. Captain Furlong agreed. He suggested that I do whatever research was necessary and to advise him of my findings/recommendations.

I found that there were many such projects that were waiting for volunteer assistance. They were officially known as COMREL (Community Relations) projects, primarily schools that were in a poor state of repair, more often than not in the worst of slum areas. The civic action system provided a means whereby local nationals submitted their requests for assistance to the Base Commander for consideration. Projects that were approved for U.S. assistance were placed on a waiting list with no guarantee of ever being accomplished. There was no such thing as a priority system. The list was made available to individuals and commands from which they could review, research, and make their selection. Some of the projects had been on the list for years, while others were only weeks or even days old.

December 12, 1975
Unexpected Visit by J. William Middendorf, II
Secretary of the Navy

After reviewing the listings, I picked out a half-dozen or so that looked interesting. I did not want to give anyone the impression that one specific project might be receiving our assistance, so when I researched each location I did so "undercover," covertly. Over a period of several days I conducted my own personal surveillance and found that some of the projects on the listings were not particularly in need of assistance. Through a process of elimination I zeroed in on one: *Balic-Balic* (which translates, "to return") Elementary School. It was not only in need of assistance, it was conveniently located well away from Olongapo City's infamous distractions.

The Captain was pleased when I reported my research and he concurred in my suggestion that we do whatever we could to improve conditions at Balic-Balic. He immediately requested funding from ComSeventhFlt

(Commander Seventh Fleet) in support of what would soon officially become the Balic-Balic Elementary School COMREL Project.

I was always one to allow, to encourage, my imagination to run the gamut in search of new ideas. I enjoyed the process of brainstorming as I took into consideration all possibilities. I then initiated action in the direction I thought of as best. This time my idea came across unexpectedly. It was anything but ordinary, outlandish at best, but I preferred thinking positive – that it had great possibilities. I prepared the Captain by advising him that what I was about to suggest would probably come as a shock.

"Skipper, I had a difficult time adjusting to the military way of life. During my early days in the Navy I was something of a rabble-rouser, an instigator, as I searched for or created one kind of problem or another. It took a great deal of understanding and encouragement on the part of many of my superiors before I really buckled down and decided that I was not only capable of doing better; I damn well had to."

He squinted ever so slightly, and his head cocked just a bit to one side. His lips had formed the beginning of a curious smile as I began laying the foundation for the unveiling of my idea.

The Captain interrupted me, "What's up, Master Chief? Your performance doesn't need your own authentication."

"Well Sir, as you know, we have a small group of restricted men aboard. It is particularly tough on them, the ship being in port, watching everyone else enjoying liberty and all."

"To the point, Master Chief; you know they deserve being restricted!"

It was difficult for me to get directly to the point without a suitable prelude, but I did as he suggested.

"I think we have an opportunity to utilize our troublemakers in a manner that would be advantageous to everyone. I am suggesting that we allow the restricted men to work on the Balic-Balic project during their off-duty hours where their interests might be meaningfully diverted. With the right type of encouragement they just might come to realize that there are other things to do besides drink, fight, and catch the clap."

The skipper looked pleased at the possibilities, but his words were more of concern. "Do you really think it would work?" he asked.

"Sir, I think it's worth a try. I will be spending a fair amount of time on the project, so it would not be as if they were totally without supervision. I also suggest that we make it voluntary; I would not want participation to

624

be mandatory where the men might think of it as punishment instead of something more in line with an undeserved privilege."

That evening I personally held muster with all restricted men. They were very enthusiastic when they learned that the Captain had approved my suggestion. Every one of them became an instant volunteer. I made it as clear as I possibly could that their behavior ashore had "damn well better be absolute perfection." I had their word, their promise that they would not let their "fellow fuck-ups" or me down. I believed that I had done a good thing and that the men would come through with flying colors. I knew intuitively that the project would be a success and that the men would benefit through increased self-esteem. I could foresee that upon completion some form of appropriate recognition would be bestowed upon the very same men who had not too long before been singled out as near misfits, restricted to the limits of the ship as I had been on so many occasions during my earlier military life. I suspected that whatever recognition they received would take place in front of the entire crew so that everyone might benefit by the reminder that there were other activities outside the main gate besides those that tested one's morality. It was, I thought at the time, one of my better brainstorms. It was not necessarily brilliant, but I believed that it was destined for success.

Balic-Balic had been on the COMREL listing for a long time. The principal was very pleased when I paid her a visit and advised her of the *Ponchatoula*'s sponsorship. I made sure that she knew our activities would be primarily on weekends, with some work being accomplished late afternoons during the week.

Arrangements were made for the base to provide the entire group, me included, with transportation out to the school, with the understanding that we would have to find our own means of transportation back to the ship. That was not considered a problem since jitneys (more frequently called jeepneys in the Philippines) were cheap and plentiful.

After introducing all of the men to the teachers at the school we immediately began leveling the ground inside one of the classrooms where the floors consisted of uneven, well-trodden and hardened, claylike dirt.

As the men worked they expressed their appreciation for my confidence in them, and for having gained the command's trust and approval in allowing them to participate in the project. They were surprised to see that I was working alongside them; not as an observer or supervisor, but as an equal

625

participant in the task at hand. Seeing that, they put forth an even greater effort. It was, as it always was in the Philippines, terribly hot and humid, and I reminded the men to take periodic breaks; that we did not need any cases of heat exhaustion.

The well-meaning teachers wanted to show their appreciation in any way they could. They popped in and out, offering to assist in whatever way they could, but they were always told that we could do the work without their help. They watched us struggle and as our uniforms became drenched with perspiration and sweat dripped from our brows, they did what they thought was appropriate – but in fact was the beginning of a nightmare for me. Involved as I was in my own efforts, I had not noticed until one of the teachers offered me a cold beer that most of the men already had a beer in hand. No wonder they were happier than ever that they had volunteered for the project. Not only had I been instrumental in getting them off of the ship while they were supposed to be restricted; I had also been responsible for the process by which they were provided free booze! Not at all a good thing. Therefore I took steps to make sure the well-meaning teachers would not continue providing alcoholic refreshments. Soft drinks were also available, but they were not in demand. I advised the men that they should have known better than to have accepted beer, but since they already had, they were to limit themselves to no more than two each!

There was no way for me to monitor the beer-drinking activities other than by insisting that the teachers discontinue their generosity. I did not want to make it known that our team was comprised of misfits; trouble-makers who would not even be allowed on terra firma had I not suggested their participation in the first place. In retrospect, I probably should have cautioned the school staff in advance. Their friendly attitudes might have been a little more subservient, whereas soft drinks or just plain water might have been the offering instead of beer; especially knowing that most of these men had been without any alcoholic beverage for a long time. With the compilation of negative factors – the extreme heat, the high humidity, and the availability of cold beer – signs of our positive efforts began to deteriorate. I was not successful at stopping the men from drinking that which was not only being offered, but that which they wanted and were being encouraged to accept. The teachers had overruled my suggestion to "cease and desist" as they continued to supply the men with all the beer they wanted.

When our efforts and charitable intentions began to take on the appearance of a ship's party I knew that it was beyond time to call it a day; it was time to get the men back to the ship. I was going to have a hard-enough time explaining their beer-laden breath, and to delay longer would have been to invite dire consequences.

I had been misinformed, or I misunderstood, when I was led to believe jeepneys were plentiful out in that area. The mode of public transportation from the school to the nearest jeepney-traveled road was by "tricycle," a motorized three-wheeler similar to the Vietnamese *siclo*. The Philippine version had a covered semi-enclosed two-seat carriage mounted behind the driver instead of in front. Both versions accomplished the goal of getting passengers from one location to another via transportation that was guaranteed to be bumpy and somewhat hazardous.

Tricycle drivers freelanced. They remained with their vehicle, sometimes sleeping, while they waited patiently for anyone in need of a ride. There was no standard rate, although you could expect to pay several times more for the luxury of being chauffeured nonstop from starting point to exact destination. It was fun riding in a tricycle, downright cozy when traveling in the company of a female. Depending on traffic conditions a tricycle could be more advantageous, even more expeditious than the routed jeepneys.

While the teachers went in search of the nearest available tricycle, I instructed the group of seven men that they were *NOT*, under any circumstances, to disembark between the school and the main gate. They were to proceed directly back to the ship. I took the added precaution of personally paring the men up so that of the two men riding, one could reasonably be depended upon to make sure that there were no unnecessary delays while en route.

When the first tricycle arrived, the driver assured me that he would send more tricycles to pick up the remaining men. At this point I did not know whether to take the lead, in order to make sure the other tricycles really were dispatched, or to take the last tricycle and follow the "pack." I decided to take the last one so that upon my arrival at the ship I could conduct an immediate head count. The possibility that one or more of the men might not make it back was a consideration I could not totally ignore. I knew of the lure, of the incredible variety of temptations available, but I tried to reject the idea that the men I had accepted responsibility for would know-ingly or intentionally let me down.

I was wrong, terribly wrong! When I arrived at the ship, the OOD, a fellow chief, advised me through an evil grin that only three of the six had returned. He took pleasure at my awkward embarrassment, my state of near-panic. I later found out how adamant the entire Chief's Quarters had been opposed to my idea, and they were, without a doubt, unequivocally and unanimously correct.

I do not think I had ever been more furious as a master chief. I was angry with myself, having stuck my neck out for such a group of noncon-formist rebels. I was angry with the three who failed to return that night and I was angry knowing of the ridicule I had justifiably earned. I had let the entire crew down from the lowest-graded enlisted man up to and including the Commanding Officer. My brainstorm became more of an out-of-control nightmare that was sure to be talked about openly as well as behind my back. I would not be at all surprised if there is still a story floating around out there within the U.S. Navy about a master chief who, way back when, showed a group of restricted men the time of their lives in Olongapo City. I would also bet that the story, as it really happened, has been "enhanced" over the years to make it far worse than it really was.

The AWOL threesome returned the following morning, and each, hav-ing failed to carry out my orders, was immediately placed on report. The Captain awarded each of the offenders with severe penalties, real eye open-ers to anyone who thought the incident might be whitewashed or otherwise minimized.

The three that did follow orders were, much to the dissatisfaction of the CPOs, allowed to continue working on the project. As wrong as I might have been in suggesting that restricted men should be allowed to participate in such a project, I was not about to punish those who had proven they were men of their word. I remain confident that whatever good came by those three men, they being not at all unlike myself when I was their age, far outweighed the consequences. The 50 percent success rate wasn't all that shabby!

Ponchatoula's role in the Balic-Balic project was initially that of pro-viding the services of her men to assist in minor construction/repair of the elementary school. Upon witnessing the assistance being provided by *Ponchatoula* sailors, the local residents in the immediate vicinity became active participants in a massive self-help project. Local residents and school faculty members obtained additional materials and funding from their own pockets as well as through local government legal channels. Our volunteer efforts were primarily responsible for the eventual complete renovation of the school.

The Balic-Balic COMREL project was officially wrapped up on January 6, 1976, and there was a farewell party (financed by the command Welfare and Recreation Fund) for the teachers, students, and *Ponchatoula* participants. The party took place on the school campus where Captain Furlong and I were guest speakers. We presented the school with a ship's plaque in remembrance of the ship and crewmen who took part in that worthy cause. We had been successful in having established considerable goodwill between people from two diverse walks of life, a very satisfying experience.

One of the changes that came about during the upgrading and modernization of the Navy, the Zumwalt era, was the discontinuance of reveille. The object was to make military life more comfortable and more in line with civilian ways. *Responsibility* was the key word. It was also the excuse for many changes that were, in my opinion, responsible for a rapid deterioration in military discipline. The logic was there, but with the slackening of rules that had been strictly enforced since the Navy's inception also came a noticeable decline in the ability to enforce rules. Military law remained, which in theory meant orders had to be carried out, but the fact was that more and more frequently orders were being challenged – sometimes completely ignored. The elimination of reveille meant the men could sleep in, but they were still responsible for showing up at quarters for muster every morning. They could sleep through breakfast, the civilian way, as long as they showed up on time. Regardless of the number of changes, one fact remained constant; it was *not* a civilian world; but the men were beginning to think like civilians, as if they had the choice of obeying only preferable or acceptable orders.

I was responsible for the problems my leading petty officers were having, getting the men up in the mornings. If I couldn't depend on my petty officers getting up, how could I expect the non-rated men to get up? Finally, on one particular morning, after the word was passed to fall in, I found myself to be the *only* one standing at quarters.

I probably appeared to have completely "flipped out" in terms of the scene I created down in the berthing compartment. I was nearly uncontrollable as I ranted and raved – thereby provoking immediate results. Arms, legs, and bodies came leaping out from all directions as I informed everyone that they had exactly two minutes to report at quarters for muster!

They were a shabby-looking bunch; and the last to show up was probably a few seconds late. But I was not yet finished. After giving my men a thorough "reaming," I told them that since they could not make it to quarters at 0800 hours, "We will hold quarters twice daily – once at 0800 and again at 1800 hours; two hours after liberty call."

That did not settle very well with the men.

"Master Chief, how long will this go on?" one of the men asked.

"That depends on all of you. I hold each one of you responsible for yourselves as well as for your shipmates. If a single one of you shows up late, I will hold that second muster later each day! As long as you are all present and on time for morning muster there will be no after hours muster. Do I make myself clear?"

The general groan of understanding from the group was quickly abated as they recognized an elevated anger in my expression.

At 1600 that afternoon, right at liberty call, I asked the MPA to join me for a cold beer – off base. Fraternizing? Perhaps, to some degree, but there were times when it didn't matter, and this was one of those times.

We went directly to the Monte Carlo, a small place at the far end of the strip, where I ordered a couple of cold San Miguel brews. We sat there talking about the workload and other shipboard-related subjects. I kept close tabs on the time, and at exactly 6:00 PM, 1800 hours, I turned to the MPA and something of a devilish smile came over my face.

"Guess what M and B Divisions are doing right now, sir."

"What's up, Master Chief?"

"I think I've turned things around a bit. Right now they are waiting for me at quarters instead of me waiting for them." I laughed as I spoke.

After I explained my quarters for muster orders, the MPA asked me how long I was going to allow them to wait.

"How long do you think I would have to wait for them?" My question needed no answer; we both knew that "indefinitely" would have been the only correct response. We ordered another couple of beers and enjoyed the rest of the afternoon informally gabbing.

Not a single man ever questioned me regarding my failure to show up. They did not like having the tables turned; however, having to wait for me was clearly the medicine they needed. The problem of their tardiness never surfaced again.

Ponchatoula's men came to me for every conceivable reason. I tried to keep an open mind as I listened patiently to their problems and suggestions. One of the nonrated men came to me to discuss his affection for one of the local whores. He described how much he loved the girl and said that he fully intended on marrying her. I told him that it was extremely rare that such marriages worked out favorably. I knew the statistics and I informed him of the 5 percent success rate where sailors took Filipina whores as their brides. Not that the women were unfaithful – but because their family ties were stronger then their wedding vows. That is, they more frequently returned to the Philippines with enough alimony to retire on. I also explained the good side; that the 5 percent were extremely successful marriages. The young man was adamant in his quest to take his "lady" back to the United States as his loving, from-this-day-forward, wife.

After I spent no less than forty-five minutes counseling the man, he opened up with a bombshell that literally sat me back in my chair.

"Master Chief, right now she's living with another guy and I can't get him to leave. How do I get him out of there?"

"She's what? Are you telling me that you intend marrying someone that is nothing but a whore and she is currently shacked up with another guy?"

"Aw, Master Chief, she's not a whore, not really."

"Where did you meet her?"

"In a bar."

"Did you sleep with her?"

"Yea. I got VD from her."

I couldn't believe what he was telling me. "Did she tell you how badly she needed money – and did you give her any?"

"Yes."

"Son, all of the bar girls are badly in need of money and they sell their bodies to anyone willing to pay. That makes them full-fledged prostitutes, whores in any language. I'm not suggesting they are bad people – hell, I've grown to love a number of 'em – but they are out there for everyone's pleasure and I urge you to think long and hard before committing yourself to marriage."

"No, I really want to marry her, and I'm going to." His words, at least for the time being, overruled my advice.

631

Special Services vehicles, with drivers, were available at very affordable rates for members of all branches of the military. Since out-of-bounds places had become scarce, nearly a thing of the past, vehicle drivers had the authority to take passengers just about anywhere. There were still areas known to be safe havens for members of the NPA, the Communist-organized New Peoples Army, areas that were not to be entered by the likes of us. Passengers in Special Services vehicles were expected to compensate their driver on lengthy trips, pay for his meals, his overnight accommodations, and a generous tip at the end of the trip. Such expenses were insignificant by American standards.

On one occasion I joined several other CPOs and we rented such a vehicle, with driver. Our destination was Baguio, the high mountainous resort area. Several of the chiefs brought female companions, I brought Ludy; the widow of my Vietnam pal. Ludy and I spent a great deal of time together in Olongapo during the *Ponchatoula*'s extended repair period. She had become my companion during most of my liberty hours. Even though she was quite a bit older than I was, some thirteen years, she was a great companion, and she was exceptionally knowledgeable in terms of knowing her way around many barrios and provinces.

It was, excluding Vietnam, the most interesting journey I had ever taken. It did not have the excitement that went along with being in a war zone, but it did have beauty and charm that up to that time I did not know existed. The road to Baguio passed through some of the thickest of jungles, banana and rice plantations, and we were able to see for ourselves exactly how rural Filipinos made their living. We saw ancient methods still being utilized to plow the fields; *tamaran*, also known as water buffalo or *carabao*, pulled one-man hand-held plows through the muddy fields in preparation for planting crops. We watched as fishermen sat patiently in their compact one-man nipa huts, conveniently located in the middle of water-drenched rice paddies, where the fish were most likely to be caught or netted. There were an abundance of peddlers on the road, some with impressive strength as they single-handedly pulled their carts, whereas others had the benefit of oxen-drawn carts. Most peddlers had their carts filled precariously high, three and four times higher than their carts were wide. Most carried an assortment of bamboo, rattan, and leaf- or grass-woven ornamental items and furniture, all piled and strapped in perfect balance.

Our driver stopped the vehicle frequently so that we could more close-ly admire our surroundings as we took photographs. Up until that time we had all been under the impression that the prices in Olongapo were as cheap as could be found anywhere. It only made sense that purchasing from the actual manufacturers, from the person or people who spent their time hand making the items that would eventually find their way to more sophisticated marketplaces, would surely provide unheard-of bargains. No middleman and near-zero overhead costs! We all bought small souvenirs of one kind or another after having our pictures taken alongside some of the proud vendors and their remarkable display of wares. Vendors were always appreciative. Having Ludy along proved particularly beneficial to all of us since she could converse in every dialect that was spoken along the way --and there were many.

I never got over my fascination at the lifestyle most villagers lived. What I saw is best described as primitive, where survival was a day-by-day routine that required tremendous effort. At that time the average Filipino earned the annual equivalency of about two hundred dollars, not even close to a dollar a day. No wonder so many Filipinas relocated near military in-stallations, where prostitution was a sure bet toward making more money.

We recognized the mountain people, the *Igorots*, as we neared Baguio, they being scantily clad in their colorful native garb; similar to that of the American Indian. The Igorots were well known for their skills at wood-carving and sculpturing. They were also very talented in the manufacture of silver jewelry and other novelties. Many worked at an active silver mine not far from Baguio. Again Ludy impressed us with her ability to speak the Igorot dialect. I did not know until then that Ludy had grown up in Baguio. It was during her migration through the many provinces that she had be-come proficient in so many Philippine dialects.

Baguio was probably the most comfortable place to relax in all of the Far East. It was not a sightseeing location, although the route there was definitely spectacular. There were fewer off-base activities, but there were plenty of shops and a multitude of souvenirs from which to choose. There was also one of the most beautiful and challenging golf courses in the world at that remote location. As this was a true R and R location a person could depend on being able to relax in absolute comfort while basking in the serenity of Baguio.

Our small group was eating a meal at the cafeteria overlooking the golf course at Camp John Hay when our skipper walked in. We were all pleased to see him; surprised to learn that he had flown to that high mountain resort by helicopter. Space-A (Space Available) flights were available to assist military travelers not just within the geographical boundaries of a country, but also worldwide. I'm sure the Captain, well educated in aviation having earned his own wings, was more than knowledgeable of the more obscure Space-A flights as well as the major ones. We described our journey there and suggested that he accompany us on our return trip. We made sure that he knew he would be a very welcome passenger. Of interest and concern, the *Ponchatoula* was scheduled to get underway the following morning. Having the CO in our midst, especially one of Captain Furlong's rank and distinction, would make things a lot easier to explain in the event some unpredictable obstacle or situation delayed us. It was not our intention to be delayed, but having the Captain with us was like having the best insurance money could buy. He accepted our invitation.

The early morning of October 31st we met at the designated time and place, all of us fully prepared for the return trip to Subic Bay. Ludy suggested we take an alternate route, one that would take us by her home in Infanta, Pangasinan. I concurred in the suggestion since I had already been to her home. I knew how impressive it was and how well it fit in with the extraordinary adjacent coastline. I also knew it to be a road that was considered safe passage from elements of the NPA. After I provided the group my own description of the area, we took a vote. The decision was unanimous; we would take the alternate route without having to be concerned about exceeding any time constraints.

The road to Ludy's home was not well traveled, and there were many stretches of unpaved road studded with potholes of every imaginable size and shape. The trip down was just as interesting as the one we had experienced on the way up. The Captain seemed equally impressed as we made our way through the many villages and barrios, stopping periodically to take more pictures and to admire the most awe-inspiring of views. At one of our stops a cart-pulling vendor allowed each of us to sit on his *carabao* long enough to have our pictures taken. In appreciation we gave the kindly old man a totally unexpected but much appreciated tip.

634

Everyone was surprised when we reached Ludy's home. Even with my prior assurance that her home was anything other than typical, the group had remained skeptical. No one would have thought such a beautiful home could exist so far away from "civilization," a more cultured society. The thatch roof on her home was the only significant similarity to nearby homes. The inside was very modern by Philippine standards even though there was no electricity or running water. Just inside the front entrance, to the left, was a well-polished bamboo-and-rattan bar. The mirror at the back of the bar and the wine racks to the side made it appear more as a piece of fine art than the usable bar it was. Against the right wall in the living room there was an upright piano that Ludy played for our entertainment. The home boasted a large dining room with a huge dining table. There were two hutches; each was filled with a combination of beautiful china and crystal. The home projected an image of comfort and wealth. Ludy liked it that way, however, in reality, the wealth was more in her heart than in substance. Before his death, Rick had built and furnished the home. Ludy lived on the meager pension he left for her, an amount she was able to live on comfortably. She was well known in her community for her generosity as she shared whatever she had left over at the end of each month with many around her who were less fortunate. Ludy also farmed and was able to provide fresh vegetables for herself and her son. She was one tough gal who never shied away from hard work. She was more than deserving of what she had and she was admired in and around her community for her willingness to share with others. That hospitality was evident during our short visit at her home. Ludy presented each of us with monkeypod souvenirs, a means of ensuring that each of her guests would always have a meaningful reminder of their visit to her home.

Our visit had to be shortened since our journey to Ludy's home had taken more time than we planned and we were still faced with several hours of travel. It was late afternoon before we were back on the road heading for Olongapo. With all the souvenirs we had purchased, the number of passengers, plus the bulky monkeypod gifts Ludy had given us, the van was filled to capacity.

It was a long tiresome trip for the lot of us, but it was a trip that we would always remember as having been exceptionally interesting and thoroughly enjoyable. I was disappointed that the time away from our military duties could not have been a day or two longer. It was well into the night when we arrived at the ship. Immediately after transferring my souvenirs to the ship I headed back into town. It would be my final evening out before returning to sea and I wanted to make the best of it by treating Ludy to a late night out on the town.

Following a week at sea, the *Ponchatoula* entered waters and a port unfamiliar to me. I had heard a great deal about Thailand, especially horror stories about the extremely high VD rate in Bangkok, a favorite R and R destination for those serving in Vietnam. We anchored off Sattahip, quite some distance out, and liberty parties had to take the hour-long liberty-boat ride to and from the ship. The boat ride discouraged many of those who were not avid "liberty hounds" from going ashore more than once.

I found Thailand to be quite exotic. I was particularly impressed at the colorful pagoda-type structures and religious statues that were seen along the roadside. Taxi drivers were highly skilled but somewhat suicidal. They would follow their passengers' orders regardless of how hazardous or spontaneous. We had all been indoctrinated regarding some of the differences in Thai law and therefore had to take special precautions to make sure we did not unwittingly get arrested for something foolish. For example, if a taxi were to become involved in an accident, regardless of the conditions that might have led up to it, the passenger(s) would be held totally responsible! The almost-understandable reasoning was that the taxi would not have been where it was, and the accident could not have occurred, had it not been for the passengers' instructions. With that in mind, we would usually tell the drivers to slow down rather than hurry up (as we did in Japan). The only alternative, be it right or wrong, would have been to run like hell in the event of an accident. The deliberate, near-impulsive American reflex to the unintentional dropping of a coin has always been to immediately step or stomp on the coin to keep it from rolling away. Taking that action with a Thai coin was a crime, and those who didn't take the law seriously could expect jail time. The monarch's image was die-cast into Thai coins, and stepping on a coin was considered no different than stepping on the monarch himself. Perhaps one of the most difficult habits for Americans to break, or at least postpone, was the unacceptable manner of sitting in any position that would show the soles of either or both shoes to an observer. If a Thai could see the bottom of your shoe, then you were showing him or her disrespect by an obscene gesture that meant something to the effect that the Thai was of less value than the ground your shoes walked on. Each

636

country had its own unique laws and customs, but in my opinion Thailand was a first-place winner by being the most imaginative.

Precious stones, cut and polished or raw, could be purchased at very reasonable prices in Thailand. The down side was that few, if any, of us were jewel experts. It was chancy, buying from street vendors where prices were always the best, instead of taking the time to shop at one of the many more reputable jewelry stores. Some of the beautifully polished stones that were being offered on the street as sets were nothing more than cut and polished glass that looked every bit as good to the uninformed shopper.

I spent most of my time at the resort area known as Pattaya Beach, where, because of the heavy tourist trade, one was sure to be entertained and comfortable. Pattaya Beach was also an area heavily populated with retirees from many other countries. Many of the nightclubs were owned and operated by foreigners, Americans in particular. Had I been afforded more time in Thailand I would probably have grown to love the area as much as any place I had ever been. But time was short, so I simply relaxed at Pattaya. I enjoyed window-shopping and talking to strangers, swapping stories about countries of origin, travels, likes and dislikes. I have always wanted to return for other visits, to travel up and down the entire peninsula and learn much more about the people and living conditions there. Perhaps someday I will.

November 12, 1975, *Ponchatoula* departed Thai waters and headed straight for Subic Bay. We remained two days before returning to sea where our services were always in demand. On November 26th we again returned to Subic Bay, where we underwent a routine upkeep and maintenance period. December 14th we headed for Hong Kong, where we knew our five-day R and R visit would extend through Christmas. Understandably, Christmas in port was preferable to Christmas at sea, even though it was always difficult celebrating any major holiday away from our loved ones back home.

The CNO, Chief of Naval Operations, did his best to ensure that ship's movements were coordinated so that maximum in-port time could be scheduled over major holidays. That could not always be accomplished, nor could any Navy man ever expect it. Ship's movements were dependent upon any number of factors, each subject to unexpected change that could, and many times did, redirect fleet movements to the east and to the west. It should be easy to understand why seagoing sailors were always interested in world affairs and local weather conditions; both played a role in determining ships' movements. Sailors were always alert to reports of inclement weather, especially when they were at sea and they were anticipating an upcoming port call. If typhoon conditions became imminent, ships that were in port were directed back to sea, in which case a recall of sailors on liberty was conducted. All recalls utilized the assistance of the AFRTS, the local Military Police, and a search by other crewmen who knew the general whereabouts of fellow shipmates. Recalls were rare but they could be expected whenever there was a typhoon somewhere in the area. Ships and crew were safer at sea during typhoon conditions even though the crew might argue the contrary. It was bad enough being recalled while on liberty, but for those who were prone to overindulge in alcoholic beverages, they earned whatever discomfort they felt when we rode out the heavy seas that were always present during a typhoon.

It would be hard for the inexperienced person to comprehend the variance between strength and calm of ocean conditions. The ocean can be extremely cruel and can cause unimaginable damage to things one might think of as indestructible. I have been there and I have seen both ends of the spectrum. I've seen the surface of the ocean absolutely glasslike, where only the ship's wake broke the perfectly still water. Granted, that's a rarity and when it occurred everyone on board marveled at its unusual beauty. It was like a giant swimming pool with no one in it, a gigantic mirror perfectly reflecting the sky and clouds above. On one such occasion the Captain ordered the ship to come to rest for a brief period of time. We all had the opportunity to look over the side directly down into the depths of the ocean. It was uncanny being able to observe the entire ocean ripple free for as far as the eye could see; the horizon all around us unobstructed by any other vessels, truly awesome. I dropped a few coins into the ocean and watched them as they sank deeper and deeper into the crystal-clear water, each took such a long time before fading out of sight. The setting in which we were engulfed was bizarre.

Full dress inspections at sea were not as frequent as those held in port, nonetheless all hands were required to always be prepared. I never questioned the Captain's or the Exec's motives for canceling so many scheduled at-sea inspections. I knew that the crew was frustrated and angered at having to time and again prepare – only to be told the inspection was canceled. Several scheduled inspections were canceled only minutes before all hands were supposed to fall in. Even the CPOs were irritated at what was beginning to look like policy: the scheduling, the preparation, and finally the cancellation. Patent-leather shoes, shoes that sparkled all the time and never needed shining, had not yet been authorized as a part of the Navy uniform. It took time and effort shining shoes with wax polish; and the shine didn't last very long under hot and humid conditions. Inspection uniforms, particularly whites, could only be worn once, and then one had to remain standing until after inspection for fear of creasing the well-starched trousers and shirts. The hardworking snipes, that committed group of men who were continuously subjected to the discomforts associated with working and standing watches in engineering spaces where they were always ravaged by the roar of the main engines and auxiliary machinery and where the heat was practically unbearable; a world comprised of grease, oil, and their own perspiration, should never have had to contend with any kind of harassment – intentional or not. That dedicated group of men spent a minimum of eight hours a day down in the "hole," surrounded by a maze of pressurized steam lines. They generally ignored the many burns they suffered as a result of accidentally bumping hot bare metal. They disregarded the devastating consequences should a steam line or fuel line develop a serious leak or, worse yet, become disjointed or fracture. That same group of men could be depended on to work around-the-clock to effect necessary repairs so that the ship could meet her commitments. Those men needed uninterrupted periods of free time to relax, certainly not to prepare for inspection after inspection only to find that they had wasted their time.

I decided to insist that one inspection not be canceled. I told the Executive Officer that if the upcoming scheduled inspection was canceled I would require my men to fall in anyway. They deserved to be inspected after having prepared time and time again – and if the command elected not to appreciate their efforts then I would. In the event of cancellation, the Exec assured me he would accompany me to inspect my men.

Sure enough, the inspection was canceled, but not for my division. My men fell in at quarters without regard as to who represented the inspecting party. Once the men had fallen in, I went directly to the XO's stateroom.

"Sir, M Division has fallen in and is ready for our inspection."

Much to my disappointment (I probably should have expected it), the Exec said, "No, Master Chief, you go ahead. It wouldn't be right for me to inspect one division without inspecting all of them." I contained myself as

I thanked the XO for having considered accompanying me in the first place, and I excused myself.

I returned to my division – in my finest uniform – and called the men to attention. A passing member of the crew made an uncalled-for snide comment: "Gee, I wish I had to stand inspection."

"Well surprise, sonny – you do! Report back to me within ten minutes in your best set of dress whites." My response, the orders I issued, should have been expected. The grumbling sailor stepped away lively.

My men were not happy about having been singled out. They had outdone themselves and I preferred to think it was for me rather than for the command. They were the sharpest bunch of serious-looking sailors I had ever seen, and I let them know it.

The "outsider," having reported back as directed, was included in my after-inspection remarks: "You are all men, the finest anywhere in the Navy." I had a flashback of my boot camp days, when I had failed to attend church services, as I continued. "You have prepared yourselves for inspection time and again, only this time you were required to carry out the orders. You have passed my inspection, as I knew you would, and I commend you on your efforts. In time you will fully understand my reasoning for insisting that you men stand before me in this manner today. You are all professionals and I am extremely proud of each and every one of you."

I went on for nearly twenty minutes, making sure that they were not only commended on their appearance but also making sure they knew that I was far more aware than they thought in regards to the demands placed upon them and the tireless efforts they were known to expend on a daily basis. I singled out several of the most deserving within the group and recognized them for their outstanding work, something they thought had gone unnoticed, and they stood tall.

Christmas Eve we pulled into Hong Kong Harbor. I was anxious to revisit the British colony, so I "hit the beach" early. I paid more attention to my surroundings as I tried to make some sort of comparison to the Hong Kong of old that I visited some twenty years before. Over that period of time the skyscrapers had taken over and had severely limited the view of hillside greenery as I recalled it. The huge SAN MIGUEL neon light, high over the center of town and known as a beacon of welcome to all ships entering the harbor, was no longer there; it too, had been replaced by high-rise structures. The old antiquated double-deck buses had been

640

replaced with a newer vintage. They still made their presence known with the unmistakable roar of their engines as they made their rounds on the same old routes. The older generation of beggars had been replaced with a younger generation, only their manner of pleading for a handout remained unchanged. I was surprised that all of the high-rise apartments that were there on my first visit remained intact, but they showed signs of aging and were in need of fresh paint and other maintenance. The custom of hanging garments and lines over the outside railings was unchanged. I recalled how much the buildings took on the appearance of a huge patchwork quilt years back – and I thought about how that quilt had retained its color and shape remarkably well over time. The bar scene was no longer the strip of past. There were a few bars and nightclubs, and they were all spacious and modernized; quite impressive and comfortable. The nuisance of having to contend with hustling hookers was a thing of the past. They were no longer exhibiting/soliciting their profession as openly as they had in the past.

I chuckled to myself as I recalled the shoe stores as they once were. Boots were a specialty and were custom fit. Many sailors had their feet measured on the day of arrival so that the finished product (as with customized clothing) would be ready for pickup a day or two prior to departure. Enlisted men could not normally carry civilian clothing on board – the exception being those garments we purchased in Hong Kong. We could not wear them, legally, until we were safe ashore back on the far side of the "pond," across the ocean in CONUS. I smiled openly as I laughed to myself at the memory of those boots, true works of art, comfortable beyond expectation and extraordinary in every impressive detail – but not quite what they appeared to be. Many, though not all, of the shoemakers were highly skilled at making shoes and boots out of paper products! To the unskilled, uneducated, novice shoe shopper, the footwear looked, felt, and wore like a product worth far more than the price paid. But sooner or later (usually sooner but far away from Hong Kong) the otherwise happy boot buyer realized he had been taken. Once the boots or shoes came in contact with water they began falling apart like a wet cardboard box. I recalled my hearty laughter, not so much at their humiliation having spent their money so unwisely, but at their pathetic footwear as it fell apart right in front of taunting onlookers. Even if one was lucky enough to return to the same store a year later, the proprietor (who would have been difficult to identify) would flatly deny any wrongdoing. They would insist that the items must

641

have been purchased down the street at a place that looked similar. The days of such deceptive practices were a thing of the past.

New Years Eve, 1975, we returned to Subic Bay, where the *Ponchatoula* remained tied up at pierside for a week. I knew that this would be my last time to visit with the Hernandez family, since my naval career was rapidly coming to an end. Any future visits, should I be so fortunate, would have to be by space-available military hop or at my own expense. Only time would tell whether or not I would ever enjoy their hospitality again. I spent a lot of liberty time visiting at their beautiful home, reminiscing nostalgically over the years of friendship that we had nourished so positively. I was deeply saddened at the thought of never seeing any of them again, and my watery eyes left little doubt in the family's minds of my deep affection and gratitude for all they had done for me. I made them a promise, a very famous promise that they were quite familiar with.

"I, like General MacArthur, shall someday return." I did return – many times over the following years.

Ponchatoula had but one remaining port call before returning to Hawaii, and that was Yokosuka, Japan. It would be my last visit to any Far Eastern country while I was in the U.S. Navy; by coincidence, one of the first foreign ports I had visited in May 1955, fresh out of boot camp. I was anxious to see what changes had taken place over the near ten-year gap between June 1966 (my most recent visit while on R and R from Vietnam) and January 1976 – my final visit.

The *Ponchatoula* was scheduled to remain tied up at Yokosuka Naval Shipyard from January 22 until February 12, sufficient time for me to revisit most, if not all, of the places I remembered as favorites.

There was little evidence of change on the base. The Enlisted Men's Club, the Petty Officers' Club, and the Chiefs' Club were all in the same locations. I had never been inside the CPO Club and decided to make that my first stop.

Intentionally I entered the club with my hat on. In every Chiefs' Club throughout the world an unobstructed sign clearly spelled out the crime and punishment for entering as I had: HE WHO ENTERS COVERED HERE SHALL BUY THE HOUSE A ROUND OF CHEER. Depending on the size of the club, BAR was sometimes substituted for HOUSE. Affixed behind the bar, always within short reach of the bartender, was the customary brass bell that was loudly rung whenever someone recklessly entered without first removing his hat. The line hanging from most bell clappers could usually be reached by anyone foolish enough to take it upon himself (or herself) to ring it. While in a drunken state, chiefs were known to ring the bell several times during an afternoon or evening. Buying the bar or the house a round of cheer was simply a way of expressing one's desire to share their happy mood with others. When that bell was rung at the Yokosuka CPO Club, everyone sitting at the bar was assured a free duplicate drink of whatever he or she was drinking. I had purposely entered the club with my hat on; it was my way of introducing myself while saying farewell at the same time. When that bell rang and the group sitting at the bar realized it was an E-9 who had entered while covered, there was a roar of delight among them. Only when I refused to immediately remove my hat did they realize my demeanor had been intentional. They appreciated my unexpected gesture and for the next hour or so I had a tough time consuming the reciprocal favors that I was being provided. It was a fine club, and I had a great time. I rang the bell one final time as I prepared to leave. I had not done anything that had never been done before, but I felt good about myself and therefore provided my new acquaintances the opportunity to enjoy one final round at my expense.

Yokosuka changed dramatically and I was a bit overwhelmed by the unfamiliar metropolis it had become. No words can adequately express my disappointment, but that's the price one must pay after such a long time between visits. Club Alliance, the downtown club I had spent so many hours in as a "youngster" was still there, but it was no longer the meeting place where sailors in uniform had at one time crowded into – a favored watering hole. The club was practically empty, and I wondered how in the world it managed to stay in business. I left the Alliance in anticipation of returning to my old hangout, the White Hat Club, it being but a stone's throw away, around the corner and down an alley.

I strained my eyes as I looked for the bar in which I recalled drinking myself into oblivion; where I had foolishly tried to out-drink more seasoned sailors. The things and places I was surrounded by did not click in my memory banks even though I knew I had to be walking over ground I had traversed numerous times during my early Navy years. My eyes scanned the entire area as fast as they could, quickly darting from one location to another in hopes of catching a glimpse of something or someone I might recognize. Then, above me, swinging slowly in the gentle breeze I saw the familiar but very old WHITE HAT CLUB sign as it dangled awkwardly by a single remaining strand of wire. It was barely recognizable as it blended in with the ghost-town appearance of the entire alleyway. The front door was boarded up, as were the upstairs windows overlooking the alley; the windows at which I had spent so many evenings and nights watching the thick crowds of sailors, girls, and vendors below. For the moment I forgot the decrepit appearance of the club and that so many years had passed, and I began pounding on the boarded doorway in hopes that someone, anyone, might be there to welcome me back. My mind was playing tricks on me as I refused to believe that my favorite memories of my genesis in the Navy were nothing more than precisely that: memories.

Upon seeing my apparent desperation an older Japanese gentleman approached and very gently stroked my arm. He looked into my eyes through the tiniest of slits under his eyelids, and I sensed that he, too, was suffering a similar touch of bewilderment.

"I know; I know," the kind old man said, as if he truly understood my anguish.

"All gone now, no more, so sorry." He continued, "All old GI come back, look see, feel same-same bad!" (Over the years many English-speaking Japanese learned to pronounce the "L" sound).

The old man hit the nail square on the head; he had read me like a book as he probably had done with countless others.

"I buy you drink?" I spoke to him in a manner I felt he would best understand.

Slowly he bowed gratefully to me, "Okay, I show you nice place."

His words triggered instant memories of the many times I had heard similar offers. Offers of the "best price," the "best hotel," the "prettiest," the "youngest," the "cheapest," and so on. But for some reason I took the man at his word and I was pleasantly surprised as a result.

Within a couple of minutes' walking distance he stopped abruptly, pointed and said; "Here, you like!" His assurance was fully qualified.

Again, with a typical polite bow of courtesy, he allowed me to enter the very small, poorly lighted bar first. As my eyes adjusted, I could see that beautiful Oriental posters, placards, and carvings of excellent quality surrounded me. There were two small booths and two bar stools at the bar; barely sufficient room to accommodate the furnishings. Without my asking, but to my pleasure, we were immediately served a small container of hot saki as two miniature saki cups were ceremoniously placed in front of us. In appropriate tradition, I poured for the aging gentleman and he poured for me. *Kampai*, we toasted each other in unison.

Shortly I learned that Mama-san, the bartender, was actually the man's wife, and the compact bar was the front of what extended into their small home in the back. I assumed that they did not have many customers, but those that did make their infrequent appearances were most likely treated with familylike hospitality. The old gentleman and I spent a couple of hours talking about changes that had taken place over the years, the welcomed changes as well as those that were not easily accepted. His stories went back before my time and I listened intently as he spoke of his younger days – and of the (atomic) bomb(s) that had ended the war. I was thankful for our by-chance meeting and I assured both Mama-san and Papa-san (as I respectfully addressed each) that I would visit them again before my final departure. They were pleased.

As I reminisced within my wandering mind, I realized that it had been fifteen years since I last saw Kimiko at Hotel Green Heights. The memory of our honest relationship coupled with a great deal more than simple curiosity made my decision easy, to attempt locating her. There could never have been anything truly serious between us, but I knew that I would always care about her life in general.

Black Market Alley, Souvenir Street, en route to Hotel Green Heights, was about the only place that had retained any similarity to my recollection of years past. Similar only in that the street was still narrow and there were souvenir shops from one end of the alley to the other, a distance of about two stateside city blocks. There were only three or four bars along the alley, quite unlike the neon strip of nightclubs I remembered; none had retained names that were familiar to me. There I was, on my old "stomping ground," but my feelings were those of visiting the gravesite of a long lost friend. Time changes everything, but I was not prepared for the magnitude of changes that had seemingly been thrust upon me so abruptly.

I could see the hotel as I walked the narrow cemented pathway leading up the side of the mountain. Through the fading paint on the side of the structure, the paint that was supposed to cover the huge but barely visible letters, I was able to distinguish the familiar words: HOTEL GREEN HEIGHTS. Having seen so many changes that had taken place, I should not have been surprised that the hotel had changed too. I knocked at the front entrance. A Japanese man about my age answered the door, but he barely

645

spoke English. Since asking for Kimiko by her "professional" name did not bring about favorable results, I asked for her by her birth name, Akemi. The man assured me that no one by either name lived there and that many years had passed since any women had lived there. His inability to speak much understandable English made it near-impossible for me to comprehend all that he told me, but from what I gathered the Hotel Green Heights had been converted to something of a male dormitory.

My disappointment and my sentiment encouraged me to continue my search even though I had no idea where to begin. I momentarily considered placing an ad in a local Japanese newspaper but quickly realized that might not be appropriate – after all, Kimiko would most likely not want her past brought to light.

I approached an aging lady tending to her garden at the base of the hotel/dormitory with little hope that she would be able to help me any more than the man had. The possibility that she had lived there for a long time, that she might have known Kimiko, was remote indeed – but it was as good a place as any to continue my search. She was very polite and she spoke English remarkably well. I was in luck – the old woman had lived there practically all of her life, and she knew things about the hotel and its occupants that would make for a most interesting book of its own. She knew the old Mama-san and she recalled the names of most of the "business women," those that had worked there for more than brief periods of time. Yes, she recalled Kimiko – in fact, they had been good friends! Much to my surprise, the old woman also knew of me: "Paul-san, the special American sailor who never returned."

Well, I had returned and I wanted to see Kimiko one last time. I wanted to wish her all the best things that life had to offer – and I wanted to thank her for having been a part of my growing-up process.

"Very sorry, Paul-san. Kimi-chan [diminutive for "sweet Kimiko"] die two years already!"

"Oh no!" I heard myself whisper. For the moment I managed to hold back my tears even though my voiced quivered as I asked, "What happened?"

"Cancer." One word said it all.

I didn't think to ask of Kimiko's life, was she married, did she have children, was she otherwise happy, etc. . .

"Where is she buried? Where are her remains?"

646

The woman had the same look of bewilderment, that same subtle sensitivity to my feelings, that Papa-san had shown only the day before. She was almost apologetic, certainly sympathetic, when she told me, "Very sorry, Paul-san, Kimi-chan very far away in her prefecture."

The old woman offered me the hospitality of her small home, a bit of solace I probably could have used, but I knew that my tears would flow heavily within the confines of those protective walls.

"Thank you, Mama-san, but I better be on my way."

I immediately turned to hide the uncontrollable grimace that was quickly forming on my face. I am unable to describe the inner pain and the frustration I was feeling. Kimiko had been there at the beginning of my Navy career, and I had it in my mind that she would be there at the end.

Luck was back by my side as I wandered aimlessly through the side streets of Yokosuka. I happened to glance down another alley-type walkway and saw a familiar sign: RED SLIPPER.

The Red Slipper had been one of the favorite hangouts for many USS *Colahan* snipes. I headed straight down the alley fully expecting the door to be sealed, just another dead remnant of the past, but instead the door swung open at my touch. I entered another dimension, a world that had remained intact, untouched by time. The place had not changed – even the same mama-san was there, although I didn't recognize her right away.

I sat at a booth, ordered a large Kirin beer, and submerged myself deep within memories that the Red Slipper had provided me. I wondered how many other memories I might have been absorbed with or preoccupied by had I not suffered periods of blackouts, the expected result of overindulgence.

Mama-san and I were the only ones in the bar. She had her dog with her; a small feisty thing that she cautioned me against petting. Dogs and I normally got along just fine; where others were incapable of approaching one, I had some kind of dog-acceptability ambience about me. I never had the misfortune of approaching a truly hostile dog. So I walked over and picked her dog up, petted it gently, and talked to it as if it were an old friend. The dog didn't quite know what to make of it all as it looked at me suspiciously. Mama-san was flabbergasted. Never before had an American GI been able to get near the dog, let alone pick it up. She stood there with her mouth agape, not knowing whether to be angry at the dog or happy at my having been accepted by it. The acceptance by that dog opened the door to conversation that lasted all evening, right up to the time Mama-san closed her bar that night. After having been so disappointed up to that point, I was elated when during our question-and-answer session she sat back abruptly and announced that she remembered me! At last, someone remembered me!

"Paul-san!" she exclaimed with a higher-than-normal pitch of excitement in her voice. She sucked in a deep breath, having been caught a bit off guard, and repeated, "Paul-san. Now I remember you! Oh, you bad boy-san. Too much all time fight-fight," she said half laughing, half scolding. Mama-san proceeded to remind me of not only those encounters I had recollection of, but also some I had long ago forgotten. Yes, I had been a bad boy-san, but I assured Mama-san that those days were no longer part of my life. I showed her my military ID card verifying I had achieved the grade of master chief. She sat back in her chair, slapped her hands together, and told me how proud she was of my accomplishment. I was surprised to learn that Mama-san had never met an E-9 although she knew they existed. She compared master chiefs to admirals; why would the likes of either find the time or the desire to venture into the alleyways of Yokosuka to the Red Slipper?

I became something of an instant celebrity in Mama-san's eyes, almost to the point of embarrassment. I assured her that I was the same Paul-san she had known in the past, that I had only been able to achieve my degree of success having exercised better judgment as I matured.

That night I relived a bit of my youth in the company of a very old acquaintance enveloped by old but familiar surroundings. At some time during the evening, Mama-san's face became familiar to me, and with her encouragement we were both able to relive some rather obsolescent events.

After my night at the Red Slipper I continued thinking in terms of the past. I needed to buy a few things, a futon for sure, so I began window-shopping along Souvenir Street. It was immediately apparent that bargain prices were no longer evident in Japan. Prices had become competitive with whatever the market would bear – similar and oftentimes higher than the same item might have sold for in the United States. I went through the old but familiar bartering stage with the proprietor of the first store I entered: her firm twenty-five-dollar price, then my fifteen-dollar counteroffer. I knew the price was negotiable; it *always* was. But she stood her ground, assuring me that her price was the "best price" that I would find. I'd heard that before, all too often, so I stood my ground almost as well as she stuck to her twenty-five dollar figure although I did slowly increase my bid by five dollars, a dollar at a time. She would come down sooner or later – I thought. When she absolutely refused to negotiate with me I politely told her I would purchase my futon elsewhere – at a more reasonable price.

"I no think so," she said.

I spent the better part of the day trying to find a better price only to discover that *everywhere* the price was thirty dollars – an equally nonnegotiable figure! Tail between my legs I returned to my starting point.

"Okay, you win, I'll buy a futon for your price; twenty-five dollars," I said.

"No, sir, now thirty dollar!" And she meant it! I couldn't help but admire her as I thought about how, over the years, the tables had been turned. I was tired of the one-sided bartering game, so I reluctantly gave her the thirty bucks. I had no mind to start all over only to find that the prices everywhere else had also become outrageously inflated.

Bar prices had also become unreasonable – and the beautiful young hostesses that had always been readily available to provide whatever degree of company and intimacy one might be desirous of, and willing to pay for, were no longer there. They had been replaced by older women who did not seem to care whether they made a living or not. I figured they were probably the residuals, those who refused to get on with their lives in some other profession, probably still of the opinion that they were as youthful and desirable as they at one time may have been. They were a far cry from it, although they probably had their special customers; probably retirees who had grown old along with them – not realizing how time had taken away their greatest selling features, their physical assets.

It snowed while we were at Yokosuka. I had never seen it snow in Japan, never even thought of it as a place one might see snow (other than on Mount Fuji). All of my previous visits had been during other seasons. I liked the chill in the air. I particularly enjoyed sitting in a bar beside one or another kind of *kamado*, a Japanese-style stove or heater. Kerosene-fired heaters, they being more efficient and easier to cram larger numbers of people around, had replaced the old charcoal-fired *kamados*.

Shipboard routine remained constant. There was enough work to keep everyone busy, and we were in port long enough for everyone to get their fill of liberty. With my knowledge and experience of the past, I wondered how the younger sailors occupied their liberty time. Would picture taking satisfy their desire to enjoy themselves ashore? Many *Ponchatoula* sailors imposed a kind of base restriction upon themselves. Few, after that first in-town experience, elected to go beyond the recreational facilities that were abundant and more conveniently located on the base. I have always felt privileged having been exposed to a time and to places when things were quite different.

Our final day in port, and at the suggestion and urging of the XO, I decided to move from the CPO Quarters (crowded and somewhat antiquated) up to a vacant single-occupancy officer's stateroom. It was intended as the doctor's stateroom, but since the ship no longer carried a doctor it had remained vacant for some time. Much to the disapproval of the CPOs, I decided that during my off-duty time I would live more as an officer for the remainder of my military service, so I moved my things into the stateroom. At once I realized how great it was having and enjoying the privacy of my own room. The furnishings were more than adequate. The single bunk bed had a very comfortable mattress, and there were plenty of drawers in which to stow my personal belongings. I no longer had to walk from CPO berthing to the head to wash up and shave; I had my own washbasin. I also had my own private locking desk with a combination safe inside as well as my own phone that gave me immediate access to the Captain's stateroom, the XO's stateroom, and the engineroom. I appreciated the knock on my stateroom door by officers as well as enlisted men, the customary prerequisite to entering.

Most of the other chiefs took a strong disliking to me, perhaps thinking that I felt I was better than they were. I was much better *off*, certainly no better as an individual. They were well aware that newer and larger ships were designed to accommodate senior and master chiefs with staterooms – but they still thought I should have continued living among my own kind. I knew that many CPOs did not like the idea that I had become a seasoned E-9 at an early age. Some were jealous of my achievement. They were known to scrutinize my each and every move, always on the lookout in hopes of finding some degree of fault, regardless of how insignificant. I valued their opinions as related to shipboard functions, however, I never allowed their opinion(s) of me personally to interfere with my responsibilities.

Officers aboard the *Ponchatoula* all lived on the 0-1 level, one level above the CPO quarters. They readily accepted me although I was never completely comfortable with the knowledge that I was the only enlisted

650

man living among them. As a matter of convenience living in Officers' Country also meant that I would have access to their head and showers. At first that was awkward for me, but within days it became as natural as it had been for me among the chiefs. I had known since my days in boot camp that officers lived a better life than enlisted men, but until I moved into the doctor's stateroom I had never actually experienced it.

Having a phone connected directly to the engineroom was an added bonus. I wired a small speaker system to the phone as a means of monitoring everything that was taking place within the spaces for which I was responsible. No one ever figured out how I became so knowledgeable of everything that was going on in engineering. When it became so apparent that I invariably responded promptly whenever there was a situation within the engineering plant that needed my attention, they accused me of having telepathic capabilities. Note: Telephone circuitry on that vessel was a party-line system on which anyone picking up a phone on the same line could listen in or join the ongoing conversation. Therefore, what I did was not exactly in violation of anyone's right to privacy. I could have accomplished the same goal had I simply held the phone to my ear – somewhat inconvenient but it would have provided me with the same result.

It was while listening in on my speaker system that I learned of the surreptitious titles by which my men referred to me. I was most often called the "Admiral" or "Two Stars" (referring to the two stars that identified me as a master chief), which I didn't mind a bit. To my knowledge those terms were never used derogatorily, rather they were used as terms of devotion and admiration, characterizations and qualities with which I was proud to be associated. During my career I knew of CPOs that were known as "Chief Dumb Shit," "Chief Asshole," "that prick," and any number of other degrading or derogatory terms. In consideration of that, I was pleased being referred to by my men in that manner.

February 12, 1976, *Ponchatoula* departed Japanese waters and headed home. The two weeks' travel time between Japan and Pearl Harbor seemed to me as a much longer period of time. I was filled with anxieties and was apprehensive about the approaching end of my military career. On the other hand and somewhat in conflict, I was extremely anxious to get it over with. I spent all of my final four-hour underway watches hoping that the plant would function properly and that there would be no serious malfunctions

651

that could not be effectively and efficiently handled without escalating as a danger to my men or to me.

The ship was about halfway between Japan and Hawaii, and I was on watch. I had been through the routine of roaming around engineering spaces thousands of times. Surrounded by an environment in which I was so thoroughly familiar, it was easy to pick out numerous discrepancies while making my rounds, some of which I took note of, whereas the very minor ones I intentionally overlooked. It would have accomplished nothing by insisting that the spaces be maintained at levels approaching perfection. There was not sufficient manpower nor were there enough hours in the day for me to insist on the accomplishment of work beyond that which was already being done. The men were fully occupied as they struggled to keep up with steam, oil, and water leaks – problems that never ended.

I noticed that the main-engine oil pressure was fluctuating between low and dangerously low, a situation that if allowed to continue might very well leave us without propulsion and at the mercy of the sea. Rather than rely on the lower level watch, I decided to investigate the problem myself. I had a flashback of the time Marcel and I had tricked MM1 Charlie Boyd by manipulating the oil pressure gauge, and I hoped that the situation would, as it had done in that instance, correct itself. I told the throttleman to stand by for a loss-of-lube-oil casualty and I reminded the other watchstanders of their responsibilities should that occur.

On the lower level of the engine room, I stood looking at a lube oil pump unlike anything I had personally worked on. I knew that all pressure-regulating valves operated on the same principle, so I reached over and twisted the valve wheel clockwise, the direction all regulating valves were turned to increase the output pressure. I was confident that the other watchstanders, the throttleman in particular (he being directly responsible for stopping the propeller shaft within seconds of losing oil pressure), were alert and prepared to react if the oil system continued to lose pressure. I barely touched the valve wheel when it and its accompanying valve stem disjoined into my hand! Instantly oil pressure dropped to zero and a real casualty to the plant was imminent, one all engineroom snipes were well trained to control and to recover from, but also one that few men ever experienced *for real*! The high wailing pitch of the loss-of-lube-oil siren was screaming as I worked frantically with both of my oil-drenched hands, attempting to replace the entire adjusting mechanism as oil spewed in all directions. Within seconds, much quicker than I would later recall, I managed to screw the stem back

652

into the threaded yoke and adjusted the pressure back to normal. Casualty control procedures had been followed by my men with collective precision. Recovery also went smoothly, and I congratulated the men on their quick response. They thanked me for having used my so-called telepathic intuitive powers, for warning them in advance and for reminding them of their responsibilities. I'm sure they would have responded just as well without my warning – but I'm glad that I took that small extra step of precaution. Such was the life of a snipe, always looking for, or responding to, some kind of deficiency and/or malfunction.

February 26, I stood my final watch, the 0400-0800 shift. I relieved a Chief Machinist's Mate from his "mid-watch" and I accepted responsibility for the entire engineering plant for the last time. I made the following entry to the engineering log, the official record that contained all pertinent information as to the configuration and operation of the engineering plant:

04-08: Underway as before except; the end of the Adkisson Era of underway watch-standing is rapidly approaching. After 20 years of chasing mysterious feedwater losses/shortages I will soon be directing my attention toward other but equally important tasks. It has been a real joy serving in the "pit" with so many hard charging snipes; however, I have serious doubts that I will miss the intrigue and suspense normally associated with underway watches in Engineering. I suspect this, my final underway watch in the United States Navy, will be equally rewarding as the thousands stood in the past. I give myself a "well-done" for having survived.

During that four-hour watch I also made other entries to the document; the taking of chloride tests, shifting of machinery, shifting and cleaning lube oil strainers, and other significant modifications or changes to the plant configuration. I knew that I would be relieved early – for breakfast – and that I would not be returning to the engineroom to stand another watch, not ever! My final entry to the log closed a chapter in my career:

Made routine tests and inspections. Conditions as noted. @0710 Properly relieved by ENC Brooks. It's over!

I have that original log only because the MPA was kind enough to mail it to me along with the following personal letter dated March 29, two days prior to my discharge.

> Dear Master Chief,
>
> I want to give you something from the Ship that may have some meaning for you. I certainly hope so.
>
> I have not really taken the time to express to you what I feel now that you have left the Ship. I must tell you, whether I showed it or not, I have learned many things from you. Perhaps most importantly, patience. I have a rather mercurial nature and you quite often listened to my utterings and then helped me see where I should go.
>
> I thank you for your steadiness and attention to duty and the other little things that are always forgotten but mean so much in the end. Here is wishing it could have been a longer more pleasant tour of duty.
>
> Master Chief, may I say thanks again for those, the ones who benefited the most, for all you left with us.
>
> May the deck rise up to meet your foot and the wind be to your back and happiness be your lot.
>
> > Respectfully yours,
> > [Signed]
> > David Bradley

I truly appreciate that "Mister" Bradley took the time to send me those laudatory remarks.

At 0734 hours, while eating breakfast aboard a Navy vessel for the last time, I heard the 1-MC blast out the words; "Now set the Special Sea and Anchor Detail."

Ponchatoula edged her way into port at Pearl Harbor and I remained topside to enjoy the view one final time.

Captain Furlong acknowledged my last official request by favorably approving my early release from his command. I did not want a lot of phony hubbub from *Ponchatoula* chiefs at a retirement ceremony they would not enjoy attending. Besides, such ceremonies were more often spontaneous.

In any event, recognition for retirement was never arranged by the retiree – it was usually done by a fellow CPO, sometimes by an officer, with or without the knowledge of the retiree.

March 15, my final day aboard the USS *Ponchatoula*, I attended my final Officers' Call in the wardroom, the usual procedure while in port. That was when and where the XO, a newcomer to the ship, issued his orders to the Division Officers. They, in turn, carried those orders to their subordinates. It was at that final meeting, when I told Mr. Bradley about a portion of the POD that contained misinformation about me – and I did not intend on having that portion read at Quarters that morning. I acknowledged that the errors were unintentional. Responsibility for errors in the POD rested with the XO. In his effort to honor my service, to pay me tribute, the XO had failed to pay attention to details. For example, the POD stated it had taken me two years longer to attain the grade E-9 than it had actually taken. It also stated I was being transferred directly to the Fleet Reserve on a date two weeks premature, and there were other discrepancies as related to my career. Mr. Bradley understood and he nodded his head in agreement.

Unexpectedly the Exec then walked directly up to me with a harsh scowl on his face and said, "I heard what you said. You will report to my stateroom immediately following Quarters."

Somewhat bewildered, I replied, "Aye-aye, sir."

As I stood at Quarters with my men for the final time I told the chief who normally read the POD to disregard the paragraph that contained any reference to me. In retrospect I should have ignored the whole thing – but I was too much of a stickler for accuracy. If I was being recognized for something, for anything, I felt it should have been accurate – something I *really* did, or something I was *really* going to do. The BT Chief agreed and he skipped the part about me.

Following Quarters I went to the XO's stateroom as directed, knocked on his door, and entered. He was sitting at his desk pretending to read some lower-rated enlisted man's quarterly evaluation while he completely ignored my presence. I stood there like some kind of fool, not knowing what was taking place and feeling quite uneasy at the total lack of recognition. The XO's obvious and intentional failure to exert the slightest bit of courtesy was absolutely uncalled for. A full minute or more passed and I was within seconds of excusing myself and walking out when the XO dropped the paper in his hand, scooted his chair back away from his desk, and as he glared at me said, "I understand that you never allow the POD to be read at Quarters and that you are particularly displeased with today's POD!"

He got it half right and I was not the one to assist him in being wrong again. "You're right in that I thought the remarks about me should have been accurate, however, you are wrong about reading the POD – I *insist* that the POD is read *everyday* at Quarters—"

The XO interrupted me, "I heard you in the wardroom when you said the POD is never read to your men."

"No, sir, you misunderstood—"

Again I was interrupted. "Bull! I know what I heard, you know-it-all Master Chief."

"Well, sir, you've shown me absolutely no respect, and from this point on I'll show you the same. You've had me standing here in silence like a goddamned boot camp recruit while you pretend to read something as insignificant as that piece of shit on your desk without so much as recognizing my presence. If you haven't noticed, sir, or were not aware, I am still the Master Chief of this command!"

"Yeah, I know all about you master chiefs," he said, as if we were all some kind of a joke.

"My record speaks for itself," I responded.

"And I know all about those phony records you master chiefs boast of. You're lucky you never served under me because you'd never have made it; you'd never have been recommended for chief."

The entire conversation was beginning to get out of hand, and I was truly out of character – but I had the "hammer," so to speak, since I knew that I was within days of retirement. I was thinking, *Who the hell is this guy, he's so wrong – and I'm letting him ruin my last day on my last ship? Why is he so against my success?* I really didn't want to know the answers; I only wanted to get out of his stateroom, pick up my transfer orders, and be on my way. By then my anger had taken control and I blurted out my true thoughts. "You think you're a tough guy, that you'd be tough to work for? Well, I've made it under guys that would make you look and sound like a fuckin' tenderfoot pussy." I surprised myself at my choice of words, but I felt relieved having said them. My insubordination went right over his head --or else he intentionally ignored my words.

"So what's wrong with the POD?" he demanded.

I tried to explain, but when I realized that I was not going to convince him that he was wrong, I grumbled, "To hell with you," and I walked out.

The XO truly believed that he had heard something that was never, he had formed a distinct aversion to me, someone he had not, up until that very day, so much as conversed with. I had serious thoughts of sympathy for the unfortunate enlisted men that would have to serve under him –. I decided that the skipper should be informed of the entire ordeal. He deserved to know of the XO's questionable performance. It was reasonable to assume that he would treat other enlisted men, from the most junior through the most senior, in a similar manner.

The Captain was a good listener. He thanked me for sharing my experience and assured me that he would be on the alert for any similarities in the XO's future contacts with enlisted men. Having had my say, I picked up my orders from the Ship's Office, stopped in to say goodbye to Mr. Bradley, and headed for the gangway – the final path that would detach me from ship and relocate me ashore. The XO happened to be heading in the same direction, and he was in close proximity to me when much to my surprise he said, "Good luck, Master Chief – I really mean it."

"Fuck you! See if you can misunderstand that!" I glared into his quickly reddening face and never broke my stride. It was fortunate for both of us that he allowed my remarks to go "unnoticed" as I walked across the gangway, no longer attached to that command, en route to my next.

It is a rare situation when an enlisted man is honored by the tune of a boatswain's pipe. The single most important instance is when he leaves a command for the final time, destined for retirement. He is then honored by a number of "side boys." Side boys were a part of the quarterdeck ceremonies when an important person or high-ranking officer arrived or departed a ship. The custom of having side boys originated centuries ago in the Royal Navy when officers were hoisted aboard in a sort of basket and, since senior officers usually weighed more than junior, more boys were needed on the line. When the side is piped by the Boatswain's Mate of the watch, from two to eight side boys, depending on the rank of the officer, will form a passageway at the gangway. They salute on the first note of the pipe and finish together on the last note. Interestingly, there was nothing in Navy regulations stating that side boys had to be male; in ceremonies ashore when side boys are required, enlisted women could be, and were, detailed as side boys.

In the instance of a retiring CPO, fellow chiefs normally volunteer as side boys. They all render that final salute formally honoring the departure

...ief. It is an honor that brings tears to the eyes of many a hard-
of a fel as they depart for the last time.

enedre were no side boys, chiefs or otherwise, as I departed the
chatoula. I missed out on an honor I had looked forward to for such
long time. I expected someone to accept traditional responsibility and
to make the same arrangements that I had made many times as a devoted
chief. I would not have felt quite so offended at my departure had I, at very
least, heard the farewell sound of a boatswain's pipe.

My orders were specific, I was transferred to U.S. Naval Station, Pearl
Harbor, Hawaii, "for separation and retirement." With me went my final
evals, the overall evaluation that would describe my final days in the Navy.
I am proud to include that evaluation as written and approved:

MASTER CHIEF ADKISSON IS CURRENTLY ASSIGNED
AS M DIVISION CPO, MASTER CHIEF PETTY OFFICER OF
THE COMMAND AND ADMINISTRATIVE ASSISTANT TO
THE EXECUTIVE OFFICER.

MASTER CHIEF PETTY OFFICER ADKISSON HAS
PERFORMED ALL ASSIGNED TASKS IN AN OUTSTANDING
MANNER. UNDER HIS LEADERSHIP AND SUPERVISION,
THE OVERALL SKILL LEVEL OF THE PROPULSION
MACHINIST'S MATES AND THE MATERIAL CONDITION
OF THE ENGINEROOM MACHINERY HAVE IMPROVED
SIGNIFICANTLY. HE HAS DEMONSTRATED EXCEPTIONAL
MANAGERIAL AND LEADERSHIP SKILLS AS THE
COMMAND SENIOR ENLISTED ADVISOR. HE HAS EARNED
THE RESPECT AND TRUST OF ALL HANDS BY HIS SOUND
COUNSELING AND SINCERE CONCERN FOR THE WELL
BEING AND ADVANCEMENT OF HIS SUBORDINATES.

MASTER CHIEF PETTY OFFICER ADKISSON IS AN
OUTSTANDING CAREER PETTY OFFICER WHO HAS
PROVIDED A COMMENDABLE EXAMPLE FOR ALL
HANDS. HE HAS BEEN ABLE TO MEET AND EXCEED
THE REQUIREMENTS OF ALL ASSIGNMENTS GIVEN
HIM. HIS APPEARANCE AND MILITARY BEARING ARE
IMPECCABLE. AS SENIOR ENLISTED MAN ON BOARD,
HE HAS SERVED WELL AS SENIOR ENLISTED ADVISOR

AND ADMINISTRATIVE ASSISTANT TO THE EXECUTIVE OFFICER, BOTH POSITIONS REQUIRING CONSIDERABLE DIPLOMACY AND TACT IN COORDINATING INTERDEPARTMENTAL EFFORTS. HIS RELIABILITY AND INITIATIVE ARE BEYOND QUESTION; WHEN GIVEN AN ASSIGNMENT, HE CAN BE TRUSTED TO COMPLETE ALL REQUIREMENTS IN A TIMELY AND THOROUGH FASHION, AND HAS FREQUENTLY PRODUCED RESULTS THAT FAR EXCEEDED REQUIREMENTS. HIS CONDUCT HAS BEEN EXEMPLARY. HE HAS THE ABILITY TO MAKE THE MOST EFFECTIVE USE OF AVAILABLE RESOURCES AND HAS INTRODUCED SEVERAL WATCHSTANDING AND ORGANIZATIONAL INNOVATIONS WHICH HAVE IMPROVED THE EFFICIENCY OF M DIVISION. MASTER CHIEF ADKISSON IS A FIRM LEADER BUT POSSESSES THE JUDGMENT TO DETERMINE WHEN EXPLANATION AND ENCOURAGEMENT WILL PRODUCE BETTER RESULTS THAN DIRECTIVES. HIS SERVICES AS COUNSELOR AND ADVISOR HAVE BEEN INVALUABLE TO THE COMMAND. THEY HAVE SOLVED MANY PERSONAL PROBLEMS AND HAVE HELPED MANY CREWMEMBERS THROUGH DIFFICULT TIMES. HE SERVED AS COORDINATOR OF A COMMAND SPONSORED COMMUNITY PROJECT WHILE THE SHIP WAS DEPLOYED IN THE SUBIC BAY, R.P. AREA. THE PROJECT CONSISTED OF THE RENOVATION OF AN ELEMENTARY SCHOOL IN THE OLONGAPO AREA AND THE GENERATION OF INTEREST ON THE PART OF LOCAL INHABITANTS IN DEVELOPING A SELF-HELP PROGRAM TO CONTINUE THE PROJECT. MASTER CHIEF ADKISSON WAS HIGHLY SUCCESSFUL IN BOTH ENDEAVORS. LARGELY THROUGH HIS EFFORTS, A LASTING BOND OF FRIENDSHIP AND GOODWILL WAS DEVELOPED BETWEEN TWO WIDELY DIVERSE GROUPS, A TRIBUTE TO HIS SKILL AND TACT. HE IS AN EXCEPTIONALLY FINE LECTURER WHO CAN GET HIS POINT ACROSS CLEARLY AND DIRECTLY. HIS WRITING SKILLS ARE OUTSTANDING. MASTER CHIEF PETTY OFFICER ADKISSON HAS SERVED THE NAVY WELL THROUGH A LONG AND SUCCESSFUL

CAREER. HE HAS BEEN AN INVALUABLE ASSET TO THIS COMMAND AND IS A CREDIT TO THE NAVY.

19

THE LAST MAIN GATE

The retirement of any CPO, regardless of his pay grade, was always cause for celebration by those among whom he or she last served. I had not only participated in numerous such celebrations; I had been instrumental in formulating many. Everywhere I served, as long as I had the title and was vested with the obligation and authority of Mess President, I never allowed my personal feelings or the personal feelings of other chiefs within any given mess to override the recognition due a fellow CPO for having served twenty or more years honorably. It was not only a matter of tradition; it was a moral obligation. It was also a time to put aside any ill personal feelings that may have at one time come between CPOs. Retirement was a time to be celebrated by all, first and foremost in recognition of those departing the military service, but also in anticipation of the day those remaining behind would be similarly honored. It was a day filled with envy by most and a day of awakening for the retiree.

Regardless of whatever image I might have portrayed throughout my career, somehow I retained the same sensitive feelings I had at the time I entered the service. My emotions were not always easily concealed, particularly those feelings of loneliness or nostalgia. I was sentimental but I did my best to conceal it. There was always a lump in my throat and tears in my eyes at gatherings where Taps was played in remembrance of those who had already experienced that ultimate and final surrender to the Almighty.

It had been my choice, the result of my own request, that had removed me from the USS *Ponchatoula* and those chiefs with whom I would last serve. I did not want them to feel at all put out; that they were under any obligation to piece together a farewell party. It would have appeared ludicrous, insincere, and artificial had *Ponchatoula* CPOs gone out of their way for me. Besides, I knew that if there was a party, at some time during a moment of recognition I would probably break down right in front of the very chiefs who thought more of me as someone who had no feelings – a person who probably had never cried in his life.

I had very little to do while I was attached to the naval station. The command knew that I would only be there for a couple of weeks, so there was no need for me to establish myself. Usually I was allowed to call in for morning muster. A couple of times the command had me personally hold muster on groups of men that were waiting for transportation to their next duty stations, to remind them with the voice of authority of their responsibilities while attached to the naval station. In other words, I was to demand of them that which the command had been unable to accomplish. It was only during those very few mornings that I issued orders in a manner I had never before found necessary. The command insisted that I instill the fear of God in those men – so I ranted and raved about rules and regulations in my best simulation of a grouchy, threatening voice of which even a Chief Bos'n would have been envious. I demanded and I threatened, and I grabbed their undivided attention while in the back of my mind I knew that within days I would be nothing more than history to the U.S. Navy and that my voice would no longer carry with it the authority I had become so used to exercising.

The last week of March, I received a message that Captain Furlong was trying to get in touch with me. When I returned his call he asked me to come to the ship, that he had something for me. Within the hour I crossed the brow and boarded the *Ponchatoula*. On the way there I had thought of all the possible reasons the skipper might have for inviting me back – none of which made a great deal of sense. When I last departed that vessel I had no intention on ever boarding her again, and I was in hopes that my stay would be short.

The OOD welcomed me on board, and I proceeded directly to the Captain's stateroom. I knocked.

"Enter," came the Captain's distinct voice.

Captain Furlong seemed genuinely pleased to see me. We sat in his comfortable furnishings and talked about things in general for nearly thirty minutes. He then presented me with the ship's plaque, a letter of appreciation, and a briefcase.

"The plaque was an oversight; the chiefs should have made arrangements to present you with one." He smiled broadly and continued, "The briefcase is for you to carry all of the money you will make as a civilian, and the letter speaks for itself."

I thanked the skipper for having thought so highly of me and for having backed me in every single decision I had made during my tour of duty under his command. Everything good that was ever written about me would have applied to an even greater extent to that outstanding naval officer and I tried, during that very brief period of time, to convey those thoughts to him.

We said our final farewells and I headed back to the quarterdeck. There were no chiefs at the quarterdeck, but there were several officers. I was completely overcome with a sense of pride when I realized that officers standing in as side boys were honoring me. I heard the boatswain's pipe sound and saw the snappy salutes executed in unison by the officers and the quarterdeck watch. After I returned their salute I walked slowly down the gangway; real tears streaming down my cheeks – unseen by those honoring me – and I heard the words coming from the 1-MC "Master Chief departing." Not until that moment did I realize the real purpose Captain Furlong had invited me. It was his understanding and enforcement of naval tradition that ensured I was recognized as a retiring master chief. I felt a little sad that it had not been the work of fellow CPOs, but at the same time I realized how lucky I was being honored and saluted by such a fine group of officers. I had dreamed of that day, and it had finally become a reality.

April 1, 1976, was just another typical day in Hawaii. It was to be my last day of active military service. I felt a little strange, uneasy at best, when I realized that I was being handed my final set of orders, my final separation into a completely different civilian environment, by an E-4, a petty officer third class. I thought to myself how much more appropriate it would have been if someone a little more senior, right up to the Base Commander, had taken a minute out of that day just to shake my hand and wish me well. In the back of my mind I was secretly hoping that a small group of CPOs, some or even all from the *Ponchatoula*, might be gathered outside, waiting for me to exit with outstretched hands, or in formation saluting me, as I had done so many times for other retiring chiefs. But, as expected, there was

663

no one there as I walked out of the headquarters building into the Hawaiian sunshine.

As I walked the relatively short distance from the administration offices toward the main gate, my final set of official orders under my arm, I experienced a strange but familiar sensation, feelings I had not been very sensitive to for well over twenty years. I was once again acutely aware of the gentle breeze and the variety of bird calls that surrounded me; déjà vu not at all unlike the manner in which my senses had peaked on my final day at high school. Thoughts of many military experiences raced through my mind with incredible speed, as if I was making some meaningless attempt at prioritizing my entire career. I recalled myself as an awkward youth, so very intent on leaving home. I thought of boot camp and of the chief who guided Company 046 to graduation. I glanced down at my chest and took notice of the five rows of ribbons that represented medals and awards I had earned, and I silently recounted the qualifications for each. At top center represented the Navy Achievement Medal, with Combat "V" (for valor) followed by and in order of precedence: the Combat Action Ribbon, the Navy Unit Commendation with one bronze star, and the Meritorious Unit commendation, all earned while serving in Vietnam; the Good Conduct Medal with three bronze stars, the Navy Expeditionary Medal first earned while serving on the USS *Cowell* and earned a second time while serving on the USS *Seadragon*; the China Service Medal earned while on the USS *Colahan*, the National Defense Medal earned for service during the period December 1955 to November 1958; the Armed Forces Expeditionary Medal, the first earned while attached to the USS *Colahan* and a second earned while attached to the USS *Cowell*; the Vietnam Service Medal with two silver and two bronze stars earned by virtue of having participated in thirteen different campaigns in Vietnam; The Republic of Vietnam Gallantry Cross Medal (also known as the Republic of Vietnam Armed Forces Meritorious Unit Citation), another foreign award earned twice; and the Vietnam Campaign Medal with Device, the third foreign award that was also earned twice. I chuckled to myself as I recalled being laughed at by fellow chiefs during full dress inspections because, according to them, I stood with a forty-five-degree port list caused by the extreme weight of the medals I wore. I thought of the different ships I had served on, of the different personalities I had come in contact with, and of the many friendships I had acquired in faraway places. I thought of the times and the coordinated effort it must have taken when someone managed to set off all the different alarm systems at precisely midnight on several New Year's Eves. I recalled that I had made a total of twelve Western Pacific deployments on board Navy ships, each averaging six months in duration – and I thought of the two years I spent in Vietnam. I realized that during my military service I had spent thirteen years outside the continental United States, eight of which were within the geographical boundaries of foreign countries. I recalled my volunteer efforts that had always been coordinated toward improving the standards of living, habitability, safety, and general welfare of needy children, and I realized how those experiences had contributed immeasurably toward my overall education. I remember thinking how strange it was that I had no unpleasant thoughts; all were of enjoyable and fascinating experiences, all of which would be missed significantly. Many of those thoughts are contained somewhere within the pages of this book. It was a most interesting career and one that I am not only extremely proud of, but one that provided me with an education based on actual experiences that would never have otherwise been possible.

I paused briefly before passing the main gate. I turned and slowly surveyed all that I could see in my final appraisal of that which had been and in anticipation of that which would be. I looked beyond the gate and thought of the civilian world I was about to enter, and I passed through the gate. The tremendous weight of responsibility instantly fell from my shoulders, and I breathed in deeply of fresh air.

Last Day on Active Duty – Retired April 1, 1976

APPENDICES

Appendix A

RESEARCH SOURCES

All Hands, the Bureau of Naval Personnel Information Bulletin, April, September, 1957; June, July 1967.

Anchor, The. United States Naval Training Center, Company 046, class book. Dallas, TX: Taylor, 1955.

Bourke, ENS Bill, JO2 Dale Pitman, and NSA Public Affairs Division, eds. *1965/66 Annual, U.S. Naval Support Activity, DaNang, Vietnam*. Tokyo: Dai Nippon, 1966

Crossroads, October 13, 1967.

Eiben, RD2 Jim. 1971 WestPac Cruise Book, USS *Preble* (DLG-15). Anaheim, CA: Allen, 1971

Lott, Arnold S., Lieutenant Commander, U.S. Navy (Retired), ed. *The Blue Jackets' Manual*, 19th ed. Annapolis, MD: Naval Institute Press, 1973.

Moku Nuhou, ARD-30 ship's newspaper, 1970.

Naumann, YN2 S. P., ed. *1971—1973 Cruise Books*, USS *Preble* (DLG-15), Anaheim, CA. Allen, 1973

Naval Support Activity, Civic Action, DaNang, Newsletter 1, no. 6 (October 1968).

1966/67 Annual, U.S. Naval Support Activity, DaNang, Vietnam. Tokyo: Dai Nippon, 1967

1968 Annual, U.S. Naval Support Activity, DaNang, Vietnam. Tokyo: Dai Nippon, 1968.

1969 Annual, U.S. Naval Support Activity, DaNang Vietnam. Tokyo: Dai Nippon, 1969.

Oudine, John A., ed. *All Hands, Rights and Benefits*. Washington, DC: Bureau of Naval Personnel, 1972

Personal notes, 1955—76.

Service Force, U.S. Pacific Fleet, Information Bulletin, August 1966; November 1968.

Ship's History, USS *Seadragon* (SSN 584), Handout.

Ship's History, USS *Tecumseh* (SSBN 628) handout, n.d.

Slagle, RD2 L. L., ed. *1956 Cruise Book.* USS *Colahan* (DD-658), San Diego, CA: Mirror-graphic Yearbooks, Jack Davidson, 1956.

Vaughn, ENS Phillip D., OS2 Daniel Frantz, SHSN Timothy A. Graham, and JOSN Robert W. Lewis, eds. *1975 Cruise Book,* USS *Ponchatoula* (AO-148). N.p., n.d.

Welcome Aboard, USS *Chipola* handout, 1971.

Welcome Aboard, USS *Colahan* (DD-658) handout, 1955.

Welcome Aboard, USS *Tecumseh* handout, n.d.

Wright, David A., BTCS, USN-Ret, Consultant

Appendix B

GLOSSARY

AFDL	A 288-foot-long floating dry dock. Not capable of self-propulsion.
AFRTS	Armed Forces Radio and Television Service. Commonly referred to as "A-farts."
Ao Dai	Vietnamese outer garment. Translation: "Long shirt."
ASAP	As soon as possible.
ASW	Anti-Submarine Warfare.
Awards, Service	Awards made to those who took part in designated wars, campaigns, or expeditions or fulfilled specified requirements in a credible manner. *See* Decoration.
AWOL	Absent Without Leave.
BM	Boatswain's Mate: trains, directs, and supervises personnel relating to marlinespike deck, boat seamanship, painting, maintenance, and upkeep of ship's external structure, rigging, deck equipment, and boats.
Brow	A form of gangway used when the ship is moored alongside a pier or nested alongside other ships. Note: Brow, gangway, and gangplank mean basically the same thing.
BT	Boiler Technician: operates and repairs all types of marine boilers and fireroom machinery.
Buoy	There are many different types of marker buoys, each serves a special purpose. There is only one kind of buoy referenced herein; a large floating device that is used by ships as a mooring instead of dropping anchor.

Called away	Navy jargon for "passed the word" or "announced" usually over the 1-MC, the ship's public address system.
Captain (1)	Officer pay grade 0-6, *See* Captain (2), Skipper, and CO.
Captain (2)	Also known as the Commanding Officer. The line officer in actual command of a ship whether or not his pay grade is that of 0-6. In case of absence or death his duties are assumed by the line officer next in rank – usually the Executive Officer. Also, the complimentary title given to anyone in charge of a vessel.
Channel fever	Insomnia caused by excitement. Usually associated with returning home following a lengthy overseas deployment. Also suffered by some men the night before visiting a country or port for the first time.
Chief	Chief petty officer. Specifically pay grade E-7 but sometimes incorrectly used when addressing senior chief petty officers and master chief petty officers.
Chocho	Japanese for "butterfly." As a butterfly flies from flower to flower, sailors and/or their Japanese acquaintances were known to *chocho* – go from acquaintance to acquaintance. A *chocho* was one who was unfaithful.
CID	Criminal Investigation Division
CMAA	Chief Master At Arms: responsible for the internal discipline of the crew. *See* MAA.
CNO	Chief of Naval Operations.
CO	Commanding Officer: the line officer in actual command of a ship. In case of absence or death his duties are assumed by the line officer next in rank – usually the Executive Officer.
Cold iron	An engineering term that means the ship is being provided an external source of steam and electricity.
CONUS	Continental United States.

Coxswain	The most responsible member of a boat crew; has full charge and is responsible for the appearance, safety, and efficient operation of the boat.
CPO	Chief Petty Officer: pay grade E-7. With the promotion to this grade came a complete change of uniform to one similar to that of officers.
CPO Club	Chief Petty Officers' Club. More frequently referred to as the Chiefs' Club. Reserved for enlisted men pay grades E-7 and above. Officers welcomed as guests only.
Crow	Navy slang for rating badge.
Cumshaw	Overused by Navy men as a term meaning to beg, borrow, trade for, or steal from one location to serve another.
Decoration	A medal awarded to an individual by name for exceptional courage, bravery, skill, or performance of duty. *See* Awards, Unit and Awards, Service.
Detailer	That person at the Bureau of Naval Personnel directly responsible for assigning all enlisted men within a specific rate and rating.
Dream sheet	A form filled out by naval personnel and sent to the Bureau of Naval Personnel. Used to designate first-, second-, and third-choice duty assignment preferences. One's detailer took the preferences into consideration when individuals were due for rotation.
EM (1)	Enlisted man/men. *See* EM (2).
EM (2)	Electrician's Mate: operates and maintains electrical equipment, circuits, distribution switchboards, generators, and motors.
EM Club	Enlisted Men's Club.
EN	Engineman: operates, maintains, and repairs internal combustion engines, main propulsion machinery, gas turbine engines, and auxiliary equipment.
Engineer Officer	Responsible for the operation and maintenance of all propulsion and auxiliary machinery, damage control, the maintenance of boat machinery, the re-

	pair of the hull and its fixtures, and all repairs beyond the capacity of other departments.
ET	Electronics Technician: maintains and repairs radio and radar equipment used for communications, detection, ranging, recognition and countermeasures, calibrates, tunes, and adjusts equipment.
Exec	Slang for Executive Officer: the line officer next in rank to the Captain. The Exec is responsible for all matters relating to the personnel, routine, and discipline of the ship. All orders issued by him are considered as coming from the Captain.
FBM	Fleet Ballistic Missile.
FN	Fireman: pay grade E-3. Cares for and operates boilers, operates pumps, motors, and turbines, records readings of gauges, and maintains and cleans engineering machinery and compartments. Stands security, engineroom, and fireroom watches.
Gedunk	A snack. Also used to describe a place that sells snacks, such as the PX or the Base Exchange.
GQ	General Quarters. The same as Battle Stations.
Hat, The	Common expression used by chief petty officers to describe someone working toward or having been promoted to chief petty officer. "Earning the Hat" meant promotion to pay grade E-7.
Head	Navy term for bathroom, restroom, washroom, etc.
Hien Binh	Vietnamese. Also known as QC or Quan Canh, Republic of Vietnam Military Police.
HN	Hospitalman: pay grade E-3. Arranges dressing carriages with sterile instruments, dressings, bandages, and medicines; applies dressings; gives morning and evening care to patients; keeps medical records. Commonly referred to as corpsman.
IH	International Hold. Initiated primarily in the Philippines, although available to any foreign government, whereby one surrenders his or her passport as a guarantee he or she will remain in the country until legal matters pending are resolved to

	the satisfaction of the foreign government. Usually the result of a lawsuit against the alien visitor.
JAG	Judge Advocate General: the senior law officer of the command, also known as the "Legal Officer." The office of the JAG has cognizance of all major phases of military administrative, legislative, and applied law incident to the operation of the naval establishment.
Lagging	Lagging and lagging pads were the insulating materials that surrounded steam lines. The primary ingredient (at that time) was asbestos.
LCM	Landing Craft, Mechanized. Commonly called "Mike boat" or "M boat."
Liberty hound	A sailor who seldom allowed a liberty day to go by without going ashore.
MAA	Master At Arms: performs security duties, enforces law and order; investigates incidents and offenses; trains personnel in police duties; assists local law enforcement agencies; contributes to welfare of Armed Forces personnel; prepares records and reports.
MAF	Marine Amphibious Force.
MCPO	Master chief petty officer: pay grade E-9. Usually referred to as Master Chief.
MCPOC	Master Chief Petty Officer of the Command. Usually referenced by the shorter and equally acceptable Master Chief of the Command, and/or Command Master Chief.
Mike boat	Designated as LCM, Landing Craft, Mechanized.
Military time	The day is divided into twenty-four hours instead of twelve hours. Time starts at 0001 (one minute after midnight). Zero one hundred hours equates to 1:00 A.M. – thirteen hundred hours equates to the thirteenth hour of the day, hence 1: 00 P.M.
Missing movement	Also, to miss movement. Failure to be on board when the ship embarks.
MM	Machinist's Mate: operates, maintains, and repairs ship propulsion machinery and auxiliary equip-

674

	ment, outside machinery and refrigeration and air conditioning equipment.
MPA	Main Propulsion Assistant: subordinate to the Engineer Officer. In charge of the main propulsion plant and such additional machinery as may be assigned him. He is responsible for its upkeep and for training the men who operate it.
MPC	Military payment Certificate.
MSTS	Military Sealift Transportation Service. Vessels owned by the Navy but are civilian-operated.
Mustang	Navy slang for an officer who worked his way through the enlisted ranks.
Muster	To call a body of people together. A roll call. Usually held at quarters. *See* Quarters.
MWB	Motor Whale Boat: round-bottomed, double-ended, twenty-six foot-long, diesel-powered boat used as lifeboat and shipboard utility boat. Many small ships use them as gigs and officers' motorboats, in which case they have metal or canvas canopies.
NEC	Navy Enlisted Classification Code: a number that indicates "outside-the-rate" aptitudes, skills, and qualifications. There are several hundred of them, and every enlisted member is coded. Some had a primary and a secondary code. NEC 3355 designated engineers as nuclear-trained.
Nonrated	Enlisted personnel who are in pay grade E-3 and below.
Nose-coner	Slang term used on nuclear submarines to identify those who were not nuclear-trained.
NPA	New People's Army: the Communist-organized Philippine military.
NSA	Naval Support Activity.
NTC	Naval Training Center.
Nuke	Short for nuclear. Also slang on nuclear-powered Navy vessels used in identifying those who were nuclear power trained.
Nuoc mam	Vietnamese. A type of salty sauce made from fish.
"O" Club	Officers' Club.

Old Man	When not referring to an aging person it meant the senior man assigned to a ship or shore station – usually the Commanding Officer or the Captain.
1-MC	The public address system that broadcasts information or orders throughout the ship. Slang: "Squawk box."
OOD	Officer of the Day (Deck).
Open gangway	Nonduty status. The privilege of determining one's own liberty hours.
PCS	Permanent Change of Station. Official orders issued denoting the next permanent duty station to which one is being assigned.
Personnel officer	Responsible for the administration of all enlisted men's records and other administrative matters as may be assigned.
PMS	Preventative Maintenance Schedule.
PNA	Pass(ed) but Not Advanced. Under the quota system there were many instances where enlisted personnel were PNAd. They successfully passed the written examination, but because of quota limitations they were not advanced/promoted.
POD	Plan of the Day: Also known as "the word." The daily schedule of events, prepared and issued by the Executive Officer. The POD names duty officers and various watches and includes such information as changes or additions to the normal routine and orders of the day – drills, training schedules, duty section, liberty hours, inspections, etc.
QC	*Quan Canh,* also known as the *Hien Binh* – the Republic of Vietnam Military Police.
Quarters	When used as a Navy term, it designates a specific place to muster. *See* Muster.
Rank	Pay grade of a naval officer.
Rate	Pay grade of a Navy enlisted member.
Rating	The specialty field within a rate.
Rating badge	Worn by enlisted members of the Navy. Worn on the left arm, consists of an eagle perched with wings expanded, tips pointing upward, head to eagle's

	right, chevrons indicating the wearer's rate, and a specialty mark indicating the rating. *See* Crow.
SEA	Senior Enlisted Advisor.
RHIP	Rate Has Its Privileges. The higher the rate/grade, the more privileges one normally received. RHIP did not always hold true, but in general it was widely accepted as unwritten law where there was no specific policy governing it.
Ribbons	For decorations and awards – worn on the left breast of a dress uniform. Ribbons are worn in order of precedence from the wearer's right to left and from top down.
RVN	Republic of Vietnam. Usually used when referring to Vietnamese military troops or police.
Senior chief	Senior chief petty officer. Pay grade E-8
Short-time	In the Far East the expression usually meant an hour or less of sexual pleasure.
Siclo	Vietnamese three-wheel man-pedaled transportation. Similar to the Philippine tricycle but without a motor.
SJAG	Staff Judge Advocate General. *See* JAG.
Skipper	Commanding Officer.
SN	Seaman: pay grade E-3; keeps compartments, lines or rigging, decks, and deck machinery in shipshape condition; act as lookouts, members of gun crews, helmsmen, and security and fire sentries. Deckhands.
Snipe	A slang term (not derogatory) for all personnel assigned to the Engineering Department, most frequently engineroom and fireroom personnel.
SP	Shore Patrol. Naval term for Military Police.
Special Sea Detail	Whenever a ship gets underway from a pier or anchorage and goes to sea or returns from sea to an anchorage or mooring, the detail is set. Men assigned to the detail must be well trained and experienced, for moving a ship into or out of a crowded harbor, can be a difficult and, at times, dangerous operation.

677

Squawk box	Any public address speaker system.
Steamer	Engineering term for liberty hound. Also used to describe one who indulged in excessive drinking while on liberty.
Striker	An enlisted member who is in pay grade E-3 or below and has been designated to train for a particular rating.
Supply Officer	Heads the Supply Department. Responsible for the procurement, receipt, stowage, issue of, and accounting for equipment, repair parts, and consumable supplies required by the ship. Also responsible for disbursing government funds, payment of bills, paying the crew, and accounting for funds.
Throttle board	A watch station in the engineroom where all plant parameters can be monitored from a central location. The station where the speed and ahead/astern direction of the ship is controlled. Note: under normal conditions all ships and boats were steered by rudders.
U boat	Utility boat.
UCMJ	Uniform Code of Military Justice. The law under which all members of the armed forces are governed.
VD	Venereal Disease.
WesPac/WestPac	Western Pacific – the Far East.
Whale boat	Also known as MWB (Motor Whale Boat). Round-bottomed, double-ended, twenty-six-foot-long, diesel-powered boat used as lifeboat and shipboard utility boat. Many small ships use them as gigs and officers' motorboats, in which case they have metal or canvas canopies.
Whitehat(s)	All enlisted sailors of pay grade E-6 and below.
XO	Executive Officer; usually the line officer next in rank to the Captain. The XO is responsible for all matters relating to the personnel, routine, and discipline of the ship. All orders issued by him are considered as coming from the Captain.
YD	A floating crane with minimal repair capabilities.

| YR | A fully equipped but relatively small repair craft. Not capable of self-propulsion. |

ABOUT THE AUTHOR

Paul L. Adkisson was born December 18, 1937, in Bakersfield, California, where he attended Bakersfield High School up until the time he joined the Navy. During a break in his military career he furthered his education at Bakersfield College. He entered the U.S. Navy January 20, 1955. On April 1, 1976, after two decades of dedicated service, he retired from the military life to which he had become so devoted.

The author's second career began where his first left off, as an executive in a sensitive security position with an agency of the Department of Defense. His travels continued much in line with his military career, in that his responsibilities required his presence on military installations throughout the United States and the Orient. He again retired in 1985 and made his home in Santa Maria, California.

In 1987, finding full retirement unacceptable, the author returned to the work force and accepted employment with a California corporation specializing in industrial security. In November 1994, as Vice President of the Santa Maria corporate branch, he once again opted to retire at which time he began to write of his military experiences. *Anchors and Eagles* is the result of that venture.

The author's travels have taken him to sixteen countries. He has exhibited exceptional compassion for and has spent much time with orphans and underprivileged children, particularly in the Philippines and Vietnam. Paul often ventured away from beaten paths, always preferring to mingle with and share the customs and traditions of the true, host country, natives.

Much of the author's adult education is based on actual experiences. He traveled to foreign lands and met the inhabitants in their own environment, he tasted strange and unusual foods prepared by local nationals, and he learned about and shared in the customs and traditions of which most people only read or hear.

The author has led a most unusual and exciting life. He has not committed himself to specific future plans; however, it is his desire to return to many of the places he previously visited, to renew old friendships, and to continue exploring other new and totally unfamiliar places as he gains new friendships. The author and his lovely wife Toni have settled in Fredericksburg, Texas, the heart of Texas Hill Country, where they currently enjoy full retirement.

Printed in the United States
127976LV00004B/77/P